# Biographical Dictionary
# of the
# American Left

# BIOGRAPHICAL DICTIONARY OF THE AMERICAN LEFT

EDITED BY
BERNARD K. JOHNPOLL AND
HARVEY KLEHR

GREENWOOD PRESS
New York • Westport, Connecticut • London

**Library of Congress Cataloging-in-Publication Data**
Main entry under title:

Biographical dictionary of the American Left.

  Bibliography: p.
  Includes index.
  1. Socialists—United States—Biography—Dictionaries.
2. Communists—United States—Biography—Dictionaries.
I. Johnpoll, Bernard K.  II. Klehr, Harvey.
HX84.A2B56  1986  335′.0092′2  [B]      85–27252
ISBN 0–313–24200–3 (lib. bdg. : alk. paper)

Library of Congress Catalog Card Number: 85–27252
ISBN: 0–313–24200–3

First published in 1986

Greenwood Press, Inc.
88 Post Road West, Westport, Connecticut 06881

Printed in the United States of America

The paper used in this book complies with the
Permanent Paper Standard issued by the National
Information Standards Organization (Z39.48–1984).

10 9 8 7 6 5 4 3 2 1

For Leonard Klehr and Robin Klehr Avia,

and to the memory of Alexander C. Johnpoll and Paul Kirtzman

# CONTENTS

*Introduction*                                                                            ix

**Biographical Dictionary of the American Left**                                           1

Appendix A: Chronology of Key Events                                                     437
Appendix B: Major Radical Party Affiliation and Year of Entry                            441
Appendix C: Place of Birth                                                               447
Appendix D: Birthdate (with Date of Death)                                               453
Appendix E: Those Who Abandoned the Radical Movement                                     459
Appendix F: Ethnic Origin                                                                461

*Index*                                                                                  465

*Contributors*                                                                           491

# INTRODUCTION

The American Left has represented a vast collection of diverse movements stretching over a long period of time. The movements have ranged from the absolute anti-statism of the individualist anarchists to the authoritarianism of the various Leninist organizations. Between the two extremes there have been democratic Socialist organizations, rambunctious syndicalist groups, radical pacifists, and Communist anarchist segments. None of these achieved the political power such organizations would acquire in Europe, but almost all had an influence out of all proportion to their size.

Millions of Americans—and aliens living in the United States—went into and withdrew from left-wing organizations. In 1912 the Socialist Party had more than 135,000 members, making it the largest radical party in U.S. history. A year later the party had lost more than 40,000 members, and five years later there were 50,000 fewer Socialists. The Industrial Workers of the World reached the apex of radical syndicalist membership during the latter period of the second decade of the twentieth century when it enrolled more than 40,000 workers in its ranks. At its peak the communitarian movement of the nineteenth century attracted thousands—at least 20,000 were vaguely affiliated with the Fourierites during the first half of the nineteenth century. Anarchist statistics are almost impossible to ascertain; record-keeping was not a notable attribute of the movement. So too with Edward Bellamy's loosely organized Nationalist Clubs. The Communist Party enrolled around 80,000 members at its height in 1939, with 20,000 more in its youth group. The New Left of the 1960s included tens of thousands of students.

Because there was a huge turnover of membership in all the left-radical groups, most experts agree that as many as 2 million residents of the United States belonged to Socialist, Communist, syndicalist, or anarchist units at one time or another. These millions affiliated with particular groups, which attracted members by their ideology or by the leader who enunciated it.

It is these leaders who are described in this biographical dictionary. Each is placed in the ideological context of his or her time, place, and milieu. Not all the leaders that make up this volume were or are Americans by birth. Some were foreigners who lived in the United States intermittently; others were aliens who refused to become U.S. citizens. Some of the alien radicals dreamt of changing their homelands, to which they hoped to return permanently; others hoped to create in America the Utopia of their dreams. No matter what their national allegiance, all these radical leaders had some effect on American thought and behavior.

In each era of U.S. history a unique brand of radicalism dominated the Left. The most prevalent ideology of each period was a reflection of the cultural, economic, and social milieu of the time. The key factors that determined the ideology of the Left were the industrial system then in vogue, the dominant ethnic makeup of the working population of the nation, the theological and social status of religion in the United States, the extent of egalitarianism inherent in American society at a particular time, and finally the relationship of the Left to foreign movements.

In early- and mid-nineteenth-century America, when the United States was still basically an agrarian nation, libertarian individualism and voluntary communalism dominated the Left. With the growth of industry after the Civil War, democratic socialism, in various forms, became the primary radical ideology. Even many of those who called themselves anarchists had, after 1880, abandoned libertarianism. They were, in fact, militant Socialists who labeled themselves anarchists. During the twentieth century, when industry became the absolutely dominant economic force in the United States, anarchism virtually vanished. Socialism (democratic or otherwise), syndicalism, communism, and welfarism became the dominant movements of the Left.

Prior to 1830 the vast majority of residents of the United States were Anglo-Saxon or Scottish in origin, and so were most of the immigrants coming to America. Most came seeking religious, political, and economic freedom, issues which dominated British thought between the mid-seventeenth and mid-eighteenth centuries. During the 1840s the ethnic makeup of the U.S. population began to change. Germans, fleeing a failed revolution against an oppressive landed Junkerdom, and Irish peasants on the brink of starvation, fled to the western hemisphere. They were quickly absorbed into the growing industries of the nation and turned into city-dwelling proletarians. Thus, while the earlier Americans called for "free thought and free land," the new immigrants called for better conditions in the factories, mills, and mines in which they worked and for a restructuring of the economic system in order to give the workers control of their means of earning a living. Moreover, the issues of religious and political freedom, which had dominated the earlier period, were for historical reasons far more important to the English-Scottish-Welsh people than to the people from Germany and Ireland.

During the last decade of the nineteenth century and the first three decades of the twentieth, immigration into the United States changed again. Millions of newcomers arrived from central, eastern, and southern Europe. Most were fleeing economic woes. Only one group of these immigrants—Jews from Russia—was seeking political, cultural, and religious freedom, for they were the victims of religious, cultural, and political persecution unequaled up to that time. From this immigration came the members of the Marxist movements—the Socialists and Communists of the twentieth century.

The United States has never been an egalitarian republic. Black Americans have historically been denied equal status, and even among white Americans there has been a long history of political, social, and economic inequality. As equality of opportunity has advanced during the past two hundred years, the issues raised by radical leaders have changed from decade to decade. During the fight against slavery and the fight for industrial reform and equality—when the church accepted the Social Gospel—there was a major movement for Christian Socialism which attempted to give Christianity a radical-Left coloration and socialism a Christian, ethical caste.

The leaders of the disparate American left-wing movements between 1820 and the present make up this volume. If one movement dominates, in sheer number of entries, it should be noted that the role of leadership varied from movement to movement: some eschewed leadership, others thrived on it. Moreover, the number and turnover of leaders varied from group to group. These variations were generally due to divergent philosophies.

There are a great number of differences, as well as points of similarity, between the various tendencies of the American Left. Anarchists, for example, consider the state to be an absolute evil, the cause of all that is wrong in society. Syndicalists believe that government and the political state are irrelevancies in a basically economic conflict. They agree with the anarchists that by its very nature the state must represent the interests of the class in power, the capitalists, against the enemies of capital, the working class.

On the contrary, Socialists and Communists of all stripes assume that the state can be controlled by the working class and can thus become an instrument for revolutionary change. Socialists insist that the state must be democratic, with a legal and respected opposition. The Communists would bar organized opposition and would establish a dictatorship of the Communist Party under the appellation "dictatorship of the proletariat."

All the radical factions agree in their opposition to the capitalist system, or to any socioeconomic system based on competition. They all would replace it with a system based on cooperation—a noncompetitive economic order. They agree that the world's woes are the result of a class structure in which a small group that owns the means of production and distribution rules over a large group of people that owns nothing but their own labor and that a struggle exists between these classes—a struggle that will end only when classes vanish in society. Some leftists see this class struggle as a necessary result of historical fact; others see it as an unfortunate aberration of history.

As for tactics, radicals universally proclaim that they hope to avoid violence, although, except for a small pacifist wing, none would shy away from violence, if it was deemed necessary. Syndicalists expect to seize power in a peaceful general strike, although most expect the capitalists to instigate violence. Even followers of the violence-prone anarchists Johann Most and August Spies declared that they favored peaceful revolution even though they doubted it was possible. Socialists, the least belligerent of the radicals, want to change society by the ballot, although many doubt that the capitalists will allow such nonviolent change. Even communitarians, many of whom were devout Christians, had grave doubts that the capitalists would turn the other cheek.

For all its accomplishments and the nobility and heroism of many of its supporters, American radicalism has been a failure. No radical group has ever seriously contended for power in the United States, much less gained it. Yet radicals have had a major impact on American life—sparking or participating in movements for black rights and women's rights, unionization, political reform, and many others. Particularly in the twentieth century, American radicalism has had an influence far out of proportion to its numbers.

In choosing those to be included in this volume, we tried to balance the need to recognize key figures in America's radical history with our interest in presenting material on some neglected but important people. Because of space limitations, we were unable to include many of the fascinating, colorful characters that populate our radical past. Unless they seemed to have some substantial importance to the history of American radicalism or some other noteworthy accomplishment, we reluctantly did not include them. We also omitted most radical intellectuals, except for those who were actively involved with and important to radical political movements. Finally, while we included a number of radicals prominent in the New Left of the 1960s, we did not attempt to cover that movement as comprehensively as we covered those from earlier in the twentieth century. Not only was the New Left a more amorphous and less coherent radical movement, but obtaining biographical details about many of its leaders is extraordinarily difficult.

Our choices have provided a representative cross-section of the leadership of the American Left which will give scholars and general readers a sense of who was in charge of various radical parties and from what social or ethnic stratum these parties drew their vitality. Each entry contains certain standard biographical material, if it is available, including birthdate and birthplace, other names used, year of immigration to the United States (if applicable), religious and ethnic background, father's occupation, the individual's occupation, political affiliations, and major roles in the radical movement. Depending on the individual's importance, there may also be an assessment of his or her contribution to American radicalism. The sources at the end of some entries direct readers to more complete biographical information, usually either a biography or an autobiography. For many of the entries, however, there is no good comprehensive source for biographical information.

Several appendices at the end of this volume list the biographies by their political party affiliation, birthplace, birthdate, and ethnic origin. Another appendix lists those who abandoned radicalism.

In compiling these entries, we were fortunate to have the aid of dozens of scholars and experts. Without their willingness to suggest names that needed to be included, to ferret out obscure facts, and to write many of the entries, this project would not have been possible.

Particular thanks are due to Linda Boyte of Emory University, who typed the manuscript, to the librarians at the Milwaukee, Bridgeport, Norwalk, and Reading public libraries, the Montana, Minnesota, and Wisconsin State Historical Societies, the Tamiment Collection at New York University, and the State Library of New York in Albany.

# Biographical Dictionary of the
# American Left

# A

ABERN, MARTIN (1898–1949). Martin Abern (Abramowitz) was a founder of the American Communist movement, of the American Trotskyist movement, and of the Workers Party, holding major positions in each group. He was born on December 2, 1898, in the Bessarabian area of Romania, and was brought to the United States in 1902 at the age of 4 by his Jewish parents. The family settled in Minneapolis, where Abern attended elementary and high school and the University of Minnesota.

At age 15, Abern joined the Industrial Workers of the World and the Young People's Socialist League. He was a tolerated "campus radical" at the university because he was a star member of the championship football team. When the United States entered World War I, Abern refused military service on political grounds and was expelled from the university after less than three years of attendance. He was sentenced to a six-month term in prison.

A supporter of the Russian Revolution, Abern joined the Left Wing faction when it split off from the Socialist Party at its 1919 convention. At an underground convention in 1920, Abern, at age 23, was elected as the youngest member of the Communist Party Central Committee. During 1920–1921 he was secretary of the Workers Party of Minnesota, the legal organization of the underground party. He then transferred his activities to Chicago, where he was made national secretary of the Young Workers League.

In 1922 Abern was present at the Fourth Congress of the Communist International. He was also a delegate to the Second Congress of the Young Communist International in Moscow and became a member of its Executive Committee. As a member of the Central Committee of the Communist Party from 1923 to 1928, Abern was a leading member of the James Cannon (q.v.) faction, which was particularly influential among the youth. When Cannon became national secretary of the International Labor Defense (ILD), Abern joined him as assistant national secretary and helped build the ILD into a mass organization.

Along with Cannon and Max Shachtman (q.v.), he was expelled from the Central Committee and the Party in November 1928 for supporting Leon Trotsky and the Russian Left Opposition. They were joined immediately by Maurice Spector, a founder and leader of the Canadian Communist Party.

Together with their supporters in both countries, Cannon, Shachtman, Abern, and Spector formed the Communist League of America in Chicago in May 1929. Abern was a member of the National and Political Committees of the new organization until 1934, when it united with the American Workers Party, led by A. J. Muste (q.v.), and then was a member of the National and Political Committees of the newly formed Workers Party until it dissolved in 1937, when its members entered the Socialist Party.

The brief stay of the Trotskyists in the Socialist Party ended in their expulsion when they challenged the party's critical support of Largo Caballero's Popular Front Spanish government with the Communists. In 1938 the expelled Trotskyists formed the Socialist Workers Party, and Abern served on its National and Political Committees until the split in 1940 between the Trotsky-led Cannon leadership and Shachtman over the nature of the Soviet Union. Abern was an active participant in this struggle; he was elected to the National Committee of the Shachtman-led Workers Party in April 1940. He remained among the leadership until he died of a heart attack in April 1949 at the age of 50.

SOURCES: Solon DeLeon, *The American Labor Who's Who* (1925); Theodore Draper, *American Communism and Soviet Russia* (1968); Max Shachtman, "Martin Abern: An Obituary," *Labor Action*, May 9, 1949.

*ALBERT GLOTZER*

**ALLEN, DEVERE (1891–1955).** Devere Allen was a leading Socialist-pacifist and journalist. A native of Providence, Rhode Island, where he was born in 1891, Allen graduated from Oberlin College in Ohio in 1917, less than two months after the outbreak of World War I. An opponent of the war on primarily ethical and religious grounds, he joined the newly organized Fellowship of Reconciliation, a leading Anglo-American pacifist organization, and soon became one of its leaders. In 1922 he succeeded Norman Thomas (q.v.) as editor of the Fellowship's official publication, *The World Tomorrow*, and turned it into the leading Christian Socialist weekly in the United States. He remained editor of the journal until its demise in 1934. He had earlier been editor of *Young Democracy*, a pro-Socialist publication.

After the demise of *World Tomorrow*, Allen became an associate editor of the *Nation*. He was for a short time also a foreign correspondent for the North American Newspaper Alliance. In 1933 Allen formed the No-Frontier News Service, a feature syndicate for pro-Socialist and anti-war publications throughout the world. He was also a director of World-Over Press, which provided international news coverage for newspapers and magazines. Both news organizations were friendly in the anti-war movement of the United States during the pre–Pearl Harbor period. Allen's opposition to U.S. participation in World

War II did not prevent him from vehemently opposing fascism. He was particularly active in the League Against German Fascism, an organization that aided Jewish and Christian victims of Hitler's rule. Allen argued that ends could not justify means; he thus opposed war as the means for eradicating fascism and Nazism.

Allen was the author of more than twenty books and pamphlets—almost all of them pacifist. His most famous book was *The Fight for Peace* (1930). Allen was also an editor for the publications of the Pro-Socialist League for Industrial Democracy and for the pacifist War Resisters League.

From 1929 to 1936 Allen was active politically. He was on the board of the League for Independent Political Action (1928–1932), an attempt at creating a powerful Social Democratic movement in the United States. He was the Socialist candidate for U.S. Senator from Connecticut in 1932 and 1954 and the party's candidate for governor of Connecticut in 1936. During the internal strife that rent the Socialist Party between 1932 and 1936, Allen was in the pro–Norman Thomas militant wing. He challenged Bridgeport Mayor Jasper McLevy (q.v.) for control of the state party in 1936, but lost. He was also active in the League for Industrial Democracy, the American League for India's Freedom, and the Authors League of America.

Later Allen taught at the Williamstown (Massachusetts) Institute of Politics and was on the staff of the Wellesley Summer Institute for Social Progress. He died in Westerly, Rhode Island, in August 1955.

*BERNARD K. JOHNPOLL*

**ALLEN, JAMES (b. 1906).** James S. Allen was an organizer, writer, and editor for the Communist Party (CPUSA). An expert on the South, he helped develop and popularize the Party's position on the Negro question in the United States. Later he served as president and editor-in-chief of the CPUSA's publishing house, International Publishers.

Allen was born Sol Auerbach in Philadelphia on August 6, 1906, the son of Russian Jewish immigrants. His father had participated in the Revolution of 1905 and, after a pogrom in Odessa, where he was active, emigrated to the United States, where he became a clothing worker and later an insurance agent. The younger Auerbach received a B.A. degree from the University of Pennsylvania and taught philosophy as a doctoral candidate there in the mid–1920's. During the summer of 1927 he traveled with the first American student delegation to the Soviet Union. Upon his return to Philadelphia he gave a public lecture on education in the USSR. The university's administration ordered his expulsion for radical activities in 1928. That same year he joined the Communist Party. He began writing for its newspaper, the *Daily Worker*, and edited the *Labor Defender*.

In 1930 he adopted the pen name James S. Allen and founded and began editing the *Southern Worker*, the first Communist weekly ever published in the South. It circulated on an underground basis. As a member of the CPUSA's southern district committee, Allen played a prominent role in all the Party's major regional activities during the early 1930s: the organizing of Alabama sharecroppers, the Harlan (Kentucky) miners strike, and the Scottsboro case. Allen interpreted black liberation as a question of national oppression, not merely a part of the class struggle. This expanded on and applied specifically the Communist International's doctrine, announced in 1928, demanding "the right of self-determination of the Negroes in the Black Belt." Allen wrote two important books on the subject, including *Reconstruction: The Battle for Democracy* (1937).

The strain of underground existence caused Allen to leave the South in 1931. In the late 1930s he was CPUSA representative in the Philippines, where he helped achieve the merger of the Communist and Socialist parties, which established the basis for the Huk guerrilla resistance to the Japanese invasion. During World War II he served as the *Daily Worker*'s foreign editor until being drafted into the infantry in 1944 at age 37. During the Cold War years he became foreign editor of the *Sunday Worker* and was subpoenaed before the House Un-American Activities Committee and Senator Joseph McCarthy's committee.

In 1962 Allen was named head of the financially troubled International Publishers. Anticipating both the rise of the New Left and the impact of the paperback revolution, he introduced New World Paperbacks, which made available the classics of Marxism-Leninism at modest prices and tapped the burgeoning university market of the era. Allen retired in 1972. He lives in New York City and is completing an autobiography.

SOURCE: James S. Allen, *Negro Liberation* (1938).

*JAMES GILBERT RYAN*

**AMERINGER, OSCAR (1870–1943).** Oscar Ameringer was a Socialist editor, publisher, organizer, and leader of the powerful Oklahoma Socialist Party during the first three decades of the twentieth century. Ameringer was born in 1870 in Laupheim, Bavaria, Germany, of a working-class family. He attended the local school until he was 15, at which point his parents sent him to the United States to join an older brother in Cincinnati, Ohio.

In the States, Ameringer soon became embroiled in trade union activity. At age 17 he helped lead a futile strike in a furniture factory where he was employed. After the strike Ameringer found himself blacklisted by all employers in the furniture trade. Fortunately, he was an able cornet player and joined one of the innumerable German bands which played in beer halls and theaters in southern Ohio. Under the name of Oscare Americolini, Ameringer eventually became part of a short-lived Italian band that played in vaudeville theaters. He then turned to painting landscapes on screens for barrooms, still lifes on wooden bowls, butterflies on white slippers, and portraits of Ohio farmers. He was financially successful as an artist, although his work failed to win any critical acclaim.

With the money he earned as an artist, Ameringer returned to his native Bavaria in 1890. There he spent most of his time reading, studying, and attending Social Democratic meetings in local beer halls. Among the speakers who made an impression on his thinking was Wilhelm Liebknecht, leader of the Marxist wing of the German party. Although Ameringer was sympathetic to the Socialists by the time he returned to the United States in 1895, he was not a member of any party.

His first job on his return to the United States was as a musician in the band that greeted visitors to the home of William McKinley during the Ohioan's successful "front porch" campaign for the presidency in 1896. Ameringer recalled that campaign with disdain and claimed that the vapidity of McKinley's speeches turned him into an active Socialist.

For about a year Ameringer drifted through the Southwest, working occasionally as a press agent for a purported health resort. Along the way he read *Progress and Poverty* by Henry George, *Looking Backward* by Edward Bellamy (q.v.), and other American Socialist classics. He also discussed socialism and social problems with many social activists and labor leaders. He was most impressed with the pro-Socialist arguments of a German Catholic priest, a Monsignor Soenthgerath, who convinced him to become a Socialist.

Soon thereafter Ameringer turned to labor editing and organizing. His first editing job was in Columbus, Ohio, where he directed the trade union weekly. In the first decade of the twentieth century he edited labor weeklies in the South and Midwest and helped lead union-organizing drives in those areas. He was instrumental in organizing the New Orleans brewery and dock workers, although his efforts at organizing both black and white workers into single unions in those trades failed; each of the racial groups acted as strikebreakers when members of the other race went on strike. By 1908 he had moved to Oklahoma, where he became a leader of the Socialist Party and editor of its newspaper. His ideological position in the party was somewhat ambiguous; he supported both left-winger Eugene V. Debs (q.v.) and right-winger Victor Berger (q.v.) and was friendly with both. The party in Oklahoma generally reflected his position.

Ameringer was not known as a leading theoretician or ideologue. He was primarily an innovative organizer. He organized camp meetings of impoverished farmers. These meetings resembled religious encampments prevalent in the Midwest and the Prairie States, with gospel sings and prominent orators. They helped build a party that was the largest per capita in the United States by 1910. In 1911 Ameringer came close to winning the mayoralty of Oklahoma City.

In 1914 the Oklahoma Socialists reached the apex of their strength, electing six representatives and a senator to the state legislature from the western end of the state. Two years later they were all defeated for reelection and the party went into decline. The party had fallen victim to a short-lived farm prosperity which followed the outbreak of war in Europe.

During the national convention of 1912, Ameringer abandoned his longtime friendship for Debs to support Emil Seidel (q.v.) for the presidential nomination, which finally went to Debs. His action and the failure of the Socialists to maintain their legislative strength in the state led to a rupture in the Socialist ranks. A large number of Eastern Oklahoma party members abandoned the Socialist ranks to join the ultra-left, violence-prone Working Class Union. When the United States entered World War I, the Working Class Union attempted, against the advice of Ameringer, an open armed rebellion. This tragi-comedy, called the Green Corn Rebellion, was a failure, and persecution followed. The rebellion, which Socialists generally and Ameringer in particular opposed, helped destroy the once-powerful Socialist Party in Oklahoma.

Soon after the failure of the uprising, Ameringer was called to Milwaukee by Berger to join him in an effort to save the daily *Milwaukee Leader*, which was then under attack by the federal government: its mailing privileges and rights were revoked, its editor was arrested and charged with sedition, and its advertisers and readers were threatened with official economic boycott. The newspaper was finally saved, though much weakened by the government's actions.

The war turned Ameringer into a pacifist, a position from which he would never vary. Immediately after the war, Ameringer returned to Oklahoma and tried to revive the Socialist Party by publishing a new daily newspaper there. Both the party and the paper failed, although a Socialist-Progressive coalition demonstrated some power in the early 1920s. By 1921 Ameringer had moved to Illinois, where he edited the anti–John L. Lewis *Illinois Miner*, the official organ of the Progressive Miners of America. He held that post for ten years.

In 1931 Ameringer began publishing the *American Guardian*, a Populist-Socialist weekly (which absorbed the *Oklahoma Leader*, a quasi-Socialist weekly published from 1914 to 1931). The *Guardian*'s circulation was primarily in the Prairie West. It favored militant Socialist organization and moderate Socialist ideology. The *Guardian* collapsed because of Socialist disagreement over World War II. An editorial by Ameringer's son Siegfried supporting the war after Pearl Harbor (Oscar Ameringer was ill at the time) led many pacifist-isolationist Prairie Socialists to cancel subscriptions. The *Guardian* went out of existence in early 1942.

Oscar Ameringer died in Oklahoma City on November 5, 1943.

SOURCES: Oscar Ameringer, *If You Don't Weaken* (1940); Henry Burbank, *When Farmers Voted Red* (1976).

*BERNARD K. JOHNPOLL*


**AMTER, ISRAEL (1881–1954).** Israel Amter, one of the founding members of the American Communist Party, was a leading Party functionary into the 1940s. Never at the very pinnacle of power, he nonetheless held numerous important positions and was regarded as one of the most dedicated and ascetic revolutionaries in the movement.

Amter was born on March 26, 1881, in Denver, Colorado, to Jewish immigrant parents. His mother came from Germany and his father, of Russian descent, had been an alfalfa farmer and then a tradesman. After finishing high school, Amter, influenced by a series of miners' strikes, joined the Socialist Party in 1901. He moved to Germany in 1903 and remained there until 1914, editing the *German*

*Export Review* for several years, studying music at the Leipzig Conservatory of Music from 1906 on, and participating in the German Social Democratic Party.

Returning to the United States just before World War I, Amter did not rejoin the Socialist Party until 1917. He was a professional musician in New York until he joined the Communist movement at its inception in 1919. For several years he was a leading advocate of an underground party and used the pseudonym J. Ford, while also heading the Unemployed Council of New York and holding an important post in the Friends of the Soviet Union. After he was won over to a fully legal movement, Amter held a variety of responsible Party posts, including district organizer in Chicago and Cleveland, and served as American representative to the Comintern from 1923 to 1925.

As the Communist Party's district organizer in New York in 1930, Amter was arrested and sentenced to six months in prison for his part in the huge March 6, 1930, unemployment demonstration. Soon after his release he took charge of Party work on behalf of the unemployed as national secretary of the Unemployed Councils and oversaw Communist efforts to pass unemployment insurance legislation. In 1936 he became chairman of the New York State Communist Party. Amter served on most Party Central Committees from 1922 to 1945.

By the late 1940s Amter was suffering from Parkinson's disease and was no longer very active. The federal government indicted him for violation of the Smith Act in 1951, but he was severed from the case due to illness. He died on November 24, 1954.

SOURCES: FBI File 100–19685; *New York Times*, November 25, 1954, p. 29.

*HARVEY KLEHR*


**ANDREWS, STEPHEN PEARL (1812–1884).** Stephen Pearl Andrews, a nineteenth-century individualist anarchist, was born in March 1812 in Templeton, a farm community in central Massachusetts. He studied law in Massachusetts and passed the bar there after challenging some obsolete laws. Soon after passing the Massachusetts bar examination he moved to Houston, Texas where he resumed his practice at age 27. While in Houston he worked on a plan to free the slaves by government purchase from the slaveowners. His proposal roused the ire of his pro-slavery neighbors, and in 1843 he was forced to flee Houston with his wife and infant son to evade lynching.

Andrews went first to London, where he made a futile effort to raise money to buy out the slaves. While in London, he became interested in the shorthand system developed by Sir Isaac Pitman, which he imported into the United States (he called it phonography). He also became interested in a new universal language called Alwato, a precursor of Esperanto.

For the first few years after his return from England, Andrews divorced himself from political movements. In 1850 he met Josiah Warren (q.v.) in the United States and was won over to the latter's individualistic anarchism. In 1851 Andrews wrote *The Science of Society*, which he claimed to be an irrefutable scientific explanation of Warren's social system. Andrews drew on the then-developing social science to expound the system. His argument began with the biological assumption that no two individuals were exactly alike. This he argued was a natural law—the law of individuality—and since natural law cannot be violated, and must be obeyed, it followed that each individual had to be sovereign over his own individuality. Under these conditions no man had a right to own or control another. Thus slavery was illegal, a violation of the natural law which he dubbed sovereignty of the individual. Also in violation of this natural law were the army, the navy, nationalism, taxes, and commercial restrictions. And since a criminal is an individual exercising his right to his own sovereignty— albeit a sick individual—Andrews denounced capital and corporal punishment, although he favored restricting such a person.

The ideal government, Andrews opined, was one that did not rule at all. Rule by majority was wrong, he believed, because it could ignore the rights of the minority. No man-made law could be superior to the individual. Andrews agreed that the ideal political system which Warren postulated could hardly be achieved instantaneously. He proposed that an economic system based on the Warren proposition that cost should be the limit of price would be necessary before government would disappear. This economy could be achieved by turning over all state power to private—ostensibly nonprofit—corporations.

In 1851 Andrews and Warren founded the Modern Times colony in Brentwood, Long Island. Although organized as an individualist Utopia, Modern Times founders did try to screen those who were admitted. They also charged each member $120 for a home and a piece of land. But neither the screening nor the fee kept eccentrics out of the community. Because the colony officially allowed total freedom, rebels linked to all sorts of unique social mores became members. Some women wore men's clothing, and others wore bloomers (a socially brazen act in the Victorian period). Many of the members of the colony lived on peculiar diets—one colonist starved himself to death by eating only beans for months.

The most serious breach from the socially accepted norms was the view of sex and marriage held by some of the residents of Modern Times. Many of the members believed that sex was a private matter and practiced and preached free love—sex without the bonds of matrimony. Andrews was among those who preached—but did not practice—free love. The sexual views of the colony's residents created a scandal in the New York area. A debate in writing between Andrews, Henry James, and Horace Greeley was printed in the *New York Tribune*. This led to internal strife at Modern Times. So serious was the disagreement and the scandal that the community had to change its name in 1864 to Brentwood.

The Civil War also helped split the community. Andrews became virulently anti-Southern. He called for all-out war against the South. He virtually abandoned anarchism and individualism in his hawkish view of the war. Some of the settlers were opposed to all war; others were for the war, albeit moderately. The splits over the war and sexual mores made the position of the community untenable. It fell apart.

After the war Andrews became active in the New Democracy, an anti-Marxist affiliate of the First International. There he wrote virtually all the articles and speeches for Victoria Woodhull (q.v.), who was the spokesperson for the organization. She would later denounce him for these articles, especially those that attacked marriage.

Andrews spent his last years writing articles in small anarchist journals. He died in 1884 at the age of 72.

SOURCES: James J. Martin, *Men Against the State* (1970); Eunice Minette Schuster, *Native American Anarchism* (1932).

*LILLIAN KIRTZMAN JOHNPOLL*

# B

**BARTEL, HEINRICH L. (1875–1968).** For fifty-eight years Heinrich Bartel was an editor of German-American labor and Socialist newspapers. Bartel was born in 1875 in Austria, where he was raised and educated. He completed no more than the sixth grade in schools there, but from his earliest years he was an avid reader.

In 1904 he and his wife—the daughter of Austrian Socialist leader Josef Schiller—emigrated to the United States, settling first in Lawrence, Massachusetts, an industrial city with a large working-class German population. He soon joined the staff of that city's German newspaper. Tired of the provincial life in Lawrence, Bartel moved to Chicago, where he became a writer and editor of the *Arbeiter Zeitung* (Workers Paper). He later moved to Sheboygan, Wisconsin, where he edited another German newspaper. In 1911 Victor Berger (q.v.) invited Bartel to edit the Milwaukee Socialist German-language newspaper, *Vorwaerts* (Forward). Berger was leaving the German daily to become editor of the English-language daily *Milwaukee Leader*. Bartel remained editor of *Vorwaerts* for twenty-two years, until its demise in 1932.

From 1919 on Bartel was a major intellectual leader of the German Socialists in the United States, actively lecturing in the Milwaukee area and editing the *Freie Wort*, the publication of the *Freie Gemeinde* (Free Thinkers). Bartel's private library of more than 3,000 volumes was donated to the Milwaukee County Historical Society at the time of his death in 1968, at age 93.

*JAMES E. INGBRETSON*

**BEDACHT, MAX (1883–1972).** Max Bedacht was a founder of the Communist movement in the United States. He briefly served as Party leader before leading a major Communist auxiliary during its heyday. Bedacht was born in Munich, Germany, on October 13, 1883, the illegitimate child of a cook. Raised as a Catholic, he ended his formal schooling at age 13. Four years later he moved to Switzerland, where he worked as a barber, becoming president of the national union in the trade in 1907 and joining the Swiss Socialist Party in 1903. He immigrated to the United States in 1908 and soon was associated with the German Socialist movement in Yorkville in New York City while working as a barber. Beginning in 1912 he edited German-language Socialist newspapers in Detroit and San Francisco.

Active in the Socialist left-wing in California, Bedacht was elected as a delegate to the 1919 Socialist Party convention. However, he was denied a seat and took part in the Communist Labor Party's convention, being chosen to be on the National Executive Committee. He represented his party on the Executive Committee of the Communist International in the early 1920s, using the alias "Marshall." Bedacht was a fixture on the Party's National Committee during the 1920s, identified with the Lovestone (q.v.) faction. In 1929 he capitulated when Stalin ousted Jay Lovestone and was rewarded by being named acting secretary of the Communist Party (CPUSA) in mid-year. His tenure was not very successful, and in June 1930 he was removed from the Party secretariat, replaced by Earl Browder (q.v.), and became director of agitation and propaganda work. In 1932 he was shunted off to direct the International Workers Order (IWO), a fraternal insurance agency dominated by the Party. Under his direction its membership jumped dramatically from 20,000 to 150,000 prior to World War II. He was also accused by Whittaker Chambers of being an important figure in the Party's illegal work, a charge he denied.

By the end of the 1930s Bedacht was no longer an important factor in the Party. After the war he challenged the Party's nationality policy, which encouraged separate ethnic units of the IWO as "bourgeois nationalism," and he was expelled in 1948. Moving to New Jersey, he became a chicken farmer. Bedacht was reinstated in the CPUSA a few years before his death on July 4, 1972.

SOURCE: Max Bedacht, "On the Path of My Life" (unpublished manuscript, Tamiment Library, New York University, New York City.

*HARVEY KLEHR*

**BELLAMY, EDWARD (1850–1898).** Edward Bellamy was the author of *Looking Backward*, a Utopian novel that more than any other book influenced democratic Socialist thought in the Western world. Born in a Baptist parsonage in the Western Massachusetts industrial city of Chicopee Falls on March 25, 1850, Bellamy was of Puritan stock. Many of his ancestors had been Congregational and Baptist clergymen. During the Civil War, while he was a young boy, Bellamy became enamored of the military life. Unfortunately, he was frail, and could not pass the physical examination for the U.S. Military Academy at West Point. Instead, his family sent him to Union College in Schenectady, New York. Bellamy stayed there for only a year and then dropped out of college permanently. When he was 18 years old he went to Europe, where he explored England and Germany.

His travels included visits to the poor sections of both countries' major cities. The suffering of the working-class population won Bellamy's sympathies. On his return in 1869, Bellamy read law and was admitted to the Massachusetts bar in 1871. He soon discovered that he hated the practice of law and became instead a journalist, at first as an editorial writer for the *New York Post*, which was edited by William Cullen Bryant, a noted Western New England poet. He then accepted the post of associate editor of the Springfield (Massachusetts) *Union*.

While serving on the *Union*, he wrote several novels, the most notable of which, *The Duke of Stockbridge: A Romance of Shays' Rebellion*, appeared originally in 1879 as a series in the *Berkshire Current* of Great Barrington, Massachusetts. Essentially a potboiler, similar in many ways to what would later be euphemistically called proletarian literature, the novel has been cited as the first indication that Bellamy was a Socialist long before he wrote *Looking Backward*. This assumption is at best faulty. The book offers no Utopian hope. It merely indicated that Bellamy generally supported the radical point of view. Actually, Bellamy told both Abraham Cahan (q.v.) and William Dean Howells that he knew little of socialism before 1887, when he completed *Looking Backward*. He later admitted that he had read Laurence Gronlund's (q.v.) *The Cooperative Commonwealth* before he wrote his own magnum opus.

*Looking Backward* did poorly when it first appeared in 1887, but a year later it became a major success—a genuine best-seller. Its sales reached 10,000 a month by 1889, and total sales during the first seventy-five years of the book's publication have run into the millions. *Looking Backward* is a fantasy, an early version of science fiction. The story begins in the year 2000. It tells of a Bostonian who awakens after a 113-year sleep and finds his native city completely changed. From a competitive, almost anarchic society controlled by and serving rapacious capitalists, the new society he discovers in Boston is a well-ordered city of cooperation in which all industry is socially owned and whose sole aim is to serve the needs of society.

The revolution that led to this change involved no violence or strife. It came about peacefully. Neither the Socialist political parties nor the labor unions of the period played any role in this revolution. In fact, the revolution came about by what was tantamount to universal consensus. Bellamy rejected the theory of the class struggle. He argued that the revolution which brought Utopia to Boston was favored by all classes. Monopolies, which were the bugbear of American radicals in the last quarter of the nineteenth century, were the instruments through which the revolution was made possible, according to Bellamy. The monopolies remained in place after the revolution; only their purpose had been changed. Instead of profit, their aim was the production for use. Instead of competition their aim was cooperation. Instead of greed their aim was social betterment.

The new society was run like an industrial army organized along military lines. All citizens between 18 and 45 years of age would be enrolled in the industrial army. Each would be assigned his role—some to do physical labor, others to do intellectual work, still others to be in positions of command. All retirees would be allowed to vote in elections—no others would. The actual day-to-day control of the operation of Bellamy's Utopia would be in the hands of civil servants. It is significant that the press would be free, privately owned—albeit nonprofit. The editors would be elected by the readers, and the editors would decide what a newspaper would publish. The book's description of the Boston of the year 2000 includes many developments that would become realities within fifty years, for example, radio and credit cards.

The huge sale of the book resulted in the organization of Nationalist Clubs dedicated to making the fantasy a reality. Most of those who joined the Nationalist Clubs were intellectuals, and they generally came from upper-class society. All opposed any militancy. By 1890 the Nationalists were deeply involved in politics. The leaders of the Socialist Labor Party, who had previously been friendly to the Nationalists, now turned against them. This was especially true after Daniel DeLeon (q.v.) seized control of the Socialist Labor Party about 1891—even though the Nationalists and the Marxian Socialists disagreed on only two points: (1) the class struggle, which the followers of Bellamy considered an inaccurate description of society and thus irrelevant, and (2) whether the workers could emancipate themselves (the Bellamyites believed the workers would need leadership from intellectuals). On this issue, most Marxists agreed with the Nationalists, but they could not bring themselves to say so openly.

From the beginning, the Nationalists did not do particularly well in elections in the East. They did especially poorly in Massachusetts, Rhode Island, and New York. In California the Nationalist candidates, most of whom would later become Socialist leaders, did far better than expected. In 1891 the Nationalists went into the People's Party, but they had little effect. By 1896 Bellamy was disgusted with the Populist support of William Jennings Bryan for President. That year Bellamy wrote a new, more nearly Marxist book, *Equality*, but it was a failure. All that is remembered generally of the book is the "Parable of the Water Tank," which Socialists republished in pamphlet form as late as the 1960s.

In 1897 Bellamy considered joining the new Social Democracy of Eugene Debs (q.v.), but he was too sick to be politically active then. He died in Chicopee Falls, Massachusetts, in 1898.

SOURCES: Edward Bellamy, *Looking Backward*, (1887); Arthur E. Morgan, *Edward Bellamy* (1944).

*BERNARD K. JOHNPOLL*

**BENJAMIN, HERBERT (1898?–1983).** Herbert Benjamin was a Communist Party functionary from the early 1920s to the mid–1940s, best known for his activities during the 1930s as an organizer of and spokesman for various unemployed workers and relief client groups—most notably the Communist-sponsored Unemployed Councils in the early 1930s and later in the decade the Workers Alliance of America, which the Party came to dominate.

He was born Benjamin Greffenson in Vilna, Lithuania, in either 1898 or 1900, the youngest of fourteen children of whom only six survived. His Jewish parents brought the family to Chicago around the turn of the century. The family's circumstances were limited (his father was a watchmaker), and Herbert left grade school in Chicago in 1912 to work as an errand boy at $4.00 a week. During the next years he briefly joined the Young People's Socialist League, bummed around the nation, and did a stint with the Industrial Workers of the World (IWW). He joined the underground Communist Party in 1921 and was a delegate to the supposedly secret Bridgman convention, which was raided. It was at this time that he assumed the name Herbert Benjamin.

During the 1920s Benjamin held a succession of Party posts. He served as a functionary in Ohio, Buffalo, and Philadelphia. In the fall of 1929 he was assigned to be organizational secretary in New York City. Until then he had considered himself a "Lovestoneite," but like so many others in the Party, when the Comintern forcefully made its preferences known Benjamin abandoned Lovestone (q.v.).

Actively involved in the Party's activities in New York City (including the spectacularly successful demonstration on the Communist-organized International Unemployment Day, March 6, 1930), Benjamin fell out of favor with the Comintern representative and was reassigned to Ohio. After a short stay there his health broke, and in the summer of 1931 as part of his recuperation he was sent overseas to participate in an international unemployment conference and to spend six weeks in Moscow, where he worked on a Comintern resolution dealing with unemployment in the United States.

Benjamin returned to the States in October 1931 and for the rest of the decade was director of Party work in the unemployed field. As such he was the chief spokesman for the Communist-sponsored Unemployed Councils, which despite a flashy start in 1930 had by the time Benjamin was put in charge of the organization failed to find a mass base despite the increasing number of jobless. Benjamin represented the Unemployed Councils before Congressional committees dealing with joblessness and unemployment benefits, at relief investigations studying what had and could be done, in front of rallies agitating for aid to the out-of-work, and on hunger marches (most of which were ill-fated propaganda demonstrations despite the dedication of those involved).

With the advent of the Popular Front in 1935, the Party line changed dramatically, and in 1936 Benjamin oversaw the merger of the Unemployed Councils into the Workers Alliance (created in 1935 as a result of the coming together of various unemployment and relief client groups). Benjamin was subsequently elected secretary-treasurer of the Alliance. He handled its day-to-day operations and continued his Party functions.

Changes resulting from the Nazi-Soviet Pact in August 1939 quickly exposed the Party's domination of the Alliance. Its non-Communist president and founder, David Lasser (q.v.), forced the resignation of Benjamin. But at the showdown between Lasser and the Communists in mid-1940 over who would dominate, Benjamin, even though he was no longer an Alliance officer, directed the executive board meeting, which ended with Lasser leaving the organization he had helped to create.

In 1940 Benjamin went to the International Workers Order, and in 1942 he was sent to St. Louis as the Party's district organizer. By the end of World War II he had left the Party and gone into business. From 1953 until his retirement in 1978 he ran a store, the Pottery Fair, in the Georgetown section of Washington, D.C. Benjamin died of a heart ailment May 13, 1983, at the Hebrew Home in Rockville, Maryland.

*DANIEL LEAB*

**BENSON, ALLAN L. (1871–1940).** Allan L. Benson was a journalist and writer who was the Socialist candidate for U.S. President in 1916. Born in Plainwell, Michigan, in 1871, of Pilgrim and pioneer stock, he was educated in the public schools of Otsego, Michigan. Beginning in the early 1890s, Benson worked as a journalist on daily newspapers in Chicago, Salt Lake City, and San Francisco.

After 1897 he was managing editor of major metropolitan newspapers, including the *Detroit Journal* (1897–1901), the *Detroit Times* (1901–1906), and the *Washington (D.C.) Times* (1906–1907). He resigned from the *Washington Times* in 1907 in order to devote full time to writing articles for the progressive, pro-Socialist *Pearson's Magazine* and for the Socialist weekly newspaper *Appeal to Reason*. The combined circulation of both publications amounted to almost one million. During this period Benson also wrote several pamphlets and books, which sold millions of copies. His major works while he was a Socialist included *Socialism Made Plain* (1904), *The Usurped Power of the Courts* (1911), *The Growing Grocery Bill* (1912), *The Truth About Socialism* (1913), *Our Dishonest Constitution* (1914), *A Way to Prevent War* (1915), and *Inviting War to America* (1916).

His articles in mass circulation publications made Benson a household name among American Socialists. Thus when Eugene V. Debs (q.v.) refused to be the Socialist candidate for U.S. President in 1916 and the party's National Executive Committee decided to choose its candidate for President by referendum instead of convention, Benson was nominated.

The campaign turned out to be a disaster. Benson was a lukewarm Socialist who claimed to have been converted by reading an article on socialism by British playwright George Bernard Shaw—a member of the British Fabian Society—in the Encyclopaedia Britannica. He campaigned primarily on the war issue. His only major campaign proposal was a suggestion that the U.S. Congress be prohibited from declaring a war of aggression without support by popular referendum. Moreover, many Socialists, left wing and right wing, were backing Democrat Woodrow Wilson in his reelection campaign. In the end Benson polled 585,000 votes nationally.

When in 1917—soon after war was declared by Wilson—the Socialist Party convention decided to oppose American participation in the war, Benson objected. He now favored the war. As the Socialist candidate for U.S. President at the election immediately preceding, Benson attempted to use his influence within the party to have it reverse its stand. When it became apparent that the Socialists would not change their position, Benson resigned from the party with a stinging attack on its leadership [as quoted in *Revolutionary Radicalism*, vol. I, pp. 546–547]:

The present foreign-born leaders of the American Socialist Party, if they had lived during the Civil War would doubtless have censured Marx for congratulating Lincoln.

...I now take leave of the Socialist Party a year after I ceased to agree with it. It seemed to me that having been at the head of the national ticket, two years ago, it was particularly my duty to wait and see if the party would not right itself. It has not righted itself. I, therefore, resign as a protest against the foreign-born leadership that blindly believes a non-American policy can be made to appeal to many Americans.

After the war, Benson founded a short-lived magazine in Baltimore, wrote popular books about Henry Ford, Daniel Webster, and geology, and wrote articles about popular, nonpolitical subjects until 1930. He died in August 1940 in Yonkers, New York.

SOURCES: Joint Legislative Committee Investigating Seditious Activities, *Revolutionary Radicalism* (1920); *National Encyclopedia of American Biography*; David A. Shannon, *The Socialist Party of America* (1955).

*BERNARD K. JOHNPOLL*

**BENSON, ELMER (1895–1985).** Elmer Austin Benson served as Minnesota U.S. Senator and governor and a national chairman of Henry Wallace's Progressive Party. He brought the Communist Party into mainstream Minnesota politics and aided left-wing causes throughout his life.

Benson was born of Norwegian immigrant parents in Appleton, Minnesota, on September 22, 1895. His father owned a general store and farm in that small rural town. Elmer was raised in the Norwegian Lutheran Church but attended only occasionally in later life. In 1915 he entered the St. Paul College of Law, but was drafted during World War I and served in Europe in a noncombat post. After discharge he was admitted to the bar. He returned to Appleton to become a partner in a clothing store and to marry. Later he became the manager of a local bank.

Benson was active in Minnesota's Farm-Labor movement in the early 1920s. In 1933 Governor Floyd Olson (Farmer-Labor) made Benson his banking commissioner. In December 1935 Olson appointed Benson to the U.S. Senate to serve out the term of an incumbent who had died. As U.S. Senator, Benson called for social ownership of key industries and introduced the Antiwar Propaganda Bill, which made it a crime to publish false information inciting war, and the National Youth Act, providing for a massive youth aid program.

Benson ran for governor of Minnesota in 1936 and defeated his Republican opponent by 225,000 votes. As governor, Benson controlled the Farmer-Labor Party, welcomed Communists into the Farmer-Labor movement, and became a national spokesman for Popular Front causes. Benson's legislative program was an ambitious collection of advanced New Deal measures, but only a portion became law. Although he was an eloquent spokesman for social justice, Benson was an inept governor. His uncompromising personality offended many Farmer-Labor constituencies. In 1938 a Republican buried Benson's reelection bid by a 292,000-vote margin. After leaving office, Benson became wealthy through land speculation.

In 1940 he took the leadership of the Farmer-Labor Party's Popular Front wing in its battles with an anti-Communist faction and became chairman of the Farmer-Labor organization in 1941. In 1944 he played a decisive role in the merger of the Farmer-Labor Party with the Minnesota Democratic Party to form the Democratic-Farmer-Labor Party (DFL). In 1944 he also became chairman of the National Citizens Political Action Committee (NCPAC), the nation's largest left-wing political organization. Later the NCPAC became the Progressive Citizens of America and the foundation of Wallace's Progressive Party. In 1946 Benson's faction took control of the Minnesota DFL Party and in 1948 attempted to make it the Progressive Party state affiliate. Benson was defeated by the DFL's anti-Communist wing under Hubert Humphrey.

In the early 1950s Benson contracted encephalitis and was forced to reduce his public activities. However, he continued to support left-wing activities. He died in 1985.

SOURCES: John E. Haynes, *Dubious Alliance: The Making of Minnesota's DFL Party* (1984); James M. Shields, *Mr. Progressive: A Biography of Elmer A. Benson* (1971).

*JOHN E. HAYNES*

**BERGER, META (1873–1944).** Meta Berger was a leading Milwaukee Socialist official, a feminist, and later a pro-Communist. Born Meta Schlichtling in Milwaukee in 1873, of upper middle-class parentage, she married Victor Berger (q.v.), leader of the Socialist Party in that city, shortly before the turn of the century.

Meta Berger played a leading role in Socialist political campaigns between 1902 and 1936. She was elected to the Milwaukee school board in 1919 and served for the next thirty years, retiring in 1939. She also served on the Wisconsin state board of education from 1917 to 1919 and on the board of regents of the State Normal School (now the University of Wisconsin at Milwaukee) from 1928 to 1934.

During most of her life Meta Berger was an active Socialist, serving for more than twenty years on the Milwaukee City Central Committee and the Wisconsin State Committee of the Socialist Party between 1907 and 1934. In 1929 she succeeded her husband on the National Committee of the party. Meta Berger was also a delegate to virtually all Socialist Party national conventions between 1909 and 1937. The Socialist Party leadership attempted to nominate Meta Berger as its vice-presidential candidate in 1928. She refused the nomination, supporting instead James H. Maurer (q.v.) of Reading, Pennsylvania.

During the first two decades of the century, Meta Berger was also active in the women's suffrage movement in Milwaukee, and she was a leading member of numerous women's civic organizations in that city. Beginning in 1930 she evinced considerable sympathy for the Soviet Union and the Communist movement. By 1936 she agreed with most of the Communist Party political line, although she remained a member of the Socialist Party. At the 1937 convention of the Socialist Party, Meta Berger called for "collective security" with the Soviet Union and the "other democracies" against the threat of fascism, which was then the official position of the Communist Party. This action alienated her from the pacifist Socialist leadership. When, with the signing of the Hitler-Stalin Pact of August 1939, the Communist Party line changed to one of militant isolationism, Meta Berger also changed her position. In June 1941, after Hitler invaded the Soviet Union, the Communist line changed to extreme interventionism, and she shifted her line and proclaimed her support for the war in strident terms. She had by this time left the Socialist Party (May 2, 1940). Two years earlier she had reportedly joined the Communist Party.

Meta Berger died in Milwaukee on June 16, 1944.

SOURCE: *Dictionary of Wisconsin Biography* (1960).

*JAMES INGEBRETSEN*

**BERGER, VICTOR L. (1860–1929).** Victor L. Berger was a founder of the American Socialist Party, a controlling force in the powerful Milwaukee Socialist organization, leader of the right wing of the national party during the period of its greatest strength, a member of the U.S. House of Representatives from 1911 to 1913 and from 1923 to 1929, and editor of the most powerful Socialist newspaper in the United States, the *Milwaukee Leader*, from 1911 to 1929.

He was born in 1860 in the small city of Nieder-Rehbach in the Hungarian-Ukrainian-German region of the Austro-Hungarian Empire. Berger considered himself an ethnic German who was born a Jew. He graduated from a German-language gymnasium and studied at, but never graduated from, the Universities of Budapest and Vienna.

In 1878 his father suffered severe financial reverses, and Berger found it necessary to leave Austria-Hungary for the United States. After short stays in New York and Chicago, he finally settled permanently in Milwaukee in 1880. During his early years there he worked as a metal polisher and as a teacher in the public schools and at B'nai Jeshurun synagogue.

Soon after arriving in Milwaukee, Berger joined the South Side *Turnverein* (gymnastic union), where he came in contact with German Socialists who then dominated the intellectual life of the city. Berger's ability as an organizer was recognized almost at once by the other members, and he was elected president of the union.

Converted to socialism in the *Turnverein*, Berger immediately devoted all his free time to his new ideal. Because of his organizational and writing ability, he was named editor of the weekly *Arbeiter Zeitung* and later of the new Socialist daily, *Wisconsin Vorwaerts*.

The Milwaukee Socialists were a purely local organization. They refused to affiliate with the Socialist Labor Party (SLP), then under the control of the acerbic, vindictive, and vituperative Daniel DeLeon (q.v.). They affiliated instead with the then-powerful, loosely organized social reformist People's (Populist) Party. The Socialists also had a close relationship with the local affiliate of the American Federation of Labor—the Federated Trades Council of Milwaukee. In the 1893 municipal election, the joint Socialist-Populist ticket came close to capturing the city, but within three years the alliance collapsed over the presidential nomination.

Berger led the Milwaukee delegation to the 1886 Populist national convention in St. Louis. He attempted there to win the presidential nomination for Eugene V. Debs (q.v.), leader of the American Railway Union (ARU), whom he had converted to socialism, but the convention nominated instead the Democratic candidate, William Jennings Bryan, on a free silver platform.

The Debs-Berger friendship had begun in 1894, when Berger visited Debs in jail, where he was serving a sentence for defying an injunction during the ARU strike against the Pullman Company. At these meetings Berger convinced Debs of the efficacy of socialism as an instrument for liberating the working class from "wage slavery." He also convinced Debs to turn the ARU into a Socialist organization. Debs refused to act until after the 1896 election, in which he supported Bryan.

The next year Debs reorganized the ARU into the Social Democracy of America (SDA), committed to a form of Owensian (see Robert Owen) communitarian Socialist scheme. The SDA hoped to set up communities in a single sparsely-populated state which would eventually be turned into a Socialist Utopia. Berger and his Milwaukee followers joined the new organization but rejected its communitarian dream. They hoped to wean it away from the colonization scheme and turn it into an electoral organization.

At the 1898 convention of the SDA, Berger convinced Debs and the Eastern Social Democrats—mainly Jews and Germans who had bolted DeLeon's Socialist Labor Party a year earlier—to withdraw from the SDA and form the new Social Democratic Party. The new party tasted electoral victory within a few months. Two of its members were elected mayors, three were elected state representatives in Massachusetts, and the Milwaukee party polled a respectable 5 percent of the total vote cast in the 1898 municipal election. The Massachusetts election victories proved to be ephemeral. The Milwaukee party, under Berger's tutelage, remained a political power for more than half a century.

In 1900 the Social Democrats joined with a new group, which had withdrawn from DeLeon's party in 1899, to run Debs for U.S. President. A year later the two groups merged into the Socialist Party of America. Berger, who had opposed changing the party's name from Social Democratic to Socialist and who had little faith in the recent converts from the SLP, was at first unhappy with the merger, although he accepted its inevitability. He soon found allies among the former SLPers, many of whom became his lifelong friends. But he insisted that the Wisconsin party retain the name Social Democratic.

During the next ten years, Berger turned the Milwaukee party into a powerful political machine. He developed neighborhood canvassing teams that spread Socialist propaganda door-to-door throughout the city. He also arranged for a continuing political liaison between the party and local labor and ethnic organizations. Berger himself ran for office virtually every year and polled large votes in most municipal elections as a candidate for mayor or alderman. In the Socialist sweep of Milwaukee in 1910, Berger was elected first to the board of aldermen and then to Congress, where he served for eight of the next eighteen years.

Besides electoral activity and Socialist journalism, Berger devoted himself primarily to the labor movement. As a regular delegate to conventions of the American Federation of Labor, he opposed the "business" unionism of Samuel Gompers as well as the dual union policies of DeLeon and the Industrial Workers of the World.

He and Gompers exhibited personal animosity toward each other. Gompers disliked Berger's linking of the Milwaukee city federation of the American Federation of Labor (AFL) and the local Socialist organization. And the labor leader strongly opposed Berger's philosophy of government intervention in labor relations even on the side of the trade unions. Berger, on the contrary, believed that Gompers' philosophy, especially his nonpartisan approach, was against the best interests of the trade union movement. He argued that American unions should support a party of their own—the Socialist Party—thus emulating their European counterparts.

Despite his antipathy for Gompers, the Milwaukee Socialist fought vigorously against the organization of any competing union federation—even one dedicated to socialism and Socialist political action. Thus, in 1905, Berger refused to participate in the organizing meeting of the Industrial Workers of the World (IWW). For this he was assailed by most "revolutionary" Socialists of the time, although Debs—himself an anti-AFL left-winger and a participant in the founding convention of the IWW—refused to condemn Berger's action. In fact, Debs himself soon left the IWW.

Berger's antagonism for the IWW did not prevent him from aiding striking members of the radical union organization. He used his position in the House of Representatives to aid the IWW textile strikers in Lawrence, Massachusetts, in 1912. By a series of parliamentary maneuvers he turned a committee hearing on the advisability of an investigation of the strike into a full-scale probe of the conditions that led to the strike and the repression during the strike. He thus scored a major public relations victory for the hard-pressed strikers.

His other activities in Congress during his first term included introduction of major social reform legislation. Among the bills he offered were proposals for old-age pensions, health insurance, unemployment insurance, women's suffrage, public ownership of radio-telegraphy and railroads, public works to alleviate the distress caused by unemployment, and the withdrawal of American forces from Mexico.

The bills proposed by Berger were invariably defeated, but they formed the foundation for much of the social legislation that was passed under Democratic President Franklin D. Roosevelt more than twenty years later. Old-age benefits were part of the Social Security legislation enacted during the 1930s; child labor was outlawed at the same time; public works as a means of alleviating unemployment was effectuated by Roosevelt in the Public Works Administration, the Civilian Conservation Corps, and the Works Progress Administration. Women won the right to vote in 1919, and health insurance for the poor and the elderly was enacted in the 1960s. Only on the issues of public ownership and use of American troops in Latin America have Berger's proposals been ignored.

The legislation Berger proposed was based on his overall Socialist philosophy. He believed that socialism would come into being gradually—over a long period of time, possibly a century or more—because of economic and social forces rather than political forces. In a 1909 article in the *Saturday Evening Post*, he rejected the assumption that a Socialist victory would usher in the new system. Only historical development could, he argued, result in socialism.

The primary role of the Socialist Party was to ease the path of society into socialism. This could be achieved primarily by enacting social reform measures that would make life on earth more palatable. Moreover, these reforms would all be socialistic in essence and would thus make the Socialist system itself more humane. The only other role of the party that Berger recognized was educational: developing among workers an understanding of their role in history, in society, and in the system they would help build and control.

Berger rejected the hide-bound political "Marxism" that dominated the Socialist thought of the time. As early as 1901, within two years after it had been first published in German, Berger published Eduard Bernstein's major work in revisionist thought, *Evolutionary Socialism*, in his newspapers. But Berger did not totally abandon Marx or his teachings. Like Marx, he accepted the thesis that capitalism was a necessary step in history. "The capitalist system was a step in . . . evolution . . . but only a step. It has now outlived its usefulness. . . . Therefore it must pass away."

The socialism that Berger believed in was basically the socialism that most of the so-called Marxists of the early years of the twentieth century favored. His definition of a socialist system was "collective ownership of all the social means of production and distribution in the interest of the whole people . . . carried out gradually and logically." It was to be carried out under basic political liberty, the right of free expression and of dissent.

Berger was a man of the early twentieth century, and he held many of the prejudices of that period. Like most other white Americans of the period, he assumed that blacks were inferior, but he was not at all a virulent racist. He believed, for example, that the inferiority came from environment rather than inheritance and that blacks would be fully equal to whites once socialism was established—for he believed that socialism was the cure for all society's ills.

He held a classic Socialist view of his fellow Jews. Although he never denied that he was of Jewish origin, Berger considered himself to be a German-American by culture. He vehemently rejected all religion and any sort of nationalism. However, he modified his view during World War I and the period immediately thereafter, when Jews suffered from pogroms in Poland, the Ukraine, Russia, and the rest of Eastern Europe. Then, like Debs, he supported the idea of a Jewish homeland, where Jews would be safe from persecution, in Palestine.

After his defeat in the 1912 election, Berger maintained his leadership of the Wisconsin party and the national party's right wing. And he continued to edit the daily *Milwaukee Leader*.

The outbreak of the war in Europe in 1914 placed Berger in a dilemma. The area in which he lived was strongly pro-German. He was personally opposed to any war and to the Kaiser's regime. But his strong opposition to the autocratic czarist regime in Russia led him to defend—but not support—the action of the German Social Democrats who backed the Kaiser's declaration of war. Germany, he maintained, was facing an invasion from Russia and there was little else that Social Democrats could do. Likewise, Berger explained away the sinking of the arms-laden British passenger liner *Lusitania* as a necessary, if brutal, act of war. Most other Socialists were horrified by the torpedoing and the loss of life by what Debs called "this barbaric act."

When the United States entered the war in April 1917, the Socialist Party passed an anti-war resolution that Berger backed wholeheartedly. As a result of the declaration, there was almost immediate persecution of Socialists as pro-Kaiser opponents of the war effort. Berger was among those most severely persecuted. His *Milwaukee Leader* was denied all mailing rights by the postal authorities, and advertisers in his newspaper were virtually forced by the government to withdraw from its pages. The *Leader* thus suffered severe losses in circulation and advertising revenue; only the devotion and sacrifice of Milwaukee's Socialists and their leader kept the newspaper alive for another twenty-one years.

Berger and four other party leaders were arrested and sentenced to twenty years each for opposing the war. At his sentencing Berger refused to bow from his position. He told the court that

Socialism taught that modern wars were mostly struggles over business and commercial interests. Socialists held that these struggles should not interest the modern working class in any country. The wage-workers—the men and women who work with brain or brawn—were mainly interested in peace and in improving the conditions of their class, which formed the overwhelming majority of every civilized nation.

Judge Kennesaw Mountain Landis' harsh sentence was overturned by the Supreme Court in 1921. During the war years, Berger scored his most spectacular electoral feat. More than 114,000 Wisconsin voters—almost one in four—sup-

ported him in a special election for the U.S. Senate in February 1918. It was
the largest vote ever cast for a Socialist in Wisconsin. Several counties, which
had previously been considered rock-ribbed Republican, were carried by Berger.
In November 1918 Berger was again elected to the House of Representatives
from his Milwaukee district, but he was denied his seat by the members of the
House because of his opposition to the war. In a special election, he was again
elected, and again was denied his seat—even though the war was over by then.

In 1922 the voters of the district again sent Berger to the House. This time
he was allowed to serve. He was reelected in 1924 and 1926. He used his position
in the House to send out Socialist propaganda under his Congressional mailing
frank, and he again proposed and fought for social reforms and pro-labor-union
legislation.

Berger's career in Congress ended with his defeat in the 1928 election, caused
in great part by the refusal of the Socialist Party national convention or its
presidential candidate, Norman M. Thomas (q.v.), to call for repeal of the
Eighteenth Amendment to the Constitution, which prohibited the production and
sale of all alcoholic beverages (brewing was a major industry in pre-Prohibition
Milwaukee).

On August 29, 1929, less than ten months after his defeat, Berger stepped
into the path of a streetcar and was killed. Thousands of Milwaukeeans attended
his funeral.

SOURCES: David Shannon, *The Socialist Party of America* (1955); Marvin Wachman,
*History of the Social Democratic Party of Milwaukee* (1945); Victor Berger's speeches
and editorials appear in *The Voice and Pen of Victor Berger: Milwaukee Leader* (1929).

*BERNARD K. JOHNPOLL*

**BERKMAN, ALEXANDER (1870–1936).** Alexander Berkman was, with Emma
Goldman (q.v.), the leading anarchist in the United States between 1906 and
1918. Born in Vilno, Russia, in 1870, of wealthy Jewish parents, Berkman was
raised in St. Petersburg, the imperial capital. His family was permitted to live
in the capital—normally barred to Jews—because of his father's status as a
leading businessman. His mother's brother, Mark Natanson, had been a leader
of the Narodnaya Volya, the Populist anarchist revolutionary underground society
that plotted the overthrow of the czar. Natanson was Alexander's lifelong hero.

From his earliest years Alexander was precocious and rebellious. He was
ousted from school because he was refractory and uncontrollable. His father died
when Alexander was 13 years old. The family was forced to move to Kovno
because the law barred them from St. Petersburg once the father was dead.
Within four years of his father's death, Alexander's mother also died. Young
Berkman left Russia—and Europe—for the freer United States. He arrived in
the United States three months after the execution of the four condemned
Haymarket anarchists.

Berkman was repelled by the brutality of the state's action in the Haymarket
affair and affiliated almost immediately with the Jewish anarchist group and the

firebrand anarcho-terrorist Johann Most (q.v.). At this time he also met and became enamored of his lifelong partner in revolution, Emma Goldman (q.v.). In 1892 he, Emma, and an artist friend opened a small lunchroom in Worcester, Massachusetts.

At the same time, a strike of steelworkers broke out in Homestead, a suburb of Pittsburgh. The plant's managing director, Henry Clay Frick, had employed a private army of Pinkerton thugs and state militia to put down the strikers in bloodshed. Berkman was incensed by the brutal attack on the striking steelworkers and pledged revenge. He went to Pittsburgh, somehow gained admission to Frick's private office, and there tried to shoot the steel magnate to death. But the 22-year-old Berkman was a poor shot. He barely injured Frick. Berkman was arrested, tried, and convicted of the shooting. He served in the state penitentiary from 1892 until 1906—to age 36.

Berkman's attack on Frick was in keeping with his political philosophy—a combination of libertarian anarchism and romantic bravado. Life without a high purpose, without revolutionary ideals, was worthless, he argued. Only a life dedicated to the creation of a just society without government was, for Berkman, worth living. He insisted that man-made law was at the root of all social maladies. The sole purpose of such law, he said, was to "enslave and oppress humanity." Because he opposed man-made law, he also rejected the whole concept of legal justice. "What a travesty! They are mutually exclusive terms."

He rejected more than the law; he also rejected the idea of a universal morality. For example, murder might be considered immoral under such normal conditions, but for the revolutionist it was an ethical, moral act because the end justified the means. "All means are justified in the war of humanity against its enemies." And to those who would argue that he had made those who loved him suffer, Berkman denied that the true revolutionist could love any other human being, as he argued in his 1929 work, *Now and After*:

The revolutionist has no personal right to anything. Everything he has or earns belongs to the cause. Everything even his affections. Mere human sentiment is unworthy of the real revolutionist. . . . The soldier of the revolution must not be lured from the field of battle by the siren song of love.

Released from prison in 1906, Berkman was still an anarchist, but a much-changed revolutionist, for he had now lost his faith in violence and terrorism. In prison he had read most of the classics and had a more humane view of revolution and of society. He spent the first ten years of his freedom helping Emma Goldman edit her journal *Mother Earth* and her book *Anarchism and Other Essays*, which appeared in 1911. He also helped found and run the Modern School in New Jersey, which was named for the Spanish libertarian educator Francisco Ferrer (who was executed in 1909 by the clerical, authoritarian Spanish government). In 1912 Berkman used his talents to raise money for the textile strikers in Lawrence, Massachusetts, and two years later he raised funds for the homeless victims of the Ludlow massacre of union miners families in Colorado.

Unhappy in New York, Berkman went to California to edit his own newspaper, *Blast*, which he started in 1916. It was as editor of *Blast* that he again gained national prominence as he led the struggle that eventually saved Thomas Mooney (q.v.) from execution for a dynamiting in which he played no role. (Mooney and his co-defendant Warren K. Billings [q.v.], who was given life in prison, were freed in 1939.)

With war raging in Europe and threatening to engulf the United States, Berkman and Emma Goldman founded the No-Conscription League. Once the United States became involved in the war, the League was suppressed. Berkman continued his agitation against the draft, advising young people to refuse to be forced into the army. For this he was arrested and sentenced to two years in federal prison.

Upon his release from prison Berkman was deported—along with Emma Goldman and others—to Russia. Although he went to Russia full of hope, he soon became totally disillusioned, as Bolsheviks arrested all dissenters, dispersed the army of peasant leader quasi-anarchist Nester Makhno, and created an overbearing bureaucracy. Finally the crushing of the rebellion of the Kronstadt naval barracks convinced Berkman to leave Russia. He went first to Stockholm, from there to Berlin, and finally to France.

In 1925 Berkman published a book on Russia under the Bolsheviks called *The Bolshevik Myth*. Boni & Liveright, the publishers, refused to publish the final chapter because it was too strongly anti-Bolshevik, so Berkman arranged to have it published as a separate short work. In the larger work, Berkman declared that "The embers of hope had died out. Terror and despotism had crushed the life born in October, 1917. Dictatorship had trampled the masses underfoot. The revolution was dead."

In 1929 he was approached by the Jewish Anarchist Federation of New York to write a primer for the anarchist-Communist movement. The result was the standard twentieth-century work on anarchism, *Now and After: The ABC of Anarchist Communism*, a simplistic attack on capitalism and political socialism and communism. In almost Marxian terms Berkman argued that labor had created everything. And, he added, all the wealth of the world had been stolen from the workers by the capitalists. What is needed, he concluded, was a new system of free workers communes, producing for use and not for profit, in a world devoid of compulsion. It was a dream of a world in which all would share in the world's bounty. To those who argued that Berkman was describing the perfect Christian society, as Norman Thomas (q.v.) would three years later, Berkman answered that Christianity could not achieve his ideal because it is "the greatest sham and shame of humanity . . . a complete failure because the Christian appeal is a lie."

*Now and After* would be his last work. Soon Berkman became extremely ill. The pain and his debilitation (he had lost his eyesight) became too much to bear, and at age 66 he committed suicide in June 1936.

SOURCES: Works by Alexander Berkman: *The Bolshevik Myth* (1925), the concluding chapter of which had to be published by Berkman in Berlin as a separate pamphlet:

*Now and After: The ABC of Anarchist Communism* (1929); *Prison Memoirs of an Anarchist* (1912), several later editions of which were published in paperback. Berkman's personal papers are at the Institute for Social History in Amsterdam, the Netherlands. See also Richard Drinnon, *Rebel in Paradise* (1961); Emma Goldman, *Living My Life* (1931); James Joll, *The Anarchists* (1964); George Woodcock, *Anarchism* (1962).

*LILLIAN KIRTZMAN JOHNPOLL*

**BERRIGAN, DANIEL (b. 1921) and PHILIP (b. 1923).** Daniel and Philip Berrigan were activist priests who played an important role in the New Left movement of the 1960s. The names of the Berrigan brothers were constantly before the public from 1967 through 1972. They were sons of Tom Berrigan, an Irish immigrant, and Freida Fromhart, a German immigrant. Their father was a union organizer and their mother was a devout Roman Catholic.

Daniel, born on May 9, 1921, in Virginia, Minnesota, was accepted at the Jesuit seminary in Poughkeepsie, New York, at age 18. After spending time at Woodstock College in Maryland, he was ordained in 1952. After a year in Europe, primarily in France, where he became interested in the worker-priest movement, he returned to the United States as a teacher in the Brooklyn Preparatory School, where he became associated with the Young Christian Workers program of social work in the Brooklyn slums. In 1956 he became a professor of religion at Le Moyne College in Syracuse, where he once again became active in anti-poverty groups.

Philip, born on October 5, 1923, in Two Harbors, Minnesota, entered St. Michael's College in Toronto, Ontario, in 1942 but was drafted and spent the duration of the war in the army. After the war he entered Holy Cross College, graduated in 1950, and was ordained in 1955. In 1956 he was teaching at a Catholic high school in New Orleans.

Beginning in the mid–1950s the brothers took up the cause of civil rights in the South, where they participated in demonstrations. By 1964 both had returned to New York—Philip had a parish in Newburg, and Daniel was in New York City editing *Jesuit Missions*. In 1964 they were among the founders of the Catholic Peace Fellowship, the first anti–Vietnam War group founded by Catholics. Both became outspoken critics of the Vietnam War, and in 1967 they began to pursue more direct action. Daniel, who had moved to Baltimore in 1965, was arrested during the October 22 march on the Pentagon. Philip was arrested on October 27 after he and a group of supporters poured blood over the records of a Baltimore draft board. Neither was sent to jail for those incidents, but on May 17, 1968, both were arrested after they entered the draft board offices in Catonsville, Maryland, seized records, and burned them before newsmen. Their 1968 trial for the Catonsville incident provided a forum for expression of their anti-war views. For his actions Philip spent more than three years in federal prison; Daniel spent eighteen months. Daniel was released in February 1972; Philip was paroled in November 1972.

Philip was the subject of another newsworthy trial in early 1972 that stemmed from federal indictments gained against him and seven others, the so-called Harrisburg Eight, for plotting a bombing and the kidnapping of Henry Kissinger. An additional charge against Philip was that he had smuggled letters into prison; he was subsequently convicted of the last charge only. His conviction, and that of cohort Sister Elizabeth McAlister for the same offense, were the only convictions arising from the trial of the Harrisburg Eight. Philip left the priesthood in 1973 after revealing that he had married McAlister in January 1972 while he was in Danbury Prison.

Daniel continues to work with New York peace groups, and also counsels victims of Acquired Immune Deficiency Syndrome. Philip remains active in peace and anti-nuclear activities and has continued to publish works of social and religious commentary.

SOURCES: Daniel Berrigan, *The Trial of the Catonsville Nine* (1970); Philip Berrigan, *Prison Journals of a Priest Revolutionary* (1970) and *Widen the Prison Gates* (1973); Richard Curtis, *The Berrigan Brothers: The Story of Daniel and Philip Berrigan* (1974).

*TOM WILLIAMS*

**BILLINGS, WARREN K. (1893–1972).** Warren K. Billings was a trade union activist and Socialist who, along with Thomas Mooney (q.v.), served more than twenty years in prison for the bombing of a San Francisco Preparedness Day parade in 1916. Billings was born in Middletown, New York, in 1893, of working-class parents. He was raised in Brooklyn, where he received a grammar school education. In 1913 he moved to San Francisco and soon became active in the shoeworkers union. During a strike in which he acted as a spy for the union, he was shot and wounded by a strikebreaker.

He was then elected president of the local shoeworkers union and a delegate to the San Francisco Labor Council. He was considered a good organizer and helped lead that union during a strike. At that time he assisted Mooney during an organization drive among employees of the Pacific Gas and Electric Company. Billings was arrested and subsequently convicted of carrying a valise full of dynamite. There is considerable evidence that the dynamite was planted on him by anti-union forces. He served fourteen months for that affair.

In the spring of 1916 Billings worked with Mooney in organizing and leading a futile strike of San Francisco streetcar workers. Later that year he and Mooney were accused of bombing a Preparedness Day parade in San Francisco; ten people were killed and fifty were injured.

Despite strong evidence that they were some distance away at the time of the bombing, Mooney and Billings were convicted. Mooney was watching the parade from a roof more than a mile from where the explosion occurred, and Billings was sabotaging strikebreakers' autos—far from the parade—for the Mechanics Union, which was then on strike.

Mooney and Billings were both finally sentenced to life in prison. The federal Wickersham Commission, composed of conservatives, later investigated the case and found that neither the police nor the district attorney had made any effort to find the actual perpetrator of the bombing. It said the sole aim had been to convict Mooney and Billings, whether they were guilty or innocent. Efforts by President Woodrow Wilson to have the two men freed were ignored, and they were imprisoned from 1917 until 1939. While in Folsom Prison, Billings taught himself the watchmaker's trade.

Following worldwide protests, Mooney and Billings were released in 1939, but Billings was refused a pardon. He was finally pardoned in 1961 by California Governor Edmund M. Brown. After his release Billings worked as a watchmaker in the San Francisco Bay area and served on the executive board of the Watchmakers Union. He withdrew from radical politics. Billings died in Redwood City, California, in December 1972.

*BERNARD K. JOHNPOLL*

**BITTELMAN, ALEXANDER (1890–1982).** Alexander Bittelman was one of the founders of the Jewish Communist movement in the United States, an important figure in the Communist Party's factional wars in the 1920s, and an important theoretician for many years before his expulsion for revisionism.

Bittelman was born on January 9, 1890, in Berdichev in the Ukraine. His father was a shoemaker. Alexander grew up in Berdichev and Odessa. He attended a Jewish school for several years before being apprenticed to a printer. At age 13 he joined the Jewish Bund and participated in strikes and anti-government demonstrations. When anti-Jewish pogroms broke out in 1905, Bittelman was active in forming self-defense units. That same year he became a Bund functionary.

After a brief trip to Paris with his father, Bittelman returned to Russia, working in the printing industry and continuing his union and Bund activities. He was frequently arrested and finally sent into exile to Archangelsk for two years in 1909. Facing induction into the army and continued political persecution, he left Russia and arrived in the United States early in 1912.

Settling in New York, Bittelman worked as a printer and attended Cooper Union. Early in 1915 he joined the Jewish Socialist Federation and became active in its work. In Russia, Bittelman had been torn between the positions of the Bolsheviks and Mensheviks, although leaning toward the former. In 1919 he became one of the leaders of the pro-Bolshevik left wing in the Socialist Party and editor of its organ, *Der Kampf*. He led the Left out of the party that year and became secretary of the Jewish Federation of the largely foreign-language Communist Party of the United States (CPUSA).

Bittelman was one of the few leaders of the foreign-language federations who successfully made the transition to general Party work in the 1920s. In fact, he was briefly expelled from the CPUSA in early 1921 for supporting unity with the more Americanized United Communist Party. Early in the decade Bittelman became allied with William Z. Foster (q.v.) in a Party faction that opposed first Charles Ruthenberg (q.v.) and then Jay Lovestone (q.v.). Foster, defensive about his lack of background in Marxist theory, relied on Bittelman as his theoretician and interpreter of Soviet policies.

As Foster's chief henchman, Bittelman was a key figure in the factional battles that convulsed the Party and to punish the Foster faction was briefly dropped from the Political Committee in 1925 on orders from the Comintern's representative in the United States. When the dispirited Foster hesitated to embrace dual unionism, which had been ordered by the Comintern in 1928, Bittelman led the assault on his old chief and was briefly recognized as the new leader of the opposition to the Party leadership.

Bittelman had been one of the leading opponents of Lovestone's advocacy of American exceptionalism, arguing against it at the 1928 Sixth World Congress of the Comintern. He did not benefit, however, when the Comintern intervened in the CPUSA and removed Lovestone from power in 1929. One of its decisions was to withdraw Bittelman, one of the leading factionalists, from the United States. Appointed vice-chairman of the Far Eastern secretariat, Bittelman went to India early in 1930 as a Comintern representative. The British soon expelled him.

Bittelman returned to the United States in 1931 in poor health and without being welcomed back into the Party leadership. After brief service with the Anti-Imperialist League, he moved to Southern California, where he aided the district Party. In the summer of 1934 Bittelman returned to New York to work in the propaganda department. He was soon given greater responsibility, supervising the "Questions and Answers" column in the *Daily Worker* and, beginning in 1936, writing a monthly "Review of the Month" to lead off every issue of the theoretical magazine, *The Communist*. He also resumed his position on the Party's Politburo.

Bittelman frequently clashed with Party leader Earl Browder (q.v.) during the Popular Front years, pushing for more militant policies and warning against embracing Franklin Roosevelt and John L. Lewis too enthusiastically. After the Nazi-Soviet Pact of 1939, Bittelman and Foster led the faction in the Politburo most anxious to break with the New Deal and return to the ultra-left policies of the early 1930s.

During World War II, Browder, once again firmly in control of the Party machinery, shunted Bittelman aside. Bittelman became the Communists' overseer of work among Jews. In 1948 he obediently purged the Party's Jewish schools for children of their Jewish content in response to Soviet policies attacking Jewish institutions. Early in the 1950s he was one of the "second-string" Party leaders indicted and convicted in New York on charges of violating the Smith Act. After his release from prison, Bittelman called for a reevaluation of Party policy and a less doctrinaire approach to socialism. In a series of articles entitled "I Take a Fresh Look," he adopted some of the very positions he had so fervently denounced when they had been held by Lovestone and Browder. His views angered the Party leadership, and in 1959 Bittelman was expelled from the

Communist Party. He lived quietly in Croton-on-Hudson, New York, until his death in 1982.

SOURCES: Theodore Draper, *American Communism and Soviet Russia* (1960); Harvey Klehr, *The Heyday of American Communism* (1984).

*HARVEY KLEHR*

**BLANSHARD, PAUL (1892–1980).** Paul Blanshard was a leader of the Socialist Party and the pro-Socialist labor movement for eighteen years—from 1915 to 1933. He was especially active in its municipal reform campaign in New York City. In the early 1940s he led the anti-Communist wing of the American Labor Party. During the 1950s and 1960s, he was also a major critic of the Roman Catholic Church.

Paul and his twin brother Bland Blanshard were born in Fredericksburg, Ohio, a village of about 600 people, in 1892. Their father was an impoverished, sickly Congregational minister. The family lived in various Midwestern towns during Paul's early life. Both his parents died when Paul was a child. He was raised by his paternal grandparents (his grandfather was a Methodist minister). Blanshard was educated in Detroit public schools, the University of Michigan (from which he graduated in 1914), the Harvard Divinity School, and the Union Theological Seminary in New York. He later also graduated from the Brooklyn Law School.

Blanshard became active in the Socialist Party and the Clergymen's Socialist Alliance during 1915 while he was serving as head minister of the Maverick Church in East Boston. The church, located in a working-class area of the city, had a long history as a Social Gospel pulpit. Blanshard's predecessor was another Socialist, Albert Rhys Williams, who would later become a major American spokesman for the Russian Bolshevik Revolution.

In 1916 Blanshard moved to Tampa, Florida, where he was minister of the First Congregational Church, which also had a large Socialist membership. Much of Blanshard's energies in Tampa were devoted to opposing America's entry into World War I. Blanshard continued to oppose the war even after the United States had entered it. As a result, he and his church were ostracized and, despite pleading by his congregation, he resigned his pulpit. At this time Blanshard decided that Christianity was a fraud, and he wrote an article (under an assumed name) in the prestigious journal *Open Court* assailing his old religion.

Late in 1917 Blanshard moved to New York, where he attended Union Theological Seminary. After the war he accepted an appointment as an organizer with the Amalgamated Textile Workers Union (an offshoot of the Amalgamated Clothing Workers of America [ACWA]). He led that union's futile strike of mainly foreign-born workers in Utica, New York. He was fined $100 and served thirty days in Oneida County Jail during the strike for contempt of an anti-picketing injunction. After the strike was lost, Blanshard took a job as a presser in a unionized men's clothing factory.

A few months later he was named educational director of the ACWA in Rochester, New York, where he founded the Rochester Labor College, which offered lectures by Socialist, Communist, syndicalist, and civil-libertarian leaders. He also wrote pamphlets and articles in the *Outlook*, the *New Republic*, the *Nation*, and the *Survey*. He was active in the Socialist movement in Rochester, where he worked for formation of an American labor party similar to the British Labour Party. In 1923, after a summer in Great Britain, he wrote his first book, *An Outline of the British Labor Movement*. It was a paean of praise for that country's Labour Party and its leaders.

Blanshard was named field director of the pro-Socialist League for Industrial Democracy (LID) in 1924. The League was directed by Norman Thomas (q.v.) and Harry W. Laidler (q.v.). Blanshard organized its lecture tours and was himself sent on tour. Blanshard toured Soviet Russia and China while working for the LID. His reports from China in the *Nation* were generally anti-imperialist, but they also doubted the Russian Communist dedication to a free China. He was impressed with the Soviet Union's new social mores, which Stalin would soon abrogate, but he was distressed by the lack of civil rights and liberties in that country.

In 1926 Blanshard took a summer job on the editorial staff of the *Nation*. He remained "on and off" with the leading liberal magazine as a part-time and later full-time editorial associate until 1929. Blanshard's most important reportage for the *Nation* during the 1920s was a series of firsthand stories about the harsh realities of work in Southern textile mills.

In 1929 Blanshard became a director of the Socialist-led anti-Tammany movement, which named Norman Thomas as candidate for mayor. He helped Thomas amass a record 175,000 votes in that mayoralty campaign. The next year he was named executive director of the City Affairs Committee, a Socialist-led anti-corruption organization in New York. While serving as director of the committee, he co-authored *What's the Matter with New York* with Norman Thomas. The committee was the instigator of the Seabury investigation, which resulted in the ouster of Mayor Jimmy Walker in 1932 and began the process by which Tammany Hall was destroyed as a controlling political force in New York City.

During this period Blanshard was a member of the pro-Thomas "Militant" faction of the Socialist Party and was active in Thomas' 1932 presidential campaign. But a year later he left the party to support Fiorello LaGuardia, the victorious Fusion-Republican candidate for mayor. There were two reasons for Blanshard's support of LaGuardia. The first was his dislike for Charles Solomon (q.v.), the Old Guard Socialist Party candidate for mayor. The second reason was that he had reached the conclusion that reform could not be achieved without political victory. And he saw no chance of the Socialists winning a national, New York state, or New York city election in the foreseeable future.

LaGuardia named Blanshard his commissioner of accounts in 1935. In that post Blanshard forced out all the old Tammany officials, sending several to prison. He resigned his city post in 1937 to practice law in New York. During World War II, which he supported, Blanshard served with the State Department as an analyst of Caribbean affairs. Between 1939 and 1944 Blanshard was active in the American Labor Party in New York City, where he led the vain fight against Communist domination of the party.

After the war, Blanshard began research into church-state relationships. The result was his 1949 best-seller *American Freedom and Catholic Power*, some of which had first appeared in articles in the *Nation* in school libraries throughout the country. The book itself was denied advertising space in the *New York Times* and most other major dailies. Despite the ostracism, the book and its successor, *Communism, Democracy, and Catholic Power*, sold in the hundreds of thousands of copies. Michael Novak, the Roman Catholic social thinker, would later declare that Paul Blanshard had become something of a Catholic prophet. But the book itself and its author were considered an anathema by church leaders.

Blanshard spent the last ten years of his life as a writer and lecturer. He had, he wrote in his autobiography, become an absolute atheist, a secularist, and "a standard, socialistic pragmatist, infested with some non-violent dreams, non-Marxist dreams" who had become "skeptical about any ideological system." He died in St. Petersburg, Florida, in 1980.

SOURCE: Paul Blanshard, *Personal and Controversial: An Autobiography* (1973).

*BERNARD K. JOHNPOLL*

**BLISS, WILLIAM D. P. (1856–1926).** William Dwight Palmer Bliss was the leading Christian Socialist organizer and publicist at the end of the nineteenth century and beginning of the twentieth. The son of Congregational missionaries, he was born in Constantinople, Turkey, in 1856 and educated at Roberts College (an American college in Constantinople) and at Amherst College and the Hartford Theological Seminary in the United States.

Upon graduating from the Hartford Seminary in 1882, Bliss was ordained in the Congregational Church. He held only two Congregational pastorates: one in Denver, Colorado, and the other in South Natick, Massachusetts. While serving in the South Natick church in 1884, he resigned from the Congregational Church and became an Episcopalian. He converted to Episcopalianism because he favored its centralized, hierarchical form of organization, as opposed to the loose structure of Congregationalism. He was also impressed with the intellectual freedom that prevailed in his new church.

At the same time that he changed churches, Bliss was also converted to socialism. He used his position, first as layreader and then as deacon of the Episcopal church in the poor Western Massachusetts industrial town of Lee, to further the cause of socialism. In 1886 he organized a lodge of the Knights of Labor in that town.

Ordained an Episcopal priest in 1887, Bliss was immediately named rector of Grace Church in Boston. While serving in that parish, he organized the first Christian Socialist Society in America and began publication of a Socialist monthly, *The Dawn*, which he issued for the next seven years. While at Grace Church he was also instrumental in organizing the Church Association for the Advancement of the Interests of Labor, which propagandized for labor unions, cooperatives, profit-sharing, the eight-hour day, civil service reform, the Australian ballot, and land reform. He also joined the first of the Nationalist Clubs that evolved from Edward Bellamy's (q.v.) *Looking Backward.* He left that organization because of the ethereal nature of the Theosophist leadership of the club. In 1890 he organized the nondenominational Christian Socialist Church of the Carpenter in Boston.

Bliss' socialism was basically a combination of Christian and prophetic Judaic social teachings. He opposed nationalization of industry for its own sake. The lot of the workers would deteriorate under most governments then in existence should industry be nationalized, he argued. The objective of Bliss' socialism was to promote the brotherhood of humanity as Jesus had preached it. One of his followers aptly described Bliss' socialism as pre-Nicaean Christianity.

Although he was a Socialist who had addressed meetings of the Socialist Labor Party (SLP) before 1891, Bliss refused to join the party. By 1892 he was strongly opposed to its leadership, particularly Daniel DeLeon (q.v.), and openly opposed the SLP thereafter.

Bliss was active politically in the People's Party from 1892 until 1896. He was a delegate to the 1892 Populist convention and was active in its campaign, especially in the East and Midwest. Although disappointed in the Populists' failure to work for women's suffrage, he continued to support the party. In 1896 he worked for William Jennings Bryan and condemned Socialists for refusing to support "the Great Commoner." After the election of 1896, Bliss was inactive in electoral politics, although he supported Eugene V. Debs (q.v.) during his campaigns for U.S. President.

In 1895 Bliss edited the short-lived *American Fabian* and attempted unsuccessfully to organize an American Fabian Society. Thereafter he wrote and edited a number of Socialist books and compendia; held pastorates in Long Island, New Jersey, and Southern California; was president of the National Social Reform Union; was an investigator for the U.S. Department of Labor; and during World War I directed the educational work among interned French and Belgian troops in Switzerland.

After the war he was rector of St. Martha's Church in New York from 1921 to 1925. He died in New York City in 1926.

SOURCES: Bernard K. Johnpoll with Lillian Johnpoll, *The Impossible Dream* (1981); Howard H. Quint, *The Forging of American Socialism* (1953).

*BERNARD K. JOHNPOLL*

**BLOCK, S. JOHN (1880–1955).** A leading Socialist and labor attorney and administrator, S. John Block served in many official capacities in Socialist organizations between 1910 and 1936. Block was born in Cleveland, Ohio, of upper-middle-class parents in 1880. He was educated in the Cleveland public schools and entered New York's Columbia University in 1897, where he received a B.A. degree with distinction in 1900. The next year he was awarded an M.A.

degree from the same university. Three years later he graduated from the New York Law School and was admitted to the New York bar.

Block's interest in socialism began while he was a student at Columbia; he joined the Socialist Party in 1902. Block held many posts in the party, including chairmanship of the New York organization from 1916 to 1925. During his early years in the party, Block was important primarily because he was the counsel for many trade unions, including the New York locals of the Amalgamated Clothing Workers. With the entry of the United States into World War I, which he opposed, Block became a leading legal defender of the New York party, its members and its institutions, from the repression unleashed by Woodrow Wilson's wartime administration.

He defended the *New York Daily Call* from an attempt by the federal government to close it down in late 1917. Although Block failed to prevent the postmaster-general from revoking the daily's mailing privilege, his efforts helped prevent the immediate destruction of the paper. He also defended Scott Nearing (q.v.) and the Socialist Rand School at their trial for violation of the Espionage Act. After the war, Block served as counsel for the five Socialist members of the New York State Assembly in the 1920 proceedings that led to their ouster.

Between 1911 and 1924 Block was president of the Workingmen's Co-operative Publishing Association, which published the *New York Daily Call*. He also served on the board of the American Socialist Society, which operated the Rand School, the leading Socialist educational organization. The Socialist Party nominated him for many public offices, including attorney general of New York state and justice of the New York Supreme Court (in 1927, 1928, 1932, and 1933).

In 1934 Block sided with the more moderate wing of the party in its struggle against Norman Thomas (q.v.) and his more militant, younger followers. When the militant wing won control of the party in 1936, Block withdrew and supported the American Labor Party and Franklin D. Roosevelt in the 1936 election.

Block was named by New York Mayor Fiorello LaGuardia in 1935 to the New York City Charter Revision Commission. There he was instrumental in the enactment of proportional representation in the election of members to the city council. Mayor LaGuardia also named him an interim justice in the Court of Domestic Relations in 1942. He served for only thirty days.

An avowed anti-Communist, Block was a vice-president of the National Lawyers Guild for a short time. He was also a president of the Labor Press Association during the 1920s and served on the executive board of the American Civil Liberties Union during the 1920s and 1930s. Poor health forced him to retire from public life in 1946. He died on May 31, 1955, in New York City.

*BERNARD K. JOHNPOLL*

**BLOOR, ELLA REEVE (1862–1951).** Ella Reeve ("Mother") Bloor was a dedicated organizer, speaker, journalist, party official, and candidate for public office whose long years of activism spanned the development and decline of both the Socialist Party and the Communist Party. She was an ardent reformer who was more concerned with organization results than accumulation of personal power. She rose in the Communist Party to be one of the most visible women in its history.

Mother Bloor was born Ella Reeve on July 8, 1862, on Staten Island. The daughter of a prosperous druggist and his wife, she was the oldest of their twelve children. A member of a Yankee family with deep American roots, she traced her activism to ancestors who fought in the Revolution and the Civil War as well as to relatives who worked in the abolition and Greenback movements. Ella attended public school and, for a short time, finishing school before she was withdrawn to continue her education at home.

Ella Reeve Bloor's three marriages and the raising of her eight children were closely linked to her growing political awareness and commitments. Her first marriage to cousin Lucien Ware and her second marriage to Socialist Louis Cohen produced six children and two children respectively, and both ended in divorce. Bloor's third marriage to farmer and Communist candidate for Congress Andrew Omholt came in 1932 when the pair were working together in North Dakota. Two of her children followed her into active work in the Communist Party. Harold Ware (q.v.) worked on farm issues for the Communist Party until his death in an automobile accident in 1935. He previously had been awarded the Order of Lenin by the Soviet Union for his role in modernization of that nation's agriculture in the 1920s. Her youngest child, Carl Reeve, became a labor journalist who edited the *Labor Defender*.

Bloor started her activism in the temperance and suffrage movements. In her twenties she wrote and organized for the women's vote and was president of her local Women's Christian Temperance Union chapter. Her association with radical parties started with her membership in the Socialist Labor Party (SLP) in 1897. Bloor help organize the 1900 SLP convention and was a member of the executive board of its labor affiliate, the Socialist Trade and Labor Alliance. She jumped to the Socialist Party in 1902.

Between 1902 and 1919, when she left the party, Bloor was a devoted adherent who spoke and organized widely for the Socialist Party. She was an articulate and popular speaker at party gatherings and in strike support work on behalf of the party. She worked as an organizer for a number of state and local party branches, including New York, Ohio, and Connecticut, and twice ran for statewide office on the Socialist ticket. Ella was also a union organizer at home among miners, streetcar workers, and members of the needle trades. With Elizabeth Gurley Flynn (q.v.), she organized the Workers Defense Union, a legal-aid organization that assisted Socialists and radicals jailed during and after World War I.

At various times in her life, Ella Reeve Bloor worked as a journalist. Besides her work for radical newspapers, she also wrote articles on child labor, women's issues, and the conditions in the Chicago stockyards for such mainstream periodicals and newspapers as *Wilshire's Magazine, Pearson's Magazine*, and the Waterbury (Conn.) *American*. At Upton Sinclair's (q.v.) request, she testified before a Congressional delegation checking the validity of his novel, *The Jungle*, and later worked undercover for an exposé on noncompliance with meat inspection laws. When she traveled to Chicago in 1906 to give testimony in the company of friend and fellow Socialist Richard Bloor, Sinclair suggested that she appear as "Mrs. Bloor" to avoid any damaging scandal. Though she claimed no romantic association with Bloor, his name stuck and has remained as her most familiar surname.

Ella Reeve Bloor attended the 1919 Socialist Party convention as a left-wing delegate from Kansas City, Missouri. When both the convention and the left wing split, she became a founding member of the Communist Labor Party and served as its eastern district organizer in Boston. After the Workers Party was formed in 1921, she attended its convention in 1922 and the secret Bridgman, Michigan, meetings of the same year. Ella worked throughout the 1920s to build a Communist presence in the labor movement, especially through her work with the National Miners Union and in support of the Gastonia strikers, and to aid political prisoners, as in her work to free the Italian anarchists Sacco and Vanzetti (q.v.). Though not given to heavy factional fighting, and until recently a backer of William Z. Foster (q.v.), Bloor did travel to the Soviet Union as part of the delegation from the U.S. Party's sixth convention in 1929 to appeal the Comintern's decisions concerning Jay Lovestone (q.v.) and the direction of the Party's efforts. She was personally denounced by Stalin for holding out in her support of Lovestone and finally capitulated.

In the 1930s Ella Reeve Bloor worked with both her son, Harold Ware (q.v.), and her new husband, Andrew Omholt, in organizing the Depression's agrarian unrest for the Communist Party. She helped build the membership of the United Farmers League and its successor, the Farmers National Committee for Action (FNCA). She was arrested in connection with her work for the FNCA in Nebraska and was imprisoned for thirty days at the age of 72. Though she had been arrested numerous times, this was her longest stay in jail.

Bloor served as a delegate to the first and second congresses of the Red International of Labor Unions and also was a delegate to the first international meeting of Communist women. In 1937 she traveled as an honored guest to the Soviet Union for the celebration of the twentieth anniversary of the Bolshevik Revolution.

Ella Reeve Bloor and her husband "retired" from their work for the Communist Party to an apple farm in eastern Pennsylvania in 1937. She continued to serve on the Party's national committee, a position she held from 1932 to 1948. She was chair of the Pennsylvania state Party and ran for Congress on the Party's ticket in 1940. During World War II, Mother Bloor did her last speaking tour for the Communist Party to rally support in "winning the war against fascism." She died after suffering a stroke on August 10, 1951, at the age of 89.

SOURCE: Ella Reeve Bloor, *We Are Many* (1940).

*JOHN P. BECK*

**BOHN, FRANK A. (1879–1975).** Frank A. Bohn was the intellectual leader of the Industrial Workers of the World (IWW) during the first ten years of its existence. A native of Warrensville, Ohio, born in 1879, Bohn received his education at Ohio State University and the University of Michigan, from which he received a Ph.D. in economics at the turn of the century. He served in the Spanish-American War.

In 1900 Bohn joined the Socialist Labor Party (SLP), then dominated by Daniel DeLeon (q.v.). He remained in the SLP for only four years, breaking with it in 1904 because he objected to DeLeon's total domination of the organization. That same year Bohn was among the participants in a meeting at which the IWW was conceived. A year later he participated in the founding convention of the IWW and was one of its chief defenders.

Three years later he joined William Haywood (q.v.) in writing the definitive theoretical work of the quasi-Socialist syndicalism which was the hallmark of IWW ideology. That pamphlet, *Industrial Socialism*, which appeared in at least four editions in English and another twelve in foreign languages, delineated the difference between the political socialism of the Socialist Party and the industrial socialism of the IWW. The essential argument of that work declared that the enemy was industrial and could be overcome only by industrial means. It was essentially a plea for trade union action to overturn the capitalist system and replace it with a socialist system in which the unions, organized by industry rather than craft, would serve as management.

In 1910 Bohn became disillusioned with the IWW membership, which he feared was losing its perspective. In an article in the June 11, 1910, issue of the left-wing *International Socialist Review*, he declared that the IWW was dead. He remained a member of the IWW and the Socialist Party for the next five years, but he was no longer active in the former.

By 1913 Bohn had withdrawn from Socialist activity, resigning from the party four years later. During the period from 1913 to 1917 he was a correspondent in Germany and Austria for the *New York Post*. After the war, Bohn wrote for the *New York Times Magazine*, lectured at the University of Southern California, co-authored, with Richard Ely, *The Great Change* (1935), and directed the evacuation of refugees from the war zone in 1940.

He retired during the 1950s and died in a West Virginia veterans facility in 1975 at the age of 96.

SOURCES: Obituary in the *Washington Post*, August 1, 1975 (ignores his radical years); Donald Drew Egbert and Stow Persons, *Socialism and American Life*, vol. 1 (1952) (esp. pp. 313, 498).

*BERNARD K. JOHNPOLL*

**BOUDIN, KATHY (b. 1943).** Kathy Boudin was an active member of Students for a Democratic Society (SDS) during the 1960s and belonged to the radical faction of the SDS, Weatherman, that went underground in 1970. She was born in 1943, the daughter of Jean Boudin, a poet, and Leonard Boudin, a civil libertarian and constitutional lawyer. After she graduated from Bryn Mawr College in 1965, she worked in the SDS Economic Research and Action Project (ERAP) in Cleveland, assisting welfare mothers. She took part in the protests in Chicago during the 1968 Democratic national convention and worked with the National Mobilization Committee to End the War in Vietnam. Boudin became a prominent member of Weatherman after it took control of the national office of the SDS in the summer of 1969. During that summer she went to Cuba as part of an SDS delegation.

After the December 1969 SDS "War Council" in Flint, Michigan, she went underground with the cadre of Weatherman who proposed to conduct bombings of government buildings. On March 6, 1970, she escaped from an explosion in a Weather Underground bomb factory in a New York townhouse in which three members of the group were killed. In April and July, federal grand juries in Chicago and Detroit indicted Boudin and eleven other Weatherman leaders on conspiracy charges. Boudin made the FBI's "Ten Most Wanted List."

In the mid–1970s, when Weather Underground devolved into the Prairie Fire Collective, which favored resurfacing, and the May 19th Coalition, which wanted to remain underground and become part of a black terrorist army, Boudin remained with the latter organization. On October 20, 1981, she and two other May 19th Coalition members joined members of the Black Liberation Army in a robbery of a Brink's truck in Nanuet, New York. A guard was killed during the robbery, and two policemen were killed at a roadblock near Nyack, New York, by the group. Boudin and several others were arrested. On April 26, 1984, Boudin pleaded guilty to murder and robbery charges at her trial in White Plains, New York, and on May 3 was sentenced to twenty years to life in prison.

SOURCE: Lucinda Franks, "The Seeds of Terror: How Children of Privilege Became the Weather Underground," *New York Times Magazine*, November 11, 1981.

*MART STEWART*


**BOUDIN, LOUIS B. (1874–1952).** Louis B. Boudin was the leading theoretician of the left wing of the American Socialist Party before the 1919 Communist split. He was also a leading labor attorney, civil libertarian, scholar of constitutional law, and critic of the U.S. Supreme Court and its members.

Born in Russia in 1874 of middle-class parents, Boudin migrated at age 17 to the United States because of legal disabilities suffered by Jews in the czarist empire. He went to school almost immediately upon his 1891 arrival in New York City and earned a master's degree from New York University Law School in 1897. He was admitted to the New York State bar in 1898 and the federal bar twenty-one years later.

Boudin joined the Socialist Party shortly after it was formed at the turn of the century. He became a major writer for party organs by 1905 and composed the standard Socialist work on Marxism in 1907, *The Theoretical System of Karl Marx in the Light of Recent Criticisms*. That book is still used in university classes of Marxism as one of the major works in the field.

He argued in this book—and in articles in Socialist journals of the period, particularly the *International Socialist Review* and the *Class Struggle*—that political systems reflected the means of production of a given era. As the mode of production changed, the political system would change. New tools, Boudin maintained, made new political and social systems imperative.

Ideas, Boudin believed, were not independent entities devoid of historical and social influences; they were the result of social conditions. But these ideas fired the imagination of the revolutionary class—in this instance the working class—and helped it effectuate the revolution. Because he argued that the working class would have to be convinced of the Socialist ideal before the system could be developed, Boudin opposed Lenin and his vanguard thesis. His opposition to the Leninist theory of dictatorship of the proletariat and the rule by the vanguard party led him to assail the Bolshevik seizure of power in late 1917 and to resign from the editorial staff of the left-wing Socialist journal *Class Struggle*, which supported the Bolshevik coup.

Boudin also opposed revolution by a working class unprepared to rule democratically. He thus refused to join either of the two Communist parties formed in 1919. He declaimed at the opening convention of the Communist Labor Party, as he walked out, "I did not quit a party of crooks to join a party of lunatics."

Two years previously Boudin had proved his devotion to Marxian socialism by refusing to support the Hillquit (q.v.)–Ruthenberg (q.v.) anti-war St. Louis Declaration of the Socialist Party, despite his vehement opposition to American participation in the world war. He argued that the resolution was theoretically vague. Instead, he offered a resolution of his own, which attempted to explain opposition to the war on the basis of Socialist theory. He had two years earlier written a Socialist explanation of the causes of war under capitalism. The St. Louis Declaration won overwhelmingly. During the war he defended Socialists and other radicals who were arrested for opposing U.S. intervention.

By 1919 Boudin began to divorce himself from political socialism. He devoted himself, instead, to legal work and scholarship, and he veered more and more toward moderate social democracy. By 1924 his writings indicated that he favored a new American party fashioned after the British Labour Party. He believed that neither the Socialist Party nor the Communist Party served any purpose as then organized. By 1940 he had turned strongly against the Communists, although he defended their civil liberties.

In 1932 Boudin produced his legal magnum opus, *Government by Judiciary*, in which he assailed the power "usurped" by the anti-labor, anti-reform judiciary. He cited the social origins of the members of the U.S. Supreme Court to explain its conservative bent. The two-volume work became a standard tome in constitutional law studies and jurisprudence. It is still cited in legal briefs more than fifty years after publication and used in advanced courses in graduate law schools.

As a labor attorney, Boudin won several major cases. He argued the case in which labor unions in public utilities won the right to be covered by the terms of the Wagner Act. He won the right of white-collar workers in New York State to use the facilities of the State Labor Relations Board. And he was the lawyer for a Teamsters Union local that won exemption for labor unions from anti-trust laws.

After withdrawing from political activity, Boudin devoted his energies to helping European Jews from the effects of the pogroms that followed World War I and the Holocaust of World War II. He was an active leader of the World ORT (Organization for Rehabilitation through Training) organization at the time of his death in 1952.

SOURCES: By Louis Boudin: *Government by Judiciary* (1932); *Socialism and War* (1915); *The Theoretical System of Karl Marx in the Light of Recent Criticism* (1907). See also the Louis Boudin Papers at Columbia University, New York City, and Robert Hyfler, *Prophets of the Left: American Socialist Thought in the Twentieth Century* (1984).

*BERNARD K. JOHNPOLL*

**BOURNE, RANDOLPH (1886–1918).** Randolph Silliman Bourne was a leading figure in the Greenwich Village renaissance and a spokesman for the youthful assault on middle-class culture at the beginning of the twentieth century. Bourne's opposition to U.S. intervention in World War I and his critique of Wilsonian liberalism made him a legendary figure after his death in 1918.

Bourne was born in Bloomfield, New Jersey, on May 30, 1886. His father, Charles Bourne, succumbed to drink and left the family in the hands of Sarah Barrett Bourne, who relied on her brother, a wealthy Newark lawyer, for support. Randolph was badly disfigured by a forceps delivery, and the spinal tuberculosis he contracted in 1890 left him a hunchbacked dwarf. Raised a Presbyterian, he turned bitterly against his family's religion as an adult.

In 1909 Bourne enrolled at Columbia University and studied with Charles Beard and John Dewey, among others. While an undergraduate, Bourne wrote essays on youth and generational conflict which were later collected in *Youth and Life* (1913). A disciple of Nietzsche, Henri Bergson, William James, and Dewey, Bourne attacked Victorian conventions in the name of "the experimental life." Upon graduating in 1913, he received a Gilder Fellowship, which allowed him to travel in Europe in 1913–1914. Bourne returned to New York in 1914 and joined the staff of the *New Republic*, for which he wrote essays on education, sociology, literature, and urbanism. His essays on progressive education formed the basis of *The Gary Schools* (1916) and *Education and Living* (1917).

During the years 1916–1917, Bourne's views on Wilson's foreign policy diverged sharply from those of most Progressives, and he turned to the Seven Arts to publish his most famous essays, a series of attacks on liberals who collaborated with the war effort. Bourne charged that Progressive intellectuals had given up critical thought for the exercise of power and the "easy rationalization of what is actually going on.'' Opposition to the war brought Bourne close to the positions of the Industrial Workers of the World and radical Socialists. After his death from influenza on December 23, 1918, Bourne's friends discovered his unfinished manuscript entitled ''The State.'' There Bourne traced the making of the American state, concluding that ''war is the health of the state.'' Bourne's memory has since been resurrected by later generations of young radicals as a symbol of moral intransigence and intellectual courage.

SOURCES: Olaf Hansen (ed.), *The Radical Will* (1977); John Adam Moreau, *Randolph Bourne: Legend and Reality* (1966).

                                                                    *CASEY BLAKE*

**BRAY, JOHN FRANCIS (1809–1896).** John Francis Bray was a Socialist printer and publisher for more than sixty-five years in the United Kingdom and the United States. Born in 1809 in Washington, D.C., of a British father and an American mother, Bray spent his teen years in Great Britain. He accompanied his father—a music-hall performer—to Leeds, England, when he was only 13. His father died almost immediately after arriving, and John was raised in Leeds by an aunt. Bray was educated in the grammar school in Leeds and was apprenticed to a printer at age 15.

After completing his apprenticeship, he became a tramp printer working on usually illegal Chartist publications throughout the United Kingdom. While working for these publications between 1835 and 1836, Bray wrote letters to various newspapers in Leeds. Most of the missives were anti-monarchist. They won the admiration of the members of the pro-Chartist Leeds Workingmen's Association, who chose him as their leader.

Lectures he delivered to that association were the basis for his most famous book, *Labour's Wrongs and Labour's Remedy* (1839). Karl Marx cited the book in his 1847 polemic against Proudhon, *The Poverty of Philosophy*, and erroneously called Bray an Englishman. The *Leeds Times* assailed the book as Utopian, a charge Bray answered by writing a new book, *A Voyage from Utopia to Several Unknown Regions of the World*. A heavy-handed satire, it described a fanciful trip by a resident of Utopia to Brydon (the United Kingdom), Franco (France), and Amerco (the United States of America). Bray used the book to describe the hunger, inequality, and degradation he believed existed in these countries at that time and to place the blame on private control of the means of production and distribution. It is significant that the book was not printed until 1957, more than one hundred years after it had been written.

At age 22 Bray returned to the United States, landing in Boston in 1842. He remained there for a few months and then moved to Michigan, where he spent the rest of his life working as a printer, farming, and agitating for socialism.

His first effort at pamphleteering in the United States took the form of two polemics. The first was an effort to debunk spiritualism, then popular among radicals and ex-radicals. His second effort was by far more significant: a pro-Southern polemic against the Union in the Civil War. Bray argued that the states of the South had a right, under the Constitution, to secede from the Union. He also charged that the North, by opposing the secession, was acting against the basic tenets of the American Revolution and the Constitution.

Moreover, Bray argued that chattel slavery was not the real burning issue in the United States; wage slavery in the North was more pernicious and a more significant evil. He doubted that the blacks wanted their freedom; they were at least guaranteed basic food, clothing, shelter, and care so long as they were chattel. The wage slaves, on the other hand, had no such guarantees and were thus in a far less favorable position than the chattel slaves. Bray's position was not totally unique among American Socialists, but he was in the minority.

After the war Bray became active in the Socialist Labor Party (SLP), as the party was then known. He toured the nation from coast to coast during the 1870s as a lecturer for the party. In 1880 the party proposed that he be the Greenback-Labor candidate for U.S. Vice-President. However, the SLP delegates walked out of the Greenback convention before the nominations were made.

During the 1870s and early 1880s, Bray wrote articles in Socialist and Utopian journals—mainly the *Labor Standard* and John Humphrey Noyes' (q.v.) *American Socialist*. He pleaded for Socialist political action, especially during the strike wave of 1877.

Bray's socialism was an amalgamation of the individualist anarchism of Josiah Warren (q.v.), the rejection of reform that dominated the thought of Marxian Socialists of the period, Ferdinand Lassalle's political socialism, Karl Marx's view of man's becoming a commodity under capitalism, and a simplistic form of the class struggle. He believed that, under socialism, workers would work voluntarily in communes that they would set up themselves. Amelioration of conditions under capitalism, he argued, would be useless so long as men worked for the advantage of others—the capitalists. Under those conditions, they must be mere commodities. Only socialism could free humans from that fate.

He believed that a class war did exist between the workers and the capitalists. In that war, he argued, the working class was destined to win. In the first place, they represented the vast majority of the population. In the second place, they would win in any military confrontation because the majority of the military came out of the working class.

After the 1880 Greenback-Labor election debacle, Bray became disillusioned with the working class. In 1882 he called the workers apathetic and slovenly. He remained active in the SLP and worked within the Knights of Labor—whose Pontiac, Michigan, unit was named the John Francis Bray Assembly. But he no longer expected labor unions to succeed or a Socialist government to be formed in the foreseeable future.

Bray was somewhat more optimistic in 1892 when the Populist candidate for U.S. President polled a large vote. By 1894, at the age of 85, he again pleaded for independent labor political action, this time via the People's Party. He was still a Socialist, albeit an old and sick one. He worked for the nomination of Eugene V. Debs (q.v.) as Populist candidate for President.

Before Bray could see his last hope for socialism in his time fail, he died in Pontiac in 1896—prior to the Populist convention vote to back the Democratic candidate for President, William Jennings Bryan.

SOURCES: John Francis Bray, "A Brief Sketch of the Life of John Francis Bray, Social, Political, and Religious Reformer," Handwritten manuscript at London School of Economics Library (microfilm copy at State University of New York at Albany Library); (ca. 1860); M. F. Jolliffe, "Fresh Light on John Francis Bray, Author of *Labour's Wrongs and Labour's Remedies*," *Economic History* 3 (February 1939); H. E. Wade, "John Francis Bray" (Ph.D. diss. St. Louis University, 1967).

*BERNARD K. JOHNPOLL*

**BRIDGES, HARRY (b. 1901).** Harry Bridges was leader of the International Longshoremen's and Warehousemen's Union in San Francisco and a leading labor radical on the Pacific Coast for forty years. Bridges was born Alfred Renton Bridges in Australia on July 28, 1901. His father was a well-to-do real estate agent, in whose employ as a rent collector Bridges had his first direct contact with economic deprivation. He went to sea when he was 16, at which time he was first exposed to organized labor activity as a member of the Australian Seamen's Union. On April 8, 1920, Bridges legally entered the United States in San Francisco.

After his involvement in the 1921 seamen's strike in New Orleans, Bridges turned away from the American Federation of Labor, which he accused of having "sold out" the strike, and briefly joined the Industrial Workers of the World (IWW). Finding their refusal to sign contracts too anarchistic, Bridges dropped out of the IWW before settling in San Francisco as a longshoreman in October 1922. Because of his reluctance to join a company "blue book" union and because of his involvement in efforts to reorganize the International Longshoremen's Association (ILA) on the San Francisco docks, Bridges periodically found work hard to come by during the 1920s. By the middle of the Depression, Bridges was involved in the publication of *Waterfront Worker*, a newspaper begun in 1932 and close to the Communist Party. In 1933, as a new movement to revive the ILA on the Pacific Coast gathered strength, Bridges aligned himself with the union's "Albion Hall" group, the most militant of its three main factions.

An ILA strike over wage issues beginning in May 1934 was marked by Red-baiting by employers and public officials and by violence on both sides of the picket line. With Bridges among the leaders of the strike committee, a general strike in San Francisco was organized briefly during July. Eventually arbitration led to an overwhelmingly pro-union settlement. During the following two years the ILA began to recruit members among warehousemen as well as longshoremen. In 1935 Bridges formed the Maritime Federation of the Pacific to organize and coordinate united job actions among the various components of the waterfront work force. Having alienated the conservative AFL and the national ILA leadership by his militance and independence, Bridges in June 1937 led the Pacific Coast division of the ILA into the Congress of Industrial Organizations (CIO), reconstituting the union as the International Longshoremen's and Warehousemen's Union (ILWU). Shortly thereafter he was named Pacific Coast regional director of the CIO.

Between 1939 and 1953 Bridges had to fight back three efforts to have him deported. Such efforts were ostensibly because of his Communist Party connections and sympathies, but in part at least also because of his aggressive labor advocacy. Twice, in 1945 and 1953, the U.S. Supreme Court overruled orders to deport him and, in the latter instance, declined to revoke the U.S. citizenship Bridges took out in 1945. During World War II, Bridges followed the Communist Party's policy to maximize waterfront efficiency in handling war materials while minimizing labor conflicts. Beginning in 1944 the ILWU under his direction began to organize Hawaiian sugar and pineapple plantation laborers, a move that gained the union some 30,000 members in two years. Bridges opposed the American drift into the Cold War, and in 1950 the CIO expelled the ILWU during its purge of Communist-dominated unions.

Ironically, in his final two decades in power Bridges was often accused of having dissipated his youthful radicalism. One element of this argument was his increasing respectability in the eyes of employers. Another was the Mechanization and Modernization Agreement he negotiated with shippers in October 1960, which recognized the inevitability of automation in the shipping industry but built wage, safety, and pension protections into the process to try to minimize labor dislocations. The failure of the ILWU to attempt to organize California farmworkers, in striking contrast to its Hawaiian efforts of twenty-five years earlier, was often interpreted as a loss of drive on Bridges' part—a charge he hotly denied.

Harry Bridges retired from the presidency of the ILWU on July 1, 1977, and continues to live in San Francisco.

SOURCES: Charles P. Larrowe, *Harry Bridges: The Rise and Fall of Radical Labor in the United States* (1972); Charles A. Madison, *American Labor Leaders* (1950).

*ED SHOEMAKER*

**BRIGGS, CYRIL (1887–1966).** Cyril Valentine Briggs, founder and leader of the militant African Blood Brotherhood and one of the most important and original of the Communist Party's theoreticians on the "Negro question," was born on the island of Nevis, Leeward Islands, on May 28, 1887, the son of Louis and Marion Briggs. He was educated at Wesleyan and Baptist parochial schools at Basseterre, St. Kitts. After leaving school at the age of 16, he worked for a year as a subreporter with local Basseterre newspapers.

Briggs landed in the United States in 1905. Between 1912 and 1915 he worked for the *New York Amsterdam News* in various capacities. He resigned in 1915 to found his own short-lived magazine but rejoined the *Amsterdam News* in June 1916, becoming editor in all but name. However, after the United States entered World War I, Briggs wrote a series of editorials that were critical of black

American support for the war effort and was forced to resign in March 1918. Briggs launched the *Crusader* in September 1918, and in 1921 it became the "Organ of the African Blood Brotherhood" (ABB), the formation of which it had announced in October 1919. In addition to Briggs, who held the position of "Paramount Chief" of the Supreme Executive Council, other ABB charter members included such West Indian radicals as the Burrell brothers (Theophilus and Benjamin), Richard B. Moore, W. A. Domingo (q.v.), Otto Huiswoud (q.v.), and Claude McKay.

Organized through a system of "posts" (e.g., the New York "Menelik Post") and possessing benevolent and fraternal features, the ABB described itself as a "revolutionary secret Order." It also became the first, and for some time the only, black radical group to challenge the dominance of Marcus Garvey and his Universal Negro Improvement Association (UNIA). In response to criticism, Garvey charged that Briggs, who was undeniably light-complexioned, was "a white man . . . claiming to be a Negro for Convenience." (*Negro World*, Oct. 8, 1921). Briggs sued Garvey for criminal libel. At a court hearing on November 11, 1921, Garvey was forced to retract his statement and to publish a formal apology.

*The Crusader* ceased publication at the start of 1922, however, and for the next two years Briggs ran the Crusader News Agency as a means of distributing radical propaganda to the black press. In March 1923 Briggs set about organizing a United Negro Front Conference, which eventually became subsumed under Kelly Miller's All-Race Conference (commonly known as the Negro Sanhedrin) that met in Chicago the week of February 11, 1924, with Briggs in the position of secretary.

In the early 1920s the rival factions of the Communist movement vied eagerly for the support of the ABB. Briggs attended the second annual conference of the Workers Party in December 1921 as one of two ABB representatives. In 1922 he went to work for the national office of the Friends of Soviet Russia and was also elected a subdistrict organizer of the Yorkville branch of the Workers Party.

The ABB was dissolved in 1924. Thereafter, Briggs participated in the Communist Party's various auxiliaries for blacks. He was editor of the official organ of the American Negro Labor Congress, *Negro Champion*, and its successor, the *Harlem Liberator*. In 1936 he was appointed a contributing editor of the *Negro Worker*, the Paris-based organ of the International Trade Union Committee of Negro Workers, which had been founded in 1930 under Profintern auspices.

In 1938 Briggs became embroiled in a dispute with James W. Ford (q.v.), at that time the leading black figure in the Communist Party (CPUSA), but he continued to be a member of the party's Negro Commission. The following year, however, the CPUSA expelled Briggs, along with Richard B. Moore and other black party members, for their alleged "Negro nationalist way of thinking."

In 1944 Briggs moved to Los Angeles. He rejoined the Communist Party in 1948, and for a time during the height of the McCarthy era witch-hunt in 1951 he functioned as a leader of the Party underground in the Los Angeles area. He was a member of the Southern California District Communist Party's Negro Commission. During the late 1950s he was employed as an editor with the *Los Angeles Herald-Despatch*. Briggs died of a heart attack on October 18, 1966, at the age of 78.

SOURCES: Theodore Draper, *American Communism and Soviet Russia* (1960), Robert A. Hill (ed.), *The Marcus Garvey and Universal Negro Improvement Association Papers*, vol. 1 (1983); Theodore Vincent, *Black Power and the Garvey Movement* (1971).

*ROBERT A. HILL*

**BRISBANE, ALBERT (1808–1890).** Albert Brisbane was the leading exponent of the quasi-Socialist ideas of Charles Fourier. Brisbane was born in Geneva, New York, in 1808, of wealthy merchant parentage. He was educated in boarding schools of Long Island and by private tutors in New York City. At 18 he went to Europe, where he studied under French philosopher Victor Cousin, French historian François P. G. Guizot, and German Philosopher Georg W. F. Hegel. He then traveled to Constantinople and returned to Paris, shortly after the revolution of 1830, and immersed himself in studying thought reform. He first studied the works of Claude Saint-Simon, whom he found disappointing. Brisbane then turned to Fourier, whose philosophy he found to be practical and "just and wise." For the next two years he studied under Fourier and became his devoted disciple.

Brisbane returned to the United States in 1834. Five years later he helped organize a Fourierite society in Philadelphia. It soon developed a nationwide following. In 1840 he published his first major Fourierite work, *Social Destiny of Man: or Association and Reorganization of Industry*. Brisbane's system— in essence an American modification of Fourier's—called for the establishment of communities called "phalanxes." Composed of approximately 2,000 residents, each phalanx would border on a forest and a city. The first would assure the community of timber, the second would assure it of a market. Most of the residents of the communes would be employed in agricultural pursuits, but there would also be industries and transportation. Children would do the most menial, demeaning, and filthy work. There would be class distinctions in the phalanxes, with capital and management receiving seven-twelfths of the total income, and labor receiving only five-twelfths.

Brisbane's writings soon made Fourierism popular, especially among intellectuals. By 1844 Brook Farm, a community of literary and intellectual elites near Boston, became a phalanx (it went bankrupt in 1846 after two years).

Brisbane's activity for Fourierism continued for the next forty-four years. He edited the movement's short-lived newspaper, composed a column for the daily *New York Tribune*, helped edit the Fourierite journal *Phalanx* and wrote for the radical Democratic journal *Plaebeian*. He also wrote two more expositions of

Fourierism—the more important, *General Introduction to Social Sciences*, was published in 1874.

Brisbane died in Richmond, Virginia, in 1890.

SOURCES: Arthur Eugene Bestor, Jr., "Albert Brisbane: Propagandist for Socialism in the 1840s," *New York History* 28U (April 1947); Albert Brisbane, *Social Destiny of Man: Or Association and Reorganization of Industry* (Philadelphia, 1840); Redelia Brisbane, *Albert Brisbane, a Mental Biography, with a Character Study by His Wife, Redelia Brisbane* (Boston, 1893).

*BERNARD K. JOHNPOLL*

**BROWDER, EARL (1891–1973).** Earl Russell Browder, a veteran of numerous Midwestern radical movements, led the Communist Party (CPUSA) from 1934 to 1945. Displaying a nativist orientation, Browder stressed his Kansas origin and called Communists heirs to American revolutionary and abolitionist traditions. Though offensive to Marxist purists, this brought the CPUSA influence far beyond its scant 100,000 members. In 1943, when Joseph Stalin disbanded the Communist International as a maneuver to placate Westerners, Browder took the dissolution literally, proclaimed independence from the Soviet Union, reconstituted his Party as a leftist lobby, and advocated postwar détente. After Moscow forced his ouster in 1945, U.S. Communists rushed headlong into political oblivion.

Browder was born in Wichita, Kansas, on May 20, 1891, the eighth of ten children. His mother was Scottish-American and his father, William, traced his ancestors to two Welsh brothers in seventeenth-century Virginia's Dinwiddie County. William, a Unitarian, tried farming, but saw drought ruin his crops and disease claim two of his children's lives. He later taught elementary school, but in 1900 he became an invalid, possibly from a nervous breakdown. This forced Earl to leave school at age 9. As a youth he worked as an errand boy and a telegraph messenger, and then went from office boy through clerk to accountant for a wholesale drug company. William tutored him at night, giving him an elementary school education. His father also imparted his Socialist politics and remnants of his previous populism. Earl joined the Socialist Party at age 16.

At age 21 Browder moved to Kansas City. Although still a Socialist in his spare hours, he entered a small business partnership manufacturing and selling brooms, which failed after only nine months. In 1913 Browder obtained an accounting position with a large private firm and completed a correspondence school law course the following year. In 1916 he found employment as an accountant and manager of a farmers cooperative outside the city.

While living in Kansas City, Browder spent time in nearly all the radical and labor movements of his day. He left the Socialist Party after it expelled the popular "Big Bill" Haywood (q.v.) in 1913. Yet Browder did not enter Haywood's Industrial Workers of the World. Instead he sought to radicalize the American Federation of Labor from within and associated with the Workers Educational League, which served as the Kansas City branch of William Z. Foster's (q.v.)

Syndicalist League of North America. That same year Browder joined the Bookkeepers, Stenographers, and Accountants Local. Elected its president in 1914, he also became a delegate to the Kansas City (Missouri) Central Labor Council. He enjoyed organizing and retained his union position after he began working for the farmers cooperative. In fact, he even found time to serve on the national council of the Grangers Cooperative League of America and to write occasionally for its journal.

Thus, between 1912 and 1916 Browder had never found a political home that could claim all his energies. Nevertheless, this era constituted a decisive, formative period in his life. It was during these years that Browder developed a keen understanding of American radical politics and nativist tendencies which never deserted him—even after he had spent more than a decade in the Russian-dominated CPUSA.

By 1917 Browder had finally found a cause that did enchant him: nonviolent resistance to World War I. His beliefs and actions cost him dearly. Refusing to register with the Selective Service brought a jail term from December 1917 to November 1918. Furthermore, the government imprisoned him in Leavenworth Penitentiary from July 1919 until November 1920 for conspiracy. News of the Russian Revolution reached Browder during his incarceration, and upon his release he moved to New York and joined the Communists. His timing could hardly have been better.

International communism had recently undergone its first historic "change of line." Previously, U.S. Communists had expected a Soviet-style uprising and had avoided association with reformers, especially the AFL. By 1920, however, V. I. Lenin had realized that except in Russia the "World Revolution" had stalled. That spring he wrote a pamphlet, "Left Wing Communism: An Infantile Disorder," which sanctioned working for reforms. When the faithful in the United States finally received a translation a year later, they found they had to bridge a chasm of ill-will between themselves and most of organized labor. Accordingly, Browder abandoned extremist tactics for more flexible ones. One Party leader, James P. Cannon (q.v.), had worked with Browder in Kansas City. He realized that Browder had more experience in the AFL than most other Party members. At that same time, early 1921, three representatives from Moscow were touring the nation, attempting to recruit an American delegation to the First Congress of the Red International of Labor Unions, or Profintern. Cannon introduced Browder to the visitors. They liked his Midwestern and AFL backgrounds and chose him to lead the U.S. delegation to the July gathering. Although Browder had obtained a lucrative position as head bookkeeper for a wholesale company on Broadway, he resigned and began rounding up delegates who could claim union support. Organizing this one project did not make Browder America's top Communist, but it did signal his arrival to at least the second stratum of leaders.

Browder's 1921 trip to Moscow had another result. William Z. Foster, who went along as an observer, decided to join the Party. Probably the nation's best-known left-wing unionist, Foster represented an important convert. He brought with him his Chicago-based Trade Union Educational League (TUEL), which became the Profintern's American section. With Russian financial backing, its power soon rivaled that of the Communist political leadership in New York. Foster entered on his own terms. Browder became his first assistant, editing the TUEL's paper, *The Labor Herald*, and serving as liaison between the Chicago and New York factions. Although he won recognition for his energy and efficiency, Browder came to be considered Foster's "man Friday." By the mid–1920s Browder seemed destined to remain little more than a high-level apparatchik.

In 1926, however, Browder's life became more exciting. The TUEL sent him to Moscow to assist the visiting Foster, and he remained there as America's Profintern delegate. But the Russians found other tasks for Browder. They asked him to lead an international labor delegation to China. In March 1927 the delegation established the Pan-Pacific Trade Union Secretariat, first in Hankow then at Shanghai. Remaining in East Asia for most of 1927 and 1928, Browder headed the organization and edited its journal, *The Pan-Pacific Monthly*. Browder's two years in China were among the most educational of his life, providing an opportunity to understand the movement in global terms. Moreover, his experiences and writings there greatly enhanced his prestige in the Communist world. Isolated from the CPUSA's factional strife, Browder began to view himself as an independent force and publicly challenged Foster for the first time.

In character with the overall history of the CPUSA, the crisis that brought Browder to the threshold of leadership concerned Russian, not American, events. In December 1927 Joseph Stalin expelled Leon Trotsky from the Soviet Communist Party. The following year he completed his consolidation of all power in the Soviet Union by engineering the ouster of Nikolai Bukharin. Stalin also purged sympathizers of both in foreign Parties. In the United States this required removal of Trotskyist James Cannon in 1928 and, more significant, of CPUSA leader Jay Lovestone (q.v.) in 1929. Numerous followers of both were also ostracized, seriously depleting the Party's top ranks. At its October 1929 Plenum, the CPUSA abolished the office of general secretary and named a three-man secretariat to run the organization, including Browder, in charge of Agitation and Propaganda. Enjoying strong support from the Communist International (Comintern), Browder made the most of the opportunity. At the Party Plenum in the spring of 1930, he delivered the main report. In June, at the CPUSA convention, he replaced Max Bedacht (q.v.) as administrative secretary.

Although Browder's title gave him nominal leadership of the Party, the other two members of the secretariat, Foster and William Weinstone (q.v.), remained contenders for power. Ultimately Browder won the struggle, aided by his own ambition, Weinstone's lengthy visits to Moscow and other parts of Europe, and Foster's heart attack and long convalescence. By 1934 Browder had full command of the CPUSA; at its eighth convention that year it recreated the post of general secretary and conferred the title upon him.

Browder seemed the ideal Communist leader during the emerging Popular Front era. Ever since Adolf Hitler's rise to power in Germany in 1933, Soviet Russia had been abandoning ideological party purity in search of allies. At the Comintern's Seventh World Congress in August 1935, the shift in tactics became official. For the first time Stalinist Parties around the world attempted to join ranks with nearly all opponents of fascism. Almost everywhere Communists campaigned for the same liberal reforms they had recently denounced as palliatives. Under Browder, the CPUSA endorsed Social Security and public works bills; it urged the people to tax the wealthy instead of overthrowing them.

Browder zealously applied the Comintern's injunction for individual Communist Parties to find links to revolutionary traditions in their respective lands. Emphasizing his own Kansas origin, he claimed kinship between the CPUSA and earlier, home-grown extremists for liberty, such as the patriots of 1776 and the nineteenth-century abolitionists. At Communist rallies, portraits of Jefferson and Lincoln accompanied those of Marx and Lenin. Opponents were likened to Tories, Know-Nothings and Confederate racists. Browder popularized the Party's ubiquitous slogan of the era, "Communism Is Twentieth-Century Americanism." Although Moscow could not accept this and forced him to drop the phrase by late 1938, Browder continued proselytizing in a similar vein. Under Browder an important turning point occurred: for the first time a majority of the Party's members were native-born.

By all definitions the Popular Front era ended with the Nazi-Soviet Pact of 1939. Communists changed their line again and maligned friends of the previous day. They stopped seeing World War II as a crusade against fascism and began denouncing it as an "imperialist" conflict. Within the Politburo, Browder briefly fought against proposals to abandon the Popular Front, but he surrendered when directives arrived from Moscow. The federal government soon unearthed an old passport violation to imprison him from March 25, 1941, to May 16, 1942. Browder, however, did not return to the rhetoric of rebellion that characterized the pre–1935 period. Instead he continued to advocate peaceful electoral change for the rest of his life, despite shifts in the Party line.

Hitler's 1941 invasion of the Soviet Union caused the Soviets to seek allies once again. As a tactic to win Western support, Stalin dissolved the Comintern in 1943. Browder, however, took the Russian premier at his word and began to see himself as the leader of an independent national Communist movement. Temporarily free from foreign interference, he tailored the CPUSA to peculiarly American conditions. Because minor parties faced dismal prospects, Browder disbanded the CPUSA in 1944. He replaced it with a Communist Political Association (CPA) to serve as an independent leftist lobby in the nation's politics. (Browder took the title of president, which sounded less foreign than general secretary.) Reconstituting the Party as a pressure group meant that Browder was abandoning hope that socialism would soon come to the United States. No other Party anywhere had ever made such a metamorphosis, and almost certainly no one in the Kremlin ordered Browder's action. Indeed, a year later Communist critics would cite this as Browder's ultimate sin.

In a final deviation from orthodoxy, Browder put forth his own foreign policy, intended for the postwar era. He contended that the 1943 Teheran Conference between Stalin, Franklin D. Roosevelt, and Winston Churchill signaled the opening of an age of East-West détente. To Browder, the Teheran agreement was not a "momentary compromise," but rather the beginning of "peaceful coexistence and collaboration" between capitalism and communism.

For Browder disaster struck suddenly in May 1945. Jacques Duclos, the second-ranking figure in the French Party, published in his Party's theoretical journal an attack on Browder's policies. It took particular exception to his transformation of the CPUSA into the CPA. Duclos also denounced Browder's plan for postwar harmony as a "notorious revision of Marxism." Finally, he excoriated him for quashing internal dissent by William Z. Foster, a fact theretofore known only among members of the CPA's national board—and in Moscow.

Astounded, American Communist leaders assumed that the article was a message from the Soviet Party. In a series of three extraordinary meetings, they called upon Browder to admit his mistakes and to endorse the Duclos article. Defiantly, Browder confessed to only the most minor of errors and refused to accept Duclos' criticisms. Foster poured oil on the flames by sabotaging a proposed compromise statement. Then Browder, after delivering a lengthy, hectoring speech at the third meeting on June 18, boycotted all discussions except for casting a negative vote. Although he temporarily retained his position as CPA president, a three-man secretariat consisting of Foster, John Williamson (q.v.), and Eugene Dennis (q.v.) was elected. Finally the Communists scheduled a "Special Emergency Convention" for late July.

The convention returned to Marxist orthodoxy by reconstituting itself as the Communist Party, USA, and added Foster's protégé Robert Thompson (q.v.) to the secretariat. It also heard Browder pledge not to form an intraparty opposition. The former leader added, however, that the final word on issues dividing them would come from "Marxists of all lands," a clear sign that he expected to take his case to a higher tribunal.

In February 1946 Browder experienced more misfortune when the CPUSA expelled him altogether. For several months he had published his political and economic views in an unauthorized bulletin, known as the *Distributors Guide*, which was subsidized by a small group of sympathetic businessmen. Three months after his ouster Browder shocked his enemies by flying to Moscow at his own expense. The Soviet government granted him a visa, and subsequently two important Russian leaders, Solomon Lozovsky and Vyzheslav Molotov, listened to his views at length. But Browder did not receive the vindication he sought. Instead he returned to the United States with the unspectacular position of distributor of Russian nonfiction literature in the United States. Sales were poor, and Browder lost his life's savings in the venture before abandoning it in 1949.

As late as 1948 Browder attempted to rejoin the CPUSA. He used the curious logic that Tito's heresy in Yugoslavia necessitated "unity of the world's movement" through Browder's readmission. The Party quickly rebuffed him. He resurfaced briefly in the early 1950s, when his refusal to inform the Senate Tydings Committee about the backgrounds of those who had expelled him led to a contempt of Congress trial. Browder conducted his own defense, based upon the correspondence school law degree he had earned forty years earlier and won acquittal.

Unlike earlier CPUSA leaders, Browder did not create an opposition faction at any time. Nevertheless, some East European regimes executed political criminals for "Browderism" during the 1950s. Browder remained a pariah, and not a single Communist Party publication in the world printed his obituary after his death on June 27, 1973.

SOURCES: Philip J. Jaffe, *The Rise and Fall of American Communism* (1975); James Gilbert Ryan, "Earl Browder and American Communism at High Tide: 1934–1945" (Ph.D. diss., University of Notre Dame, 1981) and "The Making of a Native Marxist: The Early Career of Earl Browder," *Review of Politics* 39 (July 1977).

*JAMES GILBERT RYAN*

**BUDENZ, LOUIS (1891–1972).** Louis Budenz, a longtime labor journalist and a founder of the American Workers Party, converted to communism in 1935 and edited the *Daily Worker* before converting to Roman Catholicism in 1945 and becoming a leading anti-Communist. Budenz was born on July 17, 1891, in Indianapolis, Indiana. His father was a bank cashier and a devout Catholic. Of German-Irish descent, Budenz attended a Jesuit college, St. Xavier's, from 1906 to 1910. While there he became national organizer for the Catholic Young Men's Institute and was influenced by the social doctrines of the church that encouraged labor-organizing. After a brief period studying and practicing law and editing the Carpenters Union journal in 1912–1913, Budenz moved to St. Louis to work for a Catholic social agency. In 1915 he succeeded Roger Baldwin as secretary of the city's Civic League and held the position until 1920. He then served as publicity director of the fledgling American Civil Liberties Union.

In 1921 Budenz launched *Labor Age*, an independent radical magazine, and remained its editor until 1933. He was actively involved in the LaFollette presidential campaign in 1924 and served as secretary of the Conference for Progressive Political Action in New Jersey. While carrying on his duties with *Labor Age*, he also worked as an organizer for several unions in the latter part of the 1920s.

Budenz made the transition to radical politics via A. J. Muste (q.v.). He was one of the original organizers of Muste's Conference for Progressive Labor Action in 1929 and its first national secretary. In 1933 he was a founder of Muste's American Workers Party (AWP). His forte was work among the unemployed; in 1934 Budenz was active in the Muste movement's most spectacular accomplishment, the Toledo Auto-Lite Strike. When Muste agreed to allow the

Trotskyists to enter the AWP in 1934, Budenz refused to go along. Shortly afterward, delighted by the Popular Front policy adopted by the Communist Party (CPUSA) after the Seventh Comintern Congress, he joined the CPUSA in October 1935 in New York.

Budenz moved into the Party hierarchy very quickly, becoming editor of the *Daily Worker*. He was appointed editor of the *Midwest Daily Record* in 1937. From 1940 to 1945 he was managing editor of the *Daily Worker*. He also served on the Party's Central Committee for six years. Although he had been excommunicated years before for marrying a divorced woman, Budenz remained interested in Roman Catholicism and continually urged greater sensitivity to the church. By 1943 he had decided to return to it. The Party's growing hostility to Catholicism, and the implications of Earl Browder's (q.v.) ouster as Party leader in 1945, finally precipitated his break with communism. In October 1945 Budenz dramatically announced his conversion.

During his years as a radical, Budenz had been arrested twenty-one times but never convicted. His post-Communist career was far more controversial. He remained publicly silent—although he talked to the Federal Bureau of Investigation about his Party activities—until October 1946. Then he began a career as a professional anti-Communist, appearing as a witness in at least sixty proceedings in the next decade. He also taught at Notre Dame and Fordham universities. In 1952 Budenz testified to having received more than $70,000 from lectures, books, and testimony on communism.

Budenz figured in some of the most dramatic of the government's cases against Communists and alleged Communists in the 1940s and 1950s. He was a major witness in the first Smith Act trial, where his interpretation of the Communist Party's use of "Aesopian language," as a cover for its intent to overthrow the government by force and violence, helped convict the defendants. Budenz also provided Senator Joseph McCarthy with testimony (based on what other Communist leaders had told him) that Owen Lattimore, a leading sinologist, was a Communist. This charge in particular was sharply challenged not only by Lattimore but also by a number of ex-Communists and was never proven. More plausibly, Budenz claimed to have had dealings with Soviet agents plotting Trotsky's assassination.

Budenz died on April 27, 1972.

SOURCES: Louis Budenz, *This is My Story* (1947); *New York Times*, April 28, 1972 p.
   44; Herbert Packer, *Ex-Communist Witnesses* (1962).

*HARVEY KLEHR*

**BURLAK, ANNE (b. 1911).** Anne Burlak, called the "Red Flame" of several textile strikes in the early 1930s, has been a leader in the Communist Party for some fifty years. She was born in 1911 to Ukranian immigrant parents in Slatington, Pennsylvania. Her father was a miner and a steelworker. The oldest of four children, she went to work in a silk mill at the age of 14. She was a delegate to the founding conventions of the National Textile Workers Union (NTWU) in

1928 and of the Trade Union Unity League in 1929, the year she joined the Communist Party (CPUSA) after two years in its youth organization.

Burlak became an organizer for the NTWU in 1929 and was sent to South Carolina. In 1930 she and five co-workers were charged in Georgia with violating the State Insurrection Law, which carried the death penalty. They were held in prison without bail for six to ten weeks. That law was declared unconstitutional by the U.S. Supreme Court in 1937. In 1931, Burlak was organizing textile workers in Rhode Island and Massachusetts. In 1932 she was elected national secretary of the NTWU, the youngest person and perhaps the only woman to hold such a position. She was a leader of the 1932 National Hunger March on Washington and campaigned for unemployment insurance.

Burlak became a Party organizer in 1936 and worked in Rhode Island, where she ran for public office twice on the Communist ticket. From 1937 to 1939 she helped the Congress of Industrial Organizations (CIO) organizing drive as a volunteer organizer and sought support for the Spanish Republic. In 1939 she married Arthur Timpson, a Spanish Civil War veteran.

In 1939 Burlak was elected secretary of the Party's New England District, a position she held throughout World War II. In the late 1940s she concentrated on raising her two children, on the fight for continued child day-care in Boston, and on the Party's campaign for peace. In 1954 she was indicted under the Massachusetts Anti-Anarchy Law and in 1956 under the Smith Act. Both indictments were eventually overturned.

Anne Burlak is still part of the Massachusetts, New Hampshire, and Vermont district leadership of the CPUSA.

SOURCE: Anne Burlak, Oral History, Tamiment Library, New York University, New York City.

*NORAH CHASE*

**BURNHAM, JAMES (b. 1905).** James Burnham was a leader of the circle of Trotskyist intellectuals who gave up Marxism in the early 1940s and moved after World War II to embrace conservative anti-communism. Burnham is best known for his thesis in *The Managerial Revolution* (1941) that capitalist collapse was leading not to socialism but to a bureaucratic collectivism under the direction of a managerial elite.

Burnham was born in Chicago on November 22, 1905, the son of Claude George Burnham, a wealthy English Catholic railroad executive, and Mary May Gillis Burnham. He pursued an academic career in philosophy, studying at Princeton University (B.A., 1927) and Balliol College at Oxford (B.A., 1929; M.A., 1932) before joining the philosophy department at New York University.

Burnham's political involvement began in 1930–1933 when he co-edited the *Symposium*. The plight of the unemployed and Sidney Hook's (q.v.) expositions of Marxism moved Burnham to join Hook and A. J. Muste (q.v.) in founding the American Workers Party (AWP) in 1933. That same year he served briefly as AWP secretary and wrote for *Labor Action*. In 1934 he worked to unite the

AWP and American Trotskyists in the Workers Party and also joined Max
Shachtman (q.v.) as co-editor of the *New International*. In 1936 he helped
engineer the entry of the Workers Party in to the Socialist Party. A year later
he was one of the organizers of the Joint Commission of Inquiry into Stalin's
charges against Trotsky.

Burnham's disaffiliation from Trotskyism began in 1939, when he questioned
Trotsky's thesis that the Soviet Union was a degenerated workers' state that
required defense in case of war. During 1939–1940 Burnham and Shachtman
debated Trotsky over the nature of the Soviet state and the Nazi-Soviet Pact, a
debate that ended with Burnham's resignation from the Socialist Workers Party
and rejection of Marxism in May 1940. *The Managerial Revolution* (1941)
finalized this evolution with its thesis that a new managerial class was ascendant
in the United States, the Soviet Union, and Germany. Burnham followed this
book with *The Machiavellians* (1943), where he defended realpolitik and elite
rule as safeguards against the demands of the masses for state power.

During the Cold War Burnham became a popular advocate of an aggressive
anti-Soviet foreign policy. In *The Struggle for the World* (1947), *The Coming
Defeat of Communism* (1950), *Containment or Liberation?* (1953), and *The Web
of Subversion* (1954) he joined right-wing Republicans in demanding the
"liberation" of Eastern Europe and a campaign against domestic subversion.
Burnham's controversies with liberal anti-Communists over McCarthyism led to
his resignation from the advisory board of the *Partisan Review* in 1953 and from
the American Committee for Cultural Freedom in 1954. Burnham was a founding
member of the editorial board of the *National Review* in 1955. His *Suicide of
the West* (1964) indicted liberals for a failure of nerve in opposing Soviet
expansionism. President Ronald Reagan honored Burnham's career as a
conservative polemicist by awarding him the Medal of Freedom in 1983.

SOURCES: John P. Diggins, *Up from Communism* (1975); James Gilbert, *Designing the
    Industrial State* (1972).

*CASEY BLAKE*

# C

CACCHIONE, PETER V. (1897–1947). Peter V. Cacchione, chairman of the Communist Party in Brooklyn and a member of the Party's National Committee, was the first open Communist elected to office in a major American metropolis. He served on the New York City Council from 1941 until his death in 1947. Together with Benjamin Davis (q.v.), elected Communist from Manhattan, he gave the Party a substantial presence in New York City legislative affairs.

Born on November 1, 1897, to Italian immigrant parents in Syracuse, New York, Cacchione was raised in Sayre, Pennsylvania, a railroad town in which his parents operated a small grocery and bakery. He graduated from high school, served in World War I, and worked in the operating and repair departments of several railroads during the 1920s. He came to New York City in the early 1930s and was recruited into the Communist Party via the unemployed movement on New York's Lower East Side. He was especially active in the Party-sponsored Workers Ex-Servicemen's League and in agitation for a veterans bonus.

During the Popular Front era Cacchione became head of the Party in Brooklyn and, under the new proportional representation system of election, ran for the city council. Unsuccessful in 1937 and 1939, he won victory in 1941 on a platform of "unity against Hitler." While on the city council, he specialized in fiscal matters affecting the living standards of workers, including the city sales tax and the subway fare, and he joined with Ben Davis and others to oppose discrimination in city-assisted housing and New York medical schools. He was reelected in 1943 and 1945, reflecting the Party's strength in Brooklyn during World War II.

After the war, Cacchione shifted with Party policy in the post-Browder era, offered militant opposition to increases in the sales tax and subway fare, and struggled against the growing campaign to repeal proportional representation. He died at age 50 on November 6, 1947, two days after the system of proportional representation under which he had been elected was repealed by New York's voters.

SOURCE: Simon Gerson, *Pete: The Story of Peter V. Cacchione* (1976).

                                                              *KENNETH WALTZER*

**CAHAN, ABRAHAM (1860–1951).** Abraham Cahan—journalist, author, and Socialist labor leader—was born in 1860 in the *shtetl* of Poberezya, Byelorussia, the only child of Shachne and Sarah Goldarbeter Cahan. When he was less than 6 years old, Abraham's family moved to Vilna, the capital of rabbinic learning and the seat of a growing modernization movement. Here the elder Cahan, a relatively poor shopkeeper and Hebrew teacher, and the son of an itinerant rabbi, who came to be known as the Maggid of Minsk, was torn between his desire to prepare his own son for a career through secular education or through religious school (Heder).

Abraham began with religious school and studied the tractates of the Talmud, but he also devoured the secular works in the Vilna Public Library and developed a taste for the Russian language. Mainly through independent study, Abraham Cahan mastered Russian and gained admission to the Vilna State Teachers Training College in 1878. The school was a center for student radicalism, and by 1880 Cahan had had significant contact with revolutionary students and was converted to socialism. He had read the radical student literature, which he described as "a forbidden object."

Its publishers are those people . . . who live together like brothers and are ready to go to the gallows for freedom and justice. . . . I took the pamphlet in hand as one touches a holy thing. I will never forget it.

All of this became part of my new religion, and had a great effect on my feelings. After my conversion to Socialism, I withdrew from all foolishness. I was definitely a better, more serious and philosophical man.

In 1881 Cahan was a certified schoolmaster and a member of an underground revolutionary cell. Ready to begin teaching in a school near Vitebsk in 1881, Cahan had to flee the police, whose suspicions had been aroused by the young teacher's radical associations. He joined an Am Olam group, which in the wake of pogroms in the Ukraine was going to the United States to experiment with Jewish agricultural communalism.

Cahan arrived in New York on June 6, 1882. He worked for a while in a cigar factory and then for an even shorter time in a tinshop. He found the work enervating and monotonous. His joy came from teaching rudimentary English to his East Side neighbors at night. To learn the language better himself, the 22-year-old Cahan sat among 12- and 13-year-olds (mostly non-Jews) in an elementary school on Chrystie Street.

Determined to write and eager to avoid the oppression of the shops, Cahan sent his first article—a critique of czarism—to the *New York World*. Though unsolicited, the piece was published on the front page. Cahan continued to teach

English to immigrants for ten more years and encouraged assimilation, but his main contribution came in journalism, particularly the pioneering of popular Yiddish journalism. As early as the summer of 1882, Cahan had discovered a growing immigrant audience responsive to Yiddish. Unlike many of his colleagues among the radical Jewish intelligentsia who continued to write and speak Russian to immigrants whose language was Yiddish, Cahan began to deliver popular political harangues in the so-called folk vernacular. Relatively quickly Yiddish became the primary medium of communication among Jewish radicals. Lecturing in Yiddish and English in 1884 and 1885, Cahan helped organize a Jewish tailors union and a Jewish cloakmakers union. This was the beginning of a lifelong association with the militant labor movement.

For some time the consensus continued to be that Yiddish was strictly an expedient in the conduct of Socialist labor activity and not a value in itself. Many radicals, however, came to love the "despised jargon," and Cahan would champion Yiddish to journalistic and literary heights even as he tried to transcend the Yiddish-speaking community with articles and stories in the English press and several books, among them *Yekl: A Tale of the New York Ghetto* (1896) and the classic novel of the urban immigrant experience, *The Rise of David Levinsky* (1917).

Abraham Cahan's early politics resembled an eclectic stew of European ideas strongly flavored with the ethical and moral ingredients of his Jewish religious background. After having been associated with the Am Olam, which he ultimately rejected as "Utopian," Cahan described himself as an anarchist *and* a socialist. For a while he preached the violent "propaganda of the deed" and advised the poor to "march with iron bars and axes on Fifth Avenue and . . . seize the palaces of the rich." But after the Haymarket affair in 1886–1887, when seven radical agitators were sentenced to death and four were executed for the murder of seven policemen killed by a bomb at an anarchist meeting, Cahan became convinced that the anarchists were "adventurers," and he committed himself more firmly to socialism.

In order to make the appeal to socialism effective, Cahan and other journalists, organizers, and activists believed that recruits had to see social strain and discontent and the need for collective economic and political action in terms of their own cultural heritage. Cahan constantly wove biblical references and Talmudic aphorisms into his calls to labor unionism and socialism. In the first issue of *Neie Tseit* (New Times) in 1886, he used the theme of Shevuot (the festival of weeks, associated with the receiving of the Law) to illustrate Socialist principles, and he remained interested throughout most of his career in using Jewish tradition and folk-religious forms in this way. He understood and applauded the fact that the rigid mores of Jewish Orthodoxy had already undergone a loosening in Eastern Europe and that in the United States, the *trefene medina* (unkosher land), there was further erosion. But Cahan knew how thoroughly Jewish values and traditions were embedded in the Jewish imagination, even in that of a professed atheist like himself. Ethnic attachments, in the richest sense of that term, operated even on those who thought they had discarded them as "backward," and they were certainly meaningful to the average Jewish worker who read Cahan's journalism.

In 1890 in the *Arbeiter Tseitung*, Abe Cahan began a weekly column known as the *Sedre*, the portion of the Pentateuch read each week in Sabbath services. He would begin with a formal element in the liturgy, but soon took off into a discussion of Socialist matters. Cahan's pieces proved so popular that even the anarchists tried to imitate them in the *Freie Arbeiter Shtimme* (Free Voice of Labor).

The Jewish *Daily Forward*, which Cahan edited at its founding in 1897 and to which he returned permanently in 1903, became under his leadership the educator of the Jewish immigrant masses, a critical component of the Jewish labor movement and Jewish socialism, and a defender and patron of Yiddish literature and modern culture. Among the authors sustained by the *Forward* were Sholem Asch and Isaac Bashevis Singer. At its height in 1920, the *Forward* published twelve metropolitan editions from Boston to Los Angeles, and its circulation was close to 300,000. A large part of the profits went to social causes.

Abraham Cahan was a modern Socialist whose anti-capitalist views were tempered by conditions in the United States and the excesses of Soviet authoritarianism. "Russia is free," Cahan had proclaimed at the outset of the 1917 revolution. But the *Forward* became increasingly anti-Communist in the face of militant Bolshevism. In addition, Cahan continued to be interested in the particularist oppression of Jews. As early as 1891, when Cahan was a delegate of the United Hebrew Trades at the Brussels congress of the Second International, he explained that the federation of unions he represented had "nothing to do with religion or nationality" and that the word "Hebrew" was adopted "only because of the language spoken by all its members." At the same time, however, he introduced a resolution condemning anti-Semitism.

In April 1903, when the news of the Kishinev pogrom reached Cahan in Connecticut, he was bird-watching, a hobby he had developed as a break from writing. Field glasses and bird manual in hand, he immediately rushed for a New York train. "I felt an urge to be among Jews," he explained in his autobiography. Partially in response to Kishinev, Cahan wrote his little-known novel *The White Terror and the Red*, which was published in 1905. The story, set in the early 1880s, explores the conflicts of young Jewish revolutionaries and deals with their destructive attitude toward the Jewish people and the pogroms that victimized them.

In 1925, after attending the Socialist Congress at Marseilles, Cahan visited Palestine for the first time and wept at the Wailing Wall. Jewish "crises" continued to agitate him. After the 1929 anti-Jewish riots in Palestine, which a handful of radicals applauded as the beginning of "revolution," Cahan rushed to cover the impact of the events on the Jewish community there. Although he did not consider himself a Zionist, he paid tribute to the courage and idealism of Zionist pioneers.

Throughout the 1930s and 1940s Cahan continued to be productive and creative. Only after suffering a stroke in 1946 did he stop appearing at the *Forward* office on a daily basis. He died of heart failure five years later at the age of 91.

In a series of letters written between 1883 and 1884, Abraham Cahan complained of a lack of "orientation" and a "firm foundation." He was tormented over his "divided mood." Despite his marriage to Anna Bronstein in 1886, who brought sensibilities to the relationship that helped sustain Cahan for sixty years of a turbulent career, he never completely transcended the divided mood. He was, after all, a refugee from Russia observing revolutionary sacrifice from afar, and an assertive assimilationist wedded to Yiddish journalism. Cahan as a Socialist could integrate his Old World and New World selves. But Cahan the exile—hailed along with Stephen Crane and Hamlin Garland as the harbinger of a new literature, and whose *Forward*, the largest immigrant, Jewish, and Socialist paper in the world, was described as "America's most interesting daily"—never fully came to terms with his becoming something of the "successful American." The ambivalence he continued to experience showed clearly in his semi-autobiographical novel, *The Rise of David Levinsky*. David is also a "success," but reflects: "I cannot escape from my old self. . . . David, the poor lad swinging over a Talmud volume at the Preacher's Synagogue, seems to have more in common with my inner identity than David Levinsky, the well-known cloak manufacturer." By the time Cahan died, however, this complex, often troubled man was recognized as a great journalist, a legendary teacher to a people in the process of acculturation, and an indefatigable defender of the cause of labor and socialism.

SOURCES: Abraham Cahan, *Bleter fun Mayn Leben*, 5 vols. (1926–1931); Ronald Sanders, *Downtown Jews: Portraits of an Immigrant Generation* (1969); Leon Stein (ed.), *The Education of Abraham Cahan* (1969).

*GERALD SORIN*

**CALVERTON, V. F. (1900–1940).** V(ictor) F(rancis) Calverton was the author of several important volumes of Marxist literary, sociological, and historical criticism. His most significant contribution to the American Left, however, was as founder, publisher and editor of the *Modern Quarterly*.

Originally named George Goetz, Calverton was born in Baltimore, Maryland, on June 25, 1900, the oldest of three children of Charles Goetz, a German-American merchant tailor. Calverton attended public schools and in 1918, having earned his tuition as a timekeeper for Bethlehem Steel, entered Johns Hopkins University, where he studied English, philosophy, and psychology. He graduated in 1921, and after a year of graduate work at Hopkins in psychology, he began teaching in the Baltimore public schools.

Calverton traced his political awakening to hearing his father denounce American imperialism in the Spanish-American War. World War I galvanized his radicalism, and by 1918 he was a committed Socialist. In May 1922 he and several Hopkins friends published the first and last issue of a literary magazine called *Horizons*, but out of this failure came Calverton's plans for "The Radical Quarterly," a more ambitious Socialist journal. It appeared in February 1923 as the *Modern Quarterly*, and its 22-year-old editor had taken the name V. F. Calverton, fearing that the magazine would cost him his teaching job. Calverton's characteristic political tolerance and voracious intellectual appetite were established in its first number: besides the editor himself, contributors were Upton Sinclair (q.v.), Scott Nearing (q.v.), and the poet Eli Siegel. Over the next seventeen years (from 1933 to 1938 the journal was published as the *Modern Monthly*), Calverton made good his boast to print "every left-wing liberal and radical who had artistic aspirations."

When the *Newer Spirit* appeared in 1925, Mike Gold (q.v.) hailed Calverton as the "young master of the new world" who would redeem "this stuffy bourgeois country." Similar praise from Communist leaders drew Calverton closer to the Party. He published essays in the *New Masses* and wrote a column for the *Daily Worker*, but never officially joined the Party. In the summer of 1927, at Earl Browder's (q.v.) invitation, he traveled to Russia and was warmly received in Moscow.

The Communists, however, could not long tolerate Calverton's excessive broad-mindedness, especially when he published Max Eastman's (q.v.) and Sidney Hook's (q.v.) early criticism of Stalinist dogma in the *Modern Quarterly*. In 1931 the Comintern called for his intellectual liquidation and he was reviled as a "social-fascist." In January 1933 the *New Masses* devoted an unprecedented sixteen pages to a polemic against Calverton, in which Gold acknowledged his error in praising a man he now realized was an "ideological racketeer."

Party members and fellow travelers stopped writing for the *Modern Quarterly*, but Calverton struggled to remain neutral in the sectarian battles of the late 1930s. By the fall of 1938, though, the Trotskyists and several independent Marxists had abandoned him as well. After 1939 Calverton was disgusted with radicals "who try to fit America in the Marxist pattern" and spoke of himself as a "Calvertonian."

Calverton died in New York of pernicious anemia on November 20, 1940, shortly after completing his eighteenth book, *Where Angels Dared to Tread*, a history of Utopian colonies in the United States.

SOURCES: Daniel Aaron, *Writers on the Left* (1961); V. F. Calverton Memorial Issue, *Modern Quarterly* 11 (Fall 1940).

*ART CASCIATO*

**CANNON, JAMES P. (1890–1974).** James Patrick Cannon was a founder of American Communism and a central figure in the Communist Party until 1928. Subsequently he established the American Trotskyist movement and was the most important leader of the Socialist Workers Party for several decades.

Cannon was born in Rosedale, Kansas, on February 11, 1890, the son of Irish immigrants raised in England. His father, John Cannon, worked as a laborer in a foundry and introduced his son James to the Irish nationalist tradition of Robert

Emmett, the Knights of Labor, the Populists, and the Socialist Party. Leaving school to start work at age 12, Cannon was propelled into radical politics by the Haywood-Pettibone-Moyer defense case. He briefly returned to high school, but left again to become a traveling organizer for the Industrial Workers of the World and a follower of Vincent St. John (q.v.). He later joined the Socialist Party, replacing Earl Browder (q.v.) as editor of *Workers World* in Kansas when Browder was sent to prison during World War I.

Cannon quickly became a leader of the left wing of the Socialist Party. Following the 1919 expulsion of the left wing, he joined the Communist Labor Party led by John Reed (q.v.) and Benjamin Gitlow (q.v.). When the United Communist Party was formed in the spring of 1920, he was elected to its Central Committee and assigned to be organizer of the Party's St. Louis-Southern Illinois district.

Toward the end of 1920 Cannon moved to Cleveland to edit the *Toiler*, a Party organ, and in 1921 he transferred to New York to participate in the top leadership of the Party. After an internal struggle to create a legal party and end the underground existence of the Communist movement, Cannon was elected chairman of the National Committee of the Workers Party, the new aboveground organization.

In 1922–1923 he served on the Presidium of the Communist International in Moscow, and between 1925 and 1928 he headed International Labor Defense. In that capacity he raised money and publicized the cases of the Centralia prisoners, Thomas Mooney (q.v.) and Warren Billings (q.v.) and the McNamara brothers. He also organized the International Labor Defense's Sacco-Vanzetti campaign.

During these years Cannon's group of followers, including Max Shachtman (q.v.) and Martin Abern (q.v.), formed a bloc with William Z. Foster's (q.v.) group against the faction of Charles Ruthenberg (q.v.) and Jay Lovestone (q.v.) over such issues as the attitude toward a labor party, trade union strategy and tactics, the location of the national office, and the nature and composition of the Party leadership. Cannon's reminiscences of this period were later published as *The First Ten Years of American Communism* (1962).

In the summer of 1928 Cannon attended the Sixth World Congress of the Communist International, where he received a translation of Trotsky's "Criticism of the Draft Program of the Communist International." Won over to the ideas of Trotsky's Left Opposition, Cannon and his followers were expelled from the U.S. Party in October for circulating Trotsky's views.

Cannon described the first decade of the American Trotskyist movement in *The History of American Trotskyism* (1944). Along with Shachtman and Abern, he founded the Communist League of America (Left Opposition) in mid–1929 and began publishing the *Militant* newspaper. They had only one hundred followers at first, but doubled in size over the next several years. A theoretical magazine, *New International*, was launched in 1934.

That same year members of the Communist League of America were in the leadership of the sensational Minneapolis Teamster strikes, and Cannon traveled there to provide political guidance. This success helped pave the way for a fusion of the Communist League of America with A. J. Muste's (q.v.) American Workers Party at the end of 1934. The new organization was called the Workers Party of the United States, and its newspaper was the *New Militant*.

In the spring of 1936 Cannon led the Trotskyists into the Socialist Party and then moved to California, where he edited the Socialist Party paper *Labor Action*. When the Trotskyists were expelled from the Socialist Party in mid–1937, Cannon returned to New York. The Trotskyists founded the Socialist Workers Party in January 1938 with Cannon as national secretary. The following autumn he participated in the founding of the Fourth International in Paris and was elected to the International Executive Committee. The Trotskyist movement had by now grown to over 1,000 members and had considerable authority in certain sections of the labor movement as well as among New York intellectuals grouped around the literary magazine *Partisan Review*.

In the fall of 1939 a dispute erupted between factions led by Shachtman and Cannon over questions relating to actions taken by the Soviet Union in the early days of World War II. However, at the heart of the controversy was the famous question of the class nature of the Soviet Union. Shachtman would later on embrace the position, advocated by his ally James Burnham (q.v.), a New York University professor of philosophy, that a new bureaucratic class had come to power. Cannon held to Trotsky's view that the Soviet Union, due to hostile encirclement and a totalitarian political superstructure, was a ''degenerated workers' state'' (that is, despite the lack of democracy, a post-capitalist society in transition, not yet on the threshold of socialism) and that its nationalized economy should be defended against capitalist nations. Shachtman's faction split in the spring of 1940, forming the Workers Party. Cannon recorded his version of the dispute in *The Struggle for a Proletarian Party* (1942).

In 1941 Cannon and seventeen other leaders of the Socialist Workers Party and the Minneapolis Teamsters Union were convicted under the Smith Act for their opposition to U.S. government policy during World War II. Cannon's courtroom testimony is contained in *Socialism on Trial* (1942); other writings from the early war period are available in *The Socialist Workers Party in World War II* (1975).

Cannon served thirteen months of a sixteen-month sentence at Sandstone Penitentiary in 1944–1945, as described in *Letters from Prison* (1968). Following his release, Cannon participated in a factional struggle against two of his longtime associates, Albert Goldman (q.v.) and Felix Morrow (q.v.). Writings of the late 1940s are collected in *The Struggle for Socialism in the "American Century"* (1977).

During the post-war labor upsurge, the Trotskyists grew once more to over 1,000, but they fell on hard times during the McCarthy era. In 1953 there was a fierce faction fight, recorded in *Speeches to the Party* (1973), resulting in a split in both the party and in the Fourth International. This was Cannon's last major intervention as the leader of the SWP. In 1952 he had moved to Los Angeles, and at the end of 1953 Farrell Dobbs (q.v.) took over as national secretary. Cannon became national chairman and then national chairman emeritus until his death in 1974.

In addition to having the unique capacity to hold a small party together for several decades under difficult circumstances, Cannon was a talented popularizer of Socialist ideas in his lectures and writings. This can be seen in a collection of his public talks, *Speeches for Socialism* (1971), and of his journalism, *Notebook of an Agitator* (1958). Cannon was married first to Lista Makimson, who died in 1929, and then to Rose Karsner, who died in 1968.

SOURCES: Theodore Draper, *The Roots of American Communism* (1957) and *American Communism and Soviet Russia* (1960); Les Evans (ed.), *James P. Cannon as We Knew Him* (1976).

*ALAN WALD*

**CARLSON, OLIVER (b. 1899).** Oliver Carlson, national secretary of the Socialist youth organization, headed the first American Communist youth group and worked as a Communist Party functionary before resigning in the late 1920s. Carlson was born in Gutland, Sweden, on July 31, 1899, and brought to the United States in 1902. His father, of Swedish Lutheran background, was a cabinetmaker and a Socialist. After a brief sojourn in Warren, Pennsylvania, the family settled in Muskegon, Michigan, where Oliver founded a Young People's Socialist League (YPSL) branch in 1912 and joined the Socialist Party two years later. After one year at the University of Michigan, he became fully involved in Socialist politics and was elected national secretary of the YPSL in April 1919.

Although Carlson was pro-Communist, he resisted overtures to join from both the Communist Party and the Communist Labor Party formed in 1919. A YPSL convention, held in Rochester, New York, decided to remain independent but pro-Communist. Sent as a delegate to a Young Socialist International meeting in Europe in 1921, Carlson finally decided to break with the Socialist Party. After evading police from several European countries, he and a number of like-minded young Socialists arrived in Moscow and set up the Young Communist International (YCI). Carlson was the only American delegate. After returning to the United States, he formed the Young Workers League, the first Communist youth group in the nation, and was selected national secretary and the editor of *Young Worker*.

Associated with William Foster's (q.v.) Party faction, Carlson took on a variety of tasks in the next several years, serving as district organizer in the Northwest in 1922, spending a year in Moscow as American representative to the YCI in 1923–1924 (during which time he also traveled throughout Europe as a YCI representative and reorganized Great Britain's Young Communist League), and then directing the Workers School in New York. When Foster's group lost control of the Party in 1925, Carlson was relegated to minor jobs in the educational department in Illinois and Seattle. After a stint as Western campaign manager for the Foster-Gitlow (q.v.) presidential ticket in 1928, he resigned from the Party, disillusioned with its policies and internal feuding.

From 1930 to 1932 Carlson did graduate work in political science at the University of Chicago. He taught at Commonwealth College in Arkansas and briefly worked for the Amalgamated Clothing Workers. He joined A. J. Muste's (q.v.) American Workers Party in 1934 and became its educational director, but in 1935 he gave up his radical beliefs, embarking on a career as a writer and publishing the first biography of William Randolph Hearst.

Carlson became a well-known author and essayist. He served one year as director of public relations for California's New Deal governor, Culbert Olson, and several years with the Voice of America. In 1952 he was campaign manager of Democrats for Eisenhower in Southern California. In 1985 Carlson was living in retirement in Carlsbad, California.

SOURCES: Oliver Carlson, "Recollections of American Trotskyist Leaders," *Studies in Comparative Communism*, Spring-Summer 1977. See also Oliver Carlson, Oral History Interview, March 20–22, 1978, Emory University Library, Atlanta, Georgia.

*HARVEY KLEHR*

**CARMICHAEL, STOKELY (b. 1941).** Stokely Carmichael (Kwame Toure, or Tore), who served as chairman of the Student Nonviolent Coordinating Committee and prime minister of the Black Panther Party, was a major black militant figure of the 1960s and a prominent advocate of Pan-Africanism. Carmichael was born in Port-of-Spain, Trinidad, on June 29, 1941. His Panamanian-born mother, Mabel, went to Trinidad as a teenager, married Adolphus Carmichael, a carpenter, and then emigrated to the United States during World War II. At the age of 11, Stokely Carmichael, along with other members of the family, joined his mother in Harlem. He became a naturalized citizen in 1954. After the family moved to an Italian-American neighborhood in the Bronx, Carmichael won admission to the selective Bronx High School of Science, graduating in 1960. While attending high school, he became a friend of the son of Communist Party leader Eugene Dennis (q.v.), through whom he met several veteran black radicals. Active in Socialist youth politics, he joined a Marxist discussion group and participated in demonstrations against the House Committee on Un-American Activities.

After enrolling at Howard University, Carmichael joined the Nonviolent Action Group (NAG) and participated in student protests against segregated facilities in the Washington, D.C., area. In 1961 he joined a "freedom ride" to Jackson, Mississippi, where he was arrested after entering the waiting room reserved for whites. In Parchman Penitentiary, he strengthened his ties with other movement activists and briefly considered dropping out of school to work full-time with the Student Nonviolent Coordinating Committee (SNCC), which had been formed in 1960. Convinced by his parents that he should return to Howard, Carmichael remained active in the protest movement. As an NAG representative at SNCC meetings, he stressed economic concerns rather than simply a focus on desegregation. In addition to his academic studies at Howard, his activities included freedom rides in Maryland, mass demonstrations in Albany, Georgia, and a hospital workers strike in New York.

Graduating in 1964 with a degree in philosophy, Carmichael joined SNCC's staff as director of a summer voter registration project in the second Congressional district of Mississippi. He and other black activists increasingly exhibited racial militancy, especially after Democratic Party leaders at the 1964 convention refused to unseat the regular, all-white Mississippi delegation in favor of the delegation of the Freedom Democratic Party. Though he maintained close relations with white radicals in SNCC, he became increasingly dubious about the prospects of interracial activism within the existing political structure. He left Mississippi in the winter of 1965 to help Alabama blacks form the Lowndes County Freedom Organization, an all-black, independent political group that became better known as the Black Panther Party.

In May 1966 Carmichael was elected chairman of SNCC, and soon afterward, as a result of his speeches on a march through Mississippi, he became nationally prominent as a proponent of "black power." During the following year, Carmichael delivered hundreds of speeches arguing for black unity and for a redefinition of the relationship between blacks and white liberal allies. Although he opposed the decision to expel whites from SNCC, he joined with Black Nationalists in stressing the primacy of racial unity over class unity as a basis for future black struggles. After relinquishing the SNCC chairmanship in 1967, he made a controversial trip to Cuba, China, North Vietnam, and finally to Guinea, where he conferred with exiled Ghanian leader Kwame Nkrumah, who became his Pan-Africanist mentor. Returning to the United States with the intention of forming Black United Front groups through the nation, he accepted an invitation to become prime minister of the Oakland-based Black Panther Party. His black separatist stance resulted in conflicts with other Panther leaders, including Eldridge Cleaver (q.v.) and Huey Newton (q.v.), who saw themselves as Marxist-Leninists. Despite these ideological disagreements, Carmichael remained associated with the Panthers even after the breakup, in August 1968, of the party's short-lived alliance with SNCC. During 1968 he married South African singer Miriam Makeba and later established permanent residency in Guinea. After he became the target of criticism in Panther publications, he resigned his position.

As a follower of Nkrumah, Carmichael helped to form the All-African People's Revolutionary Party (AAPRP) in 1972, which called for "the total liberation and unification of Africa under scientific socialism." On subsequent speaking tours in the United States, he argued against black alliances with white leftists and for a redirection of the energies of Afro-American radicals toward the goal of African liberation. During the 1970s, Carmichael changed his name to Kwame Toure (after Nkrumah and Guinean leader Sekou Toure). Carmichael remains active in the leadership of the AAPRP.

SOURCES: Clayborne Carson, *In Struggle: SNCC and the Black Awakening of the 1960s* (1981); Howard Zinn, *SNCC: The New Abolitionists* (1964).

*CLAYBORNE CARSON*

**CHARNEY, GEORGE BLAKE (1905–1975).** George Blake Charney was for two decades a leading Communist functionary. He was born in Ekaterinoslav, Russia, in February 1905 to Jewish parents who immigrated to the United States the following year. The family settled in Brooklyn, where the elder Charney operated first a grocery store and then a clothing store. Charney graduated from the Wharton School of the University of Pennsylvania in 1927, did one year of graduate work in economics at Harvard, and received a law degree from New York University in 1931. He joined the Communist Party in 1933. Two years later he abandoned his legal career to become a full-time Party functionary, one of many younger, American-raised Communists moving into responsible positions as the Party broke out of its isolation.

Charney's first assignment was organizational secretary of the New England district. Early in 1937 he was appointed organizational secretary in Harlem, in which post he played a key role in the Party's relationship with the American Labor Party and Congressman Vito Marcantonio (q.v.). In mid–1940 he was assigned to the New York State office of the Communist Party. After his discharge from the army in 1945, Charney became county organizer in Manhattan and a member of the New York State secretariat, one of those responsible for shaping the policies that helped isolate the Party in the late 1940s.

Charney was arrested for violating the Smith Act in 1951. Anxious to broaden the defense strategy and avoid the issue of revolution, he came into conflict with William Foster (q.v.). Convicted and sentenced to two years in prison, Charney was freed after a key witness, Harvey Matusow, admitted committing perjury. He was retried and convicted, but this decision was overturned in higher court in 1958. Charney was elected chairman of the New York Party in 1956 and also put on the National Board. Identified with the reformers around John Gates (q.v.), who hoped to democratize the Party and wean it from its close Russian ties, Charney was gradually isolated as their supporters left the Party in the wake of revelations about Stalin's crimes. He stepped down from his New York post in 1957 and resigned from the Communist Party in May 1958. Charney worked in the printing industry after his resignation. He died on December 13, 1975.
SOURCE: George B. Charney, *A Long Journey* (1968).

*HARVEY KLEHR*

**CHILDS, MORRIS (b. 1902).** Morris Childs was a longtime top functionary of the American Communist Party whose intimate knowledge of its secret work and close acquaintance with Soviet leaders made him the FBI's most valuable Communist informant ever following his secret 1952 recruitment. Born Morris Chilofsky to Jewish parents near Kiev, Russia, on June 10, 1902, he immigrated to the United States along with his three younger brothers when all were children. He became a naturalized U.S. citizen on October 18, 1927, in Chicago, where he worked as a draftsman and milk-truck driver. Before the end of the decade he had emerged as one of the Chicago Party's most promising young cadres.

Early in the 1930s Childs was sent to the Lenin School in Moscow, where he distinguished himself as a loyal supporter of Soviet preferences during factional strife. Upon his return to the United States, Childs was named district organizer in Milwaukee, and in 1935 he was promoted to Chicago district organizer and Illinois Party state secretary. In 1938 Childs was elected to the National Committee, and in 1945 he moved to New York to take over the Party's political action work. The following year he was named editor of the *Daily Worker*, and he held that post until June 27, 1947, when he was forced to step aside as a sacrificial offering by Eugene Dennis' (q.v.) majority faction to assuage complaints from the hard-line minority led by William Z. Foster (q.v.).

Childs was astounded and infuriated by his removal, and along with younger brother Jack, a longtime Communist operative, he quietly drifted away from the Party. Approached in the spring of 1952 by the FBI as part of a standing program to attempt recruitment of disaffected members, both the Childs brothers agreed to become FBI informants and to reactivate themselves within the secret world of the Party's shadowy financial operations. By the mid–1950s the two men had become central links in the chain by which Soviet financial support was furnished to the American Communist Party, and Morris regularly traveled to the Soviet Union and other Communist bloc countries, earning a private nickname as "the Ambassador" among the top inner circle of the American Party. Childs' international jaunts included a Spring 1964 visit with Cuba's Fidel Castro, undertaken at the FBI's behest so as to explore secretly possible Cuban sponsorship of Lee Harvey Oswald, assassin of President John F. Kennedy.

Married three times, the father of one son, and a longtime resident of Skokie, Illinois, Childs outlived his younger brother and compatriot Jack, who died in 1980, a year before their informant work (which the FBI spoke of by the code name "Solo") was exposed publicly.

SOURCE: David J. Garrow, *The FBI and Martin Luther King, Jr.: From "Solo" to Memphis* (1981).

*DAVID J. GARROW*

**CLAESSENS, AUGUST (1885–1954).** August Claessens was a Socialist member of the New York State Assembly and a speaker, writer, organizer, and administrator for the New York City Socialist Party. Born in 1885 in Berne, Switzerland, Claessens migrated to New York during childhood. He was educated in the Roman Catholic parochial schools of that city and worked as a newsboy while going to grammar school. In the period between 1900 and 1910, Claessens worked as a housepainter, grocery clerk, shipping clerk, and performed professionally as an elocutionist and pantomimist.

An interest in furthering his theatrical career led Claessens to study elocution at Cooper Union on the Lower East Side of New York City. His studies at Cooper Union led him to further his education at the Rand School, a major Socialist institution. While at the Rand School, Claessens became interested in socialism and the Yiddish language. Within two years—by 1909—he became proficient in Yiddish, the language of the East European Jewish immigrants to the United States. And he became a convinced Socialist. Although he was a Roman Catholic by birth, Claessens was closely affiliated with the predominantly Jewish Social Democratic movement of New York City for the next forty-five years.

By 1910 Claessens abandoned the theater for the lecture platform. He spoke throughout the United States at Socialist meetings, particularly in Jewish communities. He also lectured widely at meetings and rallies of the Workmen's Circle, the Jewish labor fraternal order.

He joined with other Socialists in opposing the war in 1917 and was threatened with arrest that same year. The Socialists, in defiance of the pro-war hysteria then sweeping the nation, nominated Claessens for the New York State Assembly from a Jewish district in the Williamsburgh section of Brooklyn. He campaigned in Yiddish and English and was easily elected in 1917. He was reelected in 1918 and 1919. But along with four other elected Socialists, he was refused his seat by the Assembly majority after his reelection in 1920. The legislative session that denied him his seat was assailed by Charles Evans Hughes, later Chief Justice of the United States, who filed a brief for the bar association opposing the action. In a bye-election, Claessens won, but he was again denied his seat. He was elected again in 1922 and seated.

That same year the party was torn asunder by the struggle with the newly formed Communist movement. Although Claessens was friendly with the Bolshevik government in Russia, he opposed the ultra-radical rhetoric and posturing of the early Communist movement in the United States. The split cost him his seat in 1923.

Between 1921 and 1936 Claessens was an administrator of the New York Socialist Party. During that period he was also active writing Socialist books, including a guide for Socialist speakers, and twelve major pamphlets, including one, *The Blue Eagle Is Dead, So What?* published in 1935, an unfriendly critique of the New Deal of Franklin D. Roosevelt.

During the internal strife between "left-wing" Militants and the more moderate "Old Guard" of the Socialist Party, Claessens supported the "Old Guard." In 1936 he withdrew from the party to help form the Social Democratic Federation, of which he was national chairman from 1936 to 1954. He joined with the other Social Democrats in supporting Roosevelt's reelection bid in 1936 under the banner of the American Labor Party (ALP). Claessens ran for office more than twenty times as a Socialist and was a candidate for several offices on the ALP ticket between 1936 and 1940.

In 1944 Claessens joined with Paul Blanshard (q.v.) and Harry W. Laidler (q.v.), among other Socialist leaders, in fighting the Communist–Sidney Hillman coalition which had captured the American Labor Party. That same year he helped form the new Liberal Party. Between 1945 and 1954 Claessens was a candidate of the Liberal Party for the state assembly from his old district. He failed to be elected, although he lost a close contest the last year of his life. Claessens died one month after the 1954 election.

SOURCES: August Claessens, *Didn't We Have Fun* (1953); August Claessens and William H. Feigenbaum, *Socialists in the New York Assembly* (1918).

*BERNARD K. JOHNPOLL*

**CLEAVER, LEROY ELDRIDGE (b. 1935).** Eldridge Cleaver was a Black Muslim leader, a radical writer and journalist, the minister of information for the Black Panther Party, the director of the International Section of the Black Panther Party in Algiers, and, since his return to the United States in 1975, a Christian evangelist. He was born on August 31, 1935, in Wabbaseka, Arkansas, to Leroy Cleaver, a waiter and piano player in a Little Rock nightclub, and Thelma Cleaver, an elementary school teacher. When his father got a job as a dining-car waiter, the family moved to Phoenix. Soon after the family moved again, this time to the Watts section of Los Angeles, his parents separated.

Eldridge had his first brush with the police in Phoenix, and in Los Angeles he was arrested for stealing bicycles and sent to reform school. An arrest when he was 18 led to a two-and-one-half year sentence to the California state prison at Soledad. Cleaver completed his secondary school education at Soledad, and continued his education in the prison library. When he was paroled in 1957, he began assaulting white women in what he later called, in his partly autobiographical book, *Soul on Ice*, "rage [as] . . . an insurrectionary act." "It delighted me," he said, "that I was defying and trampling upon the white man's law, upon his system of values, and that I was defiling his women" . . . (p. 14). At the end of the year, he was arrested and convicted on an assault-with-intent-to-kill charge. He received a two-to-fourteen year sentence and was sent to San Quentin. While at San Quentin he became associated with the Black Muslims, and although he was never formally inducted, he was considered both by himself and by others to be a Black Muslim leader.

Cleaver continued educating himself and began to write. When Beverly Axelrod—a lawyer and civil rights advocate with whom Cleaver had corresponded—visited Cleaver at Soledad, he gave her his manuscripts. He soon was writing for *Ramparts* magazine. Axelrod and other Cleaver sympathizers began working for his parole. In December 1966 he was released from Soledad on parole and began working as a senior editor at *Ramparts*.

Cleaver helped to found Black House, a cultural and social center for young blacks in San Francisco. At a meeting at Black House in February 1967, he met the co-founders of the Black Panthers, Huey Newton (q.v.) and Bobby Seale (q.v.). He joined the Panthers and became their minister of information. He edited the Black Panther newspaper and spoke widely for the party. He continued to work as a journalist for *Ramparts*, but became increasingly involved in politics. After he spoke to 65,000 people at an anti-Vietnam rally on April 15, 1967, in San Francisco, his parole board began to warn him about engaging in controversial political activities.

Cleaver met Kathleen Neal, the daughter of Ernest Neal, a U.S. Foreign Service officer, at a Student Nonviolent Coordinating Committee Conference at Fisk University in March 1967, and they were married on December 27 of that year. In the meantime Cleaver became the acting leader of the Panthers; Huey Newton was arrested for murder on October 28, 1967, and Bobby Seale was in jail. Cleaver's parole officers continued to warn him that his political activities were endangering his parole.

On April 6, 1968, Cleaver was arrested after a shootout between the Panthers and the police in which Cleaver's companion, Bobby Hutton, was killed. The California Adult Authority revoked Cleaver's parole. Two months later the Panthers' lawyer, Charles Garry, obtained Cleaver's release on a writ of habeas corpus. In mid-September, Cleaver was charged with three counts of attempted murder and three counts of assault with a deadly weapon on a police officer. December 2 was set as a trial date, and he was ordered to return to prison.

The Panthers had allied with white radicals in the Peace and Freedom Party and nominated Cleaver as their candidate for U.S. President. He continued to gather attention through the sales of *Soul on Ice* and through his many public appearances. The students and faculty of the University of California at Berkeley invited him to conduct a class on racism, and his popularity with student radicals soared. In the presidential election on November 5 he received over 36,000 votes.

Cleaver believed he would be murdered in prison and jumped bail, fleeing to Cuba in May 1969. Soon after, the Cuban authorities arranged for Cleaver to go to Algiers. The Algerian government provided quarters in Algiers for Cleaver and other fugitive Panthers. They established the International Section of the Black Panther Party, with Cleaver as head, and opened the Afro-American Information Center. In June 1969 Cleaver called himself a ''Marxist-Leninist . . . socialist.'' He claimed that socialism should not suppress civil liberties and that the United States was a good place for this kind of socialism, ''a Yankee-Doodle-Dandy version,'' to develop.

In the next two years Cleaver traveled throughout Africa, to North Korea twice, and to China, and he spent six weeks in North Vietnam. He was a part of a delegation of journalists traveling under Communist sponsorship throughout Asia, the U.S. People's Anti-Imperialist Delegation, when he went to the Far East in 1970. Recognition by the Asian Communists, especially by the North Vietnamese, lent credibility to the International Section of the Panthers and to Cleaver. The Panthers supported themselves in Algiers by trafficking in stolen passports, by counterfeiting visas, and by running stolen cars from Europe. They also received a monthly financial allotment from the Algerian government. In the summer of 1972, after the Algerian government had returned a $1.5 million ransom brought to Algeria by Panther skyjackers, Cleaver wrote an open protest letter to the Algerian president, Houari Boumedienne. After disagreements with the Algerian government mounted, Cleaver went to Paris in January 1973.

Cleaver's support in the United States had in the meantime waned. The Panthers rejected him for being too militant and too dangerous. He began to feel increasingly isolated and depressed. One evening in 1975, while in his apartment on the Mediterranean coast in the south of France, Cleaver had a religious experience, which he described later in *Soul on Fire*, published in 1978. He decided he wanted to return to the United States and began to negotiate an arrangement with U.S. authorities. In November 1975 he flew to New York and was arrested. In 1980 he received five years probation.

While out on bail Cleaver had founded an evangelical group. He soon endorsed the work of South Korean evangelist Sun Myung Moon. He began speaking on campuses, under the sponsorship of the Collegiate Association for the Research of Principles (CARP), an arm of the Reverend Moon's Unification Church. Cleaver endorsed Ronald Reagan in the 1980 presidential race, and he began telling audiences that "the United States is the best country in the world." In January 1984 he announced that he was running for U.S. Congress as an independent conservative for the seat held by Representative Ronald V. Dellums (D., Calif.), but later he dropped out of the race, citing a lack of funds.

SOURCES: Eldridge Cleaver, *Soul on Fire* (1978); *Soul on Ice* (1968).

*MART STEWART*

**CLEYRE, VOLTAIRINE DE (1866–1912).** Voltairine de Cleyre was an anarchist writer and lecturer of the late nineteenth and early twentieth centuries. She was born in Leslie, Michigan, on November 17, 1866. Her mother was influenced by the abolitionist movement. Her father was influenced by the Socialist free-thought tradition of nineteenth-century France, his native land. She was educated at the Convent of Our Lady Huron, in Sarnia, Ontario, Canada. Her reaction to the strict discipline of the convent is believed to be responsible for her hatred of authority.

Voltairine identified herself as a free thinker at the age of 19. Two years later—in 1887—she was converted to socialism after hearing a speech by Clarence Darrow. At the same time, she began the study of anarchism, principally through Benjamin Tucker's publication *Liberty*. Her revulsion at the Haymarket tragedy converted her to anarchism. She delivered a lecture or speech at each anniversary of that event during her lifetime.

De Cleyre was also an outspoken supporter of women's liberation. She strongly protested the position assigned to women, as well as the roles assigned to each of the sexes. She claimed that a married woman was no more than a chattel of her husband. True love, she maintained, was free. She never married, although she did have several lovers. She had one son.

She moved to Philadelphia in 1889 and remained there for twenty-one years. She lived among the poor Jewish immigrants, whom she admired, and taught English to a group of Jewish anarchists and learned their language, Yiddish. She wrote for the *Freie Arbeiter Shtimme* (The Free Voice of Labor), the Jewish anarchists' publication.

Voltairine de Cleyre and her contemporary, Emma Goldman (q.v.), had different opinions of both life and anarchism, although both were anarchists. De Cleyre was ascetic and believed she was a true believer whose primary concern was the poor and ignorant. She disapproved of Goldman's flamboyant lifestyle as well as her appeal to middle-class intellectuals.

De Cleyre began her public life as a pacifist. She preached peaceful propaganda and nonresistance to the evil personified by the state, but she did sympathize with those who called for social revolution. By 1907 she came to believe that violent acts were the only means for opposing exploitation and tyranny. Although she still disapproved of terrorism, she blamed the state rather than the perpetrators, that is, Alexander Berkman (q.v.) and Leon F. Czolgosz (Czolgosz assassinated President William McKinley). She admired the lofty intentions of those who committed political assassinations. The inhumane nature of developing capitalism was, she averred, responsible for the tactic of "direct action." She argued that there had to be a change within the individual if there was to be a free society.

In 1890 de Cleyre considered herself to be an individualist anarchist, as opposed to the Communist anarchism of Goldman. The latter believed in a system of cooperation; de Cleyre favored a system based on competition to be more desirable. She later changed her belief in the individualism preached by Tucker for the mutualism of Dyer D. Lum (q.v.), and she extolled the virtues of compassion for the poor and the downtrodden instead of cold intellectualizing. She believed that administration under anarchism would be similar to government and would repress individual freedom, which should be paramount.

She now subscribed to the theories of Spanish anarchists Ricardo Mella and Fernando Tarrido del Marmol, which was called "anarchism without objectives." This theory recognized that conditions differed at various times and places. Adherence to any one system would be divisive; the primary concern should be the struggle against the state and for personal liberty. Her primary interest was that there would be no compulsion in any economic community.

De Cleyre claimed that anarchism was in the American tradition, with roots in Thomas Paine, Thomas Jefferson, Ralph Waldo Emerson, and Henry David Thoreau. She argued that it would be reasonable to assume that Jefferson's political theory could lead to no government at all. She wrote that every age has a dominant force. The present era is materialistic. There are admirable persons who reject this force and defend the code of free will and personal responsibility. We should not deny the force of the idea, she asserted. But before humans can be truly free, they must give up their authoritarian notions. She wanted humans to abandon "things" and return to an austere existence. Her ideal society would be rural, with small farmers and craftsmen. She condemned the technology that benefited the employer while making life unbearable for the workers. Although she was a supporter of Francisco Ferrer and his ideas of "modern educational reform," she later became disenchanted with his idea of the Modern School.

By 1912 she had totally abandoned pacifism and called for direct action. She now sympathized with the Industrial Workers of the World, the anarcho-syndicalist labor militants, in their opposition to capitalism. She was also a staunch supporter of the Mexican peasants in their revolution of 1911.

On December 19, 1902, de Cleyre was shot by an insane anarchist. Although she was severely injured, she did survive. In keeping with her principles, she refused to identify her assailant to police. Herman Helcher, who admitted his guilt, was later diagnosed to be suffering from paranoia. De Cleyre wrote that he was deranged and should be placed in a mental hospital rather than a prison.

By 1910 De Cleyre left Philadelphia for Chicago, where she died of a brain inflammation on June 12, 1912.

SOURCE: Paul Avrich, *An American Anarchist: The Life of Voltairine de Cleyre* (1978).

*LILLIAN KIRTZMAN JOHNPOLL*

**COLLINS, JOHN A. (1810–1890).** John Anderson Collins was a pre–Civil War Socialist, a follower of Robert Owen (q.v.), and the founder of the short-lived Owenite community near Skaneateles, New York. Born in Manchester, Vermont, in 1810 of pious, upper-middle-class parents, Collins was educated at Middlebury College in Vermont and the Andover Theological Seminary in Massachusetts.

Upon graduating from seminary in 1839, Collins worked for the abolitionist movement led by William Lloyd Garrison. A devoted proponent of the abolition of slavery in the United States, Collins soon became a trusted aide to Garrison. In 1840 Garrison trusted him to become the Anti-Slavery Society's general agent in Great Britain. His primary function there was to raise and transmit money to the American society. During the year he was in England, Collins became converted to socialism by studying the work of Robert Owen, whom he met. He also met Chartists, many of whom were followers of Owen.

Collins had become an avowed Owenite Socialist by the time he returned to the United States, at which point he was named the general agent for the Anti-Slavery Society for Upstate New York, which was then the center of radical agitation in the United States. In the upstate area, known as the Burned-Over District, he worked with the famed black abolitionist Frederick Douglass. Within a year, however, Collins resigned his post and became active in spreading the Owenite philosophy.

Abolitionism, he argued, was essentially interested in curing the symptoms rather than the cause of slavery. A radical answer was needed to eliminate the evil, a solution that would reconstruct society so that no form of slavery—neither chattel nor wage—could ever again exist. Toward that end, he argued, it was necessary to abolish all private property, which he believed to be the cause of all social evil. The private ownership of property was, in his view, the cause of class strife. Economic power determined political power. A small class of entrepreneurs had seized power by usurping that which should belong to all society—land, mills, goods. That class, he believed, also gained control of the government, whose primary aim thus became the protection of the economic, social, and political power of the ruling class.

Collins denied that any individual or group of individuals was to blame for the inequities in society. Circumstances and the social system were at fault. This position signified a major break with the abolitionists, who believed that the individual slaveholder was avaricious and immoral. Collins believed that the slaveholder was merely a product of the system.

Opposed to all religion, no matter how liberal, Collins argued that all religion was based on falsehood, that the primary function of religion was to lull the people, primarily the lower class. He denied that salvation from sin was possible and that the Bible was a historical account of the world. He considered the Bible to be a lie. Organized religion, he said, was a sower of strife; it was the very negation of the peace and love it ostensibly preached.

Just as he denounced religion for spreading strife, so too did he assail capitalism for placing power in the hands of the most selfish and most unethical groups in society. It was, he said, a system which placed a premium on cant. Collins declaimed that the disparity of power and of economic possessions created two classes in society; the capitalist system encourages fraud, deception, and crime. And technology, which should have been a boon to society, had instead created crime and suffering in the hands of the capitalist system.

The solution proposed by Collins had two distinct aspects, political and economic. Both had to be affected if either was to work. First, he proposed that all economic competition and all private property be abolished. Instead there should be social ownership of the means of production and distribution. Second, he wanted all coercive government abolished. He urged his followers to refuse to pay taxes, to refuse to fight in any war—no matter how just it seemed to be— to refuse to vote, or to serve on juries, or to testify at trials, or to do business of any kind with the government. In sum, he wanted a general strike against the government's coercive power. He suggested the peaceful destruction of government. The Fourierite journal of Brook Farm, *The Harbinger*, ridiculed Collins' proposal as "no government, no religion, no business, no property, and vegetarianism."

Criticism—and there was much—did not deter Collins. He went ahead in 1845 with plans to open his community. To avoid previous debacles he required that 75 percent of the members of the community had to approve any new members. Once admitted, however, the new members were to have absolute freedom. Soon internal disputes broke out in Skaneateles, although Owen, who visited the community early in 1845, the year of its formation, praised its management. By the next year the feuding made it impossible to continue the operation and it was abandoned.

Collins was by now disillusioned with socialism. He went to San Francisco, where he became a leading attorney and a defender of the rights of dissenters. During the 1870s and 1880s he fought against the anti-Oriental agitation on the West Coast and strongly denounced the cry for an Oriental-exclusion act. He also defended the rights of free-thinkers then under attack in San Francisco and was the defense attorney in a case against *Free Thought* magazine. He charged no fee for his legal work in defense of Orientals or for the publisher of an anti-religious journal.

In 1889 he ridiculed Edward Bellamy's Socialist novel *Looking Backward*, which was then the rage of intellectual readers. "I've been there before over the past fifty years," he said.

In 1890, as he celebrated his eightieth birthday, John Anderson Collins died in San Francisco.

SOURCE: Bernard K. Johnpoll with Lillian Johnpoll, *The Impossible Dream* (1981).

*BERNARD K. JOHNPOLL*

**CONNELLY, PHILIP MARSHALL (1903-1981).** Philip Marshall ("Slim") Connelly, a Communist leader in the California union movement, was born in Everett, Pennsylvania, on December 23, 1903, the son of a working-class Catholic family. Although his father was a prominent member of the Glass Blowers Union, Connelly demonstrated little interest in unionism during his early years as a reporter on the *Los Angeles Herald and Express*, a large-circulation Hearst paper. In 1937, however, angered by management's intransigence during negotiations for a new contract, he became active in the newly formed Los Angeles Newspaper Guild, an affiliate of the Congress of Industrial Organizations (CIO). Instrumental in organizing a strong guild unit on the *Herald and Express*, Connelly's obvious leadership ability and powerful physical presence soon attracted the attention of guild activists, and in January 1938 he was elected president of the Los Angeles lodge. In the summer of 1938 Connelly played an important organizational role in the successful *Hollywood Citizen-News* strike and was recruited into the Communist Party. Shortly thereafter he was elected state president of the newly formed California CIO Council and secretary of the Los Angeles Industrial Union Council.

During the decade of his greatest influence and power in the Los Angeles and California CIO, from 1938 to 1947, Connelly attempted to maintain a non-Communist identity, repeatedly denying accusations of Party affiliation from opponents both inside and outside the labor movement. Allegations of Communist Party membership became particularly damaging during the period of the Nazi-Soviet Pact, when Connelly participated in several Communist-led organizations, including the American Peace Mobilization. The Red-baiting campaign of the early 1940s reached a peak in June 1941, when the Los Angeles CIO, headed by Connelly, gave its support to a strike at the North American Aviation plant. The strikers were accused of being part of a larger Communist campaign to sabotage the American defense effort. Shortly after the settlement of the dispute, however, the Communist Party again reversed its policy vis-à-vis U.S. participation in the war when Germany invaded Russia.

During the war years Connelly reached the apex of his power in the Los Angeles labor movement and in local Democratic Party politics, devoting his efforts both to consolidating CIO and left-wing gains and to maintaining industrial peace in the growing war economy of California. Although he played a crucial role in the postwar strikes of 1945–1946, Connelly's influence began to decline during the CIO's campaign against the Left-led unions in 1947, and in 1948 he was removed as executive secretary of the state CIO.

In the following years Connelly worked as editor of the Communist Party's *People's World*. In September 1951 he was arrested, together with several other California Communist Party leaders, under the Smith Act. Connelly received a five-year sentence in August 1952, but in 1957 the Supreme Court reversed the convictions and he returned to *People's World*. He later obtained a position with the Communist-dominated World Federation of Trade Unions, based in New York, but in the early 1960s he retired to Los Angeles and no longer participated in Communist Party activities. Connelly died on May 20, 1981.

*MICHAEL FURMANOVSKY*

**COSTIGAN, HOWARD (b. 1904).** Howard Costigan was a founder and leader of the Communist-led Washington Commonwealth Federation (WCF) and later an enforcer of the anti-Communist Hollywood blacklist. Born in Seattle in 1904, Costigan worked briefly in the mills while attending high school. In 1919 he witnessed the infamous massacre of workers in Centralia, Washington. Although radicalized by this event, Costigan did not seriously enter politics until the early 1930s, when, following a brief career as a hairdresser, he began doing "progressive radio commentary." In August 1934 he joined with members of Technocracy, the Seattle Unemployed Citizens League, and several other organizations advocating "production for use" to form the Commonwealth Builders Inc. (CBI). With an ideology and program similar to that of the California EPIC (End Poverty in California) movement, the CBI, headed by Costigan, worked within the Washington Democratic Party, and attempted to align it toward the left wing of the New Deal.

The CBI, incorporating increasing numbers of farm workers and union members, reorganized in 1935 as the Washington Commonwealth Federation (WCF) and announced its full support for Franklin Roosevelt. The Communist Party, which was banned from the WCF, initially denounced Executive Secretary Costigan as a "social-fascist." In 1936, however, the Party reversed its stance, and within a year it had successfully entered the WCF at the highest levels of leadership. In late 1936 Costigan himself was informally recruited into the Communist Party, and in the next three years the political objectives of the two organizations appeared to be virtually indistinguishable.

During the years 1937-1939 the Communist Party through careful planning and discipline won control of the WCF, with Costigan himself secretly sitting on the Party's district bureau. In 1938 he played a major role in the WCF's state election campaign and together with other members of the Federation was accused of being a Communist, a charge he denied. The elections marked the peak of WCF strength and several Federation members were elected to the state legislature.

Following the Nazi-Soviet Pact, Costigan attempted to maintain WCF support for Roosevelt and collective security. Communist control of the WCF executive board, however, ensured that the Federation's policies followed the new Party line, and in April 1940 Costigan left both the WCF and the Communist Party to support the President's reelection. In the following years he held several important administrative positions within the state Democratic Party, but in 1946 he broke with Washington Governor Mon Wallgren on the issue of communism and ran in the Democratic primaries against Representative Hugh DeLacey, who was widely acknowledged as a Communist sympathizer or member. Although DeLacey won the primary, he was defeated by his "Red-baiting" Republican opponent. After the election, the Washington Democratic Party began a campaign to expel all suspected Communists.

In 1948 Costigan voluntarily appeared before the Washington State Un-American Activities Committee as a friendly witness and later received $2,050 as payment for his work as an "undercover agent" for the committee. His anti-Communist credentials and testimony soon attracted the attention of both the Federal Bureau of Investigation and labor leader Roy Brewer, and in 1948 Costigan was employed by Brewer as secretary of the League of Hollywood Voters, made up of American Federation of Labor craft unions in Hollywood that served as a clearinghouse for Democratic candidates for public office. Costigan later worked as an assistant to Brewer in playing a major role in the blacklisting of actors and entertainment figures with suspected Communist or left-wing ties.

SOURCES: John Cogley, *Report on Blacklisting* (1956); Vern Countryman, *Un-American Activities in the State of Washington* (1951); *Investigation of Communist Activities in the Pacific Northwest Area*, Part 1, House Un-American Activities Committee, 83d Congress, 2d Session, pp. 5975-5997.

*MICHAEL FURMANOVSKY*

# D

---

**DARCY, SAMUEL (b. 1905).** Samuel Adams Darcy was a youth leader first for the Socialists and later for the Communists, and by age 25 he was a veteran Stalinist official with wide experience both in the United States and abroad. Although Darcy possessed the talents and training necessary to rise to the highest level within the Communist Party of the United States (CPUSA), for over a decade he disagreed strongly with the policies of General Secretary Earl Browder (q.v.). In 1944 he was ousted from the Party. When Moscow forced Browder's ouster the following year, many Marxists expected Darcy to return as a candidate for a leading CPUSA post, but he remained outside radical politics.

Darcy was born Samuel Dardeck on November 6, 1905, in Kamenetz, county of Podolia, the Ukraine. His father was a clothing factory worker who emigrated to the United States in 1908. Darcy attended New York City public schools, DeWitt Clinton High School, and New York University. His first job, at age 12, was as a packing machine tender. Other work during his youth included positions as a stringer for the *Bronx Home News* (which paid him the equivalent of a week's wage to change his name to Darcy to appeal to its largely Irish-American clientele), as a freight checker for a railroad, and as an office boy with a law firm.

Darcy became a Socialist early in life and rose rapidly on the Far Left, though he never commanded a large personal following. He joined the Young People's Socialist League in 1917 before his twelfth birthday and the Workers Party (later known as the CPUSA) at its founding convention in December 1921. Darcy helped organize the Young Workers League (which would become the Young Communist League) and led it from 1925 to 1927. At the same time, he also sat on the Communist Party's Political Committee (Politburo) representing the youth.

Darcy found time to marry his co-worker Emma Blechschmidt in 1926. The following year, Darcy was elected to the Executive Committee of the Young

Communist International. In Moscow he was chosen as chairman of the International Children's Committee and served for sixteen months. Before returning to the United States in 1929 he spent three months doing Comintern work in China and the Philippines. Back in New York, the versatile Darcy completed brief assignments as *Daily Worker* editor, head of the New York Workers School, and for most of 1930, leader of the International Labor Defense.

The year 1930 proved to be an important turning point in Darcy's career. On March 6, Communists around the world staged International Unemployment Day to protest the lack of work and inadequate social services in most capitalist nations. The CPUSA placed Darcy in charge of organizing New York City's demonstration. The results exceeded all expectations, bringing between 35,000 and 110,000 people to Union Square. When Darcy and William Z. Foster (q.v.) incited a march on City Hall, more than 1,000 police charged into the crowd, and Manhattan experienced its worst riot in a generation. Subsequent rallies attracted far less public support, however. Unfortunately for the militant Darcy, 1930 also brought both the rise of Earl Browder, who considered street fighting counterproductive, and a decision by the Communist International that building Party organizations was more important than violent confrontations with lawmen. In December the CPUSA exiled Darcy to distant California.

Between 1931 and 1936 Darcy headed the Party's California-Nevada-Arizona district. During this period he organized migratory agricultural workers, conducting strikes where participants displayed great courage despite massive employer violence. However, they achieved few lasting results. Darcy also led Communist involvement in the West Coast maritime strike and the San Francisco general strike; the latter idled between 100,000 and 175,000 workers in 1934.

Darcy attended the Communist International's historic Seventh World Congress in 1935. He remained in the Soviet Union afterward, serving on the Comintern's Presidium as head of its Anglo-American secretariat and in several other capacities combatting the rising Nazi and Fascist movements. He wanted the CPUSA to endorse President Franklin Roosevelt in 1936, but lost out to Browder's argument that Communist support would cost Roosevelt five votes for every one it might bring. Darcy returned to the United States in 1938 to serve as the Party's national education director and Central Committee representative for the Minnesota-Wisconsin-Dakotas district.

Although considered a leftist within the Party, Darcy readily accepted the Popular Front orientation of the mid-1930s. A vigorous Marxist-Leninist, he nevertheless believed in cooperating with and educating liberal politicians and organized labor. Darcy contends that he had achieved an informal electoral arrangement to support Upton Sinclair's (q.v.) EPIC (End Poverty in California) movement in California's gubernatorial campaign of 1934, but the Politburo rejected the plan at Browder's behest and forced Darcy to run for governor himself. In any case, after the contest Party official Robert Minor (q.v.) denounced the efforts of the California comrades in harsh terms. Darcy, who was an acquaintance of Minnesota Governor Elmer Benson (q.v.), attempted in 1938 to stop the surging anti-Communist sentiment in that state. Darcy claims that he wanted the CPUSA to make clear that while the Communists endorsed all the Farmer-Labor Association's goals, the Association did not support every objective of the Communist Party. Shortly thereafter Browder's lieutenants Gil Green (q.v.) and Eugene Dennis (q.v.) had Darcy demoted from Central Committee member to alternate. Darcy was not without friends among the Party leadership, however. A strong backer of William Z. Foster, Darcy moved to Philadelphia in 1939 and served as CPUSA state secretary for Pennsylvania until 1944.

Darcy contained his bitterness until 1944, but that year Browder proclaimed that the conference held by Roosevelt, Churchill, and Stalin at Teheran the previous November signified that the post-war years would be an age of East-West détente. He called for the transformation of the CPUSA into a political association to enable Communists to function within the two-party system. On February 8 at a Political Committee meeting, Foster and Darcy denounced Browder's interpretation of Teheran's import. The remainder of the body stuck by Browder and supported a resolution condemning Foster's and Darcy's dissent. Thereafter Darcy resigned all Party offices as a protest against Browder's policies. Subsequently John Williamson (q.v.) approached Darcy on behalf of the Political Committee, offering six months paid vacation in Florida to "think over" the new line. Darcy declined, and on April 1 the *Daily Worker* excoriated him for factionalism. Four days later the same organ announced that a Party commission, chaired by Foster, had expelled the 38-year-old Darcy.

In mid-1945 America's Communists read the infamous Duclos article and responded by removing Browder from his leadership position. Darcy visited the Party's national office and received a warm welcome. Eugene Dennis, however, insisted on seeing a manuscript Darcy had been working on for about a year, to judge its ideological correctness. Darcy resented both this request and the large number of former Browder men (including Dennis) still holding high positions in the CPUSA. He refused to rejoin the American Communist Party. He found employment in a Philadelphia lumber yard and later spent seventeen years as a successful furniture merchant. Darcy retired to a small New Jersey town. He enrolled in the Democratic Party in 1952, edited a campaign paper in 1964, and served as a member of the Ocean County Democratic Committee.

SOURCES: Maurice Isserman, *Which Side Were You On?* (1982); Harvey Klehr, *The Heyday of American Communism* (1984); Joseph R. Starobin, *American Communism in Crisis, 1943-1957* (1972).

*JAMES GILBERT RYAN*

**DAVIS, ANGELA (b. 1944).** Angela Davis, one of the Communist Party's most celebrated black activists and a prominent figure in a major criminal trial, was born in Birmingham, Alabama, on January 26, 1944. Her parents were part of the black middle class—her mother was a teacher and her father owned a service station—and active in political causes. Among their friends in such organizations as the Southern Negro Youth Congress were several prominent Communists.

When she was 15 Davis received a scholarship from the American Friends Service Committee enabling her to attend high school in New York. Living with the family of the Reverend William Melish, himself under attack for his pro-Soviet views, Davis attended Elizabeth Irwin High School, where she became acquainted with Socialist and Communist thought with the aid of left-wing students and teachers. She also attended meetings of, but did not join, Advance, a Marxist-Leninist youth group tied to the Communist Party.

Davis entered Brandeis University in 1961. In her senior year she studied with the noted Marxist scholar Herbert Marcuse (q.v.), who influenced her to study philosophy. She did graduate work at Frankfurt University from 1965 to 1967. While in Europe, Davis remained politically active. In 1962, still an undergraduate, she attended the Soviet-dominated World Youth Festival in Helsinki. In Germany she took part in anti-Vietnam War demonstrations. By 1967 she decided to return home in order to become more politically active and to study with Marcuse, who had moved to the University of California at San Diego.

Early in 1968 Davis reestablished contact with the Communist Party in California. However, she remained reluctant to join the Party, influenced by the views of the New Left. She did join the Black Panther Political Party, a group separate from the better-known black militant organization with a similar name. Her group soon became a chapter of the Student Nonviolent Coordinating Committee, then in the process of disintegrating.

Davis joined the Communist Party in July 1968. That fall, with the Party's blessings, she also joined Huey Newton's (q.v.) Black Panther Party to assist its work. In the summer of 1969 she took an extended trip to Cuba that reinforced her faith in the Communist system.

Davis became a prominent public figure in the fall of 1969. Not yet finished with her doctoral dissertation, she had been hired to teach philosophy at the University of California at Los Angeles. Then-governor Ronald Reagan protested against her employment, noting that a state law prohibited members of the Communist Party (CPUSA) from teaching at state universities. When Davis publicly admitted Party membership and was fired, a major case involving academic freedom began. The courts ultimately ruled the law unconstitutional, but Davis was not rehired for the following year.

In the fall of 1970 Davis became involved in the case of the Soledad Brothers, three black men under indictment for murdering a prison guard at Soledad Prison. The most prominent of the three was a self-proclaimed revolutionary named George Jackson. Angela Davis became his fervent defender. In August 1970 his brother Jonathan, using a weapon registered to Angela, seized hostages in a Marin County courtroom, allegedly in an effort to free his brother. In the ensuing shoot-out, Jonathan and a judge were killed. Davis became a fugitive. Arrested in October 1970 after an intensive FBI manhunt, she went on trial in 1972, charged with murder, kidnapping, and conspiracy. The prosecution charged that her love for Jackson had led to her involvement in the plot to free him. George

Jackson himself was killed at San Quentin in August 1971 during an attempted jailbreak.

The case and trial made Davis an international celebrity. The Communist Party mounted a major campaign on her behalf, forming the National United Committee to Free Angela Davis (NUCFAD). Davis was acquitted on all counts. She soon made a triumphant world tour, including the Soviet Union, where she received a heroine's reception.

After the trial the NUCFAD was transformed into the National Alliance Against Racist and Political Repression and became a major CPUSA ''front'' group, focusing on civil rights and civil liberties issues. Davis has continued to play a prominent role in this group and currently serves as co-chair. She also plays a prominent public role in the CPUSA. For several years she has been a member of the Central Committee and in both 1980 and 1984 was a candidate for U.S. Vice-President on the Party's national ticket with Gus Hall (q.v.).

SOURCES: Angela Davis, *Angela Davis: An Autobiography* (1974).

*HARVEY KLEHR*

**DAVIS, BENJAMIN (1903–1964).** Benjamin J. Davis, Jr., was an attorney, a New York City councilman, editor and publisher of the *Daily Worker*, a member of the Central (National) Committee of the Communist Party, national secretary of the Party, and a close ally of William Z. Foster (q.v.) in the Party's factional disputes of the late 1950s. He is best known as one of the top eleven Communist leaders convicted at the famous Smith Act trial held in 1949 in New York City.

Ben Davis was born on September 8, 1903, in the small southwest Georgia town of Dawson. His father, Benjamin J. Davis, Sr., was an ambitious fraternal leader whose success enabled the family to move to Atlanta when young Ben was six. In Atlanta the elder Davis became a powerful figure in the Republican Party and in the Grand United Order of Odd Fellows, as well as a successful newspaper publisher. As a result of his father's prosperity, Ben Jr. enjoyed a comfortable and relatively secure childhood. After attending public schools, he entered the preparatory program at Morehouse College, where he also completed one year of college. Davis then transferred to Amherst College, where he played varsity football and participated in many campus activities. After graduation he entered Harvard Law School and received his degree in 1929.

For the next two years Davis worked in the publishing business in Chicago and Baltimore before returning to Atlanta to practice law. Back in the Deep South after spending most of the previous ten years outside it, the sensitive young attorney became increasingly outraged at the many indignities to which Southern blacks were still subjected. In late 1932 the International Labor Defense, a Communist-influenced legal defense group, hired Davis to defend Angelo Herndon (q.v.), a young black Communist who was accused of attempting to incite insurrection against the state government under an ancient statute originally designed to punish slave revolts. In January 1933 Herndon was convicted and sentenced to eighteen to twenty years in prison at a trial marked by rabidly anti-black and anti-Communist orations from prosecuting attorneys and an emotional debate over the Communist Party's teachings on racial equality. These outbursts in court, the personal animosity directed toward Davis throughout the proceedings, and the growing frustrations of his legal practice combined to shatter his illusions about American justice and produce a major turning point in his life. As a result, an embittered Davis made the momentous decision to join the Communist Party. After spending two more years in Atlanta, during which time he became a marked man because of his continuing legal work for unpopular causes, he was summoned to New York to edit the Communist magazine *Negro Liberator*.

In the years after 1935, Davis advanced rapidly in Party ranks. He soon joined the *Daily Worker* staff, eventually becoming a member of the editorial board and serving briefly as editor. In the 1940s he was even listed as the nominal publisher of the newspaper. In Harlem he rose to become the Party's district director, and during World War II he finally achieved the distinction of being named to the powerful Central Committee of the Communist Party. Also active in Harlem politics, Davis was endorsed by the Reverend Adam Clayton Powell as his replacement on the city council in 1943 when Powell decided to run for Congress. Davis went on to post a surprising victory, joining Peter Cacchione (q.v.) of Brooklyn as the second Communist on the council. He easily won reelection in 1945, uniting black voters in Harlem with leftist voters in working-class neighborhoods across Manhattan. While on the council he was particularly outspoken on the issues of segregation in public housing and police brutality. In 1947, however, New York voters repealed the system of proportional voting under which Davis had done so well. In 1949, running for a city council seat representing the Upper West Side and part of Harlem, he was decisively beaten by Earl Brown, behind whom the Democratic, Republican, and Liberal parties had united in hopes of upsetting him.

Legal problems accompanied his political problems. In July 1948 Davis and other high-ranking Communist leaders were indicted under the Smith Act for allegedly conspiring to teach and advocate the overthrow of the U.S. government by force or violence. In 1949, following a stormy trial under Judge Harold Medina in New York City, the eleven Foley Square defendants were all found guilty. Davis received a five-year prison sentence, which he served in the federal penitentiary in Terre Haute, Indiana. Released in 1955 after serving three years and four months, plus an additional two months for a separate contempt conviction, Davis returned home and resumed his position on the National Committee. He also became chairman of the New York State district of the party.

During the fierce internal strife that racked the Communist Party following the abortive Hungarian Revolt and Nikita Khrushchev's startling revelations about Stalinism, Davis vigorously defended the Soviet Union's invasion of Hungary and sided wholeheartedly with the hard-line faction led by William Z. Foster. When the Foster group succeeded in defeating the rival faction led by John Gates (q.v.), which had proposed greater intraparty democracy, Davis was rewarded for his loyalty in 1959 with the post of national secretary. In March 1962 he and Party head Gus Hall (q.v.) were indicted by a federal grand jury under the Internal Security Act of 1950 for failure to register the Communist Party as a subversive organization. The indictments were part of the federal government's continuing efforts to outlaw the Party. Before the case was ever tried, however, Davis died in Beth Israel Hospital in New York City on August 22, 1964, following a lengthy illness. He was survived by his wife, Nina, and one daughter, Emily. Only after his death did federal authorities finally release his autobiographical notes, written while he was imprisoned at Terre Haute. They were published posthumously in 1969.

SOURCE: Benjamin J. Davis, *Communist Councilman from Harlem* (1969).

*CHARLES MARTIN*

**DAVIS, RENNIE (b. 1941).** Rennie Davis was a prominent leader and organizer in Students for a Democratic Society. He was instrumental in organizing the demonstrations that took place during the 1968 Democratic national convention in Chicago. Davis was born in Lansing, Michigan, on May 23, 1941. His father was a federal economist who served as an adviser to President Harry Truman from 1947 to 1952. Davis majored in political science at Oberlin College and received a B.A. in 1962. He continued his education at the University of Illinois, where he earned an M.A. in 1963, and at the Universities of Michigan and Chicago.

An early member of Students for a Democratic Society (SDS), he was elected a National Council member in 1963 and remained prominent in the organization until it began to disintegrate in the late 1960s. In 1964 he became the national director of the Economic Research and Action Project (ERAP). When this community organizing effort began to fail in 1965, Davis moved from Ann Arbor to Chicago, where he worked as a community organizer for the SDS project Jobs or Income NOW (JOIN). In 1967 he traveled to Czechoslovakia with a group of SDS leaders to meet with representatives of the Vietnamese National Liberation Front.

Davis organized demonstrations in Chicago during the Democratic convention in Chicago in August 1968 and was indicted with seven others by a federal grand jury in Chicago on charges of conspiracy to riot. Although found guilty, all the defendants were freed on appeal. Davis worked with several organizations protesting U.S. involvement in the war in Vietnam and was a project coordinator for the National Mobilization to End the War in Vietnam (MOBE).

In 1972 Davis became interested in the religion of the Indian guru, Mahara Ji, and he went to India the next year and became a devotee. In 1977 he was living in Denver, where he was associated with the Divine Light Mission and was selling life insurance for the John Hancock Company.

SOURCE: Kirkpatrick Sale, *SDS: Ten Years Toward a Revolution* (1973).

*MART STEWART*

**DAY, DOROTHY (1897–1980).** For over six decades Dorothy Day was an untiring activist in the struggle for peace and social justice. The initial expression of her commitments came as a journalist on the Left during World War I. The fullest and most sustained manifestation of her values began with her founding of the Catholic Worker movement in 1922. Day's vision and clarity of purpose provided the bedrock for the movement for almost half a century. Over those years Day spent her energies "comforting the afflicted and afflicting the comfortable," as a citation honoring her in the 1970s put it.

Dorothy Day was born in Brooklyn on November 8, 1897, the third of five children. Her father, a newspaper sportswriter, moved the family to San Francisco in 1904 when he changed papers, and transferred again in 1906 to Chicago. In 1914 Dorothy won a competition sponsored by the Hearst paper in Chicago and received a scholarship to the University of Illinois. Although only minimally involved in her formal studies, she found much intellectual stimulation in Urbana. She read long into the nights, joined the campus Socialist club, and wrote for the local paper. Several of her articles attacked the limited pay and job opportunities provided for the poorest students at the university. After her sophomore year, Day left Urbana and went to find work in New York City.

Her first job was as a reporter for the *New York Call*, the Socialist daily. She wrote on tenement life in New York's slums, covered strikes and the anti-war movement, and did an interview with Leon Trotsky. In April 1917, as the nation prepared to enter the war, she left the *Call* to work for the Anti-Conscription League. The following month she was hired as assistant editor on the *Masses*, working under Floyd Dell and Max Eastman (q.v.). This position came to an end when the government suppressed the journal in November 1917.

The next decade, while Day was in her twenties, was one of searching and introspection. She began nurse's training at a Brooklyn hospital but soon left that. She entered a marriage that lasted little more than a year. She continued writing, publishing an autobiographical novel, *The Eleventh Virgin*, in 1924. A Hollywood studio purchased the movie rights for $5,000, and with this money Day purchased a cottage on Staten Island. She began living there with Forster Batterham, an anarchist and marine biologist, and in March 1927 a daughter, Tamar Teresa, was born.

The birth of Tamar resolved the spiritual searching in which Day had been involved. She had been drawing closer to the Roman Catholic Church and had her daughter baptized, precipitating the breakup of her relationship with Batterham. In December 1927 Day took the vows of baptism in the Catholic Church. Her spiritual attraction toward Catholicism did not reflect any lessening of her radical social vision. Her quest, now, was to find the means of integrating her spiritual and social perspectives.

In 1932 she met Peter Maurin, beginning a collaboration that clarified for her the direction in which she should move. Maurin, a 54-year-old Frenchman, blended an awareness of the spiritual roots of society with a biting critique of capitalism. Day was initially wary of Maurin's fervent analysis. She later recalled,

"I was thirty-five years old and I had met plenty of radicals in my time, and plenty of crackpots, too; people who had blueprints to change the social order were a dime a dozen around Union Square." Maurin, however, found a more responsive Day when he urged her to start a newspaper for the unemployed. She channeled her considerable energy into realizing this suggestion, and on May Day 1933 the first issue of the *Catholic Worker* was sold on the streets of New York at a penny a copy.

Dwight Macdonald (q.v.) noted the confusion of New York radicals in identifying "this political chimera. Its foreparts were anarchistic but its hind parts were attached to the Church of Rome." The *Worker* reported on strikes and evictions, the plight of Arkansas sharecroppers, and conditions in New York's slum tenements, all from a radical gospel perspective. It provided some of the best labor coverage in that turbulent decade, with Day being one of only two reporters allowed to enter the General Motors plant during the sit-down strike.

The *Catholic Worker* soon found its audience. The initial issue, with a run of 2,500, attracted enough support and contributions for it to go on a regular monthly basis. By November 1933 its circulation was up to 20,000, by the end of 1936 it was up to 100,000, and by December 1940 it had reached 185,000. The success of the paper represented only a partial fulfillment of Dorothy Day's social vision. She sought more than a *Catholic Worker* reporting on the pain of the poor in America; she wanted a Catholic Worker movement that would respond to that pain. The paper could serve as an advocate for the poor, but the movement would be grounded on living among the poor and offering them food and shelter.

The first Catholic Worker House of Hospitality opened shortly after the paper began publication. A double tenement on Mott Street served as the paper's offices, a residence for the staff and the homeless, and a soup kitchen for the city's hungry transients. By 1938 some 1,200 people a day were being fed. Other houses opened in Boston and St. Louis in 1934, and in Chicago, Cleveland, and Washington, D.C., in 1935. By 1941 there were thirty-two Houses of Hospitality in twenty-seven cities.

The growth that had marked the Catholic Worker movement in the 1930s ended as the United States moved toward war. The *Catholic Worker*'s espousals of pacifism were read by a rapidly shrinking audience. In the wake of Pearl Harbor, circulation of the paper plummeted by more than two-thirds, to 50,000. The relatively small ranks of Catholic conscientious objectors contained a sizable portion of men who had come out of the Catholic Worker movement.

Dorothy Day, regardless of shifting public responsiveness to the concerns of the *Catholic Worker*, sustained the movement's commitment to advocacy of a radical gospel message and a daily encounter with the needs of the poor. One of those who shared her labors at the House of Hospitality in the early 1950s, Michael Harrington (q.v.), drew on this experience a decade later when he wrote *The Other America*, an analysis that helped initiate the federal government's war on poverty.

The issues of peace and social justice remained closely linked on Day's agenda. In 1955 she and other Catholic Workers began to refuse to move into shelters during the annual Civil Defense air raid drill. They were arrested and jailed for five days but returned in protest each of the following years. By 1961 this had grown into a major demonstration in New York City and other parts of the nation, and the federal government discontinued the testing program.

The peace witness of the *Catholic Worker* that had alienated so many during World War II drew additional readers in the 1960s. Day had begun writing on Vietnam in the 1950s, and the first Catholic Worker anti-war demonstration took place in November 1962. The relative isolation the *Catholic Worker* experienced as a pacifist voice in the Roman Catholic Church in the 1940s had changed considerably, due in good measure to Day's sustaining witness. Priests such as Daniel and Philip Berrigan (q.v.), and Thomas Merton, all deeply influenced by Dorothy Day, became important contributors to the revitalized peace movement of the 1960s.

In the 1970s Day maintained her active schedule, speaking and writing on public issues while remaining involved in the care of the poor at the House of Hospitality. In August 1973, at age 75, she was arrested in California while demonstrating in support of the United Farm Workers. She died on November 29, 1980, at the House of Hospitality on New York's Lower East Side, ending her days among the poor she had served so faithfully.

SOURCES: Dorothy Day, *From Union Square to Rome* (1938) and *The Long Loneliness* (1952); William Miller, *Dorothy Day: A Biography* (1982); Mel Piehl, *Breaking Bread: The Catholic Worker and the Origin of Catholic Radicalism in America* (1982).

*JOHN O'SULLIVAN*

**DEBS, EUGENE V. (1855–1926).** Eugene Victor Debs, a folk hero of the American Left, was the leading Socialist spokesman between 1897 and 1926. He helped found the American Socialist Party, was the Socialist candidate for President five times, was a founder—and later severe critic—of the Industrial Workers of the World, and was a pacifist who served more than two years in prison for his opposition to war during the 1917–1918 conflict.

Debs was born to a middle-class Alsatian immigrant family (his father owned a grocery) in Terre Haute, Indiana, in November 1855. He received his education in the public schools of Terre Haute and at a local business school. At age 15, Debs ended his formal education when he took a job as a laborer on the Terre Haute and Indianapolis Railroad. He was promoted to the position of locomotive fireman.

Although he had resigned his railroad job by 1873, Debs joined the newly formed local of the Brotherhood of Locomotive Firemen (BLF) in 1874. He was elected secretary of the Terre Haute local in 1875 and three years later, at age 20, was named associate editor of the brotherhood's monthly *Locomotive Firemen's Magazine*. During this period Debs had also become active in local Democratic politics. He was elected Terre Haute city clerk in 1879 and reelected in 1881.

Three years later he was elected to the Indiana House of Representatives. He soon became disgusted with the reality of the legislative process—the lobbying and the graft—and refused to run for reelection.

Over the next few years Debs decided that the manner in which labor unions were organized was against the best interests of the working class—and so in 1892 he resigned as secretary-treasurer of the BLF and began to organize a new, almost all-inclusive union of railroad workers: the American Railway Union (ARU). The nascent union differed in organizational principle from all the old railroad brotherhoods, for it was to be composed of almost all those who worked on a railroad, rather than only those in a specific trade.

Debs expected the new union to end the jurisdictional disputes that plagued the railroad brotherhoods, and the social stratification that permeated the ranks of railroad workers. He was especially cognizant of the jurisdictional warfare between the railroad firemen and the railroad engineers, and noted particularly the deleterious effect these internecine labor struggles were having on the railroad workers. Although there were some industrial unions then in existence—in the brewery industry, for example—the Debs ARU was the first union organized specifically as an industrial union in competition with craft unions.

The sole discriminatory clause of the American Railway Union constitution was the clause that limited its membership to all *white* workers on the railroads. The "whites only" clause was enacted by the union's first convention despite Debs' strong opposition. It would come back to haunt the ARU during the strikes of 1894, when black railroad employees, barred from ARU membership, worked despite the strike and the boycott.

The ARU won unexpectedly strong support as soon as it was organized in 1893. Early the next year the workers on the Great Northern Railroad struck successfully and forced the railroad to rescind pay cuts. The victory in the Great Northern strike turned Debs into a hero of the railroad workers. Cries of "Debs! Debs! Debs!" greeted him all along the railroad lines. The membership of the ARU reached more than 150,000 during the summer of 1894. Then catastrophe struck in the form of an unwanted and unauthorized strike.

The workers at the Pullman Company works near Chicago had had their wages cut by about one-third between August 1893 and late May 1894. They suffered great economic hardship, because rents and the cost of utilities in the company-owned town, in which virtually all the plant's workers were compelled to live, remained high. Moreover, the working conditions at Pullman were extremely harsh. The Pullman workers turned to the ARU to form them into a union. Debs was leery of the organization effort, despite his sympathies with the Pullman workers. He feared that the isolation of the Pullman employees from the rest of the industry would make them difficult to control.

His fears became realities when the unprepared Pullman workers called a strike, against the advice of Debs at the end of May. And in late June, again against the advice of Debs, the ARU convention backed the strikers by voting to boycott all railroads carrying Pullman cars. By July, when it appeared that the strike would be successful, the federal government intervened on the side of the railroads and Pullman. Attorney General Richard Olney, a former attorney for the railroads and a member of several railroads' boards of directors, made the spurious charge that Debs and his supporters were interfering with the mail by refusing to switch trains carrying Pullman cars. Olney appointed Edwin Walker, a lawyer for one of the major railroads, as a special federal attorney in charge of dealing with the strike and obtained a federal court injunction barring the union leaders from participating in or aiding the strike or boycott in any way.

On July 4 Olney prevailed on President Grover Cleveland to order out federal troops, ostensibly to protect federal property and prevent the impeding of interstate commerce, but actually to break the strike. Before the arrival of the troops the strike had been peaceful, but the troops goaded the strikers into acts of violence.

In the end, Debs and the union were forced to give up. He and the other ARU leaders were arrested and many of the strikers were permanently blacklisted. Although Debs and his fellow directors of the ARU were found not guilty of conspiracy, they were convicted of contempt of court for defying the injunction and served six-month terms in jail. The ARU was destroyed by the strike and the suppression of the strike, as well as by the secret blacklist against its members.

By 1894 Debs had become a Socialist, although he did not so proclaim himself. In August 1894 he told a presidential commission that he was not a Socialist because he was a follower of Laurence Gronlund (q.v.) and his book *Co-operative Commonwealth*. This was merely semantics. Gronlund was a Socialist—a Marxist, in fact. The book's subtitle proclaimed it to be *An Exposition of Modern Socialism*. What Debs meant was that he was not a follower of the stultified, autocratic "socialism" identified with Daniel DeLeon (q.v.) and his Socialist Labor Party.

While in the Woodstock (Illinois) jail, where he served his term for contempt, Debs read widely in Socialist literature. He claimed to have been most impressed with Karl Kautsky, the Austrian-German Socialist theoretician. He was visited in jail by Milwaukee Socialist leader Victor Berger (q.v.), who brought him a copy of Karl Marx's three-volume magnum opus *Capital*. Although Debs claimed that the work set the "wires humming in my system," there is little reason to believe that he was influenced by it—if he had indeed read it. Actually, he remained a follower of Gronlund and Edward Bellamy (q.v.) more than of the more rigid Marxists. (His socialism was always far more sentimental and Christian than hardheaded and Marxist.)

By 1896 Debs was a popular labor leader without a labor organization to support him. His work for the American Railway Union had alienated him from the old railroad brotherhoods, especially his own firemen's union. He despised Samuel Gompers, whom he considered an enemy of progressive organized labor, and he refused to become part of the minuscule, dogmatic Socialist Labor Party (SLP).

But Debs was immensely popular with the rank and file of organized labor. He drew huge and enthusiastic crowds wherever he spoke, and a faction of the

People's Party (Populist) membership—possibly a majority—favored his nomination as the Populist candidate for President. The group, led by Henry Demarest Lloyd (q.v.), included all the delegates from Illinois, Indiana, Missouri, and Ohio, plus great support from Minnesota, Wisconsin, California, and Pennsylvania. Lloyd believed that Debs could win the nomination. But Debs short-circuited the campaign to win him the Populist nomination. On the day before the nomination was to be made, Debs wired Lloyd, "Please do not permit use of my name for nomination."

Lloyd acquiesced. The convention endorsed William Jennings Bryan, whose nomination Debs had actually supported. Debs worked hard for Bryan. He issued a pro-Bryan circular to the old members of the ARU and other labor supporters, he toured the nation pleading with workers to vote for Bryan, and he defended bimetallism as the panacea for the ills that beset America's working people and farmers.

Bryan was defeated and the Populists disappeared. The 1896 defeat convinced Debs that there was little hope in simple reform measures. Two months after the election he issued an open letter to the ARU membership in which he proclaimed socialism to be the sole hope of the working people. "The issue is Socialism versus Capitalism," he wrote in the *Railway Times*. "I am for Socialism because I am for humanity. We have been cursed with the reign of gold long enough. Money constitutes no proper basis of civilization. The time has come to regenerate society—we are on the eve of universal change."

Debs' socialism was barely political, for although he condemned the Republican and Democratic parties and declared the Populists to be dead, Debs did not propose a Socialist Party as an alternative. Instead he suggested that a Utopian community be built in one of the poorly populated western states. He believed that the Utopia would be the basis for a political party that would eventually take over the reins of government in the state where the Utopia was located. The basis of the new movement would thus be another Utopian scheme, not unlike those that had preceded it for more than seventy-five years.

Two major groups of Debs' allies and supporters opposed the colonization plan: the Wisconsin Social Democrats, led by Victor Berger, and the newly formed Jewish Socialists of New York, led by Abraham Cahan (q.v.), who had recently bolted DeLeon's SLP and were forming a new Yiddish daily, *The Forward*. Debs, who abhorred internecine strife, worked out a compromise under which the Utopian proposal remained the dominant plan of the new movement, but partisan Socialist politics was also given support—albeit lukewarm.

Debs' new organization, the Social Democracy, was formed in June 1897, and he was named chairman. All the other officers were also former officers of the American Railway Union, and most of its members were former ARU members. Only a few Socialist groups, particularly the Wisconsin group led by Berger and the New York group led by Abraham Cahan, joined the Social Democracy; the rest remained in the SLP, where they fought with DeLeon for two more years before setting up their own party.

During the ensuing year Berger worked hard at convincing Debs that the Social Democracy should be turned into a political party. During the latter part of 1897 and the early part of 1898, Berger won another important ally to his case: the Socialists of Haverhill and Brockton, Massachusetts (who had just elected mayors and state legislators), left the SLP to join the Social Democracy. This new group favored electoral rather than communitarian activity. Debs and the majority of the Social Democracy's members still favored colonization. Debs' speech at the opening of the meetings was a paean of praise for the colonization scheme. But during the next two days Berger's arguments won Debs to the side of political action, and when Berger and his allies split from the Social Democracy during that convention to form the Social Democratic Party, Debs joined them, abandoning his old ARU comrades and ignoring the pleas of Henry Demarest Lloyd (q.v.) and Emma Goldman (q.v.).

Debs was little different in 1898 from the Debs who had advised caution during the strike at Pullman four years earlier. He was essentially an opponent of the more rapacious aspects of capitalism, but he rejected the Marxian concept of the class struggle and was opposed to all forms of violence under any conditions. Despite his later reputation, Debs was in 1898—as he was for the next twenty-eight years of his life—a Christian Socialist given to mouthing militant-sounding, often meaningless rhetoric.

In 1899 the Socialist Labor Party split into two separate parties. One, headed by Daniel DeLeon, retained formal title to the name, political assets, and liabilities of the party. The second, headed by Morris Hillquit (q.v.), differed little from the Social Democratic Party of Berger and Debs. But personality conflict between the leaders of the New York–centered Hillquit faction of the SLP and the Midwest-centered leaders of the Debs-Berger Social Democratic Party kept them from merging. In 1900 a temporary accommodation between the two parties allowed them to run a joint Socialist ticket in the national elections. Debs was the candidate for U.S. President; his running mate was Job Harriman (q.v.), leader of the California organization of the Hillquit-led faction of the SLP.

During this campaign Debs proved to be a tireless and effective campaigner. He spoke throughout the nation, especially in areas where there were former railroad workers, with whom he had a special affinity. The Socialist ticket of Debs and Harriman polled approximately 97,000 votes—considerably more than double the vote any previous Socialist candidates had received.

The platform on which Debs ran, and which he had helped devise, called for a mixture of socialism and social reform under capitalism—with the emphasis on reform. It paid lip service to socialism, which it proclaimed to be the party's aim—and thus the aim of its candidates. But the bulk of the platform was devoted to social reform—calls for women's suffrage, public works programs for the unemployed, direct legislation, and national laws to protect labor. His campaign speeches were laden with revolutionary rhetoric as well as practical proposals.

The campaign was poorly financed. Only one major union, the Western Federation of Miners—whom Debs had helped during its 1897 strike in Leadville,

Colorado—supported his candidacy. Moreover, there was serious friction in the coalition; for example, Harriman accused Debs of running the campaign for his personal aggrandizement. There were also serious inner-coalition disputes between the followers of Hillquit and those of Berger (Debs found these arguments distasteful, although he sided with Berger due to his distrust of the ex-SLPers).

During the last months of 1900 and the early months of 1901, a strong drive for unity of all Socialist forces—but excluding DeLeon—was under way in both Socialist organizations. Despite objections from Berger and his followers, and Debs' doubts, the two Socialist parties met in Indianapolis in the summer of 1901 and merged into the Socialist Party of America.

The debates at that convention hardly indicated a major ideological struggle between the Berger and Hillquit factions. The key debates were over a proposal by Algie Simons (q.v.) that the party delete all social reform planks from the platform. The vast majority of all pro-Berger and all pro-Hillquit delegates opposed the proposal. Debs also opposed Simons' motion. Berger's insistence that the party be named Social Democratic rather than Socialist, another point of conflict, was supported by small minorities in both factions. What differences did exist were based on factors other than previous factional loyalty. The 1901 convention would be the last that Debs would attend. After that, he avoided conventions because he found internecine party strife extremely distasteful. The party conventions were invariably scenes of internal warfare between the right, center, and left wings of the party.

After the 1901 convention the party was busy organizing itself, and Debs spent much of his time speaking throughout the nation. The party membership grew rapidly—from about 9,000 at the time of the unity convention of 1901 to more than 25,000 three years later. The greatest gains were in the western regions—Colorado, Montana, Oklahoma, Kansas, Nevada—where Debs had done most of his speaking. By 1902 the Socialists were able to boast of major vote gains in Congressional elections—nationally the Socialists had more than doubled their 1900 total. In several areas, particularly in the Mountain West—Socialists were elected to office.

But the party was again in the midst of internal conflict. Some party leaders, Berger especially, wanted a party that would campaign for reform as the road to socialism. Others, especially Louis Boudin (q.v.), favored campaigns for pure socialism. Still others—and Debs belonged to this third group—wanted Socialists to reject reform except as it helped pave the way for socialism. Debs' argument meant that Socialists could not form alliances with simple reformers or campaign primarily for reforms. He wanted Socialists to specify that they intended ultimately to establish a cooperative commonwealth.

Although Debs was considered to be in the left wing of the party, his positions differed only slightly—except rhetorically—from those of Berger of the right wing or Hillquit of the center. Like Berger, Debs did not consider trusts an absolute evil. They were, he maintained, making socialism easier to achieve by setting up central control of the economy, a key factor in his version of socialism.

Like Hillquit, he was an absolute democrat, insisting on the right of even his most vituperative opponent to have his say. And he was an absolute opponent of all war—a pacifist.

He did speak of class warfare, and he called on the working people to take the side of their own class, but he opposed the use of violence under virtually any circumstances, although he sympathized with those who disagreed with his basically pacifist stance. Unlike other pacifist Socialists, Debs put little faith in such panaceas as treaties or disarmament; only socialism would end the scourge of war by eliminating its causes—the struggle for markets and sources of scarce raw materials.

In 1904 Debs was nominated by the Socialist Party as its presidential candidate again. A printer from New York named Ben Hanford was his running mate. Debs carried the burden of the campaign; he toured the nation in one of the most active election drives Socialists had ever organized. Debs and Hanford polled more than 420,000 votes, an increase of more than 400 percent over 1900. Debs was elated. American socialism was on the road to victory, he proclaimed. But new disputes were rending the party.

In 1902 Debs was instrumental in organizing the American Labor Union (ALU), which was supposed to become a federation of Socialist trade unions. Centered in the Mountain States, the ALU was based in the Western Federation of Miners (WFM). The other affiliates were minuscule. The ALU from the start proclaimed its support of socialism and of the Socialist Party. Most of the other Socialist Party leaders were incensed at Debs for founding the ALU because it was a dual organization competing with the American Federation of Labor (AFL).

Debs despised Samuel Gompers and the other AFL leaders. His animosity for Gompers was fivefold: (1) Gompers' long-standing opposition to socialism; (2) Gompers' political creed of helping labor's ''friends'' and opposing its political enemies in the major parties; (3) Gompers' opposition to independent labor political action; (4) Gompers' support of the National Civic Federation, which called for labor-management cooperation; and (5) Gompers' refusal to permit the Chicago Federation of Labor to call a general strike to aid the ARU strikers in 1894. All the other Socialist leaders also opposed Gompers and his policies, but they objected even more strenuously to the organization of dual unions.

Within a year it was obvious that the American Labor Union was a failure, but the militants who formed it were not ready to dissolve. Instead they proposed the establishment of a new trade union federation dedicated to socialism and industrial unionism. Debs was among the founders of the new Industrial Workers of the World (IWW). So was DeLeon and a large group of anarcho-syndicalists. Almost from the start the IWW was a beehive of intrigue and internal disputes. Within a year a coalition of DeLeon and the anarcho-syndicalists drove the WFM from the union. DeLeon and his followers were soon also forced out. Debs also left the IWW early, condemning it as an anarchist organization that was not interested in electoral activity.

Large numbers of pro-IWW Socialists remained in the party; some state and a number of local party organizations were dominated by the IWW forces. In 1912 the party leadership acted to oust all violence-prone IWW members from membership. They added a clause to the party constitution barring from membership any who advocated sabotage, direct action, or violence. Debs supported the addition of the anti-sabotage clause. He even backed the ouster of IWW leader Big Bill Haywood (q.v.) from the Socialist National Executive Committee and from the party itself (although he later had second thoughts about the ouster).

Between 1904 and 1910, Debs and the party had seen a period of doldrums and slight decline, caused to a great extent by the internal party feuding. In the 1908 election, for example, Debs found himself under attack from many of the party's right wing, which objected to his role in the founding of the IWW. He was also assailed by part of the left wing, which was unhappy with his abandonment of the IWW. His campaign, which included a railroad train to take him from coast to coast (labeled "the Red Special"), and a $65,000 fund, turned out to be an abysmal failure. He gained virtually no votes over 1904.

A year earlier Debs had been named an editor of the *Appeal to Reason*, a Socialist weekly published in Gerard, Kansas, by Julius Wayland (q.v.). The *Appeal* had a circulation of more than 350,000 when Debs joined it in 1907; its circulation passed 500,000 in a few years. It was essentially a populist paper that supported the Socialist Party.

During the next four years, Debs was involved primarily in speaking and writing for the Socialist Party. He stayed out of most internal squabbles, except that he opposed an attempt to support restrictions on immigration into the United States, a proposal that was popular in the West.

In 1910–1912 the party again showed signs of growth. Socialists won control of the Milwaukee city government and elected a Socialist, Victor Berger, to Congress. A year later, Socialists carried Schenectady; New York; Butte, Montana; and Berkeley, California, among other cities. And Job Harriman, the Socialist candidate for mayor of Los Angeles, was barely defeated. The party's future appeared assured.

But the feuding at the 1912 party convention exposed the sharp divisions in the Socialist Party. The 1912 campaign itself, despite a record Socialist vote, further split the party. The anti-sabotage clause in the party constitution infuriated many Socialists, and about 20,000 of the party's 150,000 members left in protest of the clause.

Moreover, Debs was challenged as the Socialist nominee for the first time by less radical Socialists. Although he won the nomination, his running mate (former Milwaukee Mayor Emil Seidel [q.v.]) and his campaign manager (J. Mahlon Barnes) had opposed him. Debs was particularly incensed that Barnes, whose morality he questioned, had been named to direct his campaign. A vituperative battle over the Barnes issue ensued inside the party. Debs was opposed by a powerful pro-Barnes coalition, which included Berger, Hillquit, and John Spargo (q.v.). In the end the coalition won, and Barnes directed what turned out to be a successful campaign.

In this campaign, Debs polled more than 6 percent of the total vote cast—approximately 900,000 of 15,000,000—an all-time Socialist record. But there were two significant weaknesses to the vote. In the first place, a considerable part of the vote could be attributed to the fact that the Progressives nominated Theodore Roosevelt, whose progressivism was open to serious doubt, instead of Senator Robert H. LaFollette. Many of LaFollette's followers supported Debs to protest the Roosevelt nomination. The Socialist vote was shifting from the heavily populated industrial East and Midwest to the poorly populated areas of the West. Debs' vote was greatest proportionately in Oklahoma, Nevada, Montana, Arizona, Washington, and California. Added to those two weaknesses was the fact that the 1912 elections had cost the Socialists their one Congressman and the city administration in Milwaukee. More than 50,000 members, fed up with internal squabbles, had left the party in the year following.

In 1913 Debs resigned from the *Appeal* and joined Kate Richards O'Hare (q.v.) and her husband Frank as editors of the *National Rip-Saw*. The new magazine was more militantly Socialist than the old one, but it did not matter; the party was about to collapse.

The outbreak of the war in Europe in 1914 and the decision of most European Socialists to support their countries upset Debs. His discomfiture was eased slightly by the election in 1914 of another anti-war Socialist, Meyer London (q.v.), to Congress from New York's Lower East Side. And he was especially pleased that the Socialist Party leaders were pleading with their European comrades to help end the bloodshed. Debs was strongly anti-Kaiser but equally anti-czar. However, he was neither anti-German nor anti-Russian; he merely wanted both autocracies abolished. All this would change with the sinking of the ammunition-laden British passenger vessel *Lusitania* by a German submarine. He condemned the Germans' action vehemently in the left-wing *International Socialist Review*. Although he now sounded pro-Allied, Debs still opposed American entry into the war.

In 1916 Debs refused to run for President. He decided instead to run for Congress from his home district. The decision was based on the assumption that he could win the seat, as could Berger in Milwaukee and London again in New York. This would give the Socialists three voices against the war in Congress. Debs lost his bid for the Congressional seat, although he ran a respectable second; Berger also lost. Only London was reelected. Moreover, Allan Benson (q.v.), the anti-war publicist who was the Socialist candidate for President in 1916, polled only 585,000 votes. He became pro-war soon afterward.

America's declaration of war against Germany in April 1917 was roundly condemned by the Socialists then in convention in St. Louis. Although Debs was absent, he sent word as usual that he supported the anti-war declaration. But then he became strangely silent. There were even rumors in the party that he was secretly pro-Allied.

Other Socialists were suffering for their opposition to the war. Socialist newspapers—including the *Milwaukee Daily Leader* and the *New York Call*—were denied use of the mails. Socialist speakers, including Kate Richards O'Hare and Charles Ruthenberg (q.v.), were in prison. Party leaders, including Berger, Irwin St. John Tucker, Adolph Germer (q.v.), and William Kruse (q.v.), were under indictment for opposing the war, and so were more than one hundred leading members of the IWW and numerous other Socialists, anarchists, and unaffiliated radicals.

Debs decided to raise his voice against the persecutions. In the early summer of 1918 he spoke out in Canton, Ohio. The speech, which was moderate and restrained, led to his indictment and arrest for violation of the so-called Espionage Act of 1917. He was found guilty in an almost farcical trial and sentenced to ten years in jail. At the end of the trial and before sentencing, Debs delivered a speech in which he repeated his Socialist views. "I have never advocated violence in any form," he told Judge D. C. Westenhaver. And he condemned capitalism as an unfair exploitative system. He compared himself to the revolutionists of 1776 and the pre–Civil War abolitionists and then declaimed, "While there is a lower class, I am in it; while there is a criminal element, I am of it; while there is a soul in prison, I am not free." The speech was published as a pamphlet by the Socialist Party.

President Woodrow Wilson refused to consider amnesty for Debs long after the war was over. His animosity for the Socialist leader was almost an obsession. But Debs was more interested in events abroad.

The Bolshevik seizure of power in November 1917 was hailed by Debs before his incarceration. "I am a Bolshevik from the tip of my toes to the top of my head," he proclaimed. But he knew little of what the Bolsheviks stood for, and he was not pleased with the effect the Russian Revolution was having on the Socialist Party. He at first sided with the pro-Bolshevik left-wing section of the party in early 1919, but he then vehemently opposed its decision to split the Socialist Party.

In April 1919 Debs began his prison term in Moundsville, West Virginia, and was transferred to the Atlanta penitentiary in June. There he became a hero of the other prisoners, but he remained an anathema to Wilson and his attorney general, A. Mitchell Palmer.

In 1920 the Socialists again nominated Debs for U.S. President. His friend and attorney Seymour Steadman was the party's candidate for Vice-President. Debs campaigned from his cell. In the end he polled 912,000 votes, an increase in actual votes from 1912, but a sharp decrease in percentage—from 6 percent to 3.5 percent. And most of the Socialist vote was a protest against Debs' incarceration. Moreover, the Socialists were too busy fighting the Communist split to run an effective campaign.

On Christmas Day 1921 the new President, Warren G. Harding, ordered Debs released. The 67-year-old Socialist hero found himself almost immediately immersed in internal Socialist squabbling between the pro-Communist and anti-

Communist factions. By 1922 Debs was disturbed by the brutal dictatorship of the Russian Bolsheviks. He signed a cable protesting the execution of Lenin's Socialist opponents. That year he also rejected all Communist appeals that he join their party. He said that he saw no reason to leave the Socialist Party, and he assailed the American Communist obeisance toward Soviet Russia, labeling them "neither left nor right but east."

In 1923 Debs went on a speaking tour that failed to rouse much enthusiasm. He was too old, too tired, and too frail, and his speeches dealt with topics that could barely interest post-war audiences. A year later he backed the right-wing Socialists in their determination to support Progressive Senator Bob LaFollette for President. But then Debs' health had failed, and on October 20, 1926, Eugene Victor Debs died in a sanitarium near Chicago.

SOURCES: Harold W. Currie, *Eugene V. Debs* (1976); Ray Ginger, *The Bending Cross* (1949); H. Wayne Morgan, *Eugene V. Debs: Socialist for President* (1962); Nick Salvatore, *Eugene V. Debs: Citizen and Socialist* (1982).

*BERNARD K. JOHNPOLL*


**DE CAUX, LEN (b. 1899).** Leonard (Len) De Caux was a radical journalist from the early 1920s through the mid-1950s. Between 1935 and 1947 he was director of publicity for the Congress of Industrial Organizations (CIO) and edited the *CIO News* from 1937 to 1947. De Caux was born on October 14, 1899, in New Zealand. His father was an Anglican vicar. In 1912 or 1913 the family moved to England. De Caux was educated at Harrow and Oxford (Hertford College). Moved and angered by poverty observed as a youth, De Caux embraced socialism as a teenager and has remained an anti-capitalist radical. Early on he disassociated himself from his father's religious beliefs.

De Caux came to the United States in 1921. He worked in diverse manual jobs, joined the Industrial Workers of the World (IWW), and wrote for IWW newspapers. From 1922 to 1924 he attended Brookwood Labor College, where he met Caroline Abrams, a radical activist. They were married in 1927 or 1928 and were companions in many left-wing endeavors until her death in 1959.

In 1925 De Caux became European correspondent for the Federated Press. In the same year he joined the British Communist Party. From 1926 through 1933 he was assistant editor of the *Brotherhood of Locomotive Engineers Journal* (during which period he became a member-at-large of the American Communist Party). In 1934 and 1935 he was Federated Press Washington correspondent.

Soon after the Congress of Industrial Organizations was founded, John Brophy, its director, hired De Caux to direct press relations. In 1937 De Caux originated the *CIO News*, a weekly paper marked by vivid reportage and later by enthusiasm for the Popular Front. De Caux's lively weekly column shared the perspective of the pro-Soviet Left. His departure in 1947 reflected the CIO's increasingly anti-Communist orientation.

In 1948 De Caux directed publicity for the Wallace campaign's Labor Division. Between 1951 and 1953 he edited *Labor on the March*, a publication that embraced a pro-Soviet perspective. Between 1954 and his retirement in 1965, De Caux worked as a printer and linotype operator. In 1952 and again in 1954 he was subpoenaed by Congressional committees to testify about his Communist affiliations. His grudging responses earned him a reputation as an "uncooperative" witness. Since retirement he has written two vivid, unrepenting books on the history of American radicalism.

SOURCES: Len De Caux, *Labor Radical—From the Wobblies to the CIO: A Personal Memoir* (1970); Len De Caux and Caroline Abrams Papers, Walter P. Reuther Library, Wayne State University, Detroit, Michigan.

*ROBERT H. ZIEGER*

**DE CLEYRE, VOLTAIRINE.** *SEE* CLEYRE, VOLTAIRINE DE.

**DELEON, DANIEL (1852–1914).** Daniel DeLeon was the leader of the Socialist Labor Party (SLP) from 1891 until his death in 1914. During that period he was editor of its weekly and daily newspapers, *Workmen's Advocate*, the *Weekly People*, and the *Daily People*. His acerbic personality, his penchant for intrigue, and his dogmatic control of the party and its press was responsible for disintegration of the SLP and for the organization of the Socialist Party. DeLeon was also a founder of the Industrial Workers of the World and its leader for a short period.

Much of DeLeon's early life is cloaked in mystery because of his lack of candor. His name, place of birth, ancestry, religious background, and education are all matters that were misrepresented by him at various times. It is generally believed that he was born in the Dutch colony of Curaçao in the Caribbean of Sephardic Jewish ancestry, although DeLeon claimed at times that he was born in Venezuela or Surinam of Spanish grandee ancestry. No birth record of a Daniel DeLeon exists in Curaçao, or elsewhere, although the records of the Curaçao Sephardic Jewish congregation indicate that he did live there as a child. His parents, Salomon DeLeon and Sara Jeshurun DeLeon, are listed as members of the congregation.

DeLeon's father was a medical assistant, although DeLeon claimed that he had been a well-known physician. His mother was the daughter of an upper-middle-class family of tradesmen and planters. Salomon DeLeon served in the medical corps of the Dutch army in Curaçao and Surinam, where he died when Daniel was only 12 years old.

At age 14, DeLeon and his mother left Curaçao for Europe. DeLeon said they went to Hamburg and then to Hildesheim in Germany, where he claimed to have graduated from the Hildesheim Gymnasium, one of Germany's better private secondary schools. The records of the school indicate that he was never a student there. His claim of a long residence in Germany, which cannot be verified, and his German speech inflection led Samuel Gompers and other opponents to maintain that DeLeon was a German Jew whose real family name was Loeb, the German version of Leon, but there is no evidence to support or refute that.

In the early 1870s DeLeon did attend the Atheneum Illustre of Amsterdam, a lower-level college that eventually became the University of Amsterdam. He attended as a pre-medical student for only a few months and took none of the examinations required for matriculation. DeLeon would claim later that he had graduated from the University of Leyden, the prestigious Roman Catholic University of the Netherlands, but the records of the university show that he never attended the school.

From Amsterdam, DeLeon and his mother traveled to Curaçao and then to New York, where Daniel obtained short-term employment as a teacher in a private school in suburban Westchester County, New York. In 1876 DeLeon was admitted to the law school at Columbia University on the basis of his false claim of having received bachelor of philosophy and master of arts degrees from Leyden. He earned his bachelor of laws degree in 1878. DeLeon then practiced law, first in Brownsville, Texas, and later in New York. While practicing in Brownsville, DeLeon traveled back to Curaçao, where he married Sara Lobo, daughter of a leading Jewish family in that city, at the Sephardic congregation. She died five years later in childbirth, leaving DeLeon with three children.

A year later, after his return to New York, DeLeon was named a part-time lecturer in international law at Columbia's law school. He later claimed that during this period he became an activist in the Latin American liberation movement and that he edited the Cuban–North American pro-liberation newspaper. There is no evidence that he did edit such a newspaper; in fact, there is evidence that he was less than proficient in the Spanish language and its idiom. For example, in one of his more picturesque flights of fancy, DeLeon claimed he was a descendant of the explorer Juan Ponce de León. Had he been proficient in Spanish, Daniel DeLeon would have known that the explorer's family name was Ponce and not de León, the latter being his mother's maiden name.

Prior to 1886 DeLeon considered himself a Progressive Republican, although he had voted for Grover Cleveland, then a reform Democrat, in the 1884 presidential election. In 1886 DeLeon's gradual swing to the Left began. He became an active supporter of Henry George, the Single Tax land reformer, in his campaign for mayor. Although George was supported by the Socialists during that campaign, DeLeon was in the non-Socialist segment of the George party. When the Henry George movement in 1887 split, DeLeon remained active in the anti-Socialist wing.

During the campaign DeLeon listed himself as Professor Daniel DeLeon, Ph.D., but he held neither professorial rank nor a doctorate. Frederick Barnard, conservative president of Columbia, attempted to have DeLeon fired from his lectureship because of the misrepresentation and because he had listed his affiliation with Columbia in the Henry George campaign literature. The board of trustees of the university refused to accede to the president's wishes, and DeLeon was retained.

DeLeon and his followers would later claim that he was fired for his Socialist activity. In fact, DeLeon did not become a Socialist until three years after he left Columbia. He separated himself from the university voluntarily; he was never fired. DeLeon resigned from Columbia because he was refused professional status for which he had applied in 1887.

Edward Bellamy's (q.v.) quasi-Socialist novel, *Looking Backward*, introduced DeLeon to socialism. The book, published in 1888, was one of the best-sellers of the next year. DeLeon was among those who read it, and he was impressed by its description of life in a socialist utopia. He joined the Bellamy-inspired socialistically oriented Nationalist movement and became one of the leaders of its New York club. Most of the members of the Nationalist Club were, like DeLeon, intellectual professionals. He joined the nonproletarian District 49 of the Knights of Labor at the same time.

A year later DeLeon became a member of the Socialist Labor Party, then a small organization whose membership was almost completely made up of foreign-born radical workingmen. As an educated, English-speaking member, DeLeon was welcomed into the party. He soon became associate editor of the party weekly *Workmen's Advocate* and its successor, *The People*. Lucien Sanial, the editor of the newspaper, suffered from an eye disorder and had to take a leave. DeLeon was appointed his "temporary" successor in 1891.

DeLeon used his position as editor of *People* to gain control of the party and its machinery. He toured the nation establishing organizations—generally of one or two members—loyal to himself. He turned *People* into a vitriolic organ of attack on any who disagreed with him. And he proceeded to fight against any pro-Socialist newspaper he did not control. The first victim of his attack was G. A. Hoehn, editor of *St. Louis Labor*, organ of the labor and Socialist movements in that city.

*People* accused the St. Louis weekly of being dishonest, non-Socialist, and divisive. Behind the charges was the fact that the St. Louis paper printed editions in many other cities in the Midwest and had a circulation considerably larger than that of *People*. Eventually, *St. Louis Labor* and its subsidiaries lost the official blessing of the SLP. It was not affected, however. It barely lost circulation, and it continued as the leading labor weekly in that area. The SLP did lose a valuable organ in the Midwest.

The next to feel the wrath of DeLeon was British-born bibliographer and old-time Socialist, Charles Sotheran. The latter's chief crime was his failure, through a typographical error, to pay due homage to DeLeon in the 1892 Socialist picnic program he edited. The result was an incessant drumbeat of personal invective and distortion against Sotheran. Attempts by prominent party members to defend Sotheran brought the wrath of DeLeon down on them. An attempt by some of Sotheran's defenders to have *People* publish a letter in support of the Englishman was rudely rejected out of hand. When members of the party recalled to DeLeon that he had called Sotheran "true as gold," the former called them "lying fakirs." When the Executive Committee refused to oust Sotheran from the party, DeLeon used a technicality to force him out. Sotheran gained his revenge two years later.

The word "fakir" began to dominate *People*. The inference of the word was, of course, that DeLeon's opponents were dishonest "fakers." Among those called "fakirs" and worse were all trade union officials, Socialists who disagreed with him, such as Abraham Cahan (q.v.) and Morris Hillquit (q.v.). Even a Socialist trade-unionist of the stature of Eugene Debs (q.v.) was labeled a "fakir" and "a crook" in DeLeon's *People*. Nor was DeLeon above twisting names to ridicule opponents. In one case he persisted in calling an SLP opponent named Goldstuk, Mr. "Goldstunk."

By such tactics, DeLeon drove many Socialists out of the party and thus gained control of the organization. He finally forced almost all other Socialists out of the party, even those who had previously supported him. This he accomplished by his dogmatic insistence on (1) ruling or ruining the trade union movement, (2) total control of the Socialist press, and (3) absolute control of the program of the party and of its organization.

DeLeon's position on trade unions was friendly at first, but then the trade unions rebuffed him and the SLP. First came the American Federation of Labor (AFL). The Socialists in the AFL had presupposed that they were the political branch of the labor movement. They tried, often successfully, to be represented as such directly on local AFL councils. One council that did admit SLP representation was the New York Central Labor Federation (CLF). For that reason the AFL and its anti-Socialist leader, Samuel Gompers, refused to charter the CLF. When the CLF named Socialist Lucien Sanial as its representative to the AFL convention in 1891, Gompers and the convention refused to seat him. Anxious to remain in the mainstream labor movement, the CLF then ousted the SLP. DeLeon, who had previously been silent on the issue, now launched an all-out attack on Gompers and the AFL generally, an attack that lasted for twenty-three years.

Two years later, Knights of Labor District 49 joined with a Populist, James Sovereign, to wrest control of the Knights from Terrence V. Powderly and his conservative supporters, but the Sovereign-DeLeon alliance was short-lived. DeLeon claimed that Sovereign had promised the editorship of the *Journal of the Knights of Labor* to an SLP choice. Sovereign denied the agreement and pleaded that the declining Knights, whose membership had fallen from 1,000,000 to 15,000 in five years, had no money to pay an editor. DeLeon promptly declared war on the Knights, but too late to affect the organization; it was already in its death throes.

At this point Sotheran charged that DeLeon, who had forced him out of the party, was ineligible to be in the Knights because he was a lawyer and lawyers were prohibited by the order's constitution from being members. DeLeon, who was an elected delegate, was barred from attending the 1895 convention—and from membership in the Knights.

Ousted from both the AFL and the Knights, DeLeon was convinced that he could not gain control of the labor movement by "boring from within." Instead he formed a new organization, the Socialist Trades and Labor Alliance (STLA), ostensibly aimed at moving the labor movement to class-consciousness and dedication to socialism. In reality, however, it created a competing—albeit unsuccessful—labor federation. By 1896 the new organization became the center for internal disputes within the SLP and played a significant role in tearing it apart between 1897 and 1899. It is significant that the STLA never became a factor in the labor movement or the center for industrial rather than craft unions, which DeLeon claimed it would.

In the mid-1890s another major split rent the SLP, caused by a feud in which DeLeon need not have played a role. That he did merely placed him in a position that assured that the party he would control would be without membership or influence.

The SLP's East European Jewish members had founded a Yiddish-language weekly *Arbeiter Zeitung* in the early years of the 1890s. It was controlled by an independent association, the Arbeiter Zeitung Association, all of whose members were required to be members of the party. In 1894 a dispute over organizational matters broke out in the association. The primary issue was whether all party members of proven loyalty were to be admitted into the association. The bureaucracy that controlled the organization, fearing that its power would be weakened, opposed the expansion of membership rolls. A minority of the membership, led by Abraham Cahan (q.v.) and Louis Miller, both of whom would later gain fame as editors of two major Yiddish dailies, demanded that the membership rolls be opened. DeLeon, who was not involved in the dispute, interposed himself on the side of the bureaucracy, some of whom became his loyal supporters for a few years as a result.

In 1894–1895 the association was torn asunder by the feuding. The Cahan-Miller faction organized a new association for the purpose of publishing a new Yiddish Socialist newspaper, the *Jewish Daily Forward*. DeLeon reacted by having the majority of Jewish SLP members, most of whom favored the Cahan-Miller faction, thrown out of the party. The ousted members soon joined the Social Democracy, which had just been organized by Victor Berger (q.v.) and Eugene V. Debs (q.v.). The newspaper they organized, the *Forward*, would in a few years become the leading foreign-language newspaper in the United States, reaching a circulation of 275,000.

Two years after the ouster of the dissident Jewish Socialists, DeLeon engineered the ouster of those other members of the SLP who disagreed with him on the trade union issue. Foremost among them were Morris Hillquit (q.v.) and the editors of the *Volkszeitung*, the old Socialist German-language daily published in New York. A majority of the SLP membership went into the Hillquit-*Volkszeitung* wing. The new group—labeled Kangaroos by DeLeon because they had leapt out of his party—eventually joined with the Debs-Berger Social Democrats to form the Socialist Party. Within a few years almost all those who had remained in DeLeon's party during all the splits—including such stalwarts as Lucien Sanial, Joseph Schlossberg, and Hugo Vogt—had bolted the party.

Immediately after the 1899–1900 split, DeLeon reorganized *People* into a daily newspaper that he used as his personal organ. The primary tool of this unique newspaper was vitriolic polemics against any real or perceived opponent of DeLeon. DeLeon was a virtual one-man editorial board and reportorial staff news director. The circulation of the *Daily People*, which lasted from 1900 to 1914, never reached 2,000. It had little influence in the labor or Socialist movements.

DeLeon's political life was resurrected temporarily in 1905 with the birth of the Industrial Workers of the World (IWW), of which he was a founding member. At the very first IWW convention in 1905, DeLeon caused a serious dispute by demanding an inflated number of votes for his followers. That dispute was soon settled, and DeLeon and his small group of followers were admitted into the IWW. A year later, in 1906, DeLeon united with William Haywood (q.v.), Vincent St. John (q.v.), and William Trautmann to force out the more moderate wing of the organization and seize control. DeLeon assumed that this would assure him of control of the Wobblies (the popular name for the IWW) and thus of a powerful base of operations, but in 1908 his erstwhile allies had become antagonized by DeLeon's persistently antagonistic lectures and forced him out of the organization. DeLeon's followers formed a rival IWW that had few members. It led only one major strike, in 1912, among silk workers, in Paterson, New Jersey. It is significant that DeLeon played no role in that strike and denigrated its importance.

Much has been made of DeLeon's theoretical work. Unfortunately his ideas were never unified or critically analyzed. Most of his theoretical work is in lectures he delivered and in articles he wrote for his party's press. Some of it is replete with contradictions; some of it is of fleeting importance. Only a few of his ideas have any universal, long-term application.

The socialism envisioned by DeLeon was little different from the socialism anticipated by his Socialist antecedents and adversaries. Socialism would revolutionize society, he said, by establishing collective ownership of all the tools of production and the elimination of profit. And his idea of how the Socialists would gain control was not particularly revolutionary either. He, like Hillquit or Berger, proposed that working people use the ballot box to achieve the Socialist victory, calling the ballot the total of the twentieth-century revolution. But he did not rule out the use of force when necessary. It was possible, he argued, that the Socialists would triumph at the polls and the capitalists would yield to popular demand. But that was unlikely. In the more likely event that the capitalists would offer resistance or try to count the Socialists out, the SLP would dissolve into its economic organization [the pro-SLP wing of the IWW] . . . which would use force to destroy the "barbarian capitalist class."

DeLeon's view of the need for economic and political action to be used jointly to achieve socialism led him to reject ameliorative measures of reform under capitalism as an aim for trade unions or the Socialist movement. The best the honest unionist could expect from his union, he argued, in the *Burning Question of Trade Unionism* (1904), "is a brake on the decline of his conditions." Reform, which he described as a change in external things only, was useless. What was needed, said DeLeon, was revolution, which he described as internal as well as external change. So antagonistic was he to reform and simple trade unionism that in 1900, when he gained full control of the party, he barred from membership any and all officials in "pure-and-simple" labor unions and deleted from the SLP platform all reform proposals.

The labor union organization which DeLeon favored was essentially political. Its sole purpose would be to work for a new Socialist order, and when the new social order was established it was to become the state itself. In 1907 he argued in *As to Politics* that the IWW was "the embryo of the workers' republic" and would run the nation's industries for the benefit of the working class and administer the state. Although this is essentially the anarcho-syndicalist view as espoused by Dyer D. Lum (q.v.) in the United States, it differs with Lum on one major point.

Lum and the other anarcho-syndicalists favored voluntarism and a loose federation of the independently operated industrial plants. DeLeon believed in a directing authority to enforce organization. Aims were fine, he told IWW members in 1907, but without a directing organization with the power of enforcement it would be "just so much hot air."

After his ouster from the IWW DeLeon was a leader with virtually no following. When he died in May 1914, his movement was in a shambles. The *Daily People* finally went out of existence in February 1914, and membership in the SLP was down to less than 1,000. His labor union movement barely existed. Some 3,000 people attended his funeral, but few of them were his followers.

SOURCES: Socialist Labor Party Collection, Wisconsin State Historical Society (on microfilm); Works by Daniel DeLeon: *As to Politics* (1907); *Fifteen Questions About Socialism* (1914); *Socialism versus Individualism* (1914); *A Socialist in Congress: His Conduct and Responsibilities* (1912); *Socialist Landmarks* ("Reform and Revolution" [1896], "What Means This Strike" [1898], "The Burning Question of Trades Unionism" [1904], and "Socialist Reconstruction of Society" [1905]) (1952). See also Abraham Cahan, *Bleter fun Mayn Lebn* (Pages from My Life; Yiddish) 5 vols. (1926); Louis C. Fraina, "Daniel DeLeon," *New Review* 2 (July 1914); Albert Fried, "Daniel DeLeon and the Socialist Labor Party, 1890–1908" (M.A. thesis, Columbia University, 1955); Morris Hillquit, *History of Socialism in the United States*, 5th ed. (1910); Bernard K. Johnpoll, "A Note on Daniel DeLeon," *Labor History* 17 (Fall 1976); Olive Johnson, *Daniel DeLeon: American Socialist Pathfinder* (1935), an official Socialist Labor Party hagiography, replete with errors; Henry Kuhn and Olive Johnson, *The Socialist Labor Party During Four Decades* (1969), an inaccurate official history; Don K. McKee, "Daniel DeLeon: A Reappraisal," *Labor History* 1 (Fall 1960); I. Glenn Seretan, *Daniel DeLeon: Odyssey of an American Marxist* (1979). Seretan's work is the best study of DeLeon. Unfortunately, many facts are hidden in footnotes, and the thesis of the book is untenable.

*BERNARD K. JOHNPOLL*

**DELLINGER, DAVID (b. 1915).** As activist, writer, and editor, David Dellinger was a key figure in the New Left. Probably more than any other person in the movement, he provided the link between the pacifist movement of the World

War II period and the activist phase of the New Left era. Dellinger was born in Wakefield, Massachusetts, on August 12, 1915, into a family that traced its ancestry to the earliest days of New England settlement. His father, Raymond Pennington Dellinger, was a Yale graduate and a Boston lawyer. David also graduated, magna cum laude, from Yale in 1936. He was a student at New College, Oxford, during the 1936–1937 term and spent the following year studying at the Yale Divinity School. In 1939–1940 he attended the Union Theological Seminary.

Dellinger was active in draft resistance efforts during World War II. In 1945 he was the leader behind the founding of *Direct Action*, a journal of radical pacifism. In 1948 he led a section of the Committee for Non-Violent Revolution, founded two years earlier as a radical-pacifist organization, into a merger with a group led by A. J. Muste (q.v.), Dwight Macdonald (q.v.), and Milton Mayer called the Peacemakers. That group represented a wide range of concerns and approaches, many of which—participatory democracy and civil disobedience, for example—foreshadowed the New Left movement. In 1956 he helped found and became editor of *Liberation*, a journal of radical thought that provided a forum for the views of radicals such as himself and Paul Goodman (q.v.) in the late 1950s and an organ for New Left ideas in the 1960s.

Also an activist in the New Left movement of the 1960s, Dellinger was a featured speaker at the first Vietnam teach-in on the University of California at Berkeley campus, in March 1965. In 1966 he served as co-chairman of the Spring Mobilization to End the War in Vietnam, which staged massive demonstrations in the spring of 1967. He traveled to Hanoi in 1966 and met with Ho Chi Minh and had subsequent meetings with North Vietnamese officials in Paris in 1968 and 1969. His contacts with Hanoi were strong enough that the Vietnamese released three captured Americans through him in August 1969.

Following the riots that erupted in connection with the 1968 Democratic convention, Dellinger was arrested and tried for conspiracy to incite riot, along with seven others. He was convicted of the act of inciting to riot, not conspiracy. The conviction was overturned on appeal. Dellinger has remained active in radical causes, including protests against nuclear weapons and nuclear power plants.

SOURCES: Dave Dellinger, *More Power Than We Know* (1975) and *Revolutionary Nonviolence* (1970).

*TOM WILLIAMS*

**DENNIS, EUGENE (1905–1961).** For many years a Communist functionary and Comintern agent, Eugene Dennis became a national Party leader in 1938 and general secretary of the Communist Party in the United States of America (CPUSA) in 1946. After nearly a decade of legal battles with the federal government, Dennis, a colorless, cautious politician, swung back and forth between the factions fighting for control of the divided Party in 1956–1958 and presided over its collapse.

Dennis was born as Francis X. Waldron on August 10, 1905, in Seattle, Washington. His mother, the daughter of Norwegian immigrants, died when he was 11, an event that caused him to abandon Roman Catholicism. His father, the son of Irish immigrants, was a railroad worker addicted to get-rich-quick schemes that invariably failed. Dennis attended the University of Washington for a semester but dropped out to work. He was attracted to the Industrial Workers of the World before joining the Communist Party in Seattle in 1926. Almost immediately afterward he moved to the Mojave Desert for a year to recuperate from tuberculosis, working as an ironworker, a truck driver, and a salesman.

In 1927 Dennis became a teacher at a Party summer school and active in the factional wars on the side of William Foster (q.v.) in both Los Angeles and Seattle. He was appointed Southern California head of the Trade Union Unity League, the Communists' dual union organization. In December of that year he began to encourage Party attention to agricultural unrest in the Imperial Valley, and he participated in strikes there in January among lettuce workers. At the same time he was working to organize the Marine Workers Industrial League in Los Angeles. As a result of his role in a large unemployment demonstration on March 6, 1930, Dennis was arrested in Los Angeles. While on trial he heard about the arrest of Party organizers in the Imperial Valley on charges of criminal syndicalism and, correctly fearing his own indictment, he fled the country.

Using the name Tim Ryan, Dennis traveled to Moscow, where he worked in the Far Eastern Secretariat of the Communist International (CI). Beginning in the summer of 1931 he served as a CI representative to the Philippine Communist Party, remaining underground for almost a year. He then became CI representative to the South African Communist Party, which was in the throes of a split as a result of the Comintern's insistence on its support for an independent, black-controlled South Africa. Dennis returned briefly to Moscow in October 1933, but was quickly dispatched to Shanghai, where he worked with the Central Committee of the illegal Chinese Communist Party.

Returning to Moscow early in 1935, Dennis was reunited with his wife, Peggy, who had been working as a Comintern courier, and they prepared to return to the United States. However, they were not allowed to take their young American-born son with them (who later became a Soviet citizen and, as Timur Timofeev, director of the Institute of the World Labor Movement in Moscow).

Adopting the name Eugene Dennis, on his return in January 1935 he was appointed state secretary of the Wisconsin Communist Party. In that position he took advantage of the Party's more moderate policies to cement an alliance with Meta Berger (q.v.), widow of Victor (q.v.) and an important figure in the state Socialist Party and union officials in the newborn Congress of Industrial Organizations (CIO). He was made American representative to the Comintern in June 1937 and stayed in Moscow for six months. In January 1938 he met with Earl Browder (q.v.), Foster, and Comintern leaders to thrash out a dispute over the Party's support of Franklin Roosevelt and John L. Lewis. Dennis sided with Browder, urging all-out endorsement of the New Deal and the CIO, a policy known as "the democratic front." Afterward he returned to New York to direct the Party's legislative affairs and become part of its national leadership. With scant experience in American Party affairs and barely known to most Party members, he clearly owed his eminence in large part to his Comintern connections. Dennis spent considerable time in Washington, D.C., meeting with the Party's friends and allies, edited *National Issues*, a Party publication, and became Browder's closest political aide. When William Foster challenged Browder's leadership early in 1939, it was Dennis who most firmly denounced Foster and warned him that Browder's policies had Comintern support.

Dennis' loyalty was not, however, to Browder the individual. After the Nazi-Soviet Pact, Dennis broke with the Party leader when Browder attempted to continue the Communists' support for Roosevelt. He joined Foster and Alex Bittelman (q.v.) in demanding a break with the administration. When the Comintern endorsed that position, Dennis went underground, dropping from public activity for seventeen months. In June 1941 he returned to Moscow for a few weeks.

Although he had once again become Browder's staunch supporter during World War II and endorsed the Teheran policy and the dissolution of the Communist Party, Dennis quickly repudiated those positions after publication of the Duclos article in 1945 indicated Soviet unhappiness with Browder. He abandoned "Browderism," joined forces with William Foster, and was elected general secretary of the Communist Party in 1946. But Dennis resisted Foster's efforts to push the Party further to the left and into a more militant posture until the formation of the Cominform in 1947 convinced him that the international Communist movement was going in the same direction. He then began to orient the Party toward endorsing the Progressive Party candidacy of Henry Wallace for President in 1948. That decision cost the Party much of its support in the CIO and led to its further isolation.

Dennis' legal troubles also began to mount. He was convicted of contempt of Congress in 1947 after refusing to answer questions about his background posed by the House Committee on Un-American Activities and sentenced to a year in jail. In January 1949 he was one of eleven Party leaders put on trial for violating the Smith Act, charged with conspiring to teach and advocate the overthrow of the government by force and violence. After a rowdy nine-month trial they were all found guilty. Dennis received a five-year sentence plus six months for contempt of court. When the Supreme Court held in *Dennis vs. U.S.* that the Smith Act did not violate the First Amendment, Dennis and several other defendants prepared to jump bail and go underground. His arrangements miscarried, and the Party leader went to prison in July 1951. He was released in March 1955.

After his parole ended, Dennis renewed his Communist activity in January 1956 with a call to the Party to take a new look at the policies that had proven so disastrous. He openly criticized the Party's "left-sectarian" course and allied himself with forces led by *Daily Worker* editor John Gates (q.v.), which called

for sweeping changes in policy. As the fallout from Khrushchev's de-Stalinization speech spread, the splits in the Party became more severe. Dennis cautiously criticized the Soviet Union but did not go as far as Gates. Foster attacked both as revisionists. Dennis sought to placate both sides, but as the Soviets retreated from de-Stalinization and the Gates faction intensified its criticisms of the Hungarian invasion and Soviet anti-Semitism, Dennis abandoned his reform efforts and his alliance with Gates. In 1959, with the Party reduced to a shell, Gus Hall (q.v.) became general secretary. Dennis beat back a Foster-led effort to prevent his election as national chairman, but he was suffering from cancer and took little part in Party activities thereafter. He died on January 31, 1961.
SOURCE: Peggy Dennis, *The Autobiography of an American Communist* (1977).

*HARVEY KLEHR*

**DOBBS, FARRELL (1907–1983).** Farrell Dobbs, a labor organizer and leader of the Socialist Workers Party, was born on July 25, 1907, in Queen City, Missouri, the son of a coal-mine mechanical superintendent. The family moved to Minneapolis when he was 6. He attended local schools, graduating from North High School in January 1925. Employed by Western Electric, he went from telephone installer to supervisory work, quitting in 1932 over company treatment of an older worker. After a failed attempt at starting his own business, he worked as a coal heaver at Pittsburgh Coal Company in Minneapolis, where he was contacted in November 1933 by Grant Dunne and joined Teamsters Local 574.

After participating in the February 1934 Minneapolis coal strike, he joined the Communist League of America (forerunner of the Socialist Workers Party) in March 1934. As chief picket dispatcher in the 1934 Teamsters truckdrivers strike, he played a crucial role in its victory. In 1935, after holding off attempts by International Brotherhood of Teamsters (IBT) President Tobin to drive the radicals out of Local 574, Dobbs was elected recording secretary of the reconstituted Local 544.

In 1936 and 1937 he began aiding Teamster organizing drives throughout the region, which eventually led to the successful 1938 eleven-state organizing campaign. The outcome was the first area master contract, which benefited over 125,000 drivers. In this effort Dobbs and other revolutionists were able to work closely with IBT officials, including Jimmy Hoffa.

Dobbs was appointed an IBT International organizer by Tobin in May 1939. He resigned the position the next year over disagreement with Tobin's pro–World War II policy and in order to devote himself full-time to the Socialist Workers Party (SWP). He was convicted under the federal anti-sedition Smith Act in 1941 along with other Minneapolis and national SWP members as part of a Tobin-FBI-Roosevelt plan to regain control of the Minneapolis Teamsters, who were trying to join the Congress of Industrial Organizations. Dobbs served thirteen months in Sandstone Federal Penitentiary, beginning in 1944.

Dobbs edited *The Militant* (1943–1948). He was the SWP's candidate for United States President in 1948, 1952, 1956, and 1960, touring Cuba during his last campaign. He served as SWP national chairman (1949–1953) and thereafter as SWP national secretary until 1972. He spent the last decade of his life in California and died on October 31, 1983.

SOURCES: Farrell Dobbs, *Teamster Bureaucracy* (1977); *Teamster Politics* (1975); *Teamster Power* (1973); *Teamster Rebellion* (1972).

*SETH WIGDERSON*

**DODD, BELLA (1904–1969).** Bella Dodd, a member of the Communist Party National Committee, was state legislative representative for the Communist Party in New York from 1943 to 1946. Earlier, as a secret Party member, she was legislative representative for Local 5 of the New York Teachers Union. For more than a decade, she was a prominent spokeswoman for teachers union causes and a leading personality in Communist alliances in electoral politics in New York.

Born Bella Visono in October 1904 in Picerno, Italy, Dodd was the daughter of Italian immigrant parents who came earlier to the United States. She was born on a return trip by her mother, was raised abroad by foster parents, and joined her parents and siblings in East Harlem when she was six. Raised largely in the East Bronx, where her father ran a small grocery, she attended Evander Childs High School and then Hunter College, graduating in 1925. A trolley accident in 1916 left her physically scarred and with an artificial limb, but she became a vigorous honor student and activist. She began teaching at Hunter College in 1926, where she stayed for thirteen years, and she also quickly completed a master's degree in political science at Columbia University and a law degree at New York University.

Early during the Depression, Bella Dodd was a leader in the Hunter College Instructors Association and in efforts to organize New York college teachers. She encountered the Communist Party through the Classroom Teachers Association, a group associated with the Trade Union Unity League and later with the opposition in the American Federation of Teachers (AFT), Local 5. She also became attracted to the Party through involvement in the Anti-Fascist Literature Committee. Gradually, she accepted Party discipline, but did not formally join. Party leaders preferred that she remain a secret member.

During the late 1930s and early 1940s, Dodd served as legislative representative for Local 5, which the Party then dominated, and was active in the American Labor Party (ALP). She herself ran for the state assembly on the ALP ticket in 1938, and she led Local 5 in its fight against the Rapp-Coudert legislative committee investigation of Communism in the New York City schools in 1939–1940. In 1940 the Teachers Union was ousted from the AFT and the AFL, and Dodd became legislative representative for the newly created Local 555 of the State, County, and Municipal Workers Union, an affiliate of the Congress of Industrial Organizations.

In 1943 Dodd came forward openly as the Communist Party's legislative representative in New York. She also entered into her own law practice. During this era of maximum cooperation between Communists and non-Communists,

Dodd became a member of the Party's National Committee, an important figure on its New York State board, and second in charge of political campaigns behind State Secretary Gil Green (q.v.).

During the Party's post-war repudiation of Browder (q.v.) revisionism, Dodd turned out to be a reluctant Communist. Although a member of the Party's Central Committee in 1945, she remained sympathetic to Browder and eager to maintain cooperative relations in the New York labor movement and politics. She also opposed Robert Thompson's (q.v.) leadership of the New York Party. Brought up on charges herself twice in 1946, she drifted away from active involvement but remained a member. The Party expelled her in mid–1949.

Subsequently, Dodd testified before several Congressional committees and wrote a confessional autobiography. She also found a new family and movement in the Roman Catholic Church. During the late 1960s she ran for Congress on the Conservative Party ticket, calling for a U.S. victory in Vietnam. She died on April 29, 1969.

SOURCE: Bella Dodd, *School of Darkness* (1954).

*KENNETH WALTZER*

**DOHRN, BERNARDINE (b. 1942).** Bernardine Dohrn was an organizer for the National Lawyers Guild, a prominent figure in Students for a Democratic Society (SDS), and a leading force in the extremist faction of SDS, Weatherman. She was born in Chicago on January 12, 1942, to Jewish parents. Her father was an appliance store credit manager, her mother was a secretary. Dohrn earned a B.A. and an M.A. in history at the University of Chicago, and in 1964 she entered the University of Chicago Law School. While there, she joined SDS and was an organizer in its community assistance program, Jobs or Income Now (JOIN). After graduating in 1967, she went to New York and worked for the National Lawyers Guild, organizing students to resist the draft. In the fall of 1968 she was elected national interorganizational secretary of SDS.

Dohrn and other SDS members traveled to Yugoslavia in the summer of 1968 to meet with representatives of the Vietnamese National Liberation Front. When she returned, she joined a radical cadre of SDS, the Jesse James Gang. Dohrn and ten other leading members of SDS took over the national office of SDS in the spring of 1969 and began calling themselves Weatherman. By the end of the summer, she was a leading force in this group and headed the Women's Militia in the "Days of Rage," the protests in Chicago in October, planned to coincide with the Chicago Seven conspiracy trial.

During the "war council" held by SDS in December 1969, Dohrn advocated armed struggle and proposed that Weatherman go underground and conduct bombings of government buildings. After a homemade dynamite bomb killed three members of the Weather Underground in New York on March 6, 1970, Dohrn became the main leader of the group. In the spring of 1970 she was indicted by federal grand juries in Chicago and Detroit on conspiracy charges, and she made the FBI's "Ten Most Wanted List."

When the remnants of Weather Underground began to disintegrate in the mid–1970s, Dohrn began to favor resurfacing. In 1980 she surrendered and was fined and put on three years probation. In 1981 she was working as a waitress in New York City. In 1985 she was denied readmission to the bar, but continued working for a New York law firm.

SOURCE: Kirkpatrick Sale, *SDS: Ten Years Toward a Revolution* (1973).

*MART STEWART*

**DOMBROWSKI, JAMES ANDERSON (1897–1983).** James Anderson Dombrowski, Christian Socialist and civil rights activist, was a co-founder of Highlander Folk School, served as executive secretary of the Southern Conference for Human Welfare and was executive director of the Southern Conference Education Fund for nearly two decades.

Dombrowski was born on January 17, 1897, in Tampa, Florida, where his father owned a jewelry store. After completing high school, he studied jewelry-making for a time. In October 1917 Dombrowski joined the Aero Service and served in France during World War I. Following the war he entered Emory University, where he distinguished himself as a student, debater, and leading member of several campus organizations. He took a position as secretary for the Emory Alumni Association after graduating in 1923. In 1926 he enrolled at the University of California and served as assistant pastor at a Methodist church in Berkeley. He left California for Harvard University in 1928. Not satisfied with the program of study there, he enrolled at Union Theological Seminary in New York, where he developed the philosophical basis that would guide the rest of his life.

Dombrowski studied with Reinhold Niebuhr and Harry F. Ward, two of the most influential theologians and social activists of the time. His thesis, ''The Early Days of Christian Socialism,'' concluded that the Social Gospel movement was misguided insofar as it emphasized social harmony and inevitable progress while neglecting a critique of capitalism. Dombrowski argued that exploitation was inherent to capitalism and that the struggle for a more just society must therefore also aim toward a new economic order based on socialism.

As part of his course work, Dombrowski traveled south in 1929 to observe strikes taking place in several mill towns and was jailed for one night in Elizabethton, Tennessee. After receiving his Ph.D. in 1933, he returned to Tennessee and joined fellow Union Theological graduate Myles Horton (q.v.) in establishing Highlander Folk School. Highlander trained many of the organizers who led the labor movement in the South during the 1930s. Dombrowski served as staff director and taught courses in religion, economics, and organizing.

Highlander was closely affiliated with the Southern Conference for Human Welfare (SCHW), an interracial reform organization established by Southern supporters of the New Deal in 1938. Dombrowski joined the staff of SCHW as executive secretary in 1942. His skill as an administrator and fund-raiser helped revive the faltering organization during the war years. He initiated publication of a monthly newspaper, *The Southern Patriot*, which he edited.

In 1946 the SCHW board of directors established the Southern Conference Education Fund (SCEF). After a dispute over administrative authority within SCHW, Dombrowski assumed directorship of the SCEF, which became a completely separate organization. By now, he had come to view the race issue as the single greatest problem facing the South. Under the leadership of Dombrowski and Aubrey Williams, the New Orleans–based SCEF devoted itself to the fight against segregation and racial discrimination, focusing primarily on ending segregation in public schools. During the late 1950s it emphasized securing black voting rights and was an early supporter of the Student Nonviolent Coordinating Committee. Following a police raid on Dombrowski's home and SCEF offices, SCEF pursued an important civil rights and First Amendment case, *Dombrowski vs. Pfister*, which was decided by the Supreme Court in 1965 in SCEF's favor, declaring major parts of the Louisiana law on subversion unconstitutional, as well as overturning the doctrine of abstention, which required persons seeking federal constitutional protection to exhaust all state remedies before turning to federal courts. This legal practice had been used by Southern states to tie up civil rights cases in lengthy and expensive court proceedings.

Dombrowski retired from the SCEF in 1966 and began devoting much of his time to painting, a lifelong interest. He remained an active presence, however, in the struggle for economic and racial justice until his death in May 1983.

SOURCES: Anthony Dunbar, *Against the Grain: Southern Radicals and Prophets, 1929–1959* (1981); Irwin Kilbaner, "The Travail of Southern Radicals: The Southern Conference Education Fund, 1946–1976," *Journal of Southern History*, May 1983; Thomas Krueger, *And Promises to Keep: The Southern Conference for Human Welfare, 1938–1948* (1967).

*PAT SULLIVAN*


**DOMINGO, W. A. (1889–1968).** W(ilfred) A(dolphus) Domingo, black radical Socialist and pioneer Jamaican nationalist, was born at Kingston, Jamaica, in 1889. He was orphaned at an early age and raised by his uncle, Adolphus Grant, a master butcher in St. Ann's Bay. After leaving Baptist-run Calabar School, Domingo was employed in Kingston as an apprentice tailor. He joined S.A.G. Cox's National Club, the first organized body to agitate for the cause of island self-government, and for a time held the position of first assistant secretary (Marcus Garvey was second assistant secretary). He helped Garvey, the future black nationalist leader, write *The Struggling Mass* (1910), a pamphlet dealing with the Jamaican political struggle.

In August 1910 Domingo left Jamaica to pursue a medical career in the United States. He subsequently abandoned the idea and in 1912 moved from Boston to New York. When Garvey arrived in New York in the spring of 1916, he visited Domingo, who introduced him to various black political figures. In July 1917

Domingo was also instrumental in the organization of the British Jamaicans Benevolent Association.

After the United States entered World War I, Domingo declared himself a conscientious objector. With the rise of the "New Negro" movement in Harlem in 1917, Domingo developed close political ties with black Socialist Party members A. Philip Randolph (q.v.), Chandler Owen, and Richard B. Moore. In 1918 Garvey appointed him first editor of the *Negro World*, the official organ of the Universal Negro Improvement Association. Domingo was also invited to become a member of the Socialist Party's Speakers Bureau. He was fired by Garvey in July 1919 for using *Negro World* as a platform for spreading Socialist propaganda. Randolph and Owen, who were critical of Garvey's Black Nationalist program, promptly appointed him a contributing editor of the *Messenger*. In the spring of 1920, however, he teamed up with Richard B. Moore in the publication of the *Emancipator*, a virulently anti-Garvey weekly that was to fail after only ten issues. Domingo's radicalism also extended to active participation in the militant African Blood Brotherhood (his formal title was Director of Publicity and Propaganda).

In early 1923 Domingo broke with the *Messenger* group in reaction to Chandler Owen's vicious editorial attack against Garvey and, by implication, West Indians, marking the end of his involvement in the Harlem radical movement. For the next decade and a half, he devoted his considerable energy to building up a lucrative commercial business as an importer of West Indian foods in New York.

In 1936 Domingo reemerged into active political life with the founding of the Jamaica Progressive League (JPL), an organization made up of patriotic Jamaicans in New York City demanding political self-government for Jamaica. As vice-president of the JPL, Domingo visited Jamaica on a speaking tour in 1937–1938. Domingo was invited back to become the organizing secretary of the fledgling People's National Party (PNP), whose leaders he had helped advise on his earlier visit, but on his arrival on June 6, 1941, he was arrested aboard ship and placed in an internment camp. A lengthy campaign to secure his release was launched by the Jamaican lobby in New York, with legal help coming from the American Civil Liberties Union. Domingo was finally released after serving twenty months in detention, but he was forced to remain in Jamaica for an additional four years because the U.S. government refused to grant him a reentry visa.

After his return in 1947, Domingo became an outspoken critic of proposals for the ultimately abortive West Indian Federation, resulting in a political break between himself and his former PNP associates in Jamaica. Domingo favored maintaining the original ideal of Jamaican national independence. Permanently incapacitated by a stroke he suffered in December 1964, he died in New York on February 14, 1968.

SOURCES: Philip S. Foner, *American Socialism and Black Americans* (1977); Robert A. Hill (ed.), *The Marcus Garvey and Universal Negro Improvement Association Papers*, vol. 1 (1983).

*ROBERT A. HILL*

**DUBOIS, WILLIAM EDWARD BURGHARDT (1868–1963).** Scholar, human rights activist, socialist, Pan-Africanist, and peace advocate, W.E.B. DuBois was born February 23, 1868 in Great Barrington, Massachusetts. His father, Alfred DuBois, was born in Haiti in 1825 and his mother Mary Silvina Burghardt, 1831, in Massachusetts. DuBois' parents lived together for only a year after his birth. His father moved to Connecticut, and DuBois never saw him again. His mother probably worked most of her life as a housemaid. During his early youth, she suffered a stroke that left her partially paralyzed. His relatives were Episcopalians, but his mother joined the Congregational Church, where DuBois attended Sunday School. After age thirty, he eschewed all religion as the defender of color caste and the exploiter of labor.

DuBois was the first member of his family to graduate from high school in 1884, the same year that his mother died. He wanted to attend Harvard University but entered Fisk University, a black college in Nashville, Tennessee. DuBois had experienced little overt racial discrimination in his boyhood hometown. It was at Fisk, he later recalled, that "a new loyalty and allegiance replaced my Americanism: henceforth I was a Negro." He earned an A.B. degree there in June 1888, and enrolled at Harvard as a junior. Two years later, he graduated cum laude. With a fellowship for graduate study at Harvard, DuBois received a Ph.D. in history in 1896 that included two years' work at the University of Berlin. His dissertation, "The Suppression of the African Slave Trade to the United States of America, 1638–1870," was the first volume published in the Harvard Historical Studies.

While completing his dissertation, DuBois took a teaching position at Wilberforce University, a black college, in Xenia, Ohio. There he met his wife, Nina Gomer, whom he married on May 12, 1896. They had two children, a son who died in infancy, and a daughter. DuBois' first wife died on July 1, 1950, after fifty-four years of marriage. He later married Shirley Graham, a writer.

In his brilliant collection of essays, *The Souls of Black Folk* (1903), DuBois postulated that " . . . the problem of the Twentieth Century is the problem of the color line." He devoted his career, in large measure, to destroying the "color line," and produced a prodigious amount of scholarship, including nineteen books, almost two dozen edited works, and hundreds of articles.

During the first phase of his career from 1885 to 1910, DuBois sought to reveal the truth about the racial situation in America. He assumed that white Americans did not know the nature and extent of racial oppression in their country. Once they knew the truth, based on scientific study, they would improve race relations. DuBois, at this juncture, was primarily absorbed with including Afro-Americans into the mainstream of American society. He did not question the society, its values or goals. His only criticism of America was that it excluded his people.

In 1896, DuBois undertook a study of Afro-Americans in Philadelphia for the University of Pennsylvania. That work resulted in the publication of his pioneering sociological book, *The Philadelphia Negro* in 1899. DuBois was convinced that the nascent field of sociology would solve the "Negro Problem" in America. He began teaching in 1897 at Atlanta University, a black college, with a well-developed plan for the scientific investigation of black people and their relation to the larger society. The Atlanta University Publication Series under DuBois' guidance became a foundation for future studies of Black America.

DuBois held that the higher education of the "Talented Tenth," the leaders of the race, would guide Afro-Americans to a superior level of civilization. He believed that group cooperation in preserving and developing the best elements of Afro-American culture would help the race to achieve equality. Until the last phase of his career when he embraced Communism, DuBois considered culture the salvation of the race, which he defined more in historical and behavioral than biological terms.

Two developments made it difficult for DuBois to continue his scientific investigations. First, he could not remain an objective, dispassionate scholar while black people were being lynched, brutalized, and starved to death. Second, he discovered that there was little demand and support for his work. During the latter years of this first phase, DuBois became openly critical of Booker T. Washington, the founder of Tuskegee Institute and one of the most important black leaders. DuBois had tried to give Washington's program of racial conciliation a chance. By 1905, however, he recognized the need for direct protest against worsening conditions, especially in the South. Together with William Monroe Trotter and others, DuBois formed the Niagara Movement that prepared the way for the National Association for the Advancement of Colored People (NAACP) in 1910.

DuBois left Atlanta University that year to become Director of Publicity and Research for the NAACP. He edited its main publication, *The Crisis*. During the second phase of his career, 1910–1930, DuBois advocated interracial cooperation as a means to improve the status of Afro-Americans. He also recognized the important influence that African recovery from the slave trade and colonial domination could have on Afro-Americans. For twenty-four years, he edited *The Crisis* as a record of the darker races.

In 1910, DuBois also joined the Socialist Party but remained a member for only two years. He rejected the Socialists' line that the "Negro Problem" had to await the triumph of Socialism, when it would then be solved together with other specific problems. DuBois argued that the Socialists sought to submerge the race question to win white adherents in the South. Moreover, he charged that the European and American white working class did not acknowledge its own role in subjugating colonized nations. Although DuBois renounced the Socialist Party, he did not abandon Socialism, which for him was more a form of African communalism to be practiced among Afro-Americans.

In 1919, DuBois organized the first Pan-African Congress in Paris. Subsequent Pan-African Congresses were coordinated by him in London, Brussels, and Paris in 1921, in London, Paris, and Lisbon in 1923, and in New York City in 1927. Those meetings were generally marked by a large Afro-American and West

Indian presence and a small African representation. They encouraged racial equality as well as African development, participation in local government, and eventual self-rule. The Fifth Pan-African Congress in Manchester, England, October 15-21, 1945, elected DuBois its International President. George Padmore (q.v.), who arranged the meeting, hailed DuBois as the "Father of Pan-Africanism". The Fifth Pan-African Congress had a majority of Africans in attendance and demanded the immediate end of colonial rule in Africa.

In 1926, DuBois made his first trip to the Soviet Union. He called that nation the "most hopeful land in the modern world". But he did not consider Communism, at that time, the best route for Afro-Americans. The organization of industry for private profit was, in his opinion, doomed, because it drew its strength from exploitation of the colored world. The rise of socialism in America, however, would be evolutionary rather than cataclysmic. "American Negroes do not propose," DuBois warned, "to be the shock troops of the Communist Revolution, driven out in front to death, cruelty, and humiliation in order to win victories for white workers." He argued that the first step toward the emancipation of colored labor must come from white labor.

DuBois sensed greater potential for economic cooperation in the "Negro Nation Within the Nation" than in the society at large. He characterized Marxist philosophy as appropriate for Europe in the mid-nineteenth century but as unsuitable for the United States without modification. He contended that both white capitalists and the white proletariat exploited Afro-Americans. Their best defense was internal organization against both white classes.

White labor, in DuBois' view, deprived Afro-Americans of the right to vote, denied them education, excluded them from trade unions, prevented them from buying decent homes, and insulted them. And they were not the dupes of capital, because white labor in America was highly informed. DuBois maintained that Afro-Americans did not have class stratification similar to the broader society and that differences among black people were more cultural than economic. Educated Afro-Americans, according to DuBois, had more in common with the lowest members of their race than was true of any other group of leaders.

DuBois criticized the American Communist Party for suggesting that the black population consisted of a petit bourgeois minority that dominated a large, helpless, black proletariat. For him, black capital was insignificant as it was invested primarily in education, homes, and small businesses. Insurance represented the largest portion of black capital, but the industry among Afro-Americans was for mutual benefit, not exploitation.

The third phase of DuBois' career, 1930-1944, emphasized cultural and economic cooperation among Afro-Americans. He advised Afro-Americans to safeguard their culture for the eventual freedom of mankind. They constituted a "nation within a nation" in the black church, schools, and retail stores. DuBois urged them to take advantage of the segregation already present in American society and to make the most of it. Through cooperative enterprise, they could command racial equality. Even if it led to a temporary increase in race prejudice, DuBois deemed progress through self-segregation a risk worth taking.

That position caused him considerable difficulty with the NAACP. He was disturbed, however, that the NAACP offered no program beyond the end of racial discrimination. It did not even contemplate the path Afro-Americans should follow once segregation disappeared. He was forced to leave the NAACP in 1934, whereupon he returned to Atlanta University. He published one of his more important books, *Black Reconstruction*, in 1935, with a Marxist analysis of the systematic abuse of black labor. His chapter, "The Propaganda of History", excoriated white historians for their misuse of the past in explaining the Reconstruction Era and in subjecting Afro-Americans to racial oppression because of their distortion and lies.

As DuBois focused increasingly on black self-sufficiency during the Depression, he read more deeply about Communism for the first time in his career. He began to recognize the relationship between imperialism, colonialism, and racial domination. The removal of colonialism would not end imperialism nor the oppression of the colored world.

In 1944, at age 76, DuBois was unceremoniously retired from Atlanta University. He rejoined the NAACP and entered the final phase of his career, 1944–1963. This phase marked his foremost concern with preserving world peace. Colonialism and imperialism were, for him, root causes of war. He cheered the prospect of the United Nations becoming a "parliament of man" to resolve mankind's basic problems without regard to national boundaries. He was disappointed that the United States sought to replace Western Europe in dominating the colored world.

DuBois' opposition to American imperialism triggered his dismissal from the NAACP in 1948. The Council on African Affairs, chaired by Paul Robeson, invited DuBois to become its Vice Chairman, a position that he readily accepted. The federal government attacked the Council as a subversive organization. Robeson defended it as a useful group that monitored events in Africa, publicized them, and supported African liberation without regard to the religious or political beliefs of its members.

In 1949, DuBois attended the World Congress for Peace in Paris. He helped to organize the Peace Information Center in the United States. It published "Peacegrams" periodically with information on what other nations were doing to prevent war. And it circulated the "Stockholm Appeal" which garnered about two and a half million signatures to abolish the atomic bomb.

DuBois ran for the United States Senate from New York on the American Labor Party ticket in 1950. He used the campaign to challenge the assumption that war was inevitable. He gained over two hundred thousand of the five million votes cast, including about fifteen percent of the vote in Harlem. The Justice Department requested during his campaign that the Peace Information Center (PIC) register under the Foreign Agents Registration Act of 1938. The PIC considered itself an American organization and not the agent of any foreign power. On February 8, 1951, the PIC and its officers were indicted for failure to register as the agent of a foreign principal. The case came to trial in November, and the defendants were acquitted.

Although acquitted, DuBois was hounded by the federal government, denied a passport, and excluded from the college lecture circuit. He was gradually isolated from Black America, and as he put it '' . . . lost my leadership of my race.'' DuBois had hoped that the decline of segregation would foster greater cultural unity among Afro-Americans. Instead, he saw the black bourgeoisie becoming ensnared in materialism.

When Ghana became the first modern African nation to gain independence in May, 1957, the State Department refused DuBois a passport to visit, unless he signed a non-Communist affidavit. Ghana's independence was a culmination of DuBois' Pan-Africanist work, but he could not attend the ceremony. He did regain his right to travel abroad in the summer of 1958 after the Supreme Court ruled that the State Department could not require a political affidavit as a prerequisite for a passport. DuBois spent the next eleven months in Europe, the Soviet Union, and China, where he received a warm welcome.

He was particularly struck by progress in the Soviet Union and China toward combating illiteracy, poverty, and disease. He compared that progress with the stagnation of Afro-Americans. DuBois concluded that socialism was the best route for the emerging nations of Africa. He believed that Africa would lead the way to a socialist future and would influence Afro-Americans to follow the same path.

DuBois, in 1961, joined the American Communist Party. That same year, he moved to Ghana at the invitation of its President, Kwame Nkrumah, to supervise the publication of an Encyclopedia Africana. DuBois became a citizen of Ghana, where he died on August 27, 1963, the eve of the historic march on Washington in the United States. He received a State funeral and was buried in the capital city, Accra.

SOURCES: Herbert Aptheker, ed., *The Correspondence of W.E.B. DuBois*, 3 vols. (1973–78); Francis L. Broderick, *W.E.B. DuBois: Negro Leader in a Time of Crisis* (1959); W.E.B. DuBois, *The Autobiography of W.E.B. DuBois* (1968); Paul G. Partington, *W.E.B. DuBois: A Bibliography of His Published Writings* (1979).

*ROBERT L. HARRIS JR.*

**DUNCAN, LEWIS J. (1858–1936).** Lewis J. Duncan was a leading Socialist in the Rocky Mountain West. He served as mayor of Butte, Montana, from 1911 until 1915. Born in St. Louis in 1858 of working-class parents, Duncan was educated in the public schools of that city and spent one year at Hanover College in Indiana. In 1882 he was ordained a minister in the Unitarian Church. The Unitarians were at that time liberal theologically but generally conservative politically and economically. Duncan was liberal in his political and economic philosophy as well as theologically. After serving several years as a minister in

Midwestern and Rocky Mountain pulpits, Duncan accepted a call to the Unitarian church in the wide-open mining town of Butte in 1902.

During his first years at Butte, Duncan was active in moderate reform movements aimed primarily at alleviating the economic distress of the miners in the region. His reform activities early earned him the animosity of the managers and owners of the mines in the Silver Bow (Butte) County area. In 1908 Duncan used his pulpit to defend civil liberties for radicals; he offered his church to anarchist-feminist Emma Goldman (q.v.), who had been denied a meeting hall for a lecture in that city. A large number of wealthy members of the congregation resigned in protest, but a majority of the congregation supported his action.

After the Goldman affair, Duncan veered further to the left and by so doing won the support of many union miners. An official 1909 report to the American Unitarian Association headquarters in Boston voiced disapproval of Duncan's politics, but conceded that he had won considerable support for himself and his congregation from the working-class population of Butte.

The government of Butte was corrupt. Prostitution, gambling, and other forms of crime and vice were rampant. Disease was commonplace because of open sewage, poor medical facilities, and filthy conditions generally. The police force was at the disposal of the mine owners and was used often to prevent militant unions from being effective. In 1909 Duncan began a campaign to clean up the government of Butte and to make the city a decent place to live. As a result he was elected mayor of the city two years later, carrying a Socialist majority into the city legislature with him. Within a year the Duncan administration cleaned up the vice that was rampant in the city, improved sanitary conditions, sharply cut the incidence of disease and infant mortality, and reorganized the city's police—naming the first black man to the force. The Socialist regime was reelected in 1913 and continued its drive to improve living conditions.

Before 1912 Duncan was inactive in the internal dispute in the Socialist Party regarding the use of sabotage by the labor movement. A year later he led the futile fight to prevent the ouster of William Haywood (q.v.) from the party's National Executive Board for advocating sabotage. Despite these stands, Duncan opposed the Industrial Workers of the World (IWW), which was then competing with the Western Federation of Miners (WFM) for the loyalty of Butte's miners, who were organized into an independent militant union.

In 1915 a mob of Butte miners—belonging to the independent union that supported neither the IWW nor the more conservative Western Federation of Miners—broke up a rally for WFM President Charles Moyer. Someone also dynamited the WFM union hall. Duncan tried to contain the violence, but Moyer and Samuel Gompers, president of the American Federation of Labor (AFL), joined the mine owners to pressure the governor into ordering out troops to end the union rebellion. Although the governor and the AFL officials blamed the dynamiting and rioting on the IWW, it appeared that those were spontaneous acts (miners often carried dynamite for use in their jobs). Duncan pleaded with the governor not to send troops, which he feared would further infuriate the mob. The governor ignored him and forced Duncan from office. Many miners were made to flee the city, others were blacklisted by the WFM and the mine companies.

Duncan remained in Butte until August 1917, when a local mob instigated by mine officials lynched IWW organizer Frank Little. Warned that he also faced mob action, Duncan fled to Minneapolis, which had just elected a Socialist mayor. In Minneapolis, Duncan was active for a few years in the Non-Partisan League, which evolved into the Farmer-Labor Party. During the period immediately following World War I, he was also involved in the 1924 presidential election campaign for Robert M. LaFollette. Thereafter he left politics and worked as a schoolteacher in Minneapolis, where he died in 1936.

*BERNARD K. JOHNPOLL*

**DUNNE, VINCENT (1889–1970).** Vincent Raymond Dunne, a leader of the Trotskyist movement in the United States, was born on April 17, 1889, in Kansas City, Kansas, the son of an Irish railroad construction worker from County Clare and a French-Canadian shoemaker from Wisconsin. Two of his brothers, Miles and Grant, became Trotskyists, while William (q.v.) remained in the Communist Party.

The family moved to Little Falls, Minnesota, after their father suffered an industrial accident. They lived in a log cabin, and Vincent had five years of education in an ungraded school. At age 14 he went to work in a Minnesota lumber camp and then moved to the Montana camps. There he joined the Western Federation of Miners and then the Industrial Workers of the World (IWW).

After the 1907 financial panic Dunne roamed the nation and was arrested in Seattle and Los Angeles Wobblie free-speech fights. In 1908 he was on the Bogalusa, Louisiana, Saw Mill Workers Strike Committee. Settling in Minneapolis in 1910, he worked for an express company and drove one of the city's first trucks. He continued as an IWW activist, and under the influence of Carl Skoglund (q.v.) joined the newly organized Communist Party. During the 1920s he worked in a Minneapolis coal yard. He was a member of the Minnesota district committee of the Communist Party, Communist candidate for Congress (1928), active in the Farmer-Labor Association, secretary of the Minneapolis Central Labor Union (1922–1924, until the Communists' expulsion), and a charter member of the Minneapolis Office Workers Unions.

Expelled from the Party for Trotskyism in 1928, Dunne was a national leader of the Communist League of America and successor organizations. The Minneapolis Trotskyists utilized their connections with friendly Teamster officials to plan and execute the 1934 coal yard strike, then used that victory to wage the successful 1934 Minneapolis Truckers strikes. Dunne played the key political and strategic role in these campaigns.

During the rest of the 1930s, although he devoted most of his time to political action, Dunne remained active in the union movement. He was usually on the executive board of International Brotherhood of Teamsters (IBT) Local 574 (later

Local 544), was beaten by company agents in the Strutwear Knitting strike and
by Teamsters sent in by IBT President Daniel Tobin. He was active in the multi-
state Teamsters over-the-road truckers organizing campaigns. While the Trotskyists
were Socialist Party members, he was Socialist Party candidate for
Minnesota secretary of state (1936) and Minneapolis mayor (1937).

Dunne was a founding member of the Socialist Workers Party (1938) and
held discussions with Trotsky in Coyoacán, Mexico. Convicted in the 1941
Minneapolis anti-sedition Smith Act trials, he served his sentence in 1944 in
Sandstone (Minnesota) federal penitentiary. After World War II, he remained
active in Minneapolis, usually as branch organizer for the Socialist Workers
Party. Dunne died in Minneapolis on February 17, 1970, at the age of 80.

*SETH WIGDERSON*

**DUNNE, WILLIAM (1887–1953).** William Dunne was a labor organizer from
Montana who held important positions in the Communist Party throughout the
1920s. He was born on October 15, 1887, in Kansas City, Missouri. Part Irish
and part French-Canadian, the son of a railroad worker, he was a tough, hard
Midwesterner. Dunne played football at the University of Minnesota but dropped
out after a few semesters to become an electrician and eventually vice-president
of the International Brotherhood of Electrical Workers. After moving to Butte,
Montana, in 1916, Dunne quickly became vice-president of the Montana Federation
of Labor and editor of the *Butte Daily Bulletin*, its organ, and helped lead a
violent strike against the Anaconda Copper Company in 1917.

Dunne had joined the Socialist Party in 1910. He was elected in 1918 to the
Montana legislature as a Democrat on a radical platform supporting recognition
of the Soviet Union and "all power to the workers and farmers." He brought
his Butte Socialist Party branch into the Communist Labor Party in 1919 and
afterward held a series of high-level positions in the Party. His labor career,
however, ended in 1923 when he was expelled from the American Federation
of Labor convention as a Communist, the first time in history a delegate had
been removed from the floor.

For most of the 1920s, Dunne was associated with James Cannon's (q.v.)
faction in the Communist Party. He was a delegate to the Profintern in 1921 and
1928 and the Party's representative to the Comintern in 1924–1925. In addition,
he served as a Comintern representative in Outer Mongolia in 1928. He edited
both the *Daily Worker* and *Labor Unity* and was the Party's first Southern
organizer. In 1928, when Cannon founded the Trotskyist movement in the United
States, Dunne broke with him, and also severed relations with his brothers
(Vincent [q.v.], Miles, and Grant), who joined Cannon.

One of the Party's most capable leaders, with ability and ambition, Dunne
was added to the Politburo in 1929. With Earl Browder's (q.v.) rise to leadership
in the early 1930s, however, Dunne's career began to slide. He was removed
from the national leadership in 1934 and sent back to Montana. An instinctive
left-winger, Dunne was uncomfortable with the transition to the Popular Front

and protested the Party's "surrender" to John L. Lewis. By the late 1930s his alcoholism had gone out of control and his Party career was over.

Dunne worked at a variety of jobs thereafter. In 1944–1945 he was a cook in the Aleutian Islands. The Communist Party expelled him in 1946 for alcoholism and "ultra-leftism." For several years he maintained loose organizational contacts with a group of Communists who had been expelled at the same time, including Vern Smith and Harrison George (q.v.). Dunne died on September 23, 1953.

SOURCES: Theodore Draper, *American Communism and Soviet Russia* (1960); FBI File 61–130.

HARVEY KLEHR

# E

EASTMAN, MAX (1883–1969). Max Eastman edited the *Masses* and the *Liberator*. He was a leading voice among radical writers and intellectuals from World War I through the 1930s and a member of the Socialist Party's left wing, which sympathized with the Industrial Workers of the World (IWW) and supported the Russian Revolution. He was a leading proponent of Bolshevism in the United States, one of the earliest supporters of the Trotskyist Left Opposition, and a critical writer on Marxist theory and philosophy.

Eastman was born in 1883 in Upstate New York, the son of two ordained Congregational ministers. In 1907 he joined his radical, feminist sister, Crystal, in New York's Greenwich Village. Through Crystal, Max met and subsequently studied under the philosopher John Dewey. In 1909 he became actively involved in the campaign for women's suffrage. Through his first wife, Ida Rauh, Max was converted to socialism. In 1912 he joined the Socialist Party and in the same year became editor of *Masses* magazine. Under Eastman's leadership, and with an editorial board including such figures as John Reed (q.v.) and Floyd Dell, *Masses* became an extremely influential organ of the literary Left. It championed striking miners in West Virginia and Colorado; promoted free love, contraception, and women's suffrage; and published cartoons, poems, short stories, and political tracts by many of the most important thinkers and writers of the period.

In 1916 Max linked up with Crystal to oppose U.S. involvement in World War I. He quickly became one of the most visible and outspoken opponents of American militarism. In late 1917 the federal government succeeded in suppressing *Masses*, and the following year Eastman and the other editors were twice tried under the Espionage Act.

In 1918 Eastman launched the *Liberator*, which also served as a central forum for radical artists and writers. Perhaps its most important objective was to rally support for the new Bolshevik regime in Russia, which Eastman called "the most just and wise and humane and democratic government that ever existed in the world.'' Although he did not become organizationally involved in the new Communist parties, through the *Liberator* Eastman became perhaps the most influential American supporter of the Bolsheviks. By 1921, however, he began to tire of radical journalism. He turned the editorship of the *Liberator* over to Mike Gold (q.v.) and Claude McKay and set out for a trip to Russia. A few years later the *Liberator* became an official organ of the Workers (Communist) Party.

During his stay in Russia (1922–1923), Eastman mastered the Russian language, studied Marxist theory in depth for the first time, and became personally acquainted with many Bolshevik leaders. He created an international furor when, on his departure from Russia, he released to the public what became known as ''Lenin's Testament,'' in which the Bolshevik leader warned on his deathbed against the rise of Stalin's power, which he hoped to see offset by Trotsky's assuming leadership of the party. Eastman's reputation as Trotsky's foremost supporter in the West was strengthened the following year with the publication of *Since Lenin Died*, which detailed the power struggle in Russia that had followed Lenin's death.

Eastman remained in western Europe for the next couple of years. When he returned to the United States in 1927, he continued to champion the Left Opposition against Stalinism and became instrumental in the formation of the first Trotskyist group in the United States, although he again refused to take on any organizational affiliation or responsibility. Eastman's brilliant translation of Trotsky's *History of the Russian Revolution* was published in 1932, and in 1934 he published *Artists in Uniform*, which bitterly denounced Stalinist cultural policy. Eastman's influence within the anti-Stalinist Left can be gauged from the fact that in March 1938 he was singled out in the Moscow treason trials and accused of being a paid agent of British and Japanese intelligence. Stalin denounced him by name as a ''notorious crook'' and a ''gangster of the pen.''

Eastman's hopes that a true Socialist democracy could be salvaged from the Soviet Union faded in the mid-1930s. From a revolutionary anti-Stalinist, he rapidly evolved into a crusading anti-Communist. In 1941 he became a ''roving editor'' for *Reader's Digest* and began arguing that Leninism was a natural precedent for Stalinism, that Marxism was inherently authoritarian, and that socialism was incompatible with human nature. He remained associated with right-wing causes for the rest of his life, supporting the witch-hunt against the Left in the 1950s and joining a number of other ex-leftists on William F. Buckley's *National Review*.

Eastman's sincere and prolonged commitment to socialism and to Leninism was never based on a thorough assimilation of or agreement with Marxist thought. Like many intellectuals of his generation, Eastman embraced John Dewey's pragmatic philosophy of instrumentalism. He drew from Dewey a commitment to applying ''science'' and ''scientific technique'' to the solution of social problems. He dismissed the Hegelian dialectic as an unscientific and religious strain in Marx's thought. Eastman came to Lenin as an instrumentalist for whom Marxism was never more than an experiment. He saw Soviet communism as a "scientific hypothesis in the process of verification." When, in his view, dogmatic dialectics defeated scientific inquiry in Russia, the cause of socialism was lost.

Max Eastman published more than twenty books during his lifetime on a wide range of subjects. They included several volumes of poetry, a novel, and two volumes of memoirs. He died in 1969.

SOURCES: Max Eastman, *Enjoyment of Living* (1948) and *Love and Revolution* (1964); William L. O'Neill, *The Last Romantic: A Life of Max Eastman* (1978).

*JEFF BENEKE*

**ENGDAHL, J. LOUIS (1884–1932).** J. Louis Engdahl, a journalist who edited Socialist newspapers and for much of the 1920s the Communist *Daily Worker*, was born in Minneapolis, Minnesota, in 1884. His parents were of Swedish Lutheran background; his father was a carpenter. After two years at the University of Minnesota, Engdahl became a newspaper reporter. He was a city editor of the *Minneapolis Daily News* before joining the Socialist Party in 1907. Prior to World War I, he edited the *Chicago Daily Socialist* and other Socialist journals. He was also a delegate to the International Socialist Conference in Copenhagen in 1910 and the Party's candidate for Congress in Illinois in 1916. During World War I, while he was editor of the *American Socialist*, he was sentenced to twenty years in prison for opposing the draft; the sentence was later reversed.

Engdahl left the Socialist Party in 1920 after the demands of his Committee for a Third International, favoring affiliation to the Communist International, had been rejected. He joined the Workers (Communist) Party in 1921 in Chicago and became editor, first of the weekly *Worker* and then, along with William Dunne (q.v.), of the new *Daily Worker*, where he remained editor until 1928. That year he became national secretary of the International Labor Defense. He died in Europe on November 21, 1932, while on a tour to garner support for the defense of the Scottsboro Boys.

SOURCES: Solon DeLeon, *American Labor Who's Who* (1925); Theodore Draper, *The Roots of American Communism* (1957).

*HARVEY KLEHR*

# F

**FARRELL, JAMES T. (1904–1979).** James Thomas Farrell, an internationally known novelist and literary critic, was sympathetic to the Communist Party in the early 1930s. At the time of the Moscow purge trials he defended Leon Trotsky and subsequently collaborated with the Trotskyist Socialist Workers Party and then Max Shachtman's (q.v.) Workers Party until the late 1940s.

Farrell was born on February 27, 1904, into a working-class Irish-American family in Chicago. His father was a teamster and his mother worked as a domestic servant. The Farrells were so poor that at 3 years old James had to be turned over to the care of middle-class relatives. He worked his way through the University of Chicago as a gas station attendant and in other assorted jobs, but quit before graduating because he had decided to become a writer.

In 1931 he eloped to Paris, writing industriously while living in dire poverty. The next year he settled permanently in New York, witnessing a change in fortune when his first novel, *Young Lonigan*, was published by Vanguard Press. In 1935 the appearance of *Judgment Day* completed the Studs Lonigan trilogy, and Farrell was established as a major figure in American letters.

A supporter of the Communist Party from 1932 to 1935, Farrell broke with it at the time of the Popular Front and the Moscow trials. In the spring of 1936 he published *A Note on Literary Criticism*, a Marxist polemic against the political manipulation of literature practiced by the Communist Party. Later that year he helped organize the American Committee for the Defense of Leon Trotsky, and in 1937 he traveled to Mexico to observe the John Dewey commission, which took Trotsky's testimony. On his return to New York he encouraged the transformation of *Partisan Review* magazine into an organ of the anti-Stalinist literary left and contributed to it regularly for several years. In 1938 he was a sponsor of the League for Cultural Freedom and Socialism, initiated by the *Partisan Review* editors in collaboration with the Trotskyists.

Until the end of 1944, Farrell was a dependable ally of the Socialist Workers Party. Along with Columbia University art historian Meyer Schapiro and cultural critic Dwight Macdonald (q.v.), he was one of the few prominent intellectuals to oppose U.S. government policy in World War II. From 1941 to 1945 he served as chairman of the Civil Rights Defense Committee, formed to defend the trade union militants in Teamsters Local 544 and leaders of the Socialist Workers Party prosecuted as the first victims of the Smith Act.

But in 1945 Farrell grew dissatisfied with the Socialist Workers Party and switched his allegiance to Max Shachtman's (q.v.) Workers Party until the spring of 1948, when he abandoned revolutionary Marxism altogether for social democracy. After that he joined the anti-Communist Cold Warriors of the American Committee for Cultural Freedom and was chairman from 1954 to 1956. In the 1960s he became an ardent supporter of Hubert Humphrey and a harsh critic of the New Left. One year before his death in 1979, he joined Social Democrats USA.

SOURCES: Daniel Aaron, *Writers on the Left* (1961); Edgar Branch, *James T. Farrell* (1971); Alan M. Wald, *James T. Farrell: The Revolutionary Socialist Years* (1978).

*ALAN WALD*

**FERGUSON, ISAAC (1888- ? ).** Isaac Ferguson was one of the founders of American Communism. Born in 1888 in Winnipeg, Canada, the son of a Jewish butcher, Ferguson came to the United States in 1893 with his Russian-born parents. He earned a B.A. (1910) and a law degree (1912) from the University of Chicago. After graduation from law school, he left for Wyoming, where he divided his time between farming and a small law practice. During this period, he also ran for county attorney on the Republican ticket.

Ferguson first came under the influence of socialism in 1917 when he returned to Chicago and became friendly with Socialists at the University of Chicago. In 1918 he joined the Socialist Party and became the personal secretary to millionaire Socialist William Bross Lloyd (q.v.). In collaboration with Lloyd, he drafted one of the first comprehensive statements of the left wing of the Socialist Party, a lengthy brochure entitled *The Socialist Party and Its Purpose*. In November 1919 he helped form the Communist Propaganda League and was elected national secretary. Several months later Ferguson was also elected national secretary of the National Council of the left wing. When the Socialist Party split in 1919, Ferguson joined the group that became the Communist Party and was elected international delegate and member of the Executive Committee. Although he had little training in the Socialist movement, his superior organizational skills earned him a prominent place in the new party. During 1919 he was also indicted by the state of New York on a "criminal anarchy" charge along with other prominent Communists such as Charles Ruthenberg (q.v.). In the trial that followed, Ferguson served as defense lawyer and received a five-to-ten year sentence. After serving time at Sing Sing, he won his release on a technicality.

Following his release, he left the Communist movement and eventually became a prosperous Chicago lawyer.

SOURCES: Theodore Draper, *The Roots of American Communism* (1957); *The People of the State of New York Against Isaac F. Ferguson and Charles E. Ruthenberg*, 234/ NY/159, 136/N.E./327 (1922).

*JOHN GERBER*

**FLYNN, ELIZABETH GURLEY (1890–1964).** Elizabeth Gurley Flynn, a longtime member of the Industrial Workers of the World (IWW) and later a Communist, was a tireless and inspiring labor orator who traveled the United States on labor's behalf. She was born on August 7, 1890, in Concord, New Hampshire, to Thomas Flynn, a civil engineer and cartographer, and Annie Gurley, both of whom were direct descendants of Irish Catholic immigrants. She attended grammar school in the Bronx. From her parents, Flynn inherited the rebelliousness that became her trademark.

In 1906 Flynn gave her first public speech at the Harlem Socialist Club on the topic "What Socialism Will Do for Women." She was soon invited to speak elsewhere and was arrested that same year for "speaking without a permit" and "blocking traffic." She became so involved in Socialist activities and speech-making that she dropped out of high school shortly after enrolling. In 1907, at the age of 17, she attended the IWW convention in Chicago, toured several eastern cities, and in December, at the invitation of labor organizer J. A. Jones, toured the Mesabi Iron Range in northern Minnesota. She and Jones were married in January 1908 and moved to Chicago, where Flynn's first child died shortly after birth.

Soon after, Flynn was asked to go on a speaking tour from Chicago to the West Coast and northward into western Canada. In the fall of 1908 she and her husband participated in the "Free Speech" battle in Missoula, Montana, the first of twenty-six such confrontations between 1906 and 1916. The next year, though pregnant, she went to Spokane, Washington, to participate in a brutal confrontation with authorities over the right to speak on the streets. She was jailed briefly and tried for "conspiracy to incite men to violate the law," but was acquitted. She left Jones for good and returned to New York City to have her baby. A son, named Fred, was born in May 1910. She and Jones were formally divorced in 1926.

In 1912 Flynn was active in the textile strike in Lawrence, Massachusetts. While in Lawrence, she met Carlo Tresca (q.v.), an Italian-born anarchist, on May Day 1912. Although they never married, they lived and worked together until 1925. After the strike in Lawrence was settled, Flynn quickly moved on to a strike in the cotton mills of Lowell, Massachusetts.

In 1913 she was deeply involved in the Paterson, New Jersey, silk weavers strike—a brutal strike that saw the introduction of pageants held nightly in Madison Square Garden in nearby New York on the strikers' behalf.

In 1914 Joe Hill (q.v.), a Swedish immigrant migratory worker and songwriter for the IWW, was sentenced to death in the state of Utah for murder. Flynn visited him on death row, and he composed "The Rebel Girl" in her honor. She used it as the title of her work *The Rebel Girl: An Autobiography, My First Life (1906–1926)*, the story of the first part of her life, published in 1955.

In 1916, Flynn, Tresca, Joe Ettor, and other IWW organizers were involved in the Mesabi Range miners strike in northern Minnesota. Tresca and several other IWW leaders in the area were jailed in Duluth on the grounds that speeches made by them had induced a group of Croatian miners to kill a deputy sheriff and another man. The strike, which was lost, was followed by several months of legal maneuvering that ultimately secured their release. But conflicts with William "Big Bill" Haywood (q.v.), the national leader of the IWW, caused the Mesabi organizers to have doubts about the IWW and its tactics. Before she could have time to reflect on IWW tactics, however, Flynn was called to Everett, Washington, in the wake of the Everett Massacre to aid in the defense of those IWW members charged with murder. She spoke throughout the West Coast region until May 1917, when all the men charged were acquitted.

In September 1917 Flynn and Carlo Tresca were arrested in a federal crackdown on the IWW, the results of which led eventually to the trial of 166 of the group's leaders in Chicago. Tresca and Flynn refused to follow Haywood's order to all those charged to appear in Chicago and be tried as a group. Instead they filed a severance motion in New York and won. They were never tried. Of those who were tried, ninety-three received harsh sentences of five to twenty years in jail plus fines. The trial signaled the end of the IWW as a viable force in favor of workers throughout the United States.

Between 1918 and 1923 Flynn worked mostly on freeing all those who had been imprisoned during World War I and after (during the Palmer Raids in November 1919) for their radical statements and beliefs. In December 1918 the Workers Liberty Defense Union was established, and she was named an organizer. The Defense Union maintained close ties with the National Civil Liberties Bureau, and when it was reorganized in 1920 Flynn was named a founding member of the National Committee of the American Civil Liberties Union.

In 1920 Flynn became deeply involved in the Sacco and Vanzetti (q.v.) case. Throughout 1920 and 1921 she and the Workers Defense Union did all they could to publicize the "frame-up" of the two Italian anarchists, Nicola Sacco and Bartolomeo Vanzetti, for murder and robbery. Convicted in July 1921, the two appealed their cases unsuccessfully and were electrocuted in 1927. Flynn worked ceaselessly during their incarceration, conducting a nationwide tour as the newly elected chairman of the International Labor Defense organization in order to raise money for their defense and to call attention to their cases.

In 1925 Flynn and Tresca parted for good. The following year Flynn applied for membership in the Communist Party. Because of Party factionalism, her application was not acted upon, but she regarded herself as a Communist from that point on, after concluding that membership in the Party was the next logical step after the previous twenty years of her labor activities. In the mid-1930s Flynn applied for membership again and was accepted. She remained a Communist for the rest of her life.

In 1925 Flynn was involved in the Passaic, New Jersey, textile strike and was named chairman of International Labor Defense. While on a nationwide tour seeking money for Sacco and Vanzetti, she became seriously ill in Portland, Oregon, and was forced to withdraw from public life for the better part of the next decade.

The last two decades of her life found Flynn on the defensive. In 1940 she was expelled from the American Civil Liberties Union because she was a Communist. In 1952 she was tried and convicted in Foley Square, New York, under the provisions of the Smith Act. After exhaustive appeals failed, she finally served two years and four months at the Federal Women's Reformatory in Alderson, West Virginia.

She died on September 4, 1964, at age 74, while visiting Moscow to attend a Soviet Party congress in her capacity as chairman of the American Communist Party.

SOURCES: Melvyn Dubofsky, *We Shall Be All: A History of the IWW* (1969); Elizabeth
  Gurley Flynn, *The Rebel Girl: An Autobiography, My First Life (1906–1926)* (1955).

*MIKE KARNI*


**FORD, JAMES (1893–1957).** James Ford was the most prominent black Communist in the United States during the 1930s, a candidate for Vice-President of the United States in 1932, 1936, and 1940, and director of Communist Party activities in Harlem. Ford was born on December 22, 1893, in Pratt City, Alabama, near Birmingham. One grandfather had been lynched in Georgia. His father worked in steel mills and coal mines. At age 13, Ford went to work on the railroad and continued working through high school. In 1913 he entered Fisk University in Nashville, where he played football and received his degree in 1920. An army enlistee, Ford fought in France in World War I. After the war he moved to Chicago and found a job in the postal service. Active in a union, he was fired and helped found the American Negro Labor Congress, a Party auxiliary, in 1925. One year later he joined the Communist Party in Chicago.

Only a handful of blacks were then members of the Communist Party, and unlike virtually all of them, Ford had some trade union experience. His rise in the Party hierarchy was rapid. He was selected as a delegate to the Profintern Congress in 1928 and stayed in Moscow nine months, being appointed to its Executive Committee. He then organized the first International Conference of Negro Workers in Hamburg, Germany, in 1930 and became the first editor of its *Negro Worker*. By the time he returned to the States in 1931, after being expelled from Austria, Ford was being groomed as the Party's spokesman on the Negro question. He became a leader of the League of Struggle for Negro Rights and, in 1932, a Politburo member.

Ford received national attention in 1932 when he was selected as William Foster's (q.v.) running mate on the Communist Party's presidential ticket. The Communists trumpeted his selection as evidence of their commitment to Negro rights. He was also the Party's vice-presidential candidate in 1936 and 1940. Following the 1932 election, Ford was made leader of the Harlem section of the Party in an effort to bolster Communist recruitment among blacks. A few years later he became chairman of the New York County Party. In addition, he directed the Party's Negro work and served as its official spokesman on racial issues. In the mid–1930s Ford was a key figure in the formation of the National Negro Congress, a large Popular Front organization led by A. Phillip Randolph (q.v.).

Ford's prestige in the Party began to diminish during World War II. He became a vice-president of the Communist Political Association in 1944. Even though he joined in the denunciations of Earl Browder (q.v.) in 1945, Ford's role as the Party's Negro leader soon diminished, while that of Benjamin Davis (q.v.) grew. He was not reelected to the National Committee after Browder's ouster. Ford became Party chairman in Bedford-Stuyvesant and faded from the top leadership. Just before his death, he was executive director of the National Committee to Defend Negro Leadership, a Party group set up to support black Smith Act defendants. He died on June 21, 1957.

SOURCES: FBI File 100–14632; Mark Naison, *Communists in Harlem During the Depression* (1983).

*HARVEY KLEHR*

**FORMAN, JAMES (b. 1928).** James Forman, who served as executive secretary of the Student Nonviolent Coordinating Committee (SNCC) from 1961 to 1966, was one of the foremost black militant leaders to emerge from the Southern civil rights movement. Born on October 5, 1928, in Chicago, Forman spent his early years living with his grandmother on a farm in Marshall County, Mississippi. When he was 6, his parents took him to Chicago, where he attended a Roman Catholic grammar school before transferring to a public school in fifth grade. Until he was a teenager, Forman used the surname of his stepfather, John Rufus, a gas station manager, rather than that of his real father, Jackson Forman, a Chicago cabdriver.

Forman graduated from Englewood High School in 1947 with honors and then served in the air force before entering the University of Southern California in 1952. After being beaten and arrested by police at the beginning of his second college semester, Forman transferred to Roosevelt University in Chicago, where he became a leader in student politics and chairman of the university's delegation to the National Student Association conference in 1956. He graduated in 1957 and attended Boston University as a graduate student.

During the late 1950s Forman gradually became active in the expanding Southern black civil rights movement. He covered the 1956–1957 desegregation crisis in Little Rock for the *Chicago Defender*. In 1961 he left his job as a substitute elementary school teacher to go to Fayette County, Tennessee, to help sharecroppers who had been evicted for registering to vote. In the summer of 1961 he was jailed with other Freedom Riders protesting segregated facilities in Monroe, North Carolina. After his sentence was suspended, Forman agreed to become executive secretary of SNCC.

Older than most civil rights activists, Forman gained the respect of SNCC's staff of organizers because of his militancy and willingness to undertake mundane administrative chores that were avoided by other staff members. In 1964, after participating in the unsuccessful effort of the Mississippi Freedom Democratic Party to unseat the regular all-white delegation at the national convention in Atlantic City, he and other SNCC workers went to Guinea at the invitation of the African government. After his return, Forman became increasingly outspoken in his criticisms of the federal government and of cautious liberalism. Within SNCC he advocated staff education programs to make civil rights workers more aware of Marxist and Black Nationalist ideas. Critical of the black separatists who expelled whites from SNCC in 1966, Forman, who was married for several years to white activist Constancia Romilly Forman, nevertheless joined other black militants in demanding a greater role for blacks in alliances with white radicals. As SNCC's director of international affairs, he sought to build ties between Afro-Americans and revolutionaries in the Third World.

Expelled from the disintegrating SNCC in 1968, Forman joined the League of Revolutionary Black Workers. In April 1969 he and other League members took control of the National Black Economic Development Conference in Detroit, and a month later he interrupted a service at New York's Riverside Church to read his "Black Manifesto," a demand that white churches pay half a billion dollars to blacks as reparations for previous exploitation. He received a master's degree in African and Afro-American history from Cornell University and a Ph.D. from the Union of Experimental Colleges and Universities. In 1981 he published his thesis, *Self-Determination and the African-American People*, in which he advocated an autonomous black nation in the Black Belt region of the United States.

SOURCES: Clayborne Carson, *In Struggle: SNCC and the Black Awakening of the 1960s* (1981); James Forman, *The Making of Black Revolutionaries* (1972).

*CLAYBORNE CARSON AND PENNY A. RUSSELL*

**FOSTER, WILLIAM Z. (1881–1961).** William Z. Foster, an influential trade union organizer during and just after World War I, is best known for his role as a leader and public spokesman for the Communist Party USA in later years. Joining the Communist movement in 1921, he spent the next two and a half decades in a grueling battle for Party leadership, finally achieving his goal in 1945 when his arch-rival Earl Browder (q.v.) fell victim to Soviet disfavor. From 1945 until his death in Moscow in 1961, Foster presided as chairman over a declining Communist movement.

Foster was born in Taunton, Massachusetts, on February 15, 1881. His father, an Irish immigrant who worked as a carriage washer and livery stableman, was an ardent Irish nationalist who instructed his son in the perfidies of the English. His mother, an English immigrant of mixed English and Scottish ancestry, was a devout Roman Catholic who bore her husband twenty-three children, most of whom died in infancy. She had hoped to see William, one of only two sons who survived to adulthood, enter the priesthood, but Foster was of a different bent and soon abandoned the beliefs of his father and mother. Forced to leave school and go to work at the age of 10 as an apprentice to a local sculptor, he soon moved on to a series of hard and dirty jobs in a type foundry, lead works, and several fertilizer factories. According to his later account in the autobiographical *From Bryan to Stalin* (1937), he was converted to the trade union cause when he was clubbed by a mounted policeman during a streetcar workers strike in Philadelphia in 1895, and he converted to socialism after hearing a streetcorner speaker from the Socialist Labor Party criticize his earlier political hero William Jennings Bryan.

Foster joined the newly formed Socialist Party in 1901, but he did not have much opportunity to support its activities for the next few years. In 1900 he left Philadelphia and saw the world as an itinerant laborer, finding employment in a Florida lumber camp, on a New York City streetcar line, in an East Texas railroad camp, and then for three years as an able seaman aboard British merchant ships that carried him to Africa, South America, and the South Pacific. In 1904 he settled in Oregon, where he set himself up as a homesteader and worked a succession of jobs in logging camps, mines, and on the railroad.

From 1904 to 1909, first in Portland and then in Seattle, Foster was active in the Socialist Party. He grew increasingly critical of what he regarded as its reformism and electoral illusions. In 1909 he joined other Washington state left-wingers in walking out of the Socialist Party and organizing a rival Wage Workers Party, which sought to guard its own revolutionary purity by allowing only bona fide proletarians to enlist under its banners. Few did, and the Wage Workers Party soon collapsed. Foster was a man who was never comfortable without organizational affiliation, and he joined the Industrial Workers of the World (IWW) while serving a jail sentence for taking part in an IWW free-speech fight in Spokane, Washington.

Foster went to Europe in 1910, where he studied the powerful French syndicalist movement and was converted to the strategy of "boring from within" existing trade unions. After a stay in Germany and a side trip to Budapest (where he challenged the right of the American Federation of Labor [AFL] delegate to speak for American labor at an international trade union conference), Foster returned to the United States in 1911. Unable to persuade his comrades in the IWW to abandon their opposition to working within the existing unions of the AFL, Foster quit to form his own group, the Syndicalist League of North America (SLNA). The SLNA survived for two years and attracted several thousand adherents (among them the young Earl Browder in Kansas City), but never had any significant impact on the labor or radical movement. Meanwhile, Foster had shifted his political base to Chicago, where he worked in the railroad yards, was elected as a delegate to the Chicago Federation of labor, and ran the SNLA and its even smaller successor, the Independent Trade Union Educational League.

Foster was a skilled and dedicated organizer, and he attracted favorable attention from the leaders of the Chicago AFL. In 1917 he finally got the chance to move from the marginal world of radical unionism to a major AFL organizing drive. His proposal to lead a combined effort by Chicago unions to organize workers in the stockyards won official AFL approval, and in short order (thanks in part to government mediation of labor conflicts in wartime) Foster had brought 200,000 workers into the unions and won them a shorter workday and increased wages. As a result of this success, Foster had become one of the nation's top labor organizers, and in the fall of 1919 he led a similar effort to bring unions to the steel industry, the bastion of the open shop. In September 1919, some 365,000 workers walked off their jobs in the steel industry to demand union recognition. But this time the results were quite different. Employers, taking advantage of the conservative post-war political climate (and pointing to Foster's radical past as evidence of the steel strike's subversive goals), were able to defeat the strike within a few months. The AFL, stung by the defeat, showed no further interest in the kind of ambitious organizing campaigns Foster was trying to promote.

So, once again, Foster found himself adrift. In November 1920 he formed an organization called the Trade Union Educational League (TUEL), and in the spring of 1921 he set off for Moscow as part of a delegation of radical American unionists who were invited to attend the first congress of the Red International of Labor Unions (Profintern). While in Moscow, Foster joined the newly unified American Communist movement. He was a valuable recruit for the Communists because of his reputation and trade union connections, and he was immediately brought into the top leadership of the Party and put in charge of its trade union work.

The 1920s turned out to be a bleak decade for American Communists. The conservative political climate, combined with the Communists' crude sectarianism and power-grabbing, left them with few political friends. The Communists' attempt to take over a nascent Farmer-Labor Party in 1923 left that enterprise in ruins, TUEL supporters were thrown out of the organized labor movement, and Foster's two campaigns for the presidency on the Workers Party ticket attracted few votes. The Communists devoted most of their energy in the 1920s to internal faction-fighting, and Foster was second to none in these battles. Foster, an opponent of C. E. Ruthenberg (q.v.), the Party's first general secretary, and then of Ruthenberg's successor, Jay Lovestone (q.v.), always seemed to take the losing side. In 1929 his loyalty to the Comintern received its ultimate test when a new line emerged from Moscow ordering the return to a dual-union strategy, and the conversion of TUEL into an independent revolutionary labor federation to be renamed the Trade Union Unity League (TUUL). Foster went along. When Moscow ordered Jay Lovestone out of Party leadership, Foster hoped that his own hour had arrived. Instead he found himself shunted aside in favor of his onetime lieutenant Earl Browder. In the 1930s Foster did hold the post of Party chairmanship, but it carried no power. He never got over the humiliation, and for the next fifteen years he searched grimly for the opportunity that would allow him to strike back at Browder.

The public, and even most Party members, had no inkling of Foster's dissatisfaction. Foster, an able speaker with a distinguished appearance, made a useful public spokesman for the Party. It was Foster who was up front, leading the unemployed march from Union Square to City Hall in New York City on March 6, 1930. The resulting riot led to Foster's arrest and six-month prison sentence. Later that same year he appeared as the Party's representative before the Fish Committee, a forerunner of the House Un-American Activities Committee. In 1932 he published *Towards a Soviet America*, a fierce work of Communist fundamentalism that caused the Party considerable embarrassment over the next twenty years. And in November 1932 he was once again the Party's candidate for the Presidency, this time attracting almost 103,000 votes, the strongest showing any Communist candidate ever made in a presidential election.

After the campaign, Foster suffered a heart attack and spent the next three years convalescing. When he returned to active political involvement, Browder had firmly established his own control of Party policy and had no intention of allowing Foster to play a significant leadership role. Foster worked on his autobiographical writings (*From Bryan to Stalin*, followed in 1939 by *Pages from a Workers Life*), turned out a series of minor articles and pamphlets, and journeyed to Moscow every year to lobby, unsuccessfully, against Browder's policies.

The signing of the Nazi-Soviet Pact briefly strengthened Foster's hand in the inner-Party debate, but the return to Popular Front policies after the Nazi invasion of the Soviet Union once again left Foster fuming impotently on the sidelines. In January 1944 Browder disclosed plans to dissolve the Party and replace it with something called the Communist Political Association. Foster and his longtime friend and ally Samuel Darcy (q.v.) wrote a private letter to other Party leaders, taking issue with Browder's assumptions about the end of class conflict in the United States and the likelihood of continued Soviet-American cooperation in the post-war world. Browder easily turned aside this challenge, expelling Darcy and forcing Foster to chair the commission that recommended Darcy's expulsion.

In the spring of 1945 Foster finally got his long-awaited revenge. Browder was served notice from Moscow via the agency of the "Duclos article" that he had committed a "notorious revision" of Marxism, and he was in short order deposed and expelled. Foster resumed his post as chairman of a reconstituted Party, and this time he exercised decisive power over the Party's policy-making.

The Communists faced a rough time as the U.S. government geared up for prolonged Cold War with the Soviet Union, but Foster's policies exacerbated an already dangerous situation. The Communists climbed far out on a political limb with the Wallace campaign of 1948, and Foster's insistence that Communist union leaders endorse Wallace and oppose the Marshall Plan led to the expulsion of Communist-led unions from the Congress of Industrial Organizations (CIO) in 1949.

In 1948 Foster was indicted along with eleven other top Communist leaders for violating the Smith Act. Foster managed to avoid trial because of his health problems. When the Supreme Court upheld the convictions of the first group of Smith Act defendants, opening the way for further prosecutions, Foster ordered hundreds of the most trusted Communist cadres to go "underground," which served only to further disrupt and demoralize the Party.

Foster grew increasingly detached from political realities in this period. He spent much of his time turning out long historical works, including his 1952 *History of the Communist Party of the United States*. He was proud that these books were printed in large editions in the Soviet-bloc countries, even though few Americans outside the shrunken ranks of the Communist Party would ever read them.

In 1956–1958 Foster fought his last great factional war. Khrushchev's "secret speech" denouncing Stalin created a crisis that deeply shook the remaining American Communists. Some, like *Daily Worker* editor John Gates (q.v.), sought to break the Party's links with the Soviet Union and discard its Leninist structure. Initially thrown on the defensive, Foster admitted to having been guilty of serious "leftist" errors since 1945. But the Soviet suppression of the Hungarian Revolution strengthened his resolve, and he eventually emerged as the triumphant leader of a party with a few thousand members left to its name. Foster died in Moscow, where he had gone for medical treatment in 1961.

SOURCES: Theodore Draper, *The Roots of American Communism* (1957); Joseph Starobin, *American Communism in Crisis* (1972); Arthur Zipser, *Working-Class Giant: The Life of William Z. Foster* (1981).

*MAURICE ISSERMAN*

**FRAINA, LOUIS (1892–1953).** Louis Fraina was at various times a member of most American radical organizations. An early theoretician of American communism, he was one of the important instigators of the Communist Party, a rival of John Reed (q.v.), and a Comintern agent in Mexico. After breaking with the Party, he became a prominent left-wing economist and eventually a leading anti-Communist.

Fraina was born in Galdo, Italy, in 1892. His father, a Republican exile, brought the family to New York in 1895, and Louis grew up in the slums of the Lower East Side. An excellent student, he nonetheless had to quit school at age 14 after his father's death. By age 16 his Roman Catholicism had vanished and he was writing for an agnostic journal, beginning a career in journalism. He briefly worked for the *New York Herald Tribune* as a cub reporter, but radical politics soon attracted him.

Fraina was in and out of most of the radical parties of the day. He joined the Socialist Party before he was 15, but quit within six months to join the Socialist Labor Party (SLP) and write for its *Daily People*. Inspired by the Lawrence strike in 1913, he joined the Industrial Workers of the World for six months. After resigning from the Socialist Labor Party early in 1914, Fraina became editor of the *New Review*, a theoretical Socialist magazine, which suspended publication in 1916. Fraina moved to the editorship of *Modern Dance Magazine*.

World War I and the Russian Revolution were stirring the radical political waters, and Fraina was in the midst of the current. He rejoined the Socialist Party in 1917 and became a leader of its revolutionary anti-war forces as editor of the *New International*. Six months before the Bolshevik Revolution it was the first supporter of Lenin. In the winter of 1917–1918, Fraina, Ludwig Lore (q.v.), Louis Boudin (q.v.), Leon Trotsky, Alexandra Kollontai, and Nicholas Bukharin made plans to start the journal *Class Struggle*. After the Russians returned home, the three Americans became its editors. In the spring of 1918 Fraina moved to Boston to start still another influential journal, *The Revolutionary Age*, which became the national organ of the Party's left wing.

Fraina was widely recognized as the most important theorist of the left wing, and he authored the manifesto of the new foreign-dominated Communist Party in 1919 as well as becoming its international secretary. Shortly after the Party's founding, he was dispatched to Moscow to argue his group's merits over those of a competing Communist group in the United States led by John Reed (q.v.). Before he could leave, however, Fraina was accused by another Communist— himself a secret government agent—of being in the employ of the Department of Justice. Fraina was cleared after a Party hearing in which his chief defender was Jacob Nosovitsky, an undercover government agent.

Fraina finally arrived in Moscow in 1920, where he had to undergo a second trial. Again he was cleared, and he attended the Second Comintern Congress. At the end of the year he was sent to Mexico as a Comintern representative, effectively removing him from American Party affairs. His own faction had repudiated him for adopting the Comintern's position on several controversial issues. Isolated, unhappy, and ineffective in Mexico, Fraina made a brief trip to Germany, resigned from the Party, and returned to Mexico with less than $5,000 of the Comintern's money.

Early in 1923 Fraina came back to New York and worked quietly as a clerk and copyreader. In 1926 he wrote an unsolicited review for the *New Republic* under the name of Lewis Corey. He soon began another writing career, working at the Brookings Institution in 1929–1930, as an associate editor of the *Encyclopedia of the Social Sciences* from 1931 to 1934, and as a respected Marxist economist.

His relationship with the Communist Party was touchy. He joined the League of Professional Groups for Foster (q.v.) and Ford (q.v.) in 1932, but its Communist members knew of his background and remained suspicious of him. He resigned in 1933, after some of them sabotaged a League project on which he was engaged. His *Decline of American Capitalism* (1934) was attacked by the Party. With the onset of the Popular Front, Corey was once again wooed. *The Crisis of the Middle Class* (1935) was favorably reviewed, he was asked to edit a middle-class issue of *New Masses*, and overtures were made about his rejoining the Party—which he refused.

The Russian purges pushed Corey further from communism. He was briefly associated with Jay Lovestone's (q.v.) Communist splinter group in the late 1930s but soon moved in other directions. He spent six months in Washington as an economist for the Works Progress Administration. From 1937 to 1939 he was educational director of Local 22 of the International Ladies Garment Workers Union. He resigned from the Keep America Out of War Committee in 1939, and the following year was a founder and research director of the Union for Democratic Action, a forerunner of Americans for Democratic Action. The Nazi-Soviet Pact killed his faith in Marxism itself. Writing in the *Nation* in 1940, he announced that collective ownership of the means of production had totalitarian implications.

From 1942 to 1951 Corey taught economics at Antioch College in Ohio. He then became education director of the Amalgamated Butchers Union. His Communist past once again caught up with him in 1950 when the Immigration Department sought his deportation on the grounds he had once been a Party member. Ordered deported in 1952, he was fired from his union position. Corey died on September 16, 1953, two days before the government gave him permission to remain in the United States.

SOURCES: Esther Corey, "Lewis Corey (Louis C. Fraina), 1892–1953: A Bibliography with Autobiographical Notes," *Labor History*, Spring 1963; Theodore Draper, *The Roots of American Communism* (1957).

*HARVEY KLEHR*

**FRANK, WALDO (1889–1967).** The novelist and critic Waldo Frank was one of the brightest stars in the Communist Party's galaxy of literary fellow travelers during the 1930s. He campaigned for the Party's 1932 and 1936 presidential ticket, traveled to Harlan County, Kentucky, with food for striking miners, headed the American Society for Technical Aid to Spanish Democracy, and served as first chairman of the League of American Writers, one of the Party's most influential front organizations.

Frank was born in Long Branch, New Jersey, on August 25, 1889, the youngest of four children of Julius J. Frank, a successful Wall Street attorney of German-Jewish ancestry. He grew up in a prosperous middle-class home and attended DeWitt Clinton High School. In 1907, after a year at a private prep school in Switzerland, Frank entered Yale University, where he studied French drama. His academic career was brilliant. By 1911 he had received both B.A. and M.A. degrees, won two awards for literary essays, and been named a Fellow of the university. In 1913, after a stint as a reporter for the *New York Times*, Frank exiled himself to Paris and began to write and study intensively.

When he returned to New York the following year, Frank was prepared to embark on a career as a literary rebel. In the fall of 1916 he helped create *Seven Arts*, a magazine that published the ground-breaking cultural criticism of Van

Wyck Brooks and the pacifistic essays of Randolph Bourne (q.v.). Frank himself registered for the draft as a conscientious objector in 1917, the same year that his first novel, *The Unwelcome Man*, appeared, and the next year he published his own book-length cultural study, *Our America*. Throughout the early 1920s Frank wrote a series of experimental "lyric novels"—*City Block* (1922), *Rahab* (1922), *Holiday* (1923), *Chalk Face* (1924)—in which he attempted to combat artistically the spiritual malaise of capitalist culture. When in November 1925 he became a contributing editor to the liberal *New Republic*, Frank's radicalism grew more political. In August 1929 he, Sherwood Anderson, Theodore Dreiser, and other writers raised money for striking Southern textile workers. Frank toured the Soviet Union from August to November 1931 and published *Dawn of Russia* (1932), a sympathetic but critical account of the trip. In early 1932 he led the Independent Miners Relief Committee to Kentucky, where on February 10 he was assaulted by vigilantes and thrown out of Harlan County. This experience, combined with President Herbert Hoover's unsympathetic treatment of the Bonus Army, brought Frank even closer to the Communist Party. In April 1935 he addressed the opening session of the Party-organized American Writers Congress and was elected chairman of its permanent organization, the League of American Writers. He was an active supporter of the Professional Groups for Earl Browder (q.v.) and Ford in 1936, and on September 30 Frank and Browder, the Party's general secretary, were arrested while campaigning in Terre Haute, Indiana.

Frank's "integral communism," however, was more Talmudic than dialectical, owing as much to Spinoza as to Marx. He demonstrated his independence in 1935, when as a member of the International Committee for the Defense of Political Prisoners he published his minority protest against the Russian purges in the *New Republic*. A reluctant administrator at best, Frank resigned as chairman of the League of American Writers in May 1936.

The following January, while in Mexico attending the National Congress of the League of Revolutionary Artists and Writers, Frank interviewed Trotsky. After returning home he suggested in another letter in the *New Republic* that an international tribunal investigate Trotsky's charges of a frame-up. When Browder issued a harsh reply, an angry and disillusioned Frank broke off relations with the Party. At the Second American Writers Congress in June 1937, Browder denounced him again. Frank continued to work for the Spanish Loyalists, but a Party paper in Madrid declared him a Trotskyite.

Frank resigned as contributing editor to the *New Republic* in 1940 because of the magazine's policy of neutrality. His political activism remained largely dormant until he visited Cuba in the fall of 1959. Though he worried about Castro's dictatorial behavior, he accepted temporary chairmanship of the Fair Play for Cuba Committee. In October 1961 he published his final book, *Cuba: Prophetic Island*, a pro-Castro analysis. Frank died in White Plains, New York, on January 9, 1967.

SOURCES: Paul J. Carter, *Waldo Frank* (1967); *Memoirs of Waldo Frank*, ed. Alan
    Trachtenberg (1973).

                                                                ART CASCIATO

**FREEMAN, JOSEPH (1897–1965).** Joseph Freeman was one of the earliest intellectual recruits to the Communist Party and was associated with its cultural organizations and activities through the 1930s. He was born in Piratin, Poltawa, in the Ukraine on October 7, 1897, came to the United States in 1904, and grew up in the Williamsburg ghetto of Brooklyn. Active in the Zionist youth movement and the product of a Yiddish-Hebrew home, Freeman considered himself a Socialist by the time he was 15. He enrolled at Columbia University in 1916, about the time his father's real estate business became successful.

Freeman originally supported Woodrow Wilson, but the growing war hysteria radicalized him. He was an elected delegate to the People's Council of America in 1917. The group opposed American involvement in the war and turned pro-Soviet after the Russian Revolution. He also supported Morris Hillquit's (q.v.) mayoral campaign that year and was active in Columbia's anti-war movement.

After his graduation in 1920, Freeman left for Europe, where he worked on the Paris and London staffs of the *New York Herald* and the *Chicago Tribune*. Although he already considered himself a Communist, he subordinated political activities to his desire to become a poet. Returning to New York in 1922, he joined the staff of the *Liberator,* a radical journal close to the Communist Party. He agreed with the staff's decision to hand the magazine over to the Communist Party. Freeman also served as publicity director of the American Civil Liberties Union in 1924.

One of the few intellectuals who joined the Communist movement so early, Freeman moved more directly into Party work in the mid-1920s. He co-authored *Dollar Diplomacy* (1925) with Scott Nearing (q.v.). With Mike Gold (q.v.) he founded and co-edited the *New Masses* in 1926. Shortly afterward he moved to the Soviet Union and spent more than a year as a translator for the Comintern, becoming acquainted with the Soviet writers whose work he presented to America in *Voices of October* (1930). Upon his return to the United States in 1927, Freeman did not rejoin the Communist Party; he had concluded he was not a politician and should concentrate on his art. At some point in the next three years he apparently resumed his Party membership.

Freeman was a prominent figure in the Party's cultural life in the early 1930s, helping to edit the *New Masses*, organize the John Reed Clubs, champion proletarian literature, and speak on behalf of the Party. He also wrote for Tass and worked for Amtorg, the Soviet trade agency. At the first League of American Writers Congress in 1935, Freeman took the lead in castigating Kenneth Burke for having suggested that the Communists should substitute ''the people'' for ''the workers'' to appeal to Americans.

The Popular Front years coincided with Freeman's decline in Party prestige. His autobiography, *An American Testament* (1936), was published to enthusiastic reviews, but its sympathetic portrait of Trotsky and considerable detail about the bohemian culture of the 1920s got the book quietly condemned in Moscow. At Party leader Earl Browder's (q.v.) request, Freeman canceled a lecture tour and helped stifle the book. Meanwhile, he was growing restive about the purges that were destroying many of his old friends. While in Mexico as a delegate to the International Congress of Culture in 1937, he refused a Party request to return to New York to write up one of the trials. Robert Minor (q.v.) and V. J. Jerome (q.v.) attacked one of his unpublished works for deviations. In August 1939 the *Communist International* openly condemned his autobiography. Freeman never publicly attacked the Party, but he abandoned politics and announced his disillusionment in a novel, *Never Call Retreat* (1943).

Freeman went to work for the radio show "Information Please" in 1943 and as a public relations executive. He died in August 1965.

SOURCES: Daniel Aaron, *Writers on the Left* (1961); Joseph Freeman, *An American Testament* (1936).

*HARVEY KLEHR*

**FREESE, IRVING C. (1883–1964).** Irving C. Freese was the Socialist mayor of Norwalk, Connecticut, for two terms (1947–1951). He also served as an Independent mayor from 1951 to 1955 and from 1957 to 1959. Freese was born in 1883 in East Brunswick, New Jersey. He began his career as a secretary of the New Brunswick Young Men's Christian Association (YMCA) and director of its physical education department. He left his YMCA post in 1928 to become a credit manager for Norwalk Tire and Rubber Company in Norwalk. He later opened a photo shop there. In 1929 Freese became interested in socialism and joined the Socialist Party. In 1931 he became Norwalk town chairman.

Freese was impressed by the anti-corruption campaign led by Norman Thomas (q.v.) and Paul Blanshard (q.v.), which deposed James J. Walker as Tammany Hall mayor of New York City. He devoted his energies thereafter to municipal affairs, attending virtually all City Council meetings and running unsuccessfully for mayor seven times, beginning in 1933. In 1947 his persistence was rewarded with his election as mayor.

Freese believed that socialism would come to the United States in slow increments. Socialists, he argued, would first have to prove that they were responsible rulers who would give their constituents honest, frugal, and humane government. He believed that citizens would thus realize the effectiveness of Socialist municipal government and would extend the party's power to the state and eventually the federal government. Once that had been accomplished, the Socialists could bring to fruition their ideal. Freese thus saw his role to be the setting of an example of good government under the Socialist banner. He cited the Norwalk experience as proof of the efficacy of his thesis. He maintained that the example of nearby Bridgeport, Connecticut, under the Socialist regime of Jasper McLevy (q.v.) convinced Norwalk voters to elect him mayor.

As mayor, Freese lived up to his ideals, but he alienated many Socialists and trade unionists. He gave up all business interests and became a full-time mayor at $2,500 a year (the same salary paid part-time mayors previously). He kept his office open to all 49,000 residents of the city, and he investigated all citizens' complaints. He also devoted most of his time to supervising the administration of city departments. He attended meetings of city boards, often clashing with officials, many appointed by himself. He would at times check the operations of city departments by observing close up the work being done. He followed garbage trucks or rode snowplows to make sure that city employees were performing their jobs. In 1950 and 1951 he fought the Board of Education's request for an increased budget in order to increase teachers' salaries. During the latter battle he assumed chairmanship of the school board, a power, which although permitted by the city charter, had never previously been employed by a mayor.

These actions so alienated the labor unions and Socialists that Freese was forced to leave the party and form his own Independent Party in 1951. The Socialists that year supported his unsuccessful opponent. In 1955 he was defeated by a noted educator. Freese was again reelected in 1957. He lost again in 1959, when he was 76 years old. He remained active in city politics, running unsuccessfully again in 1961 and 1963. He died in Norwalk the next year at age 81.

*BERNARD K. JOHNPOLL*

**FRIEDMAN, SAMUEL H. (b. 1897).** Samuel H. Friedman, a leading member of the Socialist Party for more than seventy years, has twice been the party's nominee for vice-president. Born in Denver, Colorado, on February 20, 1897, Friedman was educated at the City College of New York (B.A., 1917), Columbia University (M.A., 1940), and New York University, where he was a Ph.D. candidate in the 1970s but was forced to withdraw because of encroaching blindness. As a 15-year-old high school student, Friedman was active in the 1912 campaign of Eugene V. Debs (q.v.) for U.S. President. Three years later Friedman joined the Socialist party, in which he has been active ever since.

For many years Friedman was employed as a newspaper man and a publicist. He served as assistant news editor and copy chief of Fairchild Publications' *Women's Wear Daily* and *Daily News Record*. He was also a founder and labor editor of the Socialist *New Leader* and was editor of the *Socialist Call*. An expert on radical songs, Friedman edited the *Rebel Song Book* (1935), the most complete collection of labor and revolutionary songs ever published. It is now considered a collectors' item.

During the internecine feuding that tore the Socialist Party asunder during the mid- and late 1930s Friedman attempted to act as mediator in the dispute. He and B. Charney Vladeck (q.v.) pleaded in vain with Norman Thomas (q.v.) and Louis Waldman (q.v.) to end the dispute.

Friedman ran for state, local, and Congressional office many times between 1920 and 1954. In 1952 and again in 1956 he was the Socialist candidate for U.S. Vice-President. Friedman was also an officer of many other labor, Socialist, and humane organizations. He is presently a member of Social Democrats USA.

*BERNARD K. JOHNPOLL*

# G

GANNETT, BETTY (1906–1970). Betty Gannett, Marxist theoretician, teacher, writer, and editor, was active in the Communist Party USA (CPUSA) for almost fifty years. When she died in 1970, she was editor of *Political Affairs* and a member of the national and political committees of the CPUSA. Gannett was born in 1906 in Poland to a Jewish family and immigrated with six brothers and sisters to New York in 1914. Reared by her widowed mother, who was a cook and a maid, Gannett completed grade school and a two-year commercial course before assuming the support of her family at age 15, when her mother died of tuberculosis.

Gannett worked as a secretary in several union locals and joined the Young Communist League (YCL) and the CPUSA in 1923. In 1927 she went with an American delegation of trade unionists to the Soviet Union and attended the Lenin School. While organizing for the YCL in Cleveland in 1928, she was arrested for criminal syndicalism and sentenced to ten years in jail, but she won her appeal. In 1929 she became national education director of the YCL, and in the early 1920s she returned to New York City to edit the *Communist* and the *Party Organizer*. After a short time as organization secretary of the Party in Pennsylvania, she became education director of the California branch. There she was one of the leaders in the struggle to organize agricultural workers, and she helped found the *Western Worker* and later *People's World*. In 1938 she married James Tormey, who was active in the California branch of the party.

From 1941 to 1944 she served as Midwest regional coordinator of the CPUSA and then as the assistant national organization secretary of the Party, becoming its national educational director in 1950. She was convicted under the Smith Act and spent two years, 1955–1956, in prison in West Virginia. In 1949 and again in 1956, the government unsuccessfully attempted to deport her. It then sought to have her report weekly to Ellis Island and to restrict her to within a fifty-mile radius of Times Square. Through litigation, she forced the government to lift these restrictions, thus setting a precedent for the civil liberties of aliens. From 1963 until her death in 1970, she was an editor of *Political Affairs*, the theoretical journal of the Party in the United States.

SOURCE: Betty Gannett Papers, State Historical Society of Wisconsin, Madison, Wisconsin.

*NORAH CHASE*

**GATES, JOHN (b. 1913).** John Gates was a top-ranking American in the International Brigades that fought against Franco in the Spanish Civil War of 1936–1939, a leader of the Young Communist League and the Communist Party for more than a quarter-century, editor-in-chief of the Party newspaper for a decade, and leading figure in a futile attempt of a party majority to liberalize the Party following the Khrushchev revelations of Stalin's massive crimes in early 1956.

Gates was born Sol Regenstreif in 1913 on Manhattan's East Side of Polish-Jewish parents. His father was, successively, a waiter, a candy store proprietor, and an ice-cream parlor proprietor. Educated in Manhattan's public schools, Gates joined the Young Communist League (YCL) in March 1931 while at City College, which he entered in February 1930. The YCL-led Social Problems Club at the college was then locked in battle with the college president on the issue of military training. Gates' political activity while in college included participation in the historic campaign around the Scottsboro case.

Early in 1932 Gates dropped out of college to work in a radio parts factory, with union-organizing as the motive. He joined the left-wing Steel and Metal Workers Industrial Union. Later that year he volunteered for full-time Party work and was assigned as YCL organizer in Warren, Ohio, a steel town. Organizing among the unemployed was included in the assignment. At this point he adopted the name John Gates and soon transferred his activities to Youngstown, Ohio, a major steel center.

After four years in the area, he went to Spain early in 1937 as a volunteer in the struggle to defend the democratic republic against the military uprising led by General Franco and aided by Fascist Italy and Nazi Germany. In Spain he rose to the rank of commissar of the Fifteenth International Brigade, consisting of an American, a British, a Canadian, and a Spanish battalion. The American (Lincoln) battalion made up about half the brigade. Late in 1938 the international volunteers were pulled out of Spain in a vain effort to win international support for the removal of foreign Fascist forces.

While still in Spain, Gates was elected to the YCL's national council. His first post-war job was as executive secretary of the Friends of the Abraham Lincoln Brigade, set up to assist Americans who had fought in Spain and Spanish Republican forces. In 1939 he was elected YCL national education director and then chairman of the New York state organization.

A week after Pearl Harbor, Gates volunteered again to fight fascism, this time in the U.S. armed forces. His combat experience led initially to promotions and repeated recommendations for admission to Officers Training School, which were denied because of his political association. When his division was sent overseas, he was pulled out and sent to the Aleutians. He pressed for reassignment to militarily active fronts, was finally accepted for paratroop training, and was sent to Europe as a replacement in the famed 101st Airborne Division, but too late to see military action. When demobilized after the war, he was a first sergeant in that division. On leave before he departed for Europe early in 1945, he married Lillian Ross, a fellow leader in the Communist youth organization.

In 1945 he was elected in absentia to the Communist Party's National Committee, and his first post-war assignment was as national director of veterans affairs. In 1947 he was named editor-in-chief of the *Daily Worker*, the Party's paper.

In July 1948 the Party's entire top leadership—its twelve-man political bureau, which included Gates—was arrested for violation of the Smith Act, enacted in 1940, during the Nazi-Soviet Pact period. The charge was conspiracy to teach and advocate the duty and necessity of overthrowing the U.S. government by force and violence. For the next seven years, Gates' life was dominated by the trial, which ran from January to October 1949 and the sentence that followed his conviction. Gates received the maximum sentence of five years in jail and a $10,000 fine, as did nine of his fellow defendants. The Supreme Court upheld the conviction in mid-1951. Gates served three years and eight months in Atlanta Penitentiary. Released in March 1955, but not permitted to engage in politics during parole, he went to work in a plastics factory.

During his incarceration, historic world and domestic developments led him and his prisonmate, the Party's general secretary, Eugene Dennis (q.v.), to question hitherto sacrosanct Party doctrine. Released from parole in January 1955, Gates and Dennis resumed their respective Party roles. They immediately proposed a thorough review of basic Party policies and doctrine. The proposal was soon followed by Khrushchev's shattering secret report to the Soviet Communist Party's twentieth congress detailing Stalin's crimes. The report caused upheavals in Communist parties everywhere, but that in the American Party was perhaps most severe. Gates took the unprecedented step of throwing the *Daily Worker* open to freewheeling discussion of the Party's faults and future direction, which endured for a full year. The Soviet intervention in Hungary in November 1956 intensified the internal Party debate, in which Gates took the lead among those who sought a drastic change of direction.

A Party convention in February 1957 generally embraced the changes advocated by Gates and most members, with minor concessions to those who, under Chairman William Z. Foster's (q.v.) leadership, sought to stem the tide of change. In general, the projected changes foreshadowed in essential respects the trend later termed Euro-communism. But in the course of the struggle many members and younger leaders who had dedicated their lives to the Party since the 1930s lost confidence in its ability to reform itself and quit.

Joined by Dennis, who supported the Soviet intervention in Hungary, Foster was thus able to regain control. He moved to force Gates out of his editorial post and compelled the paper's suspension as a daily on January 13, 1958. Gates resigned from the Party a few days later, bitterly charging betrayal of the convention's mandate for change and rendering the Party's cause hopeless.

Following his resignation, Gates resumed the college studies he had stopped in 1932 and obtained a degree from Brooklyn College. He subsequently obtained a job with the Research Department of the International Ladies Garment Workers Union, specializing in unemployment insurance problems.

SOURCE: John Gates, The Story of an American Communist (1958).

*MAX GORDON*

**GEORGE, HARRISON (1888-?).** Harrison George was a leader of the Industrial Workers of the World (IWW) who joined the Communist Party and became one of its important functionaries. He was born on June 27, 1888, in Oakley, Kansas. His father was a farmer of Anglo-Saxon background, and the family traced its American roots to the pre-revolutionary era. George went to work as a postal messenger at age 15. After ten years he moved on to a variety of odd jobs, working most steadily as a tailor and a migratory worker.

George joined the Socialist Party in 1910, was expelled with its left wing in 1913, and joined the IWW the following year. He quickly became an IWW organizer, participating in the Mesabi strike in 1916 and editing an IWW newspaper. Arrested with the rest of the Wobbly leadership in 1917, he authored the first pro-Bolshevik pamphlet in the United States, *Red Dawn*, while in Cook County Jail. Convicted of conspiracy to sabotage the war effort, he was jailed in Leavenworth Penitentiary from 1918 to 1920. In 1919 he secretly joined the Communist Party, but remained in the IWW to convert it to communism. Out on appeal, he edited the Wobblies' *Industrial Unionist*. George returned to prison from 1921 to 1923 to finish his sentence. After his release he continued to work secretly for the Party in the IWW until 1924.

In the late 1920s George worked for the Profintern's Pan-Pacific Trade Union secretariat after serving as the American representative to the Profintern in 1927. In the early 1930s he helped supervise the Party's agricultural work. His son, Victor Baron, a Comintern agent, was executed by Brazilian police in 1936. Two years later George became executive editor of the *Daily People's World*, a Communist newspaper published in San Francisco.

George was expelled from the Communist Party in 1946 after protesting the expulsion of his longtime IWW compatriot Vern Smith and others on charges of ultra-leftism. The group had urged a sharper turn to the left after Earl Browder's (q.v.) ouster as Party leader. He was briefly involved with a tiny Communist splinter group that included Smith and William Dunne (q.v.). He died sometime in the early 1960s.

*HARVEY KLEHR*

**GERMER, ADOLPH (1880–1964).** Adolph Germer, national secretary of the Socialist Party from 1916 until 1920, was sentenced to twenty years in prison in 1920 for opposing the war. Born in the German town of Welan in 1880, the son of a coal miner, Germer came to the United States at the age of 8. His family settled in Braceville, Illinois, where he attended a lutheran school for about four years before going to work in a coal mine in Staunton, Illinois. He continued his education by taking correspondence courses.

From 1894 until 1964 Germer was active in the United Mine Workers of America union (UMWA). He was an official of the union from 1906 until the 1940s, serving as local secretary from 1906 until 1907, as state legislative committeeman from 1907 to 1908, as district secretary-treasurer from 1908 until 1912, as organizer from 1912 to 1914, and as vice-president of the Illinois district from 1914 until 1916. From 1920 until 1940 he was an international vice-president of the union, and thereafter he was an organizer for the Congress of Industrial Unions. While organizing for the UMWA, Germer was a leader of the strike against the Rockefeller-owned Colorado Fuel and Iron Company in 1914.

Germer had joined the Socialist Party in Illinois in 1900 and in 1916 he was chosen national secretary of the party. Because he opposed World War I, he was an early target for persecution by the government. Germer was one of the party leaders indicted for opposing the war in 1918. In 1920 he was sentenced, with four of the other leading Socialists, to twenty years in prison. He refused to plead for mercy from Judge Kennesaw Mountain Landis, but he did appeal the conviction. The Supreme Court reversed the decision.

In 1920 Germer insisted that the Socialist Party expel the 20,000-member Slavic federations, calling them the "Soviet breed." This ouster set the stage for the organization of the Communist Party. Between 1920 and 1922 Germer was an organizer for the fast-declining Socialist Party. In 1922 he resumed his union activity, first as an international vice-president of the UMWA and later (1936–1955) as an organizer for the Congress of Industrial Organizations (CIO). He was one of the key organizers of the 1937 strike of the United Automobile Workers (CIO) against General Motors.

Germer retired in 1955 and died in Rockford, Illinois, in 1964.

SOURCE: Adolph Germer Papers, Wisconsin State Historical Society, Madison, Wisconsin.

*BERNARD K. JOHNPOLL*

**GERSON, SIMON (b. 1909).** Simon W. ("Si") Gerson is a veteran public relations man for the Communist Party USA (CPUSA). A journalist most of his life, he himself was the subject of public controversy in New York City on three occasions. In addition, Gerson has been the Party's expert on local and state politics since the 1940s and has served as the CPUSA's national campaign manager during the last three presidential elections.

Gerson was born in New York City on July 23, 1909, into a Russian-Jewish family. During his teens, Gerson joined the Young Communist League. Later, while attending City College, he first attracted public attention. Gerson and three other City College undergraduates traveled with the first American student delegation to the Soviet Union in 1927. Upon his return to campus, the Social Problems Club, a group spearheading an anti-ROTC movement, elected him president. In 1928, City College suspended Gerson. When he reassumed the club's leadership (against a faculty order) the following year, the administration expelled him.

Thereafter Gerson became a professional Communist, helping organize workers during the Gastonia, North Carolina, textile strike of 1929. When that collapsed, he began a lengthy career with the *Daily Worker*. He spent the early 1930s as a sportswriter and city hall reporter. During the heyday of the Popular Front in 1937, Manhattan's borough president-elect Stanley M. Isaacs, a LaGuardia Republican, appointed Gerson as his assistant. Despite an unceasing barrage of protests, Gerson held the position for three years until a 1940 state law forced his resignation.

Gerson thereupon rejoined the *Daily Worker*, as its Albany correspondent and a political writer. Late in 1941 he served briefly as the Party's legislative chairman for the entire state, then became CPUSA lobbyist for the New York City Council's 1942 session. He spent the remainder of World War II as an infantryman in New Guinea. After his return to civilian life, Gerson was city editor of the *Daily Worker* for a short time, and then the Party's New York state campaign manager for the 1946 off-year elections. More important, however, was his reappointment as the Party's state legislative chairman, a post he would hold continuously until 1957.

During the Cold War years Gerson became the subject of public clamor a third time. Peter Cacchione (q.v.), one of two Communist members of New York's city council, died in November 1947. The CPUSA, citing a city charter provision that in such cases permitted a party to name a successor of the same political faith, selected Gerson to complete Cacchione's unexpired term, but other council members seized on a technicality and opposed his seating. In February 1948 the legislative body voted to leave Cacchione's seat vacant until the general election that November. When autumn arrived, Gerson campaigned vigorously and garnered 150,000 votes. Although this far exceeded any total Cacchione had ever received, the 1947 repeal of proportional representation had ended the CPUSA's chances of electing any more councilmen.

In June 1951 the federal government indicted Gerson as one of fifteen "second-string" Communist leaders to be prosecuted under the Smith Act. At their trial, however, the judge directed a verdict of acquittal for Gerson and one other defendant, Isidore Begun. One of the few prominent Party figures free during the McCarthy era, Gerson headed the Party's national Civil Liberties Committee from 1955 to 1957 and was also its official spokesman to the press.

Gerson relinquished these positions in March 1957 to become executive editor of the *Daily Worker*. This newly created post represented an attempt to save the CPUSA's best-known organ, which had suffered a circulation decline, from attempts by the Party's left wing to oust its editor-in-chief, John Gates (q.v.), for his growing independence from the Soviet Union. Gerson fought a losing battle until the *Daily*'s demise on January 13, 1958. Shortly thereafter he signed an appeal to the National Committee urging the pro-Moscow majority not to purge the Party's right wing in New York State.

Because of his association with the Gates faction, Gerson maintained a low profile for the next several years, but by 1967 he had risen to membership on the National Committee. That year the Communist Party selected him to coordinate a campaign to raise one million dollars to begin a new daily paper. Gerson's efforts were successful, and in early 1968 Long View Publishing Corporation, of which Gerson had become vice-president, bought out the old *Workers'* assets and subscription lists. In July it began printing the *Daily World*, with Gerson as executive editor. Under his policies the newspaper survived and continues to express the Party viewpoint. Gerson still plays an important role in CPUSA affairs. In 1976, 1980, and 1984 he managed the Communists' presidential campaign.

SOURCES: Maurice Isserman, *Which Side Were You On?* (1982); Harvey Klehr, *The Heyday of American Communism* (1984).

*JAMES GILBERT RYAN*

**GILMAN, ELISABETH (1867–1950).** Elisabeth Gilman was the leader of the Baltimore, Maryland, Socialist Party during the 1930s and 1940s and a financial mainstay of the national party and its affiliates. Born in New Haven, Connecticut, in 1867, when her father was a professor of geography at Yale University, she moved to Baltimore when he was named the first president of Johns Hopkins University in 1875. Her mother died when Gilman was only 2 years old; she was raised by an aunt and a stepmother. During her youth, Elisabeth traveled extensively in Europe with her family. Taught at home by a governess and in a private school for girls, Gilman did not receive her B.A. degree from Johns Hopkins until she was 54.

A devout Episcopalian, Gilman was active in church-related settlement-house work. She founded a boys club in a poor neighborhood in Baltimore and helped reorganize the Open Forum, a series of discussions regarding social issues to which she brought American and European Socialist and liberal speakers. During World War I, Gilman was involved with canteens and surgical dressing units in France. While in France, she became interested in pacifism and socialism. By the end of the war she was a dedicated Christian Socialist.

In the 1920s Gilman was active in aiding striking West Virginia coal miners and in defending members of various radical unions in court actions. During the LaFollette campaign of 1924, she was one of the leaders of the Progressive and Socialist drives in Maryland. She also met and became a close friend and ally of Norman Thomas (q.v.), who was soon to become the leader of the Socialist Party. She joined the party in 1929 at his urging.

In the 1930s Gilman toured Europe several times, visiting the Soviet Union, Sweden, and other countries with Socialist governments. She was the Socialist candidate for U.S. Senator from Maryland (1934, 1938) and mayor of Baltimore (1935). Although she was in the Thomas-led militant wing of the party, Gilman's positions were generally moderate.

Her most lasting contribution to the Socialist cause was the Christian Social Justice Fund, which donated large sums of money to various Socialist organizations. She also served on the board of the League for Industrial Democracy and the National Executive Committee of the Socialist Party of the United States.

Elisabeth Gilman died after a long illness in Baltimore in December 1950.

*BERNARD K. JOHNPOLL*

**GITLOW, BENJAMIN (1891–1965).** Benjamin Gitlow was a founding member of the Communist movement, a defendant in a landmark Supreme Court case, one of the leaders of the Communist Party in the 1920s, and a prominent Lovestoneite expelled by Joseph Stalin in 1929. Gitlow was born on December 22, 1891, in Elizabethport, New Jersey. Both his parents, Russian-Jewish immigrants, were garment workers and active Socialists. Gitlow graduated from high school and studied law for two years. He clerked in a department store, eventually becoming president of the Retail Clerks Union in New York.

Joining the Socialist Party in 1909, Gitlow became active in its left wing as a result of his anti-war activities during World War I. Representing a Bronx district, he was one of ten Socialists elected to the New York legislature in 1917. From 1917 to 1919 he was associated with several radical journals. Expelled from the Socialist Party in 1919, he and John Reed (q.v.) were the two most prominent founders of the Communist Labor Party.

Gitlow was convicted of criminal anarchy by New York State in 1919 and received a lengthy sentence. In *Gitlow v. New York* (1923), the Supreme Court upheld his conviction by establishing a state's right to punish speech that had a "tendency" to produce evils. The case, however, marked the first time the Court had held that the Fourteenth Amendment applied any of the provisions of the Bill of Rights to the states. Gitlow, who had been in and out of prison on appeal, was pardoned by Governor Al Smith after the decision.

In 1922 Gitlow had opposed ending the Party's underground existence, but after his legal difficulties were resolved he joined the "liquidators" and became a leader in the Ruthenberg (q.v.)–Lovestone (q.v.) faction. He briefly edited the Yiddish-language *Freiheit* in 1923–1924 as a mediator between two factions. In 1924 and again in 1928 he was the Party's vice-presidential candidate, running with William Foster (q.v.). A longtime member of the Political Committee, Gitlow was put on the Party's three-man secretariat in 1929 and went to Moscow with Lovestone and others to oppose the Comintern's decision to oust their faction from control. Despite Stalin's demand that they capitulate, Gitlow remained defiant, threatening to fight against the Comintern decision in the United States.

He was kept in Moscow for several weeks. Returning to the States, he found a campaign against him in the Party in full swing. Gitlow was expelled.

Gitlow became the first secretary-general of Lovestone's Communist Party (Majority Group). His growing criticism of the Soviet Union led him to break with Lovestone in 1933 and form a tiny splinter group, the Workers Communist League, which soon metamorphized into the Organization Committee for a Revolutionary Workers Party. He joined the Socialist Party once again in 1935, but soon left it and moved to the right. He testified for the Dies Committee which investigated communist activities in the late 1930s and became identified with conservative causes. Gitlow died on July 19, 1965.

SOURCES: Theodore Draper, *American Communism and Soviet Russia*, (1960); Benjamin Gitlow, *I Confess* (1939).

*HARVEY KLEHR*

**GOLD, BEN (1898–1985).** Ben Gold, one of the few union leaders of the Congress of Industrial Organizations (CIO) publicly identified as a Communist, was the longtime head of the International Fur and Leather Workers Union (IFLWU). He was born on September 8, 1898, in Bessarabia, Russia. His father was a Jewish watchmaker and jeweler. Gold came to the United States in 1910 and within a year was working in a fur shop in New York. He attended Manhattan Prep School at night and briefly studied law in 1914. His energies, however, were devoted to the International Fur Workers Union (IFWU), which he joined in 1912, and the radical movement. He joined the Socialist party in 1916. Gold was elected to the New York Furriers Joint Board in 1919 and became the leader of the union's left wing. At the same time, he was active in the left wing of the Jewish Socialist Federation and became a charter member of the Communist Party in 1919.

The struggle for control of the IFWU between Communists and their foes heated up in 1924, when Gold was suspended from the union and then reinstated. Elected manager of the joint board in 1925, he led the seventeen-week 1926 general strike in the New York fur industry for the forty-four-hour week. After its failure, the American Federation of Labor (AFL) appointed a committee to investigate the Communist role in the affair. Along with others, Gold was expelled from the IFWU.

Under Gold's guidance and leadership, the Needle Trades Workers Industrial Union (NTWIU) was created as a unit of the Trade Union Unity League (TUUL) in 1928 after the Profintern had ordered the Communists to set up dual unions. It lost a big strike and much of its membership in 1929. Gold, the union's secretary, left for Europe in September 1930 and did not return until June 1931, spending much of the time at the Lenin School in Moscow.

While the NTWIU never amounted to much, the fiery and charismatic Gold retained the loyalties of most of the New York fur workers. When the TUUL was dissolved in 1934, he had enough strength to negotiate a merger with the IFWU, which gave him a predominant influence in the union. Gold led the IFWU into the newly formed CIO in 1937 and became president of the International Fur and Leather Workers Union in 1939.

During the last half of the 1930s and throughout the 1940s, Gold was one of the few avowed Communists in the union movement, serving on the Party's Central Committee. He supported Henry Wallace for President in 1948. The IFLWU was expelled from the CIO in 1950 for being under Communist domination. Gold himself publicly resigned from the Party that year, to comply with the anti-Communist provisions of the Taft-Hartley Act, but he was convicted of perjury in 1954. The conviction was later reversed. Gold resisted the Party's efforts to merge the IFLWU with the Amalgamated Meat Cutters Union in 1955. He attempted to win control of the fur division, but was beaten and once again became an ordinary fur worker. Around 1960 Gold retired to Florida. He died in July 1985.

SOURCES: Ben Gold, *Memoirs* (1985); Gary Fink (ed.), *Biographical Dictionary of American Labor Leaders* (1974); Philip Foner, *The Fur and Leather Workers Union* (1950).

*HARVEY KLEHR*

**GOLD, MIKE (1893–1967).** Mike Gold was a popular Communist writer and critic active in the Party's cultural movement. He was born on April 12, 1893, on New York's Lower East Side under the name Irwin Granich. His father, a Russian-Jewish immigrant, manufactured suspenders and peddled before he went bankrupt. Young Gold attended grammar school, but went to work when he was 12. He held a variety of jobs, ranging from night porter and clerk to carpenter's helper, before being stimulated to writing in 1914 after stumbling into an unemployment demonstration in Union Square that was attacked by the police. Gold became a prominent member of New York's bohemian world, contributing poems to *Masses* and writing three one-act plays produced by the Provincetown Players prior to World War I. He briefly attended Harvard as a special student in 1916, and remained in Boston to write for an anarchist paper. Sometime in 1917 he moved to Mexico for two years to avoid the draft. While he was there he wrote for an English-language paper and worked on a ranch and in the oil fields.

Gold became co-editor of the *Liberator*, successor to *Masses*, in 1921. He clashed with his co-editor, Claude McKay, and with Floyd Dell over editorial policy; Gold's increasing emphasis on proletarian literature and art and his increasing politicization marked the split between the old bohemianism and the new Communist influence. In 1922 the magazine was turned over to the Communist Party and became almost exclusively political. Gold himself joined the Party sometime in the 1920s.

Gold became a co-editor of *New Masses* when it was founded in 1926. Two years later he became editor and embarked on a crusade to transform it into a revolutionary organ dedicated to the working class. He championed "proletarian literature," written by, appealing to, and telling the story of ordinary workers.

His own novel, *Jews Without Money* (1930), became a classic account of the poverty of the Lower East Side. A *New Republic* article scouring Thornton Wilder for his sanitized, effete prose attracted even more attention.

Gold was a delegate to the Second World Plenum of the International Bureau of Revolutionary Literature in Kharkov, Russia, in 1930 and returned to the United States even more enthused about enlisting writers and artists in the revolutionary struggle. He played a prominent role at the first conference of the John Reed Clubs in 1932, but his plea not to drive away middle-class intellectuals leaning toward communism went unheeded, and he was left off the national board. He continued, however, to play a prominent role in Party cultural affairs and wrote a popular and slashing *Daily Worker* column, "Change the World." His increasingly shrill attacks on "renegades" (*The Hollow Men*, 1947) culminated in 1946, when he led the orthodox Communist condemnation of Hollywood writer Albert Maltz, who had suggested that Communists should recognize that art could not be judged by political merit only.

From 1948 to 1951 Gold lived in France. After returning to the United States, he lived in dire poverty in the Bronx until several Communist papers formed a small syndicate to publish his column once again. He died on May 14, 1967.
SOURCES: Daniel Aaron, *Writers on the Left* (1961); Michael Folsom, *Mike Gold: A Literary Anthology* (1972).

*HARVEY KLEHR*

**GOLDMAN, ALBERT (1897–1960).** Albert Goldman was active in several radical parties and served as Leon Trotsky's American lawyer. He was born in the province of Minsk in White Russia in 1897. In 1904, when Goldman was 7, the family moved to the United States and settled in Chicago, where Albert attended grammar and high school. In 1915 Goldman attended Hebrew Union College in Cincinnati but did not complete his studies for the rabbinate. He transferred to the University of Cincinnati, where he was captain and star of the basketball team and a member of the track team. He graduated from the university in 1919.

After graduation, Goldman's interest in socialism led him into the Industrial Workers of the World and other socialist groups. He was associated with the Workers Educational League of New York in the early 1920s, for which, using the name Albert Verblin, he wrote "The Struggle for Power," a pamphlet in answer to Morris Hillquit's (q.v.) book *From Marx to Lenin*, wherein Goldman defended the Russian Revolution and Bolshevism against Social Democracy and reformism.

In 1925 Goldman received a law degree at Northwestern University and began to practice in Chicago. For several years thereafter he had a relationship with the Communist Party and became counsel for the International Labor Defense, during which time he defended many Party and ILD members. He became disenchanted with the politics of both the Party and the Communist International, broke with them, and joined the Trotskyist Communist League of America in

1933. Shortly after joining the Communist League, he advocated its dissolution and entry into the Socialist Party. He failed to win support for his views and left to join the Socialist Party.

In the Socialist Party, Goldman formed his own group, which published an inner-party journal, *The Socialist Appeal*, which he edited. The journal advocated a more radical policy for the Party, especially in connection with the Spanish Civil War. When the Workers Party, a coalition of Trotskyists and Musteites, dissolved and its members joined the Socialist Party in 1937, Goldman and his group associated themselves with the Trotskyist faction. They were expelled from the Socialist Party in 1937 because of their intensely critical attitude toward the People's Front government of Socialists and Communists in Spain. The expelled group formed the Socialist Workers Party in 1938, and Goldman became a member of its National Committee.

Meanwhile, Albert Goldman had become attorney for Leon Trotsky and was his counsel in depositions taken from the Russian exile by the Preliminary Commission of Inquiry in Mexico in April 1937. The Commission, headed by the venerable John Dewey, America's foremost philosopher, examined Trotsky in connection with the charges against him in the Moscow trials. Goldman represented Trotsky in various legal matters, including the transfer of his enormous archives to the Houghton Library at Harvard University. He also represented Natalia Sedova Trotsky in similar legal matters.

Goldman supported Trotsky and James Cannon (q.v.) in the Socialist Workers Party during its split with the faction led by Max Shachtman (q.v.) over the Russian question in 1940. In August 1940, when Trotsky was assassinated, Goldman flew to Mexico and as attorney for Trotsky and his wife participated in the examination of Trotsky's assassin, the Spanish Communist and Russian agent Ramon Mercader. Afterward he wrote a lengthy pamphlet entitled *The Assassination of Leon Trotsky: The Proofs of Stalin's Guilt*.

In 1941 Goldman was a defendant in the Minneapolis trial of the leaders of the Socialist Workers Party indicted under the Smith Act. They were convicted and served a term in jail of twelve to sixteen months. Following the verdict, Goldman was barred from the practice of law. His closing remarks to the jury were published as a booklet entitled *In the Defense of Socialism*.

After his release from prison, Goldman resumed his role as a leader of the Socialist Workers Party until 1946, when his increasing differences with the Party and doubts on the Russian question led him and a group of supporters to join Shachtman's Workers Party. He left the Workers Party in 1949 in a dispute over the Marshall Plan, which he supported in opposition to the Party's position. Goldman had no political affiliations in the 1950s. He developed serious health problems in this period. Toward the end of the decade he was afflicted with cancer and died in 1960.

*ALBERT GLOTZER*

**GOLDMAN, EMMA (1869–1940).** Emma Goldman was the leading American anarchist during the late years of the nineteenth century and the early years of the twentieth. She was also a leading feminist, drama and literary critic, and political gadfly. Born in Kovno in czarist Russia in 1869, she spent her childhood there and in Koenigsberg, in East Prussia, and St. Petersburg, Russia. She received a German-Jewish elementary education. Although she passed her entrance examination with honors, Emma was denied entrance to a secondary school (*gymnasium*) for religious reasons.

Her father, Abraham Goldman, a rigid disciplinarian and ne'er-do-well, was disappointed that Emma was not a boy. He beat her and demeaned her often. The family lived in near poverty. Her mother, who was from a wealthy East Prussian Jewish family, was sickly during most of Emma's childhood. Rising anti-Semitism in Russia, plus the unstable economic condition of the family, led Emma and her half-sister to emigrate to the United States in late 1885. At first they attempted to live in New York City, but within a few months Emma and her half-sister left for Rochester, where an older half-sister had settled a short time earlier.

In Rochester the 17-year-old Emma went to work in a clothing factory owned by the chairman of the United Jewish Charities of Rochester. She sewed for ten-and-a-half hours a day, for which she was paid $2.50 a week. Although the factory was spacious and well lighted, conditions there were oppressive. Employees were under constant surveillance of the foreman and were not permitted to talk or move about—"One could not even go to the toilet without permission," Emma wrote in her autobiography *Living My Life* (1930) forty-one years later. Moreover, her employer was not above expecting sexual favors from his female employees.

The pay was too low and the conditions were too oppressive for Emma Goldman to remain at this factory long; so she took another job in another clothing factory run by a man named Rubenstein. Emma's pay was now $4.00 a week, and the conditions were less onerous. In Rubenstein's factory she met Jacob Kershner, a handsome young Russian-Jewish intellectual. He became enamored of the young Emma, who worked alongside him in the factory. They exchanged books and occasionally attended dances. After four months Kershner asked her to marry him. Only 18 at the time, she believed she was too young to be engaged. But Kershner persisted, and they were married in February 1887 by a rabbi in an Orthodox Jewish rite. On her wedding night she discovered that Kershner was impotent. She prevailed on him to visit a doctor, but to no avail.

Soon after the marriage, Kershner lost all interest in things intellectual. He developed a passion for poker and become jealous and argumentative. She obtained a Jewish religious divorce from him less than a year after they were married. A few months later Kershner's pleadings led Emma to marry him again, but in a short time the second marriage also failed. While married to Kershner, Emma became interested in the radical movement of the period. She was particularly drawn to the Haymarket case, especially the execution of four Chicago anarchists who were convicted of throwing a bomb that killed eleven people at a demonstration in Chicago. She became totally immersed in that case and soon was herself converted to anarchism. From that point until her death, fifty-three years later, Emma Goldman dedicated her life to the libertarian Socialist movement.

Goldman moved to New Haven immediately after her first divorce from Kershner. There she became active in an anarchist group. She participated in the long discussions of the group and attended every lecture organized by its members. She remained in New Haven a relatively short time, returning to Rochester after remarrying Kershner. When that marriage collapsed, she left again—this time permanently. In August 1889 she moved to New York.

In New York, Goldman met fellow anarchist Alexander Berkman (q.v.), with whom she would develop a lifelong attachment, and Johann Most (q.v.), the fiery petrel of the rhetorically violence-prone wing of the anarcho-Communist movement. Within six months, Most had arranged for Goldman to go on a speaking tour. During this tour, she began to question some of Most's assumptions, particularly his antipathy to social reform and especially his opposition to the eight-hour day. When she informed Most that she dared disagree with him, he flew into a rage—an act she considered the opposite of the anarchist ideal. Moreover, Goldman had been reading a German anarchist weekly published in London called *Die Autonomie*, run by an Austrian named Joseph Peukert. *Die Autonomie* and Peukert were sworn enemies of Most, who accused the latter of being a police spy. Peukert's dedication to individual and group autonomy was closer to what Emma assumed anarchism to be, and she ended her collaboration with Most.

By 1890 Goldman was a follower of the Russian anarchist thinker Peter Kropotkin. A believer in an anarcho-Socialist society, Kropotkin rejected Most's assertion that violence had to be the midwife of revolution, although he feared that it would be inevitable in any social revolution. His ideal was a society in which private property, the church, and the state would vanish and a free, socialistic society based completely on voluntarism would reign.

Berkman, who was Goldman's companion by this time, was equally rebellious as she, but he had a more explosive personality. Thus when in 1892 the Carnegie Steel Company used Pinkerton guards to enforce a lockout at its Homestead plant near Pittsburgh, the two anarchists were incensed. When the Pinkertons, on orders from Henry Clay Frick, chairman of the corporation, attempted to reopen the plant by use of arms—an attempt that cost ten workers and three Pinkerton guards their lives—their rage reached fever pitch. Berkman went off to Pittsburgh to avenge the dead workers, while Goldman attempted to gain enough money to back him. She tried to raise money as a prostitute but failed— she found herself unable to solicit. Berkman proved to be equally inept as an assassin. His attempt to kill Frick failed, although the industrialist was wounded.

Berkman was sentenced to twenty-one years in prison for his futile attempt to murder Frick. His action helped defeat the steelworkers' strike, and his deed also permanently split the anarchist movement. Most argued that the story of Berkman's act was probably a newspaper fabrication. Shortly thereafter Most proclaimed his opposition to terrorism, especially in the United States, a country with so small a revolutionary movement. Goldman was so incensed by Most's statements that she horsewhipped him in public. The former protégé of Most was now his sworn enemy, an enmity that would last until his death in 1906.

The Jewish and German anarchists, who made up the bulk of the movement in the early 1890s, joined Most to express their disapproval of Berkman's act. Goldman believed this was a betrayal of basic anarchist tenets, and in Most's case it was an act of dishonesty. In Goldman's view, violence should be avoided if possible, but if a violent act is committed the blame should be placed on the individual or groups who created the conditions that caused the act to be committed, rather than on the actual perpetrator of the deed. Most revolutionary terrorists were individuals who were supersensitive "to the wrong and injustice surrounding them," which led them to commit terrorist acts. She argued that anarchists were impelled to commit acts of violence by the tremendous pressure of conditions making life unbearable to their sensitive natures, and not by anarchist doctrine. Nor did Goldman believe that anarchist acts of violence were but a drop in the ocean when compared with governmental violence.

The Berkman affair caused Goldman serious difficulties. She was evicted from her flat after police raided it in search of evidence of her involvement in the attempt to murder Frick, and she found herself isolated even among the anarchists.

In 1893 Goldman addressed a mass meeting of unemployed. Her speech was militant, powerful, and replete with ultra-revolutionary rhetoric. But it was hardly a call for revolution or open class warfare. A few days later she was arrested, and after being offered her freedom and a large sum of money if she would turn police informer on radicals—an offer she rejected disdainfully—she was found guilty of inciting to riot and unlawful assembly and sentenced to a year in prison.

On her release from prison, Goldman decided to dedicate her life to the sick poor. She sailed for England, where she met many anarchist leaders, including Peter Kropotkin—and Austria, where she studied nursing and midwifery at Vienna's famed teaching hospital. She returned to the United States in 1895 with diplomas in nursing and midwifery and practiced both for a short time.

In 1899 Goldman again went to Europe to study medicine, but she soon became involved in the life of Europe's anarchist movement and returned to the United States in late 1900 without having attended a single class in medicine. It was a move that would cost her dearly. On September 6, 1901, Leon Czolgosz, a young Polish-American, mortally wounded President William McKinley in Buffalo. Czolgosz was a self-proclaimed anarchist. Although Goldman had met Czolgosz only once and was in St. Louis when the assassination occurred, she hurried to Chicago and was arrested and questioned about the assassination for several days. She remained steadfast in her denial of any implication in the crime. Czolgosz, despite torture, bore out her story. Even though Goldman was apparently telling the truth that she was in no way connected with either Czolgosz or the assassination, police in Rochester hounded her family, and Buffalo police tried to have her extradited to be tried—in the hysteria of the moment in a nonexistent conspiracy to kill the President.

The Czolgosz case created new problems for all anarchists, even the most passive. The New York legislature enacted a law that made the preaching of anarchist doctrine a crime. It was first used against John Turner, a British trade-unionist and libertarian anarchist who was arrested and ordered deported. Goldman organized a committee to fight for his right to be heard here. Among the members of the committee were individualist Benjamin Tucker, Socialist Gaylord Wilshire (q.v.), and Hugh O. Pentecost, a Social Gospel Baptist minister turned attorney. Pentecost defended Turner; Clarence Darrow and Edgar Lee Masters handled his appeal. After the case was heard by the Supreme Court, a year later, Turner was deported.

In 1906, a watershed year for Goldman, she began publication of her magazine, *Mother Earth*. It would continue to appear as the most prominent organ of the anarchist movement for the next twelve years. (In 1918 *Mother Earth* and its successor, *Mother Earth Bulletin*, were suppressed by the wartime government.) It was a major journal, well written by all sorts of radical literati, including Floyd Dell, Ben Hecht, Arturo Giovannitti, and Joaquin Miller.

In 1912 Goldman and her manager-companion, Ben Reitman, were the victims of mob violence in San Diego. An armed mob of businessmen kidnapped Reitman from his hotel lobby and forced him to accompany them for twenty miles, at which point they beat him senseless and tarred him before forcing him out of the area. Mob violence, and the threat of mob violence, made it impossible for Goldman to speak in San Diego for the next three years. Rowdy antagonists also threatened Goldman in other cities. Only the commitment to civil liberties of Lewis Duncan (q.v.), the Unitarian minister who later became the Socialist mayor of Butte, Montana, made it possible for her to speak there.

Goldman was an early feminist. Although she favored women's suffrage, she believed it was of little actual value for freeing women from the bonds of sexism. She considered freedom from the thralls of loveless marriages, from the taboos against birth control and sex education of more importance. Marriage, she argued, turned women from human beings into commodities in society's eyes. Absolute equality in all aspects of life was the core of Goldman's feminism. To achieve equality, Goldman believed, it was necessary for women to be freed from the burden of large families. She lectured on the forbidden topic of birth control throughout the nation. In 1915 she was arrested in Portland, Oregon, and fined (with Ben Reitman) for distributing birth control literature at a lecture (the fine was overturned on appeal). She was also jailed for fifteen days in New York City for lecturing in favor of birth control.

Goldman was also deeply involved in literature and the arts. Her lectures helped popularize the works of George Bernard Shaw in the United States, and her 1914 book, *The Social Significance of the Modern Drama*, was the seminal work in the development of a socially conscious theater. Although Goldman urged writers to reflect life as it really was, she did not favor the blatant propaganda—generally extremely poorly written—which was called "proletarian literature" in the post–World War I years. She insisted that socially conscious literature had to be well written and well thought out.

The struggle to guarantee civil liberties for all was one of Goldman's most important struggles. In 1911 she was one of the few radicals who refused to condemn the McNamara brothers, James and John, after they admitted that they had bombed the anti-union *Los Angeles Times* building. Goldman's stand would be used against her by Attorney General A. Mitchell Palmer in his successful effort to have her deported in 1919–1921. She and Berkman led the fight for Thomas J. Mooney (q.v.) and Warren K. Billings (q.v.) after they were arrested and railroaded to prison in the bombing of a Preparedness Day parade in 1916. None of the four was an anarchist or in any way a sympathizer of Goldman. The McNamara brothers were hard-line unionists and Mooney and Billings were Socialists.

The outbreak of World War I in Europe changed the direction of Goldman's activity. From 1914 until 1917 she actively opposed the war and lent all her efforts to the fight against U.S. involvement. In early 1917 she declaimed that she would refuse to support the United States should it enter the war—a precursor of the pacifist Oxford Pledge of the 1930s.

Goldman's primary interest now became opposing the draft act. She helped form the No-Conscription League and offered aid to young men who would refuse to be conscripted. As a result, *Mother Earth*'s offices were raided in June 1918—without any warrant—its records and manuscripts seized, and Goldman and Berkman were arrested for opposing the draft. She was given a two-year sentence and fined $10,000.

Goldman was sent to the penitentiary at Jefferson City, Missouri, where she met Kate Richards O'Hare (q.v.), a Socialist with whom she had disagreed vehemently for many years. In prison the two became good friends, and their attitudes generally mellowed. In August 1919 Goldman wrote her friend and comrade Louis Kramer (the letter in the Adolph Germer Papers at the Wisconsin State Historical Society in Madison): "I know that you will . . . be glad to learn the marvelous effect of a common sorrow in welding people together." Then citing how she and O'Hare, longtime political antagonists, had been drawn together personally in prison, Goldman added, "So perhaps there is more truth than fiction in the Christian attitude toward suffering."

A mellowed Emma Goldman served her full term, even though the war had ended almost a year before, but she was not freed. Instead she was ordered deported at the instigation of the American Legion, J. Edgar Hoover, and Attorney General A. Mitchell Palmer. In December 1919 Goldman and Berkman were deported to Bolshevik Russia. Emma had lost her citizenship—which she had gained by marrying Kershner, an American citizen—in 1908 under questionable conditions.

Although Goldman was pro-Bolshevik when she arrived in Russia, she was disillusioned. Her travels throughout the nation and her observations of the totalitarian dictatorship under Lenin led her to question the Bolshevik commitment to the people. Her final break came in 1921 after the Bolsheviks, under Leon Trotsky, bombarded the revolutionary soldiers at the Kronstadt naval base, killing 18,000 of them, because they had complained of the lack of freedom under Lenin. Goldman left Russia in December 1921. Her anti-Bolshevik stance made Goldman a pariah among liberals and radicals. Their journals refused to publish her articles on life in Russia. Despite offers of large amounts of money, she refused to write for the *Chicago Tribune* or the *New York World*.

Unable to be published in the left-wing press, Goldman wrote *My Disillusionment in Russia* in 1933. The most condemnatory part of the book was omitted by the American publisher. Liberals and radicals generally condemned it. A year later the deleted sections of the book appeared as *My Further Disillusionment in Russia*. In this book Goldman proclaimed that the Russian Revolution had been an utter failure. The Bolsheviks had gained power—a power they might retain into posterity—but they had achieved no genuine social revolution. No revolution, she argued, could succeed "unless the MEANS used to further it be identical in spirit and tendency with the PURPOSES to be achieved. Revolution is the negation of the existing, a violent protest against man's inhumanity to man with all the thousand-and-one slaveries it involves" (*My Further Disillusionment*). The revolution had failed because "the political power of the party, organized and centralized in the State, sought to maintain itself by all means at hand" (*My Further Disillusionment*).

Goldman's rejection of totalitarian communism followed from her basic philosophy, her antipathy for the state. "The individual is the true reality in life. A cosmos in himself, he does not exist for the state, nor for that abstraction called 'society' or the 'nation,' which is only a collection of individuals." She rejected majoritarianism, because the majority could be as oppressive as the minority. And she did not accept the view that each generation must carry on the traditions of the past. Instead, she said, "Every new generation has to fight . . . the burdens of the past which hold us all in a net" (*My Further Disillusionment*).

During her exile, Goldman lived in Sweden, Czechoslovakia, and France for short periods. Finally, in the United Kingdom, she married fellow anarchist James Colton and became a subject of the Crown. She then moved to Canada, in 1926, where she was active in the futile campaign to save the lives of Nicola Sacco (q.v.) and Bartolomeo Vanzetti (q.v.), two anarchist immigrants who were executed in a controversial holdup-murder case. In Canada her meetings were disrupted by Communist Party groups in Montreal and Toronto, and her efforts to lecture in the United States were barred by the U.S. immigration authorities. In 1928 Goldman went to St. Tropez, on the French Riviera, where she wrote her two-volume autobiography, *Living My Life* (published by Alfred A. Knopf in 1931).

As early as 1933 Goldman tried to warn the world of the grave danger that Adolf Hitler, the anti-Semitic Fascist dictator of Germany, posed to the world. In 1934 she was finally permitted to lecture in the United States, but only about literature. In 1936 she visited the anarchist and syndicalist forces in Spain, after which she returned to Canada.

Goldman died in Toronto on May 14, 1940, three months after she had suffered a stroke. She was buried in the Waldheim Cemetery in Chicago, near the Haymarket martyrs.

SOURCES: Works by Emma Goldman: *Anarchism and Other Essays* (1911); *Living My Life* (1930); *My Disillusionment in Russia* (1923); *My Further Disillusionment in Russia* (1924); *The Social Significance of the Modern Drama* (1914). Richard Drinnon, *Rebel in Paradise* (1961), is by far the best work on Emma Goldman. Manuscript sources include the Emma Goldman–Alexander Berkman Papers at the International Institute for Social History, Amsterdam, the Netherlands; the Emma Goldman Collection at the New York Public Library, New York City; the Adolph Germer Collection at the Wisconsin State Historical Society, Madison, Wisconsin; and the Labadie Collection at the University of Michigan, Ann Arbor, Michigan.

*LILLIAN KIRTZMAN JOHNPOLL*

**GOODMAN, PAUL (1911–1972).** Paul Goodman taught at the University of Chicago, Black Mountain College, and the University of Wisconsin. He was a novelist and poet as well as a social commentator and one of the most influential members of the New Left. Goodman was born on September 9, 1911, in New York City's Greenwich Village section, the son of Barnett and Augusta Goodman. His father deserted the family when Paul was an infant, so his childhood was spent in very modest circumstances except in regard to education: he attended Hebrew school and graduated from prestigious Townsend Harris High School in 1927. He attended City College, receiving a B.A. in 1931, and entered graduate school at the University of Chicago, which he left in 1940 without his Ph.D. He finally received the doctorate in 1955.

In his 1960 work, *Growing Up Absurd*, Goodman argued that the lack of meaningful work for the young was producing frustration that carried the potential for a revolt. He also delivered an attack on post-war American life, which he saw as overly commercialized, devoid of a sense of community, and oblivious to basic problems. He was particularly concerned with the way progressive education was being implemented in the public schools. He charged that it weakened standards and taught merely adjustment to prevailing assumptions. His criticism of education continued in such works as *Compulsory Mis-education* in 1964.

Goodman took an active role in the anti–Vietnam War movement, attending demonstrations like those in Washington, D.C., in 1967 and as an editor of *Liberation*. His early identification with youth and revolt stemming from *Growing Up Absurd* made him a celebrated figure among youth activists of the 1960s. Despite his place in the movement, Goodman gradually became a critic of the 1960s youth revolt. He was an academic, and as early as *Growing Up Absurd* he made it clear that one of his principal concerns was academic standards. In his *New Reformation: Notes of a Neolithic Conservative* (1970) he found fault with many of the tendencies of the youth movement—particularly its anti-intellectual strain. He died on his farm at North Stratford, New Hampshire, on August 2, 1972.

SOURCES: Paul Goodman, *Compulsory Mis-education* (1964); *Growing Up Absurd* (1960); *New Reformation: Notes of a Neolithic Conservative* (1970).

*TOM WILLIAMS*

**GRAHAM, JAMES D. (1873–1951).** James D. Graham was the leader of the Montana Socialist Party for the first half of the twentieth century and president of the Montana Federation of Labor from 1929 until his death in 1951. Graham was born in Greenock, a seaport suburb of Glasgow, Scotland, in 1873. He and his parents migrated to the United States when he was 16. They settled in Livingston, Montana, where his father worked as a machinist on the Northern Pacific Railroad. Graham himself was an apprentice machinist with the railroad in his youth, but he was more interested in trade unionism than in the machinist's trade. He thus read in engineering, mathematics, law, and labor economics and history. He became an expert in labor economics before the turn of the century, and by 1900 he became editor of the state labor newspaper. In 1901 he was named to the executive board of the state Federation of Labor.

At about the same time, he joined the Socialist Party, then a major political force among the state's miners and railroadmen. He helped organize the whistle-stop campaign of Eugene Debs (q.v.) of 1908, which was labeled the "Red Special." Although they disagreed on many major issues, Graham and Debs were fast friends during the latter's life. Graham's chief interest in the party and the labor federation during the early years of the twentieth century was amelioration of the working conditions of the working class. From 1911 onward he was particularly active in fighting for unemployment and old-age pensions. Early in the debate over Social Security, he argued that the fund had to be properly financed and worried publicly about its precarious fiscal position.

Despite his lack of formal education, Graham was considered a learned man by the union and political leaders of Montana. He was chosen vice-president of the state federation in 1927, and two years later he became its president. During the 1920s Graham pleaded with the Socialist Party to renew its organizing in the Mountain West. But the party was in such poor condition that it was unable to do any organizing. During the 1930s, when the Socialist Party was again torn by internal dissension, Graham attempted to mediate the struggle but failed. He remained a Socialist until his death, but he withdrew from party activity after 1936.

In 1934 he was named associate director of the state employment service, a post he held for six years. He was chairman of the Montana Selective Service Appeals Board from 1941 until 1949. During all this time he remained president of the Montana Federation of Labor. Despite serious illness during the last year of his life, Graham remained an active trade union leader. He died in Helena, Montana's state capital, in June 1951.

*BERNARD K. JOHNPOLL*

**GREEN, GIL (b. 1906).** Gilbert Green was a youth leader in the 1930s for the Communist Party USA (CPUSA) and a leading Politburo member for years. A fugitive from the Smith Act during the McCarthy era, Green was principal organizer of the Communist underground and its most authoritative director. After five years he surrendered to federal officials; when he finally emerged from prison, he accepted another high CPUSA position. Today Green remains an important Party figure despite previous differences with current Party leader Gus Hall (q.v.).

Green was born Gilbert Greenberg in Chicago on September 24, 1906, the son of Russian-Jewish immigrants. His father, a tailor, died when he was about 10. His mother supported her three children by working in the needle trades. Greenberg graduated from high school as class valedictorian and president in 1924, but instead of attending college he joined the Young Workers League (later known as the Young Communist League) and, within a year, the CPUSA. He supported himself through a succession of unskilled positions: member of an oil company's shipping department, postal employee, and metalworker. By 1927, after experiencing blacklisting and anti-Semitism while seeking jobs, he had shortened his name to Green.

Green's career as a Party professional began in 1927, when he became the Young Communist League's (YCL) district organizer in Chicago. In 1928 he spent several months in New Bedford, Massachusetts, raising funds for striking textile workers. Later in 1929 the CPUSA brought him to New York to serve as a full-time youth functionary. He served as editor of the *Young Worker*, was promoted to New York state organizer of the YCL in 1930, and became its organization secretary a year later. In 1932 the Party appointed Green national secretary of the YCL, the League's highest position. He remained there for the rest of the decade, implementing Earl Browder's (q.v.) Popular Front policies.

Under Green the YCL trained a whole generation of second-level cadres. It also achieved major influence in the American Youth Congress (AYC), an organization representing genuine non-Communist groups claiming 1,700,000 members and enjoying the patronage of scores of distinguished Americans, including Eleanor Roosevelt. Green's YCL accomplishments brought acclaim both at home and abroad. The CPUSA awarded him a seat on its Political Committee (Politburo). In 1935 he attended the Comintern's historic Seventh World Congress. The gathering elected him as a youth representative to the Executive Committee of the Communist International. At the same time, Green also won appointment to the YCL Executive Committee and its secretariat.

Green became head of the New York state party in 1941 and was regarded as Browder's vigorous and vocal backer. In January 1944 Browder proclaimed that the recent Teheran Conference between Franklin Roosevelt, Churchill, and

Stalin guaranteed post-war détente. That May, Browder wanted a messenger to warn perennial opponent William Foster (q.v.) against any public challenge to his Teheran Thesis; Green performed the task. Twelve months later an article written by Jacques Duclos of the French Communist Party arrived in New York. It excoriated Browder's post-war projections as a "notorious revision of Marxism." Although Party leaders at first were unsure how to respond, Green immediately expressed anguish over speeches he had given and articles he had written in support of the Teheran line. Within two months virtually all American Communist officials had turned on Browder, their most successful leader, in a similar manner, ousting him in a frenzied search for proletarian purity.

As an act of penance for his previous aid to Browder, Green returned to Chicago, seeking closer contact with the supposedly healing qualities of the industrial working class. By becoming the CPUSA's Illinois secretary, he paved the way for Robert Thompson's (q.v.) rise to the New York state Party leadership. Green was dropped from the National Board (the new name for the Political Committee) but remained on the larger National Committee. By 1947, however, the CPUSA considered Green sufficiently rehabilitated and reinstated him to the National Board. One year later a federal grand jury indicted the entire body, charging it with violating the Smith Act.

In 1940 Green and ten other members were convicted after a spectacular trial. Except for Thompson, each received a fine of $10,000 plus a five-year prison sentence. The Supreme Court upheld the decision in 1951, and seven of the defendants began serving their terms. Green and three others disappeared, however, forfeiting $80,000 in bail. For the next fifty-five months Green lived as a fugitive, organizing the Communist Party's underground.

In early 1956 Green surrendered to authorities in New York, claiming not to have seen his family for half a decade. In a contempt-of-court proceeding one month later, a federal judge added three years to Green's sentence because of his flight. Isolated in prison, Green thereby missed the internal paroxysm that nearly destroyed the CPUSA after the Hungarian uprising and Soviet invasion in the autumn of 1956. Green was incarcerated for five years and five months before being freed on accumulated good behavior credit in July 1961. Conditions of his release barred him from associating with other Communists until expiration of his full sentence.

By 1966, however, Green was again politically visible. As head of the New York Communist Party, he gave the main report at its convention, calling for a broad movement to resist the draft and the Vietnam War. Within two years he had also once more become a member of the CPUSA's National Committee. Green received attention in the capitalist press in 1968, when he denounced the Soviet Union's invasion of Czechoslovakia as "a very serious blunder" that was "totally unwarranted" and publicly rejected General Secretary Gus Hall's defense of Soviet actions. Despite his disagreement with Hall, Green was reelected to the National Committee in 1969. Presently Green lives in New York City and remains one of the Party's elder statesmen.

SOURCES: Gil Green, *Cold-War Fugitive* (1984); Maurice Isserman, *Which Side Were You On?* (1982); Harvey Klehr, *The Heyday of American Communism* (1984); Joseph R. Starobin, *American Communism in Crisis, 1943–1957* (1972).

*JAMES GILBERT RYAN*

**GRONLUND, LAURENCE (1846–1899).** Laurence Gronlund was a leading Socialist writer during the 1880s and 1890s. Born and educated in Copenhagen, Denmark, in 1846, he was a 19-year-old law student when he migrated to the United States immediately after the Civil War. He settled in Milwaukee, where he taught school and read law in an attorney's office. Admitted to the Illinois bar in 1869, he practiced law for about a year in Chicago before abandoning the law for journalism, pamphleteering, and lecturing.

In 1870 Gronlund joined the Socialist Labor Party, in which he was active for almost twenty years. During that time he wrote his two major polemics for socialism. The first, a pamphlet called *The Coming Revolution*, was essentially an outline for the *Co-Operative Commonwealth* (1884), his definitive work on socialism.

In this book he outlined his view of society as it had been, as it is, and as it would become. In the societies of the past, he argued, masters owned slaves who did all their work, in exchange for which the master had responsibility for their food, housing, and clothing. In the present system, workers are essentially slaves to capitalists, who have no responsibility to the workers. The capitalist is thus in essence a robber who steals the product of the worker's labor. Capitalism, he declared, is a moral crime. The system of the future, according to Gronlund, would be one in which all workers owned the means of production as a social entity and in which competition would be replaced by a cooperative society. Socialism was thus a moral—as well as an economic—necessity.

Gronlund accepted much from Marx: his theory of history, albeit in a much oversimplified manner; his thesis of the class struggle (a position Gronlund would drop by 1890), and his vision of the new state. Government and the whole political structure were, he believed, needless and oppressive appendages to society. He wanted government—legislative, executive, and judicial—abolished and the administration of production and justice turned over to experts, essentially the bureaucracy. As for social relations, Gronlund was anti-feminist. He argued that women were intellectually and physically inferior to men.

In 1890 Gronlund withdrew from the SLP and became a follower of Edward Bellamy (q.v.). He called himself a Nationalist and not a Socialist. Four years later Eugene V. Debs (q.v.) denied that he was a Socialist because he was a follower of Gronlund and not of Marx.

From 1890 on, Gronlund worked on New York and Chicago newspapers as an editorial writer. He also wrote two major books that bolstered his argument in *The Co-Operative Commonwealth*. Gronlund died in 1899 in New York.

SOURCE: Stow Persons, "Introduction," in Laurence Gronlund, *The Co-Operative Commonwealth* (1965).

*BERNARD K. JOHNPOLL*

**GROTTKAU, PAUL (1846–1898).** Paul Grottkau was one of the leaders of the Socialist Labor Party in the Midwest and on the Pacific Coast during the 1880s and the early 1890s. Born in Berlin, Prussia, in 1846 of working-class parents, Grottkau went to work as a mason while still young. An active member of the German stonemasons union, he joined the Lassallean political action wing of the Social Democratic Party of Germany in 1871.

Grottkau soon became a leading party activist in Berlin and found himself persecuted and jailed by the anti-Socialist government of Otto von Bismarck. In the late 1870s Grottkau fled Germany and came to the United States, settling in Chicago. In 1883 he was named editor of the *Arbeiter Zeitung*, a labor newspaper, in Milwaukee. That same year he helped found the Socialist Labor Party (SLP) of Milwaukee.

The party Grottkau joined was basically a reform-oriented organization. Its platform called for such ameliorative measures as the eight-hour day, a ban on child labor, free and compulsory education, equal pay for women, the graduated income tax, and free administration of justice. It was also a party that had as its ultimate aim a Socialist society, calling for social ownership of the means of production. Moreover, the SLP had a revolutionary rival in the anarchist International Working People's Association (IWPA), headed by firebrand Johann Most (q.v.). In 1884 Most and Grottkau debated the comparative worth of the two movements. In this debate Grottkau delineated his position on the political state and clarified the distinction between the two philosophies.

Grottkau favored the abolition of government under socialism. Government would, he argued, be unnecessary in a Socialist society. Wasn't government the executive committee of the class in power? he asked rhetorically. Would not all classes be abolished under socialism? In a society in which there was no class to hold power, government would serve no purpose. But, unlike Most, Grottkau suggested that marriage, the family, and other social organizations should continue. They were, after all, moral institutions and not class organizations, as was the state. Grottkau also assumed that the working class would, as a class, make the revolution. He thus opposed Most's theory of a revolutionary vanguard leading the way to Utopia. And he objected to violence—which the IWPA leaders favored—and the "transitional" dictatorship, supported by Most and his followers.

Although he disapproved of violent means, Grottkau was a militant Socialist. In 1886 he led the Rolling Mill demonstration of Milwaukee unemployed. A so-called Labor mayor of Milwaukee had him arrested for leading the protest. Sentenced to a year in prison, Grottkau appealed successfully and was freed after serving one month. Grottkau left Milwaukee in 1889 and moved back to Chicago. He later moved to San Francisco, where he was a leader of the West Coast German Socialist organization.

Because Grottkau never learned English well, he was suspect as a foreigner and his influence did not spread beyond the German areas where he lived. In

1898 he went on an organizing tour for the SLP. While passing through Milwaukee
he became seriously ill and died there on June 4, 1898.

SOURCE: Paul Grottkau and Johann Most, *Discussion über das Thema Anarchismus
oder Socialismus* (Debate on the Theme of Anarchism or Socialism) (1884).

*JAMES E. INGBRETSON*

# H

HALL, GUS (b. 1910). Gus Hall is a lifelong Communist, onetime labor organizer, and presently general secretary of the Communist Party of the United States of America. He has served in that capacity longer than any other person in the Party's history. Hall was born Arvo Halberg, the fifth of ten children to Matt and Susan Halberg on October 8, 1910, in the community of Iron, Minnesota, not far from Hibbing on the Mesabi Range, Minnesota's most important mining region. His parents had immigrated to Minnesota from Finland and in the years before World War I had been members of the Industrial Workers of the World (IWW). When the Communist Party was established after the war, they both had been charter members and remained members all their lives.

At age 15, Hall went to work as a woodsman in northeastern Minnesota and soon joined a union. At age 17 he joined the Young Communist League (YCL), and at 18 he determined to become a lifelong revolutionary. He soon became an organizer for the YCL in the mining communities of northern Minnesota, Wisconsin, and Michigan. In 1932 he left the Mesabi Range and moved to Minneapolis, where he became deeply involved in that city as a YCL organizer, participating in the hunger marches and farm protests of the early 1930s. In 1934 he participated in the brutal Teamsters' strikes in Minneapolis, which were won by the workers. He served six months in jail for strike-related activities. After the Teamsters strikes, he was assigned by the YCL to the Pennsylvania-Ohio region.

In 1935 he went to work at Youngstown Sheet and Tube (and for the first time used the name "Gus Hall") and contributed to the successful organization of the plant in conjunction with the Congress of Industrial Organizations. During the same year he met and married Elizabeth Turner, a Hungarian-American who was a member of the YCL. In 1936 he became field organizer for the Steel Workers Union and led the Warren-Youngstown-Niles area in the 1937 Little Steel Strike. After the Little Steel Strike of 1937, Hall resigned his union post and became head of the Communist Party in the Youngstown area. In 1937 he became the full-time Communist Party section organizer in eastern Ohio, and two years later became the leader of the Cleveland Party organization.

In 1942 Hall joined the U.S. Navy and served as a machinist's mate on the island of Guam in the Pacific. While he was serving overseas, the Party elected him to the National Committee in 1944, and within a year after his return to the States in 1946 he was elected to the National Executive Board of the Communist Party.

In 1948 Hall and ten others were indicted under the Smith Act for conspiracy to advocate and teach the overthrow of the U.S. government by force. In 1949 he was convicted and sentenced to five years in prison. While out on bail that same year, he was elected a member of the national secretariat and served as national secretary. Rather than go to prison when his appeal failed, Hall went underground. He was caught in Mexico City and returned to the United States, where he was sentenced to an eight-year term in a federal penitentiary.

In 1959, upon his release, he returned to the Party and was elected general secretary, the post he has held since, ousting Eugene Dennis (q.v.). He and Benjamin Davis (q.v.) were arrested and indicted for failure to register as Communists under the McCarran Act in the early 1960s, but major portions of the act were ruled unconstitutional by the U.S. Supreme Court, and the case was dropped. Since 1972 Hall has run regularly for President of the United States.

*MIKE KARNI*

**HALL, ROB (b. 1908).** Rob Hall was a founder of the National Student League, district organizer for the Communist Party in Alabama, and Washington correspondent for the *Daily Worker*.

Hall was born in 1908 in Alabama into a white Anglo-Saxon Protestant family. He attended Columbia University during the early years of the Depression and joined the Communist Party around 1929. Along with other left-wing students, he founded the National Student League (NSL) and served on its first Executive Committee. In March 1932 Hall led a delegation of students to Kentucky in support of striking miners in Harlan County. The group's trip was aborted at Cumberland Gap by Tennessee law enforcement officials, who arrested the students and escorted them back to the state border.

While a student of agricultural economics at Columbia, Hall worked with Hal Ware (q.v.) and Lem Harris (q.v.) in the Farm Research Bureau. The Bureau, established in 1932, was an effort on behalf of the Communist Party to support and help organize protest among farmers devastated by the Depression. Hall edited the Bureau's *Farm News Letter* and later edited a newspaper, *The Farmer's National Weekly*.

By the mid–1930s Hall was sent back to Alabama as district organizer for the Communist Party. In numerous articles published in the *Communist* and other Party publications, Hall presented the Communist case for the United Front and its successor, the Popular Front. He attended the 1938 founding of the Southern Conference for Human Welfare and remained an active participant in that organization for several years.

In 1943 Hall became the Washington correspondent for the *Daily Worker*. Distraught over the revelations of Stalin's crimes, he dropped out of the Party in 1957. Until his retirement he edited a newspaper in Upstate New York.

*PAT SULLIVAN*


**HALONEN, GEORGE (1891–1954).** George (Yrjo) Halonen, education director at Central Cooperative Wholesale—a Finnish consumers' cooperative in Superior, Wisconsin—became the center of a controversial battle for control of the CCW between Communists and nonaligned members of 1929–1930. He was expelled from the Party and led the nonaligned members to victory.

Halonen was born in Helsinki, Finland, on December 15, 1891. While he attended Helsinki University in 1911, he became associated with Socialist groups in central Helsinki. The next year he emigrated, settling first in Port Arthur, Ontario (now Thunder Bay), as an editor of *Tyokansa* (The Working People). He then joined the editorial staff of *Raivaaja* (The Pioneer) in Fitchburg, Massachusetts, and worked for five years as editor of its monthly political journal, *Sakenia* (Sparks). He supported communism after the Russian Revolution and moved to *Tyomies* (The Worker) in Superior, Wisconsin, where he emerged as a popular leader among Finnish leftists in the western Great Lakes region.

In 1924 Halonen became the education director of Central Cooperative Wholesale (CCW) and was one of the people responsible for the cooperative's growth during the 1920s to sales of well over one million dollars per year. During the period of "Bolshevization" in international Communist parties, a controversy arose over the CCW's role in financing local Communist activities. Halonen and General Manager Eskel Ronn were singled out by those loyal to the Party as the two main impediments to stronger Communist control. A heated delegate battle arose during the winter of 1929–1930, culminating at the CCW's annual meeting in the spring. The Communists' candidates for Halonen's and Ronn's positions, supported directly by the Finnish Communist Party (in exile in Moscow) and the Comintern, were voted down, and twenty cooperative stores that remained under Communist control were expelled from the CCW. Halonen emerged in the forefront of the rapidly growing cooperative, which in the late 1930s began to appeal beyond the Finnish community.

In 1942 Halonen moved to Palo Alto, California, where he went into business. In 1952 he returned to Superior, Wisconsin, where he became one of the editors of *Tyovaen Osuustoimintalehti* (The Worker's Cooperative Journal). He died in 1954.

SOURCES: Elis Sulkanen, *Amerikan Suomalaisen Tyovaenliikkeen Historia* (1951), p. 488; *Tyovaen Osuustoimintalehti*, May 18, 1954, p. 1.

*MIKE KARNI*

**HARRIMAN, JOB (1861–1925).** Job Harriman was the leader of the Southern California Socialist Party from 1890 until 1920. Harriman was born in rural Butler County, Indiana, in 1861 of pious, middle-class parents. He graduated from Butler University, then the leading university of the Disciples of Christ church. He was ordained into the ministry of that church soon after. Harriman, who suffered from tuberculosis, moved to Denver in 1886, and then to Los Angeles. In Denver he studied law and was admitted to the Colorado bar. In 1888 he moved to Los Angeles.

A Democrat when he moved to the West, Harriman gradually changed his political affiliation to Socialist after reading Edward Bellamy's (q.v.) *Looking Backward*. He joined the Socialist Labor Party (SLP) in 1889 and ran for governor of California on the SLP ticket in 1898. A year later he joined in the rebellion within the SLP against Daniel DeLeon (q.v.). He was the West Coast leader of the rebellion, which was directed on the East Coast by Morris Hillquit (q.v.). The Hillquit wing of the SLP, dubbed "Kangaroos" by DeLeon and his followers, nominated Harriman for U.S. President and Max S. Hayes (q.v.) of Cleveland, for Vice-President, in 1900. Then the Social Democratic Party—another Socialist group—nominated Eugene V. Debs (q.v.) for U.S. President. In a move to unite the anti-DeLeon Socialist forces, the two parties chose Harriman as Debs' vice-presidential running mate on a joint ticket (Hayes withdrew). The Debs-Harriman ticket polled almost 100,000 votes, the highest recorded by any previous Socialist candidate.

After the 1900 election Harriman spent most of his efforts organizing Socialist branches in every district of Greater Los Angeles and worked hard at representing labor unions in the city and its environs. The Socialist organization he built was one of the most solid in the nation. His relationship with the labor union movement was very close. Unlike most other Socialist leaders, Harriman was in favor of a labor party in which the Socialists would be a major, but not the dominant, force. In Los Angeles he arranged for unions to be represented directly on the County Central Committee of the Socialist Party.

In 1911 Harriman was nominated for mayor of Los Angeles. At Harriman's insistence a black Socialist was one of the candidates for the city council. Because of the corruption then prevalent in the city, and because of the efficient Socialist trade union alliance Harriman had built, he was given an even chance at winning the election. Unfortunately for Harriman, the Socialist Party, and the Los Angeles labor movement, a bomb blew up late in 1910 in the plant of the *Los Angeles Times*, the leading newspaper in the city, whose publisher, Harrison Grey Otis, was virulently anti-labor. Twenty persons were killed in the blast. Otis blamed it on the radical labor leaders. Harriman and most Socialists blamed the explosion on Otis and were of the opinion that he had hired a gangster to set off the bomb so that he could accuse the labor men of violence and insurrection.

In early 1911 two brothers, John and James McNamara, conservative labor officials, were arrested in Indiana and taken to Los Angeles at gunpoint by private detectives. They were then charged with murder in the bombings and would face the death penalty if convicted. Harriman and world-famous criminal attorney Clarence Darrow were chosen to defend the brothers.

Harriman, who was then campaigning, made the McNamara case one of the key issues of the race. The people of Los Angeles were apparently on his side in November, when the first part of the election was run. He was first, with a huge lead. But then, only five days before the runoff election, Darrow and journalist Lincoln Steffens (q.v.) convinced the McNamara brothers to confess and save their lives. Harriman did not know about the arrangement. The confession damaged the Harriman campaign beyond repair, and he lost by a large margin. The *Times* of London—whose analysis of the election is probably the best done at the time—doubted that the McNamara case was the only, or even the most significant, cause of his defeat. The *Times* noted that he had not had a majority of the vote in the first election and that the other candidates all endorsed his opponent. It also cited the fact that women voted in the runoff and not in the first election and concluded that women were more anti-Socialist than men. In 1912 Harriman was instrumental in having the Socialist Party convention vote a ban on sabotage and violence into its constitution. He warned against a repetition of the McNamara case.

After the 1911 election, Harriman shunned electoral activity. He formed the Llano Colony, a cooperative farm in the Antelope Valley of southeastern California. The Llano Colony prospered, but it was torn by internal disputes. Moreover, the water supply at the community was inadequate for its needs. The community moved to Louisiana, where more feuds erupted.

In 1917 Harriman was a California delegate to the emergency convention of the Socialist Party at the outbreak of World War I. Harriman served on the committee that drafted the anti-war declaration, which became known as the St. Louis Declaration. During the war he was also active in the first American Conference on Democracy and the Terms of Peace and the anti-war People's Council of America.

Soon after the war, Harriman became ill again and left Los Angeles to settle in the hills northeast of Los Angeles. He died in Sierra Madre in 1925.

*BERNARD K. JOHNPOLL*

**HARRINGTON, MICHAEL (b. 1928).** Michael Harrington is a founder and national co-chairman of the Democratic Socialists of America (DSA), author of *The Other America*, and America's most well known democratic Socialist activist. He was born in St. Louis, Missouri, on February 24, 1928. His father was a lawyer, his mother was a teacher. In 1944 Harrington graduated from the Jesuit-run St. Louis University High School. He received an A.B. from Holy Cross in 1947. During the 1947–1948 academic year he studied at Yale University Law School, entering as a Taft Republican and exiting a democratic Socialist. In 1949 Harrington earned an M.A. in English literature from the University of Chicago.

Arriving in New York in 1949, Harrington assumed the trappings of a bohemian poet. In February 1951 he joined Dorothy Day's (q.v.) militant Catholic Worker organization and in December 1952 turned toward Socialist activism. In 1953 he was a section organizer for the Workers Defense League. That year he joined the Young People's Socialist League (YPSL), the youth section of the Socialist Party. Unhappy over Norman Thomas' (q.v.) critical support for the American war in Korea, Harrington led its New York branch into Max Shachtman's (q.v.) Independent Socialist League (ISL) in February 1954. Until the ISL dissolved in June 1957, Harrington served as national chairman of its Young Socialist League (YSL). In September 1958, Harrington and other ISL-YSL members began entering the Socialist Party as a bloc. Again, Harrington became a YPSL youth leader. In 1959 he was a delegate to the International Union of Socialist Youth in Berlin.

Fron 1954 to 1962 Harrington supported himself as a researcher and writer for the Fund for the Republic. He worked on studies of blacklisting in the entertainment industry and other labor-related projects. In 1960 he emerged as a leader in the Socialist Party–Social Democratic Federation (SP-SDF) and a leading spokesperson for a realignment strategy that committed the party to entering the Democratic Party in an attempt to move it leftward. Harrington was voted on to the National Executive Committee of the Socialist Party in 1960. He was also a SP-SDF delegate to the congress of the Socialist International in Amsterdam that year. From 1960 to 1962 Harrington edited *New America*, the official paper of the Socialist Party.

The New Left was emerging as a political force, and Harrington confronted Students for a Democratic Society (SDS) leaders in his role as national chairman of the League for Industrial Democracy (LID). Technically the SDS was the youth section of the LID, and Harrington locked the SDS leadership out of its office for allowing the Communist Party observer at their Port Huron convention in the summer of 1962. Harrington remained as LID chairman throughout the 1960s.

In 1962 he published *The Other America*, which became the intellectual stimulus behind the national anti-poverty programs of the Kennedy administration. In January 1964 Harrington became a consultant to Sargent Shriver's task force on poverty, which was drawing up the battle plan for President Lyndon Johnson's "War on Poverty." In 1965 Walter P. Reuther recruited Harrington to deliver the keynote address at the founding convention of the Citizens Crusade Against Poverty. By the 1968 Socialist Party convention, the party was polarized into two mutually exclusive caucuses. Harrington and Shachtman led the Realignment Caucus; the Debs Caucus, favoring a third party and a militant anti-war movement, opposed them. The Realignment Caucus prevailed, approving unification with the more rightist Democratic Socialist Federation and designating Harrington chairman of the Socialist Party. Harrington actively pushed this strategy as a National Steering Committee member of the newly formed New Democratic Coalition group.

The years 1968 and 1969 saw intense factional dispute inside the Socialist Party, primarily because of the Vietnam War issue. Divisions within the Realignment Caucus began to develop clearly between those who opposed the war, like Harrington, but could not support unconditional withdrawal, and those who, like Shachtman, gave critical support to U.S. efforts against Communist North Vietnam. At the Socialist Party's 1970 convention, Harrington's followers split from the Realignment Caucus and formed the Coalition Caucus to pursue a middle ground between Shachtman's supporters and the decimated Debs Caucus. The convention named Harrington to act as one of three national co-chairpersons. In 1972 the Democratic presidential primaries reflected the divisions within the Socialist Party. Harrington's Coalition Caucus supported George McGovern in the primaries and general election. The Realignment Caucus favored Henry Jackson and later joined the leadership of the AFL-CIO in neutrality during the race between Richard Nixon and George McGovern. Harrington resigned as national co-chairperson in October 1972. In December the built-up tensions between the Coalition and Realignment caucuses exploded into conflict at the Socialist Party's final convention. When the majority Realignment Caucus voted to change the name of the party from Socialist Party–Democratic Socialist Federation to Social Democrats U.S.A., both Harrington's caucus and the remnant Debs Caucus bolted.

In late February 1973 the Coalition Caucus created the Democratic Socialist Organizing Committee (DSOC). Harrington became its one and only national chairman. He began a new job that year as professor of political science at Queens College, City University of New York. He spent the 1970s writing and organizing for Democratic Socialism. In 1976 he initiated and coordinated a democratic left caucus—Democracy '76—at the national Democratic convention. It became a permanent program and policy coalition in the Democratic party under the name Democratic Agenda.

Making amends to the militant anti-war and anti-Leninist wing of the New Left movement, Harrington pushed for a merger of the DSOC and the New American Movement (NAM) in the late 1970s. In 1982 his efforts resulted in the formation of the Democratic Socialists of America (DSA). Harrington became its first national chairman by acclamation. In 1983, New Left Socialist feminist Barbara Ehrenreich joined him as co-chairperson. The DSA claims to be the largest Democratic Socialist organization in the United States since the Socialist Party of 1936.

SOURCES: Michael Harrington, *Fragments of the Century* (1973) and *Political Profiles: The Johnson Years* (1976).

*ROBERT FITRAKIS*

**HARRIS, LEM (b. 1904).** Lement Upham Harris was one of the chief agricultural specialists for the Communist Party in the 1930s and has remained its expert in the field. He has also been involved with Party finances. Lem Harris was born in Chicago on March 1, 1904, the son of John F. Harris, a leading commodities trader. The family later moved to New York when the elder Harris founded a major brokerage house. Harris was educated privately and graduated from Harvard in 1926. After a disagreement with his father over professions, Harris worked three years for a Quaker farmer in Bucks County, Pennsylvania. Roger Baldwin introduced him to Harold Ware (q.v.) in 1929, and Harris went with Ware to the Soviet Union. There he worked on a state farm and in factories and became an admirer of the Communist system.

Harris and Ware returned to the United States in 1931 and traveled to observe the nation's deteriorating agriculture. The following year Harris financed Farm Research, Inc., for the purpose of analyzing rural conditions. About this time Earl Browder (q.v.) invited Harris to become a member of the Communist Party.

When a major farmers strike began around Sioux City, Iowa, in early August 1932, Ware hurried to the area and gathered a group to present relief demands to a governors conference. A mass meeting voted to ask Harris to be acting secretary of a Farmers Emergency Relief Conference in Washington, D.C., in December. The meeting gave national exposure to many farm problems and presented a further series of demands to Congress. It also voted to establish a permanent organization, the Farmers National Committee for Action (FNCA), and elected Harris as its executive secretary.

Harris made the FNCA one of the Party's more successful front groups, despite the general disinterest of many leading Communists. He staged two more national conferences, where demands for mortgage moratoriums, tax relief, and land to those who worked it were publicized. Harris worked closely with Ware in trying to build a broad-based farmers' group, but they were severely criticized by the Party's sectarian agrarian secretary, Henry Puro (q.v.). Harris immediately supported the Popular Front and attended the Seventh Congress of the Communist International in 1935.

Harris melded the FNCA into the Farm Holiday Association (FHA), a non-Communist radical group, in 1936. The FHA joined with other progressives to rid the National Farmers Union (NFU) of right-wingers in 1936 and 1937, but Harris later denied that he had ever been an adviser to NFU leaders. He was successful in wangling organizing grants from the Garland Fund for the FNCA, FHA, and NFU during the mid–1930s. During that time, he lived in Minneapolis and was friendly with Governor Elmer Benson (q.v.), who was often accused of having pro-Communist sympathies.

Harris wrote columns for the *Midwest Record*, the *Daily Worker*, and later the *Daily World*. He has maintained an interest in agriculture and attends conventions of several farmers' organizations. He has also become a leading financial adviser to the Communist party, according to FBI files.

In the early 1960s Harris started an industrial insurance business and later a highly successful tour company that specializes in trips to the Soviet Union. He has been married twice, and one daughter, an actress, lives in Moscow.

SOURCES: Lowell K. Dyson, *Red Harvest* (1982); Lem Harris, *Memoirs* (forthcoming).

*LOWELL K. DYSON*

**HART, WILLIAM OSBORNE (b. 1912).** William Osborne Hart, a longtime Wisconsin Socialist activist, was born in Chicago, Illinois, on May 15, 1912. He graduated from Bowen High School in 1928 and Chicago Central YMCA High School in 1930. He later attended St. Olaf College, the University of Missouri, South Dakota State University, the University of Maine, and Bangor Theological Seminary.

Hart settled in Wisconsin in the 1930s in rural Prairie du Sac. He became interested in the policies and philosophy of the Socialist Party and soon became active in the party. In 1934 Hart made his first bid for public office, running as a Socialist Party candidate for Sauk County clerk of circuit court.

Hart had worked as a clergyman at Marcy Center Settlement House in Chicago and as a missionary to the Dakota Indians in Minnesota, as well as serving as a lay preacher in several rural Protestant churches in Wisconsin. Being from a rural area of Wisconsin, Hart did not have the base of support that the state's urban Socialists did, and yet he came to be highly regarded by his party. He was nominated as the Socialist candidate for governor in 1950 and 1974, for lieutenant governor in 1948, and for U.S. Senator in 1962, 1976, and 1982. In addition, he found time to run for such local offices as sheriff and state senator.

As a pacifist, Hart served in the Ambulance Corps in World War II, working often with Norman Thomas' (q.v.) son Evan, who had volunteered for the same duty. In 1949 Hart ran as a candidate for state supreme court justice, even though he was not a lawyer. He polled 12,574 votes, a better showing than many Republicans and Democrats had predicted for him. As a direct result, the state constitution was changed, making it illegal for any nonattorney to run for that position again.

Hart served as state chairman of the Socialist Party of Wisconsin from 1946 to 1948 and has held numerous other offices within the party throughout the years. In 1984 the 72-year-old Hart received 13,840 votes as a favorite son candidate for President in the Wisconsin presidential primary. He is still active in public affairs and hosts a weekly radio talk show over the Wisconsin state radio network. He continues to live in Prairie du Sac.

*STEPHEN K. HAUSER*

**HASKELL, BURNETTE G. (1857–1907).** Burnette G. Haskell was the irascible leader of the independent Socialist movements on the Pacific Coast during the 1880s and 1890s. He was also a founder of the Sailors Union of the Pacific and the Kaweah Cooperative Community and leader of the Bellamyite movement in California during that movement's heyday. Haskell was born in 1857 in Sierra County in far northern California. His parents were wealthy landowners and descendants of Puritans who had settled in New England in the seventeenth century. One maternal grandfather was the first settler in the California mountain region. A paternal grandfather had started the fruit-growing industry in that area. One descendant was a Revolutionary War hero.

As was the custom in those days, Haskell's parents sent him East to get an education. He first attended Oberlin College in Ohio, but remained there only one year. He then attended the University of Illinois and the University of California, each for a short period. Finally, he read law in his uncle's office and was admitted to the California bar in 1879. He soon tired of law and decided to enter journalism. Fortunately, his uncle owned a small weekly in San Francisco named *Truth*, which he turned over to Burnette.

Haskell had been a conservative up to this time. One of his assignments in running the paper was to report on the doings of the San Francisco Trades Assembly, the trade union organization. At the meetings Haskell learned three things that led to his conversion to socialism: He discovered that there was such a theory; he learned that there was a conflict between labor and capital and that the Socialist and labor movements claimed to represent labor, and he found that the San Francisco labor movement was in need of a publishing outlet and that *Truth* was in need of a cause to increase its anemic circulation. So he set to work devouring all the books available on socialism, the labor movement, and the struggle between the working people and management. Then he proclaimed himself a Socialist and a supporter of the labor movement. *Truth* was then named the official organ of the Trades Assembly, and Haskell began his career as a Socialist leader. His leadership would prove to be erratic, capricious, and irresponsible, but his accomplishments, despite his personal and organizational failings, were many.

Within a year after he had become a Socialist, Haskell formed the International Workingmen's Association (not to be confused with the long-dead IWA founded by Karl Marx). The new association was organizationally a combination of a political body and a secret fraternal society. It was replete with mystical ritual, secret insignia and handshakes, and oaths of fidelity. Its ideology was a mixture of simplistic Marxism, dedication to violence, and virulent antagonism to Orientals.

Haskell's ideological compound included one original idea. He believed that workers were always ready to overthrow the existing social order. This thesis of permanently imminent rebellion rejected a basic Marxian and anarchist assumption—that revolution required appropriate conditions. In 1883, a year after the International Workingmen's Association (IWA) was formed, Haskell organized a band of dynamiters to destroy the Western Union office in San Francisco. The dynamite was purchased, and all the IWA men, except Haskell, gathered in the appointed place. Haskell remained at home and the project was never carried out.

The organization continued for five more years, but its membership never exceeded 500. The failure of the IWA to grow led Haskell to propose a merger between the violence-prone anarchists' Pittsburgh Congress of 1883 (which he did not attend). The congress rejected the proposal, issuing instead its own manifesto. Haskell published their Pittsburgh Manifesto on the front page of *Truth* as if it were his own.

In 1885 Haskell helped organize the Sailors Union of the Pacific, one of the most honest, powerful, and long-lasting maritime industry trade unions. He directed it in a futile strike a year later, after which his power with the union waned. Haskell served as attorney, without pay, until 1889, and again in 1894, when he successfully defended one of the union's members charged with murder by dynamite.

Haskell's violent rhetoric declined with the 1887 execution of the four Haymarket anarchists. From 1887 onward he was a moderate Socialist. In 1886 he was named editor of the *Denver Labor Enquirer*, one of the major labor weeklies in the West. He turned it into a virulently anti-Chinese, pro-SLP (Socialist Labor Party) organ, hoping thus to become a leader of that party. The SLP convention of 1886 ignored Haskell's request that he be named its Western director and that the *Labor Enquirer* be named the party's official organ in the Western states. Despite the rejection, Haskell reported in the newspaper that he had been named Western director of the SLP and that the *Labor Enquirer* had been named an official publication of the party. The fraud was uncovered and he was forced out of Denver.

The Denver interlude barely affected Haskell's ego. In late 1885 he suggested to several of his followers that they found a cooperative community based on the teachings of Danish-American Socialist Laurence Gronlund (q.v.). Two years later Haskell founded such a colony in what is now the Sequoia National Park. The community, which attracted about 400 settlers, was the scene of religious and ideological bickering and virulent jealousies. Despite the feuding, its accomplishments were significant; not the least of these was a road that cut across that whole Sequoia area, which is still used. The work of the community antagonized Harry Crocker, president of the Southern Pacific Railroad and a political power in both California and the nation. At Crocker's insistence the Haskell community (named Kaweah) was incorporated into the new national park in 1890. Moreover, all the leaders of the community were fined for having cut trees in the area. The fines were eventually overturned, but the Kaweah community had ceased to exist by 1891.

Even before the final demise of the Kaweah community, Haskell had become politically active again. He was the leader of the powerful Nationalist movement, based on the work of Edward Bellamy (q.v.), in California. He wrote the Nationalist platform, which was similar to that proposed by Upton Sinclair (q.v.) and his EPIC (End Poverty in California) movement forty-five years later. The movement, a moderate Socialist political organization, soon became a target for professional politicians. Haskell stood in the way of their taking it over, so they unearthed his violence-prone past and forced him out of the Populist organization, into which the Nationalists had been merged.

Failing as a Socialist, Haskell attempted to enter politics first as a Democrat in 1890, then as a Populist from 1892 to 1896. Then he became a Republican. In 1900 President William McKinley named him notary public in Alaska. He returned to California in 1903, unable to get any work. In 1904 he attempted in vain to be named a Socialist member of the San Francisco election board. Thereafter he lived in dire poverty, working occasionally as a proofreader on the *Oakland Tribune*.

At his death in 1907 he received his only payment from the Sailors Union of the Pacific: the cemetery plot in which he was buried.

SOURCES: Ira B. Cross, *A History of the Labor Movement of California* (1935); Bernard K. Johnpoll with Lillian Johnpoll, *The Impossible Dream: The Rise and Demise of the American Left* (1981); Ruth [Ronnie Krandis] Lewis, "Kaweah: An Experiment in Cooperative Colonization," *Pacific Historical Review* 17 (November 1948); Hyman Weintraub, *Andrew Furuseth, Emancipator of the Seaman* (1959).

*BERNARD K. JOHNPOLL*

**HATHAWAY, CLARENCE (1894–1963).** Clarence Hathaway was a Communist Party functionary who held numerous responsible positions, particularly in the 1930s, when he edited the *Daily Worker* and worked closely with Earl Browder (q.v.). Hathaway was born on February 8, 1894, in Oakdale Township, Minnesota. His mother was of Norwegian descent, his father was a carpenter of English background. Despite his father's socialism, young Hathaway was a devoutly religious Protestant. After three years of high school he began working as a machinist, also finding time to play semi-professional baseball. Hathaway worked as a tool and die maker in England and Scotland in 1915–1916, where he was converted to socialism. He joined the Socialist Party in the United States in 1917 and gravitated to its left wing. Two years later he became a charter member of the Communist Party in Detroit.

Hathaway had been an active member of the International Association of Machinists since 1913, and his first years as a Communist were spent working with the labor movement. He helped organize the Michigan Farmer-Labor Party in 1920 and served on its first state committee. After moving back to Minneapolis, he was elected vice-president of the state Federation of Labor in 1923. Hathaway took an active role in the Party's maneuvering in 1923–1924 to gain control of the Farmer-Labor movement, which hoped to nominate Senator Robert LaFollette for President of the United States. These efforts culminated in the Party's capture of the movement, the withdrawal of virtually all the non-Communists, and repudiation by LaFollette of their support. Hathaway's role burned many of his bridges to the labor movement. In 1924 the Minneapolis Trade and Labor Assembly refused to seat him as a delegate.

He soon moved into new fields. From 1926 to 1928 Hathaway attended the Lenin School in Moscow as part of its first class. Returning to New York, he became the chief accuser at the Party trial of James Cannon (q.v.) for Trotskyism, repudiating his onetime factional leader. After briefly serving as editor of *Labor Unity*, Hathaway was assigned to Chicago as the Party's district organizer in the Party's largest and most important bastion. One year later Earl Browder selected him as editor of the *Daily Worker*. For most of the remainder of the decade he was one of the Party leader's closest political advisers. When Browder was ill and unable to report to the 1938 Party plenum, it was Hathaway who stood in for him and announced the Communists' new Democratic Front policy.

By late 1938, however, Hathaway's role was being usurped by Eugene Dennis (q.v.). He had to serve a brief jail term in 1940 as a result of a successful criminal libel suit against the *Daily Worker*, and he was expelled from the Party in October 1940 for alcoholism. Hathaway moved back to St. Paul, Minnesota, worked as a machinist, and became active in the United Electrical Workers, a Party-dominated union. He was readmitted to the Communist Party in Minnesota sometime after World War II. Hathaway would doubtless have remained in obscurity had it not been for the severe leadership losses sustained by the Party in 1956–1958. As a result of the resignations of numerous functionaries, he was elected to the National Committee in 1959 and in 1960 made chairman of the Party's New York district. By mid–1961 severe illness ended his political career. He died on January 23, 1963.

SOURCES: FBI File 100–9158; Harvey Klehr, *The Heyday of American Communism* (1984).

*HARVEY KLEHR*

**HAYDEN, THOMAS (b. 1939).** Tom Hayden was born of Irish-American parentage in Royal Oak, Michigan, in 1939. He is a well-known former campus activist, past president of Students for a Democratic Society, an early New Left organizer, and a Chicago Seven defendant. In the early 1970s he shifted his political focus away from radicalism and became active in electoral politics.

Hayden entered the University of Michigan in 1957. Originally apolitical, Hayden's social consciousness was awakened by the Greensboro lunch counter sit-ins of February 1960. By the summer of that year, Hayden had been named editor of the *Michigan Daily*, the University of Michigan's student-operated newspaper. Hayden spent that summer traveling to various college campuses, most notably the University of California at Berkeley, where his nascent radicalism was crystallized through a series of encounters with local activists. The connections made at Berkeley were to provide the foundation for much of Hayden's subsequent activity.

In January 1961 Hayden took part in the organization of Students for a Democratic Society (SDS). Later that year he accepted a position as SDS field secretary in Atlanta, where he acted as SDS liaison to the Student Nonviolent Coordinating Committee (SNCC). At the SDS convention in 1962, Hayden was influential in the drafting of the widely read Port Huron Statement, an unofficial manifesto of New Left principles. He was also elected SDS president at that meeting. During this period, SDS was primarily involved in the struggle for civil rights for blacks, and Hayden reflected this focus by creating the Economic Research and Action Project (ERAP). One of ERAP's major projects was the Newark Community Union Project (NCUP), and Hayden spent three years living in the ghettos of Newark as a staff member and activist for the NCUP. The Newark race riots of 1967, however, forced ERAP workers to recognize that the ghetto blacks were no longer receptive (if indeed they ever were) to the perceived solicitous charity of middle-class whites.

The SDS had organized anti–Vietnam War protests as early as 1962, and Hayden had traveled to North Vietnam with Staughton Lynd (q.v.) and Herbert Aptheker in the winter of 1965. The trip made Hayden something of a media personality. He and Lynd recounted their experiences in *The Other Side*, one of the earliest treatises against U.S. involvement in Southeast Asia. It was not until the aftermath of the 1967 summer riots, however, that Hayden focused on the Vietnam War as the issue of primary significance.

In April 1968 Hayden took part in the student takeover at Columbia University and then moved on to Chicago to work with the National Mobilization to End the War in Vietnam in preparation for planned protests at the Democratic national convention scheduled for August. His role in the protest and subsequent police riot led to his indictment and conviction for conspiracy and incitement to riot as one of the famed Chicago Seven. Hayden was the defense coordinator for that group, and their convictions were later overturned on appeal.

Hayden then moved to Berkeley to form the Red Family, a commune based on principles of anti-privatism and group consensus on all actions. Hayden was later purged from the Family in a factional power struggle based on charges (by his lover) of bourgeois privatism and elitism. Soon thereafter, Hayden met actress/activist Jane Fonda at an anti-war rally, and they quickly developed a working rapport that culminated in their marriage in 1973. This period also represented a turning point in Hayden's political tactics. In 1972 he and Fonda worked for George McGovern's presidential campaign. This represented the first instance of Hayden's new concentration on electoral politics.

In 1976 Hayden made an unsuccessful yet highly respectable attempt at unseating then-incumbent Senator John Tunney in the Democratic primary. Hayden received nearly 40 percent of the votes cast, based on the slogan ''The radicalism of the sixties is the common sense of the seventies.''

The remnants of Hayden's campaign organization formed the basis for his next project, the Campaign for Economic Democracy (CED), which was financed largely through Fonda's considerable income as an actress. Hayden focused on CED activities for the next several years, and in 1982 was elected as a representative to the California State Assembly.

*ROBERT RUSHIN*

**HAYES, MAX S. (1866–1945).** Max S. Hayes was a pioneer labor editor and a leading Socialist trade unionist between 1900 and 1917. Hayes was born in a cabin in rural Havana, Ohio, in 1866. His parents were pioneers who had reached Ohio by canal and ox-team through the wilderness. At the age of 16, Hayes became an apprentice printer on the *Cleveland Press* and a member of Local 53 of the International Typographical Union (ITU). He remained active in that union for the next fifty-five years.

In 1891 he founded the *Citizen*, one of the first labor weeklies (as of 1985 it was the oldest labor weekly still published in the United States). By 1895 the *Citizen* was recognized as the voice of the American trade union movement.

The American Federation of Labor (AFL), led by Samuel Gompers, Hayes' antagonist inside the labor movement, was thus forced to publish its own journal, *The American Federationist*. The alternative would have been to name Hayes' *Citizen* the official organ of the federation.

Hayes joined the old Socialist Labor Party (SLP) in the late 1890s. In 1899 he joined in the revolt against Daniel DeLeon (q.v.) led by Morris Hillquit (q.v.) and helped form the so-called Kangaroo SLP. In 1900 he was nominated for U.S. vice-president by the Hillquit faction of the SLP, but withdrew in favor of Job Harriman (q.v.) after the Hillquit-SLP and the Social Democratic Party, led by Eugene V. Debs (q.v.) and Victor Berger (q.v.), agreed to run a joint ticket headed by Debs.

Hayes and Debs became close friends after the two parties merged in 1901. They had only one major disagreement: in 1905 Debs supported the organization of the Industrial Workers of the World (IWW), which Hayes opposed vehemently. By 1906 even that disagreement was forgotten as Debs moved further away from the IWW. In 1912 Hayes was asked to oppose Debs for the Socialist presidential nomination, but he refused. He supported Debs for the nomination and was active in his election campaign.

In 1911 Hayes, a delegate from the ITU, challenged Gompers for the presidency of the AFL. Hayes' platform was primarily a demand that the AFL proclaim its belief in socialism and political action. Hayes polled 30 percent of the delegate vote at the 1911 convention. It was the high point of Socialist influence in the AFL. Hayes broke with the Socialist Party in 1918 when the forces led by Charles Ruthenberg (q.v.), who later helped found the Communist Party, gained control of the Ohio Socialist organization. Hayes was an implacable foe of the Communists for the rest of his life.

In 1920 Hayes was nominated by the Farmer-Labor Party (FLP) as its candidate for U.S. Vice-President. The FLP polled more than 300,000 votes, mainly in Western agrarian states (the presidential candidate was Parley Christensen, a Utah lawyer and a Progressive). The Socialist candidate for U.S. President, Debs, polled almost a million. Four years later, Hayes was active in the Conference for Progressive Political Action in its campaign to elect Robert H. LaFollette as President. The huge LaFollette vote in Cleveland was attributed in great part to *Citizen*'s strong stand in his favor.

Hayes remained the active editor of *Citizen* until 1939, when ill health forced him to restrict his activity. He was honored at a dinner in 1941 marking the fiftieth anniversary of the weekly.

Max Hayes died in Cleveland in October 1945 at the age of 79.

*BERNARD K. JOHNPOLL*

**HAYWOOD, HARRY (1898–1985).** Harry Haywood was the leading advocate of the Communist Party's doctrine of self-determination for blacks, a policy to which he remained faithful for more than fifty years. Haywood was born Haywood Hall on February 4, 1898, in South Omaha, Nebraska. Both his parents had been born slaves and were Methodists. His father worked as a janitor in a packing company. Haywood dropped out of school at age 15 after racial threats led the family to move to Minnesota. He was a dining-car waiter when he joined the army in 1917 and saw action in France. He was recruited into the African Blood Brotherhood, a secret Black Nationalist organization and then the Young Workers League, the Communist Party's youth group, in 1923 by his older brother, Otto Hall.

In 1925 he joined the Communist Party itself. Only a handful of blacks were Communists at the time, and after a brief stint as organizer for the American Negro Labor Congress, Haywood was sent for study in Moscow in 1926 at the University of the Toilers of the East and then at the Lenin School, where he was the first black student. Under the tutelage of N. Nasanov, a former Russian representative to America's young Communists and with the covert support of Stalin, Haywood became the major American champion of the theory of self-determination for blacks in the Southern "black belt." At the Sixth Congress of the Communist International (CI) in 1928, he alone of the black delegates supported the idea that Communists should support the right of Southern blacks to secede from the United States and set up a black republic. He played a major role in drafting both a 1928 and 1930 CI resolution mandating Communist support for the policy as vice-chairman of the Negro subcommission of the eastern secretariat.

Haywood returned to the United States in November 1930 to a position of prominence. He was regarded as the Party's chief theoretician on the Negro question. He wrote the draft manifesto for the first conference of the League of Struggle for Negro Rights (LSNR), became national organizer for the Trade Union Unity League, and helped direct the Party's first campaign against "white chauvinism" in its own ranks. He was added to the Central Committee in 1931 and put in charge of Negro work. In 1934 he became national secretary of the LSNR and joined the Politburo. Shortly afterward, however, his Party career began a downward trajectory. He was assigned to Chicago as Southside organizer and chairman of the Cook County Party, where his rigid policies helped drive novelist Richard Wright out of the Party. Meanwhile, the Party's decision to downplay the issue of self-determination for the sake of the Popular Front dismayed Haywood.

In the winter of 1937 he served in Spain as an adjunct political commissar with the International Brigades. Even though he was the only member of the Party Politburo there, Haywood was given few responsibilities and was sent home amid charges of cowardice after six months. His standing eroded, he was removed from the Politburo and Central Committee in 1938. In 1939 he directed Party Negro work in Maryland but was removed within a year. A heart attack followed, and he moved to Los Angeles and rank-and-file Party work.

Haywood enlisted in the merchant marine in 1943 and served as a messman and pantryman. Following Earl Browder's (q.v.) ouster as Party leader in 1945, he hoped to return to favor, but he was rebuffed. He did publish *Negro Liberation* in 1948, thanks to a subsidy by Paul Robeson and the Party's renewed commitment to self-determination. By 1949, however, Haywood was once again out of favor, and he remained critical of Party policies through the 1950s. In 1956 he even criticized William Foster (q.v.) and Ben Davis (q.v.) for being opposed to self-determination and being "right wing." He joined the insurgent Provisional Organizing Committee for a Communist Party and was elected its co-chairman in 1958. The group expelled him that same year, and he was also expelled from the Communist Party in 1959.

Haywood lived in Mexico City from 1959 to 1963. In the 1970s he turned up as a leading figure in the Communist Party (Marxist-Leninist), headed by Michael Klonsky, which supported the Deng Xiaoping government in China. The group also called for self-determination for blacks in the Black Belt. It disbanded in 1982. Haywood died in 1985.

SOURCE: Harry Haywood, *Black Bolshevik* (1978).

*HARVEY KLEHR*

**HAYWOOD, WILLIAM D. (1869–1928).** William D. ("Big Bill") Haywood was the symbol and personification of Western radicalism and industrial unionism between the turn of the century and the end of World War I. His talents for plain speaking and sound organization were evident in his years as an official in both the Western Federation of Miners and the Industrial Workers of the World. He served as an articulate spokesman for socialism, favoring action based in the workplace rather than the polling place. He ended his career in the American labor and radical movements by escaping to the Soviet Union during the post-war Red Scare in the United States.

William Richard Haywood was born on February 4, 1869, in Salt Lake City, Utah. Named for his father and his uncle Richard, the younger Haywood would later adopt his father's middle name, Dudley. Haywood's father was a miner who married the daughter of his boardinghouse landlady. While the elder Haywood could trace his family history back to Colonial America, his wife was a recent immigrant from South Africa. A whittling accident when Haywood was 9 took the sight from his right eye. Rumors that the eye had been lost in a mine mishap or in a fight with strikebreakers added to Big Bill's Wild West image. Haywood quit public school at the age of 12 to start work, and left home three years later in 1883 to become a miner.

For his first mining job, Haywood traveled to the remote Ohio mine in northeastern Nevada. Bill used the time off the job to continue his education through reading and in the bunkhouse discussions of politics and economics. After three years of mining, he stayed on as a watchman at the mine to be close to Nevada Jane Minor, the daughter of a local rancher. The couple wed on October 24, 1889. Nevada Jane was afflicted with a severe case of rheumatoid arthritis that kept her bedridden or in a wheelchair much of her life. The apparent contradictions between her interest in the healing possibilities of the Christian Science teachings of Mary Baker Eddy and Bill's hard-drinking, hard-fighting lifestyle drove the couple apart in later years. Though the two were never formally divorced, they lived the majority of their time apart after 1910. The marriage produced two daughters, Vernie (b. 1890) and Henrietta (b. 1897). Nevada Jane preceded her husband in death in 1920.

After an unsuccessful attempt at becoming a cowboy, the newly married Haywood homesteaded land at the U.S. Army's abandoned Fort McDermitt in northern Nevada. When the army reclaimed the land, Haywood joined the thousands unemployed in the wake of the 1893 depression. He moved through a number of temporary jobs before he finally found stable employment in the mines of Silver City, Idaho. In August 1896 Bill became a charter member of Local 66 of the Western Federation of Miners (WFM) in Silver City. Started three years earlier, the WFM represented metal miners and smeltermen through the Western states. Organized industrially, the union brought all workers connected to the mines together in one union regardless of their craft. Haywood joined the Silver City local and quickly rose to the post of financial secretary and from there into Local 66's presidency. Big Bill's rise to national prominence in the WFM was also meteoric. He was elected as a delegate to the 1898 WFM convention, took a seat on the union's national executive board, and finally was elected to the WFM's number-two post, secretary-treasurer, in 1901. At this time Haywood shared the leadership of the WFM with the more conservative president of the union, Charles P. Moyer. Haywood's first years in national union office were punctuated by a series of strikes in the Rocky Mountain mining camps of Telluride, Cripple Creek, and Silver City, among others, in which he somewhat eclipsed Moyer as the leader of the WFM. Haywood's creative direction of tactics and publicity, along with his charismatic presence, dominated the intense and often violent conflicts.

Terming it the ''continental congress of the working class,'' Haywood chaired the founding convention of the Industrial Workers of the World (IWW) in June 1905. The IWW was founded with great support from Haywood and the WFM to champion industrial unionism against the narrow craft unionism of the American Federation of Labor. The new union was dedicated to the proposition that all workers must struggle together against the bosses and owners, with whom they have nothing in common, until one side was defeated. Many of the political leaders attending the convention, most notably Daniel DeLeon (q.v.) of the Socialist Labor Party, wanted the IWW to affiliate with their parties. Haywood was a strong advocate of nonaffiliation, the policy that carried the convention. Big Bill was nominated to the IWW's presidency at the founding, but he declined the office.

The bombing death of Frank Steunenberg on December 30, 1905, set off a chain of events that catapulted Haywood into the national spotlight and made him a cause célèbre. The arrest of drifter Harry Orchard, an ex-WFM member, sparked rumors that the union was behind the murder of the former governor, who had opposed the WFM in its drive to organize Idaho's mining camps. These rumors turned into charges against Haywood, Moyer, and former WFM member

George Pettibone when Orchard compiled a massive "confession" implicating them. Outside of Idaho jurisdiction, the trio were kidnapped in a plan worked out between Idaho and Colorado state officials and the Pinkerton chief, James McParland, who had engineered Orchard's story. The kidnapping produced national outrage. Angered by their state's complicity in the case, Colorado Socialists ran Haywood for governor in 1906, and he received over 16,000 votes. After fifteen months in jail, Haywood became the first to stand trial in May 1907. On July 28 the jury found Haywood innocent, after an extremely spirited trial including Orchard's monumental but contradictory testimony, which linked him to the present crime as well as to numerous other murders and acts of sabotage as a tool of the WFM leadership. Though vindicated and acclaimed, Haywood lost his power base in the WFM during the Idaho ordeal. Moyer's conservatism led the WFM to withdraw from the IWW in 1908, and Haywood was fired from his job as a union representative with the backing of younger WFM officials who viewed the colorful Haywood as a liability.

Though his career in the WFM virtually ended with the Idaho acquittal, Haywood's stature in Socialist circles grew with the trial and his subsequent tours on the fund-raising lecture circuit. Haywood was a forceful and articulate speaker who wooed audiences with simple examples and apt metaphors. To many of his Socialist party contemporaries, Big Bill was everything they were not: an American-born radical at home in the working class whose power they wanted so badly to tap. In his four short years of involvement as a major figure in the Socialist Party (SP), Haywood was a frequent and popular speaker on party podiums, served on the national executive board, and traveled as a party delegate to the 1910 Second International meetings in Copenhagen. In December 1911 Haywood made an angry speech condemning evolutionary Socialist political action as overly cautious and slow. To the Socialists having success as candidates in state and local elections, Haywood's denunciation came in the midst of victory. Though he retracted his remarks, various Socialist groups early in 1912 began to press for Haywood's removal from the national party board. In this conflict Haywood was simply the symbol of the IWW, which had turned totally away from political action, calling in their 1908 convention for a strictly workplace-based socialism. The SP's move to distance itself from the IWW's direct-action philosophy came to a climax at the 1912 national SP convention in Indianapolis. At the convention a proposed bylaw change that called for the expulsion of any member opposing political action or advocating the use of sabotage or other violent means of economic change was introduced. After long and bitter debate, the new bylaw, a thinly veiled attack on the IWW, was passed. Under its provisions, its most important intended victim, Haywood, was removed from the party board in a 1913 mail vote of SP members.

The conflict in the Socialist Party over the IWW came at a time of great success for the radical union. The IWW won an impressive victory for the woolen workers of Lawrence, Massachusetts, in their long 1912 strike. The IWW had taken control of the strike at the request of its local leaders, and Haywood was one of the IWW luminaries who took a late but leading role. The success of the Lawrence strike led Haywood and the IWW to embrace a similar strike involving silk workers in Paterson, New Jersey, in 1913. During the ultimately unsuccessful Paterson strike, Haywood spent much of his time fund-raising across the Hudson among the artists and writers of Greenwich Village. New York's bohemians welcomed the Stetson-topped Haywood, who became a mainstay in the salons of such cultural leaders as Mabel Dodge Luhan. Haywood was one of the main speakers in the financially disastrous Paterson pageant organized by John Reed (q.v.) and other Greenwich Village strike supporters.

Haywood was elected secretary-treasurer of the IWW at the union's 1914 convention. In this new role, he took pains to clean up the union's badly organized finances and threw himself into efficient and sound office management. Big Bill supported the union's new efforts starting with the convention to organize the migratory Western lumberjacks and farmworkers who were to become the backbone of the IWW in the next five years.

World War I and the suppression of radicals that accompanied it and lingered in its wake signaled the virtual end of the IWW and of Haywood's involvement in the U.S. labor movement. Based on the belief that workers could not fight in a class war and in nationalistic contests, the IWW had pressed American workers to fight their real enemies, capitalism and imperialism, during the buildup that preceded the U.S. entrance into the European conflict. Viewing the situation with growing foreboding, Haywood feared that continued vocal opposition to the war would not be tolerated, and he pulled back IWW propaganda that opposed U.S. involvement. Though Haywood was successful in containing IWW radicalism, his actions did not stop the suppression that finally came on September 5, 1917, when federal agents launched a coordinated attack on IWW halls and offices around the nation. Arrested at the Chicago headquarters, Haywood was charged along with 165 other IWW members and officials with obstructing the war effort. The massive trial of *United States v. William D. Haywood et al.* ended on August 17, 1918, with guilty verdicts for all defendants in the four-month trial. The harshness of the sentences surprised all the IWW defendants, including the nearly 50-year-old Haywood. Sentenced to twenty years in Leavenworth prison, Big Bill spent nearly a year in jail before he was released on appeal bond late in July 1919. Haywood was rearrested by federal agents early in 1920 as part of the government's attempt to stop the spread of Russian-style revolution and Communism. Haywood was charged with criminal syndicalism and conspiracy to overthrow the government, but was released on bond to continue his fund-raising on behalf of the other IWW defendants.

Haywood was slow to support the Russian Revolution, that had stimulated the newest round of federal charges. Cautious at first about the political leadership of the new Soviet Union, Haywood ultimately became its advocate when the IWW was considering affiliation with the Communist Red International of Labor Unions. Haywood's position lost when the IWW board voted against affiliation in 1920. Haywood became interested further in the new Soviet state when Russian agents approached him, along with other IWW leaders, with offers to help him escape and of asylum. With little chance of a Supreme Court reversal of the lower-court convictions, Haywood skipped bail aboard a steamer bound for Stockholm and Russia on March 3, 1921. One month after his exodus, the Supreme Court ruled against the IWW and ordered all defendants, including Haywood, back to jail. Haywood's escape left over $50,000 in bail money forfeited. It was never repaid, as promised, by the Communists.

Haywood found himself somewhat isolated in his newly adopted home and lacked a clear purpose or project until late 1921, when he started work on the Kusbas colony, an industrial colony that Haywood and co-workers set up in Siberia, to which American workers would bring their labor and technical know-how. Haywood's connection with the colony ended when conflicts forced him to leave the board of the project in 1923.

Haywood married a second time in 1926. A Russian woman who spoke little English, Haywood's wife stayed with her badly disillusioned husband until his death on May 18, 1928. Though Haywood dreamed of spending his last days in the United States, he died in Russia from a series of strokes. Big Bill Haywood was cremated; half his ashes are buried in Chicago and half in Moscow. The release and publication of his autobiography, *Bill Haywood's Book*, by the Communist Party after his death met with questions about the book's authenticity and authorship.

SOURCES: Peter Carlson, *Roughneck: The Life and Times of Big Bill Haywood* (1983); Melvyn Dubofsky, *We Shall Be All* (1969); William D. Haywood, *Bill Haywood's Book* (1929).

*JOHN P. BECK*


**HEALEY, DOROTHY RAY (b. 1914).** Dorothy Ray Healey, post-war leader of the Southern California Communist Party and lifetime political activist, was born in Denver, Colorado, on September 22, 1914. Her mother was a Russian-born Jew and a founding member of the American Communist Party. Growing up in Oakland, California, Healey was recruited into the Young Communist League (YCL) in 1928 and experienced her first arrest at a May Day demonstration in 1930. A year later, at age 16, she dropped out of high school to work as a union organizer. Healey was active in three agricultural strikes in 1933–1934. In the third and most violent of these, involving Mexican lettuce workers in the Imperial Valley, she was arrested and spent six months in jail.

Healey later worked for the United Cannery, Agricultural, Packing, and Allied Workers of America (an affiliate of the Congress of Industrial Organizations). She remained in Los Angeles to become county organizer for Labor's Non-Partisan League. In 1940 she was appointed a state deputy labor commissioner in the liberal Democratic administration of Governor Culbert Olson. Only the second woman ever to hold the position, Healey was then ''on leave'' from the Communist Party (CPUSA).

In 1941 she was called before the California Un-American Activities Committee and testified at length on her past Communist Party organization work in agriculture. Despite the ensuing attacks on her by the press, she remained with the labor commission until 1943, when she returned to Los Angeles to become international representative of the left-wing local of the Mine, Mill, and Smelter Workers Union (MMSWU).

Healey was an early opponent within the Party of Earl Browder's (q.v.) "Teheran" line and his subsequent conversion of the Party into the Communist Political Association. She also began to question the CPUSA's ultra-patriotic "no strike" pledge within Communist trade union circles. Although she did not make her opposition to Browder's policies open, Healey benefited from her early questioning of the dissolution of the CPUSA and in 1945 became the compromise candidate for organizational secretary of the Los Angeles Communist Party. In the following two decades she established herself as the leading Communist functionary in Southern California.

Although frequently dissatisfied with and critical of the undemocratic methods of the CPUSA leadership in New York, Healey remained loyal to the Party during the numerous crises of the post-war years. However, the Los Angeles Party did demonstrate an unusual degree of flexibility in its day-to-day functioning, and in fact increased its membership from 3,200 in 1945 to 5,000 in 1948. The Party also maintained its leadership role in the Los Angeles Congress of Industrial Unions until the CPUSA's decision to support the Progressive Party against Truman in 1948. Increasingly critical of the Party's misuse of "democratic centralism," Healey and other Los Angeles Communist leaders privately campaigned in upper Party circles against the CPUSA's decision to oppose Helen Gahagan Douglas in her unsuccessful campaign against Richard Nixon in 1950.

In 1950 Healey, together with Party leaders throughout the nation, went underground and was promoted to acting chairman of the Los Angeles Party. She surrendered to face trial under the Smith Act in 1951. Healey and her fellow defendants, together with their attorneys, initiated a plan to use the First Amendment as their prime defense strategy, an approach that was strongly opposed by some Party leaders. In addition, Healey and several other defendants began to privately question the CPUSA's "Five to Midnight" line, which predicted the imminent rise of fascism in the United States.

Although sentenced in 1952 to five years in prison, Healey and other California leaders served only a few months. In 1957 the Supreme Court threw out their convictions in a landmark case that gutted the Smith Act. During these critical years, the Los Angeles Communist Party, unlike many other local parties, continued to function relatively normally, and in the mid 1950s it played an important role in the struggle against residential segregation and institutionalized racism in the city.

During the ideological debates that followed the Khrushchev speech of 1956, Healey opposed the "orthodoxy" of William Foster (q.v.), the "revisionism" of John Gates (q.v.), and the "centrism" of Eugene Dennis (q.v.), advocating instead a democratization of the Party that would allow differing points of view to coexist. Despite the Party's failure to distance itself from the Soviet Union and to democratize its decision-making process, Healey remained in the CPUSA, focusing her energies on Southern California. In the early 1960s she became increasingly well known, speaking frequently on college campuses and, from 1959 on, conducting her own weekly radio program.

Unlike other local Communist parties, the Southern California district played an influential role in the burgeoning anti-war and black radical movements of the mid- and late 1960s. Such independent activities led to increasing friction between Healey and the national leadership of the CPUSA, and in 1969, having taken a critical stand on the Soviet invasion of Czechoslovakia, she declined to stand for reelection to the CPUSA National Committee or the Southern California Party leadership. However, she remained in the Party as a protagonist of Party renewal and change until her resignation in 1973. In the late 1970s Healey became a leading figure in the New American Movement (NAM), gradually assuming the status of the elder stateswoman of the California Left. Despite her self-description as a "Communist," she supported the merger of the NAM with the Democratic Socialist Organizing Committee, and in 1982 she was elected a vice-president of the newly formed Democratic Socialists of America.

SOURCES: Dorothy Ray Healey, *Freedom's Chains Have Bound Us*, UCLA Oral History (1982); *Los Angeles Times*, June 6, 1983; Jon Wiener, "The Communist Party Today and Yesterday: An Interview with Dorothy Healey," *Radical America* 2 (May-June 1977).

*MICHAEL FURMANOVSKY*

**HEATH, FREDERIC F. (1864–1954).** Frederic F. Heath, a founder and first chairman of the Social Democratic Party, was a Socialist official in Milwaukee government for forty-two years. Born in Milwaukee of Yankee parentage in 1864, Heath was educated in that city. He became a wood engraver and worked at that trade for several years. It was while working as an engraver that he discovered he had artistic ability, so during the 1880s he turned his skill to sketching and photography. Between 1888 and 1928 he worked on Milwaukee newspapers—the *Journal*, *Sentinel*, and *Leader*—as a reporter, columnist, and artist. He was on the staff of the *Leader* at the time of its demise.

Heath was a member of the Socialist wing of the Populist movement in Milwaukee during the 1890s. When that wing split off to form the Social Democracy in 1897, Heath was one of the leaders of the move. Because he was of native American stock in a party dominated by Germans, Heath soon rose to a position of leadership in the party. He was also a talented speaker and writer for the Socialist cause.

In 1898 the Social Democracy of America, with which the Milwaukee organization affiliated immediately after its formation, split over the issue of political action. Heath was, with Eugene Debs (q.v.) and Victor Berger (q.v.), in the leadership of the political action group. They formed the Social Democratic

Party. The quasi-official party book, *The Social Democracy Red Book* (1900), was edited by Heath, and he was the party's first national chairman. He was also editor of the party organ, the *Social-Democratic Herald*.

Heath was a moderate Socialist. During the 1898 meeting at which the Social Democratic Party was formed, Heath proposed platform planks, developed by Berger and himself, which were to become the basis for all future "immediate demands" (ameliorative proposals) in Socialist platforms. The platform called for social insurance, minimum pay, maximum hours, political equality for women, international arbitration to replace war, and the initiative and referendum. A strong supporter of the trade union movement and an opponent of dual unionism, Heath was strongly critical of the organization of the Industrial Workers of the World in 1905. His stand infuriated Debs, who charged, incorrectly, that Heath had never worked for a living.

In 1904 Heath was elected to the Milwaukee board of aldermen; he served for two years. In 1909 he was elected to the board of school directors, a post he resigned the next year to become a member of the Milwaukee County board of supervisors. He was reelected for the next 38 years, retiring at the age of 74.

Heath helped organize the Milwaukee County Historical Society in 1935 and served as its first president from 1937 until 1951. He died in 1954 at the age of 89.

SOURCES: *Dictionary of Wisconsin Biography* (1960); Ray Ginger, *The Bending Cross* (1949); Davis A. Shannon, *The Socialist Party of America* (1955).

*JAMES INGBRETSON*

**HENDERSON, DONALD (1902-?).** Donald Henderson joined the Communist Party in 1931 and was soon a key figure in several front groups. He was president of the United Cannery, Agricultural, Packing, and Allied Workers of America (UCAPAWA) from 1937 to 1949. Henderson was born in New York City in 1902, the son of a dairy farmer. By the mid–1920s he had gotten his bachelor's and master's degrees from Columbia University, and in 1926 he began work on a doctorate while serving as an instructor in economics.

In 1932 Henderson became executive secretary of the National Student League after resigning from the League for Industrial Democracy, and a little later he became executive director of the American Committee for the Struggle Against War. His wife was Communist Party candidate for Congress in 1932. Both served on the boards of several other Party organizations. After several warnings from Rexford Tugwell about lack of progress toward his degree, Columbia University terminated his employment in 1933, despite protests by student radicals.

The following year Henderson organized the Committee for the Unity of Agricultural and Rural Workers. With the advent of the Popular Front, he urged his scattered units to seek affiliation with the American Federation of Labor (AFL). By 1936 he claimed seventy-two locals and sought a charter at the AFL convention in December. His plea was lost in the battle between John L. Lewis and his opponents.

During the spring of 1937, Henderson shifted his allegiance to the new Congress of Industrial Organizations (CIO). In July he got a charter for the UCAPAWA, which included the Southern Tenant Farmers Union (STFU). With a healthy subsidy from Lewis, Henderson began a nationwide organizing campaign and soon claimed well over 100,000 members. An angry dispute led the STFU to secede in 1939.

After a series of other defeats, Henderson dropped further organizing of field-workers in 1942. He concentrated on processing workers, and reorganized his union in 1946 as the Food, Tobacco, Agricultural, and Allied Workers (FTA). In the post-war period, his adherence to the Communist line and his support of Henry Wallace in 1948 became increasingly unpopular. The CIO convention, in November 1949, voted to investigate the FTA. It was expelled in March 1950. Henderson left union work, and his later days are obscure.

SOURCES: Lowell K. Dyson, *Red Harvest* (1982); Harvey Klehr, *The Heyday of American Communism* (1984); James Wechsler, *The Age of Suspicion* (1953).

*LOWELL K. DYSON*

**HERBERG, WILL (1909–1977).** Will Herberg had two careers, one as a Communist leader, the second as a leading Jewish theologian. Herberg was born in New York City on August 4, 1909. He received B.A., M.A., and Ph.D. degrees from Columbia University in 1928, 1930, and 1932 respectively. While still a college student in 1926, he joined the Communist Party. He was aligned with the leadership of Jay Lovestone (q.v.), and when the Lovestoneites were expelled from the Party on orders of the Stalinist leadership of the Communist International late in 1929, Herberg was one of those expelled. He subsequently became one of the principal leaders of the dissident Communist group led by Lovestone between 1929 and 1941.

During his years with the Lovestoneites, Herberg specialized in putting forth the ideological position of the group. After the defection of Benjamin Gitlow (q.v.) late in 1932, Herberg was generally recognized as the third most important figure in the Lovestoneite ranks, after Lovestone himself, and Bertram Wolfe (q.v.).

When the Lovestoneites began to move away from their general endorsement of Soviet internal and foreign policy after 1937, and even to question the basic tenets of Marxism-Leninism, Herberg was one of those who took a lead in this direction. His articles in *Workers Age* first raised the question as to whether the developments in the Soviet Union to which the Lovestoneites were opposed had their origin during the period in which Lenin had been the Soviet leader, rather than during the Stalinist period.

In 1935, through his connections with the Lovestoneite group, Herberg was named educational director of the International Ladies Garment Workers Union. He continued to hold that position until 1948. Between 1948 and 1955, Herberg was a free-lance lecturer and writer. Meanwhile, he had become reconverted to Judaism, the religion in which he had been raised. He became one of the most important Jewish theologians of the post–World War II period and published a number of books setting forth his ideas in that field, including *Judaism and Modern Man* (1951), *The Writings of Martin Buber* (1956), *Four Existentialist Theologians* (1958), *Protestant–Catholic–Jew* (1960), and *Community, State, and Church* (1960). He also was an editor of the conservative *National Review*.

From 1955 until his death on March 27, 1977, Herberg was a professor at Drew University in Madison, New Jersey.

*ROBERT ALEXANDER*


**HERNDON, ANGELO (b. 1913).** Angelo Herndon (Eugene Braxton) was an organizer for the Unemployed Councils, a Communist youth leader, and the famous defendant in a controversial political trial in Georgia during the 1930s. He was born on May 6, 1913, in southern Ohio, the son of a coal miner. Raised in poverty, he left school at an early age and worked as a miner and manual laborer in Kentucky and Alabama. During the summer of 1930 he joined the Communist Party in Birmingham, Alabama, and later moved to Atlanta, Georgia, to form a chapter of the Unemployed Councils.

In June 1932 the 19-year-old Herndon successfully organized a large, interracial demonstration demanding resumption of relief payments to Atlanta's jobless workers. Soon thereafter the young black Communist was arrested and charged under an old Georgia statute with attempting to incite insurrection against the state, a capital offense. The International Labor Defense (ILD), a Communist-influenced legal defense organization, came to his aid and hired two black attorneys, Benjamin J. Davis, Jr. (q.v.), and John Geer, to defend him.

In January 1933 Herndon was convicted and sentenced to eighteen to twenty years in prison at a dramatic trial marked by the prosecution's impassioned pleas to white supremacy and anti-communism. During the next two years the ILD publicized the affair widely and made it into a national cause célèbre symbolizing Southern injustice toward blacks. Although the U.S. Supreme Court initially declined to review the case, it eventually agreed to hear an appeal. On April 26, 1937, the Court overturned the conviction and ruled that the Georgia insurrection law, as applied and construed, was unconstitutional because it unduly restricted free speech (*Herndon v. Lowry*).

The widespread publicity surrounding the legal proceedings and publication of his autobiography in early 1937 briefly made Herndon a minor celebrity. Settling in New York City, he worked on various Communist projects, occasionally wrote articles for the *Daily Worker*, and served as national vice-president of the Young Communist League. During the early 1940s Herndon helped edit a small literary journal, the *Negro Quarterly*. Toward the end of World War II he became disenchanted with communism and left the party, eventually moving to the Midwest, where he abstained from further political activities.

SOURCES: Angelo Herndon, *Let Me Live* (1969); Charles H. Martin, *The Angelo Herndon Case and Southern Justice* (1976).

*CHARLES MARTIN*

**HICKS, GRANVILLE (1901–1982).** Granville Hicks was a leading Marxist cultural critic in the 1930s, a prominent figure in the Communist Party's cultural work, and later an active anti-Communist. Hicks was born on September 9, 1901, in Exeter, New Hampshire. His father was superintendent of a small factory, and the family was Unitarian. Hicks graduated from Harvard University in 1923. He spent two years studying for the ministry in the Universalist Church at Harvard. He began teaching in the Bible Department at Smith College in 1925 when his labors on behalf of Sacco and Vanzetti (q.v.) first involved him in radical politics. He returned to Harvard in 1928 to do graduate work in English and began teaching at Rensselaer Polytechnic Institute in Troy, New York, in 1929. In the meantime he was becoming well known for his reviews in New York intellectual journals.

In 1931, along with his friends Newton Arvin and Robert Gorham Davis, Hicks began to study Marxism, convinced that the Depression revealed the failure of capitalism. Sympathetic to the Communist Party, he joined the League of Professional Groups for Foster (q.v.) and Ford (q.v.) in 1932, became active in the John Reed Clubs, and toured with a delegation from the National Committee for the Defense of Political Prisoners. A year after publication of his *Great Tradition* (1933), a Marxist interpretation of American literature, he became literary editor of *New Masses*.

Hicks formally joined the Communist Party in the winter of 1934–1935 in New York and quickly became the Party's leading cultural spokesman, presiding at the first congress of the League of American Writers that spring. He was fired by Rensselaer at the end of the year, ostensibly for economic reasons, occasioning a series of protests. Hicks remained a prolific author, producing a biography, *John Reed*, in 1936 and *I Like America* (1938) during the Popular Front days.

The Nazi-Soviet Pact in 1939 came as a great shock to him. He resigned from the Communist Party in a public letter and failed in an attempt to organize a group of left-wing intellectuals opposed to it. As the years passed, Hicks became increasingly anti-Communist. He appeared before the House Un-American Activities Committee in 1953 and named other academics whom he had known as Communists when he taught at Harvard in 1938–1939. He continued to write criticism for a variety of magazines, living in a farmhouse in Grafton, New York. He died on June 18, 1982.

SOURCES: Daniel Aaron, *Writers on the Left* (1961); Granville Hicks, *Part of the Truth* (1965) and *Where We Came Out* (1954).

*HARVEY KLEHR*


**HILL, JOE (1882–1915).** Joe Hill was the troubadour of the Industrial Workers of the World and the organization's most famous martyr. He was executed for a double holdup murder in Salt Lake City. Hill was born Joel Emmanuel Hoagland in Sweden in 1882. Little is known of his early life except that he had worked as a seaman aboard North Sea vessels and that he had studied English in a Swedish YMCA. At the age of 20 he came to the United States and changed his name first to Joe Hillstrom and then to Joe Hill. Why he changed his name twice is still a mystery, although it was common at that time for immigrants to "Americanize" their names.

Hill was a drifter who rarely held a job for more than a few days. Sometime around 1910 he joined the Industrial Workers of the World (IWW) in San Pedro, the seaport of Los Angeles. Although he was active in the IWW, Hill was barely known among the organization's rank-and-file membership. He was active in the San Diego free speech fight of 1912 and in the San Pedro dock strike within the next year. He was also involved in an effort to aid revolutionists in Baja California, Mexico.

In 1913 Hill went to work in a copper mine in Utah. He attempted to organize the other miners there into an IWW union, but he was not an official organizer for the "Wobblies," the name by which IWW members were known. He would later claim that his arrest and conviction were revenge by the mine owners for his work in organizing the mine workers.

In January 1914 two masked men held up a grocery store in Salt Lake City. In the course of the holdup the robbers shot and killed the grocer and his son. Before he died, the son shot and apparently wounded one of the robbers. Two hours later Hill visited a physician, who treated him for a bullet wound. The physician reported him to the police, and Hill was arrested in his room late at night.

Hill was known to the leadership of the IWW largely as a writer of songs that were extremely popular among radicals generally, although he was personally virtually unknown to them. (Twenty-one of his songs are reprinted in Joyce L. Kornbluh's *Rebel Voices* [Michigan University Press, 1964], pp. 127–149). He also wrote a few articles for pro-IWW journals.

The Wobbly leaders were convinced that their bard had been framed, and they decided to make his arrest and later conviction a cause célèbre. During the trial the fact that Hill had been shot became a crucial item in the prosecution's case. Hill testified that he had been shot in a quarrel over a married woman with whom he had been having an affair and that for reasons of chivalry he would not divulge her name. After a perfunctory trial, the court found him guilty and he was condemned to death. Pleas to spare Hill's life came from many of the nation's leaders, including President Woodrow Wilson, Samuel Gompers, president of the American Federation of Labor, and Virginia Snow Stephens, daughter of the president of the Mormon Church, the major religious and political power in Utah; the Swedish ambassador also intervened. But all was to no avail. The governor of Utah and the state Board of Pardons refused to take any action. On November 19, 1915, twenty-one months after the crime, Hill was executed by firing squad.

His last message, a telegram to IWW leader William ("Big Bill") Haywood (q.v.), concluded: "Don't waste any time in mourning. Organize!" His ashes were buried next to the Haymarket martyrs in the Waldheim Cemetery in Chicago.

SOURCES: Vernon Jensen, "The Legend of Joe Hill," *Industrial and Labor Relations Review* 4 (April 1951); Joyce L. Kornbluh (ed.), *Rebel Voices* (1964); James O. Morris,

"The Joe Hill Case" (M.A. thesis, University of Michigan, 1951); Wallace Stegner, "Joe Hill: The Wobblies' Troubadour," *New Republic* 118 (January 5, 1948).

*LILLIAN KIRTZMAN JOHNPOLL*

**HILLQUIT, MORRIS (1869–1933).** Morris Hillquit was the leading theoretician of the American Socialist Party from its organization in 1901 until his death in 1933. Hillquit was born Morris Hillkowitz in Riga, in Russian-ruled Latvia, of assimilated Jewish parents in 1869. He was educated at a Russian gymnasium, one of the few Jewish students admitted to the school. Because of economic difficulties, Hillquit's father, Benjamin Hillkowitz, came to the United States with Morris' older brother Philip in 1885. Two years later, Hillquit came to New York, in steerage, with his mother and the rest of his family. They settled in the Jewish ghetto in the Lower East Side of the city. Young Morris went to work in the garment industry almost immediately.

Morris also became active among the Russian-Jewish intellectuals of the Lower East Side. Converted to socialism while still a student in Riga, Hillquit joined a Russian-speaking, mainly Jewish branch of the Socialist Labor Party (SLP) in 1887 (the SLP was primarily composed of foreign-language branches at that time; there was no English-speaking section of the party in New York in 1887).

Almost immediately Hillquit became a leading party activist. He helped organize the United Hebrew Trades, a federation of Jewish labor unions in New York City, and helped found new trade unions among Jewish working people of the city. He believed that unions were instrumental in developing a Socialist movement because they educated the workers about socialism. When the unions brought about an improvement in the conditions of labor workers, they would be better able to organize a new social order—socialism.

In 1890 Hillquit was named manager of the new Yiddish-language Socialist newspaper, *Arbeiter Zeitung* (Workers Newspaper). He remained on that job while he studied at the law school of New York University. He graduated in 1893 and passed the New York State bar examination that same year. His first clients were mainly workers injured on the job who sued for lost earnings.

Daniel DeLeon (q.v.) had joined the SLP shortly after Hillquit. He proceeded to reshape the party in his own image. An acerbic, dictatorial, basically dishonest man, DeLeon used invective to force anyone who disagreed with him out of the party. He immediately caused dissension in the SLP. Hillquit, who was studying law at the time, was not involved in the feuding of the period. The majority of Jewish Socialists refused to accept DeLeon's dictates about the organization of a Yiddish daily, and in 1895 they bolted the party and began organizing their own daily under the leadership of Abraham Cahan (q.v.) and Meyer London (q.v.). Although he disliked DeLeon, Hillquit remained in the party at that time.

However, a series of events between 1895 and 1899 forced Hillquit to formally break with the DeLeon SLP. First, DeLeon formed a new union federation in 1895–1896 called the Socialist Trades and Labor Alliance (STLA), which he pictured as a noncompeting organization to spread the ideas of socialism among union members. Then he turned the STLA into a dual union that declared war against the American Federation of Labor. In 1899 Hillquit (who had changed his name from Hillkowitz in 1897) led a split in the SLP in which a majority of the membership went into Hillquit's so-called Kangaroo SLP.

In 1900 the Hillquit faction of the SLP ran a joint ticket with the Social Democratic Party, formed in 1897 by Eugene Debs (q.v.) and Victor Berger (q.v.). A year later the Hillquit SLP united with the Social Democrats to form the Socialist Party of America. Hillquit, Debs, and Berger formed the triumvirate that led the new party. Within the party hierarchy, Hillquit normally took a so-called centrist position—considerably more revolutionary than Berger's moderate position, the so-called right-wing stance, and less rhetorically revolutionary than the quasi-syndicalist views of the party's left wing, of which Debs was considered a member.

Hillquit called the Socialist movement revolutionary because it favored the complete overthrow of the capitalist system. He declared that socialists were out to overthrow the entire capitalist system which he blamed for international wars, violence, profiteering and oppression. He doubted that the capitalist system could remain in power solely by legal, electoral means. Hillquit, who abhorred war all his life, declared in 1913 that the only battle in which the workers would be justified in taking up arms would be the struggle of the working class to free itself from economic exploitation and political oppression.

Hillquit opposed the 1905 formation of the Industrial Workers of the World, despite his antipathy toward the existing trade union federation. He did not believe that a dual union would serve any purpose except the disruption of the labor movement, both economic and political. What he did favor was organization of the unskilled working people by the existing unions. As the American Federation of Labor (AFL) was organized, he argued, skilled workers unions represented only a single group within the oppressed and exploited working class. Unions under the craft system, which dominated the AFL, thus created craft solidarity rather than the class solidarity that Hillquit considered essential for the liberation of the working class.

Even though he was opposed to the conservative trade union system, Hillquit was the target of considerable vituperation from the party's pre-war left wing. In 1909, for example, William English Walling (q.v.), intellectual leader of the party's syndicalist left wing, accused Hillquit of joining with John Spargo (q.v.) and Victor Berger, among others, in an attempt to form a national labor party that would absorb the Socialist Party. The charge was untrue—especially with regard to Hillquit, who had only six years previously fought his friend Job Harriman's (q.v.) attempt to have the California Socialist Party become absorbed into the United Labor Party of California.

Hillquit ran for Congress in 1906 in the heavily Jewish Lower East Side of New York City. In 1906, despite the support of many prominent Americans and of the popular Russian writer Maxim Gorki, who spoke for him, he lost the election. An examination of registration and voting records proved that his defeat was due to the large number of Jewish immigrants who had not yet become citizens. In 1908 Hillquit again polled a high vote, but again he lost, although he ran considerably ahead of the rest of the Socialist ticket.

He was active in 1907 in the defense of William Haywood (q.v.), George Pettibone, and Charles Moyer, militant Western labor leaders who were accused of murdering an ex-governor of Idaho. Four years later, however, he criticized Haywood, who was then president of the IWW, for advocating sabotage and violence. The disagreement between Hillquit and Haywood, at times exceedingly acrimonious, shook the Socialist Party from 1911 until 1913. Hillquit won the struggle when the 1912 Socialist convention voted to proclaim the party's rejection of sabotage. In 1913 Haywood was ousted from the National Executive Committee for continuing to preach sabotage.

During the 1912 election campaign the party was again shaken by an internal squabble. A Hillquit protégé, J. Mahlon Barnes, was named campaign manager even though he was opposed by the party's presidential candidate, Debs, and had been involved in a morals scandal and ousted as national secretary of the party the year before. Hillquit defended Barnes, who remained on the job until after the election. The Barnes affair demonstrated Hillquit's power within the party. That same year Hillquit suffered from his first attack of tuberculosis and was forced to spend a large part of the next year in Bermuda.

Between 1900 and 1913 Hillquit wrote two major works, which delineated his philosophy prior to World War I. The first, *The History of Socialism in the United States*, first published in 1903 and revised in 1910, indicated Hillquit's sympathy with the early Socialist and communitarian movements in the United States and demonstrated his Marxian outlook. He argued that before the latter part of the nineteenth century the United States had not been ready for a genuine Socialist movement. His second work, *Socialism in Theory and Practice*, published in 1912, was essentially an attempt to popularize Marx's ideas. Although it was greatly oversimplified, it served to introduce many Socialists to Marxism.

A major turning point in Hillquit's life came in 1914 with the outbreak of World War I. The war, he charged, was caused by European capitalism. He pleaded with his fellow Socialists in the United States and abroad to oppose the war. A month after the outbreak of hostilities, Hillquit composed an appeal "To the Socialist Workingmen of the Warring Countries of Europe," which was adopted by the Socialist National Executive Committee. The appeal called on the European Socialists to bring about the war's end by refusing to support it financially or politically.

Hillquit was soon sorely disappointed—and dismayed—by the actions of the German, French, Austrian, and British Socialists, a majority of whom formally backed their countries by voting in favor of military appropriations in parliaments or by proclaiming their support for the country's war actions. He denied the German Social Democrats' claim that their country represented culture, and he derided the British and French claim that their countries were fighting for democracy.

He explained the actions of the European Socialists by blaming their close ties with the trade unions. He denied that it was their attachment to parliamentarianism which was to blame for what he termed a betrayal of trust. Actually, he wrote, the Socialists in Parliament faithfully expressed the sentiments of their constituents. In countries where the unions and the Socialist parties were most closely linked, he observed, the Socialists invariably supported the war. In countries where the unions and the Socialists were distanced from each other, the party remained true to its Socialist opposition to war. In Germany, France, Austria, and Great Britain the links between party and union movement were too close, so the Socialist and Labour parties invariably supported the war. Even in such cases where individual members opposed the war, they were almost always intellectuals, for example, Kautsky, Bernstein, and Lederbour in Germany. After the United States entered the war, Hillquit's argument was reinforced, for in the United States the party and the American Federation of Labor were far removed. And in the United States, where the AFL leadership, especially Samuel Gompers, was the most avid jingo, the Socialists opposed the war and suffered persecution for their opposition.

Besides explaining the European "betrayal," Hillquit was active in attempting to end the war, especially between 1915 and 1917. In 1915 he helped formulate a plan, much like the Fourteen Points, which President Woodrow Wilson would enunciate more than a year later. The Socialist program called for no indemnifications, no annexation without support of the population of the area involved, no international court, a league of nations, neutral internationalized waterways, an extension of democracy, a solution to the economic causes of war, disarmament, and a referendum before a nation could be involved in an "aggressive" war. Late in 1915 Hillquit, Debs, and James H. Maurer (q.v.) met with Wilson, who assured them he was in agreement with most of their proposals, especially the no indemnities, and no annexation planks.

When in 1915 a German submarine sank the British liner *Lusitania* with a loss of 1,100 lives—128 of them American citizens—Hillquit joined Debs and other Socialists in condemning the German action. But Hillquit warned against allowing American revulsion at the torpedoing to lead the nation into the war. During the next year and a half, Hillquit helped organize the Emergency Peace Federation and the People's Council of America. The latter was fashioned after the pre-Bolshevik Russia soviets of workers, peasants and soldiers, which played a major role in the overthrow of the czar in April 1917. The Council counted among its members many liberals who opposed the war.

By early 1917, with the United States about to enter the war, the Socialist Party leadership appeared to be divided. Some favored strict neutrality, others wanted to join the Allied crusade, especially now that czarism had been abolished in Russia. To decide the party's position formally, an emergency convention was called for early April. It opened on the day after war had been declared. At the opening session, Hillquit delivered a rousing anti-war speech. He then joined Algernon Lee (q.v.) and Charles Ruthenberg (q.v.) in fashioning the defiant anti-war St. Louis Declaration, which was adopted by the convention 140 to 5, with 31 delegates supporting Louis Boudin's (q.v.) centrist proposal.

Hillquit was soon thereafter nominated by the New York City Socialist Party as its candidate for mayor. He and the other Socialist candidates ran as opponents of the war. Many prominent non-Socialists supported him. Although he was not elected, Hillquit polled a record 21.3 percent of the total vote. He helped elect ten Socialists to the New York State Assembly and seven members to the New York City board of aldermen.

But two events that year were responsible for tearing the party asunder. The first was the persecution of Socialists by federal and local governments under the Espionage Act. Socialist publications were closed or denied mailing privileges, even publications that did not overtly oppose the war. Other Socialist publications found themselves censored. Socialist leaders were arrested—Debs, Berger, and Adolph Germer (q.v.), among others. Hillquit helped prepare their defense. He also defended non-Socialist radicals, including the anarchist Alexander Berkman (q.v.).

The second event, the Bolshevik seizure of power in November 1917, had a longer, more far-reaching effect. Greeted by most Socialists with accolades, it soon turned out to be a catastrophe for the party. Hillquit headed the legal bureau of the Bolshevik government in the United States in the early days. He worked tirelessly for the success of the Soviet government's Bolshevik rule, but when a group of so-called left-wingers tried to split the party in 1918, Hillquit fought them. The left-wingers—a majority of whom were foreign-born and few of whom had bothered to become U.S. citizens—formed a party within the party. This "Left-Wing Section" of the Socialist Party, as it was called, held its own conventions, issued its own declaration of principles, opened its own office, elected its own officials, disrupted meetings, and attempted to seize the Socialist machinery by honest or dishonest means. Hillquit, who was then ill with an attack of tuberculosis, wrote an article in the New York *Call* (May 21, 1919) demanding a split in the party.

Let them [left-wingers] separate honestly, freely, and without rancor. Let each side work in its own way, and make such contributions to the Socialist movement in America as it can. Better a hundred times to have two numerically small Socialist movements, each homogenous and harmonious within itself, than to have one big party torn by dissensions and squabbles, an impotent colossus on feet of clay. The time for action is near. Let us clear the decks.

Four months later the party did split into three warring political movements. Within the Socialist Party, infighting continued. In 1920 the issue was which international the American Socialist Party should join—the Socialist (the Second International) or the Communist (the Third International). Hillquit favored joining neither. He opposed the Second International because of its failure to oppose the war, and he rejected the Third International because it was monolithic and controlled completely by the Russians. In opposing the Third International,

Hillquit argued that the methods by which a party gained power depended on conditions in a given nation and could not be dictated from abroad. According to Hillquit, each revolution develops its own methods, fashioning them from the elements of the inexorable necessities of the case.

During 1920 Hillquit also defended the five Socialist members of the New York State Assembly who were ousted by the Assembly leadership. His defense was assailed by the Communist wing because he did not use the platform to proclaim against capitalism and for socialism but instead defended the five assemblymen's right to their seats on constitutional grounds.

In 1921 Lenin specifically barred Hillquit from membership in any party that was admitted to the Third International. A small group of Socialists accepted Lenin's dictate and went over to the Communist Party. A larger group remained in the Socialist Party. But neither party amounted to much—their total membership was less than one-fourth what the Socialist Party membership had been in 1919.

By 1921 Hillquit had become disillusioned with the Soviet Union. Two years later he wrote *From Marx to Lenin*, in which he opposed Leninism on Marxian theoretical grounds. His final break with the Russian brand of "socialism" came in 1928, when, in a discussion reported in the February 4, 1928 *New Leader*, he called the Soviet regime a failure and "the greatest disaster and calamity that has occurred to the Socialist movement."

The decline of the Socialist Party after World War I led Hillquit to reconsider his position on politics. From 1922 to 1925 he worked unceasingly for the organization of a labor party in the United States. Labor parties were on the rise in the United Kingdom, Australia, and New Zealand. Admittedly these were not Socialist parties in the Marxian sense, but there were major Socialist elements in the programs of each of the parties. In the United States a third party, fashioned to a considerable degree after the British Labour Party, was being organized. It was being formed from trade union and Progressive movements, including the Railroad Brotherhoods, the Amalgamated Clothing Workers of America, the International Ladies Garment Workers (of which Hillquit was general counsel from 1914 until his death in 1933), most of the Non-Partisan League, and pro-Socialist organizations. In 1922 Hillquit represented the Socialist Party at the Conference for Progressive Political Action (CPPA), which organized the new party. The CPPA also adopted a program that was generally fashioned after the immediate demands in the Socialist Party program.

In 1924 the CPPA nominated Robert LaFollette, a Progressive Wisconsin Republican, for President, and Burton Wheeler, a Progressive Montana Democrat for Vice-President. Despite his ambivalence about the candidates, Hillquit led the Socialist Party into the Progressive camp—arguing privately that the Socialists had no alternative, that they were too weak to field their own candidates. Moreover, he hoped that the LaFollette campaign would give birth to a genuine labor party in the United States. LaFollette polled 4,826,471 votes, almost 17 percent of all cast. But neither the LaFollette supporters nor most of the unions involved believed that a labor party was feasible at that time. So in 1925 the CPPA abandoned the Progressive Party, and the Socialists resumed their independent existence. In 1928, Hillquit led the campaign in the party to nominate Norman Thomas (q.v.) as Socialist candidate for U.S. President. The election was a disaster as far as vote totals were concerned, but it gave the Socialists a new leader and brought many educated young people into the party.

The Socialists continued to drift until the Great Depression created a near-revolutionary situation in the United States. Hillquit led the party drives in 1930, which saw major increases in the party's electoral strength. But many of the educated young members of the party who had joined after 1928 wanted more militant, new leadership. The result was new, intense inner-party squabbling from which the party never recovered.

Hillquit was the target of the militants' attack. In 1932, at age 63, he was national chairman of the party. He was also a foreign-born Jew and a New Yorker. There were strong anti-Semitic and nativist anti–New York feelings in some sections of the Socialist Party. William H. Henry, national secretary of the party, was so anti-Semitic that Norman Thomas insisted on his ouster in 1928. And Kate Richards O'Hare (q.v.), Socialist firebrand of the Prairies before the war, wrote in 1945 that she despised Hillquit because he was an Easterner—a New Yorker—born in Europe who had built the New York party "entirely on European concepts."

At the 1932 convention the anti-Semitic nativist wing of the party joined new young and educated militants in an effort to oust Hillquit as national chairman. There were others who opposed Hillquit as national chairman: Norman Thomas, who feared that Hillquit's Marxism would prevent the party from winning new American recruits; B. Charney Vladeck (q.v.), manager of the Jewish *Daily Forward*, who saw Hillquit as a basically parochial leader; and Daniel Hoan (q.v.), mayor of Milwaukee, who questioned Hillquit's ability. During the convention debate Hillquit answered his critics, telling them sarcastically that he "apologized for having been born abroad, being a Jew and living in New York, a very unpopular place." Hillquit was reelected national chairman.

During the 1932 election campaign, the mayor of New York, James J. Walker, was ousted for corruption that was first uncovered by two Socialists, Norman Thomas and Paul Blanshard (q.v.). In the election to fill that post, the Socialists nominated Hillquit. He polled 251,056 votes, despite ill-health. By 1933 the party that Hillquit had helped build was in the process of disintegrating as left-wing "Militants" battled the moderate "Old Guard," to which Hillquit belonged. That year too the German Social Democratic Party, which had been the model Hillquit hoped to emulate in the United States, was destroyed by Hitler, its leaders slain or forced to flee.

In October 1933, shortly after his autobiography, *Loose Leaves from a Busy Life*, appeared, Morris Hillquit died of tuberculosis.

SOURCES: Morris Hillquit, *Loose Leaves from a Busy Life* (1933); The Morris Hillquit Collection at Wisconsin State Historical Society, Madison, Wisconsin. New York State

Joint Legislative Committee Investigating Seditious Activity, *Revolutionary Radical-ism*, vols. 1 and 2 (1920); Socialist Party Papers at Duke University, Durham, North Carolina.

*BERNARD K. JOHNPOLL*

**HOAN, DANIEL WEBSTER (1881–1961).** Daniel Webster Hoan was the second Socialist mayor of Milwaukee, Wisconsin. He was born in suburban Milwaukee on March 12, 1881, the son of Daniel W. Hoan, Sr., and Margaret Augusta Hoan. While young Dan was still a boy, his father showed much sympathy for the labor movement. This spurred Dan's own political interests.

Hoan received a B.A. degree from the University of Wisconsin in Madison in 1905 and studied at Chicago Kent College of Law from 1905 to 1906. He set up his first law practice in Milwaukee in 1907 and in 1908 became an attorney for the Wisconsin State Federation of Labor. During his two years in the Federation's employ, he wrote and directed the implementation of the State Workmens Compensation Act, the first such piece of legislation to be passed in the United States.

During this time Hoan became active in the new Milwaukee Socialist Party. He was elected city attorney on the party's ticket in the Socialist landslide of 1910 and was reelected in 1912 and 1916. He developed a reputation as a city attorney who would not tolerate vice. In 1916 Hoan was persuaded to run for mayor and was elected, becoming the second Socialist to serve in that position. He was a fiery public speaker and soon became a popular local political figure. He was reelected mayor in 1918, 1920, 1924, 1928, 1932, and 1936, finally going down to defeat in 1940. Hoan was nominated to be the Socialist Party of America's national chairman in 1932; but he lost the election to Morris Hillquit (q.v.) of New York at the national convention.

While mayor, Hoan retired Milwaukee's municipal debt and put the city on a pay-as-you-go basis, established a local civil service system, instituted harbor improvements and a vast city park system, introduced competitive bidding on city contracts, established adult night schools, and created a branch-oriented public library system to serve the various city neighborhoods.

After his 1940 defeat in the mayoralty race, Hoan left the Socialist Party. He ran as a Democrat for governor, U.S. Senate, Congress, and, in 1948, mayor, but was unsuccessful in all these attempts. Although he was widely respected and retained much of his personal popularity, he was unable to translate it into votes at the ballot box. Mayor Frank P. Zeidler (q.v.) later appointed him to the city's harbor commission.

Hoan was the author of two books, *The Failure of Regulation* (1913) and *City Government* (1936). He died in Milwaukee on June 11, 1961, after being in poor health for a number of years.

*STEPHEN K. HAUSER*

**HOFFMAN, ABBIE (b. 1936).** Abbie Hoffman was one of the most prominent members of the counterculture during the 1960s. He was born into a Jewish family on November 30, 1936, in Worcester, Massachusetts and attended Brandeis University (B.A., 1959) and the University of California. In 1967 he came to national attention as the co-founder of the Youth International Party—the Yippies. Hoffman's activities to 1967 had been typically liberal; he wrote for left-wing journals and newspapers and participated in the civil rights movement in the South. In 1967, however, he opted for cultural politics and gained notoriety for his invasion of the New York Stock Exchange and his attempt to levitate the Pentagon during the October anti–Vietnam War demonstrations. His 1968 book, *Revolution for the Hell of It*, spelled out a doctrine of pointing out the absurdities of American life. In Chicago in 1968 the Yippies held a mock convention and nominated Mr. Pigasus, a pig, for U.S. President.

Hoffman was one of the defendants in the Chicago Eight trial of 1969 and was convicted of inciting to riot, but his conviction was overturned on appeal. In March 1974 Hoffman dropped from public view to avoid facing charges of selling cocaine to an undercover officer. For the next six years he was a celebrated fugitive who occasionally, through journalists, commented on the status of the movement. In 1975 he declared that it was time to end the emphasis on sex, love, and individuality; he described his new approach as more orthodox Communist. He resurfaced in September 1980, having spent many of the intervening years under the name Barry Freed living in Fineview in upstate New York. As Barry Freed, a concerned environmentalist, he appeared frequently on local television and testified at government hearings—once before a U.S. Senate subcommittee.

SOURCES: Abbie Hoffman, *Revolution for the Hell of It* (1968) and *Steal This Book* (1971).

*TOM WILLIAMS*


**HOLMES, JOHN HAYNES (1879–1964).** John Haynes Holmes was a leading pacifist, Socialist, and political reformer. He was born in Philadelphia of wealthy parents in 1879, educated at Harvard University (B.A., 1902) and Harvard Divinity School (bachelor of sacred theology, 1904), and was ordained a Unitarian minister in 1904. After serving for three years as minister of a Unitarian church in Dorchester, Massachusetts, he took over the pulpit of the liberal Unitarian Church of the Messiah in New York. He renamed it the Community Church, severed his denominational ties, and served this church for the next forty-two years.

While at the Community Church Holmes was an active advocate of democratic socialism, pacifism, liberal religion, and civic reform. One of the original signers of the call for the conference at which the National Association for the Advancement of Colored People (NAACP) was organized, he remained active in the NAACP almost all the rest of his life, serving as its vice-president for many years. He also helped found the American Civil Liberties Union in 1918.

Holmes was an outspoken opponent of ecclesiastical opulence. He roundly condemned the Protestant Episcopal Diocese of New York for building the huge Cathedral of St. John the Divine. He charged that "the tomb of marble" cost millions, while the Tuberculosis Society needed funds, child labor prevailed, "and so much remains to be done."

During World War I and World War II, Holmes was an opponent of U.S. intervention. Pro-Soviet during the Bolshevik regime's first eighteen years, Holmes turned anti-Soviet at the time of the purge trials of the 1930s. In 1935 he derided pro-Soviet liberals, remarking, "I am unwilling to condemn ghastly horrors in Nazi Germany, and denounce dreadful crimes in my own country, and then remain silent when I see these horrors and crimes, or even worse, being perpetrated in Russia."

Holmes was also active in the destruction of the corrupt Tammany political machine in New York. He, Paul Blanshard (q.v.), Rabbi Stephen S. Wise, and Norman Thomas (q.v.) organized the City Affairs Committee which in 1928–1932 exposed much of the corruption in the city and led to the ouster of Mayor James J. Walker and the end of Tammany rule.

Holmes' health failed him in the late 1950s. He died in New York City in April 1964.

SOURCES: John Haynes Holmes, *I Speak for Myself* (1955); Bernard K. Johnpoll, *Pacifist's Progress* (1970).

*BERNARD K. JOHNPOLL*

**HOOK, SIDNEY (b. 1902).** Sidney Hook was a leading American Marxist philosopher and writer throughout the 1930s. He helped rally support for the Communist Party in the early 1930s, became a radical critic of Stalinism in the mid–1930s, and late in the decade worked with the Socialist Party and wrote for its journals. Subsequently he broke with Marxism and moved to the Right.

Hook was born in 1902 in New York City to Jewish parents. One of John Dewey's students at Columbia University, Hook received his Ph.D. in 1927 with a dissertation embracing the scientific basis of pragmatism. He then traveled to Europe, studying briefly in Germany and at the Marx-Engels Institute in Moscow. He began teaching in the philosophy department at New York University, where he remained until his retirement in 1970.

Hook was a principal organizer of an effort to enlist the support of artists and writers for the 1932 Communist Party presidential campaign of William Z. Foster (q.v.) and James Ford (q.v.). The League of Professional Groups for Foster and Ford managed to gain the endorsement of a significant number of influential intellectuals. However, Hook did not join the Party, and he remained critical of its style and theoretical stance. He came to criticize the "third period" Communist analysis of fascism that equated social democracy with Hitlerism, and he argued in favor of "workers' democracy" against the consolidation of Stalin's rule in the Soviet Union.

In the mid–1930s Hook joined a number of notable left-wing intellectuals in an effort to organize an anti-Stalinist radical movement. With Louis Fraina (Lewis Corey; q.v.), V. F. Calverton (q.v.), James Burnham (q.v.), Louis Hacker, Meyer Shapiro, and A. J. Muste (q.v.), he helped found the American Workers Party, which led an independent existence for a few years before merging with the Trotskyists. Hook sharply denounced the Moscow purge trials and, along with Dewey, was active in the Commission of Inquiry that cleared Trotsky of Stalin's charges.

It was in his books and articles that Hook was most influential. Like his fellow Dewey student Max Eastman (q.v.), Hook sought a common ground for Marxism and pragmatism. Unlike Eastman, however, Hook tried to incorporate dialectical materialism into this fusion. In a series of lively though bitter articles in *Modern Monthly* in the early 1930s, Eastman and Hook presented their views. Hook refuted Eastman's charge that the Marxist dialectic left little room for human thought and activity. He felt that dogmatic, "orthodox" Marxists had developed a deterministic view that was alien to Marx. Consciousness and practice formed a single, inseparable continuum that was always in the process of adjusting to the level and nature of human input. Consequently, Hook's dialectic was open, free of any single goal or purpose. It was scientific and experimental, and consistent with Dewey's instrumentalism. Hook's most important Marxist works are *Towards the Understanding of Karl Marx* (1933) and *From Hegel to Marx* (1936). Few books by American Marxists in the 1930s stand up as well as these two studies. The influence of George Lukács and Karl Korsch is both evident and acknowledged in them.

Hook's disenchantment with communism, under the impact of the purge trials in the Soviet Union, led him into an open break with Marxism and socialism by 1940. In the early 1950s Hook argued that Communist party members were part of an international conspiracy and should therefore not be allowed to teach in American universities.

SOURCES: Cristiano Camporesi, "The Marxism of Sidney Hook," *Telos* 12 (Summer 1972); Richard H. Pells, *Radical Visions and American Dreams* (1973).

*JEFF BENEKE*

**HOOPES, DARLINGTON (b. 1896).** Darlington Hoopes was a leader of the Socialist Party in Reading, Pennsylvania, a Socialist member of the Pennsylvania House of Representatives, national chairman of the party, and Socialist candidate for U.S. President in 1952 and 1956. Hoopes was born on a farm in northeastern Maryland in 1896 and attended school in Maryland and Pennsylvania between 1902 and 1913. He studied at the University of Wisconsin, read law in Pennsylvania, and was admitted to the Pennsylvania bar in 1920. He practiced in Norristown, near Philadelphia, between 1921 and 1927, and in Reading, Pennsylvania, thereafter.

In 1914, while a student at the University of Wisconsin, Hoopes joined the Socialist Party. By 1928 he became a leader of the Reading (Pennsylvania) party and was elected as its candidate for state legislature in 1930. While a member of the State House of Representatives, Hoopes led the unsuccessful fight for ratification of the Child Labor Amendment to the U.S. Constitution. He was also a leader in the fight for unemployment insurance, and, with fellow Socialist representative Lilith Wilson (q.v.), for women's rights. The Association of Pennsylvania Newspaper Reporters voted him the outstanding state legislator in 1935.

The Socialist Reading party, led by Hoopes, withdrew from the national party in 1936 when the more radical wing, under Norman Thomas (q.v.), won control. Hoopes then became a member of the National Committee of the Social Democratic Federation (SDF), composed of Socialists who left the party at that time.

A Quaker and a pacifist, Hoopes objected to the pro-war, interventionist position that the SDF had accepted in 1940, and supported the anti-war isolationist posture of Thomas and the Socialist Party national organization. He led the Reading party back into the national group. In 1944 Hoopes was the Socialist candidate for U.S. Vice-President. During the 1940s he was also the Socialist candidate for district attorney in the Reading area, a judge of the court of common pleas, and a member of Congress. Among his other activities, Hoopes was also active in the struggle for racial equality. He served on the Community Race Relations Council in Reading, as chairman from 1944 to the 1970s. He was also on the State Council for a Fair Employment Practices Act and on the Pennsylvania Equal Rights Council.

In 1950 Hoopes and Norman Thomas found themselves again at opposite ends of an internal struggle for control of the Socialist Party nationally. Hoopes opposed a proposal by Thomas that the party announce it would no longer nominate candidates nationally but would instead become a purely educational organization, endorsing occasional non-Socialist candidates for public office. The national convention of the party that year backed Hoopes, who was elected to replace Thomas as national chairman.

Two years later Hoopes was the Socialist nominee for U.S. President, polling more than 40,000 votes in thirteen states. It is significant that Thomas and his followers gave minimal support to that campaign. During the next four years Hoopes attempted vainly to heal the rift in the party. In 1956 he was again nominated for U.S. President, but the internal party struggle had intensified and Hoopes polled only 2,192 votes nationally. That campaign spelled the end of the Socialist Party as a national electoral organization.

During the next decade Hoopes remained national chairman of the party, which was then in the process of disintegration. In the late 1960s and early 1970s, when the Socialist Party disintegrated into three small groups, Hoopes joined the most left wing of the groups—the Socialist Party USA.

He withdrew from active Socialist work in the late 1970s. In 1986 he was residing in Reading, Pennsylvania.

*BERNARD K. JOHNPOLL*

**HORTON, MYLES (b. 1905).** Myles Horton was a founder of Highlander Folk School, a center for labor-organizing and civil rights activities in the South, and its director for four decades. He was born on July 9, 1905, the eldest son of Perry and Elsie Fall Horton, former schoolteachers who made a living as sharecroppers after World War I. In 1924 Horton enrolled in Cumberland University in Lebanon, Tennessee, where he majored in literature and took active part in the Young Men's Christian Association (YMCA). During the summer of 1927 he organized vacation Bible schools for the Cumberland Presbyterian Church in the eastern mountain communities of Tennessee. Horton became deeply concerned about the failure of conventional religion and education to speak to the needs and experiences of poor mountain people. After graduating from Cumberland, Horton enrolled at Union Theological Seminary in New York in search of background and ideas for establishing an education program relevant to their lives.

Reinhold Niebuhr, Horton's mentor at Union Theological Seminary, took an active interest in Horton's plan for a school, as did fellow students John Thompson and James Dombrowski (q.v.), who would later join him in establishing Highlander. During 1930–1931, Horton studied at the University of Chicago and was a frequent visitor at Jane Addams' Hull House. He completed his training in Denmark, where he spent several months observing that nation's world-renowned system of folk schools. In 1932 Horton returned to Tennessee and, along with Don West, founded Highlander Folk School on Monteagle Mountain, north of Chattanooga.

At the peak of the Depression, Highlander provided a center for economically distressed people to meet, discuss their problems, and work collectively toward a solution. Horton believed that this was the key to effectively challenging the system of economic and racial exploitation in the South. Invigorated by the New Deal and the organizing drives of the Congress of Industrial Organizations (CIO), Highlander became a regional base for labor-organizing activities and training. Horton also participated in the Southern Conference for Human Welfare, an interracial organization dedicated to achieving economic and political democracy in the South. This fragile coalition of labor and reformers fragmented in the wake of the Cold War. Horton and the Highlander staff maintained their traditional nonexclusionary policy and refused to exclude Communists. After expelling the left-wing unions in 1949, the CIO severed relations with Highlander.

Early in the 1950s Highlander responded to the emerging civil rights movement by sponsoring citizenship education programs and annual workshops on desegregation for black leaders. Horton and the school continued to be harassed by Red-baiters and segregationists. In 1954 Horton was subpoenaed to testify before Senator James Eastland and the Senate Committee on Internal Security. Three years later a photograph of Martin Luther King, Jr., attending Highlander's twenty-fifth anniversary was publicized throughout the South with the caption "Martin Luther King at the Communist Training School." In 1961 the state of Tennessee confiscated Highlander's property after school officials were convicted of illegally selling alcohol and operating the school in violation of Tennessee segregation law. The property was sold at public auction.

Highlander relocated to Bays Mountain near Knoxville. During the 1970s its main focus turned to educational programs for community leaders in rural Appalachia and the Deep South. Although Horton passed along the directorship to younger staff, he has remained actively involved in the school.

SOURCES: Frank Adams, *Unearthing Seeds of Fire: The Ideal of Highlander* (1975); Anthony Dunbar, *Against the Grain: Southern Radicals and Prophets, 1929–1959* (1981).

*PAT SULLIVAN*

**HOWE, IRVING (b. 1920).** Irving Howe is one of America's leading literary critics, a vice-chairman in the Democratic Socialists of America (DSA), and a founder and co-editor of the influential Socialist journal *Dissent*. He was born on June 11, 1920, in New York City. His family migrated to the East Bronx Jewish community after the failure of his father's grocery business in 1930. His father found work as a garment presser; his mother became a sewing-machine operator. In 1934 Howe joined the Young People's Socialist League (YPSL), the youth arm of the Socialist Party. He was a soapboxer in the East Bronx during Norman Thomas' (q.v.) 1936 presidential campaign. That same year, he entered City College and, over the course of the next four years, emerged as a Socialist youth leader and organizer among the anti-Stalinist students.

In 1937 he fell under the spell of Max Shachtman (q.v.), a brilliant and charismatic Trotskyist. When the Trotskyists were expelled from the Socialist Party late in 1937, Howe reluctantly left with them. In January 1938 he entered the newly formed Socialist Workers Party (SWP). In 1940 Howe received his B.A. degree from City College. That year Shachtman and his supporters split from the SWP and founded their own party, the Workers Party (WP). At the age of 21, in 1941, Howe became the editor of the Workers Party official paper, *Labor Action*. In 1942 he was drafted into the army and stationed in Alaska. Unable to follow WP policy and make contact with "the masses," Howe read literature prodigiously. Returning from the army, he resumed the editorship of *Labor Action*. In 1946 he began to write literary criticism for "bourgeois" publications like *Commentary*, *Partisan Review*, *Nation*, and *New Republic*. Howe became a *Time* literary reviewer in 1948 and remained there for four years.

As the Workers Party faded in the late 1940s, Howe became less and less active. In March 1949 it downgraded its status to a mass propaganda group and renamed itself the Independent Socialist League (ISL). In 1949, with fellow Shachtmanite B. J. Widick, Howe published his first book, *The U.A.W. and Walter Reuther*. In 1953 Howe became an associate professor of English at Brandeis University. He resigned from the ISL that year, giving critical support to the U.S. war efforts in Korea, which Shachtman opposed. Howe immediately founded *Dissent* as a new vehicle for democratic Socialist expression. He published several works in the 1950s, the most important being *Politics and the Novel* (1957).

In 1963 Howe returned to New York as a professor of English at Hunter College of City University of New York. During the 1960s he was politically associated with the National Committee for a Sane Nuclear Policy (SANE) and the League for Industrial Democracy (LID). He frequently criticized the escalation of New Left radicalism in the pages of *Dissent* and in public addresses. In 1968 he became actively involved, for the first time since 1936, in electoral politics by backing Eugene McCarthy in the Democratic Party primaries.

Michael Harrington (q.v.) persuaded Howe to give organized Socialist politics one last chance in 1973. Howe joined Harrington's Democratic Socialist Organizing Committee (DSOC). Within DSOC, he served on the National Executive Committee during the 1970s, acting as a leader of the right wing, which strongly supported the State of Israel and work within the Democratic Party. In 1977 his widely acclaimed *World of Our Fathers* became a best-seller and it was awarded the National Book Award in History. He actively opposed the merger of the DSOC with the New Left anti-Leninist New American Movement (NAM). His Mainstream Caucus "extended their hands," but vowed to "retain the use of their feet" after the DSOC voted for merger in 1981. At the first political convention of the newly formed Democratic Socialist of America (DSA), in October 1983, Howe helped write a compromise resolution on Israel and was elected a vice-chairman.

SOURCE: Irving Howe, *A Margin of Hope: An Intellectual Autobiography* (1982).

*ROBERT FITRAKIS*

**HUDSON, ROY (1904–1982).** Roy Hudson, director of the Communist Party's trade union work in the late 1930s, was born on April 9, 1904, in Tonepah, Nevada. He was of Anglo-Saxon descent, but no information is available about his parents. After finishing eighth grade, Roy left home and became a seaman, serving in the navy from 1919 to 1923 and as a merchant sailor thereafter. Hudson joined the Communist Party around 1929 and soon became a Party organizer. He visited the Soviet Union in 1931. From 1932 to 1936 he was national secretary of the Marine Workers Industrial Union (MWIU), the Party's dual union for seamen.

Many of the MWIU organizers obtained key positions in the National Maritime Union (an affiliate of the Congress of Industrial Organizations), but Joe Curran, the union's president, feared Hudson as a rival and kept him out of power. Hudson shifted into the Communist Party's own bureaucracy and by 1937 was supervising the Party's trade union activities. He remained in charge of that key sector of Party work. In 1944 he became vice-president of the new Communist Political Association.

Hudson was closely allied with Earl Browder (q.v.). When Browder came under attack from French Communist Jacques Duclos for "revisionism," Hudson at first abstained on a resolution denouncing Browder. Although he later changed his vote, his fatal hesitation proved costly. He was sent to Pittsburgh in 1945 as district organizer. In 1948 he was dismissed from that position and moved to San Francisco, where he worked for the Party on the waterfront. Hudson was expelled from the Party around 1951 as a "Browderite" and because of Party suspicions that his wife was a government agent. He found work as a housepainter. Subpoenaed later in the decade by the House Un-American Activities Committee, he refused to testify and sank into obscurity.

*HARVEY KLEHR*

**HUGHAN, JESSIE WALLACE (1875–1955).** Jessie Wallace Hughan, dedicated to the causes of pacifism and socialism, founded the War Resisters League in 1923 and served it unstintingly until her death in 1955. Born in Brooklyn, New York, in 1875, Hughan attended Northfield Seminary in Massachusetts and received her bachelor's degree from Barnard College in 1898. Her senior thesis, "Recent Theories of Profits," began a lifelong focus on the profit motive as the underpinning of injustice. The following year she earned a master's degree in economics from Columbia University, writing a thesis entitled "The Place of Henry George in Economics." She then began teaching in the public school system, the first year in Naugatuck, Connecticut, and subsequently in the New York City school system until her retirement in 1945.

Over the next decade, while pursuing her teaching responsibilities, Jessie Hughan became progressively more involved in the American Socialist movement. She integrated her political and academic interests, joining the Socialist Party in 1907 while conducting research for her doctoral dissertation on socialism. She received her Ph.D. in economics from Columbia University in 1910 with a dissertation entitled "The Present Status of Socialism in America."

Hughan's commitments to pacifism and socialism deepened as war erupted in Europe. She helped organize the No-Conscription League in 1915 and joined the newly formed Fellowship of Reconciliation. That same year she ran on the Socialist Party ticket for the office of New York City alderman. This was the first of a series of unsuccessful campaigns for Hughan as a Socialist, with subsequent contests in New York for secretary of state (1918) and lieutenant governor (1920) and for U.S. Senator (1924).

In 1923 Hughan created an organization that reflected the particular focus of her pacifist commitment. The War Resisters League (WRL), which evolved from a committee of the Fellowship of Reconciliation, sought to bring together those war objectors who were uneasy with the Fellowship's religious orientation. Although it remained one of the smaller peace organizations during the interwar period, the WRL constantly sought to win adherents to its pledge: "War is a crime against humanity. We therefore are determined not to support any kind of war and to strive for the removal of all causes of war." By 1937 more than 12,000 Americans had signed the WRL's statement.

During the years of World War II, Hughan publicly defended the integrity of the pacifist witness in a nation increasingly mobilized for military victory. Although still a small segment of the peace movement, the War Resisters League more than doubled its ranks during these years, growing from less than 1,000 in 1939 to 2,300 in 1945.

As early reports of Hitler's final solution arrived in the United States, Jessie Hughan called for an armistice to save European Jewry from destruction. An immediate end to hostilities offered the only hope, she insisted, since increasing military pressure on Germany would only accelerate the rate of extermination. "Victory," she warned, "will not save them for dead men cannot be liberated." Hiroshima and Nagasaki furnished the ominous backdrop for Hughan's insistence in 1946 on the necessity for war resistance:

Never before has Victory yielded such bitter fruits; never before has it left men so terrified and aghast at the monster they have created for their defense. It is for us to transform this bitterness and terror into hope and courage, into the high resolve to cast aside weapons of death and risk all for Peace. We now know that only this untried adventure can save our civilization.

Jessie Hughan, now 70, still devoted herself to the struggle against war. She had stepped down as secretary of the War Resisters League in 1945, but continued her nay-saying to war as honorary secretary and member of the executive committee of the WRL up until her death in 1955.

SOURCES: Works by Jessie Wallace Hughan: *The Present Status of Socialism in America* (1911); *A Study of International Government* (1923); *Three Decades of War Resistance* (1942). See also Charles Chatfield, *For Peace and Justice: Pacifism in America, 1914–1941* (1971); *Notable American Women* (1980); Lawrence S. Wittner, *Rebels Against War: The American Peace Movement, 1941–1960* (1969).

*JOHN O'SULLIVAN*

**HUISWOUD, OTTO (1893–1961).** Otto Eduard Gerardus Majella Huiswoud, a black charter member of the American Communist Party and the first official black delegate to the Comintern in Moscow, was born at Paramaribo, Surinam, Dutch West Indies, on October 28, 1893. He was educated in the colony's Roman Catholic school. At the age of 19 he was hired as a scullion aboard a banana boat and arrived in the United States in 1913, finding work as a salesman of tropical products from Puerto Rico.

As World War I drew to a close, Huiswoud became active in the Harlem branch of the Socialist Party, which he left in 1919 to join the Communist Party at the time of its formation. This act bestowed on him the distinction of being both a charter member and the first black to enlist. Huiswoud also became the national organizer of the militant African Blood Brotherhood (ABB) and was the group's main contact with left-wing trade union leadership.

In 1922, under his party name "J. Billings," Huiswoud attended the Fourth Congress of the Communist International as an official American delegate, traveling to Moscow via Shanghai and Siberia. At the congress, he was elected permanent chairman of the Negro Commission, which drafted the first Comintern Theses on the "Negro question." Huiswoud's report, delivered before the full congress on November 25, 1922, argued that the "Negro question" was simultaneously part of the colonial question as well as a phase of the class struggle in the United States.

After arriving back in the United States on March 1, 1923, Huiswoud was appointed the first black member of the Central Executive Committee of the Party. He also resumed his active role as national organizer of the ABB as well as a member of its Supreme Council. However, Huiswoud's influence was soon eclipsed by the rising star of Lovett Fort-Whiteman, who was being groomed to take over Negro work for the Party, which he did after attending the Comintern's Fifth Congress in 1924. During this period Huiswoud attended printing school in New York City. In 1925 he was called on to help organize the American Negro Labor Congress, becoming a member the following year of its provisional committee.

Huiswoud spent most of the 1930s out of the United States. In 1929 he attended the Comintern's hearings in Moscow, at which Jay Lovestone (q.v.) was deposed as Party leader, and also served as the Comintern's representative to Marcus Garvey's Sixth International Convention of the Negro Peoples of the World in Jamaica. In 1920 he returned to Jamaica, where he attempted to organize, with little success, a Jamaica Trades and Labor Union. He was expelled from Jamaica, Trinidad, and British Guiana as a Communist agitator.

Back in the United States, at the Party's national convention in June 1930, Huiswoud voted against the line handed down at the Comintern's Sixth Congress in 1928, declaring "the Right of Self-Determination for Negroes" in the Black Belt area of the American South. Like several other blacks who voted against the resolution, Huiswoud lost his position on the National Negro Committee. Called to Moscow the following year, where he was enrolled at the Lenin School, Huiswoud was assigned to the Negro Bureau of the Red International of Labor Unions, or Profintern. In addition, he was appointed the Comintern's representative to the South African Communist Party, a position he held for about six months.

From 1931 to 1939 Huiswoud lived in Germany, Belgium, Holland, and France. For a time around 1932 he was put in charge of the International African Bureau in Berlin. He also succeeded James W. Ford (q.v.) as chairman of the Profintern's International Trade Union Committee of Negro Workers (ITUC-NW). In 1933, following George Padmore's (q.v.) resignation, he took over the production of the *Negro Worker*, the official ITUC-NW organ. The following year Belgian authorities expelled Huiswoud and his wife from Antwerp, where he was a Comintern organizer. Huiswoud moved to Amsterdam and then from 1936 to 1937 he lived in Paris, where under the name Charles Woodson he took over editorship of the *Negro Worker*.

Huiswoud returned with his wife to the United States in 1939 and took up his old profession of salesman of tropical products. He was also hired as an instructor at the Harlem People's School. Early in 1941 Huiswoud returned to Surinam, but he was immediately interned by the Dutch governor. He was released in 1942, but at the end of the war he was refused reentry into the United States.

In 1947 he went to live in Holland, where he had relatives and where he was joined by his wife, who had remained in the States. He was employed as a clerk with the National Post and Telegraph Service in Amsterdam in 1952. As chairman of the association Ons Suriname between 1953 and 1957, he helped influence its growing nationalist and left-wing character. In 1959, at the age of 66, he attended the Second International Congress of Negro Writers held in Rome. He died in Amsterdam sometime in the latter part of 1961.

SOURCES: Billings (Otto Huiswoud), "The Report on the Negro Question," *The International* (South Africa), March 2, 1923; C. B. (Cyril Briggs), "Otto Huiswoud," *Daily Worker*, December 31, 1961; Harry Haywood, *Black Bolshevik* (1978).

*ROBERT A. HILL*

# J

**JAMES, C. L. R. (b. 1901).** C. L. R. James has been a leading thinker and activist in the Pan-Africanist, West Indian independence, and Afro-American liberation movements. He is a Marxist theoretician, historian, novelist, playwright, sportswriter, and politician who has maintained a lifelong commitment to the cause of socialism.

Cyril Lionel Robert James was born in Trinidad in 1901 into a family of modest means. He developed an early love for literature and the game of cricket. James moved to the United States in 1938 from England, having established himself as a founder of the self-government movement in Trinidad, a leader of the embryonic African liberation movement, and a notable writer and historian (*World Revolution* [1937] and *The Black Jacobins* [1938]). He spent the next fifteen years in the United States as an illegal resident who was unable to play a public role but who nevertheless left a profound mark on American radicalism in a number of realms.

Having been a Trotskyist leader in England, James joined the Socialist Workers Party in the United States. In 1939 he held a stimulating series of discussions with Leon Trotsky in Mexico on the relationship between Marxism and black liberation. James insisted that the revolutionary Left was required to support an independent black movement, free from programmatic and organizational control by the revolutionary party. However, James soon broke with Trotsky's analysis of the nature of the Soviet Union and joined the new Workers Party. Under his pseudonym, J. R. Johnson, he wrote regularly for *Socialist Appeal* and the *New International*.

James utilized his Third World perspective to support his sharp opposition to U.S. intervention in World War II. The brutal and oppressive role of the Allies in the colonial world, he maintained, belied their claim to be defending democracy against tyranny. Throughout the 1940s James and a small number of followers developed a critique of Trotskyism that centered on a rejection of the concept of the vanguard party. They also criticized Trotsky's characterization of the Soviet Union as a "degenerated workers' state." Basing their conclusion on a "concrete analysis of labor" rather than following Trotsky's emphasis on nationalized property, the "Johnson-Forest Tendency" (James and Raya Dunayevskaya) declared that the Soviet Union was "state capitalist" and that Stalinism represented the final stage of capitalism.

For James and his followers, vanguard parties, sectarian factional disputes, and endless programmatic polemics—all of which tended to characterize much of the radical movement—were a waste of time. Socialism could only be the result of the self-activity of the working class itself. Therefore it was the life of the working class, at work and at leisure, that constituted the only subject worthy of concern for Marxists. James strongly supported the 1956 uprising in Hungary and actively campaigned for the Solidarity movement in Poland in the early 1980s.

In 1953 James was expelled from the United States. He was able to return only in the 1970s, when he taught at Federal City College (the University of the District of Columbia) and at Howard University. During his absence small publications such as *News and Letters*, *Correspondence*, and *Facing Reality* continued to publicize many of the views of James and his co-thinkers. His ideas also influenced the editors of *Radical America*, which was formed in the midst of the New Left in the late 1960s. James currently lives in London, where he is writing his autobiography.

SOURCES: Paul Buhle (ed.), "C. L. R. James: His Life and Work," *Urgent Tasks* 12 (Summer 1981); Cedric J. Robinson, *Black Marxism: The Making of the Black Radical Tradition* (1983).

                                                                                    *JEFF BENEKE*


**JEROME, VICTOR J. (1896–1965).** Victor Jeremy Jerome (Jerome Isaac Romaine), cultural director of the American Communist Party and editor of its theoretical journal, *The Communist*, was born in Poland in 1896. His Jewish parents emigrated first to England, where Jerome attended high school, and later to the United States, where he studied at New York University. At the university, Jerome joined the Communist Party while supporting himself as a bookkeeper, tutor, and printing salesman. Following his graduation in 1930 he became a writer for the Communist Party's theoretical journal and a follower of one of its leading intellectuals, Sidney Hook (q.v.). Three years later he denounced Hook for "revisionism" in *The Communist*, the first in what would be a series of denunciations of Communist intellectuals who deviated from the Party line.

In the early 1930s Jerome was elected to the Central Committee of the Communist Party and given the position of educational director. A few years later, in 1936, he was sent to Hollywood as Party organizer. In addition to raising money for the Hollywood Anti-Nazi League (HANL) and other Popular Front groups, Jerome coordinated activities with the Los Angeles Communist Party, recruited several entertainment figures into the Hollywood branch, and lectured to small groups of writers and actors on the role of the artist in the struggle against Fascism. Although his organizational abilities played a major role in the growth of the Popular Front in Hollywood, Jerome soon won a reputation for his unbending dogmatism and in 1940, following the collapse of the Popular Front, he published his first book, *Intellectuals and the War*, an attack on "pseudo-Marxists" who "did not see integration with the working class as a privilege," but rather as "a pedestal on which to rise."

As chairman of the Communist Party's Cultural Commission during the 1940s, Jerome wrote extensively in the Communist press on the political role of the Marxist intellectual and artist in capitalist society and regularly denounced those who advocated greater artistic license. Jerome also wrote on the film industry, his most notable work being *The Negro in Hollywood Films*, an attack on racism in the industry. In 1951, shortly after taking the Fifth Amendment before the House Un-American Activities Committee, he was arrested together with twelve other Party leaders under the Smith Act. After a nine-month trial, Jerome was convicted, and in 1955 he began his jail sentence. He was released in 1957 and subsequently spent several years in Poland and the Soviet Union editing a collection of Lenin's works. Jerome died in New York in 1965.

SOURCES: Larry Ceplair and Steven Englund, *The Inquisition in Hollywood* (1980); *HUAC, Communist Infiltration of Hollywood Motion Picture Industry: Part 1*, 82d Congress, 1st Session, pp. 56–70; V. J. Jerome Papers, Yale University Library, New Haven, Connecticut.

*MICHAEL FURMANOVSKY*

**JOHNSTONE, JACK (1880–1942).** Jack Johnstone was for many years closely associated with William Z. Foster (q.v.), following him into the Communist Party and holding a variety of second-echelon positions, primarily in the trade union field. Johnstone was born on November 21, 1880, in Scotland. He left school at 15 to go to work, and later fought in the Boer War. Shortly afterward, in 1902, he came to the United States. For several years Johnstone moved back and forth between Canada and the United States as a housepainter. He joined the Socialist Party in Canada in 1902. In 1906 he became a member of the Industrial Workers of the World (IWW) and participated in their activities on the West Coast, including the free-speech fight in Spokane, Washington, in 1909–1910. In the IWW Johnstone came under William Foster's influence and, while living in Nelson, British Columbia, became a founding member in 1912 of Foster's Syndicalist League of North America, which believed in "boring from within" existing unions to win them to revolutionary principles. Thereafter Johnstone's public career was linked to Foster's. When the latter began to organize packinghouse workers in Chicago in 1917, Johnstone served as Foster's assistant and became secretary of the Chicago Stockyards Labor Council in 1919. A co-founder of Foster's Trade Union Educational League in 1920, he followed his mentor into the Communist Party the following year and, like him, was arrested at the Party's secret Bridgman Convention in 1922.

During the 1920s Johnstone was a key underling in Foster's faction of the Communist Party, specializing in trade union affairs. He also found time to undertake several Comintern assignments—in Mexico in 1924–1925 and in India in 1929 with the All-America Anti-Imperialist League. The British jailed and deported him on the latter mission. In 1928 Johnstone chaired the American delegation to the Profintern plenum, where J. Lozovsky won approval for his demand that the Americans form dual unions. Ever since 1912 Johnstone had resisted "dual union" policies, but at the Comintern's Sixth World Congress in 1928 he joined other members of Foster's faction in savagely attacking their leader for hesitating to embrace them. He became national organizer of the newly established Trade Union Unity League (TUUL) in 1929.

After several futile years with the TUUL, Johnstone became the Party's district organizer in Pittsburgh and spent the latter half of the 1930s as Party chairman in Illinois. From 1927 until his death on April 18, 1942, he served on the Party's National Committee.

*HARVEY KLEHR*

**JONES, MARY HARRIS (1830–1930).** Mary Harris ("Mother") Jones was a syndicalist labor agitator and organizer. She was born into a poor family in County Cork, Ireland, in 1830. She was educated in Toronto, Ontario, Canada, to which her family migrated, completing normal school. Her first job was as a teacher in a Roman Catholic convent school in Michigan. She later worked as a dressmaker in Chicago and taught school in Memphis, Tennessee. Her husband and four children died in the yellow fever epidemic in that city in 1867. Jones returned almost immediately to Chicago, where she became active in the Knights of Labor. Her home was destroyed in the Great Chicago Fire of 1871. During the railroad strike of 1877, she went to Pittsburgh to help the strikers.

Beginning in 1880 Jones was an itinerant labor organizer. In the 1890s she was an organizer primarily for the United Mine Workers (UMW). During 1902 and 1903 she was active in the anthracite strikes in eastern Pennsylvania. She led the mine wives in the much publicized mop-and-broom brigades that routed strikebreakers, especially in 1902. The general settlement of those strikes, which was arranged by President Theodore Roosevelt, was opposed by Jones because it did not include formal recognition of the UMW. After the anthracite strikes, Jones organized the workers in the bituminous fields of West Virginia. She then went to Colorado, where she helped organize a mineworkers strike. When UMW president John Mitchell disavowed that strike, Jones resigned from the UMW.

In 1898 she was a founder of the Social Democratic Party, and in 1905 she helped organize the Industrial Workers of the World, but she was active in neither for any length of time. In fact, she campaigned for a Democratic ticket in Indiana endorsed by the American Federation of Labor in 1916. Despite her radical views on most issues, Jones opposed women's suffrage, which she considered a sideshow to keep women from organizing industrially.

In 1911 she was again organizing for the UMW in West Virginia. In 1913 she was convicted by a West Virginia militia military court of conspiracy to commit murder during the 1912–1913 mine workers strike. The sentence was revoked by a new governor before Jones served any time. In 1914 she was at Ludlow, Colorado, where twenty members of strikers' families were killed by machine-gun fire. Her description of that massacre was so vivid that President Woodrow Wilson pleaded with mine owners and the union to create grievance procedures.

Jones continued to organize and work with unions into her eighties and nineties. She helped streetcar and garment strikers in New York and West Virginia coal miners. She also helped the Progressive Mine Workers Union of Illinois after a falling out with John L. Lewis of the UMW. Mother Jones died in Silver Spring, Maryland, in December 1930.

SOURCE: *Notable American Women* (1980).

*LILLIAN KIRTZMAN JOHNPOLL*

# K

KELLEY, FLORENCE (1859–1932). Florence Kelley was a Socialist, feminist, consumer advocate, opponent of child labor, settlement-house worker, author of factory laws, and translator of Friedrich Engels' major work. Born into an upper-class Quaker family in Philadelphia in 1859, Kelley was educated at Quaker schools in Philadelphia, Cornell University (B.A., 1882), the University of Zurich in Switzerland, and Northwestern University Law School (evening division), from which she graduated in 1894.

After being turned down by the Graduate School of the University of Pennsylvania because of her sex, Kelley toured Europe before enrolling at the University of Zurich. There she became involved with an international Socialist students group and became an active advocate of socialism herself. While still at Zurich she translated Friedrich Engels' *The Condition of the Working Class in England in 1844* from German into English. There also she met and married Lazare Wishnewetzky, a Russian medical student, in 1884. She and her husband sailed to New York the next year with their son. The couple soon joined the German-dominated Socialist Labor Party. Mrs. Wishnewetzky was not trusted by the other Socialists because she rejected their European orientation. And, although she supported the party in the 1886 election, she and her husband were ousted from the party in 1887 for minor infractions of discipline.

In 1891 she and Dr. Wishnewetzky were divorced; Florence won custody of their three children and resumed her maiden name. Immediately after the divorce she became a worker at the Hull House in Chicago while her children lived in the home of Henry Demarest Lloyd (q.v.). She soon became a member of the inner circle of the Hull House and a close friend and associate of Jane Addams.

As early as 1889 Kelley had written a pamphlet assailing child labor. In 1892 she was hired by the Illinois Bureau of Labor Statistics to study the sweatshop system in the garment industry. Meanwhile the federal commissioner of labor, Carroll D. Wright, asked her to take part in a study of slums. Her work in these reports was instrumental in the Illinois legislature's passage of the 1893 Factory Act limiting hours of labor for women and prohibiting child labor and tenement workshops. Part of the act was declared unconstitutional in 1895.

In 1893 Kelley was appointed chief factory inspector by Governor John Peter Altgeld, but was fired four years later by his conservative successor. After her dismissal she moved to New York City, where she became active in the Henry Street Settlement. At the same time, she formed the National Consumers League, whose aim was to boycott goods of manufacturers who employed children. In 1905 she proposed a national wages and hours law, which was enacted some thirty years later. She also persuaded Louis D. Brandeis, then a noted Boston constitutional attorney, to join the defense staff in the Oregon ten-hour law case (*Muller v. Oregon*). She worked with Brandeis (often supplying him with valuable data) and with Felix Frankfurter (who replaced Brandeis after he was appointed to the Supreme Court). Kelley was also founder of the National Child Labor Committee.

In 1909 she joined with Mary White Ovington (q.v.) in founding the National Association for the Advancement of Colored People. She joined the Intercollegiate Socialist Society in 1911 and served as its president from 1918 to 1921. In 1912 Kelley became a member of the Socialist Party.

A birthright Quaker, Kelley was a pacifist who opposed American intervention in World War I. She helped found the Women's International League for Peace and Freedom in 1919. For the rest of her life Kelley fought for women's suffrage (although she opposed the equal rights amendment), for a child labor amendment to the Constitution, and against imperialism and war. After 1926 her health declined. She died in early 1932 in Philadelphia.

SOURCES: Harry W. Laidler, "Florence Kelley: Social Pioneer," *L.I.D. Monthly*, March 1932; *Notable American Women* (1980).

*BERNARD K. JOHNPOLL*

**KESTER, HOWARD (1904–1977).** Howard Anderson Kester was Southern representative for the Fellowship of Reconciliation, executive secretary of the Committee for Racial and Economic Justice, a leader of the Southern Tenant Farmers Union, a member of the National Executive Committee of the Socialist Party, and director of the Fellowship of Southern Churchmen. Kester was born in Martinsville, Virginia, on July 21, 1904, the son of William Kester, a master tailor from Pennsylvania, and Nannie Holt, daughter of a Virginia plantation overseer. In 1921 he enrolled in Lynchburg College on a ministerial scholarship from the Presbyterian Church. Kester became a leading figure in the college Young Men's Christian Association (YMCA) and worked to end the policy of separate organizations for black and white YMCA members. During the summer of 1923 he participated in a student pilgrimage to Europe, where he observed the devastation left by World War I. He became a lifelong pacifist.

After graduating in 1925, Kester briefly attended Princeton Theological Seminary, then returned to Virginia and continued his YMCA work. In the fall of 1926 he enrolled in Vanderbilt University School of Religion and studied under Dr. Alva Taylor, a leading exponent of the Social Gospel. Taylor challenged his students to realize the teachings of Christ by striving for a more just social order.

Kester's studies at Vanderbilt were interrupted in 1927, when he lost his job with the YMCA after leading a protest against Allied intervention in the Chinese rebellion. He accepted a job as youth secretary for the New York–based Fellowship of Reconciliation (FOR), an international pacifist organization. In 1929 he returned to Nashville as Southern secretary for the FOR and completed his bachelor of divinity degree in 1931.

In 1931 Kester joined the Socialist Party and established a local party organization in Nashville. The following year he ran for Congress on the Socialist Party ticket, which was headed by presidential candidate Norman Thomas (q.v.). During this time Kester's participation in a miners strike in Wilder, Tennessee, caused him to move beyond pure pacifism and accept the possible necessity of violent revolution to end class exploitation. The FOR opposed any concessions to violence, and Kester was forced to resign. Reinhold Niebuhr, Elisabeth Gilman, (q.v.) and several other national leaders resigned as well. In February 1934 they formed the Committee on Economic and Racial Justice (CERJ) in order to continue support for Kester's efforts in the South.

Kester became involved with a variety of organizations during the 1930s. He personally investigated a number of lynchings for Walter White and the National Association for the Advancement of Colored People. Kester devoted much of his time to the Southern Tenant Farmers Union (STFU) as a speaker, organizer, fund-raiser, spiritual adviser, and publicist. By the late 1930s he was a nationally known figure in Socialist Party circles and was elected to the party's Executive Committee in 1937. That year he became embroiled in a major factional dispute when the Trotskyists tried to take over the Socialist Party. Kester sided with Norman Thomas in voting for their expulsion.

While active in union and party work, Kester maintained his base in the religious sphere. He devoted increasing amounts of time to the Fellowship of Southern Churchmen (FSC), a group of liberal clergy striving to make the church more responsive to social issues in the South. In 1942 the CERJ formally dissolved and transferred its remaining funds to the FSC. Budgetary problems, however, caused Kester to accept a position as principal of the Penn Normal and Industrial School in St. Helena, South Carolina, the first school for black children in the South. Kester resumed directorship of the FSC in 1948. During the 1950s he organized several major conferences for clergymen in the South to focus their leadership on ending segregation.

Kester left the FSC in 1957 and worked primarily as a college teacher and administrator until his retirement in 1970, at which time he was dean of students at Montreat-Anderson College in North Carolina. He died in 1977.

SOURCES: Anthony P. Dunbar, *Against the Grain: Southern Radicals and Prophets, 1929–1959* (1981); Howard A. Kester, *Revolt Among the Sharecroppers* (1969); Howard A. Kester Papers, Southern Historical Collection, University of North Carolina, Chapel Hill, North Carolina.

*PAT SULLIVAN*

**KONIKOW, ANTOINETTE (1869–1946).** Antoinette Konikow, a Russian-born physician, was a prominent member of the Socialist, Communist, and Trotskyist movements in the United States from the mid–1890s to the mid–1940s. During the same period she was a pioneer of the birth control movement. Born in central Russia in 1869, she spent much of her youth in the Black Forest region of Germany and entered medical school in Switzerland in the late 1880s. At the age of 17 she joined the Emancipation of Labor Group, Russia's first Marxist organization, founded by G. V. Plekhanov. She attended the founding congress of the Second International in Paris in 1889. Although she had a Lutheran background, she married a Jewish medical student named William Konikow. They emigrated to the United States in 1893, settling in Boston, and their home became a center for Russian intellectuals (Maxim Gorki stayed there during his American tour) and for Socialists of all nationalities. They had two children, but were divorced in 1910.

Joining the Socialist Labor Party (SLP), Konikow served on the party's Massachusetts state committee and was a delegate to its national convention in 1896. An opponent of Daniel DeLeon (q.v.), she was expelled from the SLP in the following year. In 1901 she joined the Socialist Party of America (SP), led by Eugene V. Debs (q.v.). Multilingual, she was particularly active in organizing the SP's foreign-language federations. She was a delegate to numerous state and national meetings and was one of the five members of the SP's Women's Commission.

A member of the SP's left wing, Konikow was especially close to Ludwig Lore (q.v.), head of the party's German-language federation and editor of the Socialist daily *New Yorker Volkzeitung*. With the split in the SP in the wake of the Russian Revolution of 1917, she joined in the creation of the American Communist Party, playing a role in the Trade Union Educational League and in Russian relief work.

In 1902 Konikow had graduated with honors from Tufts College and began to practice medicine. It was in this period that she began disseminating information on birth control, defying Massachusetts' repressive laws on such matters. Within this movement she opposed arguments for eugenics and "population control" that were often used to justify birth control. Konikow attended the first American birth control conference in 1921, and in 1923 she published a birth control manual entitled *Voluntary Motherhood*, which sold over 10,000 copies in its first three editions. She gave annual lectures on "Sex Hygiene and Sex Problems" and was arrested in 1928 for exhibiting contraceptives in public (the case was dismissed). With her son-in-law John G. Wright, a chemist and political radical, she developed an inexpensive contraceptive jelly. In 1931 she authored *A*

*Physician's Manual of Birth Control* to assist doctors in giving advice to their patients.

Konikow visited the Soviet Union in 1926, in part to share her knowledge of birth control methods. During this visit she became disturbed by growing signs of repression and bureaucracy there. She had earlier been a vocal critic of Gregory Zinoviev's heavy-handed methods in his leadership of the Third (Communist) International.

In 1928 Konikow was expelled from the American Communist Party for defending Leon Trotsky. She and five co-thinkers in Boston formed the Independent Communist League, which soon merged with the Communist League of America, led by James P. Cannon (q.v.), Max Shachtman (q.v.), and Martin Abern (q.v.). In addition to being a mainstay of the Boston branch of the Trotskyist movement, Konikow contributed articles to its national press, including discussions of birth control. She participated in the fusion of the Trotskyists with A. J. Muste's (q.v.) American Workers Party in 1935, and in the following year she entered the Socialist Party along with other Trotskyists. After expulsion of the SP's left wing, the Socialist Workers Party (SWP) was founded in 1938 and immediately affiliated with Trotsky's Fourth International. Konikow became an honorary member of the SWP's National Committee. She visited Trotsky in Mexico for a month before his assassination in 1940.

Following World War II and her retirement from her physician's practice, Konikow chaired the American Committee for European Workers Relief, to send food, clothing, and medicine to anti-Fascist workers who had been in prisons and concentration camps during the war. She died in 1946.

SOURCE: Dianne Feeley, "Antoinette Konikow: Marxist and Feminist," *International Socialist Review*, January 1972.

*PAUL LEBLANC*

**KRUMBEIN, CHARLES (1889–1947).** Charles Krumbein, a key Communist functionary for nearly thirty years, was born on February 10, 1889, in Chicago. Both parents were of German descent; his father, a housepainter, was an immigrant. Krumbein dropped out of grammar school to start work at age 11 as a baker's apprentice. Later he attended an evening high school. He eventually became a steamfitter and an active participant in the Chicago labor movement. He became a Socialist in 1910, was partial to its left wing, and joined the Communist Labor Party in 1919. One year later he was convicted of conspiracy to overthrow the government in a sedition trial and sentenced to a year in prison. He served one day and was pardoned.

Krumbein was part of a strong Communist presence in the Chicago labor movement in the early 1920s. He was a delegate to the Chicago Federation of Labor in 1921 from the Plumbers Union and worked closely with independent radical Chicago unionists to build a farmer-labor movement. The effort collapsed in 1923. Krumbein was shifted to New York as district organizer in 1924 when William Foster's (q.v.) faction won control of the Party. One year later the

Comintern stripped the Fosterites of their majority and Krumbein was replaced. Expendable in the United States, he was selected to attend the first class at the Lenin School in Moscow in 1926.

Krumbein carried out a series of sensitive assignments for the Comintern in the late 1920s and early 1930s. Active in China from 1927 under the name of Isadore Dreiser, he was arrested in 1930 in Great Britain and served a total of six months in prison for using a false passport. After his release the Soviet consulate issued him travel documents and he proceeded to Moscow. Back in China in 1930–1931, Krumbein allegedly had ties to the Sorge spy ring and served as a Comintern representative. His past caught up with him in 1934. He was arrested in the United States and served fifteen months in prison for using a false American passport.

After his release from jail, Krumbein served as the Party's district organizer in New York. In 1938 he became the Party's treasurer, retaining this sensitive position until his death on January 20, 1947.
SOURCE: FBI File 100–17433.

*HARVEY KLEHR*

**KRUSE, WILLIAM (1893–?).** William Kruse was an important fuctionary in the pre-war Socialist Party and in the first decade of the Communist Party's existence. Kruse was born of German-Lutheran parents in Hoboken, New Jersey, in 1893. As a teenager he joined the Young Peoples Socialist League. A few years later he was its head, forsaking college for a career as an activist. His important and visible position within the Socialist movement led to his indictment and conviction under the Espionage Act of 1917 for obstructing the draft.

Kruse did not immediately switch his allegiance from the Socialist Party (SP) to the Communist Party, but remained in the SP's left wing in 1920 and 1921 as an important lieutenant to J. Louis Engdahl (q.v.). Like Engdahl he hoped the Socialist Party would join the Communist International, and he disapproved of the Communist Party's underground status. With the formation of the Communists' legal arm, the Workers Party, in December 1921, Kruse joined, and was immediately made an alternate to its first executive committee.

In 1923 Kruse became a full-fledged representative to the Central Executive Committee. A few years later (1926–1927) he was among the first contingent of Americans at the Lenin School in Moscow, a reflection of his promise as a leader. In Moscow, Kruse was also widely considered to be the main representative of the Jay Lovestone (q.v.) leadership faction. When Kruse returned to the United States, he became a district organizer for the Party in Chicago.

Kruse held this position when he was expelled from the Communist Party in 1929 for refusing to denounce Jay Lovestone. After his expulsion, Kruse faded from the radical scene and did not take an active role within the Lovestoneite group. Instead, he became the educational director for Bell and Howell Films. When last heard from, he had opened his own film service in Chicago, William Kruse and Associates.

*JUDY KUTULAS*

**KRZYCKI, LEO (1882–1966).** Leo Krzycki was a vice-president of the Amalgamated Clothing Workers of America, a Socialist alderman in Milwaukee, the national chairman of the Socialist Party during the 1930s, and a leader in left-wing Polish-American organizations during and after World War II. Born and educated in Milwaukee, Krzycki was elected president of his local in the Amalgamated Lithographers Union at the age of 22 in 1904. The same year he became active in the Socialist Party in Milwaukee. Krzycki was one of the few Polish-American Socialist leaders—the party in that city was heavily German. In 1912 he was elected an alderman from one of the Polish wards of the city, serving for four years. In 1918 he was named an undersheriff for Milwaukee County, serving until 1920.

During the 1920s Krzycki was named an organizer for the Amalgamated Clothing Workers Union. Although on the payroll of the Union, Krzycki also did work for other unions in the Milwaukee area, especially in organizing Polish workers. He was an effective orator and organizer during that period and was much in demand as a speaker. In 1932 he was one of the leading forces in both the Socialist Party and the Labor League for Thomas and Maurer (the Socialist national ticket). He was also active in the campaign for Morris Hillquit (q.v.), the Socialist mayoralty candidate in New York. Elected to the National Executive Committee of the party in 1932, Krzycki was named national chairman of the party late the next year.

Krzycki presided over the party at the time of its most severe decline. Internal disputes rent the party. By adopting many of the reform measures previously proposed by Socialists, Franklin D. Roosevelt had won over many former supporters of the party. Ex-Socialist trade union officials now backed Roosevelt.

Immediately preceding the 1936 convention of the party, Krzycki told Norman Thomas (q.v.), the party's titular head, that he would support the party in the forthcoming election. A few days after the convention adjourned he informed Thomas that Sidney Hillman, president of the Amalgamated Clothing Workers, had forced him to support Roosevelt. He resigned from the Socialist Party in 1936.

Krzycki was later active in the union and in Polish-American associations in Milwaukee. In a further split with his old Socialist comrades, he supported the pro-Communist faction in Poland at the end of the war. In 1950 he retired from union affairs. Krzycki died in January 1966 in his native Milwaukee.

*JAMES INGBRETSON*

# L

**LAIDLER, HARRY W. (1884–1970).** Harry W. Laidler was executive director of the Intercollegiate Socialist Society (renamed the League for Industrial Democracy in 1921) for forty-seven years (1910–1957), a member of the New York City Council from 1939 to 1941, and an internationally known labor economist. Laidler was born into an upper-middle-class family in Brooklyn, New York, in 1884. His father was a pillar of the Plymouth Congregational Church of Brooklyn, where Henry Ward Beecher was minister. The younger Laidler was educated at Wesleyan University, Middletown, Connecticut (B.A., 1907), Brooklyn Law School (LL.B., 1910), and Columbia University (Ph.D., 1913). His parents were liberal but hardly radical. One of his uncles, who influenced young Laidler, was a Socialist trade union leader. Laidler was won over to socialism while still a teenager.

Laidler attended the September 1905 meeting in New York at which the Intercollegiate Socialist Society, (ISS) was formed. The executive committee of the Society chosen at the meeting did not include a single student, so Benjamin Feigenbaum of Columbia University nominated Laidler as an additional member to represent undergraduates. When Laidler was added to the board he began his sixty-five-year association with the Society (later the League for Industrial Democracy).

The ISS was not an overtly Socialist organization. Its objective was to study socialism, ''as has been done for several years at Harvard, where there is a full course on Methods of Social Reform—Socialism, Communism, the Single Tax.'' Despite its formal refusal to propagandize for socialism, the ISS was condemned by anti-Socialist groups—most especially the National Civic Federation. Laidler was active as an executive board member during the first five years of the Society's existence. During that period he attempted to organize Socialist study groups, including one at Wesleyan, with limited success. In 1910 he was named executive director of the ISS, a position he held for forty-seven years.

Under Laidler's direction the ISS became the chief instrument for converting intellectuals to socialism. Among those who were converted were Paul H. Douglas, who would later become a Democratic senator from Illinois; Talcott Parsons, a leading sociologist; the philosophers Sidney Hook (q.v.) and Walter Lippmann, the poet Babette Deutsch, and black leader W. E. B. DuBois (q.v.).

Between 1912 and 1917 the ISS held conferences and published pamphlets and journals by leading experts in socialism. Although American Socialists were almost universally opposed to U.S. participation in the war raging in Europe after 1914, the ISS took no formal position. In 1917, when the United States declared war against Germany and its allies, the Socialist Party formally denounced the action and called for what was tantamount to resistance. A considerable number of Socialists supported President Woodrow Wilson's declaration of war and left the Socialist Party. Many of them were members of the Society and threatened to split the ISS as well. Laidler saw his main task to be prevention of a fissure in the ISS. He believed it was vital that ISS members promote an intelligent interest in Socialism; and that they do not turn their groups into pro-war or anti-war, pro-conscription or anti-conscription organizations.

The attempt by Laidler to avoid confrontation over the war issue was to no avail. Most of the pro-war Socialists resigned from the ISS. The government cracked down on it, breaking up ISS meetings and preventing the organization from using the mails for even the most moderate of materials, much of which was seized and destroyed. The effects of the war and the revolution in Russia virtually paralyzed the ISS. Only the perseverance of Laidler prevented the organization from collapsing.

In 1917 another earth-shattering occurrence—the Bolshevik seizure of power in Russia—further splintered the ISS. Most of its members were enamored of the revolution. Several of them left the Socialist movement, which they considered too tepid, and joined the Communists. Among these were the poet and left-wing Socialist Rose Pastor Stokes (q.v.) and Albert Rhys Williams, a noted correspondent then in Moscow. Laidler, who generally agreed with Morris Hillquit's (q.v.) anti-Soviet position, avoided the debate until 1931, when he wrote a scathing attack against the Communists.

There was unity on a few issues. For example, Laidler was active, together with Hillquit and Norman Thomas (q.v), in the unsuccessful campaign of 1924 to elect Senator Robert LaFollette President. He was also involved in the futile effort to form a farmer-labor party in the United States.

In 1921 the ISS changed its name to the League for Industrial Democracy, (LID). The change of name signified a change in purpose as well. The LID became the cultural arm of the Socialist Party. The requirement that members had to be either university students or graduates was dropped. Instead, the organization opened its membership lists to anyone interested in spreading democratic socialism.

During the next fifteen years Laidler worked at building the LID into a major educational organization. He succeeded in setting up a significant speakers bureau and was responsible for publication of more than seventy pamphlets. Laidler remained active also in the Socialist Party, helping to direct Norman Thomas' presidential campaigns of 1928 and 1932. During this period he attempted to remain aloof from the internal party battles between the younger "Militant" faction and the older "Old Guard" group. When the party was torn asunder by that internal struggle in 1936, Laidler remained among the "Militants," although his views were essentially in agreement with the Old Guard. In 1937 he joined the American Labor Party (ALP) and became inactive in the Socialist Party, although he remained a member.

During the 1920s and early 1930s Laidler had run unsuccessfully for various public offices as a Socialist. In 1939 he accepted the ALP nomination for membership on the New York City Council. For the first time Harry Laidler was elected to office. In the city council Laidler fought for slum clearance and good low-cost housing, for public ownership of electric power generation, for a more scientific tax system, for consumer protection, and for an expansion of social services.

By 1939 Laidler disagreed with his old friend Norman Thomas on America's position with regard to the war then beginning in Europe. Thomas was basically an isolationist; Laidler favored U.S. aid to the Allied powers. In the 1940 presidential election Laidler refused to support Thomas, although he did not openly oppose him. This roused Socialist antagonism against him in the 1941 election. His refusal to leave the Socialist Party annoyed the ex-Socialist directors of the *Jewish Daily Forward*, a powerful force in the American Labor Party at the time. And his refusal to hail the Soviet Union during the period of the Hitler-Stalin Pact earned for him the animosity of the Communists—who had by 1939 become a major force in the ALP. After the German invasion of Russia, Laidler refused to become a supporter of Stalin and his policies despite his support of the Soviet war effort. He thus became the chief target of the Communists' ire in the 1941 election.

The combined opposition of the *Forward* and its followers, of the Communists, and of Norman Thomas and the official Socialists helped defeat Laidler in 1941 despite his strong record in the city council. In 1944 Laidler joined with other Socialist and labor leaders to form the Liberal Party in opposition to the American Labor Party, which the Communists had seized with the assistance of Sidney Hillman.

For the next fifteen years Laidler was active in the post-war reconstruction of the LID. In 1957 he retired from his post, although he remained a member of the LID. He spent the next eleven years writing a history of socialism, which was based on his earlier book, *Social-Economic Movements* (1944). The new book was published in 1968.

In 1970 Harry W. Laidler died at age 86 in a Brooklyn hospital near the home where he was born.

SOURCES: Bernard K. Johnpoll and Mark Yerburgh, *The League for Industrial Democracy: A Documentary History* (1980), esp. the introduction and the eleven pamph-

lets by Laidler reproduced in the 3-volume work; Carmela Ascolese Karnoustos, "Harry W. Laidler and the Intercollegiate Socialist Society" (Ph.D. diss., New York University, 1974); "Harry W. Laidler," *Current Biography* 31 (October 1970); David A. Shannon, *The Socialist Party of America* (1952); Mina Weisenberg, *The L.I.D.: Fifty Years of Democratic Education* (1955).

*BERNARD K. JOHNPOLL*


**LANNON, AL (1907–1969).** Al Lannon, a Communist leader among seamen and waterfront workers, was born Albert Francesco Vetere in Brooklyn, New York, on October 3, 1907. His parents were working-class Italian-Catholic immigrants. He had less than one year of high school. In 1926, using the name Lannon, he enlisted in the coast guard but was discharged for being under age. A sailor for several years, Lannon joined the Communist Party (CPUSA) in October 1931 after being impressed by a stopover in the Soviet Union. He became an organizer for the Marine Workers Industrial Union (MWIU), a CPUSA dual union, in 1933, but was in attendance at the Comintern's Lenin School in Moscow from 1933 to 1935. After another stint at sea, Lannon became a waterfront organizer for the Congress of Industrial Organizations.

During World War II, Lannon shifted back into Party work. In 1942 he became the CPUSA's New York state organization secretary. From 1943 to 1946 he was Party secretary in the Maryland–District of Columbia district and then became chairman of the New York waterfront section. Lannon also served for several years on the National Committee. Along with fifteen others, he was convicted in 1951 on Smith Act charges and sentenced to prison. After his release, Lannon was a vociferous supporter of William Foster (q.v.) in the internal warfare that gripped the Party from 1956 to 1959. Soon, however, even Foster's leftism and militancy proved too weak, and Lannon, once again on the National Committee, became leader of the extreme left caucus at the 1957 national convention. But he refused to go along with many of his comrades, who quit the Party to form a more revolutionary group. Lannon died on May 31, 1969.

*HARVEY KLEHR*


**LARKIN, JAMES (1876–1947).** James Larkin was an Irish labor leader and revolutionary nationalist who, living in the United States for less than a decade, became a leader of the Socialist Party left wing and helped found the Communist Party before being jailed and deported. Larkin was born on January 21, 1876, in Liverpool, England, to poor Irish Catholic parents. His father, a fitter in an engineering firm, died when he was 11, and after just three and a half years of schooling James worked at a variety of occupations, including, at age 17, as a sailor who shipped out to Argentina and America.

Larkin joined the Independent Labor Party, a Socialist group led by Keir Hardie and Tom Mann, in 1893. He was arrested and fined several times for speaking against the Boer War. A foreman on the Liverpool docks, Larkin stayed out on strike with his men in 1905 and became an organizer for the National

Union of Dock Labourers. He was elected general organizer of the union in
1906 and began to devote more and more of his time to strikes in Ireland, where
the union was straining to establish itself. Late in 1908 the English-dominated
union suspended him, and the following year Larkin founded and became general
secretary of the Irish Transport and General Workers Union, destined to become
the dominating influence in the Irish union movement. By 1913 the union
encompassed most of the unskilled workers in Dublin and led a bloody tram
strike.

Larkin's political views veered in the direction of syndicalism. Together with
James Connolly, Larkin dominated the Irish Socialist Party. He edited the *Irish
Worker* and was elected to the Dublin City Corporation. After the 1913 strike
he served two and a half weeks of a seven-month term for seditious libel and
broke with the British Labour Party for its refusal to go out in a sympathy strike.
To his fervent Irish nationalism, devout Catholicism, and radical socialism he
also added an insistence on temperance.

Larkin arrived in New York in November 1914 for a lecture tour and remained
in the States for more than eight years. Fervently opposed to World War I, he
quickly fit in with the left-wing American Socialists. His Irish nationalism also
led him to flirt with agents of the German government and take money from
them. Early in 1918 he formed the James Connolly Socialist Club in New York
(named after his old comrade, who had been executed by the British after the
Easter Rising) and was allied with John Reed (q.v.) in the Socialist left wing.
He was a charter member of the Communist Labor Party. Larkin was convicted
of criminal anarchy in New York in 1920 and served almost three years before
being pardoned and deported in 1923.

Back in Ireland, Larkin lost control of the Transport Union and was hurt by
his public reputation as a Communist. He did win election to the Dail in 1927
but was denied his seat because of bankruptcy. He had been a delegate to the
Fifth Comintern Congress in 1924 and had been elected to the Executive Committee
of the Comintern. By 1934, although he never made a public statement, he had
drifted out of the Communist orbit. He was elected to the Dail again as an
independent in 1937 and joined the Irish Labor Party, which he had long castigated,
in 1941. He died on January 30,1947.
SOURCES: Emmet Larkin, *James Larkin* (1965); Bertram Wolfe, *Strange Communists
I Have Known* (1965).

*HARVEY KLEHR*

**LASH, JOSEPH P. (b. 1909).** Joseph P. Lash moved from a series of leadership
positions in radical and Socialist student groups during the 1930s to the reform
liberalism of the Americans for Democratic Action after World War II. The son
of Russian Jewish immigrants Samuel and Mary Lash, Joseph Lash was born
in New York City on December 2, 1909. His father died when Lash was 9 years
old; his mother operated a neighborhood grocery. Lash graduated from the City
College of New York in 1931 and earned his M.A. from Columbia University

the next year. In 1932 he also became an officer in the Student League for Industrial Democracy (SLID), a Socialist youth organization. He served from 1933 to 1935 as editor of *Student Outlook* and in 1935 played a major part in leading the SLID into the American Student Union, an alliance of Socialist and Communist student activists. From 1936 through 1939 he served as SLID national secretary and moved very close to the Communist Party.

Although initially sympathetic to the Soviet Union and willing to accept political cooperation with the Communist Party, Lash like many others was disillusioned by the Nazi-Soviet Pact in the summer of 1939 and began increasingly to seek out a leftist stance in politics that would be independent of Communist associations. Paradoxically, in November 1939 Lash was among a group of student radical leaders summoned to appear before the Dies Committee to answer allegations of pro-Communist sympathies. On this trip to Washington, Lash met Eleanor Roosevelt, who was to influence strongly his subsequent political and scholarly career.

Lash was general secretary of the International Student Service from 1940 until his induction into the army air force in 1942. After service in the South Pacific, Lash participated in the establishment of Americans for Democratic Action (ADA) with other New Deal leftists eager to distance themselves from the Communist-influenced Progressive Citizens of America and the presidential hopes of Henry Wallace. He served as ADA's New York secretary for two years, after which he helped Elliott Roosevelt edit the papers of Franklin D. Roosevelt from 1948 through 1950. In 1950 Lash joined the staff of the *New York Post* as United Nations correspondent, a position he held until becoming assistant editorial page editor in 1961. During these years he continued to remain active in Democratic reform politics in New York.

Since leaving the *Post* in 1966, Lash has produced a series of books covering the period of his political activism, with attention to the life and career of Eleanor Roosevelt. The best known of these works, *Eleanor and Franklin*, was awarded the Francis Parkman Prize of the Society of American Historians, the National Book Award, and the Pulitzer Prize for biography.

SOURCES: "Forward" in Joseph P. Lash, *Eleanor and Franklin* (1971); *Who's Who in America*, 42d ed. (1982–1983).

*ED SHOEMAKER*


**LASSER, DAVID (b.1902).** David Lasser had a multifaceted career as an architect and officer of organizations of the unemployed, as a federal employee, and as a union official. He achieved national prominence in the 1930s as an organizer and officer of the Workers Alliance of America, which he helped bring into being in 1935 and which he headed until 1940. Born in Baltimore, Maryland, on March 20, 1902, Lasser was one of five children. His parents were Jewish immigrants from Russia; his father was a tailor, the mother the daughter of a rabbi. He grew up in straitened circumstances, leaving school at age 14 to become a bank messenger. During World War I, Lasser enlisted in the army, saw action in France, and was gassed. Despite his limited formal education, the ambitious Lasser managed to return to school and in 1924 graduated from the Massachusetts Institute of Technology with a degree in industrial engineering. After a succession of jobs in various fields, Lasser found employment in the early 1930s as an editor with Gernsback Publications, a pioneer publisher of science fiction, and organized the American Interplanetary Society to promote the possibility of space travel.

The socially conscious Lasser joined the Socialist Party in the early 1930s, having voted for Republican Herbert Hoover in 1928. As the Depression worsened, Lasser became involved on a full-time basis with Socialist efforts to organize the jobless as a means of alleviating their plight. He was soon executive secretary of the Socialist-controlled New York Workers Committee on Unemployment. In March 1935 a national convention of mostly Socialist-controlled unemployed groups created the Workers Alliance of America and elected Lasser its president. The Communist "rule or ruin" tactics of the Third Period precluded inclusion of what was left of the Communist Party's Unemployed Councils. Indeed, Lasser initially rejected overtures for their inclusion in the Workers Alliance.

As a result of the Communist Party's Popular Front approach (which moved into high gear during 1935), Lasser's attitude changed, and in April 1936, with his support, the Councils were merged into the Workers Alliance. A fervent Popular Fronter, Lasser visited the Soviet Union in 1937 and the next year resigned from the foundering Socialist Party. The energetic Lasser served the Workers Alliance membership well. He was a vigorous spokesman and able in his dealings with the Roosevelt administration—his capacity to do so being especially important because the Workers Alliance quickly had evolved from an organization lobbying for more relief to one serving as a kind of collective-bargaining agency for the relief clients employed by the Works Progress Administration (WPA).

The fortunes of the Workers Alliance were tied closely to those of the WPA, and when it began to decline in the late 1930s, so too did Lasser's organization. But the demise of the Workers Alliance was in the main a result of changes occasioned in the Communist Party line by the Nazi-Soviet Pact of August 1939. Adoption of these changes by the Workers Alliance despite Lasser's opposition made clear Communist domination of the organization. In June 1940 a disillusioned Lasser resigned from the Workers Alliance and started another unemployed organization, the short-lived American Security Union.

During World War II and immediately thereafter, Lasser held several government posts (including director of the Labor Advisory Committee of the War Production Board and labor consultant on the Marshall Plan), but in both 1941 and 1950 Lasser was blacklisted from government on charges he was a security risk. He joined the staff of the International Union of Electrical, Radio, and Machine Workers in 1950, from which he retired in 1968 as assistant to the president for economics and collective bargaining.

*DANIEL LEAB*

244                                                                  LAUKKI, LEO

**LAUKKI, LEO (1880–?).** Leo Laukki (born Leo Lindqvist), a teacher at *Työväen Opisto* (Work People's College) in Duluth, Minnesota, became a leader among Finns in the Upper Midwest who espoused the precepts of the Industrial Workers of the World (IWW) before World War I. Born to working-class parents in Helsinki, Finland, in 1880, Laukki managed to attend Helsinki University for one year and worked abroad in Germany and Russia before returning to Finland to attend Hamina Military Academy. Upon graduation he joined the Russian cavalry and reached the rank of lieutenant.

Laukki participated in the Viapori military revolt in the fortress in Helsinki harbor. When the revolt was suppressed, he went underground and worked briefly for the Social Democratic newspaper *Kansan Lehti* (People's Tribune) in Tampere, Finland. In 1907 he came to the United States and joined the staff of *Raivajaa* (The Pioneer) in Fitchburg, Massachusetts, and later moved to Hancock, Michigan, where he worked for *Työmies* (The Worker).

In 1909 he began teaching at Work People's College in Duluth and later, with another Finnish exile (Yrjo Sirola) helped push the school leftward from its parliamentary socialistic base. While in Duluth, Laukki wrote and lectured extensively and became chief editor of *Työmies* in 1911. He immediately raised concern among his readers by advocating that workers had a right to destroy tools of production as a means of winning demands from employers. He was censured at the 1912 Finnish Socialist Convention but continued to speak as before. In 1914 a majority of midwestern Finnish Socialist locals, made up of Laukki followers, were expelled from the national Finnish Socialist organization. They quickly reorganized as adherents of IWW philosophy. In 1915 Laukki took over the editorship of *Sosialisti* in Duluth and in a short while made it an organ of the IWW. Due to his influence, the faculty and philosophy of Work People's College also supported the IWW.

Arrested as one of the "Chicago 166" in 1918 during World War I, Laukki became an enthusiastic supporter of the Bolshevik Revolution while in prison waiting trail. Free on bail, he fled to Russia, where for a short period he served as secretary to the Finnish Communist Party (in exile). He was later an instructor in the Western Minorities University in Leningrad. The last known contact any American had with him was in 1930. He was at that time a correspondent for *Tass* in Tashkent. No one knows what happened to him or when he died.

SOURCES: Elis Sulkanen, *Amerikan Suomalaisen Työväenliikkeen Historia* (1951), p. 493; John Wiita Collection, Immigration History Research Center, University of Minnesota, St. Paul, Minnesota.

*MIKE KARNI*

**LEE, ALGERNON (1873–1954).** Algernon Lee was a Socialist educator and editor who also served on the New York City board of aldermen from 1918 until 1922. Born in Dubuque, Iowa, in 1873, Lee was educated in the public schools of Fishkill, New York, and Minneapolis, Minnesota, and the University of Minnesota, from which he graduated in 1897.

Lee joined the Socialist Labor Party in 1895. Four years later he joined the anti-DeLeon (q.v.) "Kangaroo" organization led by Morris Hillquit (q.v.) and helped found the Socialist Party led by Hillquit, Eugene Debs (q.v.), and Victor Berger (q.v.) in 1901. He was named editor of the Minneapolis Socialist weekly, *The Tocsin*, in 1898. A year later he became editor of the New York Socialist weekly *Worker*, which later became the *New York Call*. He edited the *Call* from 1908 until 1909, when he was named educational director of the Rand School, the Socialist educational institution in New York City. He retained that position for more than forty years.

Lee was a follower of Hillquit and a centrist in intraparty factionalism. Although he was dedicated to democratic, nonviolent methods, he believed that more militantly aggressive action might at times be necessary. This was especially true of his view of the general strike, which he defended in 1916. "Very frequently the general strike is used to back up political action," he declared. But this was not always so, he added. If necessary, he said, Socialists were prepared to call a general strike and use it to achieve their political aims.

Lee was elected to the New York City board of aldermen in 1917 and was named leader of the ten-member Socialist delegation. In the 1919 election he was declared the loser and his Democratic opponent was seated in his place. However, the New York Supreme Court recounted the ballots and declared in November 1921 that Lee had in fact been reelected. He was then finally seated for the last two months of his term.

Lee was an avowed opponent of U.S. participation in World War I. He, Charles Ruthenberg (q.v.), and Morris Hillquit were the authors of the anti-war St. Louis Declaration passed by the Socialist convention a day after war was declared. On the board of aldermen, Lee opposed the purchase of war savings stamps, but he did not oppose the purchase of Liberty Bonds, and he voted for the construction of the soldiers' memorial arch. He also proposed city ownership of the transit lines, which was finally achieved some fifteen years after he left the city legislature. After his term on the board of aldermen, Lee resumed his work in the Rand School and edited *The Essentials of Marx*, an anthology of Marxian writings. He also wrote pamphlets and articles in the *New Leader*, the post-war Socialist weekly.

In the early 1930s a split developed in the Socialist Party between the Old Guard faction and the younger Militant faction. Lee became one of the leaders of the Old Guard. When the party split in 1936, Lee went into the Social Democratic Federation, leaving the Socialist Party he had helped found thirty-five years previously. He also became a member of the executive committee of the American Labor Party (ALP) of New York. He resigned from the ALP when the Communists gained control in 1944. Thereafter he was an active member of the Liberal Party.

Lee was among the Social Democrats who opposed the attempt in 1937 by Norman Thomas (q.v.) and his Socialist Party followers to enter the ALP. His opposition was based on Thomas' pacifism in the face of the threat from Fascism.

Lee, the World War I pacifist, had become a strong interventionist in the years immediately preceding U.S. entry into World War II.

Lee remained active in the Rand School and the Liberal Party for the rest of his life. He died in January 1954 in Amityville, a small city on Long Island, New York.

SOURCES: Evans Clark and Charles Solomon, *The Socialists in the New York Board of Aldermen* (1918); Joint Legislative Committee Investigating Seditious Activities, *Revolutionary Radicalism* vols. 1 and 2 (1920).

*BERNARD K. JOHNPOLL*

**LENS, SIDNEY (b.1912).** Sidney Lens has been a central figure in the labor and peace movements in Chicago for forty-five years. As labor organizer, writer, educator, and leader in the resistance to the Vietnam War and the nuclear buildup, he has attempted to merge labor and anti-military activists into a more general, unified radical movement. Lens was born Sidney Okun in Newark, New Jersey, on January 28, 1912, the only child of Russian immigrants from a small village near Minsk. His father, who worked as a pharmacist and a shopkeeper, died when Sidney was 3 years old; his mother was a garment worker. Sidney received his elementary education in Hebrew schools but soon turned away from the Jewish tradition and completed his formal education at age 17 in the New York public schools.

In 1934 Lens joined the Trotskyist Communist League of America, which was under the leadership of James P. Cannon (q.v.). That December the organization merged with the American Workers Party, led by A. J. Muste (q.v.), to form the Workers Party of the United States. By 1936 Lens was associated with a Trotskyist splinter group, the Revolutionary Workers League.

In 1941, after several years of mostly unsuccessful organizing efforts in Chicago, Lens undertook a campaign among retail clerks in direct competition with the AFL's Retail Clerks International Protective Association. These efforts led to the establishment of Local 329 of the United Services Employees Union, an affiliate of the Congress of Industrial Organizations (CIO). Lens became director of Local 329 in September 1942. He opposed U.S. participation in World War II. Believing his organization to be overly isolated and powerless as a CIO affiliate, he moved Local 329 into the AFL's Building Services Employees International Union in 1946.

During the 1950s and 1960s Lens engaged in a series of increasingly literary and educational activities. The first of his thirteen books, *Left, Right, and Center: Conflicting Forces in American Labor*, was published in May 1949, and during the 1950s, in addition to further writing, he was involved in the founding of *Dissent*, with Irving Howe (q.v.), and *Liberation*, with A. J. Muste. In May 1957 Lens became national secretary of the ultimately unsuccessful American Forum for Socialist Education. Three years later he was asked to become a founding member of the Fair Play for Cuba Committee.

At this time Lens also began to concentrate on "outreach" activities that might involve workers in the budding peace movement. His involvement in Labor Leadership for Peace during the early 1960s and in cooperative activities with the American Friends Service Committee put him in position to help found the Chicago Peace Council in 1965 in response to the escalation of the war in Vietnam. He soon became a senior leader of the movement to resist the war and the nuclear arms race. He was co-chairman of the National Committee to End the War in Vietnam, and especially since his retirement from Local 329 in 1966 he has written extensively about the nuclear weapons buildup. In the past two decades Lens has also run unsuccessfully both for the U.S. House of Representatives (in 1962) and the U.S. Senate (in 1980). In the 1980s he was active in founding and guiding an anti-nuclear group, Mobilization for Survival.
SOURCES: Sidney Lens, *Unrepentant Radical* (1980); *Who's Who in America*, 42d ed. (1982–1983).

                                                                *ED SHOEMAKER*


**LLOYD, HENRY DEMAREST (1847–1903).** Henry Demarest Lloyd was a Populist, a Socialist writer, and a muckraking journalist. Born in New York City in 1847 of devout conservative Calvinist parents, he was educated at Columbia University (M.A., 1869) and admitted to the New York State bar in 1869.

Lloyd was active during the 1870s in the Free Trade League, founded by William Cullen Bryant. He also helped found the Young Men's Municipal Reform League of New York City, which helped destroy the Tammany Hall machine led by "Boss" Tweed.

In 1872 Lloyd tired of the practice of law and moved to Chicago to join the *Tribune* as an editorial writer and financial editor. He remained at the *Tribune* for nine years. In 1881, after a tour of the United States to examine the industrial situation, he wrote a series of muckraking articles for the *Atlantic* in which he cited the perils caused by the monopolies. As a result of this tour, Lloyd became a nonparty, pro-labor-union Socialist. He also became active in the movement to free the Haymarket defendants; his appeal was crucial in the commutation of the sentences of two of the accused.

During the 1880s and early 1890s, Lloyd was particularly active in aiding strikers, especially in the Spring Valley coal walkout and in the Pullman strike. During the latter he met and became a supporter of Eugene V. Debs (q.v.). In 1894 he also wrote his most famous work, *Wealth Versus Commonwealth*, in which he denounced the dangers of monopoly and the lack of social responsibility that permeated large corporations. The book had a major influence on Populist thought.

During the 1892 presidential campaign, Lloyd was an active supporter of the People's Party. In 1896 he supported Eugene Debs for the Populist nomination for President. When the Populists named William Jennings Bryan the Democratic standard-bearer as their candidate, Lloyd left the party and supported a Socialist candidate.

Lloyd remained active as a supporter of municipal ownership and of labor organization. In 1903 he joined the Socialist Party, led by Debs, Victor Berger (q.v.), and Morris Hillquit (q.v.). In September 1903, as he prepared to attend a Chicago city council meeting as a delegate from the Municipal Ownership League, Lloyd died suddenly.

SOURCE: Caro Lloyd, *Henry Demarest Lloyd* (1903).

*BERNARD K. JOHNPOLL*

**LLOYD, WILLIAM BROSS (1875–1946).** William Bross Lloyd exemplified the "millionaire socialist" of the early twentieth century. Born on February 24, 1875, the son of writer Henry Demarest Lloyd (q.v.) and the grandson of the former Illinois governor and founder of the *Chicago Tribune*, William Bross, Lloyd received a B.A. and later a law degree from Harvard University. His earliest contact with radical ideas came during his childhood in his father's home, a frequent gathering place for reformers of various persuasions.

While traveling in Europe with his father, Lloyd met many of the leaders of European socialism, including Friedrich Engels. In 1905 Lloyd affiliated with the Socialist Party. Prior to 1917 Lloyd played an active role in the Chicago branch of the Socialist Party, standing as a candidate in several state and local elections, but refrained from participating in the national affairs of the party. A major shareholder in the *Chicago Tribune* and independently wealthy from a trust fund, Lloyd frequently posted bail for arrested Socialists (including William Haywood [q.v.] after his 1918 espionage indictment) and was a major financial supporter of several Socialist publications, including the *Chicago Daily Socialist* and the *Liberator*.

Following American entry into World War I, he began to play an active role in national party affairs as an opponent of the war. In 1918 he gained national notoriety when he was arrested for refusing to remove a red flag from his chauffeur-driven limousine while parked in front of the Palmer House in Chicago. Later that same year he was the Socialist Party's Illinois candidate for U.S. Senate, but he received only 37,000 votes out of nearly one million cast.

Under the impact of the Russian Revolution, Lloyd moved steadily to the left. In 1918, in collaboration with his private secretary Isaac Ferguson (q.v.), he drafted one of the first comprehensive statements of the Socialist Party's left wing, a lengthy pamphlet entitled *The Socialist Party and Its Purpose*. In June 1919 Lloyd was elected chairman of the National Council of the party's Left Wing. Several months later he became one of the founders of the Communist Labor Party and served as sergeant-at-arms at its founding convention. In 1920 Lloyd and thirty-eight others were indicted by the state of Illinois for sedition. Although ably defended by Clarence Darrow, he received a sentence of one to five years, but the sentence was commuted in November 1922 by Governor Len Small after he had served only eight days. Lloyd's trial marked the beginning of a long process of disillusionment with the Communist movement. Shortly after his pardon he left the Party. By the 1930s he had been transformed into a

conservative Republican and an ardent opponent of the New Deal. He died on
June 30, 1946.

SOURCE: Forbert Reynolds, ''The Millionaire Socialists: J. G. Phelps and His Circle
of Friends'' (Ph.D. diss., University of South Carolina, 1974).

*JOHN GERBER*

**LONDON, MEYER (1871–1926).** Meyer London, lawyer, Socialist, and labor
leader, was born in 1871 in the town of Gora Kalvaria in the province of Sulvakie,
Russian Poland. His mother (Rebecca Berson) was a devout daughter of a rabbi,
and his father (Ephraim London), a lifelong student of the Talmud, was an
agnostic and a radical in his politics. This rich mix of the traditional-religious
and the modern-secular appears often in the social backgrounds of East European
Jews like Meyer London who went on to become Socialists. Meyer, the oldest
of five sons, had himself attended Heder (religious school), learned Hebrew,
biblical interpretation, and Talmud, and then went on to Russian school, where
he received a secular education.

Economic instability was also a factor. Ephraim London occasionally wrote
for Hebrew periodicals but had no regular source of income. He tried his hand
as a grain merchant in Zenkov, Poltavia, before he left for what he thought
would be better opportunity in America in 1888. Here Ephraim London ran an
unprofitable anarchist print shop and published a small Yiddish paper.

Meyer London had been left behind in Russia and was expected to go on with
his education. Later he described these years there:

I was poor, of course. We were all poor together. I was able to keep up my studies by
teaching boys who did not know as much as I did. I belonged to a crowd of young fellows
who talked a lot about revolution and had not the least idea what revolution really meant.
My father in America heard of my inclination and wrote me that under no condition
whatever... was I to commit myself on revolutionary matters. I must study, think,
observe, and wait until I knew very much more about conditions in the world. (Quoted
in Hillel Rogoff, *An East Side Epic* [1930].)

When Meyer London came to New York in 1891 to join his father on Suffolk
Street in the heart of the Lower East Side, he was immediately drawn into radical
politics. Immigrant Jews were already giving growing and disproportionate support to the Left, and the elder London, who maintained a close and abiding
relationship with his son, was deeply involved with Socialist and anarchist groups.
But Meyer's developing activism and commitment did not prevent him from
continuing his voracious reading or his formal education. He tutored youngsters
and worked in a library to put himself through high school, and then in 1896
he entered New York University Law School at night. He was admitted to the
bar in 1898. The same year that London began his legal education, the Socialist
Labor Party nominated him for the New York State Assembly. By 1897 he found
himself at odds with the leadership of Daniel DeLeon (q.v.) and went over to
the newly organized Social Democratic Party. Ultimately, working with Eugene

V. Debs (q.v.), Victor Berger (q.v.), and Morris Hillquit (q.v.), Meyer London became one of the founders of the Socialist Party of America in 1901.

London was a Socialist who acknowledged the legitimacy of ethnic demands as well as class needs, and local interests as well as the interest of the generalized proletariat. He recognized the reality of particularist oppression within the broader context of economic exploitation. This was surely one of the reasons that London, on the densely Jewish East Side, was successful in his bid for a Congressional seat. In 1910 he replaced Hillquit as the Congressional candidate of the Socialist Party. Hillquit had lost the election in 1908, and his defeat had been unexpectedly heavy. At the first rally of his campaign Hillquit had said that if elected he would "not consider [himself] the special representative of the . . . special interests of this district, but the representative of the Socialist Party . . . and . . . the working class of the country."

This was put forward at a time when East Side residents were upset by a police commissioner's report that implied that Jews were responsible for 50 percent of the crime in New York City, when the "special interest" issue of immigration restriction was being hotly debated in Congress, and when the position of the Socialist Party on that issue, favoring some restriction, did not seem positive to East Side Jews who still had relatives desiring to escape from pogrom-ridden Russia.

Meyer London, unlike Hillquit, openly identified as a Jewish Socialist and allied himself with the interests and vital movements of the East Side. "I deem it a duty of the Jew everywhere," he said, "to remain a Jew as long as in any corner of the world the Jew is being discriminated against." Though failing to be elected in 1910, London garnered 33 percent of the vote and outran his own Socialist Party ticket two to one. By 1914 he won 47 percent of the vote and was victorious. He went on to be elected twice more, in 1916, despite fusion between the Republicans and Democrats, and in 1920.

London did not substitute ethnic interests for class interests. He combined them. He was not elected *despite* his socialism, but because to the Jewish immigrant masses he was very much *their* Socialist. London told a crowd of 15,000 after his initial election:

I do not expect to work wonders in Congress. I shall, however, say a new word and I shall accomplish the thing that is not in the platform of the Socialist Party. I hope that my presence will represent an entirely different type of Jew from the kind that Congress is accustomed to see.

In the same speech, which met with the same enthusiasm, London also said, "We shall not rest until every power of capitalism has been destroyed and the workers emancipated from wage slavery."

London went on in the House of Representatives to introduce bills described as "wild socialist schemes" by his Congressional colleagues. "When I made my first speech," London remembered, "one of the most extreme of the Republicans made his way across the House and peered into my face as if to discover what kind of a weird creature from some other world had found its way to this planet."

During his three terms, London advocated measures against child labor and the use of injunctions in labor disputes. He supported nationalization of the coal industry, improved salaries for government workers, unemployment insurance, and old-age pensions. He opposed immigration restriction, protectionism, and property qualifications for voting in Puerto Rico. One bill that he introduced, protecting employees of bankrupt firms, became law.

London continued to render service to the Bund, the most important organization of Russian-Jewish Socialists. He favored the March Revolution of 1917 in Russia and criticized the general Allied failure to encourage and support the provisional government there. After the Bolshevik takeover, he spoke on moral and political grounds against the policy of intervention and blockade. In the same years, Meyer London was sharply critical of the "bread and butter" unionism of the American Federation of Labor, and he served the Socialist needle-trades unions as legal counsel, adviser in matters of union policy, and spokesman in negotiations.

Although all this made London a "moderate" leftist, he was nonetheless the target of virulent anti-Socialist attacks. He also endured critical blasts from his own party, particularly in 1917–1918, for refusing to resist *all* wartime activity. London was clearly anti-war. He had earlier opposed intervention in Mexico and budget increases for the army and navy. He strongly resisted U.S. entry into World War I and voted against the conscription and espionage laws, and he vigorously fought efforts to curb civil liberties during the national crisis. He was convinced, however, that the Socialists' St. Louis Declaration, insisting that all workers refuse to heed their respective governments' calls for help, was too extreme, and once the United States was at war he voted "present"—a way of abstaining but not impeding the nation's military measures. For this the Socialist Left never forgave him, but he was also severely attacked by non-Socialists for his lack of "war patriotism."

London also ran afoul of the Labor Zionists when he evaded a request to introduce a resolution supporting the Balfour Declaration and warned against "forcible annexation" of Arab land. No longer the representative of a solidly coherent constituency, London failed to be reelected in 1918. He did run and win again for the last time in 1920. But in 1922 the Republicans and Democrats once more united against him and his district was gerrymandered in such a way that his defeat was assured. He never ran again.

Meyer London married Anna Rosenson in 1899. They had one daughter, who remembered a home with little material embellishment but filled with love and support and many books. London was a modest man who lived his whole adult life on the East Side and shared the values of his plebian constituency. He served them as adviser, advocate, and sometimes "banker." In his law office, amid his own unpaid bills, London handed over the entire $35 balance in his bankbook to strikers in 1912. It was neither the first nor the last time he would do this kind of thing. He made little contribution to Socialist theory, but he was loved and respected by the denizens of the East Side as the finest example of Socialist man. In 1926, while crossing Second Avenue and fingering in his jacket pocket a collection of Chekhov's short stories, Meyer London was struck by a taxi and fatally injured.

SOURCES: Melech Epstein, *Profiles of Eleven* (1965); Hillel Rogoff, *An East Side Epic: The Life and Work of Meyer London* (1930).

*GERALD SORIN*

**LORE, LUDWIG (1875–1942).** Ludwig Lore edited a major organ of German-American socialism, helped found the Communist movement, and represented its more moderate tendencies until his expulsion from the Party in 1925. Lore was born on June 26, 1875, in Friedberg, Germany, to Jewish parents. A graduate of Berlin University, he worked in the textile industry from 1892 to 1903 and was active in the German Social Democratic Party. He came to the United States in 1903 and worked in Colorado, where he joined the Industrial Workers of the World, and in New York as a journalist. Active in the Socialist Party, Lore was converted to the left wing by Leon Trotsky during his 1917 sojourn in the States. Even though Lore sympathized with the Left, he hesitated to break with the Socialist Party, on whose National Executive Committee he sat in 1919, but finally did so. Lore also was pardoned that year after serving ten days of a one-to-five year sentence in Chicago for syndicalism.

Lore's hesitation was prompted by his inability to reconcile his enthusiasm for the left wing with his rather orthodox German Marxism. Even though he held important positions in 1919 (he was the executive secretary and dominating force of the German Socialist Federation and had just become editor of the *New Yorker Volkszeitung*), his Communist colleagues were suspicious of his revolutionary bona fides. Elected to the National Executive Committee of the Communist Labor Party, he was removed because Party leaders doubted his doctrines and feared the rival Communist Party would use his election to embarrass them. Such slights continued in the 1920s. Lore led a faction of the Workers Party, which included Juliet Poyntz (q.v.) and Moissaye Olgin (q.v.). His group formed an alliance with that led by James Cannon (q.v.) and William Foster (q.v.). Lore opposed the Party's attempt to attach itself to the LaFollette movement in 1924. Despite the Comintern's eventual endorsement of just such a policy, he came under fierce attack from Moscow as a Social Democrat. He was also accused of being a supporter of Trotsky. At the 1925 Party convention, Poyntz alone opposed a motion expelling Lore from the Party. When the Party's German Federation refused to oust Lore as secretary, his supporters were expelled and replaced by more pliant figures, and Lore was removed.

Lore continued to regard himself as an independent Communist. He flirted with the Trotskyists in 1928 and may even have briefly joined them, but his refusal to submit his newspaper columns to party discipline ended the relationship. He gave up the editorship of the *Volkszeitung* in 1931 to become a free-lance writer. In 1934 he joined the editorial staff of the *New York Post* and wrote a daily column, becoming increasingly anti-Stalinist. He nonetheless had become enmeshed with Soviet intelligence agencies. Shortly before his death he informed the Federal Bureau of Investigation about the activities of Whittaker Chambers, with whom he had dealings. Chambers' revelations later led to exposure of Alger Hiss as a Soviet agent. Lore died on July 7, 1942.

SOURCE: Theodore Draper, *American Communism and Soviet Russia* (1960).

HARVEY KLEHR

**LOVESTONE, JAY (b. 1898).** Jay Lovestone has had three different careers. He was a major leader of the Communist Party of the United States; he was head of his own dissident Communist group in the United States and internationally for almost a dozen years; and then he was virtually the minister of foreign affairs for the American Federation of Labor and the AFL-CIO. Lovestone was born Jacob Liebstein in 1898 in Lithuania, then part of czarist Russia. He migrated with his Jewish parents to the United States when he was 9 years old. He studied at City College in New York City, where he was head of the Socialist Club in 1917.

Lovestone sided with the Socialist Party's Left Wing faction, and at the founding congress of the Communist Party of America in September 1919 he was elected to its Central Committee. When conflicting Communist factions joined forces in May 1921, Lovestone was again elected to the Central Committee of the united organization and became editor-in-chief of the underground newspaper, the *Communist*. In September 1921 he was chosen as deputy secretary, and in January 1922 he was named national secretary. He subsequently became organizational secretary and attended the Fifth Enlarged Plenum of the Executive Committee of the Communist International in Moscow in March 1925.

Meanwhile, the Communist Party was characterized by bitter factionalism. Lovestone was the principal lieutenant of Charles Ruthenberg (q.v.), leader of the faction that became the majority group after the Comintern in 1925 decided in its favor, and against the rival element led by William Z. Foster (q.v.) and James Cannon (q.v.). As Ruthenberg's major aide, Lovestone became deputy secretary-general of the Party. Upon Ruthenberg's death in the spring of 1927, Lovestone became head of the majority faction as well as general secretary of the Communist Party.

Within the Communist International, Lovestone and his faction within the U.S. Communist Party were particularly aligned with Nikolai Bukharin, who was president of the Comintern from 1927 to 1929. Lovestone played an important role in the Sixth Congress of the Comintern in 1928 and was elected to the presidium of the Executive Committee of the International at the Sixth Congress.

Soon afterward James Cannon, who had also been a delegate, announced—together with Max Shachtman (q.v.) and Martin Abern (q.v.)—his conversion to support of Leon Trotsky. Lovestone thereupon brought about the expulsion of the Trotskyist trio as well as a thorough purge of their supporters throughout the Party. Nevertheless, as an ally of Bukharin, Lovestone himself soon came under the attack of Joseph Stalin. Lovestone had the support of 90 percent of the delegates to the sixth convention of the U.S. Party in March 1929. However, his support of Bukharin and his espousal of "American exceptionalism," the argument that European and American development was different and required different tactics, led to trouble. Lovestone and his principal aides were summoned to Moscow in May 1929 for a "trial" by the new leadership of the Communist International. There, after a bitter personal confrontation with Stalin, Lovestone was removed from leadership of the U.S. Party.

Upon returning home, Lovestone found himself also expelled from the Communist Party. In the next few weeks all those who remained loyal to him were also expelled. Lovestone then undertook to establish the dissident Communist Party (Majority Group). In spite of its name, it rallied only a small minority of the Communist Party members and leaders. Subsequently, it changed its name various times, to Communist Party (Opposition), Independent Communist Labor League, and finally Independent Labor League. Throughout the existence of the group, Lovestone served as its national secretary. He also was its principal public spokesman and organizer, and he wrote regularly for its periodical, *Workers Age*.

The "Lovestoneites," as they were frequently referred to in the 1930s, constituted a major opposition group to the Stalinist Communist Party of the United States. During this period, they had considerable influence in the International Ladies Garment Workers Union, Auto Workers, United Shoeworkers, and other unions. In the United Auto Workers (UAW) Lovestone futilely attempted to help its president Homer Martin eliminate his Communist, Socialist, and radical opposition.

Lovestone was also a leading figure in the International Communist Opposition (ICO), the international organization of Communist elements in various countries that had been more or less in sympathy with Bukharin in the internal quarrels of the 1920s and thereafter in the Soviet Union. He attended various conferences of the ICO and made several trips to Europe in connection with ICO activities.

During most of this period, Lovestone remained a strong critic of Stalinist policies within the Communist International, but generally supported Stalin's internal policies in the Soviet Union as well as his foreign policy. However, the Moscow purge trials, especially the trial in which Bukharin was the major defendant, as well as Stalinist persecution of the Lovestoneites' counterpart in Spain, the Partido Obrero de Unificación Marxista (POUM), during the Spanish Civil War, made Lovestone and his followers turn completely against the Stalinists. By 1939 they had concluded that they were no longer Bolsheviks but democratic Socialists. As a result, the final conference of the Independent Labor League in January 1941 decided to dissolve the organization. Shortly before its dissolution, the Lovestoneite group had come out in support of U.S. aid to Great Britain in its struggle against the Nazis after the fall of France.

Lovestone became head of the Free Trade Union Committee (FTUC) soon after the dissolution of the Independent Labor League. The FTUC was an organization that at its inception was supported principally by the International Ladies Garment Workers Union, of which ex-Lovestoneite Charles Zimmerman (q.v.) was by then a vice-president. At first, the FTUC was devoted principally to rescuing European trade unionists and Socialists from Nazi-dominated Europe.

After World War II, however, the Free Trade Union Committee, with the support of AFL Secretary George Meany and several other major leaders of the American Federation of Labor, including its vice-president Matthew Woll, came to be in charge of the overseas activities of the AFL. Jay Lovestone, as head of the committee, became the principal author and executor of the foreign policies of the AFL, particularly in Europe, Africa, and Asia.

During this period Lovestone helped organize free trade union movements in such countries as Germany and Japan. In several cases Lovestone relied on former members of his onetime opposition Communist group as his aides. Under Lovestone's leadership, the Free Trade Union Committee also backed anti-Communist elements in other European countries. It gave extensive aid to establishment of Force Ouvrière in France and Social Democratic and Christian Democratic trade union groups in Italy. It also helped organize labor movements in various Third World Nations, including Tunisia, Morocco, Indonesia, Ghana, and Kenya.

When the AFL and the CIO (Congress of Industrial Organizations) were united early in 1955, Lovestone was briefly demoted. Within a short period, however, he became director of the International Department of the AFL-CIO and steered it on a strongly anti-Communist course until his retirement late in the 1970s.

Both in the AFL and in the AFL-CIO, Lovestone was particularly closely connected with George Meany. He wrote most of Meany's speeches on international affairs and he had major responsibility for drafting statements in that field for the conventions and executive committee meetings of the organizations. For many years he edited the *Free Trade Union News*, first as the organ of the Free Trade Union Committee and then as the organ of the AFL-CIO, which was a major source of information on the international labor movement. However, Lovestone made relatively few public appearances.

SOURCES: Robert Alexander, *The Right Opposition* (1981); Theodore Draper, *American Communism and Soviet Russia* (1961).

*ROBERT ALEXANDER*

**LUM, DYER D. (1839–1893).** Dyer D. Lum was a leading anarchist-syndicalist of the 1880s. He was an advocate of violence and of trade unionism between 1880 and 1892 and a prominent left-wing intellectual and publicist. Lum was born in Geneva, New York, in 1839, of Scot-Yankee descent. One of his ancestors was a revolutionary war soldier, several others were active in the abolitionist movement, and one uncle was a U.S. Senator and an avowed free-thinker. Lum was raised and educated in New York State's "Burned-Over District," an area stretching from the vicinity of Utica to the neighborhood of Jamestown which was the center of religious and social radicalism in that state during the period immediately preceding the Civil War.

Like most other young people in that section of the state, Lum was an active abolitionist. With the outbreak of the Civil War in 1861, Lum volunteered. He served as a front-line infantryman and cavalry soldier for the full four years of the war. Twice he was taken prisoner, and twice he escaped. Years later a disillusioned Lum would say that he had fought to free the black man only to discover that he had merely helped enrich white entrepreneurs. With the end of the war, Lum apprenticed himself to a bookbinder, becoming a journeyman in two years. Although he did not work for long at the trade, Lum played a leading role in organizing the bookbinders of the East into a union.

By 1871 he became an organizer for the nascent trade union movement in western Massachusetts. This was at a time of anti-Oriental agitation among American workingmen. He opposed the anti-Chinese agitation by the trade unionists, and in North Adams he used his influence to prevent rioting. His anti-discrimination stance led him into a major debate in the columns of the Denver *Labor Enquirer* with the leading anti-Chinese radical of the period, Bernette G. Haskell (q.v.) of California, who wanted the Orientals thrown out of the United States. Lum was prepared to concede that the Chinese were lepers, rat-eaters, and semi-human, but he insisted that they were not to blame for their migration. The real villains, he argued, were the capitalists who imported them into the United States as a cheap commodity. Lum's answer to the problem of Chinese "coolie labor" in the States was to organize these "subhuman monsters" so they would no longer be used as strikebreakers. His stance won strong support in New England.

In 1876 the Greenback-Labor Party of Massachusetts nominated Lum as its candidate for lieutenant governor. He was defeated. A year later Lum was named by Representative Benjamin Butler to be secretary of a Congressional committee to investigate the "depression of labor." And three years later Lum was named to a Knights of Labor committee to propagandize and lobby for the eight-hour maximum work day. On this committee he met and became fast friends with Albert W. Parsons (q.v.), who converted him to anarchist-syndicalism. In the same period Lum served also as secretary to Samuel Gompers, who was then organizing a new federation of trade unions of skilled workmen.

In 1884 Lum was converted to the "propaganda of the deed"—violence—as preached by Johann Most (q.v.). He also began writing for anarchist journals in both wings of the movement: *Alarm*, the Chicago organ of the pro-Most wing, edited by Parsons, which advocated a Communistic anarchism, terror, and violence; and *Liberty*, the organ of the pacifistic individualist brand edited by Benjamin Tucker and Victor Yaroslavsky, who as Victor Yarros became a renowned teacher of philosophy. In one of his articles "To Arms: An Appeal to the Wage Workers of America," published in *Alarm* a week prior to the Haymarket bombing of

1886, Lum called on the workers of the United States to arm themselves, arguing that only violence could end wage slavery.

When in May 1886 a bomb exploded at a rally of anarchists in Haymarket Square in Chicago, Lum became an active supporter of the leaders of the demonstration who were arrested. He wrote a book describing the events leading up to the explosion and defending the accused. A year later, when it became obvious to him that all peaceful efforts to save the accused had failed, Lum called in vain for the use of terror, the only way "to save the Haymarket victims." He urged the condemned men not to plead for clemency, which would be seen as an admission of wrongdoing. He is believed to have smuggled a dynamite-filled cigar to Louis Lingg, one of the condemned men, who committed suicide with it. The others—August Spies (q.v.), Albert Parsons, George Engell, and Adolph Fischer—died on the gallows on November 11, 1887. Lum took over the editorship of *Alarm* from Parsons and called on the workers of Chicago to avenge the executions. He called dynamite "the resource of civilization."

With the passage of time, Lum became less violent in his rhetoric. When Alexander Berkman (q.v.) made his futile attempt to kill (anti-labor) steel magnate Henry Clay Frick, Lum hailed his act. But he no longer advocated violence. In fact, by 1892 he had become a moderate syndicalist. In that year he published a major treatise defending conservative trade unionism and outlining the philosophy that would dominate the American Federation of Labor (AFL). The short book, *A Philosophy of Trade Unions*, was reprinted by the AFL for many years thereafter.

Lum, who lived alone on the Bowery (then New York City's theater district) was addicted to opium and whiskey during the last year of his life. By late 1892 he became depressed with the state of the world and with what he perceived to be his own failings. In April 1893 Dyer Lum, aged 54, took poison and died a suicide.

SOURCES: Paul Avrich, *An American Anarchist: The Life of Voltairine de Cleyre* (1978); Dyer D. Lum, manuscript autobiographical sketch, May 13, 1892, copy in Ishill Collection, University of Florida, Gainesville, Florida; Dyer D. Lum, Letter in *Labor Enquirer* (Denver), July 9, 1887.

*BERNARD K. JOHNPOLL*


**LUNN, GEORGE R. (1873–1948).** George R. Lunn was a Social Gospel Presbyterian minister who served as Socialist mayor of Schenectady, New York, from 1912 to 1914 and for part of 1916. Born on a farm in southwestern Iowa in 1873, he attended public schools in that state. After completing his high school education, Lunn worked as a teamster in South Omaha, Nebraska, for three years before enrolling in Bellevue (Nebraska) College. Upon graduation, he enlisted in the army to fight in the Spanish-American War.

At the end of the war, Lunn enrolled first in the conservative Princeton Theological Seminary in New Jersey and then at Union Theological Seminary in New York, the center of Social Gospel Protestant theology in the eastern

United States. He received his bachelor of divinity degree from Union in 1903. (He was awarded an honorary doctorate of divinity by Union College in 1905.)

After a short stay as assistant at the Lafayette Avenue Presbyterian Church in Brooklyn, New York, Lunn accepted a call to the prestigious First Presbyterian Church in Schenectady, New York, a heavily industrial city of almost 75,000 inhabitants, including 12,000 employees of the rapidly growing General Electric plant and 10,000 in the American Locomotive Works.

During his pastorate at the Schenectady church—which counted among its congregants most of the leading industrialists of the city—Lunn preached his own version of the Social Gospel. He argued that the Bible was more than a mere refuge for an individual in time of personal need, that it was a plea for social justice and a pathfinder on the road to a perfect society based on total human cooperation in place of competition. He differed with other Christian Socialist leaders of the period in only two respects. Lunn's sermons were more closely linked to the New Testament than were the preaching and writing of Walter Rauschenbusch (q.v.) or Stitt Wilson whose sermons were more closely tied to the Old Testament. Lunn also believed in immediate action to oppose the depredations of the existing social system at the local level, rather than proposing a universal solution. He agreed with other Social Gospel leaders in his views of the Bible as the key to social betterment and of the church as the agency for social action.

In his first major confrontation with the social order in Schenectady, Lunn did battle against the Vanderbilt-owned transit system when it raised fares in 1907. Lunn lost that fight, but he won great popular support for his stand— although the transit line's general manager, a financial mainstay of the church, resigned from the parish. Two years later Lunn forced the local gas company to cut its rates. That same year he fought an attempt to cover up corruption in the Republican-run government in Schenectady County. He secured the support of Progressive Republican Governor Charles Evans Hughes in that effort and won the indictment of several high county officials. Many wealthy members of his congregation resigned in protest of his actions.

His popularity at a high point, Lunn left the wealthy Presbyterian church and formed his own People's United Church, which became his personal platform for social reform. In 1910 he founded his own weekly newspaper, *The Citizen*, with which he further declaimed against the "malefactors" of the county and city. It was in this newspaper that the term "silent majority" appears to have been first used as a description of ordinary citizens.

Lunn joined the Socialist Party in December 1910, well after he had begun his campaign for social reform. His popularity in the city was so great by that time that he was named the Socialist candidate for mayor nine months later, despite a party bylaw that required two years of membership for any Socialist nomination.

In the 1911 election Lunn enunciated his political philosophy. Private ownership of industry, he declared, could exist only so long as the owners recognized that they had a moral obligation to society. Without that recognition, private ownership of the means of production and distribution would have to be replaced by public ownership. In this campaign he also demanded playgrounds in a city that had none, free textbooks for public school students, a municipal electric light plant, and an end to corruption.

His campaign was one of the most effective in the history of the city. Not only did he sweep Schenectady, carrying nine of its thirteen wards, he also brought in with him a majority of the city council and the county's assemblyman, the first Socialist elected to the New York state legislature.

At his inauguration Lunn declared that, although it was impossible to establish socialism in Schenectady alone, "We can, and will, demonstrate to all the spirit of socialism and the application of Socialist principles insofar as possible in the light of the handicap of laws framed to sustain capitalism."

Lunn attempted to carry out his pledges. He expanded city services, even attempting to set up a municipal coal and ice service and a municipal grocery— all of which failed because of legal and fiscal inhibitions. He also set up a city-run employment service and municipal lodging house and farm. The playgrounds he inaugurated were still in use more than seventy years later. Lunn won plaudits from the labor movement when he was arrested and jailed for four days for helping textile strikers in nearby Little Falls in 1912. And he forced General Electric to rehire two union leaders fired in a dispute over organizing tactics.

His primary difficulties as mayor were with the members of his own party. He refused to name only Socialist Party members to policy positions, although he did name many—Walter Lippmann was his secretary for four months—to the most important posts. His insistence on hiring the most capable, regardless of politics, led to an eventual schism in the party. In the 1913 election Lunn increased his vote, but he was defeated by a fusion of Republicans, Democrats, and Progressives. Two years later Lunn again won the mayoralty as a Socialist. The only other Socialist elected with him was the world-renowned electrical wizard, Charles Steinmetz, who won the presidency of the city council. The feuding over Lunn's appointment policy became so heated at the start of his second term that he was forced to resign from the party. He remained mayor, but as a Democrat.

Lunn was elected to Congress as a Democrat in 1916, but he was defeated for reelection in 1918. The next year he was again mayor of Schenectady and served until 1923. He was then elected lieutenant governor under Alfred E. Smith. In 1931 he was named to the Public Utilities Commission, on which he served for eleven years. His decisions on the commission became more conservative during his later years. He then supported rate increases for utilities.

In the last years of his life, Lunn served as commander-in-chief of the United Spanish War Veterans. He died in California in 1948.

SOURCE: Kenneth E. Hendrickson, Jr., "Tribune of the People: George R. Lunn and the Rise and Fall of Christian Socialism in America," in *Socialism and the Cities*, ed. Bruce M. Stave (1975), pp. 72–89.

*BERNARD K. JOHNPOLL*

**LYND, STAUGHTON (b. 1929).** Staughton Lynd has been a revisionist historian, a leader in the organized anti-war movement of the Vietnam era, and a lawyer oriented toward labor activism and community-organizing.

Born in Philadelphia on November 22, 1929, Lynd is the son of trailblazing sociologists Robert S. and Helen M. Lynd. He graduated from Harvard in 1951 and entered the U.S. Army in 1953, but he received an undesirable discharge in 1954 because of his radical associations in college. The Supreme Court reversed this action in 1961 and ordered the discharge changed to an honorable one.

Meanwhile, Lynd received his Ph.D. from Columbia University in 1961. He was assistant professor of American history at Spelman College in Atlanta, Georgia, from 1961 until 1966, when he joined the Department of History at Yale. As a New Left historian, Lynd emphasized in his publications the significance of economic causes and class conflict in explaining U.S. history and the need to pay further scholarly attention to the lower classes and inarticulate groups in the American past.

Lynd was director of freedom schools during the Mississippi Summer Project of 1964. Passing into the anti-war movement, he served as chairman of the first March on Washington in protest of the Vietnam War on April 17, 1965, and made a "fact-finding trip" to Hanoi at Christmas 1965 as a part of the same effort.

Lynd left Yale and attended the University of Chicago law school, from which he received his law degree in 1976. He is presently working in Youngstown, Ohio, as a legal services attorney specializing in labor law. He has represented a number of citizens and labor groups attempting to prevent industrial plant closings in the Mahoning Valley.

SOURCES: *Directory of American Scholars*, 5th ed., vol. 1: History (1969). Staughton
    Lynd and Gar Alperovitz, *Strategy and Program: Two Essays Toward a New American
    Socialism* (1973).

*ED SHOEMAKER*

# M

MACDONALD, DWIGHT (1906–1982). Dwight Macdonald, a well-known cultural critic, was an editor of *Partisan Review* magazine from 1937 to 1943 and the editor of *Politics* from 1944 to 1949. Born in New York on March 12, 1906, Macdonald was the son of a lawyer. He graduated from Yale in 1928 and began his journalism career by writing for *Fortune* magazine in 1929. By 1936 he had become a sympathizer of the Communist Party and resigned from *Fortune* in protest over changes made in an article on the steel industry.

A year later Macdonald became interested in Trotskyism. He joined the editorial board of the new *Partisan Review* when it was relaunched as an independent Marxist journal in December 1937, and he began writing for the Trotskyist journal *New International* in 1938. In the fall of 1939 he became a member of the Socialist Workers Party, but quickly sided with Max Shachtman (q.v.) when Shachtman's followers split to form the Workers Party in the spring of 1940. Within a year Macdonald had also broken with Shachtman, complaining that the Workers Party had refused to publish his unorthodox writings on the economy of fascism.

In the early 1940s Macdonald found himself in conflict with Philip Rahv (q.v.), the strongest political personality on *Partisan Review*, who began to reconsider the magazine's opposition to U.S. policy in World War II. After Rahv published a polemic in the magazine against the revolutionary-internationalist views of Macdonald and art critic Clement Greenberg, he decided that the magazine should take no position on the war. Believing that the other editors were retreating from radical politics and that his own anti-war opinions were being suppressed, Macdonald broke with *Partisan* in 1943 and founded *Politics* in 1944. Although a one-man operation, *Politics* attracted a great deal of attention from writers and intellectuals who later became quite prominent, including C. Wright Mills, Daniel Bell, Hannah Arendt, and Paul Goodman (q.v.). Macdonald evolved politically from Trotskyism to anarchopacifism.

After the magazine folded, Macdonald became less politically active during the 1950s, working as a staff writer for the *New Yorker* from 1951 to 1966 and as a film critic for *Esquire* from 1960 to 1966. During the Vietnam War, however, he became a radical activist once more, joining the War Resisters League and advocating draft resistance. He remained involved in left-wing causes until his death in 1982.

SOURCES: James B. Gilbert, *Writers and Partisans* (1968); Dwight Macdonald, *Memoirs of a Revolutionist* (1958).

*ALAN WALD*

**MARCANTONIO, VITO (1902–1954).** Vito Marcantonio, an ally of the Communist Party, served as representative from East Harlem in Congress for fourteen years. Marcantonio was born in East Harlem in December 1902, the offspring of Italian-American parents from Picerno, Italy. Raised in the ethnic slum, Marcantonio never lived more than a few blocks from his birthplace. He attended DeWitt Clinton High School and New York University Law School, became campaign manager in 1924 for Representative Fiorello LaGuardia, and then was elected Republican Congressman in 1934 after LaGuardia became New York's mayor. Already a radical, Marcantonio quickly positioned himself left of the New Deal, cooperated with Communist efforts to build a farmer-labor party, and after defeat in 1936 came back successfully in 1938 as the elected Congressman of the American Labor Party (ALP).

Marcantonio's ties to the Communist Party were close, but they were never formalized. Above all else, he was a politician, and he cooperated with the Party as much because it helped organize political power in East Harlem as because he shared its ideological worldview. The relationship became most fully developed early during the Popular Front, when Marcantonio served as president of the Party-dominated International Labor Defense and as officer of numerous Party front organizations. From then on he worked intimately with Party leaders at the national level, including Earl Browder (q.v.), and in the New York district and the unions. Simultaneously, he worked with local leaders in the Republican and Democratic parties, enabling him to run on the Republican as well as the ALP ticket through 1944 and also on the Democratic ticket from 1942 to 1946.

Marcantonio sometimes hesitated at sharp turns in the Party line, but he nonetheless followed Party policy loyally. After the Nazi-Soviet Pact, he became a critic of Roosevelt's foreign policy and of efforts to turn the United States into a "military reservoir" of British imperialism. Following the Nazi invasion of the Soviet Union, he became a critic of the Truman Doctrine and the Marshall Plan, and he was a leader in the Progressive Party campaign in 1948. His militant stands hurt him little in East Harlem, where he continued to be viewed as a "people's politician" and friend of his constituents, for whom he ran an elaborate service operation, and where he continued to organize the fragments of power by complicated deals involving the major parties.

Ultimately, Marcantonio failed to be reelected in 1950. Republican Party representatives in the state legislature gerrymandered his district in 1943, adding Yorkville to East Harlem, and Governor Dewey signed into law in 1947 a measure tightening party control of access to party primaries. In 1948 Republican and Democratic leaders shut off cooperation with Marcantonio, and in 1950 they entered a coalition candidate, who defeated him.

For a time Marcantonio remained active in New York politics as ALP state chairman, but he came into increasing conflict with Communist Party leaders, who were abandoning third-party politics. Marcantonio resigned in anger from the ALP in a dispute with the Party in November 1953. He died shortly after, on August 9, 1954, in the midst of preparations for an independent comeback.

SOURCES: Alan Schaffer, *Vito Marcantonio: Radical in Congress* (1966); Kenneth Waltzer, "American Labor Party" (Ph.D. diss., Harvard University, 1977).

*KENNETH WALTZER*

**MARCUSE, HERBERT (1898–1979).** Herbert Marcuse, the "Guru of the New Left," was a neo-Marxist political philosopher whose writings have been credited with giving the radical movement of the 1960s whatever theoretical base it may have had. Marcuse was born on July 19, 1898, in Berlin, Germany, of wealthy Jewish parents. He was educated at the University of Berlin and later at the University of Freiburg, from which he received his doctorate in 1922. While at Freiburg, Marcuse joined the Social Democratic Party of Germany (SPD) and became active in its non-Communist left wing. He left the party two years later, but remained active in the intellectual Marxist movement, especially the so-called Frankfurt Group, from which neo-Marxism developed.

When, in 1933, Adolph Hitler became ruler of Germany, Marcuse fled to Switzerland. He taught at the University of Geneva for a year before emigrating to the United States. His first American appointment was at Columbia University. In 1940, while teaching at Columbia, he became a U.S. citizen. During the war, Marcuse served in the Office of Strategic Services. After the war he taught at Brandeis and Harvard universities and at the University of California at San Diego. One of his students there was Angela Davis (q.v.), who would later become a leader in the U.S. Communist Party.

Marcuse's political philosophy was a combination of the theories of Marx and Sigmund Freud. He accepted most of the concepts Marx proclaimed, but he rejected the assumption that the primary aim of a Socialist revolution should be improved creature comforts and material goods for the working masses—a basic tenet of Socialist doctrine. He assailed the working class for generally adopting middle-class values—"high wages and hi-fi sets, split-level homes, the backyard barbecues and the second car." These values, he said, developed in the working class an unwillingness to risk their "relative prosperity" for abstract and Utopian ideas. During the 1960s Marcuse declared that radical students, alienated intellectuals, urban blacks, and people from underdeveloped Third World countries comprised the real revolutionary class. This class, he claimed, would unite with and thus awaken in the working class a need for a revolution that would end all oppression.

The two best known of Marcuse's books are *Reason and Rebellion*, which he wrote in 1941, and *One Dimensional Man*, authored in 1964, which were the bibles of the student radicals of the late 1960s.

Marcuse retired from teaching in 1970 at the age of 72. He was visiting at the Max Planck Institute in West Germany when he died in late August 1979.

*BERNARD K. JOHNPOLL*

**MATTHEWS, J. B. (1894–1966).** J(oseph) B(rown) Matthews was the archetypal fellow traveler of American communism in the early 1930s while he was in the Socialist Party. By the end of the decade he had been transformed into a fierce anti-Communist, and he devoted the rest of his life to battling the Left in association with Martin Dies and Senator Joseph McCarthy.

Matthews was born in Hopkinsville, Kentucky, in 1894. His father was a businessman and a devout Methodist. After graduating from college in 1914, Matthews earned a Ph.D. in Oriental languages at the University of Vienna and taught for several years in Chinese schools in Java. Studying for the ministry at the Union Theological Seminary in New York in 1921, Matthews came under the influence of the Social Gospel movement. While teaching at Scarritt College in Tennessee, he supported the 1924 LaFollette presidential campaign, became active in pacifist, labor, and civil rights causes, and was encouraged to resign his teaching post in 1927.

In 1929 Matthews became executive secretary of the pacifist Fellowship of Reconciliation and held the position for four and a half years, until he was ousted for advocating class warfare. His political activities became increasingly concentrated on the Socialist Party, which he had joined in November 1929. When the Communist Party began a "united front" campaign in 1933, Matthews quickly became one of their prize catches and a staple in scores of Party "fronts" ranging from the Tom Mooney Defense Committee to the United States Congress Against War. He presided over the first such congress in September 1933 and became national chairman of the American League Against War and Fascism, one of the largest and most successful of the Party's united fronts.

His activities drew increasing ire from his own political party, which suspended him for one year. Undaunted, Matthews became chairman in 1933 of the Revolutionary Policy Committee, a radical faction of the Socialist Party with close ties to the Communist splinter group led by Jay Lovestone (q.v.). His radical activities continued into 1935, despite shifting sympathies toward the Lovestoneites (he broke with them in 1934) and the Communists (he resigned as chairman of the League Against War and Fascism (LAWF) in 1934).

Matthews' political views began to change in 1935 when a strike that he considered Communist-led took place against Consumers' Research, of which he was vice-president. Denounced by his old comrades, he swiftly moved to the political right. He testified as a friendly witness before the Dies Committee investigating communism in 1938 and then became its chief researcher. Matthews devoted the rest of his life to exposing Communists and insisting that there was little difference among liberals, radicals, and Communists. Appointed staff director of Senator Joseph McCarthy's Government Operations Subcommittees in 1953, he was fired after the Eisenhower administration was embarrassed by his claim that Protestant clergymen were the largest single American group supporting communism. He later served as a private consultant to the Hearst newspapers and by the 1960s was associated with the John Birch Society. Matthews died on July 16, 1966.

SOURCES: Walter Goodman, *The Committee* (1968); J. B. Matthews, *Odyssey of a Fellow-Traveller* (1936).

*HARVEY KLEHR*

**MAURER, JAMES HUDSON (1864–1944).** James Hudson Maurer was a leader of the Socialist Party for more than thirty years. He was the Socialist candidate for U.S. Vice-President twice (1928, 1932), a member of the Pennsylvania House of Representatives for six years (1911–1913 and 1915–1918), and president of the Pennsylvania Federation of Labor for seventeen years (1912–1929).

Maurer was born in 1864 in Reading, Pennsylvania, the son of a poor shoemaker. He received only one year of formal schooling. At the age of 9 he was forced to go to work as a newsboy. At age 16 Maurer became an apprentice machinist.

In 1880 he became active in the labor movement, joining the Knights of Labor in his native city. It was in the labor movement that he discovered the world of books. He taught himself to read and became an avid reader of political, social, and economic works. His reading, particularly of Utopian works, won him over to socialism. After completing his apprenticeship Maurer became a member of the Plumbers and Steamfitters Union in Reading. He was elected an officer of the local in 1886 and remained one for the rest of his life.

Maurer joined a Nationalist Club, composed of disciples of Edward Bellamy (q.v.), about 1890 and became a member of the Socialist Labor Party (SLP) in 1898. Four years later he and virtually all the other members of the Reading SLP resigned and joined the newly formed Socialist Party. By 1906 Maurer was the Socialist candidate for governor of Pennsylvania. Five years later he was elected to the State House of Representatives from Reading. Defeated in 1913, he was again elected in 1915 and in 1917. In the state legislature he led the fight for workmen's compensation and for abolition of the brutal and often lawless Coal and Iron Police. During this time he also helped build the powerful Socialist organization in Reading.

Maurer opposed American participation in World War I. His stance won him the enmity of Samuel Gompers and other leaders of the American Federation of Labor. Despite that enmity, Maurer, who was first elected to his AFL post in 1912, was reelected during the war years (1917–1918). He held the post until 1929, when he retired at age 65.

Maurer also served as chairman of the Pennsylvania Old-Age Assistance Commission, was a founding member of the national board of the American Civil Liberties Union, was on the board of the non-Communist left-wing Brookwood Labor College, was president of the Labor Age Publishing Company, and was a member of the National Committee of the Conference for Progressive Political Action, which directed the presidential campaign of Robert M. LaFollette in 1924.

Maurer was sympathetic with the Bolshevik regime in Soviet Russia until 1930, when the persecution of Mensheviks and Left Social Revolutionaries turned him against the regime.

The Socialist Party conventions of 1928 and 1932 nominated Maurer to be the running mate of Norman M. Thomas (q.v.) in the presidential campaigns. He was an aggressive candidate in both campaigns, but in the latter campaign he and Thomas were alienated by their differences in the internal party struggle. In 1936, when the Thomas wing of the party won control, Maurer resigned from the Socialist Party and with most Reading Socialists joined the new Social Democratic Federation.

Maurer remained active in the Reading Socialist movement until 1940, when his health and encroaching blindness made it impossible for him to continue. He died in Reading on March 16, 1944.

SOURCES: Solon DeLeon (ed.), *American Labor Who's Who* (1925); James H. Maurer, *It Can Be Done: The Autobiography of James Hudson Maurer* (1938); *Reading Eagle*, March 17, 1944, p. 1.

*BERNARD K. JOHNPOLL*

**MCCREERY, MAUD (1883–1938).** Maud McCreery was an editor, speaker, teacher, and organizer for the Socialist Party and the labor movement of Wisconsin between 1912 and 1938. Born in Wauwatosa, a suburb of Milwaukee, in February 1883, McCreery began her career in the radical movement as an activist for women's suffrage. In 1917 she became an active spokesperson for the League to Endorse Peace.

During the 1920s, Miss McCreery, as she liked to be known, worked as a writer for the Federated Press, the labor and radical news service, in Chicago. In this job she came to the attention of Victor Berger (q.v.), who invited her to write for and edit a women's page on the Socialist *Milwaukee Leader*. In Milwaukee she also became an organizer for the Socialist Party of Wisconsin, the Milwaukee Federated Trades Council (the Milwaukee organization of American Federation of Labor unions), and the Wisconsin Farmer-Labor Progressive Federation, a political coalition of Socialists and Progressives who were followers of Philip and Robert M. LaFollette.

McCreery left the *Leader* in 1936 to become editor of the Sheboygan (Wisconsin) *New Deal*, a labor weekly. She resigned from that post within a year and became an organizer for the American Federation of Labor. Widely known as a dynamic speaker and parliamentarian, she was appointed the next year to the faculty of the School for Workers of the Extension Division of the University of Wisconsin, where she taught parliamentary law and public speaking. She died in Milwaukee on April 10, 1938.

*JAMES INGBRETSON*

**MCGUIRE, PETER J. (1852–1906).** Peter J. McGuire was a founder and first vice-president of the American Federation of Labor, a founder and secretary-treasurer of the United Brotherhood of Carpenters and Joiners, and a leading figure in the Workingmen's Party of the United States and the early Socialist Labor Party. He has been credited with being the originator of Labor Day and also of the first May Day.

Born of Irish immigrant parents in New York's Lower East Side in 1852, McGuire received little formal schooling before being apprenticed as a joiner. He attended evening lectures and courses at Cooper Union, and from the late 1860s he was active in radical and labor organizations. In 1874 he was a leading organizer of a mass demonstration against unemployment in Tompkins Square which was violently attacked and broken up by police. In the same year he helped form the Social Democratic Party of North America, which merged with former sections of the First International in 1876 to form the Workingmen's Party of the United States (WPUS).

The WPUS, influenced by the ideas of Karl Marx and Ferdinand Lassalle, was the first U.S. Socialist organization of national breadth. During the nationwide rail strike and uprising of 1877, the WPUS organized significant public rallies in a number of cities. That autumn, however, the organization split over the question of whether to run Socialist election campaigns or to concentrate exclusively on trade union organizing. McGuire was part of the pro-electoral majority that subsequently renamed the organization the Socialist Labor Party (SLP).

McGuire was the leading organizer of the WPUS and then the SLP in the New England area from 1876 to 1878, after which he was active in St. Louis, Missouri, for several years. During this period he played a major role in initiating Socialist election campaigns and also in trade union organizing efforts. In 1879 McGuire successfully lobbied the Missouri legislature to establish a Bureau of Labor Statistics, of which he became deputy commissioner. He helped to found the Carpenters Union in 1881, becoming its secretary-treasurer and the editor of its paper, *The Carpenter*. During that same year he represented the SLP at an international Socialist conference in Europe. In 1883, testifying before a U.S. Senate committee investigating labor relations, he proudly stressed the interrelationship between socialism and trade unionism.

McGuire initiated a militant agitational campaign for the eight-hour workday, which culminated in large nationwide demonstrations and strikes on May 1, 1886. The same year saw the founding of the American Federation of Labor (AFL). McGuire was a central figure in the creation of the AFL, along with two other veterans of labor radicalism from the Cigar Makers Union, Adolph Strasser and Samuel Gompers. In 1887 he assisted in the U.S. tour of Eleanor Marx (the daughter of Karl Marx) and Edward Aveling, and they mention him warmly in their book *The Working Class Movement in America* (1891).

While never renouncing his Socialist beliefs, McGuire had drifted out of the organized Socialist movement by the early 1890s and was associated with the "pure and simple" trade union current led by Gompers in the AFL. He played a major role in combating the AFL's chief rival, the Knights of Labor, and in helping to frustrate SLP challenges to Gompers' authority in the 1890s.

From the mid–1890s to 1902 McGuire increasingly found himself caught in contradictions as he attempted to balance his early ideals with the growing conservatism of the Gompers-led AFL. The transition from Socialist unionism to "business unionism" proved too difficult for him. Gradually he collapsed mentally and physically, sinking into alcoholism, unable to carry out his union responsibilities. A scandal over financial improprieties (probably muddled bookkeeping rather than embezzlement) forced his resignation in 1902. He died in poverty at the home of his daughter in 1906.

SOURCES: Robert A. Christie, *Empire in Wood: A History of the Carpenters Union* (1956); Philip S. Foner, *History of the Labor Movement in the United States*, vols. 1– 3 (1947–1982); Stuart B. Kaufman, *Samuel Gompers and the Origins of the American Federation of Labor* (1973).

*PAUL LEBLANC*

**MCKINNEY, ERNEST RICE (1886–1984).** Ernest Rice McKinney had a distinguished career as a black leader in education, labor, and radical politics that began with his joining the Socialist Party around 1910 and the National Association for the Advancement of Colored People in 1911 and voting for Eugene V. Debs (q.v.) in the presidential elections of 1912.

McKinney was born on December 7, 1886, in Malden, West Virginia. Both his parents were schoolteachers, and his father became a principal in Huntington, where a school was named after him. His maternal grandmother was a slave, bought out of her servitude by her future husband, Lewis Rice, a "free Negro" who had great influence on young McKinney.

When McKinney was 12 years old, his father, a staunch Republican, went to Washington to take a post in the Republican administration. There McKinney attended Dunbar and Armstrong Technical High Schools. Without getting a degree, he completed four years of study at Oberlin College. Already a member of the NAACP, he and W. E. B. DuBois (q.v.) organized a branch in 1911 at Oberlin. In later years, he also attended Carnegie Institute of Technology and the New School of Social Research.

After leaving college, McKinney went to Denver for two years to participate in a social work program for Negro youth. From there, he went to Pittsburgh, where he became boys work secretary for the YMCA, executive secretary of the Pittsburgh branch of the NAACP, and a columnist for the *Pittsburgh Courier*. In 1917 McKinney served as an infantryman in the American Expeditionary

Forces and fought in France until the war ended. After demobilization, he returned to Pittsburgh.

The Russian Revolution influenced McKinney to join the Communist Party in 1920, where he remained until 1926, when his disagreements with the political policies of the Party became irreconcilable. During those years, he met A. Philip Randolph (q.v.) and Chandler Owen, who were publishing the *Messenger*. McKinney became a contributing editor to that publication at the same time he was editing the *Pittsburgh American*. In 1929 he published his own paper, *This Month*.

Also in 1929, McKinney joined A. J. Muste (q.v.) at Brookwood Labor College to create the Conference for Progressive Labor Action, which evolved into the American Workers Party (AWP), of which McKinney was a member of the National Committee. McKinney was a member of the National and Political Committees, as well as trade union secretary of the Workers Party, formed in 1934 in the unification of the AWP and the Trotskyist Communist League of America. When the members of the Workers Party joined the Socialist Party in 1936, McKinney became an organizer for the Congress of Industrial Organizations (CIO), assigned to the Steelworkers Organizing Committee, where he concentrated his activities on black workers in the steel industry.

The Trotskyist faction, to which McKinney adhered, was expelled from the Socialist Party at the end of 1937. In January 1938 McKinney became a member of the National Committee of the newly established Socialist Workers Party, which he helped found. He served on the Party's Political Committee until the split between James Cannon (q.v.) and Max Shachtman (q.v.) over the defense of the Soviet Union, the invasion of Finland by the Red army, and the partition of Poland by Stalin and Hitler.

When the new Schactmanite Workers Party was formed in April 1940, McKinney was on its National and Political Committees and was its trade union director. He assisted the Party's trade unionists in New York, Buffalo, Detroit, Chicago, and Los Angeles and visited those cities frequently. In the mid–1940s, McKinney helped organize sharecroppers and tenant farmers in Southeast Missouri.

In 1946 McKinney ran for Congress as the Workers Party candidate in Harlem's twenty-second Congressional district. After the elections his activity in the Party declined as he developed differences with it. His dissatisfaction led to his retirement from organized politics in 1950, though by his own admission he remained "a Marxist and Leninist."

In his eighties, McKinney began a new phase of his already long career as a teacher of labor and black history at Rutgers University and elsewhere. During the 1970s McKinney helped the United Federation of Teachers in its drive to unionize and train paraprofessionals. He also became assistant to the president of the A. Philip Randolph Educational Fund. He died on January 30, 1984.

SOURCE: *Max Shachtman Archives*, Tamiment Library, New York University, New York City.

*ALBERT GLOTZER*

**MCLEVY, JASPER (1878–1962).** Jasper McLevy was Socialist mayor of Bridgeport, Connecticut, from 1933 to 1957. He was a leader in the conservative wing of the Socialist Party nationally from 1935 until 1941. One of the many turn-of-the-century Socialists converted to socialism by Edward Bellamy's (q.v.) popular futurist novel, *Looking Backward*, McLevy was one of the founders of the American Socialist Party.

Born in Bridgeport in 1878, the son of a building trades worker who died when Jasper was 14, he worked during his teens as an apprentice roofer and helped found the roofers union in his native city just prior to the turn of the century. His work for the union organization drive was so successful that the union won a nine-hour day within five years. He was rewarded with the presidency of the new union soon after its formation, the presidency of the Bridgeport Federation of Labor (in 1906), and the vice-presidency of the Connecticut Federation of Labor.

Upon joining the Socialist Party, which he was instrumental in forming in Bridgeport in 1899, McLevy became its perennial candidate for office. He campaigned twelve months a year by speaking on streetcorners from soapboxes and improvised platforms and by attending every meeting of the Bridgeport city council between 1900 and 1957.

His votes were generally meager. In 1902, running for the state assembly, McLevy polled a mere 215 votes. Five years later McLevy received only 21 votes as a candidate for the city council. By 1911 he polled more than 3,600 votes as Socialist candidate for mayor. In 1908 McLevy was a member of Eugene V. Debs' (q.v.) entourage on the campaign train labeled "the Red Special" on which Debs toured the United States.

During the period of war, repression, and schism, from 1917 to 1922, McLevy remained steadfast in his commitment to the Socialist Party. He opposed the war as a needless product of rapacious capitalism; he fought for amnesty for those who were imprisoned for their opposition to the war; and he was actively opposed to the Communist left wing within the party.

McLevy ran for mayor of Bridgeport in 1921 and garnered a record 7,966 votes. His large vote was seen generally as a tribute to his own dedication to civic betterment, for which he was an outspoken advocate. But four years later his vote fell to 745, in the face of prosperity. Four years later, in 1929 soon after the collapse of the stock market, his vote rose to only 1,968. Finally, in 1931, his thirty-year-long efforts began to yield fruit. After a heated campaign McLevy garnered 15,084 votes (almost 46 percent of the total) to 17,889 for the mayor, Edward Taylor Buckingham. For the next two years McLevy hammered away at the corruption that permeated the city—bridges built under the Democratic and Republican administrations of the past ten years had collapsed because of shoddy material. He also demanded that more jobs be made available to the unemployed in Bridgeport, an industrial city which was hard hit by the Depression.

The 1933 campaign was one of the dirtiest in Bridgeport history. His opponents called McLevy a Communist and charged that he was of German and not of

Scottish descent, as he claimed (thus supposedly explaining his opposition to the 1917–1918 war). The charges were untrue, but no lie was too brazen in that campaign. The Democrats spent $20,890 in the campaign, the Republicans spent $13,630, and McLevy and his fellow Socialists spent only $1,890. When the votes were counted, McLevy had polled 22,445, James Dunn, the Democrat had polled 16,375, and John G. Schwarz, the Republican, had 7,321. After thirty-two years of Socialist activity—of attending every meeting of the city council, of speaking out against corruption—McLevy was elected mayor of Bridgeport with a Socialist-dominated city council and administration.

As mayor, McLevy was essentially a reformer who aimed at giving Bridgeport an honest, efficient economic government. He began by ousting many incompetent, inefficient, and dishonest holdovers from the previous administration. He also gave the city an economical regime. And by ending the secrecy he ended the dishonesty that had permeated the city's affairs; he ordered that all meetings be open. The result was an efficient but conservative government. Before his election, local business leaders warned that his victory would result in dire consequences for the city—that capital would flee. In fact, McLevy won the support of the business community soon after he became mayor.

At his inauguration McLevy promised to give the city its money's worth. He began almost at once to prove that he meant what he said. First he refused to accept a chauffeured limousine offered by the city (he drove his own battered old Ford around town on official business), then he refused an invitation to lunch at the Union Club. His first actions as mayor were to straighten out the fiscal mess he had found in the city's government. When he took office, the city had $1,240,000 in its treasury and bills totaling $4,000,000. McLevy immediately cut waste at the top and reorganized the fiscal methods, centralizing control of city funds. And despite a decline in tax revenues due to the Depression, he raised the salaries of the lowest-paid civil servants (thanks to his reductions at the top). Moreover, he ordered all salaries paid in cash—they had been paid in scrip for months previous. He also ended private refuse handling at exorbitant fees, instead instituting public garbage collection. Bridgeport's beaches on Long Island Sound were cleaned and refurbished—with Federal Emergency Relief Administration and Works Progress Administration funds. He barred collusion on bids for city road work, which had been common practice in the previous administration. And he worked to win a university for Bridgeport (under his administration Connecticut Junior College became the University of Bridgeport).

In 1934 McLevy and the Connecticut Socialists were riding the crest of a wave of popularity. All five state legislators from Bridgeport were Socialists. McLevy carried the city in his race for governor, although he failed to carry the state. Because neither Republicans nor Democrats had elected a majority in the state assembly, the Socialists held the balance of power. They were thus able to win for McLevy's administration a new charter, civil service merit appointments for most city jobs, and full fiscal control by the city's government.

But in 1936 the Socialist Party nationally splintered. McLevy was with the more conservative wing of the party. When the left wing, dominated by Norman Thomas (q.v.), got control, McLevy took the Connecticut Socialist Party out of the national party and into the Social Democratic Federation. His relations with Norman Thomas and his followers worsened as Thomas became increasingly anti-war isolationist while McLevy favored the Western powers in their war with Germany. The antipathy grew so bad that the national party ran an opponent when McLevy ran for governor in 1938.

McLevy's relations with the labor union movement also began to deteriorate about 1936. Because he tried to keep administration costs down, he refused what he considered "extortionate" pay increases for organized city workers. The result was a series of confrontations between him and union officials. In 1941 the Bridgeport Federation of Labor refused to endorse him for mayor. Eight years later, after he refused to raise salaries for workers in the public school system and prevented an increase in welfare payments, the Federation backed his unsuccessful Democratic opponent.

By 1946 the Socialist national organization had readmitted McLevy. In 1948 McLevy was chairman of the Connecticut delegation, which supported the nomination of Norman Thomas at the Socialist national convention in Reading, Pennsylvania. He campaigned for Thomas. He was also active in supporting the Socialist-Zionists during their campaign for the establishment of a Jewish Socialist state. Then in 1950 McLevy was again nominated for governor—for the fifteenth time. He accepted the endorsement of Vivien Kellems, an anti-union, conservative manufacturer, who was running for Senator on the Independence Party line. Moreover, McLevy accepted a place on her ticket. The Socialist Party nationally ousted him, and the labor movement fought against him.

McLevy was reelected, albeit by decreasing majorities, in 1951, 1953, and 1955. In 1957, after twenty-four years in office, he was defeated by a coalition of Democrats and labor union members. McLevy was then 79 and he still considered himself a Socialist. He tried again for the mayoralty in 1959 but failed again.

Jasper McLevy, who had started as a Socialist in 1899, who had campaigned for social reform and socialism until he finally won office in 1933, was now a conservative who still called himself a Socialist. Jasper McLevy, who helped organize the Bridgeport labor union movement over thirty years, was by 1957 an anathema to the trade union movement of his city. His work in winning such measures as workmen's compensation and decent pay for union members was almost forgotten. His conservatism as mayor overshadowed his earlier socialism. He died in 1962.

SOURCE: The Jasper McLevy Collection in Bridgeport Public Library, Bridgeport, Connecticut.

*BERNARD K. JOHNPOLL*

**MCREYNOLDS, DAVID (b. 1929).** David McReynolds is one of America's leading pacifists, a longtime organizer for the War Resisters League, and a leader of the Milwaukee-based Socialist Party. He ran for U.S. President on the Socialist Party ticket in 1980.

McReynolds was born in Los Angeles, California, on October 25, 1929, into a middle-class Republican home. His father served as an officer in military intelligence during World War II. David McReynolds majored in political science at the University of California at Los Angeles, graduating in 1953 with a B.A. degree.

Raised a devout Baptist, McReynolds began political activity in the Prohibition Party. He became a pacifist in 1948. In 1951 he was expelled from the Prohibition Party, along with the entire youth section, as a Communist. He immediately joined the Socialist Party. He moved to New York after college and took a job as editorial secretary for *Liberation*, a radical pacifist publication. In 1954 McReynolds was first elected to the National Committee of the Socialist Party, emerging as a national leader of its pacifist wing.

During the Vietnam War era McReynolds became an important figure in the anti-war movement. He was a leader of the Debs Caucus, the faction within the Socialist Party that called for the immediate and unconditional withdrawal of all U.S. forces from Southeast Asia. In 1970 he published a collection of his political essays, entitled *We Have Been Invaded by the 21st Century*, which included an exchange with Michael Harrington (q.v.) over political tactics and Vietnam. By 1970 McReynolds and the Debs Caucus were openly building the Union for Democratic Socialism as an anti-war/civil rights organization. When the Socialist Party–Democratic Socialist Federation changed its name to Social Democrats USA in December 1972, several state organizations (such as Wisconsin and California) and locals associated with the Debs Caucus disaffiliated. In May 1973 the Union for Democratic Socialism "refounded" the Socialist Party. McReynolds is the leading figure in this new Socialist Party. Since the founding of the Party McReynolds has spent most of his time on peace issues. He currently serves on the staff of the War Resisters League and writes often on the need for the nuclear freeze movement to transform itself into a broader movement for social justice.

SOURCE: David McReynolds, *We Have Been Invaded by the 21st Century* (1970).

*BOB FITRAKIS*

**MELMS, EDMUND T. (1874–1933).** Edmund T. Melms was a municipal official in Milwaukee, Wisconsin, between 1904 and 1917, a Socialist publicist, and a party official. His work in organizing Socialist propaganda is often credited with playing a major role in building the Socialist political machine in Milwaukee during the early years of the century. Melms was born in Greenfield, Wisconsin, in 1874 and was educated in the elementary schools of that town (he completed only the seventh grade). Of working-class background, he went to work in a factory at age 14 and labored in various factories for the next seventeen years.

In 1897 Melms was among the founders of the Social Democratic Party, which was among the organizations from which the Socialist Party was developed. He served as secretary of the Milwaukee City and County Socialist Party from 1902 until 1927. It was while serving as party secretary in 1904 that he developed the "bundle brigade" technique for distributing Socialist leaflets. This technique enabled party literature to be delivered to virtually every home throughout the city in a matter of hours.

Despite his lack of formal education, Melms was a prolific writer of Socialist articles for the *Social Democratic Herald* (1900–1911) and the *Milwaukee Leader* (after 1911).

In 1904, in the first municipal election in Milwaukee after formation of the Socialist Party, Melms was elected to the Common Council. Over the next eight years he served as president of the Council. He helped found the Sane Fourth of July celebration in the city as an alternative to the dangerous and rowdy affairs that had been common previously. He also served as Milwaukee County sheriff from 1915 to 1917 and ran unsuccessfully for Congress in 1918, 1922, and 1926. Melms died in Milwaukee in 1933.

SOURCE: *Dictionary of Wisconsin Biography* (1960).

*JAMES E. INGBRETSON*

**MILLER, BERT (1891–1973).** Bert Miller, teacher and Communist Party organizer, was expelled in 1929 as a Lovestoneite and became a staff member for Congressional investigating committees. He was born Benjamin Mandel on October 2, 1891, in New York City to Russian Jewish immigrant parents. After graduating from City College of New York he became a high school typing teacher in New York.

Miller joined the Communist Party at its formation in 1919, assuming his new name. For several years he was active in the American Federation of Teachers (AFT) local in New York, becoming chairman of its membership committee and a leader in its Communist caucus. He left teaching in 1925 to become the Party's industrial organizer in New York and played an important role in the Passaic textile strike the following year. Miller served as district organizer in Boston, organization secretary in New York, business manager of the *Daily Worker*, and member of the Central Committee in the next few years, becoming a key figure in Jay Lovestone's (q.v.) faction of the Party.

Miller was expelled from the Communist Party in 1929 for refusing to repudiate Lovestone's policies. After two years in Lovestone's splinter group, he joined A. J. Muste's (q.v.) Committee for Progressive Labor Action. Finally readmitted to the AFT in 1932, he became a valuable member of its anti-Communist caucus. Under his real name of Benjamin Mandel, he joined the staff of the Dies Committee investigating un-American activities in 1938 as a researcher. Mandel remained with the committee until 1951, with the exception of two years, during which he did similar work for New York State's Rapp-Coudert Committee investigating Communist teachers. From 1951 until his retirement in 1967 he was research director for the Senate Internal Security Subcommittee. He died on August 8, 1973.

*HARVEY KLEHR*

**MINOR, ROBERT (1884–1952).** Robert Minor enjoyed a highly successful career as a newspaper cartoonist before World War I. At the height of his success he chose to devote his talents full-time to radical causes as a cartoonist and political organizer. He was an early recruit to the Communist movement and remained prominent in its leadership from the early 1920s until 1945, when he was demoted as a result of a too-close association with disgraced Party leader Earl Browder (q.v.).

Minor was born in San Antonio, Texas, on July 15, 1884, the son of an unsuccessful lawyer. He dropped out of school at the age of 14 and left home two years later for a series of jobs as a farmhand, railroad laborer, and carpenter. Minor had always enjoyed drawing, and on a whim he applied for a job as a cartoonist with the *San Antonio Gazette* in 1904. To his surprise he was hired. He moved to St. Louis in 1905, secured a position on the *St. Louis Post-Dispatch*, and by 1911 had established himself as its chief editorial cartoonist, among the best-known and highest-paid figures in the field.

Minor had joined the Carpenters Union in 1903. During his years of migratory labor, Minor had met several Socialists who attempted to recruit him to the cause. He was finally persuaded in 1907 by a radical doctor of his acquaintance to join the Socialist Party. Minor soon gravitated to the left wing of the Socialist Party and became an admirer of "Big Bill" Haywood (q.v.). In 1912 Minor went to Paris to study art. He was bored by his classes, but excited by the French syndicalist movement, and he returned to the United States the following year a convert to anarcho-syndicalism. Still highly sought after as a cartoonist, he took a job with the *New York Evening World*, which at first welcomed his dramatic anti-war cartoons. But in 1915 the paper's editorial line shifted to a pro-Allied position. Given the choice of abandoning his anti-war message or abandoning his job, Minor chose the latter course. He took a far less lucrative position as the cartoonist for the New York Socialist newspaper the *Call*, and also drew cartoons for *Masses* and other radical publications.

In 1915 Minor traveled to France as a war correspondent, and in 1916 he went to the Mexican border to cover the skirmishing between the U.S. Army and Pancho Villa's forces. In August 1916 he went to San Francisco to organize a defense committee for Tom Mooney (q.v.) and four other defendants accused of planting a bomb at a Preparedness Day parade in July. Mooney's defenders were able to provoke an international outcry over the case that probably saved his life.

In 1918 Minor went to Russia for nine months as a newspaper correspondent. He met Lenin and traveled to the front lines of the Civil War. Still an anarcho-syndicalist, he was initially repelled by the Bolsheviks harsh rule, and upon his return to the United States he wrote some critical articles about the Soviet Union. But in 1920 he underwent a change of heart, repudiated his criticisms and his anarcho-syndicalism, and joined the American Communist movement.

Minor continued to draw cartoons for the radical press, including the newly founded *Daily Worker*. But as a member of the Party's Central Executive Committee he was increasingly drawn into the inner-Party factional wars, and by 1926 he gave up his cartooning for good. Minor became a close ally of Party general secretary Jay Lovestone (q.v.). Lovestone appointed him editor of the *Daily Worker* in 1928, and in 1929, when Lovestone went off to Moscow to defend his leadership before the Comintern, Minor was appointed acting general secretary. When Minor saw that the decision in Moscow was going to go against Lovestone, he promptly turned on his old ally. Minor was briefly part of the four-man secretariat set up to rule the Party in the aftermath of Lovestone's downfall. As Earl Browder secured his own power as general secretary in the early 1930s, Minor emerged as Browder's right-hand man in the Party's ruling Politburo. Minor functioned as a combination of messenger boy and hatchetman and was never taken seriously as a political heavyweight by his fellow Politburo members. He was known for his slavish flattery of Browder and was called upon on ceremonial occasions to praise the general secretary. In 1936, nominating Browder as the Communist candidate for President, he called him a "new John Brown from Ossawatomie"; in 1940, when Browder faced trial for passport violations, Minor contributed a series of articles to the *Daily Worker* with such headlines as "Lincoln, Brown, Browder—Names Negroes Revere." When Browder went to prison in 1941, Minor again filled the position of acting general secretary until Browder's release in 1942. In 1945, when Browder's fall from official favor was signaled by the arrival of the "Duclos letter," Minor attempted to disassociate himself from Browder as he had from Lovestone, but to no avail. Like others too closely associated with Browder, Minor found himself demoted to a minor Party post: Washington correspondent of the *Daily Worker*. In the late 1940s Minor's health deteriorated, and he withdrew from active participation in political activities. He died of a heart attack in 1952.

SOURCES: Theodore Draper, *The Roots of American Communism* (1957); Joseph North, *Robert Minor, Artist and Crusader* (1955).

*MAURICE ISSERMAN*


**MITCHELL, H. L. (b. 1906).** Harry Leland Mitchell was the co-founder, executive secretary, president, and always the driving force of the Southern Tenant Farmers Union and its successors. He was born on June 14, 1906, near Halls, Tennessee, the son of James Mitchell, an itinerant timber and shipyard worker, barber, and Baptist preacher. Having observed a lynching at the age of 11, he followed a line of reading and thinking that made him a Socialist and an agnostic. Harry began working at an early age and first sharecropped at 13. He married shortly after high school and moved to Tyronza, Arkansas, where he established a successful dry-cleaning business. Mitchell helped organize a Socialist local and, in 1933, an Unemployed League. His activities led to a boycott of his business and its subsequent failure. When Mitchell brought Norman Thomas (q.v.) to speak in Tyronza, Thomas pointed out that a union of sharecroppers was a more critical need than party activity because the effect of New Deal programs had been to benefit landowners and further to impoverish tenants, even to the extent of driving them off the land.

In July 1934 Mitchell was one of seven black and eleven white men who formed the first local of the Southern Tenant Farmers Union (STFU). It soon spread across Arkansas and into neighboring states, and by 1937 it had about 35,000 members. It had become one of the largest integrated organizations in Southern history. Mitchell, as executive secretary of the STFU, developed a flair for public relations. Many bright young people, such as the Reverend Howard ("Buck") Kester (q.v.) came to work for the union because of him. His letters to and forays among affluent Northern supporters kept the STFU barely solvent. The nationwide publicity he won for occasional strikes was probably more important than their immediate results.

Mitchell established several important governmental contacts, and the STFU was gradually able to improve the lot of its members, although sharecropping itself was rapidly becoming obsolete. Mitchell sought a national union connection, but the only way he could get it was through joining Donald Henderson's (q.v.) United Cannery, Agricultural, Packing, and Allied Workers of America. After numerous clashes with his Communist-dominated union, the STFU seceded in 1939.

During World War II, Mitchell arranged for STFU members to work in New Jersey canning factories. After the war he changed the union's name to the National Farm Labor Union and got an AFL (American Federation of Labor) charter. In the late 1940s the union led a major strike against the DiGiorgio Company in California but lost. From 1955 to 1960 it was known as the National Agricultural Workers Union. It struggled to organize a wide variety of workers, but Mitchell was undermined by AFL-CIO President George Meany. When a new drive to organize migratory workers in California began, Meany grudgingly approved of the Agricultural Workers Organizing Committee, with the stipulation that Mitchell have no connection with it.

Mitchell's small union merged with the Meatcutters, and he continued organizing. Since retiring he has continued to tour the nation, speaking at colleges and with unions.

SOURCES: Columbia Oral History Collection, Interview; Donald H. Grubbs, *Cry from the Cotton* (1971); H. L. Mitchell, *Mean Things Happening in This Land* (1979).

*LOWELL K. DYSON*

**MOONEY, THOMAS J. (1882–1942).** Tom Mooney was one of the martyrs of the American Left during the first half of the twentieth century. He served twenty-three years (1916–1939) of a life sentence in a California prison for a crime which it is generally agreed, he did not commit. Mooney was born in Chicago in 1882. His father, a Socialist who had been a coal miner, died when Tom was only 12 years old. Young Mooney went to work almost immediately thereafter as an apprentice iron-molder. At age 15 he won a free trip to a congress in Switzerland of the Socialist International in a contest sponsored by a Socialist publication. He became an active Socialist on his return.

In 1908 Mooney was named an aide to the Socialist national campaign committee and a member of the staff of the "Red Special" (a special railroad train from which Eugene V. Debs [q.v.], the Socialist candidate, campaigned for the presidency). From the beginning Mooney was an adherent of the pro-syndicalist Socialist left wing. In 1912 he became an editor of the West Coast radical Socialist journal *Revolt* and was the author of many of its more hyperbolic articles. He was also an organizer for various militant unions in the San Francisco Bay area. He attempted to unionize the Pacific Gas and Electric (PG&E) monopoly, which supplied power to the growing cities of the Pacific Coast. During the course of his organizational activities at PG&E he was once charged, and acquitted, with handling dynamite. He was also active in organizing streetcar workers in San Francisco and led their strike in 1916.

In 1916, however, the key issue throughout the United States was preparedness for war. Parades calling for military strength were held in all major cities. The San Francisco parade was rocked by a bomb explosion that killed ten participants and onlookers. After a less-than-thorough investigation, police arrested Mooney, his wife Rena, his close friend and fellow organizer Warren K. Billings (q.v.), Ed Nolan, an official of the Machinists Union, and Israel Weinberg, a taxi driver, and charged them with murder. They were tried in an obvious show trial, in which perjured testimony was introduced by the prosecution (Frank Oxman, a leading prosecution witness, later testified under oath that he had given perjured testimony). Frank P. Walsh, a noted New York attorney, headed the defense and contributed $50,000 to cover legal costs. None of the other defense attorneys received any compensation.

Mooney was found guilty of first-degree murder and condemned to be hanged. Billings was convicted of second-degree murder and sentenced to life in prison. The three other defendants were acquitted. An appeal by President Woodrow Wilson won Mooney a commutation to life imprisonment. Worldwide demonstrations followed the verdict to no avail. New proof that Mooney and Billings were innocent was found, but the Supreme Court refused to intervene. Even the pleas of the trial judge and jury that they now were convinced the defendants were innocent failed to win them their freedom. Finally, in 1938, twenty-two years after their conviction, the California State Assembly asked that they be freed. On January 7, 1939, Governor Culbert Olson pardoned Mooney.

After his release, Mooney went on a short speaking tour. But his health had been broken in prison. The tour was cut short, and after eighteen months bedridden in the hospital, Mooney died on March 6, 1942 in San Francisco at age 59.

SOURCES: E. Ward Estlov, *The Gentle Dynamiter: A Biography of Tom Mooney* (1984);
Henry T. Hunt, *The Case of Thomas P. Mooney and Warren K. Billings* (1929).

*BERNARD K. JOHNPOLL*


**MORROW, FELIX (b. 1906).** Felix Morrow was a writer and activist on behalf
of the Communist Party in the early 1930s and a leading Trotskyist theoretician
until the mid–1940s. He was born Felix Mayorowitz on June 3, 1906, in New
York City, the son of Eastern European Jewish immigrants who operated a small
grocery store. His parents were Socialists, and as a boy he became a member
of the Junior Circle of the Young People's Socialist League. In 1928 he graduated
from New York University and pursued graduate study in the philosophy
department at Columbia University with a special interest in religion. He also
began a career as a journalist.

In 1931 Morrow joined the Communist Party, writing for the *New Masses*
and the *Daily Worker* under the name George Cooper. He was also active in the
League of Professional Groups for Foster and Ford, the 1932 Communist Party
presidential ticket. Disillusioned by the Communist Party's tactics in Germany
during the time of Hitler's rise to power, Morrow moved toward Trotskyism in
1933 and joined the Communist League of America. In 1934 he became secretary
of Non-Partisan Labor Defense, a committee initiated by the Trotskyists and
their intellectual allies. In 1938 he was elected to the National Committee of the
Socialist Workers Party. From 1940 to 1942 he edited the Trotskyist newspaper,
first called *Socialist Appeal* and then the *Militant*. From 1942 to 1943 he edited
the theoretical magazine *Fourth International*. Convicted in 1941 under the Smith
Act with other leaders of the Socialist Workers Party who opposed U.S. government
policy during World War II, Morrow served a prison sentence in Sandstone
Penitentiary in 1944–1945.

Following his release from prison, he collaborated with Albert Goldman (q.v.)
in a political struggle against party national secretary James P. Cannon (q.v.)
over prospects for the Socialist movement in the post-war era. In 1946 he was
expelled from the Socialist Workers Party for unauthorized collaboration with
Max Shachtman's (q.v.) Workers Party. Subsequently Morrow went into
publishing and became an ardent Cold Warrior and anti-Communist. During the
1960s he became a leading figure in the modern occult boom through his publishing
house, University Books, Inc., and his associated Mystic Arts Book Society,
often writing introductions under the pseudonym John C. Wilson.

SOURCES: James P. Cannon, *The Struggle for Socialism in the "American Century"*
(1977); Alan M. Wald, *James T. Farrell: The Revolutionary Socialist Years* (1978)
and "The *Menorah* Group Moves Left," *Jewish Social Studies* 38 (Summer-Fall 1976).

*ALAN WALD*


**MORTIMER, WYNDHAM (1884–1966).** Wyndham Mortimer was a leader
in the early years of the United Automobile Workers (UAW), serving as vice-
president from 1936 to 1938. His sympathies with pro-Soviet elements made

him a controversial figure throughout his union career. Mortimer was born on March 11, 1884, in Clearfield, Pennsylvania. His father was a miner and a union member. Wyndham Mortimer was a Protestant in early upbringing, but he carried no religious affiliation into adult life. After work in the coal mines beginning at age 12, Mortimer moved to Ohio in 1905. He worked in steel mills, on railroads, and as a streetcar conductor, and was a strong, if dissident, trade unionist. Initially attracted to socialism by Eugene V. Debs' (q.v.), magnetism, he remained an anti-capitalist radical throughout his life.

In 1917 Mortimer began work at the White Motor Company, a Cleveland truck manufacturer. In 1932–1933 Mortimer led in the organization of White employees to the Auto Workers Union, an affiliate of the Communist Party's Trade Union Unity League. In 1933 he helped bring the Cleveland union into the American Federation of Labor (AFL). Mortimer pressed for the establishment of an industrial union for autoworkers. After the AFL chartered the UAW in 1935, he urged affiliation of the new union with the Congress of Industrial Organizations (CIO). In 1936 he was elected UAW vice-president and was international representative in Flint, Michigan. He soon came to oppose the erratic UAW president, Homer Martin, who expelled him and four others from the executive board in 1938. In 1939 Mortimer appeared to be the leading contender for the union's presidency, but that eventually went to R. J. Thomas. In 1940 Mortimer moved to California and was UAW representative in an aircraft workers organizing drive. In 1941 he supported workers' demands in the North American Aviation strike, during which he and UAW national officers exchanged recriminations over the wisdom and conduct of this strike in a key defense plant.

Mortimer left the UAW in 1941, and in 1945 he retired from active involvement in the labor movement. Until his death on August 15, 1966, he remained a vocal opponent of the UAW leadership. Critics believed him to be an apologist for the Soviet Union and a faithful ally of the Communist Party. Mortimer denied party affiliation, but after his death Communist leaders reported that he was a Party member.

SOURCES: Wyndham Mortimer, *Organize! My Life as a Union Man* (1971); Victor G. Reuther, *The Brothers Reuther and the Story of the UAW: A Memoir* (1976).

*ROBERT H. ZIEGER*


**MOSES, ROBERT PARRIS (b. 1935).** Though he avoided publicity and rarely spoke to large audiences, Robert Parris Moses became one of the most influential black leaders of the Southern civil rights struggle and of the New Left during the 1960s. Born on January 23, 1935, in New York City, Moses spent his early years in a public housing project near the Harlem River. In 1952 he graduated from Stuyvesant High School and won a scholarship to Hamilton College. He earned an M.A. degree in philosophy in 1957 at Harvard University. Forced to leave college by the death of his mother and the hospitalization of his father, he returned to New York and became a mathematics teacher at Horace Mann School.

During the late 1950s Moses became increasingly active in the nascent black protest movement. In 1958 he helped veteran black activist Bayard Rustin (q.v.) with the Second Youth March for Integrated Schools, and in the summer of 1960, at Rustin's suggestion, he went to Atlanta to work with Martin Luther King's Southern Christian Leadership Conference (SCLC). Moses left Atlanta to seek participants for the fall conference of a new organization, the Student Nonviolent Coordinating Committee (SNCC), that Ella Baker, onetime executive secretary of SCLC had helped to found.

Moses returned to Mississippi in 1961 to become the head of SNCC's project in McComb and ultimately director for the Council of Federated Organizations (COFO), a federation of civil rights groups in the state. Seeking to develop leadership among poorly educated blacks at the bottom of the Southern social order, he influenced civil rights activists searching for alternatives to hierarchical and manipulative political modes. Moses' goal was to develop self-reliant organizations and leaders who could continue the struggle after organizers had departed. His fear that others would become dependent on his leadership led Moses and his wife, Donna Richards, to leave Mississippi after the massive 1964 summer project.

Temporarily changing his name to Bob Parris, he participated in several rallies against the Vietnam War, but by the end of 1965 Moses had ended his relations with white activists. After separating from his wife in 1966, he went to Canada to avoid the military draft. In June 1968 Moses and his new wife settled in Tanzania. They returned to the United States with their four children in 1976. Avoiding public attention, Moses resumed his graduate studies in philosophy at Harvard and in 1982 received a MacArthur Foundation award to continue his studies.

SOURCE: Clayborne Carson, *In Struggle: SNCC and the Black Awakening of the 1960s* (1981).

*CLAYBORNE CARSON*


**MOST, JOHANN (1846–1906).** Johann Most, the "Stormy Petrel of the American Left," was the leading left-wing advocate of political terrorism in Germany and the United States during the late nineteenth century. He was also an editor, speaker, and organizer for the violence-prone wing of socialism and anarchism in the United States, Austria, Germany, and England.

Born in Augsburg, Germany (then the independent kingdom of Bavaria), in 1846 into a working-class family, Most received a ninth-grade education in that city. His mother died when he was less than 10 years old, and he was raised by a stepmother who considered him a needless burden in her life; she beat him often and hard. Most was apprenticed to a bookbinder at the age of 12 and five years later became a journeyman. When he was 13 years old he developed mouth cancer, which required radical surgery and left his face twisted into a hideous shape.

After completing his apprenticeship at age 17, Most traipsed all over Europe for five years before settling in Vienna in 1868. In the Austrian capital Most joined a trade union and became active in the labor movement as an agitator. His hyperbolic rhetoric landed him in jail for more than a year and led to his expulsion from Austria. In 1871 Most returned to his native Bavaria, where he became a leading member of the Social Democratic Party. Because the Bavarian party was too quiescent, he transferred to the Saxon party, in Chemnitz, where he edited the local Social Democratic newspaper. He was jailed for strike activity in the Saxon city. While in prison he wrote a popular synopsis of Karl Marx's *Das Kapital*. Soon after his release in 1874, Most was elected to the Reichstag. Four years later he moved to Berlin, where he became editor of the *Berliner Freie Presse*, a Social Democratic Party organ. He was also active in a movement against the church, particularly against the Reverend Adolf Stoecker, an anti-Semitic nationalist, and his Christian Socialist Party. Most's activity against the church and its political arm led to his expulsion from Berlin.

His oratorical vehemence made Most an object of police harassment all over Germany and the rest of continental Europe. He was forced to flee to London, which already had a considerable radical German emigrant population. In London he began publishing his personal revolutionary organ, *Freiheit*. This newspaper abandoned all pretense at Social Democratic restraint and became the organ of the anarcho-Communist social-revolutionary movement. Most was ousted from the Social Democratic Party of Germany in 1880. The next year he wrote an editorial in *Freiheit* hailing the assassins of Russia's czar Alexander II, a first cousin of Queen Victoria. He was arrested, spent more than a year in jail, and then moved to the United States.

Most landed in New York in December 1882 and was hailed by crowds of American, German, and Russian anarchist refugees. He set out almost immediately on a speaking tour to all the major cities in the eastern half of the United States. In the course of the tour he helped organize anarchist-Communist organizations throughout the nation. During his Chicago stopover, Most engaged in a debate on socialism versus anarchism with the German-American Socialist intellectual leader, Paul Grottkau (q.v.). In the debate Most insisted that more than organized government had to be abolished before humanity could be free. He wanted marriage, which he called immoral interference by the state in a purely private affair, to be abolished, and he called for abolition of the family, which he called a repressive institution that was the model from which the state was designed. The result of human mores and laws was, he said, an exploitative society in which vice, crime, exploitation, and inequality were nurtured. Moreover, Most argued, disease was caused by working conditions under the capitalist system. All these evils would disappear only when their root cause, government, was abolished.

In 1884 the representatives of the social-revolutionary clubs of the United States gathered in Pittsburgh under Most's leadership. The meeting adopted a manifesto that articulated Most's philosophy of anarcho-communism. It called for a totally free society with all of the economy organized into voluntary socially operated and managed industries that would produce for use and not for profit. Before that Utopia could come into existence there would unfortunately have to be a "short" transitional period. During that period there would be a veritable reign of terror against remnants of the privileged classes of the old society. Capitalists would be massacred, churches would be turned into propaganda mills for the new society, and the press would be forced to become organs of the revolution. Dissent would be dealt with severely. The organizers and rulers of the new society would be members of the "vanguard of the working class"— a small dedicated group of professional revolutionists.

Most took a job in a dynamite factory in order to learn how explosives were made. And then he wrote and published the *Science of Revolution*, a handbook for manufacturing high explosives. Then in 1886 someone took his advice and threw a bomb into a crowd at a Chicago demonstration to support the strikers in the Harvester plant. Eleven men and women died, and over one hundred were injured. More than a year later four anarchists died on the gallows after an unfair, prejudiced trial. Most's manual was one of the key exhibits used by the state in its successful prosecution. Immediately after the four were hanged, Most was arrested after delivering a fiery speech denouncing executions.

In 1889 he met Emma Goldman (q.v.) at a meeting hailing his release from prison. She was enamored of him until 1892, when he denounced Alexander Berkman (q.v.) for attempting to murder anti-union steel magnate Henry Clay Frick. Goldman was so incensed that she horsewhipped him publicly.

In 1897 Most turned to the theater, producing and playing the lead in plays by Hauptmann, Strindberg, and other radical playwrights. He continued to edit the *Freiheit* and also edited, for a year, the Buffalo *Arbeiter Zeitung*. He also lectured on anarchism throughout the nation, drawing huge and sympathetic crowds.

Most was jailed again in 1901 because of a tragic coincidence. He published an old article of his called "Murder for Murder," a call for retribution against exploiters, on the day after Leon Czolgosz assassinated President William McKinley. Czolgosz was pictured in the press as an active anarchist, which he was not.

Freed in 1903, Most continued to edit the *Freiheit* in New York until his death in 1906.

SOURCES: Emma Goldman, "Johann Most," *American Mercury*, June 8, 1926; Frederic Troutmann, *The Voice of Terror: A Biography of Johann Most* (1980).

*LILLIAN KIRTZMAN JOHNPOLL*


**MUMFORD, LEWIS (b. 1895).** Throughout a long career as a sociologist, philosopher, cultural historian, and polemicist, Lewis Mumford has been a prominent radical critic of industrial organization. Mumford's chief legacy to the Left is his vision of a participatory, ecological democracy and his defense of a core of humanistic values as central to any project of radical change.

Mumford was born in Flushing, New York, on October 19, 1895, the illegitimate son of Elvina Mumford, a German-American housekeeper. Baptized an Episcopalian, he received no formal religious training. Mumford sporadically attended City College and other New York universities between 1912 and 1919, but he never received a bachelor's degree. He first became a leading figure in New York's literary Left in the aftermath of World War I, when he identified himself with the urban regionalism of Scottish sociologist Patrick Geddes and the hopes for American cultural renewal held by the so-called Young Intellectuals— Randolph Bourne (q.v.), Van Wyck Brooks, Waldo Frank (q.v.), Paul Rosenfeld, and Harold Stearns.

Mumford's prolific work as a writer explored four general themes. In cultural criticism he followed Brooks' call for the rediscovery of America's "usable past." In urbanism, Mumford's theory of a decentralized regionalism balancing rural and city cultures made him the dominant intellectual force within the Regional Planning Association of America (1922–1923). In history and sociology, he analyzed the rise of destructive technologies and the industrial "megamachine" in Western civilization. In moral and religious philosophy, he upheld the integrity of the creative individual against technological determinism, which he believed had become the hegemonic creed of advanced capitalism.

Though never enrolled in a leftist party, Mumford has been affiliated with many left-liberal journals and organizations. He was an associate editor of the *Dial* (1919), co-editor of the *American Caravan* (1925–1927), and a contributing editor of the *New Masses* (1926–1930), the *New Republic* (1927–1940), and *Liberation* (1956–1968). Mumford was a member of the League of American Writers and the Congress of American Artists (1935–1940), resigning from both over the Nazi-Soviet Pact. During 1938–1941, Mumford was an outspoken critic of American isolationism, joining the Committee to Defend America by Aiding the Allies (1940) and the Fight for Freedom Committee (1941). Unlike other liberal critics of appeasement, Mumford became a consistent opponent of U.S. foreign policy after 1945 and an advocate of nuclear disarmament.

He presently lives in Amenia, New York.

SOURCES: R. Alan Lawson, *The Failure of Independent Liberalism 1930–1941* (1971); Lewis Mumford, *Sketches from Life* (1982).

*CASEY BLAKE*

**MUSTE, A. J. (1885–1967).** A. J. Muste was prominent in non-Communist Left affairs, first as an officer of radical pacifist organizations, then as a sachem in the Conference for Progressive Labor Action and as founder of the American Workers Party, and subsequently as titular leader of the Workers Party. Returning next to the pacifist camp, he was a post–World War II crusader for nuclear disarmament and a spokesman in anti-Vietnam War coalitions of the 1960s.

Abraham Johannes Muste was born at Zierikzee, in Holland, on January 8, 1885. His parents were Dutch Reformed Church members. Muste's father, employed in Holland by a Zeeland nobleman, moved his family from that country to Grand Rapids, Michigan, in 1891. There Abraham attended public schools until he enrolled at the Reformed Church of America's preparatory school at Hope, Michigan. He earned a degree at Hope College in 1905 and joined for the next year the faculty of Northwestern Classical Academy at Orange City, Iowa, a Reformed Church–related institution.

He then matriculated for two years at the Reformed Church's graduate theological seminary at New Brunswick, New Jersey, supplemented his seminary instruction with courses at Columbia University, and received a B.D. degree at Union Theological Seminary in 1912. Meanwhile, the Reformed Church ordained him in 1909. He occupied pulpits continuously from 1909 to 1915 in a Reformed institution—Fort Washington (New York) Collegiate Church—and at Central Congregational Church of Newtonville, Massachusetts, for three more years.

While a clergyman, Muste's views on world peace matters were initially inchoate, though his formal education had included instruction in the Social Gospel, and pacifist and Socialist anti-war arguments had not escaped his notice. Then the United States entered World War I in 1917, and Muste responded with preachings that emphasized brotherhood, nonviolence, and pacifism. He joined the Fellowship of Reconciliation chapter at Boston, later became a national vice-chairman of the Fellowship, and organized another pacifist group, the League for Democratic Control. To continue these new activities without impediments raised by his conservative parishioners, Muste exchanged his Newtonville pastorate in 1918 for a Society of Friends ministry and Quaker Fellowship House domicile at Providence, Rhode Island. There the laity applauded his pacifism as well as his post-war teachings on preserving world peace, and they approved of Muste's concerns for civil liberties and work as national committeeman of the American Civil Liberties Union. At the same time, however, many questioned Muste's labor-organizing activities. He surrendered his pastorate in 1919, but he retained ties to pacifist entities, most notably by remaining a Fellowship of Reconciliation officer until 1931.

In the post–World War I years Muste organized experimental labor cooperatives, conducted worker education classes in New Jersey and Massachusetts, and participated in a textile industry strike at Lawrence, Massachusetts, one outcome of which was the founding of the Amalgamated Textile Workers (ATW) union. Muste shared the organizational work incident to launching the ATW, which claimed at its height the allegiance of 25 percent of all textile factory workers in the United States. From 1919 to 1921 Muste edited the ATW's official journal, *New Textile Worker*, and was elected general secretary and treasurer of the union until the ATW foundered during an ensuing economic recession. The union also failed partly because its besetting sin was, in the eyes of the American Federation of Labor, the ATW's resort to dual unionism.

Muste next became director of Brookwood Labor College in 1921. While administering this Katonah, New York, institution for the next twelve years, he regularly contributed his writings to *Labor Age*, principal journal of the Labor

Publications Society, and he immersed himself in other non-Communist Left affairs. Among his offices, he sat on the executive board of the Workers Education Bureau and, after 1931, was chairman of the Conference for Progressive Labor Action (CPLA). In the 1930s he also organized unemployed leagues under CPLA auspices, these bodies gaining notoriety for supporting the urban poor in their conflicts with landlords, merchants, and state and federal relief bureaucracies.

Meanwhile Muste had clashed with his Brookwood College faculty because he demanded the faculty's unswerving support of the CPLA. Muste resigned from his college post in 1933 and, later in the same year, founded the American Workers Party (AWP). Under his leadership, this avowedly Marxist-Leninist party proclaimed anti-communism, pictured itself a better alternative than communism or socialism, and intervened in several labor-industry conflicts. Muste and his AWP organizers played significant roles in the Auto-Lite strike of 1934 at Toledo.

In 1934 Muste merged the AWP with Trotskyist organizations, producing the Workers Party. Muste was party national secretary until 1936, at which time Trotskyists persuaded the Musteite faction of the party to acquiesce in a tactic called the French Turn, which sent Party members scurrying into the Socialist Party. Though Muste disagreed with such practices, he joined the Socialist Party. He conferred with Leon Trotsky in 1936 and subsequently claimed that Trotsky and other European leaders of Trotsky's movement had agreed with Muste's protestations that the French Turn had not served the best interests of American radicals.

Muste disavowed Marxism-Leninism in 1936, citing a profound religious experience that induced him to return to the Christian fold. In 1937 he was director of the Presbyterian Labor Temple in New York City for nearly the whole year. More important, he quickly reestablished his prominence in Christian pacifist circles. Muste rejoined the Fellowship of Reconciliation (FOR), where he held subordinate staff positions in the organization from 1938 to 1940, and he simultaneously accepted a place on the executive committee of the War Resisters League (WRL). He withdrew at last from WRL leadership in the 1950s but retained membership in the League until his death.

Meanwhile, Muste accepted a place on the *Presbyterian Tribune* editorial board in 1938, but he failed to realign this journal exclusively on the side of the FOR's Utopian and pacifist ideas. At the same time, Mohandas Ghandi's teachings on nonviolence interested Muste, who then urged labor unions to adopt tactics of nonviolent resistance. And in 1941 Muste created the Nonviolent Direct Action Committee to teach Gandhi's precepts. In the same period, Muste wrote pacifist treatises, among them *Nonviolence in an Aggressive World* (1938) and *Not by Might* (1947).

Appointed executive secretary of the FOR in 1940, Muste administered this society until 1953. During his tenure he was often preoccupied with opposing conscription, with guardianship of conscientious objectors' rights in wartime, and working for post-war disarmament. The FOR grew from about 4,000 to approximately 15,000 members during Muste's incumbency, only to decline in the Cold War years. Finally, Muste accepted the FOR's professional retirement plan benefits in 1953, though surrendering his FOR offices was at no diminution of his influence in pacifist circles.

Again a critic of sociopolitical conventionality and the nation's Cold War verities after 1953, Muste joined Peacemakers, a group that resisted conscription, declined to pay federal taxes, and advocated civil disobedience. He personally practiced tax withholding until a federal court forced his compliance. He also edited *Liberation* magazine for a decade; establishment of this journal was Muste's main achievement when he attempted to expand the nation's radical and pacifist press. As titular missioner of the Church Peace Mission (CPM) from 1953 to 1962, Muste incurred other reverses. Under his leadership the CPM's principal goals were not reached—neither were pacifist rationales strengthened by generating more sophisticated anti-war and nonviolence theologies, nor were the historically adamant "peace" churches persuaded to march unitedly with the CPM.

Opposed, meanwhile, to American use of atomic weaponry in World War II and threats of nations to resort again to such arms, Muste was a founder of the Committee for Nonviolent Action (CNVA). Besides writing and lecturing widely, as a CNVA activist he practiced nonviolent but sometimes confrontationist opposition to nuclear warfare. He also participated in activities of the World Peace Brigade, personally explaining the newest pacifism and nonviolence ideas in Europe and Third World nations. On another front, Muste supported the newest civil rights movements in the United States. To himself he ascribed the role of grandparent to the Congress of Racial Equality. He extended his support to organizations such as the Southern Christian Leadership Conference and the Student Nonviolent Coordinating Committee.

Because of Muste's post–World War II activism, FBI Director J. Edgar Hoover accused him of acting in the company of the Communist Party's front organizations, but Muste persisted in the ways to which Hoover had objected. Moreover, he criticized the federal government's Vietnam policy in the 1960s, and frequently he acted as mediator among the politically diverse components of the anti-Vietnam War coalitions. Muste traveled in North Vietnam on January 9–19, 1967, and on returning to the United States he transmitted to President Lyndon Johnson his understanding of Ho Chi Minh's views on ways of achieving a cease-fire in the Vietnam War.

Muste died in New York City on February 10, 1967.

SOURCES: Nat Hentoff, *Peace Agitator: The Story of A. J. Muste* (1963); Jo Ann Ooiman Robinson, *Abraham Went Out: A Biography of A. J. Muste* (1982); "Sketches for an Autobiography," in *The Essays of A. J. Muste*, ed. Nat Hentoff (1967).

*HUGH T. LOVIN*

# N

**NEARING, SCOTT (1883–1983).** Scott Nearing was a teacher, anti–World War I activist, Socialist, Communist, and prominent ecologist during his long life. He was born on August 6, 1883, in Morris Run, Pennsylvania, a small coal town dominated by his grandfather, an implacable opponent of unions. Raised in luxury by his Anglo-Saxon Baptist parents (his father was a broker), Nearing graduated from the University of Pennsylvania in 1905 and, having been influenced by the Social Gospel, became secretary of the Pennsylvania Child Labor Committee while studying for his Ph.D., which he received in economics in 1909. He then taught at Penn's Wharton School. Nearing's liberalism was further nurtured by his residence in the single-tax colony of Arden, Delaware. His growing involvement in municipal reform politics led to strains with the university administration, and he was fired in 1915, the same year he declared himself a Socialist. Nearing's next academic position, at the University of Toledo, ended in the same fashion. In constant controversy because of his outspoken views, he was ousted in 1917 over his denunciations of U.S. preparations for World War I.

Nearing actively participated in organizations opposing American involvement in the war. He was elected executive chairman of the People's Council of America and joined the Socialist Party in 1917 just as most of its intellectuals were leaving it to support the conflict. Indicted in 1918 for writings critical of the war, he was one of the few prominent radicals who won acquittal. As he moved further to the Left, he became associated with *Revolutionary Age*, the organ of the party's left wing. His pacifism kept him out of the Communist movement in 1919, but his sympathy for the Bolsheviks led to his resignation from the Socialist Party in 1922.

Nearing remained an independent but pro-Soviet radical for several years, during which time he served as president of the Garland Fund (1924–1926), a foundation created to aid radical causes, directed the Rand School's Department of Labor Research, and co-authored *Dollar Diplomacy* with Joseph Freeman (q.v.). Visiting Russia in 1925, Nearing was enthralled and applied for membership in the Communist Party, USA. Because he was so prominent and nonproletarian, he was asked to respond to a lengthy set of questions on his views. Rejected on the grounds that he wanted the Party to be merely a propaganda sect, he was accepted a year or two later. Nearing's Party career was uneventful. He traveled to China and Russia, spoke at rallies, and ran for governor of New Jersey. In 1930 he submitted the manuscript of *Twilight of Empire* to International Publishers and was informed that Moscow objected to its contents. He had the book published anyway, resigned from the Party in a friendly letter, and was then expelled as an enemy in January 1930.

The Party's treatment of him did not stay Nearing's enthusiasm for it or for the Soviet Union. During the 1930s he remained active in a variety of Party fronts. He even tried to rejoin, but was rejected. Nor did the Nazi-Soviet Pact cool his ardor for Russia. Through the 1950s he continued to praise the social achievements of Stalinist rule and he applauded the crushing of the Hungarian Revolution.

After his expulsion, Nearing did change his lifestyle. He became a subsistence farmer in Vermont (later in Maine), selling maple sugar and syrup, eschewing such "luxuries" as meat, telephones, and modern tools and emerging for part of the year to lecture. Always dogmatic, he became increasingly cranky and self-consciously contradictory as he neared 100 years of age. In the 1970s his and his wife's account of their lifestyle, *Living the Good Life*, became a Bible for many advocates of the counterculture. Nearing died on August 14, 1983.

SOURCES: Scott Nearing, *The Making of a Radical* (1972); Stephen Whitfield, *Scott Nearing: Apostle of American Radicalism* (1974).

*HARVEY KLEHR*

**NELSON, STEVE (b. 1903).** For three decades Steve Nelson was an important Communist Party leader: a blue-collar organizer, a commander in the Spanish Civil War, a member of the National Board of the Party, and a Smith Act victim. Nelson was born Stjepan Mesaros in 1903 in a farming region of Croatia, now Yugoslavia. His family on both sides came from generations of millers. Barely literate after five years of grammar school, he arrived in Philadelphia in 1920 and ran the gamut of semi-skilled jobs until he joined the Carpenters Union.

A Serbian worker introduced Nelson to the Socialist Labor Party, but Nelson soon was more attracted by the Communist Party and joined the Young Workers League. In 1923 in Pittsburgh, Nelson married Margaret Yaeger, who was from a Steel Valley radical family. About 1925, as part of an effort to Americanize the Party, he took the name Steve Nelson. The couple spent four years in Detroit, where Nelson worked in several automotive plants and took over organizing the Fisher Body section.

In 1928, Nelson became a citizen and soon joined the Communist Party USA. He briefly attended the Workers School in New York City and then became a full-time Party organizer in Chicago, serving as secretary of the Unemployed Council. After a police beating and attempts to charge him with sedition, Nelson was sent to Illinois by the Party to work with the National Miners Union and to the Pennsylvania anthracite mining region.

In 1931 he attended the Lenin School in Moscow. Separately, the Nelsons worked as Comintern couriers to parts of Europe and China. By late 1933 they were back in Pennsylvania, where Steve Nelson ran for the state legislature. He fought in Spain with the Abraham Lincoln Battalion, became battalion commissar, and was wounded.

From 1939 until 1945 Nelson worked in California as a general troubleshooter, as a link with the Japanese Bureau of the Party, as chairman of the San Francisco branch, and as Oakland County organizer. During a short period underground in 1940, Nelson write *Volunteers*, about the Spanish Civil War (not published until 1953). After World War II he was elected to the National Board of the Party and was given responsibility for nationality group work; he spoke Serbo-Croatian and could follow conversations in six related languages.

Nelson moved to Pittsburgh in 1948 to become the Party's district organizer. There he was convicted of sedition under a state law and sentenced to twenty years in prison. In 1951 he was charged under the federal Smith Act. In 1952 he began serving the state sentence. The Pennsylvania Supreme Court, however, overturned the sedition conviction on the grounds that the Smith Act superseded the state's law and the U.S. Supreme Court upheld this decision. Nelson's Smith Act conviction of 1953 was also eventually overturned. In these long legal struggles, Margaret Nelson acted as his co-counsel and organizer of his defense committee.

After his release from prison and the Khrushchev revelations about Stalin, Nelson worked for reform within the Party but left it in 1957. He renewed his active role in the Veterans of the Abraham Lincoln Brigade and in 1963 was elected national commander of the Brigade, a post that he still holds.

SOURCE: Steve Nelson, James R. Barrett, and Rob Ruck, *Steve Nelson: American Radical* (1981).

*NORAH CHASE*

**NEWTON, HUEY P. (b. 1942).** Huey Percy Newton was the co-founder and leading figure in the Black Panther Party. He was born in New Orleans on February 17, 1942. His father was Walter Newton, a man variously described as a sharecropper, railroad worker, or Baptist minister, and his mother was Amelia Newton. The family left Louisiana for Oakland, California, when Huey, named for Governor Huey Long, was one year old. Newton attended and graduated from the Oakland public schools and then graduated from Merritt Junior College in 1965. He spent eight months studying at San Francisco Law School.

Newton became a disciple of Malcolm X and read widely while in college, eventually adopting a Marxist outlook. In October 1966 Newton and Bobby Seale (q.v.) founded the Black Panther Party, with Newton as president. Newton was the single most important figure in the organization. Under his leadership the party preached a doctrine of self-help and self-defense. It rejected Black Nationalism in favor of opening lines of contact with all oppressed people, black or white. When armed Panthers appeared on the streets of Oakland's ghettos, inevitable clashes with the police took place. On the evening of October 28, 1967, Oakland police stopped a car in which Newton was riding. In the altercation that followed, Newton was shot five times and one policeman was killed and another wounded.

Although he continued to run the Panthers from jail or exile, Newton had serious legal problems for much of the next decade. He was tried in 1968 for murder, assault, and kidnapping on charges arising out of the October incident of the previous year. Found guilty of voluntary manslaughter, he was sentenced to two to fifteen years in prison, but he was released from prison in 1970 after a second trial, ordered on appeal, ended in a hung jury. He left the United States for Cuba in 1974, fleeing prosecution on charges following the shooting of a young woman. He returned to the United States in 1977, and again charges against him ended with a hung jury in 1979. Through it all, and despite a power struggle with Eldridge Cleaver (q.v.), Newton retained the preeminent role in the Black Panthers. In 1980 he received a Ph.D. from the University of California at Santa Cruz. His dissertation was "War Against the Panthers: A Study of Repression in America."

SOURCES: G. Louis Heath (ed.), *The Black Panther Leaders Speak* (1976); Albert Moore, *A Special Rage* (1971); Huey Newton, *Revolutionary Suicide* (1973).

*TOM WILLIAMS*

**NOVACK, GEORGE (b. 1905).** George Edward Novack is an internationally known Marxist writer and has been a leading theoretician of the Socialist Workers Party since the 1930s. Novack was born Yasef Emmanuel Novograbelski on August 5, 1905, in Boston. His parents were Jewish immigrants from Eastern Europe. His father, who ran a Turkish bathhouse in Boston, changed the family name to Novack for business reasons; the son Anglicized his first and middle names after entering school.

Novack attended Harvard from 1922 to 1927, studying literature and philosophy, but he moved to New York City before graduation to begin a successful career as an advertising executive in the publishing industry. Originally sympathetic to the Socialist Party, he became active in 1932 in the National Committee for the Defense of Political Prisoners, an affiliate of the Communist Party's International Labor Defense. In 1933 he joined the Trotskyist Communist League of America and worked for the Non-Partisan Labor Defense.

Having abandoned his career in publishing, Novack contributed copiously to the Trotskyist theoretical magazine *New International*. From 1937 until 1940 he was secretary of the American Committee for the Defense of Leon Trotsky, and in the spring of 1937 he went to Mexico to observe the hearings of the John Dewey Commission of Inquiry into the Charges Against Leon Trotsky in the Moscow trials. From 1941 until 1950 he was national secretary of the Civil

Rights Defense Committee. Its most important case was that of the eighteen members of the Socialist Workers Party and Minneapolis Teamsters convicted under the Smith Act for their opposition to U.S. government policy during World War II. A member of the National Committee of the Socialist Workers Party from 1940 to 1973, Novack was twice treasurer of the Party's presidential campaign committee.

In the 1950s, 1960s, and 1970s, most of Novack's activities were literary. From 1965 to 1974 he was associate editor of the *International Socialist Review*, and he has written numerous works on Marxist philosophy. As of 1986, he remains a member of the SWP.

SOURCES: George Novack, "My Philosophical Itinerary," in *Polemics in Marxist Philosophy* (1978), and "Radical Intellectuals in the 1930s," *International Socialist Review* 29, no. 2 (March-April 1968); Alan M. Wald, *James T. Farrell: The Revolutionary Socialist Years* (1978).

*ALAN WALD*

**NOYES, JOHN HUMPHREY (1811–1886).** John Humphrey Noyes was a leading Christian Utopian Socialist and the founder and director of the most successful innovative Socialist community in U.S. history. Born in Brattleboro, Vermont, in 1811, the son of a leading politician in that state, John Humphrey Noyes was educated at Dartmouth (B.A., 1832), Andover Theological Seminary (1834), and Yale Divinity School.

At Yale he was converted to Perfectionism, a quasi-Christian sect. Perfectionists argued that humans had been excused of all sin in A.D. 70, when ostensibly the Second Coming of Christ had occurred. Humanity was, they believed, capable of absolute perfection, because the Second Coming had occurred. Most Perfectionists, including Noyes, were vehemently opposed to slavery and favored a violent revolution, if necessary, in order for Christ to ascend his earthly throne. During the early 1840s Noyes published a tract in which he argued that marriage and exclusive sex were both sins. The book generated virulent antagonism from the established churches after it was quoted in a religious journal. He then attempted to organize a community dedicated to pre-Nicaean Christianity, absolute communism, and free sex. He also ordained birth control among his followers.

Opposition to his ideas grew so vehement, however, that Noyes was forced to flee to Shelton, New York, in 1847. There he organized the Oneida Community, which was successful for the next thirty years under Noyes' dictatorial rule. In the Oneida Community all goods, even those that would normally have been considered purely personal, belonged to the community generally. There was no private property. Exclusive love or friendship was not tolerated. At work, the sexes mingled. Genetic breeding was practiced—it was called stirpiculture. Open criticism and censure were the means for punishing offenders. Most of the younger members, especially those born in the community, received university educations. During twenty years, 1851–1871, membership of the community rose from 150 to 170.

In the 1870s Noyes' interest shifted to Socialist politics. He organized a weekly, *American Socialist*, and proclaimed his support for a Socialist political party, although he opposed the Socialist belief in a class struggle.

The Oneida Community was economically successful; so successful that the younger members of the community, who were not imbued with its original ideals, reorganized it into a stock corporation. Noyes then moved to the Niagara frontier, where he attempted, at age 68, to organize a new colony. It failed, although Noyes remained an active Socialist and pacifist until his death in 1886.

SOURCES: Allerton Parker, *A Yankee Saint: John Humphrey Noyes and the Oneida Community* (1936); Constance Noyes Robertson, *Oneida Community: An Autobiography, 1855–1876* (1970).

*BERNARD K. JOHNPOLL*

# O

O'HARE, KATE RICHARDS (1877–1948). Kate Richards O'Hare Cunningham, known generally as Kate Richards O'Hare, was a leading Socialist agitator and organizer during the first twenty-five years of the twentieth century. She was also an active prison reformer between 1925 and 1948. Kate Richards was born into a farm family in Ottawa County, Kansas, in 1877. She was educated in the public schools of Kansas City, Missouri, and at a Nebraska normal school. At the age of 15 she went to work as an apprentice machinist and became one of the rare women members of the Machinists Union. While working in the machine shop, she thought of becoming a minister in the Disciples of Christ Church. She was also active in temperance work and at "saving" fallen women. At the same time, she read and was impressed with the Socialist and Populist literature of the period. She was finally converted to socialism by Mary Harris ("Mother") Jones (q.v.) in 1899.

She joined the Socialist Party in 1901 and soon became active in the party on the Great Plains—Kansas, Missouri, and Oklahoma. The organization there was more populist than Marxian, and she rejected Marxian dogma all her life. In 1901 she attended a seminar in Girard, Kansas, sponsored by the popular Socialist weekly *Appeal to Reason*. There she met Francis P. O'Hare of Iowa, whom she married the next year. They spent their honeymoon organizing and speaking for socialism in Kansas, Missouri, and the Oklahoma Territory.

She and her husband toured the Western states, organizing and agitating for the Socialist Party until 1917. They helped develop the camp-meeting style— with Oscar Ameringer (q.v.). This type of agitation was extremely effective, especially in Oklahoma. Her lectures were often reprinted into pamphlets that helped spread the word of socialism throughout the prairies.

Kate O'Hare also tried her hand at writing popular Socialist fiction—one novel had considerable circulation in 1904. About 1912 she and her husband were named editors of the *National Rip-Saw*, a Socialist weekly aimed at prairie farmers. In 1910 she ran for Congress. She also served on the National Executive Committee of the Socialist Party during the period 1912–1918 and was a delegate to the 1913 meeting of the Socialist International.

O'Hare was essentially an expert organizer among farmers because her theoretical base was closely tied to the agrarian Populist movement. She believed that action should precede theory. Moreover, as was typical among Western Populists, Kate O'Hare had a distaste for Easterners generally. She could thus proclaim her friendship for Victor Berger (q.v.) of Wisconsin and her dislike for Morris Hillquit (q.v.), admitting that her feelings were in great part due to the fact that Berger was a Midwesterner and Hillquit was a New Yorker.

In 1917 O'Hare chaired the Socialist convention committee which proclaimed the Socialists' opposition to the war a day after the United States declared war. Three months after the convention she was arrested for supposedly seditious remarks at a meeting in Bowman, North Dakota. Investigations by serious scholars indicate that she never made the remarks, that she was a victim of a frame-up. However, she was convicted and sentenced to five years in prison. After fourteen months in the Missouri state penitentiary she was freed, at the suggestion of Attorney General A. Mitchell Palmer, in the spring of 1920. While in prison, O'Hare became friendly with fellow prisoner Emma Goldman (q.v.), who wrote in a letter that she was "a woman of simplicity and tender feeling. We quickly became friends, and my fondness for her increased in proportion as her personality unfolded itself to me." Kate O'Hare's letters to her husband appeared in the *St. Louis Post-Dispatch* and soon resulted in improvements in the prison conditions, for example, a library and hot food. Unfortunately, she suffered physical breakdown in prison.

Upon her release she became active in the movements to free anti-war prisoners and to improve prison conditions. She was an organizer of the children's crusade to free their parents from prison, and two of her books, written while still in prison—*Kate O'Hare's Prison Letters* (1919) and *In Prison* (1920)—influenced prison reform. She was influential in winning enactment of a national law that eliminated the worst aspects of convict labor.

O'Hare was vigorously opposed to the Communist movement from its inception. With the near demise of the Socialist Party which followed the war and the Communist split, she devoted her life to prison reform. She helped organize Commonwealth College, a quasi-Socialist school, in Mena, Arkansas, during the mid–1920s. In 1928 she and Frank O'Hare were divorced. She married a California attorney and engineer, Charles Cunningham, and moved permanently to California.

In 1934 she made another foray into radical politics, working for Upton Sinclair's End Poverty in California (EPIC) campaign. In 1937 she joined the Washington staff of Representative Thomas P. Amlie, a Wisconsin Progressive. In 1939 she was appointed by California Governor Culbert Olson to be assistant director of the California Department of Penology. In her new job she helped reform the state's prison system. She remained active in the prison reform movement until her death in 1948 of a heart attack.

SOURCES: Emma Goldman, *Living My Life* (1931); H. C. Peterson and Gilbert C. Fite, *Opponents of War, 1917–1918*, (1957). Frank O'Hare's personal papers are at St. Louis University. Kate O'Hare's papers are spread throughout the United States in various collections; many are in the Tamiment Institute Library at New York University, New York City.

DOROTHY SWANSON

**OLGIN, MOISSAYE (1878–1939).** Moissaye J. Olgin, a participant in the Russian revolutionary movement, was for many years one of the Communist Party's leaders in Jewish affairs. He was born on March 14, 1878, near Kiev, Russia. His father was a lumber camp employee. Olgin first became active in the revolutionary student movement at the University of Kiev, from which he graduated in 1904. He soon became a functionary in the Jewish Bund. After the failure of the 1905 revolution he moved to Heidelberg, where he attended the university from 1907 to 1909. He returned to Russia, but settled in Vienna in 1913 to write poetry and literature and edit a Bund publication. In 1915 he moved to the United States, where he wrote for the *Jewish Daily Forward* and earned a Ph.D. at Columbia University in 1918.

At first Olgin was a bitter enemy of the new Bolshevik regime in Russia. Active in the Jewish Socialist Federation ever since his arrival in the United States, he strongly opposed its left-wingers and expressed his admiration for the Mensheviks. A visit to the Soviet Union in 1920 left him an admirer but still no Communist. Not until 1921 did he break with the Socialist Party, along with the majority of the Jewish Socialist Federation, and support affiliation with the Workers Party, as the Communists were then known. He became the editor of the Party's new Yiddish-language daily newspaper, *Freiheit*, in 1922 and remained its most important figure until his death.

Olgin's Party career was notable for his ability to adapt himself to unexpected shifts in the balance of internal power or in policies. He was at first associated with Lugwig Lore's (q.v.) faction in the Party. Sent to Moscow in 1923 to represent his group's interests, he deserted the sinking Lore to join Charles Ruthenberg's (q.v.) faction. Following Jay Lovestone's (q.v.) disgrace in 1929, Olgin pledged his loyalty to the new Party regime. Long an admirer of Trotsky, Olgin was best known in the Party for his pamphlet denouncing the Russian after he became Stalin's enemy. Likewise, after he blamed the Arab uprising against Palestinian Jews in 1929 on British imperialism and labeled it a pogrom, Olgin came under fire from factional enemies led by Alexander Bittelman (q.v.). He quickly did an about-face and blamed Zionists for Jewish deaths, leading to angry attacks on the *Freiheit* in the Jewish community.

During the Popular Front period, Olgin admitted that the Communist Party had alienated the Jewish masses and that its fight against Zionism, although correct, had been unnecessarily harsh and conveyed the impression that Jews in

Palestine were enemies. He called for greater respect for Jewish tradition. After the Nazi-Soviet Pact he exulted that it had enabled the Soviet Union to liberate the Jews of eastern Poland. He died on November 23, 1939.
SOURCE: Melech Epstein, *The Jew and Communism* (1959).

*HARVEY KLEHR*


**ONEAL, JAMES (1873–1962).** James Oneal was a Socialist editor, organizer, and writer from 1898 until his death in 1962. Oneal was born into a working-class home in Indianapolis, Indiana, in 1873. He was educated, up to the sixth grade, in public schools of that city. After leaving school, Oneal became an apprentice iron and steel worker. He was admitted into the Iron and Steel Workers Union in 1897. That same year he joined the Social Democracy, led by Eugene V. Debs (q.v.), his neighbor in Terre Haute, Indiana.

Oneal became active almost immediately in the Socialist movement. He joined in the bolt of the political Socialists, led by Victor Berger (q.v.), which formed the Social Democratic Party in 1898, and he was active in the first presidential campaign of Debs. In 1901 he was active in the formation of the Socialist Party by the merger of the Social Democratic Party and the "Kangaroo" faction of the Socialist Labor Party led by Morris Hillquit (q.v.).

Beginning in 1901, Oneal became a major speaker, writer, and editor for the Socialist Party. Shortly after the organization of the new party, Oneal was named an editor of the Socialist weekly, *The Worker*, which was merged into the *New York Call* nine years later. In 1911 he completed his magnum opus, *Workers in American History*, one of the first economic interpretations of U.S. history. More than five editions of the book were published between 1911 and 1921. In 1913 Oneal wrote a short work defending the ouster of "Big Bill" Haywood from the Socialist National Executive Committee, *Sabotage: Socialism Versus Syndicalism*. It was a major attack on the Industrial Workers of the World and its tactics.

Oneal opposed U.S. entry into World War I. Although he was threatened with arrest several times, he escaped jail.

Oneal was at first enamored of the Bolshevik seizure of power in Russia. When some Russian Socialists in the United States argued against the dictatorship and the violence engendered by Lenin's followers, Oneal answered that a revolution was not a tea party and that its success would require harsh measures. But he did oppose the attempt by American followers of Lenin to split the Socialist Party in 1919. He was at that time secretary of the Socialist Party in Massachusetts, and he used that position to oust all left-wing locals, which were mainly in the Latvian, Russian, and Finnish Socialist federations. That same year, Oneal was sent as an observer to the meeting of the Socialist International in Berne, Switzerland. He returned determined to keep the Socialist Party of America out of both the Socialist (Second) and the Communist (Third) Internationals. His position was accepted by a majority of Socialist Party members in 1921.

As information of the persecution of Socialists in Soviet Russia reached Oneal, he turned against the Russian regime. In a 1921 debate with Robert Minor (q.v.), he explained his opposition thus: "I favor all power to the working class, not all power to a handful of dictators, which is something different—all power to the working class, not all power to a clique that assumes to have super-human knowledge, that is infallible, that it cannot possibly err." [The debate was published by the Rand School in 1921.]

In 1922 Oneal was a delegate from the Socialist Party to the conference that helped set up the 1924 campaign for Robert H. LaFollette. He was active in the campaign of 1924. Oneal also worked hard for Norman Thomas (q.v.) in 1928 and 1932, although he was upset by Thomas' attempt to oust Morris Hillquit as national chairman of the party in 1932.

Beginning in 1934, Oneal and Thomas were at opposite ends of the party spectrum until 1945. Thomas was a member of the Militant wing of the party, Oneal feared a return to the Communist splits of 1919–1921. Oneal was strongly pro–Old Guard during the party fight of the 1930s. He used his position as editor of the *New Leader*, the organ of the Eastern states' Socialist organization, to oppose the Militants, especially after the pro-Thomas wing had captured the national party in 1934. The Militants retaliated by publishing their own weekly, *The Socialist Call*, beginning in 1935.

The party in New York State soon split. A primary election was necessary to determine control of the state party. The Militants won. The 1936 Socialist convention resulted in a nationwide split, with the Old Guard forming the Social Democratic Federation, which became part of the American Labor Party in New York State.

Oneal, who became editor of the *New Leader* at its birth in 1924, remained at its helm until 1940. Under his later control it became a moderate Social Democratic newspaper, a supporter of Franklin D. Roosevelt. The *New Leader* under Oneal vehemently opposed the Communists, rejected any idea of cooperating with them, and was virulently opposed to the Soviet Union, especially Stalin's slaughter of his real and imagined opponents.

Oneal retired from the *New Leader* in 1940 and moved to the West Coast. In retirement he wrote several more short works and resumed his friendship with Norman Thomas. He died in Stockton, California, on December 11, 1962.

SOURCES: "Biographical Note," in James Oneal, *Socialism's New Beginning* (1958); David A. Shannon, *The Socialist Party of America* (1955).

*BERNARD K. JOHNPOLL*


**OVINGTON, MARY WHITE (1865–1951).** Mary White Ovington was a leading Socialist, a feminist, and an enemy of racial injustice during the first half of the twentieth century. Her outstanding accomplishment was her role in establishing the National Association for the Advancement of Colored People (NAACP).

Mary Ovington was born in Brooklyn, New York, in 1865 to a wealthy Unitarian abolitionist family. She was educated by private tutors at the Packer

Collegiate Institute (a private high school for girls) and at Radcliffe College, which she attended for only two years. It was at Radcliffe that she first came into contact with Socialist ideas.

The depression of 1893 ruined her father's business, and Mary Ovington took a job as registrar of the Pratt Institute in Brooklyn. In 1895 she became the head worker at the Greenpoint Settlement, a settlement house serving immigrant families. She remained at that post for the next eight years. In 1904 she accepted a post as a social worker in Mary Kingsbury Simkovitch's Greenwich House and there worked with black youngsters. At that time she began research for her magnum opus, *Half a Man: The Status of the Negro in New York.* It took her seven years of research to produce the study, which was published in 1911. It was one of the first studies of discrimination against blacks in a major Northern city.

In 1905 Ovington joined the Socialist Party, in which she remained active for more than thirty years. Although she was a member of the left wing of the Socialist Party, writing articles in the *New Review* and other like journals, she never joined the Communist movement.

In 1908 she was the object of vicious newspaper slurs because of her friendship with blacks. The immediate cause for the attacks against her in the press was her presence at a biracial dinner sponsored by the Cosmopolitan Club in New York. The *New York Times* led the attack; most other newspapers followed suit. One Socialist who attended the meeting, John Spargo (q.v.), tried to minimize the Socialist role in the dinner. Ovington was antagonized by Spargo's statement. She insisted that Socialists should be proud to have led in the fight for social equality.

Ovington was also active during this period in other causes—socialism, women's rights, pacifism, and anti-imperialism. She opposed U.S. entry into World War I, demanded that women get equal status with men, and opposed imperialism by the United States.

She was the prime mover in the organization in 1909 of the NAACP, along with fellow Socialist William English Walling (q.v.). For the next forty years she was a leading activist in the organization's ranks. Her friends in the NAACP included W. E. B. DuBois (q.v.) and Oswald Garrison Villard, who did not like each other. She used her position to keep them apart. In 1914 Villard resigned from the chairmanship and Ovington was named his successor. She held that position for the next eighteen years.

In the Socialist Party, Ovington was particularly active in combatting racial hatred within the party ranks. She was especially disturbed by the anti-Oriental agitation within the party during the period 1908–1912, especially in the left-wing Western states, and she was antagonized by the persistent anti-black feeling, especially in the Southern and Western party locals. She wrote articles in the party press, consistently chiding her party comrades for their refusal to fight racial injustice.

Ovington and DuBois broke over the issue of integration, which she favored. She also opposed efforts to have the NAACP advocate economic radicalism, although she was still a Socialist Party member. One of Ovington's major contributions to the fight for racial justice was her insistence on educational equality and eventually the end to segregation in schools.

She retired from the NAACP in 1947 due to ill health, and she died in Newton Highlands near Boston, Massachusetts, in July 1951.

SOURCES: Charles Flint Kellog, *NAACP: A History of the National Association for the Advancement of Colored People, 1909–1920* (1967); *Notable American Women* (1980); Mary White Ovington Papers, Wayne State University, Detroit, Michigan.

*BERNARD K. JOHNPOLL*

**OWEN, ROBERT (1771–1858).** Robert Owen was a pre-Marxian British Socialist who established a Utopian community in the United States. He was born in Newtown, Montgomeryshire, Wales, in May 1771. His father was a saddler and ironmonger—and postmaster of the small town. Robert Owens' formal education was extremely limited, but he read widely as a young man, especially in Greek Stoic philosophy. By the time he was in his teens, Owen had become a successful salesman as well as an authority on fabrics. By the time he was twenty, he had become a partner in a major spinning mill in Manchester, which he helped to expand. While in Manchester he became acquainted with many of the intellectual leaders of the time, including the poet Samuel Taylor Coleridge; the American inventor of the steamboat, Robert Fulton; and Jeremy Bentham, the utilitarian philosopher. On one of his business trips to Glasgow he met Anne Caroline Dale, daughter of David Dale, the owner of the New Lanark Mills. He married her in 1799 and became the manager—and later an owner—of the New Lanark Mills.

At New Lanark he revolutionized the living conditions of the people who worked there. He set up schools for the children, up to age 12. He established a school for infants, who were admitted as soon as they could walk. All his schools were free. Children were never beaten in these institutions, and they were always addressed with respect and treated with kindness. His primary object, he said, was to make the children happy and thus to have them learn. He also improved the living conditions for the adults who worked in the mill. For example, he shut down the mill but paid the workers their full salaries for four months during the American embargo in 1806.

The basis for Owen's actions at New Lanark was his social philosophy, the basic theme of which was his assumption that human beings were the products of their environment. It was thus necessary to change the human environment in order to improve the intellectual and social relationships of human society. He believed that this could be achieved more readily in small communities than in huge urban centers. As environmental conditions improved, Owen expected parliamentary government to give way to pure participatory democracy. The revision in social conditions would require a revolution rather than an evolutionary change. The new social system would do away with all private production for profit. He also called for full equality between men and women and for the abolition of the institution of marriage, which—he argued—made women into sex objects and perpetuated class divisions.

The economic depression of 1815–1816 ended Owen's experiment at New Lanark and led to his working for a universal revolution. He believed the revolution would begin in the United States, then a new nation that was open to innovative social experimentation. After long planning, he came to the United States during the mid–1820s. He spoke to Congress twice in 1825, with Presidents James Monroe, James Madison, and President-elect John Quincy Adams in attendance.

After a long and often perilous journey he purchased the old Rappite religious community in New Harmony, Indiana. There he established one of the first nonreligious Socialist communities in the United States. His colony attracted many of the leading intellectuals of the time, and they set up some of the most progressive and successful educational institutions in the world. Unfortunately the mass of people attracted to the colony were rarely skilled or diligent workers— most were would-be intellectuals more given to debate and filibustering discussion than to hard work. As a result the community floundered and finally collapsed after less than two years. Although Owen's community failed, his ideas played a dominant role in Socialist thought in the United States and Great Britain for more than 160 years.

After the failure of New Harmony, Owen returned to Great Britain, where he was active in founding Socialist and syndicalist organizations. He also visited the United States several times after the failure of New Harmony. He once addressed the New York State constitutional convention in the late 1840s. By 1850 he had become a spiritualist. Despite his advanced age, he remained active at spiritualist and social science meetings in the United Kingdom during the decade.

Owen died in Newtown, England, in November 1858.

SOURCES: Several biographies of Owen are easily available. The best is G. D. H. Cole, *The Life of Robert Owen* (1930). Owen's own autobiography, *The Life of Robert Owen* (1851–1858), is useful until 1820 only. See also Arthur E. Bestor, *Backwoods Utopias* (1950); George B. Lockwood, *The New Harmony Movement* (1905); Robert Owen, *A New View of Society and Other Writings* (1813–1814 and other editions).

*BERNARD K. JOHNPOLL*


**OWEN, ROBERT DALE (1801–1877).** Robert Dale Owen was a leader of the Workingmen's Party in the late 1820s and early 1830s in New York. He was a member of the Indiana State Legislature, a member of the U.S. House of Representatives from Indiana, a founder of the Smithsonian Institution, a fighter for women's rights, and a major influence in the composition of Abraham Lincoln's Emancipation Proclamation.

Owen was born in Glasgow, Scotland, in 1801, the oldest son of the great British Utopian Socialist Robert Owen (q.v.). His mother was the daughter of

David Dale, who owned the New Lanark cotton mills, in Scotland, where Robert Owen first introduced his social reform innovations. Owen was educated in New Lanark, while his father managed the mill there, and in Switzerland. He taught school and helped manage the mill in New Lanark before traveling to the United States at the age of 24. The next year he and his father went to Robert Owen's Utopian colony in New Harmony, Indiana. After the failure of that community, he joined Frances Wright (q.v.) in her effort to salvage the Nashoba community near Memphis, which was supposed to prepare slaves for freedom.

With the failure of Nashoba, he and Wright jointly edited the New York anti-religious, anti-capitalist weekly *Free Enquirer*, an outgrowth of the *New Harmony Gazette*. In 1829 he directed the fight inside the Workingmen's Party to oust the egalitarian faction led by Thomas Skidmore. The struggle within the party helped lead to its demise a year later.

Owen returned to Great Britain after that political debacle. There he joined his father in editing the *Crisis*, a Utopian journal. Six months later he tired of Great Britain, returned to New Harmony, and reentered American political life, this time as a radical Democrat. In 1835 he was elected to the first of his three terms in the Indiana State Legislature. He spent most of his efforts there on obtaining more funds for public schools. A firm believer in sexual equality, Owen fought in the Indiana State Legislature and the Indiana constitutional convention to grant married women property rights and to ease divorce laws.

In 1842 Owen was elected to Congress. He was instrumental in forcing a settlement of the Oregon border dispute with Great Britain. He also introduced the bill for the Smithsonian Institution, on whose board he served at its start. Owen insisted that it become a popular institution for the dissemination of scientific information as well as for experimentation.

In the 1850s Owen served as an American diplomat in Naples, Italy. During the Civil War he represented Indiana as an agent for the purchase of arms in Europe. In 1862 he wrote a letter to President Lincoln (later printed as a pamphlet, *The Policy of Emancipation*). During and immediately after the war he fought for better conditions for the freed slaves. Owen opposed immediate enfranchisement of the ex-slaves, suggesting a ten-year period before they be granted full suffrage.

While in Italy, Owen became a spiritualist and worked diligently to develop a scientific base for his beliefs. He wrote several major pamphlets, an autobiography (1874), and a number of plays and novels. Robert Dale Owen died in Lake George, New York, in the summer of 1877.

SOURCE: Richard W. Leopold, *Robert Dale Owen: A Biography* (1940).

*BERNARD K. JOHNPOLL*

# P

PADMORE, GEORGE (1900–1959). George Padmore, international Communist organizer, Pan-African theoretician, and adviser to African political leaders, was born Malcolm Ivan Meredith Nurse on June 28, 1900, at Tacarigua, Arouca District, in Trinidad, British West Indies. His father was headmaster of the local Anglican school.

Nurse graduated from a private high school and in 1918 became a reporter with the *Trinidad Weekly Guardian*. He arrived in New York in 1924 to attend college, but was promptly recruited by the Communist Party. For the next eight years of his life he would devote himself to furthering the Party's interests. Nurse attended Fisk University for two years. He also was enrolled briefly at Howard University Law School, where he appears to have adopted the party name of George Padmore.

Padmore's rise within the American Communist Party was rapid. In July 1929 he was sent as a delegate in company with James W. Ford (q.v.) to the Second Congress of the League Against Imperialism (LAI) held in Frankfurt. Immediately upon his return, Padmore traveled to Cleveland, where he spoke as a delegate before the convention of the Trade Union Unity League (TUUL). This was a period of major upheaval in the internal functioning of the Party occasioned by imposition of the controversial "self-determination of the black belt" thesis by the Comintern's Sixth Congress. Padmore's address, which vehemently attacked the prevalence of white chauvinism and black acquiescence within the party, so impressed the gathering that William Foster (q.v.) arranged for Padmore to accompany him to Moscow for the upcoming Congress of the Red International of Labor Unions (RILU/Profintern). Padmore addressed a session of the RILU in Moscow on December 19, 1929. In addition to describing conditions among black workers in the United States, he presented a trenchant critique of the many defects inhibiting trade union organizing by the Communist Party in the United

States among blacks. The Profintern placed Padmore in charge of its Negro Trade Union Committee.

At the previous Fourth Congress in March 1928, the RILU established an International Trade Union Committee of Negro Workers, simultaneously instructing "the Executive Bureau to call together the representatives of the Negro workers for the purpose of working out immediate practical measures for carrying into effect the policy laid down in regard to the question of organizing Negro workers in the United States and in Africa." It was to Padmore, the newly appointed head of the Negro Trade Union Committee of the RILU, that responsibility for planning the First International Conference of Negro Workers was now entrusted.

In April 1930, one month after he finally notified Howard that he was withdrawing from the university, Padmore made an extended visit to Africa to recruit African delegates to the planned conference of black workers which met at Hamburg in July 1930, attended by seventeen delegates from Nigeria, Gambia, Sierra Leone, Gold Coast, Cameroon, and Jamaica. Padmore presented the main report, "Economic Struggles and Tasks of the Negro Workers."

The conference led to the establishment in Hamburg of the International Trade Union Committee of Negro Workers (ITUC-NW) and the publication of the committee's official organ, eventually under the title *The Negro Worker*. James W. Ford was the journal's first editor, but he was succeeded as editor in the summer of 1931 by Padmore.

During the committee's first year alone, Padmore authored six of the twenty-five pamphlets published by the ITUC-NW. The most significant was *The Life and Struggles of Negro Toilers* (1931), destined eventually to become a classic of the antiimperialist canon. Together, they represented a trailblazing attempt to apply the theory of class to the concrete conditions obtaining in Africa.

In December 1931 the German police occupied and searched the Hamburg ITUC-NW headquarters. For the next two months the committee was forced to operate in a semi-legal situation. Then, on February 25, 1932, Padmore was eventually deported to England after being arrested and jailed by the Hamburg city police. Padmore spent the next year or so in England. Among other activities, he embarked on a fruitful literary collaboration with the English Negrophile and Communist fellow traveler Nancy Cunard, rebellious daughter of the famous shipping family. Padmore greatly facilitated editorial preparation of her famous *Negro Anthology* (1934) by helping to recruit contributors from among his by now extremely wide range of contacts within the black literary world. Padmore himself was to contribute a total of four articles to the collection.

Following Hitler's advent to power in Germany in 1933, the Soviet Union abruptly shifted away from the policy of antiimperialism. Instead it embarked in August 1933 upon a policy of placating Britain and France as a counterweight to the growing Fascist menace in Europe. This Soviet rapprochement with the colonial powers signified "a betrayal of the fundamental interests of my people, with which I could not identify myself," according to Padmore. In August 1933 he forwarded his statement of resignation to the Comintern executive in Moscow. The inevitable denunciation, however, did not issue immediately, most likely because there was hope that attempts to get Padmore to change his mind would succeed. Thus it was not until the following year that Padmore's political sins were officially denounced and he was formally expelled by the Comintern.

In the summer of 1934 Padmore organized an ad hoc committee, under his chairmanship, to rally public opinion behind the mission of the Gold Coast Aborigines Rights Protection Society. A year later, at the time of Mussolini's declaration of war against Ethiopia, the committee was transformed into the International African Friends of Abyssinia, chaired by the West Indian Marxist C. L. R. James (q.v.), with Padmore as a member of the Executive Committee. When the latter body disbanded, however, it was succeeded in early 1937 by the formation of the International African Service Bureau (IASB), with Padmore as chairman; the Sierra Leonean trade unionist I. T. A. Wallace Johnson, later founder of the West African Youth League, as secretary; Jomo Kenyatta of Kenya as assistant secretary; the Barbadian maritime union organizer Chris Jones as organizing secretary; T. Ras Makonnen of Guyana as treasurer; and C. L. R. James as editor of *International African Opinion*, the official IASB journal. The IASB became the spearhead of anticolonial agitation in Great Britain; it would merge in 1944 into the Pan-African Federation that convened the watershed Fifth Pan-African Congress in Manchester, England, in October 1945.

Between 1937 and 1945 Padmore worked ceaselessly to further the cause of Pan-African solidarity worldwide and to advance the antiimperialist struggle. From 1938 onward Padmore assumed the role of European correspondent for a number of Afro-American newspapers, chief among them the *Chicago Defender*. He also conducted political study classes for colonial students, was a frequent contributor to the press of the non-Stalinist Left, particularly the Independent Labour Party's (ILP) *New Leader*, lectured at annual ILP summer schools, and collaborated in the activities of black groups in Great Britain, such as the West African Students Union and the League of Coloured People.

In 1956, at the height of the Cold War, Padmore's most famous work, *Pan-Africanism or Communism?*, was published. The book had two purposes: to offer an analysis of the evolution of the three major political tendencies in the development of contemporary black ideology—namely, Black Zionism, Pan-Africanism, and communism—and, on the basis of this examination, to devise a coherent political strategy for the African independent struggle that would deny the West the excuse of intervening against its forward march on the pretext of stopping the spread of communism in Africa.

The African struggle scored its first major victory with the achievement of Ghana's independence in 1957, and Padmore was among the specially invited foreign guests to attend the celebrations. That autumn he was invited by President Nkrumah to become his adviser on African affairs. However, considerable opposition against him soon arose from among Nkrumah's immediate entourage as well as within the governing Convention People's Party (CPP), the civil service, and the government.

Padmore successfully organized two major conferences: the first meeting ever held of independent African states in April 1958, and later that same year the first All-African Peoples' Conference, to which representatives of almost every African nationalist movement came, including the young Patrice Lumumba from the Congo (now Zaire) and the Martiniquian Frantz Fanon, representing the Algerian FLN.

In April-May 1959 Padmore traveled with Nkrumah on a state visit to newly independent Guinea, where the steering committee of the All-African Peoples' Organization held its first session. Shortly afterward Padmore carried out his last official act in July, when he attended the meeting of the heads of state of Ghana, Guinea, and Liberia held in the Liberian village of Saniquellie. In September he flew to London for urgent medical attention, but within days of being admitted to University College Hospital he died, on September 23, 1959. The ashes were flown back to Ghana, where an elaborate state funeral was held for him and Nkrumah called him the father of African emancipation.

SOURCES: James R. Hooker, *Black Revolutionary: George Padmore's Path from Communism to Pan-Africanism* (1967); J. Ayodele Langley, *Pan-Africanism and Nationalism in West Africa, 1900–1945* (1973).

*ROBERT A. HILL*

**PANKEN, JACOB (1879–1968).** Jacob Panken, the only Socialist ever elected to a judgeship in New York State, was a leading orator in the party and a major figure in the moderate faction of the Socialist movement during the period between the two world wars. Born of middle-class parents in 1879 in Kiev, the chief city of the Ukraine, Panken came to the United States at age 11. He was educated in the evening public schools of New York City and New York University Law School, from which he graduated in 1905. The Panken family, which fled from religious, political, and economic disabilities imposed on Jews in the czar's empire, first settled on a farm established by the Baron DeHirsch–funded Jewish Colonization Society in Chesterfield, Connecticut. The farm could not support the family, so young Jacob was forced to go to work a year after coming to the United States. He worked as a farmhand from 1891 until 1895, as a pocketbook maker from 1895 to 1899, and in the ladies garment trade from 1895 to 1901. In 1901 he became an organizer for the International Ladies Garment Workers Union (which he had helped found a few years earlier). In 1903 he was named an organizer for the Purse and Bag Makers Union.

While helping to organize unions, Panken attended the New York University Law School, graduating in 1905. Panken's early law clients were almost all labor unions that he had helped organize. In 1913 he was instrumental in organizing the Amalgamated Clothing Workers of America.

Panken joined the Socialist Party in 1903. Fourteen years later—in the Socialist sweep of New York's Lower East Side in 1917—Panken was elected a justice of the municipal court of New York City. During the next seventeen years, Panken ran unsuccessfully for many other offices, including assemblyman, U.S. Representative, U.S. Senator, governor of New York, and district attorney.

A political moderate, Panken in 1919 chaired the committee that recommended the ouster of pro-Communist foreign-language federations from the Socialist Party. Later that year these federations became the core of the new Communist Party. In 1936 he was among the leaders of the "Old Guard" faction that bolted the Socialist Party and formed the Social Democratic Federation (SDF). He also helped arrange for the SDF to affiliate with the American Labor Party. Panken was active in the American Labor Party drive to reelect Franklin D. Roosevelt.

In 1934 his old friend Mayor Fiorello LaGuardia named Panken a justice of the domestic relations court, from which he retired in 1954. He was politically inactive after 1937. Panken died in 1968.

BERNARD K. JOHNPOLL

**PARSONS, ALBERT R. (1845–1887).** Albert R. Parsons was a leading anarcho-syndicalist, labor organizer, editor, and martyr of the late nineteenth century. Born in Montgomery, Alabama, in 1845 of New England Puritan parents who died when he was still a child, Parsons was raised by a brother, who was a newspaper publisher in East Texas. At the age of 12, young Parsons was apprenticed to a printer. He soon became adept at news reporting and writing. In 1861 the 16-year-old Parsons was carried away with patriotism for his native South and enlisted in the Confederate Army. He served the entire four years of the war as a scout in combat-free areas of Texas.

At the end of the war, Parsons entered Waco (now Baylor) University, but he remained there for only a year. Sometime during his stay at Waco young Parsons became a Radical Republican who argued for equal rights for black Americans. At the same time, he began publishing a weekly, *The Spectator*. The Republican administration in Washington, D.C., also rewarded him by appointing him to various government posts in Texas.

Because Parsons was a pro-Reconstruction, equal-rights Republican, he was at serious risk in Confederate Texas. For his views, he was shunned, ridiculed, beaten, and shot at by his former Confederate comrades. He therefore closed his newspaper and took a job as traveling correspondent for his brother's publication, the *Houston Telegraph*. His job required him to visit most of Texas, report on life in the "hinterlands," and sell subscriptions to the newspaper. While on the road he met and married a woman of black, Indian, and Mexican ancestry named Lucy Ella (her last name is clouded in mystery). Soon after they were married, in 1871, Parsons resumed government work. When the Democrats regained control of Texas in 1873, he was out of a job. He returned to newspaper work, but his political views made it necessary for him to seek such work in a northern city—Chicago.

Although Parsons arrived in Chicago at a time when a long and severe depression was under way, he quickly obtained a full-time regular job as a printer on the

*Chicago Times.* He also became active in the Chicago Typographical Union. Parsons soon joined the Social Democratic Workers Party. As an intelligent, native-born English-speaking Socialist, Parsons was a rare acquisition for the predominantly German party. In 1877 he was nominated by the Socialists for a seat on the Chicago City Council. He barely missed being elected.

During the railroad strike of 1877, Parsons was active working for the unions. The strike was finally suppressed by the intervention of federal troops. For his activity in the strike, Parsons was fired by the *Times* and blacklisted in the entire Chicago printing industry. During the strike, union meetings were violently assaulted by the police. In one case, armed police fired into a group of members of the Furniture Workers Union as they were leaving a meeting. One union man was slain. Thereupon Parsons and several of his fellow Socialists reactivated the *Lehr und Wehr Verein* (Learning and Defense League), an armed association of Socialists.

During the next three years, Parsons rose to the leadership of the Socialist Labor Party (SLP), successor to the Social Democratic Workingmen's Party. He was made editor of the Socialist Weekly the *Chicago Socialist* and he was offered the party's nomination for U.S. President—a nomination he rejected because he was too young under the Constitution. He also helped found the Eight-Hour League and was its recording secretary. And he was instrumental in organizing the Chicago Trades and Labor Council.

In 1879–1880 the Socialist movement began to fall apart. First the leadership of the national party ordered the *Lehr und Wehr Verein* to dissolve. Then the party leadership decided to become part of the Greenback-Labor Party, despite a platform that was unacceptable to a large part of the membership. Parsons, Paul Grottkau (q.v.), and eight other delegates to the 1880 SLP convention were thrown out of the SLP for refusing to support the Greenbackers.

Parsons then joined the new, ultra-revolutionary, quasi-anarchist Social Revolutionary Club. In 1883 he was a delegate at the Pittsburgh Congress, where the ultra-radical anarchist groups formed a national federation named the International Working People's Association (IWPA). The leading figure in the IWPA was Johann Most (q.v.). Parsons represented the most moderate wing of the IWPA. He favored trade union organization as the central focus for the federation. Parsons was also named the editor of the IWPA's English organ, *The Alarm* of Chicago.

On May 3, 1886, a peaceful demonstration in the Haymarket area under IWPA auspices was attacked by police. A bomb was thrown into the meeting; seven policemen and four demonstrators were killed, more than one hundred people were injured. The police, who may have thrown the bomb themselves to give them an excuse for killing revolutionaries, began a manhunt. Parsons, August Spies (q.v.), Adolph Fischer, Samuel Fielden, Louis Lingg, George Engel, Oscar W. Neebe, Michael Schwab, and Rudolf Schnaubelt were charged with the bombing. Schnaubelt and Parsons fled Chicago. Schnaubelt was never found again. Parsons spent more than a month hiding in the home of Daniel W. Hoan,

Sr., in Waukesha, Wisconsin. Hoan was the father of future Milwaukee Socialist mayor Daniel W. Hoan, Jr. (q.v.) Parsons surrendered voluntarily in late June 1886.

After a trial before an antagonistic judge and jury, Parsons and six co-defendants were found guilty. Parsons and five of the others were condemned to death. Oscar Neebe was given a life sentence. Of the condemned men, only Parsons refused to ask for clemency, lest it be seen as a confession of guilt. On the night before the execution, Lingg committed suicide; the death sentences of Fielden and Schwab were commuted to life in prison. Worldwide demonstrations called for clemency for all the defendants—but to no avail. On November 11, 1887, Parsons, Spies, Fischer, and Engel were executed by hanging. Neebe, Fielden, and Schwab were pardoned in 1893.

SOURCES: Paul Avrich, *The Haymarket Tragedy* (1984); Henry David, *The History of the Haymarket Affair* (1936); Dyer D. Lum, *A Concise History of the Great Trial of the Chicago Anarchists in 1886* (1886); Lucy E. Parsons (ed.), *Life of Albert R. Parsons* (1889).

*LILLIAN KIRTZMAN JOHNPOLL*

**PATTERSON, WILLIAM (1891–1980).** William Patterson, one of the Communist Party's leading black organizers and head of the Civil Rights Congress, was born on August 27, 1891, in San Francisco. His mother, born a slave, worked as a domestic; his father, a native of the British West Indies, was a ship steward before abandoning his family to become a Seventh-Day Adventist missionary in Tahiti. Patterson had to leave the University of California to work as a boat's cook. He returned to school, was briefly suspended for objecting to compulsory ROTC (Reserve Officers Training Corp) in 1917, and finally received an LL.B. from Hastings College of Law in 1919. However, he failed the bar exam, and after an abortive effort to immigrate to Liberia he moved to New York in 1920 and began practicing law.

Patterson went to Boston with an International Labor Defense delegation to protest the Sacco-Vanzetti (q.v.) execution in 1927 and was arrested three times on a picket line. The executions drove him out of law and into Communist politics, and he joined the Party in 1927. He was selected almost immediately to attend the University of the Toilers of the East and remained in Russia until 1931, attending the Comintern's Sixth Congress and the Anti-Imperialist League's 1929 meeting in Germany.

After his return to the United States, Patterson briefly served as a Party organizer in Harlem and Pittsburgh. Asked to run the International Labor Defense in 1932 while J. Louis Engdahl (q.v.) was abroad, he became its executive director and took over direction of its campaign to save the Scottsboro Boys. In 1938 he became associate editor of the *Midwest Daily Record* and in 1940 the Party's organizer in Southside Chicago. Patterson became national executive secretary of the Civil Rights Congress in 1949. Two years later he traveled to Paris to present to the United Nations a petition he had drafted charging the U.S.

government with genocide against blacks. He served thirty days for contempt of Congress in 1954, after refusing to name the contributors to the Congress.

After the resignation of John Gates (q.v.) from the Party and the closing of the *Daily Worker* in 1958, Patterson became editor of the *Sunday Worker*. He was elevated to the Party's Politburo in the early 1960s and remained on it until his death on March 5, 1980.

SOURCE: William Patterson, *The Man Who Cried Genocide* (1971).

*HARVEY KLEHR*

**PEPPER, JOHN (1886–1938).** John Pepper was a minister in the Hungarian Soviet government in 1919, a Comintern emissary to the United States in the 1920s, and the de facto leader of the Communist Party in the United States (CPUSA) for part of the decade. Pepper was born in 1886 in Hungary. He was apparently Jewish, but little is known about his background. The family name may have been Schwartz but in Hungary he was known as Joseph Pogany. A high school teacher and journalist for the Hungarian Social Democratic Party newspaper, Pogany organized a Soldiers Council of ex-veterans after World War I. It supported the liberal, democratic regime. Along with several other Social Democrats, he switched his allegiance to the Communists in February 1919.

The following month he became commissar of war in Béla Kun's Hungarian Soviet government. Mistrusted by his new comrades, Pogany was replaced in April and relegated to a minor position. With the collapse of Kun's government, he fled to Moscow and went to work for the Comintern. He bore some responsibility for a disastrous Communist uprising in Germany in 1921. Fed up with the fractious Hungarian exiles, the Comintern shipped Pogany to the United States in the summer of 1922 to work with the CPUSA's Hungarian Federation.

Adopting the name John Pepper, he quickly dazzled the inexperienced American Communists. Part of a three-man Comintern delegation to the Party's Bridgman Convention, called to consider whether to abolish the "illegal" part of the Party, Pepper soon got himself elected to the Central Executive Committee, learned English, and convinced his credulous comrades that he was the Comintern's overseer for the whole Party. Allying himself with Charles Ruthenberg's (q.v.) faction, he urged Americanization of the Party and abolition of the underground. Building his own following, Pepper was able by 1923 to engineer a Communist break with Farmer-Labor forces—a policy opposed by both Ruthenberg and William Foster (q.v.)—and became de facto leader of the CPUSA.

The failure of Pepper's policy led to his ouster from control at a January 1924 convention. A shrewd factionalist, he quickly inaugurated the American attack on Leon Trotsky as a way of breaking up the alliance of his enemies—some of them were identified with Trotsky. At the request of Foster's faction, Pepper was kept in Moscow for several years. He was appointed head of the Comintern's Information Department and served as an American delegate to the Fifth Plenum in March 1925, where his labors helped the Ruthenberg faction regain control of the Party. Pepper's Comintern influence began to wane in 1928 as the Third

Period began and the organization adopted a more revolutionary posture. He returned to the United States, but was almost immediately recalled to Moscow. Temporarily avoiding the recall, Pepper resumed a leading role in the American party. Again ordered to return, and forbidden by the Comintern from attending the Party's sixth convention, he dropped out of sight.

Pepper warned Jay Lovestone (q.v.), Ruthenberg's successor, not to go to Moscow in 1929. Lovestone went anyway, and Stalin removed him from Party leadership. Pepper too was denounced, and finally returned to Moscow. In September 1929 the Comintern's International Control Commission expelled him from the Communist Party. An American Communist met Pepper in 1937 when he was working as a technical expert for the Soviet planning agency. Pepper disappeared in Stalin's purges and is presumed to have been executed in 1937–1938.

SOURCE: Theodore Draper, *American Communism and Soviet Russia* (1960).

*HARVEY KLEHR*

**PERRY, PETTIS (1897–1965).** Pettis Perry, one of the Communist Party's leading black cadres, was born on January 4, 1897, in Marion, Alabama. His father was a Negro sharecropper. He attended school for only fifteen months and began working in the cotton fields when he was 10 years old. He left the South at age 18 and crisscrossed the nation, working as a migrant laborer and millhand.

Perry joined the Communist Party in 1932 in Los Angeles as a result of the Party's agitation on behalf of the Scottsboro Boys, and he quickly became active in various front groups such as the Unemployed Councils and the International Labor Defense. He formed the first League of Struggle for Negro Rights branch in Los Angeles. Perry was the Party's candidate for lieutenant governor in 1934.

In 1949 Perry was appointed head of the Party's National Negro Commission and soon afterward was one of those entrusted with running the Party while the top leadership went to jail for violating the Smith Act. He helped launch a campaign to root out "white chauvinism" which further demoralized the Party.

Perry himself was convicted under the Smith Act in 1953 and served three years in prison. After his release in 1957 he resumed Communist activity in California and strongly supported the William Foster (q.v.) faction in the inner-party struggles. Perry died on July 24, 1965, in Moscow.

*HARVEY KLEHR*

**PETERS, J. (b. 1894).** J(oseph) Peters, a leader in the Communist Party's Hungarian Bureau, was organizational secretary of the Communist Party in the United States (CPUSA), in charge of its underground work, and an influential Comintern agent. He was born in Cop, Hungary, on August 11, 1894, apparently under the name of Sandor Goldberger. He was of Jewish descent, but little is known of his background. He attended college for one year, probably joined the Hungarian Communist Party in 1919 after serving in the army during World

War I, and entered the United States in 1924. Peters, as he was known in the States, also used the aliases Alexander Stevens and Isadore Boorstein.

During the 1920s he was active in the American Communists' Hungarian Bureau, eventually heading it. For a brief period in the 1930s, Peters was the CPUSA's organizational secretary, writing *The Communist Party: A Manual on Organization*, which became the best-known statement of the Party's structure. These public positions, however, did not encompass Peter's key role in the CPUSA. For many years in the 1930s he supervised the Party's underground work and maintained contacts with secret Party units composed of government employees in Washington, D.C. He represented the Executive Committee of the Communist International in America and in 1931–1932 taught at the Lenin School in Moscow.

Peters was deported in 1949 after U.S. government investigators discovered that he had used false passports to travel to the Soviet Union. He also had become involved in the Alger Hiss case; Whittaker Chambers had identified Peters as one of his underground Communist supervisors. He remained in Hungary, editing the *International Review* and working as an editor for the Hungarian State Publishing House. He was still alive in the late 1970s.

SOURCE: Alan Weinstein, *Perjury* (1978).

*HARVEY KLEHR*

**PETERSEN, ARNOLD (1885–1976).** Arnold Petersen served for over half a century as a theorist and leading spokesman of the Socialist Labor Party and played a major role in disseminating the ideas of Daniel DeLeon (q.v.). Born on April 16, 1885, in Odense, Denmark, the son of a tailor, Petersen graduated from high school and commercial college.

Fascinated by Mark Twain's travel tales, he emigrated to the United States in 1905. In 1907, while working in a paper-box factory, he joined the Socialist Labor Party and subsequently developed a close relationship with Daniel DeLeon.

Petersen's rise to prominence within the party came in 1913 when Paul Augustine resigned as national secretary and DeLeon proposed Petersen for the post. He assumed the office on February 1, 1914, and held it for fifty-five years, until his resignation in 1969. Following DeLeon's death on May 11, 1914, Petersen played a major role in restructuring the party and helped rescue it from bankruptcy. During his long tenure, Petersen played a key role in the administration of the party's organizational affairs and in the management of its agitational and educational activities.

But Petersen's greatest achievement lay in the over fifty books and pamphlets he authored, expounding and interpreting DeLeonist doctrine and defending his party's version of Marxism against competing interpretations. His most important works included: *Capital and Labor, Karl Marx and Marxian Science, Communist Jesuitism, Constitution of the United States, Daniel DeLeon: Social Architect,* and *Revolutionary Milestones.* He died on February 5, 1976.

SOURCE: "Former National Secretary Petersen Dies at 90," *Weekly People*, February 28, 1976.

*JOHN GERBER*

**PHILLIPS, WENDELL (1811–1884).** Wendell Phillips was a leading abolitionist, a fighter for equal rights for blacks, Indians, and women, a labor reformer, and a Socialist. Born in Boston in 1811 of patrician parents, Phillips was educated at Boston Latin School, Harvard University (B.A., 1831), and Harvard University School of Law (1834). In 1837 he used his considerable legal knowledge and oratorical skill to soundly denounce the Massachusetts attorney general for his defense of the lynch mob that murdered abolitionist editor Elijah Lovejoy in Illinois. Phillips was almost immediately thereafter recognized as a leading abolitionist himself.

Within the anti-slavery movement, Phillips was from the start a member of the militant wing headed by William Lloyd Garrison. Both condemned the U.S. Constitution for its institutionalization of slavery. In 1842 Phillips proclaimed, "My curse be on the Constitution of the United States." He favored splitting the United States into two nations, one of which would outlaw slavery in all forms. The only difference between Phillips and Garrison was in the latter's nonresistance philosophy. Phillips was opposed to pacifism in the face of moral wrong.

Before the Civil War, Phillips opposed the Missouri Compromise, the admission of Texas into the Union as a slave state, and the 1848 War with Mexico, a war he believed was rooted in the expansion of the slave states. Once the Civil War began, he supported it, but he was an opponent of President Abraham Lincoln, whom he considered too weak on slavery. His opposition disappeared once Lincoln issued the Emancipation Proclamation. With the end of the war, Phillips split with Garrison, who had proposed the dissolution of the Anti-Slavery Society. Phillips' opposition prevented the association from being dissolved, and he became its president.

With the end of the war, Phillips also moved into new fields. As early as 1840, Phillips—and Garrison—had pleaded for equal status for women at a meeting of the World's Anti-Slavery Convention. After the war, Phillips undertook full-scale agitation for women's suffrage and equal rights. He also worked hard for prohibition of the manufacture and sale of alcoholic beverages. He was active in the movement against the persecution of native Americans, and he was especially active in the drive for the eight-hour day. Phillips' socialism was essentially a form of social reform. Socialism, which he never defined, was to be the culmination of social reforms. He viewed both as a basically Christian obligation.

In 1870 he helped found the Massachusetts Labor Reform Party, which nominated him for governor. He polled 20,000 out of slightly more than 90,000 votes cast—slightly more than 22 percent of the total. Although he remained active in Massachusetts labor politics for the next four years, he never again received as large a proportion of the vote. He ran only once more for office and then, in 1872, he polled about one-fifth of his previous vote. An examination of official returns for the state failed to find any other mention of Phillips, although several writers have claimed that he ran again in 1876 or 1879.

Phillips continued his activities into the early 1880s. He died in Boston in 1884.

SOURCES: Anti-Slavery Collection, Boston Public Library, Boston, Massachusetts; Robert Marcus, "Wendell Phillips and American Institutions," *Journal of American History* 56 (June 1959).

                                                          BERNARD K. JOHNPOLL

**PHILLIPS, WILLIAM (b. 1907).** William Phillips has been an editor of *Partisan Review* magazine since 1934. The magazine began as an organ of the New York chapter of the John Reed Clubs and was briefly influenced by Trotskyism during the 1930s. Phillips was the son of Jewish immigrants from Russia. His father, who changed his name from Litvinsky, was trained as a lawyer but unable to sustain a practice. The son, born in New York on November 14, 1907, grew up in poverty and attended City College in the late 1920s. Inspired by the ironic skepticism of philosopher Morris Raphael Cohen and the literary experiments of the poet T. S. Eliot, he pursued graduate studies at New York University and Columbia University, teaching part-time to support himself.

At the start of the Great Depression, Phillips became a sympathizer of the Communist Party, contributing to the *Communist* and *New Masses*, and starting *Partisan Review*. In 1936 he and one of the other editors, Philip Rahv (q.v.), broke with the party over the sudden shift in literary policy at the time of the Popular Front, as well as the Moscow purge trails. In December 1937 they relaunched the *Partisan Review* under the direction of a like-minded group of writers who were quasi-Trotskyist in politics and sympathetic to the modernist avant-garde in culture.

During and after the 1940s, the magazine became less radical and published fewer articles on political matters. In 1950 Phillips became active in the American Committee for Cultural Freedom (ACCF), the U.S. affiliate of the Congress for Cultural Freedom, an international organization of Cold War intellectuals. Phillips was on the board of directors of the ACCF from 1958 until its demise in 1968, and the ACCF was for a while the legal publisher of *Partisan Review*.

In the 1960s Phillips moved somewhat left again, calling himself a Socialist and criticizing the Neo-conservatism espoused by many onetime contributors to the *Partisan Review* who gathered around Norman Podhoretz's *Commentary* magazine.

SOURCES: James B. Gilbert, *Writers and Partisans* (1968); William Phillips, *A Partisan View: Five Decades of the Literary Life* (1983).

                                                                   ALAN WALD

**POTASH, IRVING (1902–1976).** Irving Potash was a leader of the International Fur and Leather Workers Union and served on the Politburo of the American Communist Party. He was born in Kiev, Russia, on December 15, 1902. His family moved to Brooklyn in 1911, where Potash joined the Socialist Party at the age of 14. He attended the City College of New York for two years. In 1919 he entered the Communist Party. That same year he served eight months for criminal anarchy, a victim of the Palmer Raids.

During the 1920s he worked as a dental machinist, a needle-trades organizer, and an assistant to Ben Gold (q.v.), head of a Communist-dominated union of furriers. In 1931 he was sent to Moscow as a representative to the Profintern and as a student at the Lenin School. Later in the decade Potash became vice-president of the Fur and Leather Workers Union and began serving on the Communist Party's Central Executive Committee. In 1940, as part of the Roosevelt administration's crackdown on Communists, he was indicted on an anti-trust charge pending since 1933, convicted, and given a two-year suspended sentence.

Potash was still an officer of the furriers union in 1948 when he was arrested along with other radical aliens and held for deportation. While free on bail, he became one of eleven Party leaders indicted for violating the Smith Act in July 1948. Convicted, he served his term and was released, only to be rearrested on a second untried violation of the Smith Act. In March 1955 Potash agreed to voluntary deportation to Poland, in exchange for which the government dropped its case against him.

For the next two years Potash sent dispatches to the *Daily Worker* from Moscow, China, and India. When he tried to return to the United States, he was arrested for illegal reentry, convicted, and sent to the Atlanta penitentiary. Potash was released in August 1958.

Unable to work for the furriers any longer, Potash turned to Party work, serving as the Party's labor secretary in the late 1950s. The government continued to harass him, calling him before Congress on several occasions and attempting to force him to register as an enemy agent. Potash died on August 16, 1976.

*JUDY KUTULAS*

**POYNTZ, JULIET STUART (1886–1937?).** Juliet Stuart Poyntz, a Socialist educator, became an influential Communist activist in the 1920s and disappeared after preparing to break her ties with Soviet intelligence agencies. She was born on November 25, 1886, in Omaha, Nebraska, to an Irish Catholic family. Her father was a lawyer. She graduated from Barnard College, received an M.A. from Columbia, and attended both Oxford and the London School of Economics. For a number of years she held research positions with the U.S. Immigration Commission (1908–1910), the American Association for Labor Legislation (1910–1913), and the Bureau of Labor Research at the Rand School (where she was director from 1914 to 1915), and she was educational director of the International Ladies Garment Workers Union (1915–1919). She also briefly taught at Columbia.

Poyntz joined the Socialist Party in 1909. In addition to her work at the Rand School, she frequently lectured for the Party. After the Bolshevik Revolution she became active in the Committee for a Third International, a group of Socialists who, while refusing to join the new American Communist movement, sought to affiliate the Socialist Party with the Comintern. She finally joined the Communist Party in 1921 in New York. Associated with Ludwig Lore (q.v.), she came under frequent attack as a right-winger but avoided his fate of expulsion. She was a candidate for public office on the Party ticket, directed the New York Workers School, headed the Party's Women's Department, and briefly served as national secretary of the International Labor Defense, during the 1920s. Although never rising to the top level of the Party, she was regarded as the most capable woman leader.

Poyntz remained active in the Party until 1934 as an organizer for the Friends of the Soviet Union and the Trade Union Unity League. Her last public role was with the Workers Committee Against Unemployment. She then went to work for Soviet intelligence.

In 1937 Poyntz told her old friend Carlo Tresca (q.v.) that she was disillusioned and was determined to withdraw from her underground activities. She disappeared from her room in early June 1937 and was never heard from again. The Communist Party denied any knowledge of or interest in her whereabouts. Friends charged that she had been murdered and turned up evidence that an old friend in the employ of Soviet intelligence had mysteriously slipped into New York before her death and left soon afterward. Tresca speculated that the acquaintance had lured her to her death.

SOURCE: FBI File 100–206603.

*HARVEY KLEHR*

**PRESSMAN, LEE (1906–1969).** Lee Pressman was a member of the Communist Party in 1934 and 1935. He remained in close touch with Party figures in and around the labor movement between 1936 and 1948, during which time he served as legal adviser for the Congress of Industrial Organizations (CIO). He was born in New York City on July 1, 1906, to Jewish parents who had emigrated from Russia. His father was a moderately prosperous hat manufacturer. Pressman graduated in 1926 from Cornell. There courses under Sumner Slichter stimulated his interest in the labor movement. He graduated from Harvard Law School in 1929, a protégé of Felix Frankfurter. Between 1929 and 1933 he practiced law with a prestigious New York firm.

In 1933 he became assistant general counsel for the Agricultural Adjustment Agency. Later he also served as general counsel for the Federal Emergency Relief Administration and for the Works Progress Administration. Late in 1935 he left government to enter private practice in New York. While in the nation's capital, Pressman joined the Communist Party. He later testified that his only activity during his brief (1934–1935) period of formal membership was participation in a study group that included other young New Deal lawyers, notably Charles Kramer, Nathan Witt, and John Abt. Pressman dropped Party membership in 1935 or early 1936 when he left Washington, D.C.

In June 1936, CIO president John L. Lewis appointed Pressman legal counsel for the Steel Workers Organizing Committee (SWOC). Pressman aided Lewis in important early CIO negotiations, as, for example, during the 1936–1937 Flint auto strike. In 1938 Pressman became full-time legal counsel for the CIO and the SWOC. Thereafter, Pressman was a central figure in the CIO. He played a major role in day-to-day administration and formulated and phrased virtually all important convention resolutions. He drafted many of the public utterances of the CIO's second president, Philip Murray, who succeeded Lewis in 1940. Pressman conferred regularly with leading Communist Party and Communist labor figures. Anti-Communist critics charged that he used his position to shape CIO policy in accordance with Communist policies. Pressman denied these charges. Even Pressman's critics rarely questioned his legal or intellectual acuity.

The onset of the Cold War eventually separated Pressman from the CIO. In 1948 he supported Henry A. Wallace for the Presidency, a stand that soon led to his resignation as general counsel. He ran unsuccessfully for a Brooklyn Congressional seat in November.

In 1948 and again in 1950, the House Un-American Activities Committee subpoenaed him. In 1948 he invoked Fifth Amendment rights, but in 1950, having consummated a self-proclaimed ideological break with communism occasioned by the North Korean invasion on June 25, 1950, he provided carefully phrased information about some of his associates and activities.

After 1950 Pressman remained in private practice in New York City. He died on November 20, 1969.

SOURCES: Lee Pressman, Oral History, Columbia University, New York City, (1957); U.S. Congress, House Committee on Un-American Activities, *Hearings Regarding Communism in the United States Government*, 80th Congress, 2d Session, 1950 (testimony of Lee Pressman).

*ROBERT H. ZIEGER*

**PURO, HENRY (1888–1981).** Henry Puro, the alias of John Wiita, was a newspaperman, agitator, and controlling force in Finnish-American Communist affairs, especially during the late 1920s, when a split occurred among Finnish radicals over control of the Cooperative Central Exchange in Superior, Wisconsin. Wiita was born on April 27, 1888, in Ylistaro, Vaasanlaani, Finland. He came to the United States in 1905 and worked on the ore docks in Superior, Wisconsin, and in the iron mines on the Mesabi Range in nearby Minnesota. He joined the Finnish branch of the Socialist Party (SSJ) in 1907 and rose quickly to the board of directors of *Tyovaen Opisto* (Work People's College) in Duluth, Minnesota. In 1910 he was elected district secretary of the SSJ. Within three years he was named editor of *Toveri* (Comrade) in Astoria, Oregon. In 1915 he returned to Duluth, where he worked for *Sosialisti* (The Socialist). Upon that paper's endorsement of the Industrial Workers of the World, Wiita moved across the harbor to Superior, Wisconsin, and assumed editorship of *Tyomies* (The Worker).

During World War I, Wiita fled to Canada, where he assumed the name Henry Puro and worked on the editorial staff of *Vapaus* (Freedom) in Sudbury, Ontario, for four years. In 1923 he returned to the United States and joined the Finnish

Federation of the Communist Party and began to work at *Eteenpain* (Forward) in Worcester, Massachusetts. In 1927 he became one of the principal organizers of the Finnish Worker's Federation, and in 1930, during the battle that resulted in a split in Finnish Communist ranks over the issue of Party control of the Finnish consumers cooperative movement headquartered in Superior, Puro traveled to Russia to explain the problems among Finnish radicals in the United States to the Comintern political secretariat. While he was in Russia, Finnish-American Communists were voted out of power in the consumers cooperative movement.

Puro was next sent to head the Party's agrarian work, where he stayed until 1935, when he was named district secretary of the Upper Michigan district of the Communist Party. In 1939 he returned to *Eteenpain* as an editor and remained there until 1943, at which time he left the Communist Party. In the fall of 1945 he moved with his family to Brooklyn, Connecticut, where he remained until his death in 1981.

SOURCE: John Wiita, "Autobiography" (unpublished), at the Immigration History Research Center, University of Minnesota, St. Paul, Minnesota.

*MIKE KARNI*

# Q

**QUICK, WILLIAM F., SR. (1885–1966).** William Quick, Sr., was a Socialist legislator and judge in Wisconsin and the Socialist candidate for governor and Congressman. Born in Milwaukee in 1885 of a working-class family, Quick worked as a railroad section hand, bricklayer, and machinist while he studied law. He completed his studies and was admitted to the Wisconsin bar in 1921, at the age of 36.

In 1923 Quick was elected to the Wisconsin State Senate, in which he served for the next two years. He was nominated by the Socialists for the Wisconsin governorship in 1924 but was defeated. He lost his seat in the state senate the next year. He was then appointed a judge of the county civil court and held the post for two years, being defeated in 1927. Quick was appointed first assistant city attorney by City Attorney Max Raskin in 1932. He served in that post until 1936. In 1932 he also ran for Congress and came within 2 percent of the vote from being elected in Victor Berger's (q.v.) old district.

That year Quick was also involved in the beginning of the schism that helped destroy the Socialist Party. At the Socialist convention that year, Quick was the spokesman for a group of delegates—headed by Norman Thomas (q.v.) and Mayor Daniel W. Hoan (q.v.)—who opposed Morris Hillquit (q.v.) as national chairman. During the debate, Hillquit accused Quick and his allies of being anti-Semitic and thus assured his own reelection.

Quick became a law partner of Raskin in 1936. He died in Milwaukee in 1966 at age 81.

His son William F. Quick, Jr. (1908–1976) was a founder and president of the Public Enterprise Committee of Wisconsin, which was principally responsible for the election of Socialist Frank P. Zeidler (q.v.) as mayor of Milwaukee in 1948.

*JAMES E. INGBRETSON*

**QUILL, MIKE (1905–1966).** Mike Quill was head of the Transport Workers Union from 1935 to 1966. He also served in the New York City Council from 1937 to 1939 and from 1943 to 1949. He was undoubtedly a secret member of the Communist Party until 1948, when he broke with the Party over its post-war policies and contested it successfully for control of the union. Thereafter, he led the Transport Workers Union himself. Born on September 18, 1905, in Kilgarven, County Kerry, Ireland, Mike Quill, who was briefly involved with the Irish Republican Army in the early 1920s, migrated to the United States in March 1926. He worked as a gateman, a ticket chopper, and a change agent on the IRT subway, sold religious relics in western Pennsylvania, and then returned to the IRT.

During 1934, together with others connected with the Communist Party and under the leadership of John Santo, Quill helped form the Transport Workers Union (TWU). He became president of the union in 1935 and led it into the Congress of Industrial Organizations (CIO) in 1937. Under Quill, the TWU successfully organized subway, bus, and taxi workers in New York and to a lesser extent, elsewhere, achieved improved wages and working conditions, and fought for collective bargaining and the closed shop in municipal transit.

A red-faced elf of a man and a passionate, resourceful politician and mass leader, "Red" Mike Quill used his considerable skills to battle for his workers and to sustain his leadership in a conservative, Irish Catholic union. He was elected to the city council, using the position to cultivate public pressure for his union's interests in New York, even where they clashed with the American Labor Party (ALP)-backed LaGuardia administration. He also fought openly for tangible benefits for his union members, including the forty-hour week, and he sharply played up his Irish brogue and Republican experience for effect and employed Party domination and control of the TWU bureaucracy to stifle opposition.

During the post-war period, Quill and the Communist Party came into conflict over Party policy in the TWU. The issue was the Party's dual insistence that the TWU oppose a fare increase in the New York City subways, even at the cost of transit workers' wages, and that it support Henry Wallace's third party in 1948. Although reluctant to sever all ties, Quill ultimately did so in April 1948, declaring, "wages before Wallace," resigning from the American Labor Party, and denouncing Party leaders as "merchants of confusion." He then ousted Communists from bureaucratic positions in the TWU and barred them from future office. Shortly after, he cooperated with the CIO national leadership in helping drive Communist-dominated unions from the labor federation.

During the Wagner administration in the 1950s, Quill and the TWU achieved exclusive bargaining status in New York transit, and city residents became familiar with a theatrical pattern of threatened strikes, crises, and repeated last-minute negotiated settlements. Early in the Lindsay administration, however, Quill broke the pattern and took the TWU out in a massive subway strike, only the second in the TWU's history, and Quill's last. The TWU leader, who was arrested during the strike, died shortly following the settlement, from a heart attack on January 29, 1966.

SOURCES: Max Kampelman, *The Communist Party vs. the C.I.O.* (1957); Shirley Quill, *Mike Quill-Himself* (1985); L. H. Whittemore, *The Man Who Ran the Subways* (1968).

*KENNETH WALTZER*

# R

RAHV, PHILIP (1908–1973). Philip Rahv was a major literary critic who was strongly influenced by Marxism. In 1934 he founded the *Partisan Review*, originally an organ of the New York chapter of the John Reed Clubs, and he remained an editor until 1969. He was born Ivan Greenberg on March 10, 1908, in Kupin in the Russian Ukraine. His parents were early Zionists who tried to stay aloof from the Russian Revolution and civil war and who fled to Austria and Palestine at the first opportunity. At age 14 Rahv was sent from the Middle East to Providence, Rhode Island, to live with an older brother. There he learned English, which he added to the Russian, German, Yiddish, Hebrew, and French he had already absorbed.

Rahv was an autodidact who never went to college. He began work early for an advertising agency on the West Coast and passed his spare hours in the public library poring over the classics of literature, history, and philosophy. When the Depression came, he lost his job and traveled to New York City, where he stood in bread lines and slept on park benches. In 1932 he became involved in Communist Party activities and changed his name to Rahv (meaning ''rabbi'' in Hebrew).

Soon he became secretary of the monthly magazine *Prolit Folio*, sponsored by the Revolutionary Writers Federation. He published reviews in the *Daily Worker* and *New Masses*, joined the Rebel Poets group, and wrote left-wing poetry. Then, in 1934, Rahv and other activists in the New York chapter of the John Reed Clubs launched the *Partisan Review*, a journal that was mainly to be devoted to Marxist criticism. In these years Rahv's object was to foment a genuine renaissance of literature based on working-class experiences and revolutionary ideas.

By 1936, however, Rahv was disgusted by what he took to be the opportunism of the official Communists in both literary and political matters. He had come to believe that the so-called proletarian cultural line was mainly a vehicle by which the Party could supervise the content of art and the behavior of writers.

The commencement of the Moscow purge trials in 1936 added to Rahv's disillusionment with the Communist Party, and the *Partisan Review* stopped publishing for a year.

When the journal reappeared in late 1937, its revamped editorial board consisted of anti-Stalinist Marxists who had either been expelled from or broken with the Party and who also championed literary modernism: Rahv, William Phillips (q.v.), F. W. Dupee, Dwight Macdonald (q.v.), Mary McCarthy, and George L. K. Morris. Until the advent of World War II, the *Partisan Review* considered itself a Leninist publication with considerable sympathy for Trotskyism. Although Rahv and his closest associate, William Phillips, were suspicious of any organizational association, Trotskyists and Trotsky himself were among the *Partisan Review*'s contributors, and all the editors collaborated with the Trotskyists in setting up the short-lived League for Cultural Freedom and Socialism.

But wartime pressure caused a major rift in the editorial board. Two of the editors, Dwight Macdonald and the recently added Clement Greenberg, argued that opposition to fascism should not mean abandoning the struggle for socialism and endorsing the imperialist war aims of the Allies. Rahv and Sidney Hook (q.v.) wrote in favor of giving "critical support" to the U.S. government. In 1943 Macdonald felt forced to resign, and after this rupture the *Partisan Review*'s connections with the Left became even more tenuous.

Although Rahv was sharply critical of McCarthyism, he was cautious about expressing his views and was by and large politically silent during the 1950s. During the 1960s he moved sharply left again, criticizing many of his fellow intellectuals for having sold out to American prosperity. In 1969 he broke with Phillips because he believed that the *Partisan* had capitulated to the counterculture. In 1971 he published *Modern Occasions*, which lasted for only six issues. He died in 1973.

SOURCES: Arthur Edelstein (ed.), *Images and Ideas in American Culture: Essays in Memory of Philip Rahv* (1979); James B. Gilbert, *Writers and Partisans* (1968); Philip Rahv, *Essays on Literature and Politics: 1932–1972* (1978).

*ALAN WALD*

**RANDOLPH, A. PHILIP (1889–1979).** Asa Philip Randolph achieved a lengthy and varied record of accomplishments in almost fifty years of political activism on the American Left. Co-founder and co-editor of *Messenger* magazine, first president of the Brotherhood of Sleeping Car Porters, first president of the National Negro Congress, progenitor of the 1941 March on Washington movement, founder of the Negro American Labor Council, and originator of the 1963 March on Washington, A. Philip Randolph was a longtime member of the Socialist Party and one of black America's preeminent leaders for over a quarter of a century.

Born in Crescent City, Florida, on April 15, 1889, Randolph was the son of Elizabeth Robinson Randolph and the Reverend James William Randolph, an African Methodist Episcopal minister of modest circumstances who moved his family into nearby Jacksonville when Asa was 2 and his brother James was 4. Randolph completed his high school education at Jacksonville's Cookman Institute, a Methodist mission school, and after several years of working odd jobs in Jacksonville he adventurously booked passage to New York City in the spring of 1911 in search of a livelier existence and possible stage career.

Arriving in Harlem at the age of 22, Randolph worked a succession of menial jobs while taking courses at the City College of New York. He discovered the contemporary political scene both in those classes and in the streetcorner soapbox oratory that characterized Harlem's major avenues. He was strongly attracted to Socialist principles, quickly developed into an ardent admirer of Eugene V. Debs (q.v.), and late in 1916 formally joined the Socialist Party. Having wed a well-to-do widow with a prospering hairstyling business, Lucille E. Green, in late 1914, Randolph was free to devote all his time to political discussions and several short-lived attempts to launch organizations that would represent both poorly paid black workers and progressive political tenets. Along with a fellow young ideologue, Chandler Owen, Randolph attempted to build a Harlem employment agency and worker-organizing enterprise called the Brotherhood of Labor, but that too failed to prosper. Though Randolph had acquired a strong reputation as a superb streetcorner orator and had built up a discussion society, the Independent Political Council, around his forceful articulation of radical politics, it was not until early 1917, when the president of the Headwaiters and Sidewaiters Society of Greater New York asked Randolph and Owen to begin putting out a monthly magazine for the organization's membership, that Randolph finally found a firm niche in Harlem political life.

Starting out as *The Hotel Messenger*—and soon becoming simply *The Messenger* when the waiters society president withdrew his sponsorship—Randolph and Owen's journal quickly emerged as a lively and forcefully outspoken magazine of political commentary and cultural criticism. Fervently supportive of the Industrial Workers of the World, radical for that time in its demands for full black rights, and stridently critical of American involvement in World War I, the *Messenger* quickly established Randolph as one of New York's most notable black radicals. Arrested in Cleveland in the summer of 1918 for uttering Debsian-style condemnations of America's war effort, Randolph intensified his involvement with the Socialist Party when he garnered over 200,000 votes as its 1920 candidate for New York State comptroller. His firm commitment to biracial working-class radicalism led Randolph to turn the *Messenger*'s rhetorical guns on Black Nationalist messiah Marcus Garvey with stringent harshness, but by the middle of the decade Randolph's own race-consciousness had led him to an increasingly negative view of the Socialist Party, which had "no effective policy toward Negroes, and didn't spend enough time organizing them," he later declared. Displeased with the political scene and with the financially strapped *Messenger* turning more to literary and cultural concerns, by 1925 Randolph faced dimmer prospects than at any time since 1917.

In June of that year an outspoken black Pullman porter, Ashley L. Totten, asked Randolph to turn his considerable energies and powerful speaking skills toward organizing the 10,000 black porters scattered nationwide into a union that could force the Pullman Company into raising the men's miniscule wages and improving their horrendous working conditions. Despite the porters' lack of success in previous organizing efforts, Randolph looked into their situation, recognized the direct relevance of their cause to his own racial and economic precepts, and, at the first formal meeting on August 25, 1925, was named president of the new Brotherhood of Sleeping Car Porters.

Randolph began what turned out to be a twelve-year effort to win recognition of the black workers' union by the Pullman Company. Touring the nation to help stiffen members' courage in the face of repeated legal setbacks, company harassment, and mass firings of suspected Brotherhood porters, he won the respect and allegiance of the core membership despite the long and draining struggle. Finally, in 1934, New Deal political support resulted in strengthening amendments to the Railway Labor Act that eventually, after Supreme Court approval, forced the Pullman Company to sit down face-to-face with the Brotherhood leadership and pursue meaningful negotiations. On August 25, 1937, the company signed an agreement with the Brotherhood giving porters a substantial salary increase and a reduction in monthly working hours from 400 to 240.

The Brotherhood's resounding triumph thrust Randolph forward into a nationally prominent black leadership position he had never before assumed. Already named the first president of the new Communist-influenced National Negro Congress a year earlier, Randolph softpeddled differences within that congress and had little to do with its actual operation until Communist efforts to set the organization's political line became self-obvious at its third convention in April 1940. Then, with Communist representatives urging American isolationism in light of the Hitler-Stalin Pact, Randolph criticized both the Soviet regime and the policies of the American Communist Party. Many delegates walked out during his remarks, and a resolution implicitly rejecting Randolph's stance was adopted. Firmly committed to his principles, Randolph resigned the presidency and publicly condemned the congress' adherence to Soviet preferences and increasing dependence on the Communist Party.

Randolph's resignation did nothing to harm his status as a preeminent black leader, and the onset of World War II, coupled with the continuing prevalence of racial discrimination in all major American industries, led him to mount a new attack on government-condoned segregation both in the military services themselves and in private firms churning out defense hardware. On January 15, 1941, Randolph announced that a mass march of at least 10,000 black citizens would take place that summer in Washington, D.C., to protest the Roosevelt administration's continued reluctance to implement nondiscriminatory practices and establish a fair employment practices committee to monitor private government contractors. As grass-roots sentiment in support of the March on Washington movement grew steadily in black communities across the nation, to the point that Randolph increased his estimate to 100,000 marchers, President Roosevelt summoned him to a June 18 White House meeting, only two weeks in advance of the July 1 pilgrimage. Consenting to Randolph's demand that a presidential directive banning racial discrimination and establishing a fair employment practices committee be issued if the mass march was to be called off, Roosevelt on June 25 signed Executive Order 8802, commanding those two steps, and Randolph canceled the protest.

Randolph remained prominent for the following quarter-century. He rejected a request to run as the Socialist Party's 1944 vice-presidential nominee, and led repeated late 1940s efforts to convince President Truman to enforce and expand the federal anti-discrimination mandate set forth in Roosevelt's initial order. He continued his long-standing battle against racial discrimination within organized labor itself, and a heated confrontation with AFL-CIO President George Meany at the group's 1959 convention led Randolph to take the helm of a new black trade union organization, the Negro American Labor Council (NALC), established specifically to press for racial justice within the labor movement. AFL-CIO executives censured Randolph for his continued public criticisms of labor's racial shortcomings, but by 1962 relations were repaired, and two years later Randolph left the NALC presidency, decrying the same influences that had torpedoed the National Negro Congress twenty-five years earlier.

Over 70 years old by the time the civil rights movement of the 1960s emerged at the forefront of American politics, Randolph functioned as an elder statesman while symbolizing to a younger generation of activists how mass protest and grass-roots organizing, rather than the courtroom litigation preferred by the National Association for the Advancement of Colored People, ought to be the movement's predominant forms of action. Assisted by his lieutenant, Bayard Rustin (q.v.), Randolph took the lead in organizing the 1963 March on Washington for Jobs and Freedom, which drew 200,000 people and became the emotional peak of the civil rights era. With AFL-CIO financial support, Rustin and Randolph in 1964 established the A. Philip Randolph Institute and two years later called for a $180 billion federal "Freedom Budget" to provide full employment plus guaranteed annual incomes for those unable to work.

Childless and left a widower by his wife's death in 1963, Randolph in 1969 formally rejoined the Socialist Party. He later affiliated with the Social Democrats USA. One of the major figures in twentieth-century black protest, he died on May 16, 1979, at the age of 90.

SOURCES: Jervis Anderson, *A. Philip Randolph: A Biographical Portrait* (1973); William H. Harris, *Keeping the Faith: A. Philip Randolph, Milton P. Webster, and the Brotherhood of Sleeping Car Porters, 1925–37* (1977); Theodore Kornweibel, *No Crystal Stair: Black Life and the Messenger, 1917–1928* (1975).

*DAVID J. GARROW*

**RAUSCHENBUSCH, WALTER (1861–1918).** Walter Rauschenbusch was a leader of the Social Gospel movement in Protestant Christianity in the United States during the first two decades of the twentieth century. He influenced many future Socialist leaders of the mid-twentieth century, especially Norman Thomas (q.v.).

Rauschenbusch was born in Rochester, New York, in 1861, the son of German Democrats who fled to the United States after the failure of the revolution of 1848. He was educated at the gymnasium at Gutersloh (from which he graduated in 1883), the University of Rochester (B.A., 1884), and Rochester Theological Seminary, from which he was ordained into the Baptist ministry in 1886. After his ordination Rauschenbusch moved to New York City, where he served his only parish, the Second Baptist Church, in a poverty-stricken area of Manhattan populated primarily by immigrants. His work among the poor immigrants helped convert him to the Social Gospel brand of Christianity, which posited that the chief work of the church should be aimed at a social and economic reorganization directed at a more egalitarian society.

In 1891 and 1892 Rauschenbusch studied economics and theology in Germany. He also read extensively in Socialist theory. Rauschenbusch was impressed particularly with the works of Edward Bellamy (q.v.) and John Ruskin and the British Fabians. Although now a Socialist, Rauschenbusch did not join the movement, nor did he consider himself a Marxist. He claimed that the root of his political and economic views was in the Bible, particularly the Old Testament prophets.

In 1892 Rauschenbusch founded the Brotherhood of the Kingdom, an organization devoted to Christian Socialism. He remained in his New York City parish for the next five years, turning it into a major center of the Social Christian movement.

He was named to the church history faculty at the Rochester Theological Seminary in 1897 and remained there until his death in 1918. While at the seminary he wrote five books. The first, *Christianity and the Social Crisis* (1907), was the most important. With its publication, Rauschenbusch emerged as the outstanding figure in Social Gospel Protestantism.

The key to Rauschenbusch's Christian Socialism was a passage in the Gospel According to Matthew, "Thy will be done on earth . . . " (Matt. 6:10). His basic assumption held that the Kingdom of God would transform the world into a "harmony with Heaven." The prophets of the Old Testament were, he maintained, the radical minority of their time. The "Day of Jehovah" of which they spoke, Rauschenbusch argued, was the day of social revolution. And Jesus, whom he considered to be a prophet and a revolutionary, was also dedicated primarily to a great social, political, and economic transformation. The church, which he believed was in a state of decline, had failed because it refused to right the evils of the existing social order. It had not advanced Christianity, even though it had built beautiful cathedrals and monasteries. It had allowed its soul to be corroded and had become an organization completely antithetical to Christianity.

Although he rejected Marxism in general, there were significant parts of Marx's system with which Rauschenbusch agreed. Like Marx, Rauschenbusch believed that class struggles were the basic dynamic of history. These struggles were, he argued, a continuum, although each era had its own means of struggle. In the age of capitalism the working people were, he believed, limited to a single weapon: organization. By use of that organization they could gain genuine power by political action or through strikes. Besides the class struggle, Rauschenbusch also agreed with Marx that the working man was alienated from himself, his society, and his product. He described alienation as a "corrosive chemical that disintegrates [the worker's] self-respect."

In a 1916 lecture Rauschenbusch proclaimed himself a Socialist, although he did not join the party. He believed that he could do more for socialism as a nonparty thinker and activist than as a party worker. The outbreak of the war in Europe in 1914 caused him great pain. He was basically a pacifist as well as a Socialist. He refused to join the clerical outpouring of support when the United States became a participant in the war in 1917.

In 1918 Rauschenbusch died in Rochester at the age of 57.

SOURCES: M. A. McGiffert, "Walter Rauschenbusch: Twenty Years After," *Christendom* 3 (Winter 1938); W. A. Mueller, "The Life, Work and Gospel of Walter Rauschenbusch," *Religion in Life* 15 (Autumn 1946); D. R. Sharpe, *Walter Rauschenbusch* (1942).

*BERNARD K. JOHNPOLL*


**REED, JOHN (1887–1920).** John Reed sympathetically described Russia's 1917–1918 revolutionary upheavals in *Ten Days That Shook the World* and other writings. He belonged to a left-wing American Socialist Party faction that later organized the Communist Labor Party (CLP), he steered the CLP's claims to legitimacy before the Communist International, and he was appointed American representative on the Executive Committee of the Communist International.

The oldest son of native-born Americans, John Silas Reed was born on October 22, 1887, in Portland, Oregon. His father was a businessman and his mother was a descendant of a frontier era entrepreneur in Portland. Of the Episcopal faith, the Reed family barely sustained its upper-class lifestyles and social status during John's youth. He attended Portland Academy until 1904, and next enrolled at Morristown School in New Jersey. He entered Harvard University in 1906 and graduated in 1910. An indifferent scholar at Harvard, Reed excelled in collegiate literary circles and participated in the student body's social ferments, though he stayed aloof from membership in the Socialist Club.

From 1911 to 1916 Reed immersed himself in the Greenwich Village cultural movements in New York City which presumed that artistic vision and intellect could free society from its conventionalities and create a climate conducive to individual fulfillment. Reed published short fiction pieces and poetry, his verse including *The Day in Bohemia* (1913), and his first nonfiction appeared in *American* magazine in 1912. A writer and producer of the Paterson Pageant, he boosted for the side of the Industrial Workers of the World during the Paterson, New Jersey, silk industry strike of 1913; he wrote sympathetically about organized labor's viewpoints in its 1914 battles with Rockefeller corporate forces in Colorado; and he recorded the revolutionary idealism of Mexico's Francisco ("Pancho") Villa in magazine and newspaper articles and in Reed's *Insurgent Mexico* (1914). The latter ensured Reed new literary recognition outside America's cultural bohemias.

Also appointed to the editorial staff of *Masses* in 1912, Reed remained an editor and wrote extensively for *Masses* until U.S. postal authorities suppressed the publication in 1917. After 1915, however, his editorial role at *Masses* diminished and as contributing editor of *Liberator*, successor publication to *Masses*, Reed contributed minimally. While he was writing for *Masses*, one of his pieces, headlined "Knit a Straight-Jacket for Your Soldier Boy," so offended American authorities that Reed was indicted for violating the Espionage Act of 1917. He escaped punishment when a panel of jurors disagreed about his actions.

In these same years Reed strengthened his journalistic credentials. His writings on Mexico's internal strife in 1914 and labor-management turmoil in Colorado mining areas in the same year were acceptable to several commercial, high-circulation magazines and the *New York Times*. Then two assignments to report on World War I events from *Metropolitan* magazine and the *New York World* in 1915 and 1916 were less successful. Here either Reed's own inability to formulate fundamental meanings for this warfare impeded his journalism, or European authorities barred him from observing the fighting firsthand, or Reed ran afoul of demands from mainstream American publishers for pro-Allied copy. On the other hand, he published *The War in Eastern Europe* (1916), a book that received favorable reviews, and commercial publications such as *Collier's* and *Metropolitan* readily accepted his writings on American events until April 1917.

However, Reed was now heralded nationally more as a culturally innovative rebel who combined his social rebellion with adventure and reportedly with personal libertinism. Yet his distaste for America's involvement in World War I beginning in 1917 and the nation's wartime excesses in the name of patriotism and at the expense of civil liberties, which also soon proscribed Reed's commercial writing opportunities and stigmatized his Utopianism, hastened Reed's conversion to political radicalism. Besides anti-conscription activism and preparing anti-war material for *Masses*, Reed produced a Marxist interpretation of World War I in an essay, "This Unpopular War," in *Seven Arts* (August 1917).

The revolutionary potential that was surfacing in Russia in 1917 so interested Reed that he hurried abroad in September, and he remained in Russia until February 1918. There he witnessed Communist successes and joined the victorious insurgents' Bureau of International Revolutionary Propaganda. Simultaneously he wrote copy for this agency and worked with the American Red Cross Mission on famine relief. More important, his observations of the Bolshevik seizure of power at St. Petersburg supplied material for numerous articles and for Reed's

*Ten Days That Shook the World* (1919). This volume procured at last the greater
literary acclaim that had eluded Reed.

After Reed returned to the United States in 1918, he also joined the American
Socialist Party. For more than six months in 1919 he was contributing editor to
*Revolutionary Age*, and he edited two other left-wing Socialist journals, the *New
York Communist* and the *Voice of Labor*. At the same time, he belonged to a
group of left-wing Socialists who, after their expulsion from the Socialist Party,
organized the Communist Labor Party (CLP). The CLP claimed 10,000 of the
35,000 expellees; a new Communist Party asserted suzerainty over the remainder.
When both groups professed to speak for American communism, Reed traveled
to Russia in 1919, hoping to procure Communist International recognition for
the CLP. While waiting for the Communist International to adjudicate these
disputes, he published two articles commissioned for Comintern journals.

During his latest stay in Russia, Illinois civil authorities indicted Reed for
criminal anarchy. He then attempted to return to the United States early in 1920
in order to defend himself, but he was intercepted in Finland while in possession
of money and jewels belonging to the Communist International. Imprisoned by
Finnish authorities for three months, he was finally released and permitted to
return to the Soviet Union. Back in Russia, he participated in proceedings to
organize the Third International and was appointed American representative on
the Executive Committee of the Communist International. Before the year had
ended, however, he privately expressed disillusionment with communism's internal
politics. In the judgment of many recent scholars, however, Reed never repudiated
his liking for communism before his death in Moscow on October 17, 1920.

SOURCES: Richard O'Connor and Dale L. Walker, *The Lost Revolutionary: A Biography
of John Reed* (1967); Granville Hicks, *John Reed, The Making of a Revolutionary*
(1936); Robert A. Rosenstone, *Romantic Revolutionary: A Biography of John Reed*
(1975).

*HUGH T. LOVIN*

**RHODES, GEORGE M. (1898–1978).** George M. Rhodes was a leading member
of the Socialist Party of Reading, Pennsylvania, from 1920 to 1940. He served
as a Democrat in the U.S. House of Representatives from 1949 to 1969. Rhodes
was born in Reading, Pennsylvania, in 1898. He served in the army during
World War I. In 1920 he joined the Socialist Party, which was then a major
force in Reading politics.

He had been a printer, working on the *Reading Daily Eagle* from 1920 until
1928, when he was named an editor of the Socialist weekly *Reading Labor
Advocate*. He held that post until 1939, when he left the Socialist Party because
he was opposed to its stand against U.S. involvement in World War II. He then
became editor of the official organ of the Federated Trades Council, the trade
union federation in Berks County (Reading and environs).

Rhodes' withdrawal from the Socialist Party was based on tactical as well as
theoretical disagreements with its leadership. He believed that socialism in the

United States could be accomplished by electoral means only. He doubted the Socialist Party could ever gain control of the American elective process, in view of the nation's inherent two-party system. He argued that Socialists could become the dominant force in the Democratic Party, much as they had in North Dakota's Republican Party during the pre–World War I period. Rhodes thus joined the pro-labor wing of the Democratic Party in 1940. His newspaper became the mouthpiece for the pro–New Deal, anti-isolationist wing of the Democratic Party, of which he soon became leader.

In the 1948 election Rhodes, who had previously been an unsuccessful candidate for city and county office, was elected to Congress as a Democrat. Once elected, Rhodes became the leader of the right to improve Social Security, which had been proposed originally by Socialist Congressman Victor Berger (q.v.) of Wisconsin. He was also active in the drive to obtain low-cost government housing for the elderly, and he was author of the Medicare bill, which offered low-cost health care for the elderly under Social Security. His record in Congress differed little from that of the two Socialists who preceded him, but his power in Congress was much greater. He eventually became the leader of the Pennsylvania Democratic delegation.

Shortly before his 1969 retirement from Congress due to ill-health, Rhodes told an interviewer that Norman Thomas (q.v.) had suggested that Socialists do precisely what Rhodes had done: use the Democratic Party as the vehicle for social change. Rhodes died in 1978 after a long illness.

*BERNARD K. JOHNPOLL*

**RICHMOND, AL (b. 1913).** Al Richmond, longtime editor of the Communist *People's World*, was born in London, England on November 17, 1913. His mother, a leader in the Russian Jewish Bund, had just arrived from Siberian exile. His family came to the United States in 1915 but separated soon after; Al and his mother returned to Russia in 1917, while his father, working in a munitions factory, remained in the States. His mother, opposed to the total absorption of the Bund into the Communist Party, left for Poland in 1921 and finally came to the United States in 1922, where she became a garment worker. Richmond joined the Young Communist League (YCL) in 1928 while living in the Bronx. After finishing high school in 1931 he became a full-time YCL functionary in Philadelphia and Baltimore before organizing for the Marine Workers Industrial Union.

Richmond first worked for the *Daily Worker* in 1934. Three years later he was sent to San Francisco to become managing editor of the new *Daily People's World*, the Party's West Coast organ. Aside from service in the medical corps in World War II, he remained with the paper until 1969, becoming executive editor after the war. Richmond was convicted in the California Smith Act trials in 1952 and sentenced to five years in prison. His conviction was overturned and a directed acquittal was ordered by the Supreme Court in *Yates v. U.S.* in 1957.

Like much of the California Communist Party, Richmond was associated with the "reformers" in the intraparty disputes of 1956–1958. He was elected to the Party's National Committee in 1957 and remained a member until 1972. He co-authored the Party's first draft program in 1965, but soon began to run afoul of Communist orthodoxy. Sharply critical of the Soviet invasion of Czechoslovakia in 1968 (the *Daily Worker* and the Party endorsed the invasion), Richmond came under pressure from Party leader Gus Hall (q.v.) to give up his role on the *People's World*, by now a weekly. He resigned his post in 1969. After his autobiography was published without Party clearance in 1973, Richmond was publicly denounced and, even though he had previously announced his resignation, expelled from the Party.

SOURCE: Al Richmond, *A Long View from the Left* (1973).

*HARVEY KLEHR*

**ROSE, ERNESTINE (1810–1892).** Ernestine Rose was a leading Owenite Socialist, suffragette, and opponent of slavery in the United States between 1836 and 1870. The daughter of a rabbi, she was born in Piotrokow, Poland (then part of the czarist Russian empire) in 1810. Her family name was Potowsky. She was educated by her father in Jewish religious lore and the Hebrew language, and she was also well versed in Polish and Yiddish. At 16 she sued successfully in a court to allow her—a woman—to control her own inheritance.

In 1827 she left Poland forever and moved to Berlin, then to Holland, and in 1830 to Paris, where a revolution was in progress. She soon left Paris and settled in London. In Great Britain she became an active member of Robert Owen's (q.v.) Association of All Classes of All Nations, a Socialist organization. She became acquainted there with Owen and met William Rose, a jeweler and silversmith, who was also a member of Owen's organization. She and Rose were married in 1836.

The Roses moved to New York in 1836, where she became active almost immediately working for a law to allow women to own property in their own names. The law was finally passed in 1860. Ernestine Rose was also active in the free-thought movement of the 1830s and 1840s. She attended meetings, donated funds, and wrote articles in free-thought journals. She was also involved, with her husband, in the short-lived Skaneateles community founded in 1843 by John Anderson Collins (q.v.). And she joined Robert Owen in his 1845 Convention of the Infidels of the United States in New York.

Rose introduced the first proposal for an equal rights amendment at the first national women's rights convention in Worcester, Massachusetts, in 1850. She was also active in the temperance and anti-slavery movements of the period. During and immediately after the Civil War, she was active in the movement for equal political rights for blacks and women. In 1866 she worked with Elizabeth Cady Stanton and Susan B. Anthony in forming the Equal Rights Association, which became the National Woman Suffrage Association in 1869. That year

Mrs. Rose and her husband went to Europe, settling permanently in England in 1870. She died in Brighton in 1892.

SOURCES: *Notable American Women* (1980); Yuri Suhl, *Ernestine Rose and the Battle for Human Rights* (1959).

*LILLIAN KIRTZMAN JOHNPOLL*


**ROSS, CARL (b. 1913).** Carl Ross was the leader of Communist Party youth work in the early 1940s and one of the younger national leaders of the Communist Party in the late 1940s and 1950s. He was born on July 22, 1913, in Hancock, Michigan. His father, Edwin Rasi, was an immigrant from Finland, his mother was born of Finnish immigrant parents. Ross grew up in the Finnish (and Finnish Communist) community located within the neighboring cities of Duluth, Minnesota, and Superior, Wisconsin. He graduated from Central High in Superior in 1931.

In 1930–1934 Ross was secretary of the Midwest district of the Labor Sports Union, a largely Finnish and politically radical organization, and he edited the weekly English section of the daily Finnish language and Communist newspaper *Tyomies*. In 1934–1937 he served as secretary of the Young Communist League of Minnesota, participated in the Minneapolis Youth Council and Minnesota and Midwest Youth Congresses, and represented Hotel and Restaurant Workers Local 665 on the Hannepin County (Minneapolis) Farmer-Labor Party Central Committee.

From 1937 to 1943 Ross served in various capacities in the national leadership of the Young Communist League and as editor of *Clarity*. He also served on the National Board of the American Youth Congress. In 1944–1945 Ross was national secretary of the American Youth for Democracy and helped to edit *Spotlight*.

In 1946 he became secretary of the Communist Party of the Minnesota-Dakotas district and supervised extensive Communist activity within Minnesota CIO (Congress of Industrial Organizations) unions and the Democratic-Farmer-Labor Party. During the next decade he served on the Communist Party's National Committee and in a variety of important national Party positions. He was also convicted and imprisoned for harboring a Smith Act fugitive in the early 1950s. Ross left the Communist Party in 1957 when it fell into disarray in the wake of Khrushchev's confirmation of the crimes of Stalin's regime and the Russian suppression of the 1956 Hungarian Revolution.

In the 1960s Ross ceased active participation in politics and developed a successful electroplating business in Minneapolis. In the 1970s he retired from business and became an independent scholar in Finnish-American, radical, and labor history. In 1984 he became the executive secretary of the United Fund for Finnish-American Archives.

SOURCE: Oral History Interview, Minnesota Historical Society, St. Paul, Minnesota (1977).

*JOHN E. HAYNES*

**RUBIN, JERRY (b. 1938).** Jerry Rubin was one of the most visible and outspoken members of the counterculture during the 1960s. He was a representative of that part of the New Left that abandoned, indeed ridiculed, traditional political activity in favor of cultural politics. Rubin was born on July 14, 1938, into a middle-class Jewish family in Cincinnati. He attended Oberlin College for a short period but eventually graduated from the University of Cincinnati in 1961. After extensive travel abroad, he enrolled in the graduate school of the University of California at Berkeley in 1964.

Rubin was an early leader in the free-speech movement that emerged on the Berkeley campus in the fall of 1964. He was a founder of the Vietnam Day Committee, which held one of the largest of the early teach-ins in the spring of 1965. By 1967, however, Rubin had turned away from traditional political protest to cultural radicalism. In 1967 he was one of the founders of the Youth International Party, the Yippies. Rubin and his fellow Yippies protested against American society through acts of absurdity. Their often colorful garb and behavior, such as wearing outlandish costumes to House Un-American Activities Committee hearings, generated a vast amount of media attention.

Rubin was a participant in the May 1967 disruption of the New York Stock Exchange and a leading figure in the march on the Pentagon that October. At the Chicago Democratic convention in 1968, Rubin and the Yippies staged what they referred to as a festival of life—part of which included the nomination of Mr. Pigasus, a pig, for President. Rubin was charged with conspiracy to incite riot and was one of the defendants in the Chicago Eight trial of 1969. He and four of his co-defendants were convicted of the individual act, not conspiracy, of inciting to riot. He also received a two-and-a-half year sentence for contempt for his actions during the trial. As in the case of the other convicted defendants, his conviction was overturned on appeal. In the 1980s Rubin was working as a stockbroker on Wall Street.

SOURCES: Jerry Rubin, *Do It* (1970) and *Growing Up at Thirty-Seven* (1976).

*TOM WILLIAMS*


**RUSTIN, BAYARD (b.1910).** Bayard Rustin has been a lifelong activist on behalf of nonviolence and racial justice, served as principal organizer of the 1963 March on Washington, and as executive director and later president of the A. Philip Randolph Institute, and has worked during the last quarter-century to maintain close ties between organized labor and black political activists.

Rustin was born on March 17, 1910, in West Chester, Pennsylvania, one of twelve children. He was raised largely by his grandparents and was particularly influenced by his grandmother, a member of the Society of Friends and the National Association for the Advancement of Colored People (NAACP). Rustin graduated from West Chester High School, attended Wilberforce University for one year and Cheney State Teachers College for two, and then traveled around the nation doing odd jobs until the mid–1930s, when he moved to New York.

Impressed by the anti-racist activities of American Communists, Rustin joined the Young Communist League (YCL) in 1936 and two years later began taking courses at the City College of New York, where he also functioned as an organizer for the YCL. Often singing in nightclubs in order to support himself, Rustin continued his YCL activism, concentrating on building black opposition to racism in the U.S. military. In June 1941, revulsed and disillusioned when Hitler's invasion of the Soviet Union immediately led the American Communist Party to abandon its prior hostility toward U.S. interventionism and military racism, Rustin left the YCL and became a youth organizer for A. Philip Randolph's (q.v.) March on Washington movement.

When Randolph, to Rustin's dismay, canceled the scheduled July 1 mass pilgrimage following Franklin Roosevelt's signing of an executive order banning federally sponsored racial discrimination, Rustin joined the staff of the Fellowship of Reconciliation (FOR), a pacifist group whose core principles fit well with his own. In twelve years with the FOR, Rustin's experiences and activism ranged widely. Beaten by Tennessee policemen in 1942 for refusing to move to the rear of a segregated bus, Rustin the following year refused to submit to any kind of military service on account of his pacifist principles and served two and a half years in federal prison as a result. In April 1947 Rustin was one of the leading participants in the FOR's Journey of Reconciliation, a "freedom ride" precursor designed to test Southern compliance with a Supreme Court decision mandating desegregated seating in interstate transportation. Arrested in Chapel Hill, North Carolina, for refusing to leave the "white" section of a bus, Rustin served twenty-two days on a prison camp chain gang after his conviction was upheld on appeal. In 1948 he played a major role in A. Philip Randolph's League for Nonviolent Civil Disobedience Against Military Segregation, set up to pressure President Harry Truman to enforce and expand Roosevelt's earlier anti-discrimination order. Rustin also made a lengthy visit to India to deepen his understanding of Gandhian nonviolence and helped create the Committee to Support South African Resistance, which later became the American Committee on Africa.

In 1953 Rustin left the FOR to become executive secretary of the War Resisters League, and he renewed his close working relationship with Randolph. When the indigenous black boycott of Montgomery, Alabama's segregated city buses seemed to herald a new era of civil rights activism, Randolph and other supportive New Yorkers sent Rustin south to counsel the boycott's leading spokesman, the Reverend Martin Luther King, Jr., in early 1956. Along with FOR staffer the Reverend Glenn Smiley, Rustin proved invaluable to King by supplementing his natural commitment to a Christian doctrine of love with broader intellectual expositions of the philosophy and practice of nonviolence as drawn from the writings of Gandhi, Thoreau, and others.

When the Montgomery protest ended with successful legal desegregation of the city's buses, Rustin and two New York colleagues, Stanley D. Levison and Ella J. Baker, took leading roles in helping King build on the Montgomery achievement by creating the regionwide Southern Christian Leadership Conference (SCLC). Although the SCLC was slow to emerge as an influential civil rights force, Rustin remained a close and influential adviser to King until the summer of 1960, when New York Representative Adam Clayton Powell, under political pressure to derail civil rights protests planned for the Democratic and Republic national conventions by Randolph, King, and Rustin, threatened to highlight publicly not only Rustin's draft conviction and past YCL membership but also his homosexuality, including a completely false allegation of an intimate relationship between Rustin and King. While King mulled what to do, Rustin took the initiative and resigned as King's aide so that the convention protests could proceed unhindered.

Three years later, when Randolph decided the time had come for another March on Washington, this one to focus on black joblessness, Rustin again was at his side. Although both civil rights opponents, such as South Carolina Senator Strom Thurmond, and some proponents, such as the NAACP's Roy Wilkins, suggested that some aspects of Rustin's past personal record might embarrass the march effort, Randolph, King, and others stood firmly behind Rustin's appointment as chief march organizer. With a hastily assembled staff and modest budget, Rustin used his superb administrative skills to pull off a smooth-functioning demonstration that drew almost a quarter-million people to the Lincoln Memorial on August 28, 1963. Although Rustin himself hoped to prolong the March on Washington coalition as an umbrella organization for broadening the civil rights movement's agenda from anti-discrimination legislation to more far-reaching social welfare and economic policy reforms, the effort proved unsuccessful. Nevertheless, in several extremely influential and oft-cited articles, Rustin expounded his case that the movement had to broaden its goals and that doing so would require a progression "from protest to politics"—to electoral coalitions where black activists would join with labor, church, and liberal forces to pursue a wide-ranging progressive economic agenda. Though such a perspective struck some as too radical in 1963, by 1966 and the advent of "black power," many movement activists were condemning Rustin's emphasis on biracial electoral efforts as too meek and out-of-date.

Outspokenly critical of "black power," of King's Poor People's Campaign, and of local black activism in the 1968 Ocean Hill–Brownsville, New York, school controversy, Rustin's lifelong record of radical activism looked severely tarnished to many black commentators by the end of the 1960s. Securely ensconced as head of the A. Philip Randolph Institute, founded in 1964 and funded in substantial part by the AFL-CIO, Rustin increasingly was criticized as being more responsive to organized labor's interests than to those of the black underclass. Rustin opposed and publicly condemned the 1983 March on Washington. He became national chairman of Social Democrats USA in 1972.

SOURCES: Bayard Rustin, *Down the Line: The Collected Writings of Bayard Rustin* (1971) and *Strategies for Freedom* (1976); Milton Viorst, *Fire in the Streets: America in the 1960s* (1979).

DAVID J. GARROW

**RUTHENBERG, CHARLES (1882–1927).** Charles (''C.E.'') Ruthenberg was executive secretary of the Communist party in the United States almost continuously from its inception in 1919 until his death in 1927. He was a talented but somewhat colorless administrator who used his organizational skills in the building of the Cleveland and Ohio Socialist parties, the Socialist Party left wing after 1917, and ultimately throughout the splits and mergers of the fledgling American Communist movement. Ruthenberg was not as charismatic as other radical leaders in his time, but he was adept at party infighting and had a great ability to anticipate and respond to policy and personality changes in the Kremlin.

Charles Emil Ruthenberg was born on July 9, 1882, in Cleveland, Ohio. The last and only American-born child in his German immigrant family, Charles was born four months after his parents, August and Wilhelmina (Lau) Ruthenberg, brought seven other children to the United States. A cigarmaker and woodcutter prior to immigration, August found work shoveling iron ore on the Lake Erie docks. In later years he ran a tavern. All the Ruthenberg children worked outside the home except Charles, who was somewhat favored and was allowed to spend more time in reading and study. His mother wanted her youngest son to become a minister and to this end enrolled him in a Lutheran school, from which he graduated in 1896. Instead of attending seminary, however, Charles went to work in a bookstore and enrolled in Berkey and Dyke's Business College.

August Ruthenberg's death in 1898 forced Charles into his only experience with blue-collar work. He worked as a carpenter's helper in a picture-molding factory for over a year until he was transferred into a position in the firm's office. For nearly twenty years thereafter, C. E. Ruthenberg gained his livelihood from a series of white-collar jobs in businesses ranging from a publishing firm to a manufacturer of ladies' undergarments. Ruthenberg used his employment in bookkeeping, sales, and management positions to support his family, his party work, and his numerous attempts at public office. His business career also allowed him to develop the managerial, financial, and organizational skills that helped make him such a capable leader in both the Socialist and Communist parties. Ruthenberg's life in business ended in 1917, when he reputedly chose socialism over employment when presented with such a choice by his last firm's superiors. Ruthenberg worked from 1917 until his death in 1927 as a paid worker for the Socialist Party and, starting in 1919, the Communist Party.

Charles married Rosaline Nickel, also an American-born child of German immigrants, on June 29, 1904. Supportive of her husband's politics, she followed him into membership in the Socialist Party and ran the Cleveland branch of the party in her husband's place when he was jailed in 1918. Their only child, Daniel, was born on April 4, 1905.

Ruthenberg's political development started in 1901 with his support of the ''municipal socialism'' of Cleveland Mayor Tom Johnson. Spurred by his reading and arguments with co-workers over politics and economics, Charles started to call himself a Socialist in 1908 and actually joined the Socialist Party in 1909. Convinced of its historical accuracy, Ruthenberg found that socialism echoed

his personal beliefs in evolutionary reform. His shift to the left wing of the
Socialist Party came slowly and would be especially driven by his experience
with World War I.

Upon joining the Socialist Party (SP), Ruthenberg became a steady and versatile
worker. He was elected to the executive committee of Local Cleveland a few
months after he joined the party, and he continued as a leader in the local party
throughout his ten-year career as a Socialist. He served the local at various times
as full-time organizer, taking this as his paid employment in 1917. Ruthenberg
was a frequent and popular speaker at party meetings and on the streetcorner
soapboxes of Cleveland. He penned a number of articles for the city's labor and
Socialist newspapers, the latter of which he also edited. He served on the state
party's executive committee and was its recording secretary. Starting in 1910
with his campaign for state treasurer, Ruthenberg appeared on the state or local
ballot eight out of nine years on the Socialist ticket. Though his campaigns for
governor, U.S. Senator, U.S. Congressman, and mayor of Cleveland were
unsuccessful, these election attempts allowed him to present the case for socialism
to the citizens of his city and state. Some of Ruthenberg's campaigns for public
office in the World War I period were conducted while he was in jail or out on
appeal.

Ruthenberg's first national involvement in the left wing of the Socialist Party
came in the fight over the issue of sabotage at the 1912 national convention in
Indianapolis. He voted with the left-wing minority against the move to bar from
membership any persons who advocated the use of sabotage, a move directly
aimed at Socialists who were also members of the Industrial Workers of the
World (IWW). Though he had opposed the rule, Ruthenberg voted with the
majority later in a mail vote that expelled IWW leader William D. Haywood
(q.v.) from the SP's National Executive Board under the provisions of the
disputed bylaw.

The outbreak of World War I moved Ruthenberg further to the left. Ruthenberg
viewed the war as simply a device for the expansion of imperialistic capitalism
and was deeply frustrated by the inability of the Second International to stop
Socialists in the involved nations from putting patriotism above class solidarity.
He brought these sentiments to the 1917 Socialist Party convention in St. Louis
and was an effective floor leader for the victorious anti-war left wing at the
gathering. A strong anti-war resolution co-authored by Ruthenberg—calling for
Socialists not to cooperate with the efforts of the United States, now a declared
combatant, to raise funds to aid the war, to conscript young men to fight in
Europe, or to suppress dissent—was passed by the convention. With his recent
convention victory, Ruthenberg took his opposition to the war home to Cleveland,
where he wrote articles and made speeches outlining the Socialist Party position.
He was arrested in June 1917 after one of his speeches; it was alleged that he
had called on young men to resist induction into the armed forces. He was
convicted on this charge, along with co-defendants Alfred Wagenknecht (q.v.)
and Charles Baker of the state party, and all three were jailed upon the loss of

their appeal in the Canton, Ohio, workhouse from February 1, 1918, until January 31, 1919.

Ruthenberg hailed the Bolshevik Revolution when it occurred in 1917, but cautiously. He supported its result, the end to Russia's involvement in World War I, and thought that the revolution might provide an example for American Socialists to follow. Ruthenberg's time in jail, along with his growing knowledge of events in Russia, led him further to the left. When the New York left wing circulated a draft Communist manifesto in February 1919, Ruthenberg heavily endorsed it. The riot resulting from a police raid on a peaceful May Day 1919 parade in Cleveland further convinced Ruthenberg that the time for something stronger than reform socialism had come.

Ruthenberg attended the left-wing conference held in New York in June 1919 which was called in response to the Russian Revolution. At the conference the Russian-language federations split off, vowing to start a new Communist Party in the United States while the majority of the left wing united around plans to take over the upcoming SP convention and move it to the left and recognition by the Communist International (Comintern). Ruthenberg and the Ohio delegation backed the majority led by John Reed (q.v.) and Benjamin Gitlow (q.v.). After the right wing of the SP expelled the left wing and voted not to join the Comintern, Ruthenberg bolted from his support of Reed and Gitlow and their newly formed Communist Labor Party (CLP) and instead threw his support to the federations and their Communist Party. With his special standing as an American-born, organizationally capable leader of the left wing, Ruthenberg was elected executive secretary of the Communist Party.

Ruthenberg, Gitlow, and others were arrested late in 1919 for their role in the New York left-wing conference earlier in the year. Ruthenberg, among others, was found guilty of violating New York State's criminal anarchy law and was sentenced to five to ten years in Sing Sing prison. Ruthenberg served eighteen months of the sentence from 1920 to 1922 before he was released.

From the initial split in Chicago until 1923, Ruthenberg attempted to bring all factions together in a unified Communist Party. After the First Comintern Congress echoed this same desire in January 1920, Ruthenberg split the Communist Party and joined his faction to the Communist Labor Party, forming the United Communist Party (UCP) in meetings in Bridgman, Michigan. Alfred Wagenknecht, executive secretary of the CLP, emerged as the executive secretary of the merged party, and Ruthenberg became editor of the party's paper, *The Communist*. Though serving his time in Sing Sing in 1921, Ruthenberg was elected executive secretary of the fully merged underground party, the Communist Party of America, when the UCP and the Russian-language federations finally joined together under pressure from Moscow. Ruthenberg retained this position when the aboveground Workers Party was formed in December 1921.

Ruthenberg left prison in 1922 and entered the ongoing conflict over the nature of the Party. The underground Communist Party of America had been kept alive by the more radical language federations after the formation of the Workers

Party, and Ruthenberg opposed this two-party system as divisive. He led the "liquidators," the faction that worked to eliminate the secret shadow party and to centralize all Party functions in the Workers Party, against the "geese," the more radical elements who favored an underground party. Ruthenberg's war with the "geese" ended when the underground party was dissolved after American delegates to the Fourth Comintern Congress in November 1922 were told that such a final action must be taken.

In August 1922 Ruthenberg was arrested again when he attended a secret Party convention in Bridgman, Michigan. He and William Z. Foster (q.v.), head of the Trade Union Educational League, were both tried under Michigan's criminal syndicalism statute of 1919. Ruthenberg served as an "expert" witness on communism for Foster's trial. Unlike Foster, who was freed by a hung jury, Ruthenberg was found guilty in his own trial in May 1923. Ultimately, he would serve only twenty days of his sentence before he was freed when the case was appealed to the U.S. Supreme Court in January 1925.

In December 1922 Ruthenberg was denied a seat at the Conference for Progressive Political Action (CPPA), which was meeting in Cleveland to discuss a farm-labor alliance. In July 1923 Ruthenberg led the Communists to a successful takeover of the CPPA's Chicago convention, which resulted in the formation of the Federated Farmer-Labor Party. This move destroyed Foster's credibility in the labor movement and resulted in a deep factional dispute in the Communist Party throughout the 1920s. The trade union faction under Foster favored working through the workplace as the greatest locus of Communist agitation, while the faction led by Ruthenberg and backed by John Pepper (q.v.), Max Bedacht (q.v.), and Jay Lovestone (q.v.) believed that all decisions must be made on the basis of their effect on the political life of the Party. In December 1923 Foster's faction took control of the Workers Party Executive Committee at the third party convention and installed Foster in the new office of Party chairman but kept Ruthenberg in his office of executive secretary. Foster's faction lost its majority at the 1925 fourth convention of the Workers Party after attempting to remove Ruthenberg as executive secretary when the Comintern's representative, S. I. Gusev, produced a telegram from Moscow ordering the American Party to retain Ruthenberg and to give his faction control of the Executive Committee. This move came a few months after Ruthenberg returned from his first trip to the Soviet Union, where his leadership of the American Party had been affirmed by the Fifth Plenum of the Comintern.

Ruthenberg traveled again to Russia in 1926, when he was elected to the Presidium of the Comintern, a post to which he was reelected in 1927. Ruthenberg had served as a candidate member of the Comintern's Executive Committee in 1922 and was elected a full member in 1924.

Ruthenberg died on March 2, 1927, from peritonitis after an emergency appendectomy in Chicago. At his own request, he was cremated and interred in the wall of the Kremlin, joining John Reed, the only other American to be so honored.

SOURCES: Theodore Draper, *American Communism and Soviet Russia* (1960); Stephen M. Millett, "Charles E. Ruthenberg: The Development of an American Communist, 1909–1927," *Ohio History* 81 (Summer 1972); C. Oakley Johnson, *The Day Is Coming: Life and Work of Charles E. Ruthenberg* (1957).

*JOHN P. BECK*

# S

**SACCO, NICOLA (1890–1927), and VANZETTI, BARTOLOMEO (1888–1927).** Nicola Sacco and Bartolomeo Vanzetti were the cause célèbres and martyrs of the American—and worldwide—Left during the 1920s. Both died in the Massachusetts electric chair for murders most radicals were vocally certain they did not commit. Both were born in Italy, Sacco in 1890, Vanzetti in 1888.

Sacco migrated to the United States in 1908, where he became a shoeworker and security guard in Massachusetts shoe factories. An anarchist, he was a follower of Errico Malatesta—a late-nineteenth-century advocate of violent "propaganda of the deed." Sacco was an active union member and was considered an honest militant by his co-workers.

Vanzetti was educated in Italian grade school. He was apprenticed to a baker between 1901 and 1908, at which time he migrated to the United States. In the States, Vanzetti worked as a dishwasher, a chef, a quarryman, a construction worker, a cordage employee, and finally as a fish peddler. Although Vanzetti was an anarchist, he belonged to a less militant group than Sacco.

Both men were arrested while traveling on a streetcar near Brockton, Massachusetts, and charged with the May 1920 murder of a guard and a paymaster in a $15,776 payroll holdup in South Braintree, Massachusetts. Both were convicted of first-degree murder on July 14, 1921, in the Norfolk County, Massachusetts, Superior Court. The judge in the case, Webster Thayer, displayed extreme prejudice against the two Italian anarchists and against radicals in general. The conviction set off a series of riots, bombings, and demonstrations throughout the world. The U.S. Embassy was bombed in Buenos Aires, Montevideo, and Paris, and other American legations were threatened. There were riots with fatalities in European and American cities.

The case created new animosity among the various radical groups. The Sacco and Vanzetti Defense Committee leaders charged that Communists were siphoning off a large part of the contributions to the defense fund for their own purposes.

And other radicals claimed that Socialists, union officials, and others were not doing enough for the pair.

Sacco and Vanzetti remained in prison for more than six years awaiting their execution. Judge Thayer denied all motions for a new trial, even after convicted murderer Celestino Madieros swore that he had seen the Morelli gang of Providence, Rhode Island, kill the guard and paymaster. Governor Alvin T. Fuller named a commission—composed of extremely conservative university administrators and a judge—that agreed with Fuller and Thayer that the men had received fair trials.

Sacco went on a hunger strike, for which he was sent to a mental hospital in Bridgewater, Massachusetts. Vanzetti was also sent to the hospital. But both men were ruled to be sane, and they were returned to the death house of the state prison in Boston's Charlestown district. Appeals were then made to state and federal courts to overturn the guilty verdict. All the courts refused to act, generally on grounds of lack of jurisdiction. President Calvin Coolidge refused to answer appeals sent to him by foreign and American leaders. Supreme Court Justices Oliver Wendell Holmes and Harlan Fiske Stone could not act because, they said, the case was outside their jurisdiction. Chief Justice William Howard Taft reported that he was out of the country. And Justice Louis Brandeis reported he could not act because he and his family knew too many of those closely connected with the defense.

Pleas came from all over the world to the governor of Massachusetts. Among those urging him to spare the two anarchists were famed scientists David Starr Jordan and Alexander Meikeljohn, editor Oswald Garrison Villard, muckraker Ida Tarbell, writer Floyd Dell, Mayor John Hylan of New York, liberal Republican Representative Fiorello LaGuardia, noted attorney Frank Walsh, civil libertarian Arthur Garfield Hays, and Colonel Alfred Dreyfus, himself the victim of a miscarriage of justice in France. Renowned American poet Edna St. Vincent Millay wrote a poem for the pair. Almost all the leaders of organized labor in the United States pleaded with Governor Fuller to commute their sentences, but to no avail.

Shortly after midnight on August 23, 1927, more than seven years after the slayings had occurred and while hundreds of thousands demonstrated for their lives all over the civilized world, Sacco and Vanzetti were executed.

SOURCE: Francis Russell, *Tragedy at Dedham* (1962).

*BERNARD K. JOHNPOLL*

**ST. JOHN, VINCENT (1876–1929).** Vincent St. John was a leading figure in the Industrial Workers of the World (IWW) during the first nine years (1905–1914) of the syndicalist organization's existence. He was born in Newport, Kentucky, in 1876, and he lived in the Mountain States, where his father was a Pony Express rider. At age 19 St. John became a miner in Colorado and a member of the Western Federation of Miners (WFM), the radical union of metallurgical ore miners centered in the Rocky Mountain States. At 26 he became the leader of the miners' local in Telluride, Colorado, and led the strike there. During that strike the mine operators attempted to have St. John indicted in the murder of a mine manager, but their evidence proved to be too meager. In 1902 St. John was the hero in a rescue of trapped miners. He suffered serious injuries in the rescue but saved the lives of the miners. The next year he was elected to the general executive board of the WFM.

When the IWW was formed in 1905, St. John was a leader of the WFM, its largest affiliate. The next year, when the WFM decided to withdraw from the IWW, St. John remained in the new organization and within a year resigned from the WFM executive. During the bloody feuding in Goldfields, Nevada, in 1907, St. John led the IWW faction. In the course of the fighting, he was shot in his right hand and was crippled permanently.

At the 1906 convention of the IWW, St. John joined William Trautmann and Daniel DeLeon (q.v.) in ousting the moderate faction led by Charles Sherman. The triumvirate formed a temporary coalition; within two years they split over issues of ideology and tactics. DeLeon favored a politically oriented union body, St. John and Trautmann were apolitical. DeLeon lost the struggle, and the St. John–Trautmann coalition gained complete control of the IWW at the 1908 convention. St. John was named general organizer of the IWW.

St. John's views of politics and trade unions were purely syndicalist, although they had anarchistic undertones. In 1910 he wrote his most important pamphlet, "Political Parties and the I.W.W.," whose basic theme was that economic (i.e., labor union) power was the key to the workers' liberation. There could be no political power for the workers until they had achieved such economic unity. "It is impossible for anyone to be a part of the capitalist state and to use the machinery of the state in the interest of the workers." The power of the state was in the hands of the capitalist class, which controlled all the wealth. The state, he argued, was the executive committee of the capitalist class. The workers did have power, St. John maintained, but the "only power the working class has is the power to produce wealth." And the workers could win only by controlling use of their labor to be able to stop the production of wealth except upon terms dictated by the workers themselves. St. John would repeat this theme during his entire tenure as a leader of the IWW, especially in his testimony before the U.S. Commission on Industrial Relations in 1914.

Tired and disillusioned, St. John resigned from the IWW in 1915. With financial aid from labor lawyer Frank Walsh of Montana, St. John went prospecting in New Mexico and Colorado. In 1917—more than two years after he had resigned from the IWW—St. John was arrested along with more than one hundred other IWW members, leaders, and former leaders as an opponent of American participation in World War I. He was convicted and given a long prison sentence. After he was released, St. John returned to New Mexico to prospect again. But his health had given out, and Vincent St. John died in 1929—almost forgotten (except for an obituary article in the IWW publication *Industrial Solidarity*).

SOURCES: Paul Brissenden, *The I.W.W.: A Study of American Syndicalism* (1922); Vincent St. John, *Political Parties and the I.W.W.* (1910), reprinted in Joyce Kornbluh (ed.), *Rebel Voices* (1964); Fred Thompson, *The I.W.W.: Its First Fifty Years* (1955).
                                                                    BERNARD K. JOHNPOLL

**SALUTSKY, J. B. (1882–1968).** J. B. Salutsky Hardman (he added the last name in 1924) was a prominent intellectual who founded the Socialist Party's Jewish Federation, formed an alliance with the Communist Party but soon broke with them, and devoted a decade to building a radical American party. Salutsky was born on August 25, 1882, in a village near Zelva, Russia. His father owned a lumber business, where his son went to work at age 15. The young Salutsky quit in 1902 and joined the Jewish Bund. For the next several years Salutsky was a Bund activist, serving as president of a union of bank employees in Vilna and secretary of the central body of labor unions in Kiev, participating in the 1905 Russian Revolution and being imprisoned three separate times. He also briefly attended the St. Petersburg Law School.

After spending 1908 in Paris, Salutsky came to the United States in 1909 and did graduate work at Columbia University for two years. He began writing for the Yiddish press in New York and doing research for the International Ladies Garment Workers Union. Salutsky was the first secretary of the Jewish Federation of the Socialist Party, established in 1912, and he edited *Di Naye Welt* from 1914 to 1920. One of the leaders of Jewish socialism in the United States, he opposed the party's left wing in 1919 and kept the Federation from going over to the Communist Party. Salutsky opposed the Socialist Party's "conservatism" but scorned the Communists' views on revolution, unions, and illegality as dangerously leftist. He was active in the Committee for a Third International, which sought to affiliate the Socialists with the Comintern in 1920. The following year he broke with the Socialist Party and helped form the Workers Council. Salutsky continued to oppose affiliation with the Communists, but he went along anyway when the Council joined the Communists in the Workers Party in 1921 and he was placed on the National Executive Committee. By the end of the year he was avoiding meetings. Salutsky was expelled from the Communist movement in 1923 for refusing to submit to Party discipline.

For many years he was associated with the Amalgamated Clothing Workers union. He was its educational director from 1920 to 1940 and edited *Advance*, its journal, from 1920 to 1944. From 1929 to 1933 he was on the Executive Committee of A. J. Muste's (q.v.) Conference for Progressive Labor Action and actively supported its transformation into the American Workers Party (AWP) late in 1933, hoping to create an indigenous radical party. He bitterly opposed allowing the Trotskyists to join the AWP in 1934 and quit after they were allowed in, ending his active political work in the radical movement. By 1936 he was a supporter of Franklin Roosevelt.

During World War II, Salutsky (now Hardman) was president of the American Labor Press Association. Thereafter, he wrote, taught, and lectured frequently on the labor movement. He died on January 29, 1968.

SOURCES: Theodore Draper, *The Roots of American Communism* (1967); J. B. S. Hardman Papers, Tamiment Library, New York University, New York City.

                                                                    *HARVEY KLEHR*

**SAPOSS, DAVID (1886–1968).** David Joseph Saposs was a Social Democratic scholar and publicist. He served in academic, labor, and government posts from 1907 to 1968 and was the author of fourteen books. Saposs was born David Joseph Sapostnik to an Orthodox Jewish family in Kiev, Russia on February 22, 1886. In 1895 the family migrated to Milwaukee, soon thereafter adopting the name Saposs. David Saposs' father was a ragpicker. David left school after the fifth grade to help support the family, but later continued his education in business school. Early experiences in the Brewery Workers Union and the Milwaukee Socialist Party, which he briefly joined while in college, shaped his political views. Saposs entered the University of Wisconsin in 1907. He became an associate writer in the John R. Commons–directed project *History of Labor in the United States* (4 vols., 1918–1935).

In 1914 Saposs was an investigator for the U.S. Commission on Industrial Relations and in 1917–1918 for the New York Department of Labor. In 1919–1920 he investigated the steel strike for the Inter-Church World Movement. In 1920–1921 he was educational director of the Amalgamated Clothing Workers. Between 1920 and 1926 he was an instructor at Brookwood Labor College and pursued graduate study at Columbia University. In 1935 he became chief economist for the National Labor Relations Board. He resigned in 1940, following unfounded accusations of Communist sympathies. He subsequently worked for the U.S. Department of Labor and the European Recovery Program.

Saposs left government in 1952 and returned to academic life. He wrote several books on labor history, notably the anti-Stalinist *Communism in American Unions* (1959). He died on November 13, 1968.

SOURCE: David J. Saposs Papers, State Historical Society of Wisconsin, Madison, Wisconsin.

                                                            *BARBARA BARTKOWIAK*

**SCHERER, MARCEL (1899–1967).** Marcel Scherer, head of several Communist Party fronts and founder of a Communist-dominated union for professionals, was born on August 9, 1899, in Bucharest, Rumania. His father, a Jewish metalworker, brought the family to New York in 1900. Scherer joined the Young People's Socialist League while still in high school. At the City College of New York he was briefly suspended in 1917 for refusing to serve in the Reserve Officers Training Corps (ROTC) and was called "the Bolshevik chemist." He graduated in 1919, the same year he became a charter member of the Communist Labor Party.

After working several years as a chemist, Scherer became a Party functionary. He attended the Lenin School in Moscow from 1930 to 1931. On his return to the United States he became secretary of the Workers International Relief and later national secretary of the Friends of the Soviet Union. In 1933 he founded a group designed to stimulate Party work among scientists and technicians; it later evolved into a small CIO (Congress of Industrial Organizations) union, the Federation of Architects, Engineers, Chemists, and Technicians. Scherer served as its executive vice-president and from 1941 to 1943 as its organizer in California. Both he and the union were often charged with aiding and abetting the transfer of military and industrial secrets to the Soviet Union, but no charges were ever filed.

Scherer was removed from his union position in 1943 after union opponents accused him of being too solicitous of Party interests. Scherer went on to become an organizer for such other Party-dominated unions as the Office and Professional Workers and the United Electrical Workers. In 1950 he headed the Party's National Labor Conference for Peace, which pressed support of the Stockholm Peace Appeal. He died on June 5, 1967.

SOURCE: FBI File 100–107137.

*HARVEY KLEHR*

**SCHNEIDERMAN, WILLIAM (1905–1985).** For two decades, William Schneiderman directed the Communist Party's work in California. He was born on December 14, 1905, in Tsaritsyn, Russia, to a Jewish family that moved to the United States in 1908. He grew up in Chicago, where his father was a garment worker, and moved to Los Angeles at the age of 12. Schneiderman worked in a warehouse and finished high school at night. Influenced by the Bolshevik Revolution, he joined the Party's Young Workers League (YWL) in 1921 and the Workers Party (Communist Party) itself in 1923. After two years at the University of California at Los Angeles (he finally got his degree in 1926), he went to work full-time. By 1928 he was head of the YWL in California, and the following year he was made the Party's organizational secretary in the state.

Schneiderman was outside California for the first half of the 1930s, serving first as district organizer in Connecticut (1931) and then in Minnesota (1932–1934), where he got 5,000 votes in a campaign for governor in 1932. He was in Moscow from 1934 until after the Seventh Comintern Congress as an American representative to the Communist International. He returned to California in October 1935 as the Party's district organizer and remained in charge in the state for twenty-one years. Under his guidance, California Communists made impressive strides.

In 1939 the government attempted to denaturalize Schneiderman on the grounds that he had been a communist in 1927, the year he became a citizen. The lower courts stripped him of citizenship. Wendell Willkie argued his case before the Supreme Court, which ruled in 1943 that the government had not demonstrated in a clear and compelling way that Schneiderman's conduct violated his oath of allegiance to the United States. Schneiderman was being readied to take charge of the Party's national office after its leadership went to prison in 1951. However, he himself was arrested and sentenced to five years in prison on Smith Act charges in 1952.

The California Party had always enjoyed some independence from the national office because of distance and was less inclined to follow Party "diktats." Schneiderman had reservations about the Party leadership's belief that fascism was impending in the United States, and the California defendants based their appeal not on the correctness of their views but on their constitutional rights of advocacy. The Supreme Court overturned their convictions in 1957 in *Yates v. U.S.* Schneiderman died in January 1985.

SOURCES: *Schneiderman v. U.S.*, 320 U.S. 118; William Schneiderman, *Dissent on Trial* (1983).

HARVEY KLEHR

**SCUDDER, VIDA (1861–1954).** Vida Scudder was an educator, scholar, and Christian Socialist, born in 1861 in India, where her father was a Protestant minister. She was a member of the first class of Girls Latin School in Boston and received a B.A. degree from Smith College in 1884 and an M.A. from Wellesley College in 1889. She was awarded an honorary L.H.D. from Wellesley in 1922. She was a leading Franciscan scholar.

Scudder became a social radical while studying at Oxford University after attending John Ruskin's last lectures. In 1887 she accepted a position in the English Department at Wellesley College, where she remained for forty-one years. That same year she became one of the founders of what later became the College Settlement Association. Scudder took a one-year leave from Wellesley in 1891 to help officially open Boston's Dennison House, which later became a meeting place for several labor groups. She was a member of William D. P. Bliss' (q.v.) Society of Christian Socialists, a charter member of the Brotherhood of the Carpenter, and active in the Christian Social Union. In 1899 she was elected a delegate to Boston's Central Labor Union.

Scudder suffered a "breakdown" in 1901 and spent the next two years traveling throughout Europe. Upon her return, she indicated her belief that more radical solutions were needed to solve current social problems and became active in Socialist activities. She was involved in organizing the Women's Trade Union League and was a founding member of the Episcopal Church Socialist League. She joined the Socialist Party in 1911. In 1912 she published *Socialism and Character*, which attempted to reconcile the apparent differences between Christianity and Marxism. A speech she gave in Lawrence, Massachusetts, during the 1912 textile strike led to calls for her resignation from Wellesley (although she was never officially asked to resign). Her 1917 support of President Woodrow Wilson's decision to enter the war caused a break with her pacifist friends.

Scudder organized the Church League for Industrial Democracy in 1919, which brought together both liberal and radical Episcopal Church members committed to the cause of social justice. Through her activities in helping to reorganize the

Intercollegiate Socialist Society into the League for Industrial Democracy, she formed a lasting friendship with Norman Thomas (q.v.). In 1923 she lectured at the Women's International League for Peace and Freedom near Prague.

Two years after her formal retirement in 1930, she became the first dean of the summer school of Christian ethics at Wellesley. In addition, she lectured at the New School for Social Research. Her autobiography, *On Journey*, was published in 1937, and its sequel, *My Quest for Reality*, was published in 1952.

Vida Scudder died in 1954 at the age of 92 while at her home in Wellesley after choking on a piece of food.

*JANET S. GREENLEE*

**SEALE, BOBBY (b.1936).** Bobby Seale was a leading black activist during the mid- and late 1960s. He received extraordinary notoriety in the aftermath of the Chicago riots that accompanied the 1968 Democratic National convention. Seale was born in Dallas, Texas, on October 22, 1936. He served three years in the air force and was dishonorably discharged after a fight during a racial incident.

During the Cuban missile crisis of 1962, Seale was attracted to a young black speaker, Huey Newton (q.v.), who was addressing a crowd at Merritt Junior College, where both were enrolled. What captured Seale's imagination was Newton's straightforward rejection of the middle-class civil rights movement and his contention that economics lay at the root of the problem for blacks in the United States. Their relationship gradually developed over the next few years, and they founded the Black Panther Party in 1966. The Panthers, who advocated armed self-defense and an avowedly Marxist-Leninist philosophy, received much media attention in the late 1960s.

In 1968 Seale went to Chicago and participated in the demonstrations at the Democratic national convention. Along with seven others, he was charged with planning the riot that erupted. At the 1969 trial, Seale repeatedly disrupted Judge Julius Hoffman's court, so much so that he was eventually bound and gagged for appearance in the courtroom. His trial behavior made him the symbol of black anger and frustration at a time when urban ghetto riots had made black rage a major issue in American life.

Seale was convicted of contempt of court for his outbursts, but the case was eventually dropped. In 1971 he faced murder charges involving the death of a fellow Panther. The much-publicized trial ended with a hung jury and was not retried. In the years that followed, Seale and Newton moved the Black Panther Party away from its militant stance of the late 1960s toward a community-action orientation dealing with social problems of urban ghettos. He ran unsuccessfully for mayor of Oakland in 1973, the year he left the Panthers and formed the group Advocates Scene, which sponsored community action programs.

SOURCES: Donald Freed, *Agony in New Haven* (1973); Bobby Seale, *A Lonely Rage* (1978) and *Seize the Time* (1970).

*TOM WILLIAMS*

**SEIDEL, EMIL (1864–1947).** Emil Seidel was the first Socialist mayor of Milwaukee (1910–1912), a member of the city's board of aldermen for twelve years (1904–1908, 1916–1920, 1932–1936), Socialist candidate for U.S. Vice-President in the most successful national campaign in the party's history, and a leader of the party's moderate wing. He was born in the anthracite mining region near Pottsville in northeastern Pennsylvania in December 1864. His family moved to Wisconsin while he was still a baby and finally settled in Milwaukee when Emil was 4 years old. Most of his education was in the public schools of that city. He was sent to Germany as a teenager to study wood carving.

While in Germany, Seidel was converted to socialism, and upon his return he became active in the Socialist movement in Milwaukee. He was first active in the Socialist wing of the Populist Party, which broke away after the 1896 election to form the Social Democratic Party of Wisconsin. He played a major role in the founding of that party in 1897 and in the organization of the national Social Democratic Party that year. He also was active in the 1900 election campaign, in which the American Socialists ran their first presidential ticket of Eugene V. Debs (q.v.) for President and Job Harriman (q.v.) for Vice-President. Seidel supported Victor Berger (q.v.) during most of the internal debates within the new Socialist Party.

In 1902 Seidel was nominated as a Social Democratic candidate for the board of aldermen. Although defeated, he and the other Socialist candidates polled a large vote. Two years later, Seidel and eight other Socialists were elected to the board. They used their positions to attack the corruption that was endemic in Milwaukee municipal politics at that time. Seidel was reelected in 1906, but he resigned from the board in 1908 to run against the corrupt administration of Democratic Mayor David S. Rose. Although Rose was elected, Seidel polled almost one-third of the total vote. In the 1910 election, Seidel and the Socialists were swept into office. They elected twenty-one of the city's thirty-five aldermen, the city attorney, the city treasurer, and the city controller, plus a majority on the county board of supervisors. But there was little the Socialists could do once in office. Control of the city activities was in the hands of the state government, and attempts at giving the city home rule invariably were rejected by the state government. Moreover, the minority non-Socialist members of the board of aldermen were well versed in the operation of the city legislature, and the inexperienced Socialists were not.

Despite the legal disabilities under which the Socialist regime suffered, its accomplishments were many and significant. First, the Socialist administration made the government open. It also eliminated graft, and it turned a slovenly city government into one of great efficiency. Mayor Seidel hired renowned economist John R. Commons to head a commission that proposed a major streamlining of the city's operation.

The Seidel regime raised the wages and reduced the hours of work of municipal employees. It also forced the local utility—Milwaukee Electric Railway and Light Company—to reduce its rates and was generally sympathetic to laboring people in that city. In addition, Seidel's regime beautified the city, expanded and reorganized the library into one of the finest in the United States, and organized free concerts for the city's residents.

By 1912 the state legislature had changed the electoral procedures in Milwaukee, making them basically nonpartisan. Moreover, in 1912 the issue of graft had faded into the past and the Republicans and Democrats ran a joint ticket. Seidel was defeated for reelection despite a 3,000-vote increase. Most other Milwaukee Socialists were also defeated that year.

In the internal strife then buffeting the Socialist Party nationally, Seidel sided with the so-called right wing headed by Victor Berger. This faction of the party was vehemently opposed to the Industrial Workers of the World (IWW) and was friendly toward the existing trade unions in the American Federation of Labor (AFL). The perennial Socialist candidate, Eugene V. Debs, was in the left wing, which favored industrial unions and opposed the leadership of the AFL, although it was divided on the relationship between the Socialists and the IWW.

At the 1912 Socialist national convention the right-wingers decided to oppose Debs as the party's standard-bearer. They nominated Seidel as Deb's opponent (another group of moderate Socialists centered in New York–nominated Charles Edward Russell to also oppose Debs). Debs was again nominated, although Seidel polled more than one-fifth of the delegate's vote, carrying several Western and Midwestern states. To keep peace in the party, Seidel was chosen the candidate for Vice-President. The Debs-Seidel ticket polled approximately 900,000 votes (6 percent of the total cast), a Socialist record that would never be surpassed.

After the 1912 elections Seidel spent four years recuperating from various illnesses. In 1916 he resumed his political career; he was elected alderman-at-large in Milwaukee and was reelected in 1918. Two years later Seidel left the board and became secretary of the Socialist Party of Wisconsin. He resigned from the party post in 1932 and was elected that year to the board of aldermen again. He served until 1936 when, at age 72, he retired from electoral politics, but he remained active in the Socialist Party until his death in June 1947.

SOURCES: Seidel's papers are in various collections, including the Seidel Papers at the Milwaukee County Historical Society; the Milwaukee Social Democratic Collection at the same institution; and the Socialist Party of America Collection at Duke University, Durham, North Carolina (available in microfilm from Microfilm Corporation of America). See also Sally Miller, "Milwaukee: Of Ethnicity and Labor," in *Socialism and the Cities*, ed. Bruce M. Stave (1975), esp. pp. 41–55; Frederick I. Olson, "The Milwaukee Socialists, 1897–1941" (Ph.D. diss., Harvard University, 1952); Marvin Wachman, *History of the Social-Democratic Party of Milwaukee, 1897–1910* (1945).

                                                                        *JAMES INGBRETSON*

**SHACHTMAN, MAX (1904–1972).** Max Shachtman, together with James P. Cannon (q.v.) and Martin Abern (q.v.), was a founder of the American Trotskyist movement and the leading theorist in defining Soviet society as a new exploitive system of bureaucratic collectivism. For fifty years he was at the center of international social and political controversies and made significant contributions to the movements of the non-Communist Left, as a tireless agitator, an informed and formidable debater, a pamphleteer, and a brilliant and witty polemicist.

Shachtman was born on September 10, 1904, in Warsaw, Poland, and came to the United States, settling in New York City, with his Jewish parents when he was 8 months old. He entered the City College of New York in 1920 but dropped out in the first semester because of illness.

The Socialist Party was then sharply divided over its attitude to the Russian Revolution and its relationship to the new Communist International that emerged from it. Shachtman was stimulated by the controversies to read Socialist literature and the theories of Marx and Engels and to attend street meetings. Shachtman identified himself with the party's broad and diverse Left Wing. At the age of 17 he joined the Workers Councils, a U.S. version of the Russian workers soviets, led by J.B. Salutsky (q.v.) and Alexander Trachtenberg (q.v.). These supported the Russian Revolution and the Communist International but were critical of the American Communist Party.

The Workers Councils dissolved in 1922 and entered the Workers Party, the legal organization of the underground Communist Party. In 1922 too, as a member of the Communist Party, Shachtman met Martin Abern, national secretary of the Young Workers League, who had just returned from Moscow, where he had attended the Fourth Congress of the Communist International and the Second Congress of the Communist Youth International. Recognizing Shachtman's talents, Abern persuaded him to take over the editorship of the *Young Worker* in Chicago and to function in the youth leadership at the National Center. At the beginning of 1923, at the age of 19, Shachtman began his career as a "professional revolutionary."

The next six years, until 1928, was a period of political maturing for Shachtman. Upon relinquishing his posts in the youth organization, he became an alternate member of the Party's Central Committee, an editor of the *Daily Worker*, and a national spokesman for the Party. As a leading member of the Cannon faction of the Party, Shachtman became editor of the *Labor Defender*, the magazine of the International Labor Defense (ILD). The ILD grew into a large organization, and the magazine had a wide circulation. Two years later Shachtman attended the Seventh Plenum of the Comintern and the Congress of the Young Communist International. He was also a delegate to the congresses of the International Red Aid in Moscow in 1925 and 1927.

In 1928 a new stage was reached in his political life. James P. Cannon returned from the Sixth Congress of the Communist International, where he was a member of the Program Commission and had become acquainted for the first time with the views of Leon Trotsky in his struggle with Stalin. He brought back Trotsky's *Criticism of the Draft Program of the Communist International*. Cannon convinced his two closest associates, Shachtman and Abern, of the validity of Trotsky's views. As a result, the three, members of the Central Committee, were expelled first from the Committee and then the Party. Soon dozens of Party members throughout the nation were expelled for voicing support for the "three generals without an army," as the *Daily Worker* described them.

An organized Trotskyist movement made its sudden appearance in the United States in May 1929, when a conference in Chicago of the expelled representatives created the Communist League of America. The new organization published the *Militant*, which was for many years the official organ of American Trotskyism. Shachtman was its editor during the whole period of the life of the Communist League up until 1934, when it was unified with the American Workers Party led by A. J. Muste (q.v.) and took the name Workers Party.

In addition to his literary and journalistic efforts, Shachtman was a member of the National and Political Committees of the Trotskyist movement from 1929 to 1940, during which time his chief contributions were as a political leader of the movement second only to Cannon. During this period Shachtman was the first American to meet Trotsky and his wife, Natalia Sedova, after their deportation to Turkey, visiting the exiled revolutionary leader in Prinkipo in 1930 and again in 1933, when he accompanied Trotsky and Natalia from Turkey to France when they moved to that country. In 1937 he was a member of the Party that greeted the Trotskys at Tampico, Mexico, when they arrived at their last place of exile. When Trotsky was assassinated by an agent of the Russian secret police in August 1940, Shachtman flew to Coyoacán to be with Natalia Sedova on behalf of the newly formed Workers Party.

In 1934 Shachtman and Martin Abern founded the *New International*, which was issued almost without interruption until 1958. During the mid–1930s, in connection with the Moscow trials and as part of the Trotskyist reply to Stalin's charges, Shachtman wrote *Behind the Moscow Trials: The Greatest Frame-up in History*.

Prior to the convention of the Workers Party in the spring of 1936, Shachtman joined Cannon in advocating that the Party should dissolve and that its members should enter the Socialist Party, which they considered a broader arena in which the Trotskyists could function. They won the support of the majority of the membership for this proposal, and following the convention the Party dissolved and its members entered the Socialist Party. The stay of the Trotskyists in the Socialist Party was anything but peaceful, differences emerging on many questions of policy, domestic and international, especially on the question of the party's attitude to the Spanish People's Front government. The Trotskyists were expelled from the party in 1937, and on January 1, 1938, the expelled formed the Socialist Workers Party (SWP). Cannon and Shachtman, who directed the strategy of the Trotskyists in the Socialist Party, remained close politically until July 1939, when the outbreak of World War II and increased tensions on the Russian question began to separate the two.

The differences growing out of the effects of the Hitler-Stalin Pact of 1939 split the SWP down the middle, with Shachtman as the principal spokesman for The Minority, which opposed the traditional Trotskyist position of "Defense of the Soviet Union" in relation to the invasion and partition of Finland by the

Red army. Members of this opposition questioned the validity of the Trotskyist view that the Soviet Union was a workers state, degenerated or otherwise. The sharp polemics between Trotsky and the Shachtman-led Minority culminated in a split and the formation of a new Workers Party in April 1940.

The Workers Party, eventually to call itself the Independent Socialist League (ISL), expressed its new views through the *New International* and a weekly paper, *Labor Action*. Shachtman directed the discussion of the nature of the Soviet Union in the Workers party that resulted in the adoption of the unique view that Soviet Russia was a new type of exploitive and oppressive society, neither capitalist nor socialist; this new phenomenon was termed "bureaucratic collectivism." Shachtman compiled his writings on the subject in *The Bureaucratic Revolution: The Rise of the Stalinist State*, published in 1962. He made several national speaking tours and lectured frequently in these years. Most significant were his debates with Earl Browder (q.v.), deposed national secretary of the Communist Party; Alexander Kerensky, head of the provisional government in the 1917 February Revolution in Russia; and Friedrich Von Hayek, author of *The Road to Serfdom*.

In the early 1950s, Shachtman and his associates challenged the attorney general's listing of the organization and its affiliates on the "Subversive List." After several years of skirmishing with the government in hearings where Shachtman was the main witness for the Workers Party, the ISL, and their youth organization, they succeeded in winning their case and in being removed from the attorney general's list.

Though politically now poles apart from Trotsky, Shachtman nonetheless remained the American editor of his works. Despite his break with Trotsky, he had a close political and personal relationship with Natalia Sedova Trotsky, who also did not believe the Soviet Union to be a workers state. She subsequently resigned from the Fourth International because of her deep political differences with it.

Max Shachtman and his political allies continued to reexamine Socialist theory and program during the 1950s, with the aim of resolving many theoretical and political doubts that they developed following the split from the SWP in 1940. They came to reject the Leninist concept of the Party and the one-party state and held that the totalitarian degeneration of the Russian Revolution was inherent in the dominant ideology of the founder of Bolshevism and his ideological system, a view that brought them closer to the Socialist Party. Shachtman and his comrades concentrated their political propaganda on the defense of democracy against all exploitive and oppressive regimes, whether right wing or Stalinist. Having declared their views democratic Socialist, Shachtman, the ISL, and its youth wing joined the Socialist Party in 1958.

In debates and dialogues inside the Socialist Party, Shachtman stressed the idea that no democratic Socialist movement could prosper without intimate ties with the American labor movement, nor could the broad democratic Socialist organization flourish without encompassing a wide spectrum of theoretical and political views contending in open discussion.

Although he developed coronary problems in the 1950s, Shachtman did not curtail his political activities. He continued to exert a significant influence on the party. He spoke frequently and lectured at numerous universities. Shachtman's political importance was widely recognized, and over the years influenced many contemporaries, notably Bayard Rustin (q.v.) and James T. Farrell (q.v.). This influence, in one form or another, embraced many younger, developing writers, intellectuals, and labor activists, including Saul Bellow, Irving Howe (q.v.), Norman Hill, Harvey Swados, Isaac Rosenfeld, and Michael Harrington (q.v.).

In the 1960s Shachtman saw the Democratic Party as the arena of social and political struggle and the place where the labor movement and Socialists should work to move the nation toward social democracy and a freer nation. Having begun his political life attracted to the democracy of socialism, he returned to it in his later years as an advocate of democratic socialism. He died on November 4, 1972.

SOURCES: Solon DeLeon, *The American Labor Who's Who* (1925); Theodore Draper, *American Communism and Soviet Russia* (1960); Albert Glotzer, "Max Shachtman, An Obituary," *New America*, November 15, 1972.

*ALBERT GLOTZER*

**SIMONS, ALGIE M. (1870–1950).** Algie M. Simons was a Socialist writer, publicist, and editor between 1897 and 1917. He turned anti-Socialist during World War I. Born in Baraboo, Wisconsin, a small industrial city about forty miles north of Madison, in 1870, Simons was educated in the public schools of Sauk County, Wisconsin, and at the University of Wisconsin. At the university he studied under Professors Frederick Jackson Turner and Richard T. Ely. He was Ely's research assistant when the noted labor economist was dismissed for vaguely supporting workers' right to organize in unions. As student assistant to Ely, he helped research the noted scholar's seminal work, *Socialism and Social Reform*, published in 1894 by Thomas Y. Crowell. The book was a plea for social reform as an alternative to socialism.

While at the University of Wisconsin, Simons also served as Madison campus reporter for the *Madison Democrat* and the *Chicago Record*. In 1895 he delivered the commencement address for his graduating class. The address, based on the Social Gospel, called for a major reform of society. Upon graduation Simons accepted a post as an investigator–social worker in Cincinnati, Ohio. After two months he left Cincinnati and accepted a post with the Chicago Bureau of Charities.

The conditions of working people in the packinghouse district of Chicago, most of them immigrants, were unbelievably poor. Simons used his position to attempt to get aid for residents of the district. He wrote a book, *Packingtown*, which described these conditions and told of how slaughterhouse workers were shortchanged by their employers, of the physical and emotional dangers for slaughterhouse workers, and of the poor housing that permeated their lives. This book, published in 1899 by Charles H. Kerr, had a major influence on Upton Sinclair (q.v.) and was instrumental in Sinclair's writing the novel *The Jungle* in 1906.

In 1897 Simons became convinced that social work and charity could not alleviate the poverty of the working people, so he joined the Socialist Labor Party (SLP). That year he also married May Wood, his high school sweetheart, who became his lifelong co-worker.

Simons was named editor of the Chicago SLP weekly, *Workers Call,* in 1899, just as the party was being torn asunder by internal infighting. The Chicago party remained aloof from the factional struggle until it became a target for Daniel DeLeon's (q.v.) animosity over two issues. First, it attempted to mediate the struggle between DeLeon's faction and the one headed by Morris Hillquit (q.v.). DeLeon opposed any settlement with Hillquit's supporters. Second, the Chicago SLP persisted in publishing its own newspaper instead of giving DeLeon and his New York–based *Weekly People* a nationwide Socialist monopoly. By 1900 the antagonism between DeLeon and the Chicago party had become irreconcilable, and the Midwesterners affiliated with the newly formed Social Democratic Party. Simons and his wife worked that year for the Socialist presidential ticket of Eugene V. Debs (q.v.) and Job Harriman (q.v.).

By 1901 Simons was a recognized leader of the more radical wing of the Social Democratic party. At the convention that united the Social Democratic Party with the Hillquit faction of the SLP to form the Socialist Party, Simons led the left-wing "Impossiblists," who rejected all social reform measures in the party platform. He also wanted the party to make a special drive for farmers, who he argued owned neither the farms they worked nor the machinery used on them; these items of capital belonged to the banks, the railroads, and the grain elevator owners. In 1901 Simons also became editor of the *International Socialist Review*, a theoretical journal published by Charles H. Kerr. He and his wife also toured the Midwest for the party and the *Review*, and in 1903 they became the faculty of the six-year-old Socialist institution of higher education, Ruskin College, in Trenton, Missouri.

Not only were the Simonses the total faculty of Ruskin, but Algie also wrote almost all the texts and wrote articles in the *Review* and ran the correspondence courses offered by Ruskin via the *Appeal to Reason*, the largest pro-Socialist newspaper in the nation. When Ruskin College failed, Simons and Ernest Untermann formed a new, short-lived Socialist college in Chicago: the Institute for Social Studies. While working on the *Review* and teaching at Ruskin, Simons wrote his two major works: *Class Struggles in American History* (1903) and *American History for the Workers*, which first appeared in the *Appeal to Reason* in 1906. By now Simons had become much more moderate in his Socialist conviction. At the 1904 party convention he called for immediate reform demands in the party platform.

The next year, Simons participated in the meeting from which the Industrial Workers of the World (IWW) was organized. He wrote the manifesto that the participants accepted and that served as the official IWW statement of principles. By 1906, however, Simons became disillusioned with the power DeLeon held over the IWW and left the organization, as did Debs. In 1906 Simons was named to the National Executive Committee of the Socialist Party. The next year he was sent as a delegate to the meeting of the Socialist International in Stuttgart, Germany.

The electoral success of British Labour Party in 1906—Labour won twenty-nine seats in Parliament—just as the Socialist vote began to show signs of decline in the United States turned Simons, who had previously been vehemently opposed to the idea of a labor party in the United States, into a vehement supporter of the idea. He did not advertise his changed position until 1909. In the meantime, Simons was named editor of the *Chicago Daily Socialist*, a moderate organ of the party. His obvious turn from the Left, his withdrawal from the IWW, his editorship of the Chicago daily, and disquieting rumors that he was about to support a labor party in the United States led Kerr to dismiss him as editor of the *Review*.

Simons' break with the party's left wing came just before the 1908 nominating convention. At that convention Simons' name was put in nomination for U.S. President by Seymour Stedman. Simons ran fourth of the four Socialists whose names were placed in nomination; Debs was renominated. Simons helped manage Debs' campaign.

The next year, Simons wrote a personal letter to left-wing party leader William English Walling (q.v.) suggesting that the Socialists be reorganized along the lines of the British Labour Party. Walling made the letter public and charged that a conspiracy, including Socialist leaders Hillquit, Victor Berger (q.v.), John Spargo (q.v.) and Robert Hunter, was attempting to dissolve the Socialist Party and replace it with a Labor Party dominated by the American Federation of Labor. The charges by Walling, although false, caused Simons to lose his seat on the National Executive Committee.

In 1910 Simons left Chicago and the *Daily Socialist* to become editor of the Socialist literary journal *Coming Nation* in Girard, Kansas. While editing the journal, Simons wrote *Social Forces in American History*, a Marxist interpretation of U.S. history. After *Coming Nation* collapsed in 1913, Simons went to Milwaukee to help edit the daily *Milwaukee Leader*. The outbreak of the war in Europe was the beginning of his disillusionment with the Socialist movement. First, the European party leaders generally supported their own nations. Then the German Americans in Milwaukee proved to be loyal to the fatherland. And finally, his neutralist stance, calling for a total embargo of all warring nations and total disarmament, failed to win approval from the party's National Executive Committee.

Then came the sinking of the *Lusitania* and the *Milwaukee Leader*'s refusal to condemn the Germans. Accusing the Socialists of disloyalty, Simons resigned from the *Leader*, wrote an article condemning the party for the *New Republic* ("The Future of the Socialist Party," February 1, 1916), and in 1917 asked that the anti-war St. Louis Declaration be suppressed by the government. He went to work for the pro-war Wisconsin Defense League and headed the literature department of the Wisconsin Loyalty League. After the war he became a reporter for the *Milwaukee Journal* and refused to support amnesty for war opponents even after the war.

Simons then became a believer in Frederick W. Taylor's efficiency theories, taught foremen efficiency techniques, and in the 1930s joined the Bureau of Medical Economics of the American Medical Association. From 1933 he was virulently anti–New Deal. In 1945 he wrote an attack on compulsory health insurance. Simons died in West Virginia in 1950.

SOURCES: William A. Flaser, "Algie Martin Simons and Marxism in America," *Mississippi Valley Historical Review* 41 (December 1954); Robert Huston, "Algie Martin Simons and the American Socialist Movement" (Ph.D. diss., University of Wisconsin, 1965); Kent and Gretchen Kreuter, *An American Dissenter: The Life of Algie Martin Simons* (1969); The Algie M. Simons and May Simons Papers, Wisconsin State Historical Society, Madison, Wisconsin.

*BERNARD K. JOHNPOLL*

**SINCLAIR, UPTON (1878–1968).** Upton Sinclair was America's most prolific radical writer. From 1904 to 1962 he wrote more than seventy novels, plays, critical studies, and pamphlets in which he espoused democratic socialism as the solution to the problems of American capitalism. However, he is remembered almost solely for *The Jungle* (1906), his muckraking novel of the Chicago meat-packing industry.

Sinclair was born in Baltimore, Maryland, on September 20, 1878, the only son of Upton Beall Sinclair, a feckless liquor salesman from an aristocratic but impoverished Virginia family, and Priscilla (Harden) Sinclair, the daughter of wealthy Baltimoreans. In 1888 the family moved to New York City, where Sinclair entered the public schools, passing through the eight elementary grades in two years. In 1892, at the age of 14, Sinclair began courses at the College of the City of New York and graduated five years later in the middle of his class. For the next four years he studied music, contemporary politics, and romantic poetry at Columbia University and worked as a hack writer, churning out nickel novelettes. By 1900 he was producing over a million words a year, none memorable, but enough to support his mother and new wife.

Sinclair's radicalism is often attributed to the economic circumstances of his childhood and adolescence. Caught between an unsuccessful dipsomaniacal father and genteel well-to-do grandparents, Sinclair was extremely class-conscious. But little of this political awareness appears in his first efforts at serious fiction, all slight and pretentious romantic novels. It was not until 1902, under the influence of writer George D. Herron and *Wilshire's Magazine*, that Sinclair discovered socialism. Buoyed by a sense of brotherhood, he wrote *Manassas* (1904), a Civil

War novel that depicted a rich young Southerner who joins the abolitionist movement. Late in 1904 the editor of the Socialist weekly *Appeal to Reason* challenged Sinclair to write about the wage slaves of industry as he had written about the chattel slaves in *Manassas*. Accepting the *Appeal*'s $500 advance, Sinclair spent two months in the fall of 1904 investigating Chicago's meat-packing industry. Out of his conversations with workers and visits to packing plants came *The Jungle*, Sinclair's fictional portrait of the filth, degradation, and brutality of Packingtown. The *Appeal* began to serialize the novel in the summer of 1905, but the book was turned down by five publishers before being published by Doubleday-Page in 1906. Though flawed by a contrived Socialist ending, *The Jungle* became a worldwide best-seller. So powerful was Sinclair's indictment of the "beef trust" that President Theodore Roosevelt sent a federal commission to Chicago to investigate. The commission's report led to the passage of the Meat Inspection Bill in May 1906, and the book established Sinclair as an international literary figure. Most readers, however, failed to grasp its condemnation of capitalist economy. "I aimed at the public's heart," Sinclair remarked somewhat ruefully, "and by accident I hit it in the stomach."

During the next few years Sinclair's attempts to promote socialism became more practical. In 1905 he started the Intercollegiate Socialist Society (now the League for Industrial Democracy), and in 1906, with earnings from *The Jungle*, he founded the Helicon Home Colony, an experiment in communal living that burned down the following year. It was not until the Ludlow Massacre of 1914 that Sinclair again found a subject equal to his talent. He traveled four times to the Colorado coalfields, where striking miners and their families had been attacked, and three years later produced *King Coal* (1917), his novel of industrial violence in the West.

In 1917, shortly after the United States entered World War I, Sinclair resigned from the Socialist Party, troubled by its noninterventionist stance. He dramatized his political dilemma in *Jimmie Higgins* (1919), the story of a rank-and-file Socialist who feels he must enlist to fight the Germans.

During the early 1930s such eccentric books as *Mental Radio* (1930), an exploration of mental telepathy, and *Wet Parade* (1931), a pro-Prohibition tract, revealed Sinclair the faddist and puritan. His increased political activism seemed to have left little time for substantial writing. Having reconciled with the Socialist Party in 1920, Sinclair ran as its gubernatorial candidate in California in 1926 and 1930 and again as the Democratic candidate in 1934. He organized the latter campaign around the principles of the End Poverty in California (EPIC) movement that he had outlined in *I, Governor of California* (1933). After an astonishing primary win, he lost the general election, receiving nearly 900,000 votes, and as usual he incorporated his political experiences into a novel, *Co-op* (1936).

Sinclair's relationship with the Communist Party was at best troubled and erratic. In 1918, for instance, he criticized U.S. military attempts to suppress the Russian Revolution even as he spoke out against the excesses of Bolshevik discipline. During the early 1930s he was disparaged as a "social Fascist."

Robert Minor (q.v.) denounced his EPIC proposals as the most backward and pro-capitalist program put forward by any American politician in ten years. In the last half of the decade, however, during the halcyon days of the People's Front, Sinclair enjoyed the Party's favor. He was a featured speaker at the Western Writers Congress in 1936 and one of the more conspicuous vice-presidents of the League of American Writers, the Party's cultural "front organization." In 1937 he wrote *No Pasaran!*—a pro-Loyalist story of the Spanish Civil War. He resigned from the League in October 1940, citing contradictions in its anti-war policy.

From 1940 to 1953 Sinclair worked on the "Lanny Budd" books, eleven novels that recapitulate the major events of U.S. history between 1913 and 1950. Sinclair spoke throughout the series as a propagandist for American progressive liberalism, and its final volume, *The Return of Lanny Budd* (1953), was decidedly anti-Communist. Sinclair died in Bound Brook, New Jersey, on November 25, 1968.

SOURCES: William A. Bloodsworth, *Upton Sinclair* (1977); Jon A. Yoder, *Upton Sinclair* (1962).

*ART CASCIATO*

**SKOGLUND, CARL (1884–1960).** Carl Skoglund, a lifelong activist in the Socialist, Communist, and Trotskyist movements, was born in Svardlungskogen, Sweden, in 1884. After four years of school he worked in a paper mill, which he helped unionize. A member of the Social Democratic Youth (1905), he was punished for anti-militarist activity. Blacklisted after a national strike, he emigrated to the United States in 1911.

In Minnesota Skoglund was a railroad worker for Pullman. As chairman of the Brotherhood of Railroad Carmen (an affiliate of the American Federation of Labor), Skoglund was blacklisted after the 1922–1923 strike. He joined the Socialist Party's Scandinavian Federation (1914) and the IWW (1917) to recruit to the Socialist Party's left wing. Excluded from the 1919 Socialist Party convention, he was a founder of the Communist Party in the United States.

Skoglund was the district industrial director for the Communist Party in Minnesota until his expulsion for Trotskyism in 1928. He was on the first National Committee of the Communist League of America and a national leader of successor organizations. Working as a coal-shoveler, he and the other Minneapolis Trotskyists helped organize the 1934 Teamsters coalyard strike. They then led the Minneapolis Teamsters truckers strikes. Elected Teamsters Local 544 president in 1938, he was removed for noncitizenship in 1940.

In 1938, Skoglund helped found the Socialist Workers Party (SWP) and was on the International Executive Committee of the Fourth International. Convicted in the 1941 Minneapolis anti-sedition Smith Act trial, he served his sentence in Sandstone Penitentiary in 1944. Afterward he was blacklisted by the coal companies and the Teamsters union.

Skoglund remained active in the educational work of the SWP. In 1954, he was put on a boat for Sweden when a last-minute court order stopped the deportation. He died in 1960 at Mountain Spring Camp, New Jersey.

*SETH WIGDERSON*

**SOLOMON, CHARLES (1889–1963).** Charles Solomon was a Socialist legislator, speaker, and publicist. He was also a labor attorney and a magistrate in New York City. Solomon was born on New York's Lower East Side of East European Jewish parents in 1889. He was educated in the public schools of New York and the Brooklyn Law School, from which he received his degree in 1910. He was also admitted to the bar that year. While attending law school, Solomon worked as a reporter on the Socialist daily *New York Call*.

When he received his degree, Solomon began the practice of labor law. Active in the Socialist Party since 1910, Solomon ran for public office each year from 1912 onward, primarily in Brooklyn's predominantly Jewish Brownsville and East New York neighborhoods. In 1919 Solomon was among the five Socialists elected to the New York State Assembly. This was the period of the repressive Red Scare, and after a lengthy legislative hearing all five were denied their seats. In the special bye-election of 1920, Solomon was again elected against a combined Republican-Democratic candidate. He was again refused his seat. In the regular election of November 1920, Solomon was reelected and finally allowed to take his seat.

The charges against Solomon and his colleagues implied that they were dangerous radicals, but Solomon was no flaming radical. On the contrary, he was a moderate social reformer. One of his chief aims was to avoid violence in any social revolution. In 1918 he told a crowd of Socialists that education alone could prevent violence, and he told the group that Socialists should develop working-class education to prevent a violent revolution similar to the one that had just ended in Russia.

In 1921 the Socialist Party was completely splintered by the Communist schism, and Solomon and all other New York Socialist candidates were defeated. The party never recovered, and Solomon never again won an election, although he ran every year for the next sixteen years. Among the offices he sought were governor, lieutenant governor, controller, U.S. Senator, mayor of New York City, Representative in Congress, and member of the state assembly. When the Socialist Party was captured by the militant faction led by Norman Thomas (q.v.) in 1936, Solomon left the party and helped found the Social Democratic Federation and the American Labor Party (ALP). In 1944 he led the Socialist and trade union exodus out of the ALP, which had been captured by the Communists. He then helped found the Liberal Party. From 1936 until 1959 he ran every year for a state or city office on the ALP (1936–1944) or Liberal (1944–1959) line.

Solomon was named to the Magistrate's Court by Mayor Fiorello LaGuardia in 1936. He served in that post until his retirement almost twenty years later. In the Magistrate's Court he earned a reputation as an unconventional judge. Solomon lectured at the Brooklyn Law School from 1941 until his retirement.

He also served on the AFL Labor's League for Political Education. He died in December 1963 in Brooklyn.

*BERNARD K. JOHNPOLL*

**SPARGO, JOHN (1876–1966).** John Spargo was an intellectual leader of the right wing of the Socialist Party from 1902 to 1917. Born to a poor family in Cornwall, England, on January 31, 1876, Spargo had little formal education. As a child he worked in tin mines and as a laborer. While working in the mines, Spargo spent his evenings learning to read and write. At age 16 he joined Henry Hyndman's Social Democratic Federation, the leading Marxist organization in Great Britain at the time. He also became an active trade unionist.

Economic hardship and lack of opportunity for a self-educated intellectual in Great Britain led Spargo to migrate to the United States in 1901. In New York he found few opportunities and lived in penury. In 1902 he joined the Socialist Party and was befriended by a Jewish Socialist who was editing a Jewish encyclopedia, who hired Spargo even though he was a nominal Protestant.

In his first four years in the party, Spargo wrote two major works. The first, *Bitter Cry of the Children* (1906), was a vivid picture of the exploitation of children in industry and of the lack of facilities for these children and a plea for a new social system which would end such conditions. The second book, *Socialism* (1906), became the theoretical handbook of the Socialist right wing.

Spargo's 1912 book, *Syndicalism, Industrial Unionism, and Socialism*, played a major role in forcing members of the Industrial Workers of the World to leave the Socialist Party. Spargo's lectures on American college campuses, under the auspices of the Intercollegiate Socialist Society, helped win many intellectuals to the party between 1912 and 1917. He thus helped change the class structure of the Socialist Party.

Faced in 1917 with the reality of American participation in World War I, a special Socialist party convention voted to oppose the war and the administration of President Woodrow Wilson. Spargo's appeal to the convention delegates to support the war was voted down by a vote of 171 to 5. He left the Socialist Party immediately after it decided to oppose the war. From the end of the war, Spargo turned conservative and virulently anti-Socialist. He became an anti–New Deal conservative during the 1930s.

Spargo died in Old Bennington, Vermont, on August 17, 1966, at the age of 90.

*BERNARD K. JOHNPOLL*

**SPECTOR, FRANK E. (1895–1982).** Frank Efrion Spector, a longtime Communist Party organizer, was born near Odessa, Russia, on February 18, 1895, the son of Russian-speaking Jews. During the 1905 revolution he served as a courier between the battleship *Potemkin* and the mainland for the revolutionary forces. In 1911 he left Russia to escape the draft, arriving in the United States in 1913. In New York he worked as a handyman while contributing articles to

*Novy Mir*, Leon Trotsky's revolutionary paper. Affiliated with the Russian Language Federation of the Socialist Party, Spector become a founding member of the Communist Party in 1919, narrowly escaping the Palmer Raids. In 1921 he moved with his family to Los Angeles, where he soon became section organizer of the small Los Angeles Communist Party.

In 1930 Spector was arrested and convicted under the state's criminal syndicalism law for his participation in the Imperial Valley agricultural strike. Following a Supreme Court decision in 1931, he was released from jail and sent by the Communist Party to New York, where he became secretary of the International Labor Defense (ILD), directing campaigns for the release of Tom Mooney (q.v.), the Scottsboro Boys, and other "class war prisoners." Two years later he was sent by the Party to Moscow to work for the International Red Aid as coordinator of Communist Party defense work in English-speaking countries. He returned to the United States in 1935 and a year later was appointed organizer of the San Francisco section of the Party. There he presided over the burgeoning activities of the Party in the city's labor movement, as well as personally leading several major anti-Nazi demonstrations.

Under threat of deportation since an arrest in 1929, Spector took a less public role during the war years, working as a Hollywood set painter in Los Angeles and serving on the local War Manpower Commission. He did, however, participate in the 1945 Hollywood studio strike and was expelled from the AFL Painters Union in 1948. Four years later Spector became one of thirteen California Communist leaders convicted under the Smith Act. He was freed by a decision of the Supreme Court in 1957. Saved from deportation to the Soviet Union only by the latter's refusal to accept American Communist deportees, Spector remained in the Communist Party until the Soviet invasion of Czechoslovakia in 1968. He died in October 1982.

*MICHAEL FURMANOVSKY*

**SPIES, AUGUST (1855–1887).** August Spies was an anarchist revolutionary editor and martyr. Born in 1855 in Landek, Germany, the son of a forester, Spies was educated at the Polytechnical College in Cassel, Germany. His father's death forced him to abandon his studies and emigrate to the United States in 1873. While in the United States he became a skilled upholsterer.

Spies was active in the *Turner Bund* (the radical gymnastics union) in Chicago within a year after his arrival in the United States. Within three years he became a member of the Socialist Labor Party (SLP), and in 1877 he was active in rejuvenating the *Lehr und Wehr Verein* (Study and Defense League). In 1880 he was ousted from the SLP along with Albert R. Parsons (q.v.) for opposing an alliance with the Greenback Party and defending the use of violence. Two years later he helped organize the violence-prone International Working People's Association (IWPA), based on the teachings of Johann Most (q.v.). In 1884 Spies was named editor of the revolutionary Socialist daily *Arbeiter Zeitung*. He turned it into a hyperbolic voice of violent revolutionary rhetoric. Spies, who was virulently anti-Semitic, also allowed anti-Jewish articles to be published in the journal.

In early May 1886, Chicago police violently broke up a strikers' demonstration at the McCormick Reaper plant. The IWPA called a rally at the Haymarket to protest the attack and to demand an eight-hour day. On the night before the demonstration was scheduled, Spies wrote a circular—reminiscent of the "Men of England" passage from Percy Bysshe Shelley's poem "Mask of Anarchy"—calling on Chicago's workers to rise in their righteous wrath. A printer added the word "REVENGE!" at the start of the circular.

The police tried to break up the poorly attended rally despite orders to the contrary from the mayor of the city. In the melee that followed, someone—no one knows who—threw a bomb killing seven police and four demonstrators. Spies was among the eight men arrested in the bombing—even though he had called for calm. After a trial before a biased judge and a "packed" jury, he was among the seven sentenced to death. One defendant was sentenced to life in prison, another fled, never to be found.

Spies' plea for clemency was denied on the night before his execution. Two of the defendants were granted commutations to life in prison. On November 11, 1887, Spies and three of his co-defendants were executed in a major miscarriage of justice. One of the other co-defendants committed suicide on the night before he was to have been executed. The three others were pardoned six years later.

SOURCES: *August Spies Auto-Biography* (1887); Paul Avrich, *The Haymarket Tragedy* (1984); Henry David, *The History of the Haymarket Affair* (1936); Dyer D. Lum, *A Concise History of the Great Trial of the Chicago Anarchists in 1886* (1887).

*LILLIAN KIRTZMAN JOHNPOLL*


**SPOONER, LYSANDER (1808–1887).** Lysander Spooner was a leading nineteenth-century individualist anarchist. He was born in 1808 in the small Western Massachusetts city of Athol, was educated in Athol schools, and clerked in law with two former justices. He was responsible for reform of legal training in Massachusetts, making it legal to take the bar examination on the basis of clerkship alone.

Spooner first practiced law in Ohio. There he became a free-thinker who wrote pamphlets against the church in 1834–1836. He also assailed the U.S. Constitution, charging that it was being manipulated into a tool for the big interests. He argued that the same was true of the entire legislative system and that the only genuine agreements were those made between individuals. The system of incorporation was, in his view, antagonistic to a free, democratic society because it allows an entity rather than a human being to enter into a contract.

Spooner was the most extreme of the individualists. He argued that there was no such thing as society and no such thing as group rights. "Society is only a number of individuals," he argued. Since society had no existence of its own, it could have no rights. And since the group is a society, there could be no such thing as group rights. He also favored the most individualistic economic system—

absolutely unfettered competition. Even in credit and banking he favored absolute free competition. Spooner believed that competition, if it were genuinely free and unfettered, would keep interest rates low. This was even truer, in his view, in industry.

There was a contradiction in his position. He believed that, by natural law, each was entitled to "all the fruits of his labor," yet he favored a system that allowed rents and interest to be collected, thus taking from labor a part of its earnings.

Spooner defended his individualism by legal arguments. His chief point was that natural law was, under all conditions, the most authentic and enforceable law. If statute law is in conflict with natural law or with the common law, then statute law was invalid. Under these conditions, Spooner argued that statutes should not have any validity over contracts. The first is an artificial product made by man, the second is natural in origin. He also favored decentralization of the monetary and banking systems, so that they would not be hostage to statute law. And to prevent government manipulation of the value of precious metals, he argued in favor of basing monetary value on investment rather than on metals.

In 1844 Spooner attempted to fight a major government-sponsored monopoly, the U.S. Mail. He set up the American Letter-Mail Company, which carried letters by railroad between New York, Philadelphia, and Baltimore at rates considerably below those charged by the Post Office. He was sued by the Post Office. In the fight he charged that the postal monopoly violated the Constitution. He maintained that competition, if permitted free rein, would lead to a more economical postal service; moreover, he said, there was grave danger of corruption in a monopoly as great as the postal service. He lost his case, but he did force some reform. The postal service was made an absolute monopoly to prevent further attempts to compete with it.

His individualism created some serious confusion in his theory. An active abolitionist, Spooner rejected the idea that slavery was approved by society. But he also argued, in his pamphlet *No Treason*, that the institutional state was not free and therefore had no rights over the slaveholder.

Spooner was basically a pamphleteer who fought the institutional state. He wrote pamphlets almost until his death in 1887.

SOURCE: A. John Alexander, "The Ideas of Lysander Spooner," *New England Quarterly* 23 (June 1950).

*LILLIAN KIRTZMAN JOHNPOLL*


**STACHEL, JACK (1900–1965).** Jacob A. ("Jack") Stachel was a leading official in the Communist Party (CPUSA) for over forty years. An expert on youth, labor, and propaganda, Stachel was a dour, tireless factionalist and intriguer who sought power within the Party instead of public acclaim.

Stachel was born on January 18, 1900, in Oberlin, Galicia. Then part of the Austro-Hungarian Empire, the area later came under Polish control and is now part of the Soviet Union. Little is known about Stachel's family except that his parents were Jewish, Polish, and poor. They emigrated to New York City's East Side in 1911. Stachel attended public schools but left at an early age. Thereafter he held a variety of unskilled positions: peddler, patent medicine seller, longshoreman, and worker in a metal shop, a cannery, and the needle trades. At age 18 he joined the Hat, Cap, and Millinery Workers Union.

As a young adult, Stachel participated in the East Side political campaigns of several Socialist aldermen and assemblymen. In 1924 he joined the Communists (then known as the Workers Party) and soon became the New York organizer of the Young Workers League. Stachel rose rapidly within the CPUSA. As early as 1925 he sat on its Central Committee, representing the youth. A member of the Ruthenberg-Lovestone wing, he became organization secretary of the Party's New York district in 1927. Here he transformed its old foreign language federations into shop and community branches. Stachel also found time for covert work. He planned and led a December 1928 raid on the apartment of recently expelled Trotskyist James Cannon (q.v.), stealing all materials useful in the Party's factional warfare.

Stachel had sharp political skills, but an even keener instinct for survival. In 1929 the Communist International advised the American comrades to remove their boss, Jay Lovestone (q.v.). Resisting, Lovestone traveled to Moscow to argue his case, but before departing in March, Lovestone left contingency orders with Stachel and Robert Minor (q.v.). In the event of an adverse decision, they should seize all Party funds and property and sell the Party buildings. On May 14 the Comintern ruled against Lovestone. When this news reached the United States, Stachel and Minor switched sides. To save their own Party careers, they cabled Moscow on June 4 that Lovestone had given "detailed technical instructions" that would have "split" the organization.

Stachel profited greatly from supporting the Comintern's decision. For the next seventeen years he was one of the most important Communists in the United States. First he received the post of CPUSA organizer for the state of Michigan in 1929. The next year he led a march of 100,000 workers on Detroit's Cadillac Square. In early 1931 the Party appointed him assistant secretary of its Trade Union Unity League (TUUL), a dual union in competition with the American Federation of Labor. When TUUL chief William Z. Foster (q.v.) suffered a heart attack in 1932, Stachel became acting secretary and headed the League until it disbanded in March 1935.

After this, Stachel spent a decade as the Party's national organization secretary and one of Earl Browder's (q.v.) top aides. An enthusiastic champion of all of Browder's Popular Front policies, Stachel helped achieve the merger of a Communist and a Socialist-led white-collar union, which became the United Office and Professional Workers Union. During the late 1930s, when Communists gained great power within the Congress of Industrial Organizations (CIO), Stachel popularized the Party's slogan that the CIO constituted a "TUUL with muscle." Despite his seemingly intimate political relationship with Browder, Stachel's primary loyalty lay with Joseph Stalin. Thus in 1945, when the Soviet Union intervened to denounce Browder's deviations from orthodoxy, Stachel turned on his Party's leader, as did nearly all other ranking domestic Communists.

Ironically, Stachel's own decline began shortly after the Party expelled Browder in 1946. Later that year Walter Reuther drove the Communists out of the United Auto Workers. Stachel's comrades blamed him for the rout and terminated his labor union activities. He served briefly as the Party's educational director and then took a staff position with the CPUSA's newspaper, the *Daily Worker*. These demotions notwithstanding, Stachel remained important enough to merit government persecution during the Cold War era. A federal grand jury indicted him and eleven other leading Communist Party figures in July 1948, charging them with violating the Smith Act. After a spectacular trial, all were found guilty in October. Free pending appeals, Stachel had a heart attack in 1950. When the Supreme Court upheld the convictions the following year, his attorney requested a suspended sentence for health reasons, but Stachel was sent to the federal correctional institution at Danbury, Connecticut, for five years.

Upon his release, Stachel rejoined the *Daily Worker* as an editorial writer. In 1957 he displayed his factional skills in dramatic fashion one final time. He helped drive out of the Party a neo-Browderite group, numbering in the thousands, led by *Daily Worker* editor John Gates (q.v.). From then until his death on December 31, 1965, Stachel was a relic of a bygone era in an organization that had squandered virtually all its influence among the American Left.

SOURCES: Daniel Bell, *Marxian Socialism in the United States* (1967); Theodore Draper, *American Communism and Soviet Russia* (1960); Harvey Klehr, *The Heyday of American Communism* (1984).

*JAMES GILBERT RYAN*

**STEFFENS, LINCOLN (1866–1936).** Lincoln Steffens was the foremost political journalist and investigative reporter of early twentieth-century America. With muckrakers Ida Tarbell and Ray Stannard Baker, he exposed corruption throughout the political and corporate life of the United States. After 1917, however, Steffens abandoned liberal reform, extolling communism instead as the inevitable cure for social ills. Though never a Party member, he was mentor and hero to many young liberals who converted to communism during the early 1930s.

Steffens was born in San Francisco, California, on April 6, 1866, the oldest of four children of Joseph Steffens, a bookkeeper of German-Irish stock. In 1870 the family moved to solid-middle-class surroundings in Sacramento, where Steffens' father became an eminent businessman, banker, and civic leader. After an undistinguished high school career and a year's discipline at a San Mateo military academy, Steffens entered the University of California at Berkeley in 1885 and graduated four years later at the foot of his class. Unsure whether to become a writer, scientist, or philosopher, he traveled abroad and began a two-year period of intellectual vagabondage, during which he studied ethics and philosophy at Berlin, art and history at Heidelberg, and psychology at Leipzig.

In 1892 he returned to the United States and, cut off financially by his father, became a reporter for the *New York Evening Post*. Steffens' 1894 investigative pieces helped drive the Tammany Hall political machine out of New York. In 1897 he became city editor of the *New York Commercial Advertiser* and in 1901 the managing editor of *McClure's Magazine*. Steffens established the "literature of exposure" in January 1902 in *McClure's* when he published his "The Shame of Minneapolis" along with Tarbell's and Baker's exposés of Standard Oil and Pennsylvania coal mining. He collected his articles on municipal corruption as *Shame of the Cities* in 1904, the same year that his series, "Enemies of the People," began to appear in *McClure's*.

Throughout the "progressive" era, Steffens remained more reformer than radical. Politically independent, he spoke out in favor of the Spanish-American War and voted Republican as late as 1894. His leftward turn began in 1908, when he supported Eugene Debs (q.v.) as Socialist candidate for U.S. President. Steffens' socialism, however, was founded on Christian ethics rather than on Marxist dogma. He took as protégés two Harvard undergraduates, John Reed (q.v.) and Walter Lippmann (the latter formed the Harvard Socialist Club at Steffens' urging). In 1911, after his wife's death, Steffens and Reed shared an apartment in Greenwich Village, where Steffens was a regular at Mabel Dodge's "evenings" and president of the Liberal Club, a collection of radicals, anarchists, and intellectuals. He went to Vera Cruz in 1914 to investigate the Mexican Revolution and supported the constitutionalist Carranza in the ensuing battle for control of the government.

Steffens traveled to Russia in 1917 shortly after the czar's overthrow and visited twice more, once in 1919 as a member of William C. Bullitt's unsuccessful diplomatic mission. On two American cross-country speaking tours, Steffens was an uncompromising defender of the Russian Revolution. "I have seen the future, and it works," he told his audiences, radical and Rotarian alike. He popularized the view of Lenin as a benign dictator whose reign of terror would finally be replaced by economic and political democracy. He also championed women's suffrage, worked for Morris Hillquit's (q.v.) Socialist campaign for mayor of New York, and testified as a character witness for anarchists Emma Goldman (q.v.) and Alexander Berkman (q.v.) at their draft obstruction trial. In 1926 he published *Moses in Red*, a historical parable in which he saw himself as a tainted liberal unable to enter the Socialist Promised Land. When *The Autobiography of Lincoln Steffens* appeared in 1931, Steffens' age, reputation, and middle-class respectability made it "almost a textbook of revolution" (Max Eastman's [q.v.] phrase), and Granville Hicks (q.v.) claimed it arrived with "the force of revelation." After suffering a stroke in 1933, Steffens retired to Carmel, California, but still had energy enough to answer critics of the Russian purges. Steffens died in Carmel on August 9, 1936.

SOURCES: Justin Kaplan, *Lincoln Steffens: A Biography* (1974); Christopher Lasch, *The New Radicalism in America, 1889–1963* (1965); Lincoln Steffens, *The Autobiography of Lincoln Steffens* (1931).

*ART CASCIATO*

372

**STOKES, ROSE PASTOR (1879–1933).** Rose Pastor Stokes was one of the most prominent American radicals of the early twentieth century. An activist for the causes of women's suffrage, birth control, trade unionism, socialism, and communism, she also created a sensation because of her 1905 marriage to the millionaire Socialist Graham Stokes.

She was born Rose Weislander on July 18, 1879, in Augustow, a Jewish town in Russian Poland. Her father, a bootmaker, deserted the family when she was still a baby. Her mother took the family to London, and Rose attended school there. In 1890 the family arrived in Cleveland, Ohio, where her mother's second husband, a peddler named Israel Pastor, had settled. By the time she was 12 years old, Rose was forced to work as a cigar wrapper to help support the family. Responding to a request from a Jewish newspaper for contributions from workers, she began writing and moved to New York in 1903 to join the staff. An assignment to interview Graham Stokes, a millionaire reformer, led to their marriage in 1905, an event avidly covered by the New York press.

By 1906 the couple had joined the Socialist Party. Rose became a frequent lecturer for the Party, and she and Graham were leading figures in the Intercollegiate Socialist Society. She actively worked on behalf of the birth control movement and for women's suffrage, and she campaigned in support of labor organizers jailed for radical activity. The Stokeses opposed the Socialist Party's removal of Bill Haywood (q.v.) from the National Executive Committee in 1913 and were associated with the party's left wing.

The Stokeses resigned from the Socialist Party in 1917 because of their support of the Allied cause in World War I and the party's opposition to the war. Rose was active in the North American Alliance for Labor Democracy with Samuel Gompers. However, the Bolshevik Revolution transformed her into an opponent of the war. She rejoined the Socialist Party in February 1918. Just two months later she was convicted of violating the Espionage Act for writing a letter explaining that the government was for the profiteers while she was for the people. Although sentenced to ten years in prison, Rose was freed on appeal. She also grew increasingly estranged from her husband, now strongly pro-war; they were eventually divorced in 1925.

Rose Stokes was one of the founders of the Communist Party of America in 1919. She attended the Comintern's Fourth Congress in Moscow in 1922 under the name of Sasha and served on the Central Executive Committee of the Party. She married Victor Jerome (q.v.), a Party functionary, in 1927 and continued her work on behalf of the Party through the end of the decade. Stricken by cancer in 1929, she died at a German clinic on June 20, 1933.

SOURCE: Patrick Renshaw, "Rose of the World: The Pastor-Stokes Marriage and the American Left, 1905–1925," *New York History*, October 1981.

*HARVEY KLEHR*

**STUMP, J. HENRY (1880–1949).** J. Henry Stump was the Socialist mayor of Reading, Pennsylvania, for eight of the eighteen years between 1929 and 1947. Born in Reading in 1880, Stump spent almost all his life, except for two years as a child, in that city. The son of a poor cigarmaker who died when Stump was only 13 years old, the future mayor was educated only through grammar school. The death of his father made it necessary for Stump to go to work. He was first employed as a newsboy, then as a freight-handler on the Reading railroad line at fourteen cents an hour for a fourteen-hour day, six days a week, then as a cigarmaker.

In 1918 Stump joined the business staff of the Socialist weekly *Reading Labor Advocate*. In 1920 he became editor of the *Labor Advocate*, a post he held until his first election as mayor. He was later president of the People's Printing Company, which published the weekly.

An active union man, Stump was elected president of the Federated Trades Council of Reading in 1914 and held that post until his election as mayor thirteen years later. He also held office in the Berks County Reading and environs Socialist Party. In 1926 Stump led a picket line and distributed leaflets at the gate of a Reading mill that was on strike. He was fined $6.25 for disturbing the peace, although the fine was later remitted. A year later he became the city's mayor. During his long membership in the Socialist Party, Stump ran for many offices, losing especially close elections for state assembly and city councilman. He was the Socialist candidate for mayor in 1919, 1921, and 1923, being defeated in close races in each of the elections. He was finally elected in 1927 and reelected in 1929, 1937, and 1945.

During his four terms in office, Mayor Stump was instrumental in building many playgrounds for the city's children. He also extended the city's water system, built low-cost housing for the poor, developed a fine library system, improved the Reading airport, and made the fire department efficient. He saw to it that the wages of city employees were increased. To save the city money, he scrapped a plan for a new city hall and instead converted the old Boys High School into the municipal building.

During the internal feud that split the Socialist Party nationally in 1936, Stump and the majority of Reading Socialists withdrew from the Militant-controlled national party. They returned in 1938 and remained active in the Socialist movement.

With the Socialist Party nationally on the verge of collapse in 1947, the local Democrats approached Mayor Stump to serve as candidate of both the Socialist and Democratic parties. He refused. "I have been a Socialist for more than forty years," he told the Democrats, "and I am still a Socialist. I can in conscience only run on my principles." He was defeated. Shortly thereafter Stump became seriously ill and died in 1949.

*BERNARD K. JOHNPOLL*

**SWABECK, ARNE (b.1890).** Arne Swabeck, one of the founders of the American Communist Party, distinguished himself as a pioneer and prominent leader of American Trotskyism. In later years he blended his earlier convictions with admiration for the thought of Mao Tse-tung.

Swabeck was born in Denmark in 1890. His father was a lay preacher in a splinter group from the Danish Lutheran Church and combined religion with Socialist sympathies. Swabeck was encouraged to consider radical ideas and to pursue his artistic talents, though he had to earn a living as a painter in the construction trades. As a journeyman painter, he traveled throughout Europe and went on to Egypt and Palestine. In 1916 he emigrated to the United States.

Settling in Chicago, Swabeck immediately joined the Scandinavian Federation of the Socialist Party of America and became active in its left wing. He also became a member of the Industrial Workers of the World. Moving to Seattle in 1918, he was active in the Seattle general strike of 1919. In 1920, as a member of the new Communist Labor Party, he became editor of a Danish-Norwegian weekly paper of the Scandinavian Federation. With the 1921 merger of the Communist Labor Party and the Communist Party of America, Swabeck continued to hold responsible posts in the unified Communist Party (CP). He was selected to represent it on the Executive Committee of the Communist International and as a delegate to the Fourth Congress of the Comintern in 1922. Before and after his stint in Moscow, Swabeck functioned as Party district organizer in Chicago during the 1920s. He was also a leading activist in the Painters Union, serving as a delegate to the Chicago Federation of Labor. In 1923 he was involved in the ill-fated effort to form a farmer-labor party. In 1928 he was assigned to direct Party participation in the radical "Save the Union" reform movement in the United Mine Workers of America. Associated with the faction led by James P. Cannon (q.v.) within the Communist Party, Swabeck developed sympathies for Leon Trotsky's Left Opposition and was consequently expelled from the Party late in 1928.

Swabeck became a leader of the Trotskyist Communist League of America (CLA) and was elected national secretary of the organization in 1930, moving to New York City to serve in this capacity. In 1933 he journeyed to Turkey for two months of important discussions with Trotsky in the latter's Prinkipo exile. When the CLA merged with A. J. Muste's (q.v.) American Workers Party in 1935, Swabeck became assistant national secretary of the new Workers Party. In 1936 this group entered the Socialist Party. When the Trotskyist-led left wing was expelled from the Socialist Party in 1937, Swabeck helped to found the Socialist Workers Party (SWP), although he returned to Chicago to resume work as a painter and therefore played a less central role in the organization. Nonetheless, he served as a National Committee member of the SWP, continued to write articles for the Trotskyist press, and was seen as an honored member of the Trotskyist "Old Guard."

Beginning in the late 1950s, however, after retiring to Los Angeles, Swabeck developed sharp disagreements with the SWP leadership over the Chinese Revolution and Maoism. Now a conscious Maoist, he also became critical of "reformist" and "opportunist" policies of the SWP. Expelled from the organization in 1967, Swabeck became associated briefly with the Progressive

Labor Party and later with the "new leftist" New American Movement. In later years he concentrated on producing his memoirs.

SOURCES: Theodore Draper, *American Communism and Soviet Russia* (1960); Arne Swabeck, *From Gene Debs to Mao Tse-tung* (forthcoming).

*PAUL LEBLANC*

# T

**TAYLOR, CHARLES (1884–1967).** Charles E. ("Red Flag Charlie") Taylor was political boss of Sheridan County, Montana, when Communists controlled it, from 1922 to 1930. He later became chairman of the Party's United Farmers League. Taylor was born in Dodge County, Wisconsin, on February 27, 1884, the son of a frontier farmer and itinerant craftsman. After an eighth-grade education, he became a teacher, learned the printing trade, farmed, and read law.

Taylor joined the Socialists in 1907 and almost won election to the Minnesota legislature in 1910. In 1918 he offered his services to the Non-Partisan League (NPL) and went to newly settled Plentywood, Montana, to start a newspaper. *Producers News* soon became one of the liveliest and most literate country weeklies in the nation. Sheridan County had been a hotbed of left-wing Socialists. Late in 1920 most of them quietly joined the Communist Party, with Taylor as their leader. Two years later they used the NPL to take over the local Republican Party. In the general election they gained control of almost all offices and sent Taylor to the state senate. Delegates to the 1924 national convention of the Farmer-Labor Party (FLP) overwhelmingly elected Taylor chairman. Much to his disgust, the Communists later dumped the nominees of the FLP, but Taylor and his allies continued to run on that party line for the rest of the decade.

Taylor briefly dropped out of the Communist Party in 1928 out of sympathy for Trotsky. He came back in 1930 as the Depression worsened. He organized for the United Farmers League, which became a strong force against dispossession in some areas. Earl Browder (q.v.) appointed Taylor chairman of the United Farmers League (UFL) in 1932. Taylor wanted to forge a broad alliance on the left under a reborn Farmer-Labor Party. Doctrinaire opponents attacked him as a deviationist, and he was suspended as chairman of the UFL early in 1932. Two years later a regional meeting prepared to oust Taylor from the party, but he quit first.

Taylor spent most of the rest of his life as a printer and proofreader. He was an active unionist and a member for many years of the Socialist Workers Party before becoming again a Socialist. He died on April 22, 1967.

SOURCES: Columbia Oral History Collection, Interview with Charles Taylor (1965); Charles Vindex, "Radical Rule in Montana," *Montana: The Magazine of Western History* (1968); Lowell K. Dyson, *Red Harvest* (1982).

*LOWELL K. DYSON*

**THOMAS, NORMAN M. (1884–1968).** Norman Mattoon Thomas was the titular leader of the American Socialist Party from 1928 until his death forty years later. Born in the small Central Ohio city of Marion in 1884, Thomas was the son, grandson, and great-grandson of Presbyterian ministers. His father was the pastor of the Marion Presbyterian Church at the time of Norman's birth. After graduating from Marion High School in 1901, Norman Thomas attended Bucknell University for his freshman year. He then transferred to Princeton University, where he studied under such professors as future President Woodrow Wilson and Social Gospel economist Walter Wyckoff. He graduated *magna cum laude* in 1905.

Although he had entered the university as a pre-divinity student, Thomas was uncertain upon graduation whether he wanted to enter the ministry. He was also interested in a possible political career or in settlement-house work. Shortly after graduation, Thomas accepted an appointment to the staff of the Spring Street Settlement House in a poor, blue-collar section of New York City. The work at the settlement house soon dispelled Thomas' romantic view of the workingman as the yeoman of society. He discovered that the worker had interests similar to those of the members of other classes, that the worker could be as selfish or selfless as members of any other group. After a year at Spring Street, Thomas accepted an invitation from a benefactor of the institution that he join him on a trip around the world. After this voyage, which Thomas later claimed opened new horizons for him, he entered Union Theological Seminary, the center of Social Gospel education in the United States. While at Union, Thomas was appointed assistant minister at Christ Church, Presbyterian, in New York's Murray Hill section.

Upon his graduation and ordination in 1911, Thomas was named pastor of the American Parish Among Immigrants, a federation of churches serving primarily Italian and Hungarian immigrants. There Thomas combined his experience in settlement-house social work and his knowledge of the ministry. Among his major accomplishments at the Parish was the development of a camp for poor boys in the New Jersey countryside. The camp was especially valuable during the 1916 epidemic of poliomyelitis. He also organized a graduate program at Columbia University's Teachers College for the training of instructors for church schools catering to immigrants. There he met a Dutch Reformed minister and fellow pacifist A. J. Muste (q.v.), who would be his lifelong friend.

Thomas supported his former professor Woodrow Wilson in the presidential races of 1912 and 1916. In the second election he had qualms about supporting Wilson because of the President's preparedness program. By 1916 Thomas had become a pacifist, a leading member of the new Christian pacifist Fellowship of Reconciliation. That year he also wrote his first book, *The Church and the City*, which indicated his acceptance of socialism. He now called himself a non-Marxian Christian Socialist.

Upset by the poverty he found in his parish, he wrote in *The Church and the City* (1917):

I . . . came to believe that the attainment of what seemed to me to be the ethics of Jesus required the reconstruction, the revolutionary reconstruction, if you will, of our system. . . . [I concluded] that on the whole . . . the best way of attaining a world wherein it would be possible to live according to this ethical system, a world wherein the peace and well-being of men, women, and children would be realizable would be the kind of world which might be attained by Socialist economics.

The man whose writings most influenced Thomas at that time was Walter Rauschenbusch (q.v.), the leader of the Social Gospel movement. Like Rauschenbusch, Thomas argued in the *Christian Patriot* (1917) that "extreme poverty and great luxury set limits on the possible attainment of a genuine Christian brotherhood." He considered the business ethic the opposite of the Christian ethic, because "the God of business is unlimited profit, Mammon, not Christ."

As the United States drew closer to being drawn into the European war, Thomas devoted more time to his opposition to U.S. participation. He became more active in the Fellowship of Reconciliation—editing its journal *World Tomorrow*—and helped organize the No-Conscription League and the American Union Against Militarism. After the United States became embroiled in the war, Thomas was a founder of the National Civil Liberties Bureau, which later became the American Civil Liberties Union. He was also active in the struggle for the rights of conscientious objectors, one of whom was his brother Evan.

He was finally drawn into the orbit of the Socialist Party by the anti-war election campaign of Morris Hillquit (q.v.) for the mayor of New York City. Thomas' activity in the anti-war movement and for a Socialist mayoralty campaign lost the American Parish major contributions, so Thomas resigned as its pastor. In 1918, no longer tied to a church, he joined first the Intercollegiate Socialist Society and then the Socialist Party itself. He made it clear in the letter that accompanied his application for membership that his socialism was tempered by an almost anarchist commitment to individual voluntarism. He considered himself a Christian-pacifist-libertarian Socialist. The Socialists were delighted to accept Thomas into their party. He was a rare find—an educated intellectual with Ivy League credentials, an excellent speaker and writer, and a Protestant American in a party heavily populated with aliens.

The party Thomas entered was on the verge of splitting itself asunder. The Russian Revolution, which all Socialists hailed at the time, was accepted by some self-styled left-wingers as an absolute model for creating socialism in all countries, especially the United States. The left wing forced the party to split, and the internal dissension drove many members from the party, as well as from the left wing. The Red Scare, the anti-democratic raids, and attacks on Socialist Party members and officers upset Thomas. He was particularly distressed by the arrests and deportations of hundreds of Socialists and anarchists.

Although Thomas was friendly to the Bolsheviks, he was opposed to the anti-democratic philosophy that permeated the Bolshevik ideology. He also rejected the overemphasis most Socialists placed on economic causes for all social ills. For example, he argued that race hatred was social rather than economic, a stance that totally rejected the general view in the party.

During the earlier 1920s Thomas openly assailed organized Christianity as more organized than Christian. His pacifism also became less absolute—temporarily.

In 1921 Thomas resigned as editor of the *World Tomorrow* to become associate editor of the *Nation*. The next year he was named one of two executive directors of the League for Industrial Democracy, an organization of pro-Socialist intellectuals. When the Socialist daily *New York Call* closed down in 1923, Thomas was named editor of its short-lived successor, the labor daily *New York Leader*.

In 1924 Thomas was a delegate to the convention that nominated Robert M. LaFollette as the Progressive candidate for U.S. President. LaFollette was also nominated as the Socialist candidate that year, although he was no Socialist. Thomas was nominated that year as the Socialist candidate for governor of New York State. LaFollette polled more than 4,800,000 votes; Thomas polled less than 100,000. Moreover, the LaFollette Progressives failed to organize a permanent Progressive or Labor Party, as Thomas had hoped.

After the election he turned to labor organization. He was arrested and held overnight by the police in Passaic, New Jersey, in 1926 for holding a mass meeting in defense of the Botany Mills strikers.

Prosperity had cut seriously into the party membership by 1928, despite Thomas' attempt to build the party by bringing in more native-born American intellectuals. His Socialist activity, the fact that he was a native-born American—the only one among the nationally known Socialists—and his education, all played a part in the decision of the party leaders to nominate him for U.S. President that year. Thomas accepted the nomination reluctantly because he had doubts that the party could do itself or its cause any good in the campaign. He proved to be wrong. Admittedly he polled only 267,000 votes; admittedly his campaign was Socialist in title only; admittedly the party attracted few workers. But the campaign drew large numbers of intellectuals into the party and its periphery, especially through the Thomas for President Clubs. And the party platform, and Thomas' evocation of it, played a significant role in the birth and development of the New Deal five years later.

While turning the party toward reform, Thomas became more active in civic affairs in New York City. His campaign for mayor of New York in 1925—from which he polled only 40,000 votes—was a forerunner of his later activities in New York affairs. In that campaign Thomas lashed out at the crime and corruption in the city administration. He and his colleagues in the League for Industrial Democracy helped expose instances of graft in the operation of the rapid transit systems and city services. His publicizing of the corruption won him a reputation as a major municipal reformer.

His nomination for mayor in 1929 won plaudits from many non-Socialists. The Scripps-Howard *New York Evening Telegram* announced its support of his candidacy. So did the Citizens Union, a non-Socialist good government group, and a multitude of ministers and rabbis and university professors, led by philosopher John Dewey. Election Day 1929 came less than a fortnight after the collapse of the stock market. This too may have helped Thomas' candidacy. In the end, Thomas' vote went up to 175,000, some 438 percent of what it had been four years previous. Admittedly Tammany Hall's candidate Jimmy Walker was reelected, but the election results made it clear that a strong reform candidate could now win.

For the next four years Thomas continued his fight against Tammany Hall and municipal corruption. He and his friend Paul Blanshard (q.v.) wrote a book entitled *What's the Matter with New York*, which exposed the relation between the corrupt politicians and the banks and big businessmen of New York. Their work led to the formation of a City Affairs Committee, which investigated the dishonest city administration. The material they gathered was forwarded to Governor Franklin D. Roosevelt in New York with a request that New York's Mayor Walker be ousted. Despite the overwhelming evidence, Roosevelt refused to act.

In 1931 Thomas ran for borough president of Manhattan. He was again backed by most good-government reformers—this time including the extremely conservative Republican Congressman Hamilton Fish. Thomas polled 40,000 votes, more than 20 percent of the total cast. By 1932 Roosevelt had decided that conditions in New York were so bad that he had to oust Walker.

There was one major interruption in Thomas' campaign for municipal reform between 1929 and 1932. In 1930 Thomas accepted the nomination of the Socialist Party for Congress from a middle- and upper-class district in Brooklyn. He was supported by the progressive League for Independent Political Action (LIPA). During the campaign, Thomas pleaded for better statistics on unemployment, free public employment offices, retraining of workers in obsolete industries and trades, public works projects, unemployment insurance, and shorter hours— most of which were to be basic parts of the New Deal. He polled a record 22.3 percent of the total vote in an extremely conservative district. Thomas remained in left-wing politics after the election. The LIPA disappeared shortly thereafter.

In 1930 the Socialists were preparing for another of their regular schisms. This time the fight would be between two age-groups, the younger Militants and the Old Guard. Most of the Militants, who were in their twenties and thirties, were college-educated intellectuals who had been recruited into the party by

Thomas during the campaign of 1928. The Old Guards were mostly in their late fifties and sixties. The Old Guard was also more closely tied to the established labor movement and they all considered themselves to be Marxists. Because of their age, the Old Guard was less activist than the Militants. The Militants were generally pro-Soviet, whereas the Old Guard was, invariably, anti-Soviet. The Militants were also less doctrinaire than the Old Guard.

Thomas generally agreed with the Old Guard rather than with the Militants. He was, for example, repelled by the dictatorship of the proletariat as practiced in Russia. Many Militants were enthralled by it, but the Militants were his supporters, the youth of the party, and almost all intellectuals, so he supported them.

At the 1921 Socialist convention in Milwaukee, Thomas led the Militant assault against the Old Guard leadership of the party. The prime target was Morris Hillquit. Thomas and several supporters moved to have Hillquit removed from the national chairmanship of the party and replaced by Mayor Daniel Hoan (q.v.) of Milwaukee. Among those who favored the change were B. Charney Vladeck (q.v.) of New York and the leaders of the powerful Milwaukee and Reading, Pennsylvania, organizations. Behind the move were three factors: the need for a more active chairman, the perceived need for an American-born leadership, and personal antagonism for Hillquit. The charge of anti-Semitism, which Hillquit leveled against Thomas' followers, was obviously false. One of his opponents was Vladeck, manager of the Jewish *Daily Forward*. In the end, Hillquit was reelected (he died within a year). The scars of that conflict were never repaired, and the hope of a reborn Socialist Party died.

During 1932 the Socialist Party appeared to be on the rise. Membership had increased. Thomas polled a respectable, albeit disappointing vote in the presidential election—884,781. This was considerably lower than the Socialist vote in 1912 and 1920. Thomas worked and campaigned hard on a platform that barely differed from his program of 1928. He spoke to large, receptive audiences and won considerable praise but little genuine support from progressives and liberals. However, his campaign brought many new young intellectuals into the party.

By now Thomas had become totally disillusioned in both the church and the Marxist movements generally. He argued that the church had become an opiate of the masses which had failed to further Christian ethics. And he condemned the left-wing Marxian movement—especially the Communists—for arguing that all Socialists in all countries must set up dictatorships of the proletariat, as did Russia. As for the church, Thomas resigned his ordination. As for Marxism, Thomas tried to build the non-Marxist wing of the party.

Beginning in 1933, Franklin Roosevelt's New Deal cut deeply into the Socialist movement. Many of Thomas' Militant followers went into the Democratic Party and abandoned Thomas and the Socialists. Several of them, including George Rhodes (q.v.) of Pennsylvania, and Andrew H. Biemiller of Wisconsin, became New Deal Democratic Congressmen. Thomas himself generally supported the

New Deal legislation, especially the Tennessee Valley Authority. He did argue that the Roosevelt administration had failed to do more of what he thought it should.

In 1933 reformer Fiorello LaGuardia, a Progressive Congressman, was elected mayor of New York. During the campaign, Thomas refused to attack him. He barely endorsed Charles Solomon (q.v.), the Socialist candidate who was a member of the Old Guard. Once elected, LaGuardia named many Socialists, of both major wings, to court and cabinet posts. A large number of Militants thus left the party. Thomas himself was named to the Charter Revision Commission for a short term.

By 1934 the Communists had begun to change their line. They now proclaimed that they favored a united front with the Socialists. But this did not make it easy for some Communists to change their tactics. They tried to attack Thomas physically when he spoke in Lawrence, Massachusetts. In February 1934 a Madison Square Garden mass meeting to protest the slaughter of Socialists by the clerico-Fascist government in Austria was attacked by a mob of Communists inside the hall itself; some were armed with furrier knives. The meeting was broken up. After this riot Thomas decided that no united front was possible with the Communists.

Meanwhile, the Socialist Party was becoming a collection of warring factions. There were the Old Guard; a group of Westerners called the Populists; another group of independents that included Milwaukee Mayor Daniel Hoan (q.v.); Darlington Hoopes (q.v.), a Socialist assemblyman from Reading, Pennsylvania; and James Graham (q.v.) president of the Montana Federation of Labor; a strange amalgam of Communists of various denominations, including the official Communist Party, who formed the Revolutionary Policy Committee; and the loose confederation of followers of Thomas, called the Militants. A sharp struggle developed at the 1934 Detroit convention over the proposed Declaration of Principles. Devere Allen (q.v.) composed the declaration, a mixture of pacifism and extreme revolutionary bombast. The convention voted its approval and gave the Militants a working majority of the ruling National Executive Committee.

The party remained a factional battlefield. Little else was done by the Socialists—they could only fight among themselves. Efforts by active Socialists B. Charney Vladeck and Samuel H. Friedman (q.v.) to keep the party united were rebuffed by Thomas, who by now wanted the Old Guard out of the party. The split finally became total in 1936, when the Old Guard bolted, formed the Social Democratic Federation, and finally became part of the American Labor Party, which supported Franklin Roosevelt in the 1936 campaign. The 1936 Thomas campaign for President was a disaster. Several Militant Socialists, including party chairman Leo Krzycki (q.v.), resigned to support Roosevelt. Thomas polled fewer than 200,000 votes. The party was dead as an electoral force.

Thomas now proposed a new thesis based on an old concept in American politics: the all-inclusive party (an idea he had first proposed in 1919 when he suggested that a new party of the Left ranging in membership from the Industrial

Workers of the World on the left to the Non-Partisan League on the right be formed). By 1935 he wanted it also to include all Socialist and Communist factions. He thus arranged for the party to admit into its ranks the Trotskyist faction of the Communist movement, but within a year they had so sabotaged the party that it was totally paralyzed. They were then ousted from the party, taking a large group of party members with them.

With the outbreak of the civil war in Spain, Thomas lent his name and prestige to a plan to set up a Debs Column in the Spanish Loyalist army. Many of the pacifist leaders of what was left of the Socialist Party—John Haynes Holmes (q.v.), Jessie Wallace Hughan (q.v.), Elisabeth Gilman (q.v.), Mayor Hoan, and Max Raskin, Milwaukee Socialist attorney—protested the action. In the end nothing came of the Debs Column except for more animosity within the party.

Thomas toured Russia and the rest of Europe, including Spain in 1937. The trip totally disillusioned him in the Soviet Union; he found it to be an oppressive inequitable society. He also assailed the purge trials and the Communist slaughter of the leaders of the independent Marxist Partido Obrero de Unificación Marxista (POUM) and the Anarcho-Syndicalist Confederacion Nacional del Trabajo (CNT). He returned, opposed to the whole Soviet system and its leader, Stalin. By late 1937 Thomas decided that there were few if any differences remaining between himself and the Old Guard, so he began a campaign to reunite the Socialists and the Old Guard. His first move was a futile attempt to have the Militants become part of the American Labor Party. His second effort to initiate negotiations with the Social Democratic Federation took twenty years to succeed.

For the rest of the 1930s Thomas was active in fighting for civil liberties. In May 1938 he was prevented from speaking in Jersey City by the police; in 1938 he worked for the release of ex-Communist Fred Beal, who was convicted of a murder during a 1929 mill strike in Gastonia, North Carolina. And in 1940 he worked for the release of his political antagonist Earl Browder (q.v.), leader of the American Communist Party. He was also active in the organization of the Southern Tenant Farmers Union. For his activity, he was arrested, jailed, and beaten by a mob of Arkansas planters. His experience in the tenant farmers movement caused him to distrust and dislike Henry Wallace, who was the secretary of agriculture.

From 1938 until 1941, Thomas' primary interest was in his effort to keep the United States out of the European war. Still basically a pacifist and an isolationist, Thomas was anti-Hitler, but he could not accept the assumption that war was the only way to destroy the German dictator. During the same period, Thomas was active in trying to save the lives of European Jews and Socialists caught behind German lines. He was instrumental in President Roosevelt's intervention to prevent the executions by Hitler of Leon Blum, Francisco Largo Caballero, and Julian Gorkin. He failed to save Henryk Erlich and Victor Alter, Polish-Jewish Socialists murdered by Stalin.

Once the United States entered the war, Thomas announced his support of the effort. In 1942 the Communists tried to silence him because he opposed

Soviet hegemony over Europe. During the war Thomas continued his fight for civil rights and civil liberties. He tried to aid conscientious objectors, vehemently condemned the evacuation of Japanese and Japanese-Americans from the West Coast, and spoke out for racial equality. In 1944 he ran for U.S. President at the urging of the Socialists of Reading, Milwaukee, and Bridgeport, Connecticut, but he polled the lowest Socialist vote ever.

America's dropping of the atomic bomb over Hiroshima and Nagasaki horrified him. After the war he backed the United Nations charter, hoped for a farmer-labor Progressive party, and ran for President in 1948 primarily to expose Wallace's dismal record on tenant farmers as secretary of agriculture. He ran fifth, polling only 135,000 votes. He refused to run ever again, despite pleas from some Socialists. In 1952 and 1956 he supported Adlai Stevenson for President. In 1953 he redefined democratic socialism as a basically reform movement in his pamphlet *Democratic Socialism: A New Approach.*

Thomas organized the anti-nuclear organization SANE. He helped victims of the Smith Act. He spoke out against the Vietnam War after 1965. He supported John F. Kennedy for President in 1960, and in 1964 he supported Lyndon Johnson. In 1966 Thomas was seriously injured in an auto accident. Two years later he died in a nursing home in Huntington, Long Island, New York, at the age of 84.

SOURCES: Bernard K. Johnpoll, *Pacifist's Progress: Norman Thomas and the Decline of American Socialism* (1970); W. A. Swanberg, *Norman Thomas: The Last Idealist* (1976); The Norman Thomas Collection, New York Public Library, New York City.

*BERNARD K. JOHNPOLL*

**THOMPSON, ROBERT (1915–1968).** Robert George Thompson was a leader of the Young Communist League (YCL), a fighter in the International Brigades during the Spanish Civil War, an American military hero during World War II, and a major figure in the removal of Earl Browder (q.v.) from the Communist Party's top position in 1945. Thompson was nearly murdered by thugs during the McCarthy era, and he was persecuted by the federal government even beyond his death.

Thompson was born in Fruitdale, Oregon, on June 15, 1915. Details of his childhood and parents' background are lacking. At age 18 he joined the Communist Party (CPUSA) in Oakland California in 1933. He spent the next two years there working as a machinist and was active in the AFL (American Federation of Labor) Machinists Union. Years later he admitted to having used the aliases "Tomes," "Condon," "Johnson," and others. Thompson went to Moscow in 1935 to attend the Young Communist International Congress. He remained for two years, taking courses in Marxism-Leninism at the Lenin School and working at a ball-bearing plant in the Soviet capital.

In 1937 Thompson traveled to Spain to defend the Popular Front government against Franco's rebels. Wounded in February, he nevertheless went on to command the Canadian Mackenzie-Papineau machine-gun battalion as a 22-

year-old captain. The following year he returned to the United States to serve as Ohio secretary of the YCL. He transferred to the New York branch in 1941.

Nine days before Japan bombed Pearl Harbor, Thompson joined the U.S. Army. Sent to the jungles near Buna, New Guinea, he rose to the rank of staff sergeant. In January 1943 Thompson swam the rain-swollen Konombi Creek under fire, towing a rope to which the rest of his troops clung when crossing. He then led a charge that wiped out two Japanese machine-gun positions, ensuring the American advance. For this Thompson received the Distinguished Service Cross, America's second highest medal for bravery during World War II. Malaria and tuberculosis returned him to civilian life that August, with a $150-per-month disability allowance.

During the CPUSA's internal crisis over the removal of Earl Browder as Party boss in 1945, Thompson served as a protégé of William Z. Foster (q.v.). This brought appointment to the Party's National Board. Thompson personified the Communist vanguard. Never a popular figure, he was aloof and unapproachable. He inspired respect and fear. A man of relentless will, he regarded doubt or hesitation as a sign of weakness. Thompson advanced the thesis that one could not measure the Left's strength in the labor movement by numbers alone. This helped the Communists rationalize their dramatic losses during the years after Browder's ouster.

By 1948 Thompson was chairman of the New York state Party. A year later, he and ten other members of the National Board were convicted of violating the Smith Act after a sensational trial. All except Thompson received fines of $10,000 plus five-year prison sentences. The judge dealt Thompson the fine and only three years because of his war record. Temporarily free during the appeals process, he was stabbed in the abdomen by a vigilante near his home. The Supreme Court upheld the convictions in 1951, and seven of the defendants began serving their terms, but Thompson and three others disappeared. Thompson remained a fugitive for twenty-six months, until FBI agents captured him in a secluded mountain cabin near Sonora, California, in August 1953.

Thompson began serving his three-year term in Alcatraz, but shortly thereafter he was taken to New York City to stand trial for contempt of court for his flight. In October, while in a lunch line at a prison there, he suffered another unprovoked attack. An anti-Communist Yugoslav seaman, a confessed assassin awaiting deportation, struck two blows to Thompson's head with an iron pipe. The assault fractured Thompson's cranium and he lay near death for days. The brain surgery that saved his life left a permanent steel plate in his skull.

That December a federal judge sentenced Thompson to four more years imprisonment on the contempt charge. In 1955 the Veterans Administration halted his monthly disability payments. Shortly before his release for good behavior in 1960, a federal court upheld the action. Freed, Thompson returned to the Party's highest ranks.

While helping prepare a massive New York City demonstration against the Vietnam War, he suffered a fatal heart attack at age 50 on October 16, 1965.

Three months later the secretary of the army ruled that his ashes could not be interred in Arlington National Cemetery. Thompson's widow, Sylvia, led a three-year court battle to overturn this decision. A federal appeals court ruled in her favor in December 1968, and Thompson's ashes lie in Arlington today.

SOURCES: George Charney, *A Long Journey* (1968); Robert A. Rosenstone, *Crusade of the Left* (1969); Sylvia H. Thompson, *The Arlington Case: Robert Thompson Story of an Unburied Soldier*, Tamiment Library, New York University, New York City.

*JAMES GILBERT RYAN*

**TOOHEY, PAT (1904–1978).** Pat Toohey, a Communist Party organizer and activist for more than fifty years, was born on September 22, 1904, into a miner's family in Barnesboro, Pennsylvania. Of Irish Catholic descent, he followed his father and brothers into the coal mines while a teenager.

Toohey joined the Communist Party in 1920. For the rest of the decade he was active in the struggle against John L. Lewis, first as a dissident in the United Mine Workers (UMW) and then as vice-president of the Communists' dual union, the National Miners Union (NMU). The collapse of the NMU in the early 1930s forced Toohey out of mining. He served as the party's district organizer in Colorado, helped organize the Puerto Rican Communist Party in 1934, and filled Party positions in other locales for most of the remainder of his life. From 1937 to 1939 he lived in Russia. In the 1950s Toohey was state chairman of the New Jersey Communist Party while farming. After his retirement to Florida, he remained active and was elected president of the Fort Myers chapter of the National Council of Senior Citizens. He died in July 1978.

*HARVEY KLEHR*

**TRACHTENBERG, ALEXANDER (1884–1966).** Alexander Trachtenberg played a key role in the dissemination and popularization of Marxist and Leninist ideas in the United States. Born to Jewish parents in Odessa in 1884, Trachtenberg was a university student there when the Russo-Japanese War broke out. Drafted into the czarist army as an engineer, he began his political career by conducting peace propaganda in the army. Following the war, he participated in the Russian Revolution of 1905 and was subsequently imprisoned for a year.

Shortly after his release, Trachtenberg emigrated to the United States, where he attended Trinity College and earned a Ph.D. in economics from Yale University. At Yale he was active in the Socialist Party and helped form the Intercollegiate Socialist Society. In 1914 he helped organize the Collegiate Anti-Militarist League and served as its first treasurer. Upon leaving Yale in 1915, he became the director of the Rand School of Social Sciences in New York, where he organized a labor research department that served numerous trade unions and initiated the *American Labor Year Book*. During this period, he also served as a staff economist for the International Ladies Garment Workers Union, as a member of the editorial board of the *New York Call*, and as the campaign manager for Morris Hillquit's (q.v.) candidacy for mayor of New York.

An enthusiastic supporter of the Bolshevik Revolution, Trachtenberg became chairman of the Russian Soviet Recognition League in 1918 and, a year later, secretary of the American Labor Alliance for Recognition and Trade Relations with Russia. But when the Socialist Party split in 1919, Trachtenberg did not immediately join the Communists. Instead, he insisted that the Socialist Party's opposition to the war made it different from social democracy. At the Socialist Party convention of 1919, he argued that the party should affiliate with the Third International and urged all pro-Bolsheviks to rejoin the Socialist Party rather than participate in the formation of the Communist Party. When the Socialist Party rejected affiliation with the new International, Trachtenberg and others formed the Committee for a Third International as an internal caucus. In September 1921 this group left to take part in the formation of the Workers Party, the precursor of the Communist Party. Trachtenberg was subsequently elected a member of the Executive Committee of the Workers Party and later became a leading member of the Communist Party. In 1922 he was a delegate to the Fourth Congress of the Communist International. A year later he was elected to the Executive Committee of the Communist International.

Trachtenberg's major achievement came in 1924, when he founded International Publishers, where he served as president and editor until his retirement in 1962. Under Trachtenberg's direction, International Publishers became the largest Marxist publishing house in the United States and made available to American readers the basic texts of Marxist studies. Although after 1924 his energies were devoted primarily to publishing, Trachtenberg helped organize the Labor Research Association in 1927 and was later a founder of the Workers School of New York and its successor, the Jefferson School of Social Science, for which he served as treasurer. He also ran for a number of public offices, including two campaigns for Congress.

In 1952 Trachtenberg was indicted under the Smith Act. Initially sentenced to three years in prison, he was released after three months, when the principal witness against him confessed to perjury. He died on December 16, 1966.

SOURCES: Robert Dunn, "Waiting for Trachty," *New World Review*, February 1967. James Weinstein, Introduction to Alexander Trachtenberg's *The American Socialists and the War* (1973).

*JOHN GERBER*

**TRESCA, CARLO (1879–1943).** Carlo Tresca was the leading Italo-American anarcho-syndicalist in the United States. He was born in 1879 into a landholding family in the city of Sulmona in Italy's Abruzzi. Like many of the generation born following the unification of Italy, he was claimed early by socialism. As a very young man he began the practice of his lifelong trade as editor of the local Socialist newspaper. In 1904, facing a jail sentence for libel, Tresca left Italy, arriving in the United States in August of that year. He was to remain for the rest of his life. By the time he was murdered in 1943, he stood as an emblem of anti-totalitarianism, excoriating the manifestations of Stalinism and fascism, while remaining a passionate militant in the cause of social justice.

During the first eight years of his life in the United States, Tresca lived in Pennsylvania, where he first edited the organ of the Italian Socialist Federation of America. But his flamboyant and fiercely independent nature drew him to anarchism, and he soon began the first of his independent newspapers, *La Plebe*, in which he vigorously attacked the clergy, the *prominenti* of the Italian community, and the mine owners of western Pennsylvania. A number of successful libel suits were filed against him and he spent many months in jail; a less successful attempt was made to cut his throat.

In 1912 a call from the Industrial Workers of the World (IWW) took Tresca to the Lawrence textile strike. His association with the IWW continued for four years, during which time he became nationally known as a "notorious" agitator and organizer to local and federal police agencies. In 1912 Tresca also formed an alliance with Elizabeth Gurley Flynn (q.v.) which lasted until 1925. His friendship with "Big Bill" Haywood (q.v.) ended in 1916 during the Mesabi iron range strike when Haywood charged that Tresca and Flynn had made an improper deal with authorities in negotiating Tresca's release from a homicide charge in Minnesota. Tresca was indicted with the IWW leaders in 1918, but his break with the organization enabled him to stay out of jail. He also avoided deportation, though his second newspaper, *L'Avvenire*, fell victim to war fever. *Il Martello* succeeded it and survived until Tresca's death.

Tresca's attacks on fascism and Italian dictator Benito Mussolini began before Mussolini's assumption of power. At the request of the Italian ambassador to suppress *Il Martello*, the U.S. government indicted Tresca in 1923, though the only charge that could be found on which to try him was sending an "obscene" advertisement for a book on birth control through the mails. Tresca was convicted and sentenced to a year and a day, but he had served only four months when President Calvin Coolidge commuted the sentence.

Released from the Atlanta penitentiary, Tresca took up the battle against the Fascists. Throughout the 1920s he and his comrades confronted Fascist demonstrations on the streets of New York. There was violence, and a number of deaths occurred, but it was generally acknowledged that it was due to Tresca that Fascists did not dare to march in the streets. During the 1920s Tresca was also active in defending political prisoners, Sacco and Vanzetti (q.v.) among them; he was instrumental in bringing IWW lawyer Fred Moore into the case.

Tresca was often attacked by other anarchist groups as a compromiser and worse. Through the 1920s he worked with the Communists in labor and anti-Fascist organizations. But with the beginnings of the purge trials in Moscow, and the persecutions and executions of anarchists and left revolutionaries in the Spanish Civil War, he became as implacable an anti-Stalinist as he was an anti-Fascist. He joined John Dewey's American Committee to Defend Leon Trotsky, which earned him the ultimate curse of the communists, "Trotskyite," though he had, in fact, little sympathy with Trotsky.

Tresca at first opposed America's entry into World War II, but he accepted the need to defeat fascism and concentrated his energies in the anti-Fascist organizations—the Mazzini Society and the projected Italian American Victory Council—both of which would have some influence in the post-war reconstruction of Italy. With cause he feared that these organizations would be penetrated and directed by Communists or former Fascists, possibly allied, and he spoke fiercely against the tactics of both groups. On the night of January 11, 1943, he was shot to death on the corner of Fifteenth Street and Fifth Avenue in Manhattan just outside the office of *Il Martello*. The two men who personified his opposition to communism and fascism—Vittorio Vadali, a former comrade who had become an agent of Comintern policies, and Generoso Pope, the openly pro-Fascist New York publisher—were both mentioned as suspects in his murder. In the end, however, Tresca's assassination remained unsolved.

*DOROTHY GALLAGHER*

# V

VAN KLEEK, MARY (1882–1972). Mary Van Kleek was a social worker and investigator of labor conditions, especially among women, who was associated with pro-Communist organizations during the period 1933–1962. A descendant of the original Dutch settlers of the Hudson Valley, where she was born in 1882, Van Kleek was educated at Smith College, from which she graduated in 1905. Her father, a Social Gospel priest in the Episcopal Church, had a great influence on her outlook. After her graduation, she accepted a fellowship with the College Settlement on the Lower East Side of New York. Her work with the working women in the immigrant district of New York led her to write an article in 1906 describing the conditions under which the women worked and calling for legal protection.

In 1907 Van Kleek was named head of the Industrial Investigations of the non-profit Alliance Placement Bureau in New York. While working for the bureau she wrote a book, *Women in Bookbinding Trades* (1910), which was cited in a successful appeal from a court ruling which held regulations against women working at night to be illegal. The next year, she became director of the Russell Sage Foundation's Committee on Women's Work. She was affiliated with the foundation for the next forty years. In her new post she was instrumental in exposing the poor pay and conditions in the millinery and artificial flower industries. Both these industries employed mainly women who worked at home. Her reports also noted the rise of child labor in these two industries.

Van Kleek did further research on the conditions of women workers and of labor in general. Her findings were cited frequently by Louis Brandeis in court cases involving regulation of hours and conditions of labor. Her research was aided during 1914–1917 by her students at the New York School of Philanthropy (now Columbia University School of Social Work). Her studies with these students helped in the drive for social and health insurance, enacted twenty years later.

During World War I, Van Kleek served on the War Labor Policies Board and as director of the Women's Division in the War Department Ordinance Division, and after 1918 as head of the Women in Industry Division of the Department of Labor. In that position she established standards for women workers which the Labor Department accepted, and wrote the bill that established the Women's Bureau of the Department of Labor.

Returning to Russell Sage Foundation after her wartime leave, Van Kleek was instrumental in establishing health and sanitation regulations for homeworkers in New York. Her studies of Italian homeworkers in Harlem and of discrimination and poor pay for black working women helped in the enactment of labor and education regulations.

During the Depression of the 1930s Van Kleek moved steadily toward the Communist position. First she supported the Communist-inspired Worker Unemployment Insurance Bill, introduced by Representative Lundeen of Minnesota. Then she announced her support of the Stalin 1st regime in the Soviet Union. In 1933 she was named to the Advisory Council of the U.S. Labor Service, but she resigned to oppose the New Deal.

Active in the American Civil Liberties Union since its inception, she resigned after it barred Communists as members during the Hitler-Stalin Pact period. During the war, she first opposed American participation while Hitler and Stalin had a nonaggression pact. As soon as Hitler and Stalin went to war, she became an all-out protagonist of the war against Hitler.

After the war Van Kleek opposed the Marshall Plan and backed Soviet foreign policy. In 1948, the year she retired at Russell Sage Foundation, she worked for Henry Wallace and the Communist-controlled Progressive Party. She wrote pro-Soviet articles until 1962.

Mary Van Kleek died in Woodstock, New York, in 1972.

SOURCE: Dahrl Elizabeth Moore, "Mary Van Kleek: Her Life and Writings" (unpublished essay, 1982).

*DAHRL ELIZABETH MOORE*

**VLADECK, BARUCH CHARNEY (1886–1938).** Baruch Charney Vladeck, a leading Jewish-American Socialist, was the manager of the *Jewish Daily Forward* and a member of the New York City legislature from 1918 to 1922 and during 1938. He was also a member of the New York City Housing Authority from 1935 until 1938.

Born into a pious family in Dukora, a predominantly Jewish suburb of Minsk in Byelorussia, in 1886, his name was originally Baruch Charney (Vladeck was added in an effort to elude czarist police during the early years of the twentieth century). Charney's early education was in religious schools of the Chabad sect of Hasidism in his home city. An outstanding scholar, he was admitted into a yeshiva—an advanced Jewish religious school—at the age of ten. It was at the yeshiva that Charney first became interested in worldly Russian literature, which the school administration forbade students to read. His interest in Russian literature led him to attempt unsuccessfully to enter a Russian secondary school to study for one of the liberal professions. He was barred because of the anti-Jewish restrictions in both schools and professions.

Charney then studied at a free private, unaccredited school, many of whose teachers were members of the newly organized Jewish Socialist parties in Russia. The two most prominent of these parties were the General Jewish Workers Bund and the Poale Zion. The Bund favored cultural self-determination for Jews within the Russian empire. The Paole Zion favored establishment of a Socialist Utopia for Jews in Palestine. Among the subjects Charney studied with these tutors were mathematics, literature, history, and Marxism.

At age 16 Charney became a Poale Zionist and taught in a school run by the organization. He also worked in a library run by the Socialist organization. In 1903 he was arrested by the czarist police for political activity. He spent eight months in the Minsk jail. While there he met older, more radical Socialists—members of the Bund—and was converted to that organization. He was now an avowed Marxist.

At the age of 18, Charney became an itinerant organizer for the Bund. During the anti-czarist disturbances that swept the czarist empire in 1905, Charney was injured by a cossack's sword. His agitation during the disturbances of 1905 was so successful that he was called the Young Lassalle—after the German Socialist agitator Ferdinand Lassalle, who helped found the German Social Democratic Party.

He was arrested again in 1905 in Vilno; he was freed after a few months by the czar's October Manifesto. But his freedom was short-lived. He was again arrested while organizing unions in Lodz in Russian Poland. He was again held for several months and freed.

Charney was named a Bund delegate to the meeting of the united Russian Social Democratic Workers Party in 1907. At that meeting he met and was impressed with Lenin. He was the only Bund delegate to support Lenin on matters of policy, and the only Bundist to vote for Lenin as a member of the party's Central Committee. This meeting marked the end of Charney's Bund activity in Russia.

Pogroms and repression had by 1907 made the Bund's life precarious. He found it necessary to adopt a party name—Vladeck—which would become his family name a year later. But even a pseudonym did not protect him from persecution. His life had become unbearable in the oppressive czarist nation. And so in the fall of 1908 he fled to the United States, arriving in New York on Thanksgiving Day.

Almost immediately Vladeck became a member of the local Bundist branch, which was affiliated with the Jewish Agitation Bureau of the Socialist Party. Large numbers of Jews, who had been in the Bund, had emigrated to the United States after 1905. By 1908 many of them formed organizations in Jewish communities in the United States which were loosely affiliated with each other and the Socialist Party through the Jewish Agitation Bureau. Vladeck soon became a leader of the Bureau, for which he went on speaking tours throughout North America and for whose journal he did considerable writing. In 1911 he was named a correspondent for the Socialist *Jewish Daily Forward*, the largest foreign-language newspaper in the United States; he was assigned to cover all U.S. cities that he visited.

His activity included aiding the shirtwaist and cloak industry strikers in 1910–1915. He raised money and agitated among the workers. In 1910 and 1912 he directed the unsuccessful Socialist Congressional campaigns of Meyer London (q.v.) on the Lower East Side of Manhattan, and he helped organize the pragmatic, effective political organization which ran London's successful campaign in 1914.

In 1912 he was named manager of the Philadelphia branch of the *Forward*. As such he was a liaison with the labor and Socialist movement for the *Forward* in that city. He lectured and organized for the Workmen's Circle (the Jewish Socialist fraternal order), Jewish Socialist branches, and trade unions with large Jewish memberships. And he wrote for the *Forward* and the Jewish Socialist Federation's journal *Naye Velt* (New World). He also found time to attend the University of Pennsylvania. In April 1915 he was naturalized, and in November of that year Vladeck was the unsuccessful Socialist candidate for judge of the Orphan's Court of Philadelphia.

Vladeck became a patriotic American during his first seven years in the United States. He was particularly impressed with the nation's natural beauty, with the people's openness and dynamism, and with the democratic, egalitarian political system. But he was appalled by the racism and nativism he found endemic. His love of the United States led him to modify his views of socialism and of assimilationism. He no longer favored an elite vanguard as the creators of the revolution. In fact, he rejected intellectuals—who were expected to create the vanguard—as potential revolutionists. The workers themselves would have to make the revolution, when they would be prepared to make it. Moreover, he argued by 1914 that the revolution would have to be preceded by reforms, organization of the workers—by the workers themselves—and unity of the workers in their own trade unions and their own labor party. This was a major departure from his pro-Lenin stance of seven years previous.

Although he had opposed assimilation for the Jews when he first came to the United States, he now favored it in the United States. In Europe he had as a Bundist favored a separate Jewish cultural milieu, protected by law, which would grant the Jews cultural self-determination. Yiddish was to have been the language of the Jews, no matter where they lived, as the basis for developing their own culture. But by 1914 he wanted Yiddish used only as the language of agitation among foreign-born Jews in the United States. Their culture was to be the culture of the United States, a culture rooted in English. He favored the integration of the Jews into the American people. He forecast, accurately, that Yiddish would disappear as the language of American Jews within two generations.

Vladeck's view of the American Jewish outlook did not prevent him from being active in Jewish groups, many of which disagreed with his forecast. In

1914 he helped organize the National Workmen's Committee for Jewish Rights, which sent aid to the starving Jews in Eastern and East Central Europe, the eastern battlefront of the war. In domestic affairs Vladeck fought actively for women's suffrage. Experience, particularly in California, Vladeck acknowledged, had shown that women tended to vote more conservatively than men. But he insisted that Socialists were honor-bound to support women's suffrage on principle.

In the raging feud in the Socialist movement at that time between pragmatic Socialists and ideologues, Vladeck found himself supporting the pragmatists. He argued that only direct appeals for immediate needs could win the working class to the party and win votes for its candidates and supporters for its ideals. Such issues would include taxes, labor conditions, schools, parks, transit, and so on. And as for operation of the party, Vladeck wanted to follow the pragmatic methods used by Victor Berger (q.v.) and the successful Milwaukee party organization. Ideological debate was, Vladeck believed, an exercise in futility. Socialism would come when the United States was ready for a Socialist revolution, and not before. Moreover, he doubted that socialism would, of and by itself, solve all the problems of mankind—physical, cultural, and psychological. There was, he argued, no perfect Utopia.

By 1916 Vladeck had developed into a moderate Socialist, a patriotic American, and an assimilationist. That year he also became city editor of the *Forward*. The United States was then on the brink of war with the German Reich. Vladeck opposed U.S. participation in the war, especially since the United States would be on the same side as the czar.

Like the party membership generally, Vladeck supported the anti-war Socialist platform of 1916. He was horrified by the German sinking of the British passenger ship *Lusitania*, and he was incensed by the Zimmermann note, which virtually proclaimed unrestricted submarine warfare in January. With the fall of the czarist regime in March 1917, Vladeck became pro-Allied, although he still opposed U.S. intervention. He supported the Socialist anti-war declaration voted by the 1917 emergency convention in St. Louis the day after war had been declared. But he was disdainful of the anti-Allied stance of Lenin and the Zimmerwald conference. Despite his sympathy with the Allied cause, Vladeck openly opposed militarism, conscription, and the weakening of civil liberties during the war.

The Socialists turned the 1917 municipal election in New York City into a referendum on the war. Morris Hillquit (q.v.), who had authored the St. Louis Declaration and was vehemently against the war, was its candidate for mayor. Vladeck was nominated for the city board of aldermen in the Williamsburg area in Brooklyn. The Republicans and Democrats ran a joint ticket in the district, but Vladeck won with a clear majority, as did six other Socialists.

While serving on the board of aldermen, Vladeck proposed unsuccessfully that the city take over the highly profitable and poorly run Brooklyn rapid transit system and the streetcars that crossed the Williamsburg Bridge. He also asked for controls on the spiraling prices of food, fuel, ice, drugs, and milk. And he moved that city employees, most of whom were poorly paid, be allowed to unionize. In addition, he won free hospitalization for city workers, free lunches for poor schoolchildren, and free licensing of pushcart peddlers.

By the middle of 1918 most Socialists had become pro-war because of the harsh treatment of the Russians at Brest-Litovsk, but the Socialists were so persecuted that they could not call a meeting to rescind the St. Louis Declaration. The New York aldermen voted in favor of Liberty Bond sales and for a victory march to honor those who died in the war.

The 1917 Balfour Declaration, which declared for a Jewish national home in Palestine, was greeted with indifference by Vladeck. He had no objection to giving Jews and Arabs equal rights in Palestine, but he opposed any special status for Jews or any favoritism toward Jews over Arabs.

In August 1918 Vladeck became manager of the *Forward*, in charge of its daily operation. In 1919 he was reelected to the board of aldermen, and in 1920 was chosen leader of the Socialist members of the board. During his second term he fought for municipal housing and regulation of housing, and he was opposed to the use of police against unions and radicals. He lost the 1921 election because of reapportionment and the splintering of the Socialist Party. In the Socialist Party split of 1919–1921, Vladeck supported the right-wing Socialists against the left-wing Communists, whom he considered to be anti-Socialist totalitarians.

After his defeat, Vladeck was again active in relieving the distress of the Jews of Eastern Europe. He headed the People's Relief, which he helped form in 1919, and he worked with the Hebrew Sheltering and Immigration Aid Society to get Jews out of Poland. Politically, Vladeck was active in the LaFollette campaign of 1924, and in 1930 he ran as a Socialist Congressional candidate under the aegis of the League for Independent Political Action. He lost, despite a record Socialist vote.

In 1932 he was among the more militant Socialists who tried to oust Morris Hillquit as chairman of the party. But he was soon disillusioned with the Militant faction, whom he accused of attempting to split the party. He tried to avert the split, which finally occurred in 1936. Vladeck then resigned from the Socialist Party and became a founding member of the American Labor Party.

With the rise of Hitler in Germany, Vladeck devoted most of his efforts after 1933 to rescuing labor leaders, Social Democrats, and Jews from Germany and attempting to force Hitler out of power. To achieve that end, he helped organize the boycott of German goods in the United States.

In 1937 Vladeck was elected to the New York City Council as a member of the American Labor Party. He became the leader of the LaGuardia coalition in the Council. Earlier he had been named to the New York City Housing Authority.

Immediately after the Munich Pact, which virtually handed Czechoslovakia to Hitler's Germany, Vladeck joined Norman Thomas (q.v.) in rescuing Socialists and Jews from Czechoslovakia. Baruch Charney Vladeck died shortly after the Munich agreement was signed in the fall of 1938.

SOURCES: Franklin L. Jonas, *The Early Life of B. Charney Vladeck* (Ph.D. diss., New York University, 1972); Algernon Lee, ''Baruch Charney Vladeck,'' *Universal Jewish Encyclopedia* (1943).

*BERNARD K. JOHNPOLL*

# W

**WAGENKNECHT, ALFRED (1881–1956).** Alfred Wagenknecht was a pivotal figure in the formation of American communism and later played a key role in building and managing various intermediary organizations for the Party. Born on August 15, 1881, in Goerlitz, Germany, the son of a shoemaker, Wagenknecht came to Cleveland, Ohio, in 1884, when his parents fled Germany in response to the Anti-Socialist Laws.

Having inherited his Socialist convictions from his parents, he became active in the labor movement at age 17. In 1901 he joined the American Socialist Party and almost immediately became identified with the left wing. In 1908 he was active as the party's organizer in the state of Washington. During that same year a major controversy erupted at the party's national convention when he applied for the position of national organizer. In 1914 he was elected a member of the National Executive Committee, where he fought for the policies of the Left.

Following American entry into World War I in 1917, Wagenknecht emerged as a major opponent of the war. While serving as the state secretary of the Socialist Party of Ohio in 1917, his anti-war activities led to an indictment and a subsequent one-year prison sentence. In 1919 he emerged as one of the main leaders of the left wing of the party and was elected executive secretary of the alternative national executive committee, which had been created by the left wing to challenge the party leadership.

When the Socialist Party split in 1919, Wagenknecht played a prominent role in the formation of the Communist Labor Party. In addition to serving as chairman during the foundation congress, he was elected executive secretary and international delegate. Following the merger of the American Communist movement into the United Communist Party in May 1920, Wagenknecht became the executive secretary of that organization as well. A year later he emerged as leader of the so-called "goose caucus," which opposed liquidation of the underground movement. When the United Communist Party became the Workers Party of

America in 1922, he was elected to the new party's Executive Committee. Wagenknecht was also one of the original founders of the *Daily Worker* and served for a time as its business manager.

During the 1920s Wagenknecht began his career of building intermediary organizations for the Party, starting with the Friends of Soviet Russia in 1922, in which he served as secretary. Shortly afterward he became head of the American section of the Workers International Relief. In this capacity he organized strike support for numerous strikes throughout the 1920s and early 1930s, including Passaic in 1925 and Gastonia in 1929 (where he was arrested). His extensive fund-raising later led Benjamin Gitlow (q.v.) to label him the "financial wizard of the party." During the early 1930s, Wagenknecht was also active in the Trade Union Unity League and directed the Party's work among the unemployed. As a leader of the National Campaign Committee for Unemployment Insurance, he led a delegation to Washington in 1931 demanding unemployment insurance. During that same year, he also served the party as the judge at the so-called Yokinen trial, in which a Party member was tried for racism.

In 1933 Wagenknecht became executive secretary of the National Committee to Aid Victims of German Fascism. His anti-Fascist activities, however, did not prevent him from becoming a prominent figure in the U.S. Congress Against War following the Nazi-Soviet Pact. By the mid-1930s, Wagenknecht's influence in the Party began to wane and his position was largely ceremonial. From 1938 to 1941 he served as chairman of the Missouri branch of the Party. Following his move to Chicago in 1941, he served the Illinois branch of the Party in a similar capacity until 1945. In 1956 he became involved in a Supreme Court case concerning the right of Communist Party leaders to receive Social Security benefits for Party work. Wagenknecht died in Chicago on August 26, 1956.

SOURCE: V. J. Jerome, "Alfred Wagenknecht: In Memorium," *Political Affairs*, September 1956.

*JOHN GERBER*

**WALDMAN, LOUIS (1892–1982).** Louis Waldman—lawyer, Socialist, and labor leader—was born in 1892 in Yancherudnia, in the Ukraine. His father, Samuel Waldman, was a relatively poor innkeeper and self-taught Hebrew scholar. Louis remembered that his was the only home in the village with books, sacred and secular. There were also constant discussions between his father and those who stopped at the inn, and from early on Louis was "up to [his] ears" in the ethical and legal teachings of the Talmud.

Louis came to the United States in 1909, and for a few months he worked in a chandelier factory in unvarying routine from 7 A.M. to 6 P.M. One afternoon a woman co-worker had two fingers torn off by a machine, and Waldman made an effort to halt the bleeding. After he was chased back to his machine by the foreman, Louis Waldman, who had been saturated in Talmudic injunctions in the old country, refused to sign a report indicating the accident was the fault of the co-worker. He was discharged and as he put it, "I had my first lesson in labor relations."

Through the efforts of his sisters, Waldman became an apprentice to a cutter of ladies' garments. He "worked six weeks without pay but this was considered a privilege." At night he went to school to learn English, and in 1911 he entered tuition-free Cooper Union. On his way home one afternoon Waldman witnessed the infamous factory fire at the Triangle Waist Company and "saw girl after girl appear at the reddened windows, pause for a terrified moment, and then leap to the pavement below.... We all felt that the workers who had died ... were not so much the victims of a holocaust of flame, as ... of stupid greed and criminal exploitation." Waldman went to hear Morris Hillquit's (q.v.) address in the aftermath of the fire. "The word 'socialism' kept recurring.... Hillquit ... aroused my enthusiasm, and sent me off on a pursuit of knowledge." This led, ultimately, to a lifetime of association with labor and Socialist politics.

In 1917, 1919, and 1920 Waldman was elected as the Socialist Party candidate to the New York State Assembly. In his first term he introduced a water-power bill that called for a centralized and publicly owned system, and a compulsory social insurance bill that included benefits for unemployment, sickness, and death. In response to critics who accused him of blunting the class struggle, Waldman said, "The Socialist Party ... is not merely a workingclass party.... Socialists should take a position on [all] public issues of moment."

When in 1920 Louis Waldman, along with four other Socialists, claimed the seats they had won in the New York State Assembly in the 1919 election, they were escorted out of the chamber by the sergeant-at-arms, and after a hearing— in this era of the Palmer Raids, immigration restriction, and the general Red scare—the Socialists were officially expelled. The *New York World* wrote: "No more lawless act was ever enacted in a lawmaking body." In September 1920 special elections were held to fill the vacancies, and all the Socialists were reelected. Waldman, however, soon left politics to study law. He received an LL.B. from New York Law School in 1922 and was admitted to the bar in 1923. From the beginning of his practice, most of Waldman's work was as counsel and adviser to labor unions.

Returning to politics in 1924, Waldman ran as the Socialist candidate for state attorney general and in 1928 for governor. He repeated his bid for the governorship in 1930 and 1932. In both instances, in response to widespread depression, Waldman called for immediate relief measures, public works, and unemployment insurance. As Waldman put it, "[I] sought a program which was intended to solve ... immediate social problems, step by step, rather than by one all-embracing plan which involved the 'inevitability of Socialism.' I saw nothing inevitable about it."

At the Socialist Party convention in Detroit in 1934, a Declaration of Principles was issued which supported the general strike as a tool for revolution and called for "massed war resistance" and the "destruction of the Bourgeois State." Waldman rejected this "short cut to the millenium," and as New York state chairman of the Socialist Party he spoke against the Declaration. In 1936 the state party charter was revoked and Waldman was "purged" as chairman. He then went on to work out a marriage between right-wing Socialists and labor unions, which led to the birth of the American Labor Party (ALP). Waldman's autobiography, *Labor Lawyer* (1944), details his growing disenchantment with the coalition, which he believed came to be controlled by Communists, under the guise of Popular Frontism. He resigned from the ALP in 1940 and remained virulently anti-Communist, speaking and writing against the "dictatorship of the revolutionary masses" and for a "peaceful struggle," ideas he had earlier enunciated in *Socialism in Our Time* (1928).

Waldman continued to practice law, often in partnership with Bella Bernstein, his wife since 1924, and he continued to make himself heard on social issues. He served many years as special counsel to the Transit Workers Union and from 1946 to 1947 he was vice-president of the Association of the Bar of the City of New York. In 1954 he became president of the Brooklyn Bar Association. In addition Waldman served as chairman of the Committee on Civil Rights of the New York State Bar Association (1951–1955, 1957–1961), and he was a Fellow of the American College of Trial Lawyers. In 1975, three years before he suffered a stroke that forced him to retire at age 86, he wrote a book whose title could easily be his epitaph—*The Good Fight: A Quest for Social Progress.* Waldman died in 1982 at age 90.

SOURCES: Julian F. Jaffe, *Crusade Against Radicalism: New York During the Red Scare, 1914–1924* (1972); Louis Waldman, *Labor Lawyer* (1944).

*GERALD SORIN*

**WALLING, WILLIAM ENGLISH (1877–1936).** William English Walling was a leader of the left wing of the Socialist Party between 1909 and 1917. He was also a founder of the National Association for the Advancement of Colored People and of the National Women's Trade Union League.

Walling was born into a wealthy, educated family in Louisville, Kentucky, in March 1877. His maternal grandfather was the Democratic candidate for Vice-President in 1880 and came within a hair's breadth of winning that election. His father was a prominent physician. William's education was obtained in private schools, primarily in Louisville and Edinburgh, Scotland. He graduated from the University of Chicago (B.S., 1897), attended Harvard University Law School, (1897–1898) and studied economics at the University of Chicago Graduate School (1899–1900).

Almost immediately after graduating from the university, Walling became interested in labor reform. He first worked for a year as a factory inspector for the state of Illinois. On that job he observed the poor conditions under which workers labored. Between 1901 and 1905 he worked in the University Settlement House on the poverty-stricken Lower East Side of New York. There he became acquainted with other leading social workers and reformers. He also became active there in the trade union movement. In 1903 he, Jane Addams, and Mary

O'Sullivan formed the National Women's Trade Union League, whose efforts helped organize thousands of underpaid, overworked female workers throughout the United States.

While at the settlement house, Walling made friends with many Jewish Socialists from Russia. They made him aware of the brutal treatment of the common people by the autocratic czarist regime. He went there to investigate for himself the conditions in that benighted land. While doing his own investigation of conditions in Russia, he met and became a friend of many of the revolutionary figures, most of whom were in hiding. On his return he wrote an anti-czarist book, *Russia's Message*, which was published in 1908. While abroad he married a Socialist writer, Anna Strunsky.

In 1908 he and his wife witnessed a race riot in Springfield, Illinois. He became incensed that there was such virulent anti-black feeling in a northern city—especially the city of Abraham Lincoln. As a result he published two articles in the *Independent* exposing the extent of racial antagonism in northern cities. He also lent his apartment for a meeting, instigated by Mary White Ovington (q.v.), at which the National Association for the Advancement of Colored People was founded. He was one of the founders of that organization.

An adherent of the Left, pro-syndicalist wing of the Socialist Party—of which he was still not a member—Walling assailed right-wing and centrist party leaders, Morris Hillquit (q.v.), Victor Berger (q.v.), Algie Simons (q.v.), John Spargo (q.v.), and Robert Hunter for plotting the formation of a labor party that would absorb the Socialist Party. The allegation that caused a major furor in the Socialist organization turned out to be inaccurate.

Walling finally joined the Socialist Party in 1910 and almost immediately became the intellectual leader of the so-called "Left Wing." Over the next seven years he wrote five major works: *Socialism as It Is* (1912), a pro-syndicalist view of the American Socialist movement; *The Larger Aspects of Socialism* (1913), a theoretical discourse about socialism; *Progressivism and After* (1914); *Socialists and the War* (1916), a survey of Socialists' positions on the war in most countries; and the *Socialism of Today* (1916).

In 1917 Walling supported Woodrow Wilson's declaration of war against Germany. He proclaimed his pro-Allied position on the war and condemned the anti-war stance of most Socialists. He accused the party of being in the control of pro-German pacifists and resigned from the organization. After the war, Walling remained active in the labor movement and friendly to most Socialists, but he now rejected revolution and socialism. He became, by 1919, a conservative syndicalist who supported the nonpartisan stance of American Federation of Labor President Samuel Gompers. He opposed the Bolshevik rulers of Russia for their totalitarianism. In 1924 he supported the Progressive ticket headed by Robert M. LaFollette and ran for Congress as a Progressive and a Democrat.

Beginning in 1933, Walling worked with the Labor Chest to aid victims of fascism. While working for the anti-Nazi underground, he contracted pneumonia and died in Amsterdam, the Netherlands, in 1936.

SOURCES: David A. Shannon, "William English Walling," in *Dictionary of American Biography*, Supplement 2 (1958); Ann Strunsky Walling Papers at the Bancroft Library, University of California at Berkeley.

                                                          *BERNARD K. JOHNPOLL*

**WARE, HAROLD (1890–1935).** Harold Ware organized mechanized farms in Russia during the 1920s, advised the Communist farm movement in the United States in the early 1930s, and directed a group of Party members serving in the Roosevelt administration. Ware was born on August 19, 1890, the son of Lucien Bonaparte Ware, secretary to the president of the Norfolk and Western Railroad, and of Ella Reeve ("Mother") Bloor (q.v.). He spent his early years in the Single-Tax colony of Arden, Delaware. He became an avid commercial gardener. At age 19 he enrolled in the two-year agricultural course at Pennsylvania State College. After graduation he bought a farm near Downington, Pennsylvania, where he had the first tractor in the locality. He spent the war years as a shipyard draftsman.

Both he and Mother Bloor joined the Communist Labor Party in 1919, but party leaders ignored his pleas to bring radical farmers into the movement. Lenin, on the other hand, wanted current information on American agriculture and wrote acerbically: "Have you no farmers in America?" The party chiefs allowed Ware to travel for six months, after which he submitted detailed reports that Lenin praised.

Ware became concerned about the famine in Russia. He won financial support from the American Russian Famine Relief Association and bought twenty-four tractors, recruited nine young farmers, and assembled a medical team and tons of food. After various difficulties on some poorly located land in Russia, he brought in a bumper crop of 4,000 acres of rye in 1922.

He returned to the United States for another tour of its agricultural regions, but once more failed to convince party bureaucrats that farmers were organizable. In disgust, he raised more funds, bought more equipment, and recruited more people to return to Russia. There the government made him director of a 14,000-acre farm in the North Caucasus, which he made a model of modern practices. He returned briefly to the United States and convinced the eminent Professor M. L. Wilson to spend a year in the Soviet Union advising on dry-farming practices. Ware now had a huge state farm of 150,000 acres, where crews worked by shifts and mobile machine shops were always available. He set a pattern that Stalin could adopt in collectivizing peasant farms.

Ware and his protégé, Lem Harris (q.v.), came back to the States in 1930. Once more they surveyed agriculture and wrote a report, which party leaders again neglected. Harris and Ware founded Farm Research, Inc., to continue their analysis, but more important events caught up with them when a fierce farm strike hit Iowa in August 1932. Ware hurried to the area and organized a group of Nebraska farmers to present relief demands to a governors conference and also to call for a Farmers National Relief Conference to meet in Washington in December. The conference was a resounding success and launched the Farmers National Committee for Action headed by Harris. Ware and Harris tried to build a broad-based insurgent group in the farmbelt, but party hard-liners criticized them severely.

After a second national conference in November 1933, Ware returned to the scholarly precincts of Farm Research, Inc., and issued economic reports. He also organized the so-called Ware Group, mainly from young lawyers in the Agriculture Department. In later years it has been described as anything from a Marxist study club to the shadow Soviet government of America.

Ware died in an automobile accident August 13, 1935.

SOURCES: Ella Reeve Bloor, *We Are Many* (1940); Lement Harris, *Harold Ware* (1978).

*LOWELL K. DYSON*

**WARREN, JOSIAH (1798–1874).** Josiah Warren, the founder of individualist anarchism, was born in Boston in 1798 of lower-middle-class parents (a claim that he was a descendant of a Revolutionary War general has never been substantiated). After traveling around the nation, he settled in Robert Owen's (q.v.) communitarian colony at New Harmony, Indiana, in 1825, where he remained until its collapse two years later.

Warren was an active participant in the debate that ensued over the causes of the community's demise. He rejected the position of most of the residents that New Harmony's failure was due to the constant internal strife and lack of discipline there. The failure was, he argued, due to Owen's paternalism and the lack of individualism there. These factors, he claimed, stifled initiative and a sense of responsibility among the communitarians: individual initiative could have avoided the collapse.

From the failure of New Harmony, Warren attempted to draw some universal political and economic theories. What was needed for a just society, he posited, was total individual freedom—each individual to do with his or her life, property, time, and reputation as he or she saw fit, provided that the individual in question did not impinge on another person's individuality and that each person take full responsibility for his or her actions. Individualism could not be attained under the political or economic system then (or now) extant. Government was, to Warren, the chief enemy of a free and just society and should thus be abolished. In its place he proposed voluntary associations that would set minimal standards of conduct but would have little if any coercive power for enforcing such standards. Under Warren's system, each person would be a society unto himself or herself. This system—sovereignty of the individual—would make government unnecessary and would abolish all oral or written law.

The capitalist economy, he argued, was the root cause of the oppressive political system. The competitive nature of the profit system created strife and required law and government to avoid unending warfare. Under the system he proposed, all profit, interest, and rent would be abolished. Warren employed an analysis of the relationship between production and value similar to that used many years later by Karl Marx. Warren labeled the economic system he developed "equitable commerce." Under this system the only criterion for price would be actual labor cost. He rejected utility as a criterion for price: "The value of a loaf of bread to a starving man is equivalent to the value of his life, and if the price of a thing is 'what it will bring' then one might demand of the starving man his whole future life in servitude as the price of the bread."

Warren's political and economic views complemented each other. If the price of goods was exactly their cost in labor, there would be no need for administration and adjudication, because there could be no disagreement. And there would thus be no need for government.

Soon after the failure of New Harmony, Warren moved to Cincinnati, Ohio, where he established a retail store that was operated on the basis of "equitable commerce." The so-called Time Store sold goods at actual labor-value only. The sales price was thus based on the actual cost of labor used in the production and transportation of an item, plus the cost of the actual time a salesperson devoted to the single transaction. The clerk's time was measured by a stop-clock on the wall. In place of money the store used "labor checks," certificates listing the labor value of each item purchased and the value of goods received in exchange.

The store was so successful that Warren tried to extend its operation and organize a satellite establishment in the town of New Harmony. But the local merchants fought the store by selling goods at less than cost and after a short time forced Warren's store out of business. Warren then returned to Cincinnati, where he established a new Time Store as a cooperative. The new store so enhanced the value of the property that it was sold by the cooperators at a great profit. Most of the cooperators bought farms with their profits.

Returning to New York, Warren met and converted to individualist anarchism Stephen Pearl Andrews (q.v.), with whom he proceeded to establish a new community in Brentwood, on Long Island, New York. This community, Modern Times, operated under a system of total freedom and an absence of any form of government. Even though this colony of individualist anarchists attracted all sorts of eccentrics, it did extremely well. With a population of 200 it had no almshouses, no jails, no saloons, no prostitution, and no police during its ten-year life.

But there were problems—internal and external—which would eventually destroy the community. First, a reporter asked a resident whether he or the others at Modern Times believed in marriage. The communitarian indicated that he did not. As for the others, "We don't interfere; there is no . . . prying." The result was a storm of clerical denunciation and an extremely bad press. Then came the collapse of the U.S. economy in 1857, which hit the community hard, although it survived. And finally came the Civil War. The communitarians were split. Some joined the Union army (a few died); others were pacifists who considered any war an abomination. The result was persistent, internal squabbling.

Modern Times could overcome the clerical assault and the economic storm, but it could not weather the schism in its ranks caused by the war. And so it died in 1862. Warren then moved back to Boston, where he lectured and wrote tracts expounding individualism. He died there in 1874.

SOURCES: William Bailey, *Josiah Warren: The First American Anarchist* (1906); James J. Martin, *Men Against the State* (1970).

*LILLIAN KIRTZMAN JOHNPOLL*

**WAYLAND, JULIUS A. (1854–1912).** Julius Augustus Wayland was the most successful Socialist publisher in U.S. history. His outstanding publication, *Appeal to Reason*, had a circulation of more than 500,000 between 1910 and 1916. Born in Versailles, Indiana, in 1854, Wayland had only two years of formal education—almost all of it in a one-room schoolhouse. He learned the printing trade by working as a printer's devil in his hometown. At age 19, in 1873, he opened his own print shop in Versailles. Four years later he and his new bride went to her family's hometown of Harrisonville, Missouri, where he opened another print shop and also became a successful land speculator.

Unfortunately, Wayland was at this time a Republican, whereas most of the residents of Harrisonville were Democrats. Thus when Wayland began publication of a weekly Republican newspaper he roused the ire of his neighbors, who made life uncomfortable for him and his family. To add to his troubles in Harrisonville, Wayland was named postmaster of the city by President Rutherford B. Hayes, a Republican despised by the town's people. After a series of disputes with an unfriendly but well-armed Democratic sheriff, Wayland left town and returned to Indiana.

After a five-year sojourn in his native state, where he again ran a successful print shop, Wayland once more moved West, this time to Pueblo, Colorado. There he opened and operated "Wayland's One Hoss Print Shop." He also invested heavily in Colorado land, which was rising rapidly in value. In Pueblo, he also became interested in socialism after reading the British *Fabian Tracts* and the works of John Ruskin, Laurence Gronlund (q.v.), and Edward Bellamy (q.v.). He became active in the People's (Populist) Party during the election campaign of 1892. In 1892 he became an editorial writer—without pay—of the Populist newspaper in Pueblo and published Populist pamphlets by the hundreds.

Populism was on the rise in Colorado during the late 1880s and early 1890s, and in 1892 a Populist was elected governor of the state. Wayland considered organizing his own pro-Populist daily in Pueblo to spread the doctrine of socialism, but his wife became seriously ill and he was compelled to move to the warmer climate in Florida. In 1893, while in Florida, Wayland discerned that the U.S. economy was about to collapse, so he sold all his land in Missouri and Colorado and moved to Greensburg, Indiana, with about $80,000 in gold and government securities. His judgment proved to be correct; a depression swept the nation in 1893.

Now an extremely wealthy man, Wayland invested his money in a new publication he founded, the *Coming Nation*, which was an almost immediate success. Its circulation was in the thousands, and it earned a substantial profit for its sole owner—Julius Wayland. The socialism of the *Coming Nation* was a simplistic compound of quasi-Marxism and Populism. It blamed the nation's economic inequities on the bankers, stockbrokers, speculators, and foreign investors, especially the Rothschilds. It called for the socialization of all means of production and distribution as the solution for all economic problems. In mid–1894 Wayland and the staff of the *Coming Nation* formed a cooperative community in Tennessee called the Ruskin Colony. The community soon became a warring camp, and in July 1895 Wayland—who had financed the entire operation—withdrew from Ruskin. He lost a considerable sum of money on the Ruskin Colony.

From Tennessee, Wayland moved to Kansas City, Missouri, where he started a new newspaper, *Appeal to Reason*, in 1895. *Appeal* met with considerable resistance from Socialists and anti-Socialists alike. To save money, he moved *Appeal* to a small Kansas city, Girard, where costs were considerably lower. He also inaugurated a competition for subscriptions and organized an army of subscription salespeople. By the end of 1900 the circulation of *Appeal* rose to more than 100,000. One issue during the first campaign of Eugene V. Debs (q.v.) for President in 1900 reached a circulation of almost one million.

The *Appeal* grew steadily thereafter, and Wayland became a major force in the growth of American socialism. Although he had abandoned the People's Party after it nominated William Jennings Bryan for President in 1896—he favored Debs, and voted for Charles H. Matchett and Matthew Maguire, the Socialist Labor candidates of that year—his philosophy was basically more Populist than Socialist. Moreover, his primary appeal was in the Prairie and Mountain States, where Populism had been most powerful. Nor was his support of the Socialist Labor Party candidates an endorsement of the party itself or of its leadership. In fact, Wayland and Daniel DeLeon (q.v.) had little but contempt for each other. From 1899 onward Wayland supported the Socialist Party, which he joined in 1901, but he refused to make *Appeal* a party organ.

Although Wayland favored labor unions, he had little use for the political policies of most labor leaders. He accused them of being political "scabs" for voting in favor of non-Socialist, "capitalist" candidates. He was especially critical of American Federation of Labor President Samuel Gompers for his policy of supporting "labor's friends and opposing its enemies" in the two old parties.

As Socialist and reform power grew in the United States, *Appeal* grew in strength. In 1902 Wayland turned the actual editorial control over to Fred D. Warren, a Socialist journalist from Schenectady, New York. By 1910 the circulation reached 500,000.

Shortly after the 1912 election, Wayland committed suicide for unknown reasons.

SOURCES: Howard H. Quint, "Julius A. Wayland, Pioneer Socialist Propagandist," *Mississippi Valley Historical Review*, vol. XXXV (March 1949) Algie M. Simons, "J. A. Wayland, Propagandist," *Metropolitan Magazine* 32 (January 1913); Fred Warren Papers in Indiana University Library, Bloomington, Indiana.

*BERNARD K. JOHNPOLL*

**WEINER, WILLIAM (1893–1954).** Robert William Weiner, also known as William Weiner, was a top financial functionary of the American Communist Party for over twenty years. Born Welwel Warszower in Radanjenko, Russia, on September 5, 1893, Weiner arrived in Philadelphia as a 21-year-old immigrant on March 27, 1914, aboard the SS *Haverford*. In 1917, using the Weiner surname for the first time, he registered as a Russian alien to avoid the military draft. After working a series of jobs in Pittsburgh, Detroit, and Chicago and becoming a member of the Young People's Socialist League, Weiner moved to New York in the early 1920s, joined the American Communist Party, and became assistant labor editor of the Jewish daily newspaper, the *Freiheit*.

By 1927–1928 Weiner had become a Party section organizer in New York, and in late 1933 he was named the Party's financial secretary. During that decade he also served as president of the International Workers Order, as chairman of the Executive Committee of the Jewish People's Committee (initially the Jewish Committee Against Fascism and Anti-Semitism), and by 1938 was a vice-president of World Tourists, Inc., and a member of the Communist Party's National Committee.

Called before the Dies Committee investigating Communism in September 1939, Weiner acknowledged no use of other names and gave his birthdate and birthplace as September 5, 1896, in Atlantic City, New Jersey. Less than three months later, on December 4, Weiner was indicted on one count of passport fraud for having falsely asserted both U.S. citizenship and that Atlantic City birth so as to obtain an American passport in 1936. At his February 1940 trial, prosecutors documented Weiner's recurrent use of alternate identities—he had traveled to Europe as Warszower in 1932—and a sloppy attempt to forge Atlantic City birth records. Weiner's defense called no witnesses and contended that he had been confused about the circumstances of his birth until the early 1930s. Convicted, Weiner was handed the maximum two year sentence, only to succeed eventually in having it suspended due to a life-threatening heart ailment.

Although Weiner testified in 1939 that the Party received no foreign financial support, and although both his financial assignment and Party membership ostensibly ended after his 1940 conviction, he served continuously from 1933 until his death on February 20, 1954, as the Party's top financial operative, with special responsibility for handling both crucial contributions from domestic "angels" and annual subsidies secretly provided by the Soviet Union. Married, with one daughter, Weiner's expensive suits and wide-ranging travels belied his supposedly poorly paid Party posts and instead reflected the habits of a successful financier whose low-visibility skills—especially the productive investment of

Party funds in capitalist businesses run by sympathetic friends—provided the American Party with solid financial management throughout its two peak decades of life.

SOURCES: Claire Neikind, "U.S. Communism: Its Underground Plans and Its Secret Business Empire," *The Reporter* 4 (January 23, 1951); *Warszower v. United States*, 113 F.2d 100 (1940), 312 U.S. 342 (1941); Testimony of Robert William Weiner, in U.S. Congress, House of Representatives, Special Committee on Un-American Activities, *Investigation of Un-American Propaganda Activities in the United States—Hearings*, Vol. 7, pp. 4747–4810.

*DAVID J. GARROW*

**WEINSTOCK, LOUIS (b.1903).** Louis Weinstock was an important leader of the Brotherhood of Painters, Decorators, and Paperhangers, and a prominent member of the Communist Party. He was born on May 14, 1903, in Satoraljauhely Hungary, the son of a Jewish painter and decorator. He came to the United States in 1924, just shy of his twenty-first birthday. Settling in New York, Weinstock worked as a painter by day and studied at night; he also joined the Communist Party. In 1926 he married, and in 1930 he became a naturalized U.S. citizen.

Weinstock belonged to the Brotherhood of Painters, Decorators and Paperhangers (an affiliate of the American Federation of Labor [AFL]), where his radical views sometimes led to trouble with the union hierarchy. During the Depression he directed the Communist Party's push for unemployment compensation, chairing the Trade Union Committee for Unemployment Insurance and Relief, which attempted to gather AFL support for a Communist-written measure. Weinstock served a lengthy term as secretary-treasurer of the New York District Council of Painters during the 1930s and 1940s, teaching in his free time at the Workers School. In 1947, however, he was defeated for reelection, and in 1950 he was expelled altogether from the union for "disruptive activities."

Weinstock visited Hungary in 1949, returning with information from a purge trial that led to the highly publicized expulsion from the Communist Party of John Lautner on unfounded suspicions that he was an American agent. Lautner's anger at his treatment did turn him into a government witness.

In 1951 Weinstock became one of the second wave of Smith Act victims. He was charged with conspiring to teach and advocate the overthrow of the government. He was convicted and jailed, while denaturalization proceedings were begun against him. After his release, the government called him before Congressional committees as an unfriendly witness.

As a native of Hungary, Weinstock was one of the Communist Party's experts on Eastern European affairs. During the Party crisis of 1956–1957 he stood firmly behind the Soviet Union's actions against Hungary and supported William Foster (q.v.) in the inner-party fight. Weinstock taught at Party-affiliated schools during the 1950s, but he retired to California. He has today turned his attention toward the rights of elderly Americans, working with the National Council of Senior Citizens.

JUDY KUTULAS

**WEINSTONE, WILLIAM (1897–1985).** William Weinstone headed the Communist Party's New York district for nearly a decade, served on the Politburo, and challenged Earl Browder (q.v.) for Party leadership. He was born on December 15, 1897, in Vilna, Lithuania. His father, a Jew, was a carpenter. Weinstone joined the Socialist Party at age 16 and continued his political activities at the City College of New York, where he was first secretary and then president of the school's chapter of the Intercollegiate Socialist Society, succeeding Jay Lovestone (q.v.) in the latter post.

Weinstone was a charter member of the Communist movement in 1919 and almost immediately sprang into its upper echelons. During the underground period he used the pseudonym "Randolph." First elected to the Central Committee in 1921, he was briefly national secretary in 1921–1922, but he spent most of the decade as the Party's New York district organizer, interrupted by stints with the International Workers Aid and postings in Moscow. Aligned with the Charles Ruthenberg (q.v.) faction in the Communist Party, Weinstone nonetheless negotiated an agreement with the Cannon (q.v.)–Foster (q.v.) group, which supported him for general secretary after Ruthenberg's death in 1927. When this maneuver failed, Weinstone made his peace with Jay Lovestone, earning the derisive nickname "Wobbly" for his indecisiveness.

After the Comintern's ouster of Lovestone in 1929, Weinstone was once again a contender for Party leadership, serving on a four-man secretariat. Late in the year he became the Party's representative to the Comintern. When he returned to the United States late in 1931, he challenged Earl Browder for control of the Party, criticizing Communist tactics toward the Bonus Marchers. The Comintern supported Browder, and Weinstone returned to Moscow. Early in 1934 he was assigned to Detroit as district organizer, and he helped establish the Party's foothold in the United Auto Workers.

Weinstone's Party career derailed in 1938. Believing that his support for wildcat auto strikes endangered the Communists' alliance with John L. Lewis' Congress of Industrial Organizations, Browder criticized Weinstone's stewardship of the Michigan Party. On one trip to Moscow, Browder and William Foster debated the Weinstone issue before the Comintern. It supported Browder once again, and in mid–1938 Weinstone was quietly transferred into less prestigious and important Party educational work, where he spent most of the remainder of his life. He was convicted in a New York Smith Act trial in 1951 and sentenced to two years in prison. Weinstone remained active on the Party's Historical Commission into the early 1980s. He died in 1985.

SOURCES: Theodore Draper, *American Communism and Soviet Russia* (1960); Harvey Klehr, *The Heyday of American Communism* (1984).

HARVEY KLEHR

**WEISBORD, ALBERT (1900–1977).** Albert Weisbord led major Communist strikes in Passaic, New Jersey, and Gastonia, North Carolina, before being expelled. He was born on December 9, 1900, in New York City. Both his parents were Russian Jewish immigrants. His father owned a small manufacturing firm. Weisbord became interested in socialism as a young boy and active in the Socialist Party at the City College of New York, from which he graduated Phi Beta Kappa in 1921. While at Harvard Law School (LL.B. 1924), he was elected national secretary of the Young People's Socialist League in 1922. He joined the Communist Party in 1924 in Boston and, rather than practice law, organized New England textile workers. Sent to Passaic, New Jersey, in 1926, he led 13,000 textile workers in a violent, year-long strike that drew national attention. The American Federation of Labor (AFL) agreed to help end the conflict only after Weisbord stepped down as leader.

Catapulted into prominence by his success, Weisbord had prickly relations with other Party leaders, whose competence and intelligence he doubted. He held a series of Party positions in the next few years, including district organizer in Detroit, and was a delegate to the 1928 Profintern Congress. Elected national secretary of the newly organized Communist-dominated National Textile Workers Union, he helped lead the famous Gastonia, North Carolina, strike of 1929, during which his wife, Vera Buch, and other organizers were charged with murder of the local sheriff.

None of the Party factions had much love for Weisbord, and he was forced out of his union position after the Gastonia strike collapsed. During the Party's leadership crisis of 1929, there were rumors that he was in line for an important position, but they proved groundless. He was expelled from the Party in 1929 amid accusations that he had encouraged or tolerated white chauvinism in Gastonia.

Weisbord briefly flirted with the Trotskyists, but then created his own Trotskyist group, the Communist League of Struggle, in 1931. He visited Trotsky in Prinkipo, Turkey, in 1932 and worked with the Partido Obrero de Unificatión Marxista (POUM) in Spain in 1937 but finally disbanded the organization in 1937; it had never attracted more than a handful of members.

For several years Weisbord was an AFL organizer. Fired in the early 1940s, he held numerous jobs until setting up a management consultant firm during the Korean War. He died in April 1977.

SOURCE: Vera Buch Weisbord, *A Radical Life* (1977).

*HARVEY KLEHR*

**WEISS, MAX (b.1909).** For nearly three decades Max Weiss was a leader of the Young Communist League and the Communist Party, a key figure in the Party's educational apparatus, and an editor of its theoretical journal. He was born on December 5, 1909, in Newark, New Jersey, of Jewish parents who migrated to the United States from Austro-Hungary at the turn of the century. His father was a garment worker, a trade unionist, and a Socialist. Weiss attended

New York City elementary and high schools and the City College of New York for three years.

Weiss joined the Young Communist League (YCL) in 1928, initially devoting himself to the student movement at City College. He was suspended in 1930 following an arrest for distributing leaflets in behalf of the unemployed. Student protests led to his reinstatement. He became president of the Social Problems Club at the college, then involved in an anti-war campaign that stressed banning the Reserve Officers Training Corps (ROTC) from the campus. When college authorities sought to curb the club's activities, the resulting confrontation led to a second suspension for Weiss and for several other students. The drive for their reinstatement, successful except for Weiss, led to formation of the New York Student League and subsequently the National Student League.

His academic studies ended, Weiss became editor of the YCL's national publication, *The Young Worker*. He served in that post and was the YCL's education director until 1936, except for eighteen months as the YCL's New England district organizer. In 1935, at the Sixth World Congress of the Young Communist International, he was elected to the YCL's Executive Committee. The following year he became national secretary of the Young Communist League, serving until 1943, when the YCL was succeeded by American Youth for Democracy. In 1940 he was also elected to the Communist Party's National Committee, remaining a member until 1948.

After leaving the youth movement in 1943, Weiss became the Communist Party's district organizer in western Pennsylvania. In 1945 he was reassigned as national education director and an editorial board member of the Party's theoretical journal, *Political Affairs*. He later became the journal's editor. At the Smith Act trial of the members of the Party's National Political Committee in 1949, he was an expert witness on Party theory concerning the use of force and violence.

In 1951, following the Party leaders' conviction and further arrests of Communist leaders, the Party was restructured to consist of three national centers: "illegal," "unavailable," and "public." Weiss was coordinator of the three leadership centers until 1955, when he was arrested that year under the "membership" clause of the Smith Act. However, he was never tried. The government abandoned Smith Act prosecutions in 1962 following adverse Supreme Court rulings.

By 1956 the Party leadership's situation was normalized, and Weiss again functioned as national education director. He played a prominent part in the intense Party debate during 1956–1957 on the issues posed by the Khrushchev revelations about Stalin at the Soviet Party's Twentieth Congress early in 1956. He helped to draft the resolution presented to the U.S. Party's Sixteenth Convention in 1957, which sought to incorporate fundamental changes in Party theory and practice similar to those now associated with "Euro-communism." He was not reelected to the National Committee and played no further role in the Party's leadership. In 1962 he left the Party because of disagreement with important aspects of its general orientation and made his living as a machine designer and draftsman.

*MAX GORDON*

**WICKS, HARRY (1889?–1957).** Harry Wicks was one of the more shadowy and mysterious figures in a radical movement that had many figures with both characteristics. He was active in several small, ultra-radical sects until becoming a second-echelon Communist organizer. Expelled in 1938, Wicks was, for his entire Party career, an undercover agent for private investigating firms. His real name may have been Richard Proctor. By his own account, he was born on December 10, 1889, in Arcola, Illinois, to an Anglo-Saxon family. The Federal Bureau of Investigation (FBI) believed he was born in 1896 in Houghton, Michigan, and was possibly of Finnish descent. His father was probably an electrical engineer.

A printer by trade, Wicks was an organizer for the Michigan Socialist Party as early as 1915. By 1918, as secretary of the party in Portland, Oregon, he was president of the local Council of Workers, Soldiers, and Sailors and connected with the Industrial Workers of the World. In 1919 he was elected to the National Executive Committee of the Socialist Party, edited the *Western Socialist,* and at the first Communist Party convention was aligned with the Michigan Socialists. He joined with them in the Proletarian Party after they were forced out of the Communist movement, serving on the Executive Committee. Back in the Communist Party again in 1922, he quit when the underground party was dissolved. Wicks then formed the United Toilers and edited *Workers Challenge,* generally considered the most vituperative radical journal ever published. Late in 1922 he once more rejoined the Communist Party.

Wicks held a variety of Party positions, editing the *Daily Worker* several times, and in 1929 served as Communist Party representative to the Profintern while on the Central Committee. He was briefly considered as a candidate for the Party secretariat after Jay Lovestone's (q.v.) ouster, but was instead sent on Comintern assignments to Australia and the Philippines. On his return to the United States in 1932, he was exiled to Chattanooga, Tennessee, as district organizer. He continued to hold minor positions until he was suddenly expelled from the Party in 1938 as a spy.

FBI files indicate that Wicks had been working for the Illinois Steel Company and the Chicago police as an undercover informant in 1919. The following year he made a strident anti-Communist speech to a Gary, Indiana, business group about his experience at the Party's 1919 convention. When he rejoined the Party in 1923, a commission investigated the incident and cleared him. Wicks also was indicted for violation of the Illinois state sedition law in 1920 but released. In 1921 he was indicted for violation of the Mann Act involving "white slavery" in Washington, but the case was not prosecuted.

After his expulsion from the Party, he briefly joined Lovestone's splinter group and resumed his work as a printer in Chicago. His exact political status remained

unclear. Wicks cooperated with the FBI and the Immigration Service in investigations on Communism and apparently sold information on the Party to private investigators. But he occasionally balked at providing information and even told FBI agents he remained a dedicated Communist. The government finally concluded that he was an unreliable informant. He died in 1957.
SOURCE: FBI File 100–29845.

*HARVEY KLEHR*

**WILKERSON, DOXEY (b.1905).** Doxey Alphonso Wilkerson was a leading black Communist in the 1940s and 1950s. Wilkerson was born on April 24, 1905, in Excelsior Springs, Missouri, to the Reverend Alphonso and Mattie Wilkerson. He received B.A. and M.A. degrees from the University of Kansas in 1926 and 1927 and embarked on an academic career in English education at Virginia State College. His research interests focused primarily on the problems of "Negro education" in a segregated society. Wilkerson also did doctoral work at the University of Michigan in the early 1930s.

He was appointed to the faculty of education at Howard University in Washington, D.C., in 1935 and advised several government organizations and committees. In 1939 he assisted the Swedish Social Democrat Gunnar Myrdal in researching and writing *An American Dilemma*. Wilkerson's role as vice-president of the American Federation of Teachers from 1937 to 1940 and his research connection to the Myrdal project reenforced Wilkerson's belief in the validity of the Marxist interpretation of social development, and he joined the Communist Party in 1943.

In the Party, Wilkerson's primary functions were those of a theorist, polemicist, and disseminator of information. He became one of the staunchest critics of the Communist Party's early appeal to blacks on the basis of the self-determination strategy, which held the promise of several contiguous Southern areas being set aside as a separate nation for Afro-Americans. To Wilkerson, the Communist Party's reaffirmation of this idea in the 1940s had "separatist implications" regarding the Party's position on Afro-Americans. This issue, along with the Party's internecine conflict over adherence to the ideological "line" of the Soviet Union in the late 1940s and 1950s, prompted Wilkerson to resign from the Party in 1957.

After severing his ties with the Communist Party, Wilkerson resumed his career in academia by acquiring his Ph.D. at New York University in 1959 and accepting a post as professor of education at Bishop College in Texas that same year. However, an anti-Communist newspaper campaign blaming him for stirring up the campus Afro-American student protest for equal rights in the community forced him to resign from Bishop in 1960. He was employed subsequently at Yeshiva University in New York City, where he taught from 1963 to 1973, serving most of that time as chairman of the Department of Curriculum and Instruction.

SOURCES: Personal interviews with Doxey Wilkerson, August 30, 1979, and March 5, 1983; Joseph R. Starobin, *American Communism in Crisis, 1943–57* (1972); Doxey A. Wilkerson, *The Negro People and the Communists* (1944).

*MACEO CRENSHAW DAILEY*

**WILLIAMS, CLAUDE (1895–1979).** Claude Closey Williams was a radical Christian Socialist who believed that religion could be a revolutionary force for achieving racial equality and a new economic order in the South. He trained organizers for the Workers Alliance and the Southern Tenant Farmers Union, served as director of Commonwealth College in Mena, Arkansas, and founded the People's Institute of Applied Religion.

Williams was born in 1895 in Weakley County, Tennessee, the son of a tenant farmer. His family had long been members of the Cumberland Presbyterian Church, a localized fundamentalist sect. After serving as a sergeant in World War I, Williams enrolled in Bethel College, the church's seminary school in McKenzie, Tennessee. Williams completed his studies for the ministry in 1924 and accepted a pastorate in Auburntown, Tennessee. He preached as a traditional fundamentalist and became one of the denomination's most accomplished preachers. He was dissatisfied, however, and took leave to study at the Vanderbilt University School of Religion under Dr. Alva Taylor, noted exponent of the Social Gospel. Taylor's class brought Williams into contact with Don West, Ward Rogers, and Howard Kester (q.v.), all of whom would be behind a regional effort to make the church a vehicle for social change in the South.

Williams left Vanderbilt in 1929, and within a year he moved his family to Paris, Arkansas, to establish a "Workingman's Church." The church provided local miners with a center for meetings, refuge, and study. In 1932 he helped the miners organize a successful strike. Shortly thereafter the Presbyterian Church removed Williams from his Paris pastorate. He was soon arrested for participating in a Workers Alliance demonstration in Fort Smith and spent a month in jail with Horace Bryan, a Communist Party organizer. During this time Bryan taught Williams Marxism. In 1935 the Southern Tenant Farmers Union (STFU) and the Workers Alliance commissioned Williams to organize a training school for black and white labor leaders. Williams based his instruction on the Bible as the longest record of the struggle against oppression.

In 1936 Williams ran for the U.S. Senate in Arkansas on the Socialist Party ticket. The following year he accepted directorship of Commonwealth College, a labor school in Mena, Arkansas. The school's apparent pro-Communist leanings raised suspicions among Williams' associates at the Socialist-dominated STFU. Evidence implying that Williams was helping to plan a Communist plot to take over the STFU led the Executive Board to expel him from the union in 1939.

Shortly after his expulsion from the STFU, Williams left Commonwealth College and established the People's Institute of Applied Religion to train leaders of mass religious groups as organizers for the Congress of Industrial Organizations and civil rights groups. Williams led institutes in Arkansas, Missouri, and

Tennessee. His success caused the Detroit presbytery to request Williams' assistance as industrial chaplain in their racially torn city during World War II. Williams helped restore peace after the 1943 race riot. His institutes for black and white labor leaders prevented racial hostility from destroying the unions.

In 1948 the House Un-American Activities Committee (HUAC) labeled Williams' institute "one of the most vicious Communist organizations in this country." Illinois Congressman Harold Velde, chairman of HUAC, urged the Detroit presbytery to try Williams for heresy. Although he reaffirmed his belief in the basic dogmas of the church, he was tried, found guilty of heresy, and stripped of his ordination.

After the war, Williams and his wife had settled in Fungo Hollow, near Alabaster, Alabama, and devoted themselves to local community work during the 1950s. By the early 1960s they were actively involved in the civil rights movement in Alabama and Mississippi. Claude Williams died in 1979.

SOURCES: Cedric Belfrage, *South of God* (1941); Anthony P. Dunbar, *Against the Grain: Southern Radicals and Prophets, 1929–1959* (1981); Mark Naison, "Claude and Joyce Williams: Pilgrims of Justice," *Southern Exposure*, Winter 1974.

*PAT SULLIVAN*

**WILLIAMS, HOWARD Y. (1889–1973).** Howard Yolen Williams was a prominent participant in attempts to found a national left-wing third party in the 1930s. Born on January 27, 1889, Williams graduated from the University of Minnesota in 1910 and then attended the Union Theological Seminary. He was an army chaplain during World War I and then served as pastor of a Congregational church in St. Paul, Minnesota, from 1919 until 1929.

Williams worked for the League for Independent Political Action (1929–1926), the Farmer-Labor Political Federation (1933–1935), and the American Commonwealth Political Federation (1935–1937) in hopes of founding a national leftist but nonrevolutionary third party modeled on Minnesota's Farmer-Labor Party and Wisconsin's Progressive Party. He welcomed the Communist Party's turn to the Popular Front and included Communists in his activities. As a leader of the Popular Front wing of the Minnesota Farmer-Labor Party, Williams headed the state's veterans agency under Governor Elmer Benson (q.v.).

Williams was employed by the Union for Democratic Action and its affiliate, the Independent Voters of Illinois, from 1942 to 1946. In 1946–1947 he also worked for the American League for a Free Palestine. After World War II, he adopted anti-Communist liberalism and assisted Hubert Humphrey in the campaign to drive Communists out of Minnesota's Democratic-Farmer-Labor Party.

Williams served as pastor of a Congregational church in Butte, Montana, from 1955 to 1965 and then worked until 1969 for the United World Federalists. He died in 1973.

SOURCE: Howard Y. Williams Papers, Minnesota Historical Society. St. Paul, Minnesota.

*JOHN HAYNES*

418            WILLIAMSON, JOHN

**WILLIAMSON, JOHN (1903–1974).** John Williamson headed the Communist Party's youth wing, served as Party leader in Ohio, was national organization secretary, and directed Communist labor work. He was born on June 23, 1903, in Glasgow, Scotland, to a Presbyterian family. After his father, a marine engineer, died in 1913, he moved to the United States with his mother. They settled in Seattle, where she worked as a housekeeper and cleaner. Williamson dropped out of school after the eighth grade and by 1918 was an apprentice in a shipbuilding company.

Under the influence of a shopmate he joined the Socialist Labor Party (SLP) in 1918 and took part in the Seattle general strike of 1919. He became state secretary of the SLP in 1921, but resigned the next year because he supported the Bolshevik Revolution. When the Communist Party endorsed working in existing unions and ending its underground existence, he joined it in late 1922 and became active in the Young Workers League (YWL).

Williamson's rise in the Party's youth group was rapid. He attended the YWL's 1923 convention and was chosen national industrial organizer. One year later he became the group's representative on the Party Central Committee and was a delegate to the Fourth Young Communist International Congress in Moscow, where he was selected for the Executive Council. In September 1924 he became national secretary of the YWL. Within a year, however, Williamson lost his post when the Comintern turned over control of the Party from William Foster (q.v.), with whom he was allied, to Charles Ruthenberg (q.v.). He remained the Foster faction's leader in the YWL. After nine months in Russia in 1928, Williamson was dispatched to Canada to root out Trotskyists in its Young Communist League.

He began his career in the adult Party in 1929 as an assistant to William Foster in the Trade Union Educational League. Elected to the Central Committee in 1930, Williamson also served as organizational secretary in Chicago. From 1933 to 1940 he was district organizer in Ohio and supervised Party work in that important state. He moved to the national level in 1941 as the Communists' organizational secretary and oversaw the transformation of the Party into a political association in 1944. After Earl Browder's (q.v.) ouster from leadership, he served on the Party secretariat and in 1946 took charge of Party labor work.

Williamson was convicted with ten other top Party leaders in a 1949 Smith Act trial and received a five-year sentence. After his release he accepted deportation to Great Britain in 1955. He remained active in the British Communist Party, serving in a variety of positions and in 1959 winning election to its National Executive Committee. After his retirement in 1965 he was a director of the Marx Memorial Library in London. He died on July 9, 1974.
SOURCE: John Williamson, *Dangerous Scot* (1969).

*HARVEY KLEHR*

**WILSHIRE, HENRY GAYLORD (1861–1927).** H. Gaylord Wilshire, widely known at the turn of the century as the flamboyant "millionaire Socialist," was born in Cincinnati, Ohio, in 1861. As the son of a wealthy local capitalist,

Wilshire enjoyed a privileged youth, which included a year of study at Harvard. Perhaps to escape paternal dominance, in 1884 he ventured to California. There he participated in the land boom of 1886–1887, developing properties in Long Beach, Santa Monica, Pasadena, and Fullerton, where he built his own ranch and became a pioneer in citrus cultivation. Through these real estate ventures, Wilshire made his first "fortune." He made a second in the late 1890s, when he developed the Wilshire Boulevard district of Los Angeles; a third at the turn of the century, when he monopolized the Los Angeles billboard industry; and a fourth in the 1920s marketing an electric health-cure device. Yet Wilshire was never technically a "millionaire"—this was a persona he presented to gain public attention. And he spent his money almost as fast as he earned it on a gracious lifestyle, bad investments, and the Socialist cause.

Wilshire became a Socialist in 1887, after reading Edward Bellamy's (q.v.) *Looking Backward*. He organized Nationalist Clubs throughout Southern California and in 1890 became the first person to run for Congress as a Socialist. Over the years he ran under this label for other political offices in California, New York, Canada, and England, where he stood as a Social Democratic Federation candidate for Parliament until he withdrew from the race.

An uninhibited publicity-seeker, Wilshire was often condemned as an egotistic exhibitionist by more orthodox Socialists. "My proposition," he wrote, "is for Socialists to get in and let people know we are alive." He gained extensive publicity through his challenges to debate William Jennings Bryan, E. R. A. Seligman, and other notable politicians and professors. He also attracted headlines when he dramatically confronted the U.S. Post Office, which following President McKinley's assassination tried to deny various liberal and radical publications second-class mailing privileges.

Most people knew of Wilshire through his two periodicals, *The Challenge*, published out of Los Angeles in 1900 and 1901, and *Wilshire's Magazine*, published from Toronto, New York, and Bishop, California, between 1901 and 1915. Wilshire was a journalist, not a theorist. His task was to churn out, at a rapid but regular pace, articles that would entice his subscribers, who numbered close to 300,000 in 1905. Through his publications he sought to popularize socialism to a nonparty audience of middle- and upper-class Americans. Consequently he deemphasized class conflict while arguing that socialism was both inevitable and would improve the quality of life of all citizens. Seldom would readers find references to the "giants" of Socialist theory. Rather, ideas were put forth in a humorous, common-sense manner. Wilshire loved metaphors and analogies and took "reasonable" stands on divisive issues. Moreover, like other turn-of-the-century radicals he strove to unite socialism with evolutionary science.

As a Socialist publisher, Wilshire knew most of the leading radicals of the Progressive era. Upton Sinclair (q.v.), whom Wilshire converted to socialism, was his closest, lifelong friend. Wilshire vacationed with Jack London, crusaded with Emma Goldman (q.v.), and helped fund several of Eugene V. Debs' (q.v.)

speaking tours. He also served as a bridge between the American and European Left. He visited and corresponded with Leo Tolstoy, George Bernard Shaw, H. G. Wells, and Prince Kropotkin; he wrote the introduction to the first American edition of *The Fabian Essays*; he hosted Maxim Gorki on his 1906 tour of the United States; and he ranked Great Britain's Henry Hyndman as one of his closest confidants on affairs of love as well as politics.

Attempting to blend entrepreneurism with socialism in 1906, Wilshire started selling through his magazine shares in two gold mines he owned. A number of the more affluent leftists—including William English Walling (q.v.)—bought into the scheme, and Ernest Untermann, one of America's leading Marxist theorists before World War I, served as manager of the Bishop Creek, California, property. However, other Socialists, led by Victor Berger (q.v.) and Thomas Morgan, thought it incongruous that Socialists should speculate and had the party go on record against mining ventures. The capitalist press took great delight in charging Socialist business fraud when the mines failed to pay off, and the U.S. postal authorities initiated an investigation.

In 1910, amid this controversy, Gaylord departed for another extended stay in England. Here Wilshire lost faith in socialism and became increasingly enthusiastic over syndicalism. As a friend of Tom Mann, he participated in the transport strikes of 1911–1912 and even assumed editorship of the *Syndicalist* when its regular editor, Guy Bowman, was imprisoned. Wilshire finally returned to the United States in 1914 and immediately joined those on the Left who thought that the United States should enter the "Great War" on the side of England and against "feudal autocracy." Yet after 1915 Wilshire's prominence on the Left faded. For one thing, he had exhausted his fortune on his mines and could no longer afford to publish his magazine. For another, his pro-war syndicalism did not attract large numbers of fellow adherents. Still, until his death in 1927, Wilshire maintained close ties with many of his old comrades and all the while tried to rebuild his fortune through quack medical schemes.

SOURCES: Howard H. Quint, "Gaylord Wilshire and Socialism's First Congressional Campaign," *Pacific Historical Review* 26, no. 4 (November 1957), and "Challenge and *Wilshire's Magazine*," in *American Radical Press*, ed. Joseph Conlin, vol. 1 (1974).

                                                          *WARREN VAN TINE*

**WILSON, LILITH MARTIN (1887–1937).** Lilith Wilson was a Socialist member of the Pennsylvania House of Representatives from 1930 until 1936, when ill-health forced her to resign. Born Lilith Martin in Kokomo, Indiana, in 1887 and educated at public schools there, Wilson became an active Socialist about five years before the outbreak of World War I.

During her first years in the Socialist Party, she was primarily an agitator, organizer, and administrator for the party in Indiana and Los Angeles, where she was for one year the executive director of the then-powerful Socialist organization. She was later employed as a lecturer for the party throughout the nation. Between 1918 and 1921 Wilson directed the drive to win amnesty for anti-war prisoners, especially her friend, Eugene V. Debs (q.v.), who had been convicted of violating the Espionage Act of 1917 for questioning U.S. participation in the war. She had been a candidate for many offices in Indiana and Pennsylvania, invariably unsuccessfully until 1930. She was active in other Socialist campaigns, especially the drive to elect Robert LaFollette, Sr., as U.S. President in 1924.

In 1930 Wilson was elected from one of Reading's two districts (the other was won by Socialist Darlington Hoopes [q.v.]) and began her career in the state House. There she proposed bills to outlaw child labor, to enact health insurance and old-age pensions (at a time when there was no Social Security legislation on the books in either the state or nation), and to offer the unemployed jobs or relief from economic distress. She also led the floor fight in the legislature for a constitutional amendment to outlaw child labor. While serving in the state legislature, Wilson was nominated as the first female candidate for governor of a major state—Pennsylvania. She polled more than 30,000 votes. She was reelected to the state House in 1934 and 1936 and led her party's fight for reform. During her third term in office, Wilson became seriously ill and was confined to a hospital from May 1936 until early 1937. She died in July of that year at age 50. Wilson, who believed that social reform was the route to socialism, was always in the moderate wing of the party.

*BERNARD K. JOHNPOLL*

**WINSTON, HENRY (b.1911).** Henry Winston is presently chairman of the Communist Party of the United States of America. He was born on April 2, 1911, in Hattiesburg, Mississippi, where his father worked as a sawmill laborer and his mother was a housewife. They were Baptists and supporters of the Republican Party. The family moved shortly after World War I to Kansas City, Missouri, where the elder Winston obtained work in the Sheffield Steel Company.

Henry was forced to withdraw from high school in 1930 due to the Depression. He joined the National Association for the Advancement of Colored People in 1930, but out of school and unemployed, Winston began to listen more attentively to the Kansas City Communists who debated and sold copies of the *Daily Worker* on streetcorners. He took a particularly keen interest in newspaper accounts and discussions related to the Scottsboro Boys and the Angelo Herndon (q.v.) case. Winston subsequently joined both the Young Communist League and the Communist Party in New York City in 1931. From 1931 to 1933 he helped organize the Unemployed Councils while traveling extensively to Afro-American communities in Harlem, New York, and Cleveland, Ohio, to encourage blacks to join and support the Communist Party. In 1932 he served as a delegate on the Hunger March to Washington, D.C. Trips to the Soviet Union in 1933 and 1937 strengthened his faith in the Party. Winston was administrative secretary for the Young Communist League from 1937 to 1942.

During World War II, Winston joined the army and served in Europe from 1942 to 1945. Honorably discharged from the army in 1945, he resumed his activities as a Communist organizer, becoming a member of the Party's National

Committee in 1945 and national secretary and national board representative in 1946. Two years later he was indicted for violation of the Smith Act along with ten other Party leaders, convicted, and sentenced to five years in prison. Believing that the arrest and conviction of Communists in 1948–1949 meant that the United States was on the road to fascism, Winston jumped bail and went underground in 1951 after his appeals were exhausted. On March 5, 1956, he surfaced and surrendered to federal marshals in New York City and was given an extra three years in addition to his original five-year sentence. He was incarcerated in the federal penitentiary in Terre Haute, Indiana. In January 1960 the discovery that Winston had a brain tumor led to his transfer to the Medical Center for Federal Prisoners in Springfield, Missouri, where at his insistence a private physician performed surgery to remove the malignant growth. Complications from the operation and attending care caused Winston to lose his eyesight. Winston sued the Justice Department for negligence he claimed led to the loss. While the lawsuit was being pressed, President John F. Kennedy commuted Winston's sentence on humanitarian grounds. Released from prison in June 1961, Winston later dropped the suit.

Winston was feted during a visit to the Soviet Union in 1965. At the Communist Party's national convention in July 1966 he was appointed Party national chairman, and he has held the post since then. Winston rallied Communist support for Angela Davis (q.v.) during her imprisonment. He also led the movement to adopt a new Communist Party constitutional amendment barring "all forms of male supremacy." As the official head of the Party, Winston went to the Russian Embassy in Washington, D.C., in the summer of 1973 to meet with then premier Leonid I. Brezhnev while the Kremlin leader was on a state visit to the United States. On the occasion of his sixty-fifth birthday, Winston was bestowed the Soviet Union's highest civilian award, "The Order of the October Revolution," in Moscow in 1976. He is still active in Communist Party affairs as a spokesman and publicist. He currently lives in New York City.

*MACEO CRENSHAW DAILEY*

**WINTER, CARL (b.1906).** Carl Winter was an important and longtime functionary of the Communist Party in the United States. He was born Philip Carl Weisberg on September 25, 1906, in Cleveland, Ohio, the son of Russian Jewish Socialists. His father worked for the *Jewish Daily Forward*, and his mother later joined the Communist Party herself in Cleveland.

Winter first became a member of the Young Communist League in 1922 in Cleveland, working as a city organizer while attending Western Reserve College. Four years later he was head of the Young Communist League in New York and a student at the City College of New York. In all, Winter attended college for three years and worked as a draftsman.

In the early 1930s Winter served on the National Board of the Unemployed Councils, was secretary of the New York chapter, and was a leader of the first National Hunger March in 1931. His talent was organization, and he moved from place to place working where he was most needed. He was an organizer in Cleveland in 1936, becoming Ohio state educational director in 1937. In 1938 he served as an assistant to John Williamson (q.v.). Between 1939 and 1942 Winter was a district organizer in Minnesota, and from 1942 to 1945 he was secretary of the Los Angeles Party. The year 1944 marked his first election to the National Committee of the Communist Party of the United States of America.

From 1945 to 1949 Winter was chairman of the Michigan Communist Party, and it was while holding this position that he was indicted under the Smith Act along with ten other Party leaders. During the trial he was jailed for contempt because he refused to reveal whether his father-in-law was a Communist. He was convicted and jailed, as was his wife Helen, who succeeded him as the secretary of the Michigan Communist Party.

In the Party crisis of 1956–1957, Winter took a position between John Gates (q.v.) and William Z. Foster (q.v.), but ultimately remained in the Party. He served on the National Executive Committee of the reconstituted Party and became the editor of the *Daily Worker*. Winter is still an active member of the Communist Party and an organizer in Michigan.

*JUDY KUTULAS*

**WOLFE, BERTRAM (1896–1977).** Bertram Wolfe was a leader of Jay Lovestone's (q.v.) Communist Party faction during the 1920s and of the Lovestone group in the 1930s. He then became a leading expert on communism. He was born on January 19, 1896, in Brooklyn, New York, to German Jewish parents. His father was a dry-goods salesman. A 1916 graduate of the City College of New York, he was teaching English at Boys High in New York in 1917 when he was fired for refusing to sign a loyalty oath.

Wolfe was drawn to the Socialist Party in 1917 because of his opposition to World War I, which led him to activity in the People's Council and editing of an anti-war journal, *Facts*. While publicity director for the Rand School, he became a leader of the Socialist Party's radical faction and with John Reed (q.v.) wrote the national manifesto of the party's left wing.

Wolfe was one of the few American-born radicals to be a charter member of the foreign-dominated Communist Party in 1919, but illness prevented him from attending the founding convention, and he was given no official post. When the Palmer Raids began, he nonetheless went underground, adopted the name Arthur Albrecht, and moved to California, where he edited a labor paper. After evading arrest when the Party's secret 1922 Bridgman convention was raided by police, Wolfe briefly settled in Boston before moving to Mexico City to teach English.

For the next two years Wolfe was an active member of the Mexican Communist Party, concentrating on educational work for the Railway Union and being chosen by the Party as its delegate to the Comintern's Fifth Congress. He also found time to earn a master's degree in 1925 at the University of Mexico. That same year the government deported him to the United States, and his comrades appointed him head of the Workers School in New York.

Wolfe was an important figure in the Party faction led by Jay Lovestone. He was one of the initiators of the theory of "American exceptionalism," which insisted that Communist tactics take account of peculiarly American conditions, and he urged attention to U.S. culture and history. Early in 1929, sensing trouble, Lovestone sent Wolfe to Moscow as the Party's representative to the Executive Committee of the Comintern. Wolfe soon learned that his faction was in disfavor. When the other factional leaders arrived in Russia, they futilely sought to prevent the Comintern from stripping them of their leadership. Wolfe rejected an offer to become a Comintern representative in Korea, returned home, and was expelled from the Party in 1929.

For the next decade Bertram Wolfe belonged to Lovestone's small splinter group. He ran its New Workers School and traveled to Spain in 1937 on its behalf. He also earned an M.A. at Columbia in romance languages in 1931 and launched a writing career by producing books on Mexican muralist Diego Rivera. In 1929 he was one of the founders of the Keep America Out of War Congress.

Wolfe established his reputation as a historian with a classic study of Lenin, Trotsky, and Stalin, *Three Who Made a Revolution*, in 1948. He was also recognized as an expert on Spanish literature. In the early 1950s he served as chief of the Ideological Advisory Unit in the State Department. Among his many honors were three Guggenheim awards and selection as a Fellow of the American Academy of Arts and Sciences. From 1966 to his death he was a Senior Fellow at the Hoover Institution. He died from burns suffered in a fire on February 21, 1977.

SOURCES: Theodore Draper, *American Communism and Soviet Russia* (1960); Bertram Wolfe, *A Life in Two Centuries* (1981).

*HARVEY KLEHR*


**WOLFSOHN, LEO (1890?–1956).** Leo Wolfsohn was an editor of the Socialist *Milwaukee Leader* between 1915 and 1938. Born in Russia about 1890, Wolfsohn came to the United States with his parents while he was still a young child. He was educated in the public schools of Chicago and the University of Missouri, from which he obtained a bachelor of journalism degree in 1913.

Immediately upon graduating from the university, Wolfsohn joined the news staff of the *Chicago World*. Two years later he moved to Milwaukee and joined the staff of the *Milwaukee Leader*. While at the *Leader*, he served as copy-desk chief, wire-news editor, and managing editor, the post he held when the Socialist daily ceased publication in 1938. From the *Leader* he went to the *Milwaukee Journal* and later the *St. Louis Post-Dispatch*.

During World War II, Wolfsohn served in the Office of War Information in Washington, D.C., as an editor and writer. After the war he worked for other government agencies, primarily the U.S. Information Agency (USIA). While in Milwaukee, Wolfsohn was one of the organizers of the Milwaukee Civic Symphony Orchestra. He also helped initiate Garden Homes, the first public housing project in the United States. He ran unsuccessfully for the Milwaukee board of school directors in 1926.

Wolfsohn was on the staff of the USIA when he died suddenly in May 1956 in Bethesda, Maryland.

SOURCE: *Milwaukee Journal*, May 26, 1956.

*JAMES E. INGBRETSON*

**WOODHULL, VICTORIA (1838–1927).** Victoria Woodhull (Claflin) made a spectacular appearance as a radical reformer on the American political scene in the Reconstruction period following the Civil War. She was born into abject poverty as part of a family of ten children in the rural town of Homer, Ohio, in 1838. Her father was a combination of confidence man, buffoon, and petty politician. Victoria acquired theatrical and oratorical skills from him and became a leader of a band of schoolchildren.

Victoria was married before she was 16 in 1853 to Dr. Canning Woodhull, a medical doctor who was an alcoholic and a notorious roué. Her marriage relationship with the ailing Dr. Woodhull was short-lived, but he continued to live in the same household with Victoria and her new husband, Colonel Blood.

Blood recognized that Victoria, with her good looks and magnetic platform ability, could be the spokesperson for the causes he espoused: philosophical anarchism, mysticism, spiritualism, free love, and Greenbackism. Afflicted by a vaulting ambition, Victoria Woodhull did not hesitate to use her sexual wiles to attract and reap benefits from a host of prominent men. Commodore Cornelius Vanderbilt, the railroad tycoon, set Victoria and her younger sister, Tennessee Claflin, up in their own brokerage firm in the Wall Street area. They derived great wealth from the inside stock-market tips received from him.

Another great ideological influence on the two sisters was the flamboyant individualist Stephen Pearl Andrews (q.v.). Andrews was both a lawyer and a medical doctor who also espoused the doctrines of the theologian Swedenborg, who advocated a universal language called Alwato and a world government called Pantarchy. He also developed a system of stenography. The Blood-Andrews combination developed the ideas for the Woodhull sisters to take to the public.

General Ben Butler, the Union army occupier of New Orleans, was a member of Congress and the recipient of Victoria's favors. This made it possible for her to achieve nationwide notoriety. On December 21, 1870, Butler arranged for Woodhull to address a message to Congress to enact laws granting women the right to vote, a right that Victoria claimed was inherent in the Fourteenth Amendment to the Constitution. The memorandum was printed by the Congress at the insistence of Senator Harris of Louisiana and Representative Julian of Indiana. After being referred to the respective judiciary committees, the House committee held a public hearing, allowing Victoria Woodhull to testify at length on the missive.

Present at the well-publicized hearing of January 11, 1871, were representatives of the National Woman Suffrage Association (NWSA), the more radical wing of the movement led by Susan B. Anthony and Elizabeth Cady Stanton. The NWSA, which had been losing influence to the more conservative abolitionist wing led by Lucy Stone, embraced Woodhull's concept and pressed for women's suffrage on a national rather than a state-by-state basis.

Victoria's open association with the doctrine of free love began to cause some embarrassment to the Anthony forces in the suffrage movement. The May 9, 1872, convention of the NWSA in New York's Steinway Hall saw Woodhull openly attempt to capture the women's suffrage organization for her own political purposes. A motion was made to continue the convention the next day to consider setting up a national political movement. Susan B. Anthony declared the motion out of order and closed the meeting by shutting off the lights, thus causing a riot.

Appollo Hall was the scene of the continued meeting now firmly in the grip of Victoria Woodhull. Six hundred delegates cheered her as she received the nomination for President of the United States as the head of the Equal Rights Party. As her running mate the delegates chose the black abolitionist Frederick Douglass. Douglass was not present and neither was he informed of the event. There never was a campaign generated behind Woodhull's candidacy.

The platform of the Equal Rights Party is instructive in that some of the planks presaged reforms that were later enacted into law. They included universal suffrage, reform of criminals, government employment for the unemployed, the printing of fiat money, and the graduated income tax. The platform also called for abolition of war through international arbitration, world government, a new federal constitution, the use of national referendums, proportional representation, government ownership of natural resources and utilities, and the abolition of capital punishment.

*Woodhull and Claflin's Weekly*, the newspaper published by the sisters, became the public vehicle for these ideas. Woodhull's notoriety reached its peak with the publicity attached to the amatory affairs of the noted preacher Henry Ward Beecher, most notably with Elizabeth Tilton, wife of Theodore Tilton, the editor of the *Independent*, an influential church-related periodical.

In May 1871 Elizabeth Cady Stanton, Susan B. Anthony's collaborator, confided to Woodhull the story that Elizabeth Tilton had confessed to Stanton. Victoria kept this information under wraps until the Protestant establishment and the Anthony wing of the suffrage movement distanced themselves from Woodhull, most particularly over Woodhull's belief in free love. Woodhull then openly castigated them as hypocrites. She claimed that they railed against free love but practiced it in private. *Woodhull and Claflin's Weekly* of November 2, 1872, carried the full story. As a result, Woodhull was charged with sending obscene material through the mails and clapped into the Ludlow Street jail, where she languished for twenty-eight days without trial. The sensational issue of the weekly commanded the high price of $40 on the black market. Repercussions continued during the next seven months of 1875.

The Woodhull forces were part of the First International, the International Workingman's Association (IWA) led from London by Karl Marx and Frederick Engels. Section 12 of the IWA was dominated by Victoria Woodhull, Tennessee Claflin, Colonel Blood, and Stephen Pearl Andrews. The other fourteen IWA sections dissociated themselves from Section 12, which they claimed was not interested in the key question of capital vs. labor. Woodhull had incidentally denounced the National Labor Union as timid and the Paris Commune for not being truly revolutionary.

Except for quadrennial reaffirmation of her candidacy for President, which extended into 1892, Victoria and her sister Tennessee spent their later years repudiating their earlier beliefs, especially regarding free love. They claimed that they had never believed in free love. Benjamin Tucker, who experienced the free love doctrine directly at the hands of Victoria Woodhull, denounced the sisters as hypocrites.

Both Victoria Woodhull and Tennessee Claflin married wealthy men and settled down in England in luxury. Victoria married John Biddulph Martin, an Oxford graduate and a banker. She died in 1927 at the age of 90. Tennessee married an international importer, Sir Francis Cook, and settled down on a lavish estate overlooking the Thames. She and Sir Francis also had a castle in Sintra, Portugal. Lady Cook died at the age of 89.

Aside from the previous reforms mentioned in the platform of the Equal Rights Party in 1872, Woodhull played the pioneering role of a woman publicly seeking the presidency of the United States. She publicized additional reforms of some significance: free legal aid for the poor, bureaus of anthropology in all police stations to check suspects' backgrounds, pure food and drug laboratories, public housing for the poor, and labor arbitration panels. A radical-reactionary aspect of her later beliefs was her advocacy of stirpiculture, a doctrine that held that there was a genetic basis for superiority in achievement, an aristocracy of blood, equating the plight of the poor with their "inherent" genetic deficiency.

SOURCES: H. Marion Marbury, *Vicky: A Biography of Victoria C. Woodhull* (1967); Emanie Sachs, *The Terrible Siren: Victoria Woodhull (1838–1927)* (1928).

*ISRAEL KUGLER*

**WORK, JOHN M. (1869–1961).** John M. Work was a Socialist administrator and editor between 1904 and 1938. He was also a founding member of the Socialist Party of America. Work was born in 1869 in rural Washington County, Iowa, of middle-class parentage. He was educated at Washington Academy, (Iowa), Monmouth College (Illinois; Bachelor of Arts, 1891), and Columbian University (now George Washington University) Law School; Bachelor of Law, 1892). Upon graduating from law school, Work practiced as an attorney in his native Iowa. During this period, he became a follower of Edward Bellamy (q.v.) and formed an independent Socialist organization in his home state. In 1897 he led his group into the Social Democracy of America, which had been founded that year by Eugene Victor Debs (q.v.) and Victor Berger (q.v.).

During the 1900 campaign, Work was nominated as a presidential elector for Debs and Job Harriman (q.v.), the Socialist candidates. He later ran for many other offices under the Socialist banner. He was a candidate for mayor of Des Moines (1902), for presidential elector (1904), for governor of Iowa (1903, 1910), for U.S. Senator from Iowa (1908), and for alderman (Chicago, 1914) and was also a candidate for superior court justice (Chicago, 1917). Although he was never elected, he polled sizable votes in both Chicago elections.

In 1904 Work was named a national organizer by the party leadership, working primarily in the Midwest. In 1911 a scandal forced the party's national secretary, J. Mahlon Barnes, to resign. The National Executive Committee named Work as his successor. The choice was made for three reasons: (1) Work was a member of the right-wing faction of the party, closely allied with Berger and acceptable to Morris Hillquit (q.v.), leader of the moderate centrist wing of the party; (2) he was an honest man, a tee-totaler, a nonsmoker, and an outspoken opponent of sexual promiscuity—the primary charge against Barnes. And he was, unlike Barnes, an educated individual.

At times, Work interrupted serious Socialist discussions to advocate his own social creed. For example, at the 1912 convention he called for laws against drinking, smoking, sexual promiscuity, and the eating of red meat. He was ignored. As national secretary, Work led the party administration during the period of its greatest growth. Although considered an able administrator, his position was made untenable by the internal strife between the party factions. In 1914 he resigned the national secretary post and became an active member in the Chicago party.

Shortly before the United States joined the Allies in World War I, Work moved to Milwaukee, where he was named editorial page editor of the *Milwaukee Leader*. He led the paper's crusade against the war, under the tutelage of Berger. When the postal authorities withdrew mailing rights from the *Leader* because of its opposition to the war, Work and Berger helped devise means for continuing the daily's circulation. Work remained an editor of the *Leader* and its successor, the *Milwaukee Post*, for exactly twenty-five years to the week. He left the post in 1942 when the *Post* went out of business. In all that time he never missed a day.

In 1925 Work ran for U.S. Senate to succeed Robert M. LaFollette, Sr., who had died. He was defeated by Robert M. LaFollette, Jr. Work was then active in other Socialist campaigns, especially the 1926 and 1928 reelection bids of Representative Victor Berger, the campaigns of Daniel W. Hoan (q.v.) for the mayoralty of Milwaukee in 1928, 1932, 1936, and 1940, and the 1948 campaign, in which Frank Zeidler (q.v.) was elected mayor.

Work also wrote several books. The most well known, *What's So and What Isn't*, was published in 1905. The last, a novel titled *Philip and Aurelia*, appeared in 1957. He continued to write articles and to take correspondence courses from Milwaukee's universities until his death, at age 92, in 1961.

SOURCES: David A. Shannon, *The Socialist Party of America* (1955); John M. Work
Letters (1911–1957) in Socialist Party of America Collection, Duke University, Durham, North Carolina.

*JAMES INGBRETSON*

**WRIGHT, FRANCES (1795–1852).** Frances Wright was an early nineteenth-
century feminist, anarcho-Socialist, rationalist, and an opponent of slavery. Fanny
Wright, as she was commonly known, was born in 1795 in Dundee, Scotland,
of upper-class parentage. Her mother and father died when she was only two-
and-a-half years old, and she was raised by grandparents in London.

Wright first visited the United States in 1819 when she was 24 years old. She
was favorably impressed with the democracy there, and she described her visit
in her first book, *Views of Society and Manners in America*, which was basically
a paean of praise for the United States and its people. It barely mentioned slavery
or any of the other problems facing the young nation.

The book brought her to the notice of two leading radicals of the day, the
elderly Jeremy Bentham and the Marquise de Lafayette. They became her fast
friends. Lafayette won her over to the democratic revolutionary movement with
which he was affiliated. She remained an adherent for the rest of her life, even
when she became engrossed in the Owenite, anarcho-Socialist, and feminist
movements.

Upon her return to the United States in 1824, Wright visited the religious
colonies run by the Utopian Christians known as Rappites. She was repelled by
the religious, dogmatic nature of these communities. On this visit she also
observed and was repelled by slavery. Her interest led her to examine the history
of slavery and its economic repercussions. She blamed the institution on the
British, claiming that most of the Southern colonies had attempted to end the
practice before the Revolutionary War. She also decided that the abolitionists
of the time had no solution to the problem of slavery, that they merely denounced
it with no plan or proposal for how it could be eradicated. Wright herself favored
moderate abolition, which would allow the slaveholders to be paid for all freed
slaves, thus assuring that the economy of the Southern states would not be
dislocated. Moreover, she proposed that the blacks be trained in skills before
they were freed and that once freed they be sent to such unsettled areas as
California, Texas, or Haiti to develop their own culture and society.

To that end, on the advice of President James Madison's secretary, Edward
Coles, she established a community called Nashoba, near Memphis, Tennessee,
where slaves would be prepared for freedom. There were financial problems at
the colony from the start. A number of radical white friends of Wright directed
the community's operation. Wright herself worked diligently on the community
farm alongside the few slaves and the white overseers. After about a year her
health gave out, and she was forced to return to England to recuperate.

While Wright was in England, the operation of the community was left in the
hands of her white co-workers. Soon there were reports of cohabitation and

miscegenation between the blacks and the white overseers. The reports, which appeared in an anti-slavery Quaker journal, soon created a major scandal, and Wright and her friend Frances M. Trollope sailed back to the United States, hoping to quiet the uproar. But before she went to Nashoba, Wright dispatched a letter to the *Memphis Advocate and Western District Advocate* in which she proclaimed her belief in free love, called marriage a form of slavery she wanted abolished, and declared her support for a full mixing of the races.

On her return to Nashoba, Wright found it in a state of collapse. She blamed its sad state on the slaves rather than on her friends, who had been its overseers. So she closed Nashoba and sent the thirty-one slaves in the community to Haiti, where she freed them and gave them all land. After her disappointing Nashoba experience, Frances Wright—although she remained opposed to slavery—no longer trusted the blacks with full rights of citizenship. In fact, she denigrated the abilities of the blacks to live in a free society.

In 1829 Wright moved to New York, where she became active with Robert Dale Owen (q.v.) in the Guardian Educational Scheme, a proposed system of education based in large part on Plato's *Republic*, which aimed at creating an egalitarian society. She also edited the *Free Enquirer*, worked for the Workingmen's Party, fought for full sexual equality, and urged an end to organized religion.

In a series of articles in the *Free Enquirer*, Wright blamed the class struggle, which she believed was a reality, on three wrongs of society: coercive government whose power was based on violence, actual or potential; irrational religion; and inequality. The first she believed could be eliminated gradually. To end religion, she organized a rationalist meeting house called the Hall of Science, which she assumed would be a substitute for the "superstition laden" churches. To end inequality, Frances Wright favored both educational and economic reorganization of society.

Her educational revolution would place all children, no matter their social background, in the same schools. The children would all wear the same clothing and would be taught useful trades plus basic language and scientific skills. They would all thus grow up under conditions of absolute equality.

Economically, Wright wanted all nonproducing classes—lawyers, soldiers, merchants, traders, bankers, brokers, capitalists, fine ladies and gentlemen—abolished. All production of goods whose primary aim was conspicuous consumption would be eliminated. In her new society, Wright proposed, all property would be socially owned (the community would buy out all private property). There would be free, universal education; Social Security would protect the old and infirm; all income would be based on the social value of work done; the press would be run by editors elected by the people; all sexes would be equal.

At age 35, Wright went to France, where she married Phiquepal Casimir Sylvan D'Arusmont, a French educator and former follower of Robert Owen (q.v.). She had two children, one of whom died. The marriage was extremely unhappy and ended in divorce in 1850. Wright spent the rest of her life in Cincinnati. She continued to lecture and write. She died of the effects of a fall in December 1852.

SOURCE: William Randall Waterman, *Frances Wright* (1924).

*BERNARD K. JOHNPOLL*

# Z

**ZACK, JOSEPH (1897–1963).** Joseph Zack Kornfeder was a Communist Party labor leader and became a professional witness before Congressional investigating committees. Known in the Communist Party as Joseph Zack, he was probably born on March 20, 1897, in Trencsen, Slovakia. He sometimes claimed that he was born in Scranton, Pennsylvania, and taken to Europe as an infant. His father was Jewish, his mother was Roman Catholic, and he was baptized and raised a Catholic. After a high school education he emigrated to the United States in 1915, already a Socialist, and became a tailor in New York and a member of the Socialist Party in 1916. He also briefly flirted with the Industrial Workers of the World.

Zack was a charter member of the Communist Party, joining in 1919. He quickly moved into the ranks of Party functionaries, becoming trade union secretary. From 1927 to 1930 he attended the Lenin School in Moscow and was then given a Comintern mission to Colombia and Venezuela. Arrested in 1931, he had to be released from prison with the aid of the State Department. Back in the United States, Zack was placed in charge of the Trade Union Unity League's New York work, fulfilling a long-standing hostility to the American Federation of Labor. He was then transferred to Ohio. As the Party's experiment in dual unionism came to an end, Zack became increasingly disaffected and publicly challenged Communist policy. He was expelled from the Party in 1934.

Zack meandered through a number of radical groups in the next few years, founding a syndicalist organization, the One Big Union Club, and briefly joining the Trotskyists. After losing hope of getting his wife and son out of the Soviet Union, he appeared as a friendly witness before the Dies Committee investigating Communism in 1938. After World War II he was a frequent witness in proceedings against Communists and became associated with extreme right-wing views. He was employed as a salesman. Zack died on May 1, 1963.

SOURCES: FBI File 100–221869; Harvey Klehr, *The Heyday of American Communism* (1984).

*HARVEY KLEHR*

**ZEIDLER, FRANK P. (b.1912).** Frank Zeidler was the third Socialist to be elected mayor of Milwaukee. He was born on September 20, 1912, in the Merrill Park neighborhood of Milwaukee, the son of Michael W. Zeidler and Clara N. Zeidler. His father operated a successful barbershop in the city. Frank graduated from a Milwaukee high school and attended the University of Wisconsin in Madison for three years.

He joined the Socialist Party during the 1930s, and became active in writing, speaking, organizing meetings, and helping party candidates for public office. In 1938 Zeidler was elected on the Farm-Labor-Progressive Party ticket as Milwaukee County surveyor. (The Socialist Party of Wisconsin was in a coalition with the Progressive Party of Wisconsin from 1936 through 1941.) Zeidler was defeated for Wisconsin state treasurer as a Progressive in 1940 and as the Socialist Party nominee for governor in 1942. He was, however, elected to the Milwaukee school board in 1941 and was reelected in 1946.

In April 1940 Frank's older brother, Carl, was elected mayor of Milwaukee as an independent Republican. The two brothers disagreed on many issues, and Frank publicly criticized his brother's positions. The election drew new attention to the Zeidler family. Carl resigned as mayor when World War II broke out and subsequently was lost at sea off the coast of South Africa while serving in the U.S. Navy.

In 1944 and 1946 Frank ran unsuccessfully for mayor of Milwaukee and for Fifth District U.S. Congressman. Two years later, in 1948, Frank Zeidler was elected Milwaukee's third Socialist mayor. He defeated his Democratic opponent, Henry S. Reuss, 56 percent to 44 percent. The soft-spoken, scholarly Zeidler proved to be a popular mayor. He succeeded in doubling the size of the city through annexation and campaigned on the issues of ensuring an adequate city water supply, improving mass transit, abolition of secret government meetings, and lower utility rates. In 1952 he was elected to a second term with 72 percent of the vote.

Zeidler also took a strong stand on civil rights. He argued that blacks must be guaranteed equal protection under the law and should be allowed to live anywhere in the city they chose. He proposed and implemented scattered-site public housing developments for veterans and poor families. The race issue hurt him seriously during the 1956 campaign, but he still was reelected with 56 percent of the vote.

In 1960, claiming he was tired, Zeidler declined to seek a fourth term. In 1963 Governor John Reynolds appointed him to head the Wisconsin Department of Resource Development in Madison. He served a two-year term in that position, retiring in 1965. Although Zeidler retired from government service at that time, he remained active in the Socialist Party and in his community. He served as secretary to the Milwaukee Public Enterprise Committee in the 1960s, 1970s, and 1980s and worked as a self-employed labor arbitrator. He also taught local history classes at Milwaukee area colleges.

In 1976 Zeidler was nominated as the presidential candidate of the Socialist Party USA. He drew 6,045 popular votes, mostly from Wisconsin. He continues to live in the city of Milwaukee with his wife, Agnes, and family.

*STEPHEN K. HAUSER*

**ZIMMERMAN, CHARLES (1896–1983).** Charles S. Zimmerman was for half a century a major leader of the International Ladies Garment Workers Union, during which period he was also an important figure in the Communist Party, the dissident Communist group the "Lovestoneites," and finally in the Socialist Party–Democratic Socialist Federation.

Zimmerman, known almost universally as "Sacha," was born to Jewish parents in Kiev, Russia, on November 27, 1896, and emigrated to the United States in 1913. Before coming to the United States, he had an education equivalent to two years of high school in Russia. On arrival in New York City he went to work in a garment factory.

Zimmerman immediately joined the United Garment Workers Union, and in 1914 was a founding member of the Amalgamated Clothing Workers Union when it broke away from the United Garment Workers. In 1916, however, he transferred to the women's garment industry and joined the International Ladies Garment Workers Union (ILGWU). Before the end of World War I, Zimmerman was chosen secretary-manager of ILGWU Local 22, and in 1924 became an organizer for the joint board of the Dress and Waistmakers Union of the (ILGWU).

Zimmerman was a member of the Communist Party from its formation in 1919. In the 1920s he was one of the principal leaders of the Communists' effort to win control of the ILGWU. As a result of this struggle, he was expelled from the union in 1925. Nonetheless, he was named head of the Joint Action Committee organized by left-wing ILGWU locals to lead an unsuccessful cloakmakers strike in 1926. When the Communists (on orders from the Comintern) organized their own "dual union" in the garment industry in 1929, he was one of the major leaders of the resulting Needle Trades Workers Industrial Union.

Within the Communist Party, Zimmerman was aligned with the Ruthenberg (q.v.)–Lovestone (q.v.) faction. In May 1929 he was part of their delegation to the special Comintern meeting in Moscow to consider "the American question," because of his presence in the Soviet capital to attend a conference of the Red International of Labor Unions, where he had opposed the effort to impose "dual unionism" on all Communist parties.

Upon returning home, Zimmerman was expelled from the Communist Party as a leading Lovestoneite. Between 1929 and 1941 he was the principal trade union leader in the ranks of the Lovestoneite opposition Communist group. He returned to the ILGWU in 1931 and was soon elected head of Local 22 and general manager of the Dress Joint Board. In 1934 Zimmerman was chosen as a vice-president of the ILGWU, a post he held until his retirement in 1972.

After the dissolution of the Lovestoneite group in January 1941, Zimmerman served as head of the Trade Union Council of the American Labor Party (ALP) in New York State. After the ALP was taken over by the Communists, he joined the Liberal Party, in which the ILGWU played a major role. He served as a member of the Liberal Party's administrative and state executive committees.

Zimmerman served on the national board of the Americans for Democratic Action. In 1957 he was named chairman of the AFL/CIO Civil Rights Committee, and in 1968 became president of the Jewish Labor Committee. In 1972 Zimmerman was chosen as co-chairman of the Socialist Party–Democratic Socialist Federation. He died on June 4, 1983.

*ROBERT ALEXANDER*

# Appendix A: Chronology of Key Events

1817 Robert Owen's *New View of Society* published in Philadelphia *Aurora*—first Socialist work published in United States.

1819 Owenite Society for the Promoting of Commonwealths formed in New York.

1824 Robert Owen arrives in United States to organize Socialist community.

1825 Owen addresses Congress twice.
Owenite community formed at New Harmony, Indiana.

1826 New Harmony community dissolves due to persistent bickering among settlers.
Frances Wright founds Nashoba community near Memphis, Tennessee, for training slaves to be free.

1828 Series of "free love" scandals leads to disintegration of Nashoba community. Slaves are given freedom and shipped to Haiti.
First labor party in America—the Workingmens Party—formed in Philadelphia. It is short-lived, polling few votes.

1829 Workingmens Party of New York elects one member to state legislature and polls significant vote.

1830 Internal feuding causes Workingmens Party of New York to collapse.

1832 Labor Party formed in Massachusetts. It proposes reforms calling for a ten-hour day, a mechanics lien law, abolition of debtors jails, an end to the militia system, and universal suffrage. Polls large vote.

1833 Democrats name Labor candidate for lieutenant governor of Massachusetts as its own. Labor Party of Massachusetts collapses.

1834 Ely Moore elected to Congress as Workingman from New York. Reelected in 1836, then becomes a Democrat

1840 Albert Brisbane's Fourierite *Social Destiny of Man* is published.
Brook Farm organized by Transcendentalists.
Horace Greeley proclaims his conversion to Fourierism.

1844 Brook Farm becomes Fourierite phalanx.
John A. Collins founds Owenite community near Skaneateles, New York.

1847 John Humphrey Noyes flees Vermont and sets up Oneida Community near Utica, New York

1848 German Democratic revolution fails. Many Socialists flee to America
1850 Individualist anarchist community Modern Times founded in Long Island.
First Marxist Socialist organization formed by German emigrés.
1855 John Francis Bray publishes first pamphlet written by an American Socialist.
1861 Civil War causes major split among radicals. Some, like Bray, argue that North has no right to control the South. Others, like Andrews, are vehemently pro-Northern.
1867 American branch of Marx's International Workingmens Association formed.
1868 Socialists run ticket in New York City election.
1870 Wendell Phillips, Labor candidate for governor of Massachusetts, polls more than 20 percent of vote.
1873 Socialists draw thousands to rallies for relief for unemployed in New York and Chicago.
1877 Railroad strikes sweep nation. Socialists lead strikers in near-rebellion in many cities, most notably St. Louis.
Socialist candidates poll massive votes, elect many officials in industrial centers.
1878 Almost all Socialist officials defeated for reelection.
1880 Socialists support Greenbacker national ticket. Socialistic Labor Party is split.
1881 Chicago Socialists call for armed struggle against capitalism, as do many New York Socialists.
1882 Johann Most arrives in United States.
1883 Pittsburgh Congress founds International Workingpeople's Association.
1886 Henry George runs for mayor of New York with Socialist support.
Bomb at anarchist meeting in Chicago's Haymarket Square kills seven police and four demonstrators.
1887 For their part in Haymarket affair, four anarchists hanged and two get life terms. One kills himself.
1888 Nationalist Clubs formed to spread socialism of Edward Bellamy's *Looking Backward*.
1891 Daniel DeLeon seizes control of Socialist Labor Party.
1892 People's Party (Populists) nominate full ticket in national campaign. Call for social reform. Win huge vote, supported by nonparty Socialists and Bellamyites.
1894 American Railway Union, led by Eugene V. Debs, strikes against Pullman. Strike broken by federal troops. Debs jailed. Debs proclaims himself a Socialist.
1897 Social Democracy formed by Debs and Victor Berger. Jewish Socialists quit Socialist Labor Party (SLP), join new Social Democracy.
1899 SLP splits into pro- and anti-DeLeon organizations. Morris Hillquit leads the latter.
1900 Social Democracy and Hillquit-led SLP faction run joint presidential ticket, poll record Socialist vote.
1901 Social Democracy and Hillquit-led SLP unite to form Socialist Party.
1905 Industrial Workers of the World formed.
1910 Socialists elect mayor of Milwaukee and Congressman in Milwaukee.
1911 Socialists elect mayors in scores of small cities, more than 1,000 state and municipal officials.
1912 Socialist Party membership hits record 135,000 members; no radical party had ever reached that large a figure before, or since.
1914 Socialists actively oppose support for either side in World War I.

1917  Socialists proclaim opposition to American entry into World War I after war is declared.
1918  Scores of Socialists arrested for opposing war. Among those arrested: Eugene Debs, Victor Berger, Charles Ruthenberg, Kate Richards O'Hare.
Left wing calls for closer ties to Bolsheviks in Russia.
1919  Socialist Party splits into Socialist and two Communist parties.
1920  Debs, in prison, polls more than 900,000 votes as Socialist presidential candidate.
1921  Workers Party, legal arm of underground Communist Party, formed.
1923  Communist Party abolishes underground.
1924  Socialists support Progressive candidate Robert M. LaFollette for President.
1928  Communists expel supporters of Leon Trotsky. Form dual unions to compete with American Federation of Labor.
1929  Communist International expels Party leader Jay Lovestone and his followers.
1930  Earl Browder emerges as Communist Party leader.
1932  Socialists poll 850,000 votes for President. Franklin Roosevelt elected.
William Foster gets 100,000 votes for Communists.
1934  Socialists split again.
1935  Communists drop hyperbolic radicalism for Popular Front rhetoric.
1938  Communist Party at peak of influence.
1939  Communist Party supports Hitler-Stalin Pact. Once again launch attacks on Franklin Roosevelt and New Deal.
1941  Soviet Union invaded. Communists back war with no reservations.
1944  Communist Party becomes Communist Political Association.
1945  Earl Browder deposed as Party leader. Communist Party reestablished.
1948  Communists support Henry Wallace for President.
1956  Khrushchev discloses reign of terror under Stalin. Communist Party rent asunder by revelations. Thousands of members, including many leaders, resign.
1960  Formation of Student Non-Violent Coordinating Committee.
1962  Students for a Democratic Society issues Port Huron Statement. First program of New Left.
1968  Students for a Democratic Society splinters into several Marxist-Leninist factions.
1972  Socialists end partisan life.
1984  Communists poll about 30,000 votes nationally.

# Appendix B: Major Radical Party Affiliation and Year of Entry

## SOCIALIST PARTY

Abern, Martin (1913)
Allen, Devere (1918)
Ameringer, Oscar (1901)
Amter, Israel (1901)
Bartel, Heinrich L. (c. 1905)
Bedacht, Max (1903)
Benjamin, Herbert (c. 1915)
Benson, Allan L. (1904)
Berger, Meta (1901)
Berger, Victor L. (1901)
Billings, Warren K. (c. 1914)
Bittelman, Alexander (1915)
Blanshard, Paul (1915)
Block, S. John (1902)
Bloor, Ella Reeve (1902)
Boudin, Louis B. (1902)
Browder, Carl (1907)
Burnham, James (1936)
Cahan, Abraham (1901)
Calverton, V. F. (1918)
Cannon, James P. (c. 1910)
Carlson, Oliver (1914)
Claessens, August (1909)
Darcy, Samuel (1917)
Day, Dorothy (1914)
Debs, Eugene V. (1901)
Domingo, W. A. (c. 1917)
DuBois, W. E. B. (1910)
Duncan, Lewis J. (1909)

Dunne, William (1910)
Eastman, Max (1912)
Engdahl, J. Louis (1907)
Ferguson, Isaac (1918)
Foster, William Z. (1904)
Fraina, Louis (1907, 1917)
Freeman, Joseph (c. 1912)
Freese, Irving C. (1930)
George, Harrison (1910)
Germer, Adolph (1901)
Gilman, Elisabeth (1929)
Gitlow, Benjamin (1909, 1935)
Gold, Ben (1916)
Goldman, Albert (1934)
Graham, James D. (1901)
Halonen, George (c. 1912)
Harriman, Job (1901)
Harrington, Michael (1953)
Hart, William Osborne (c. 1930)
Hathaway, Clarence (1917)
Hayes, Max S. (1901)
Haywood, William D. (1901)
Heath, Frederic F. (1901)
Hillquit, Morris (1901)
Hoan, Daniel Webster (c. 1908)
Hoopes, Darlington (1914)
Howe, Irving (1934)
Hughan, Jessie Wallace (1907)
Huiswoud, Otto (c. 1917)
Jones, Mary Harris (1901)

Kelley, Florence (1912)
Kester, Howard (1931)
Konikow, Antoinette (1901)
Krumbein, Charles (1910)
Kruse, William (c. 1910)
Krzycki, Leo (1904)
Laidler, Harry W. (c. 1901)
Larkin, James (1914)
Lash, Joseph P. (1932)
Lasser, David (c. 1930)
Laukki, Leo (1907)
Lee, Algernon (1901)
Lloyd, Henry Demarest (1903)
Lloyd, William Bross (1905)
London, Meyer (1901)
Lore, Ludwig (1903)
Lovestone, Jay (c. 1917)
Lunn, George R. (1910)
Matthews, J. B. (1929)
Maurer, James Hudson (1902)
McCreery, Maud (1912)
McKinney, Ernest Rice (1910)
McLevy, Jasper (1901)
McReynolds, David (1951)
Melms, Edmund T. (1901)
Minor, Robert (1907)
Mitchell, H. L. (c. 1930)
Mooney, Thomas J. (1901)
Morrow, Felix (c. 1915)
Muste, A. J. (1936)
Nearing, Scott (c. 1915)
O'Hare, Kate Richards (1901)
Olgin, Moissaye (1915)
Oneal, James (1901)
Ovington, Mary White (1905)
Panken, Jacob (1903)
Potash, Irving (1916)
Poyntz, Juliet Stuart (1909)
Poro, Henry (1907)
Quick, William F., Sr. (date unknown)
Randolph, A. Philip (1916, 1969)
Reed, John (1918)
Rhodes, George M. (1920)
Ruthenberg, Charles (1909)
Salutsky, J. B. (1909)
Saposs, David (c. 1907)
Scherer, Marcel (c. 1915)
Scudder, Vida (1911)

Seidel, Emil (1901)
Shachtman, Max (c. 1920)
Simons, Algie M. (1901)
Sinclair, Upton (c. 1905, 1920)
Skoglund, Carl (1914)
Solomon, Charles (c. 1910)
Spargo, John (1902)
Spector, Frank (c. 1914)
Stokes, Rose Pastor (1906)
Stump, J. Henry (c. 1914)
Swabeck, Arne (1916)
Taylor, Charles (1907)
Thomas, Norman M. (1918)
Trachtenberg, Alexander (c. 1907)
Tresca, Carlo (1904)
Vladeck, Baruch Charney (1908)
Wagenknecht, Alfred (1901)
Waldman, Louis (c. 1911)
Walling, William English (1910)
Wayland, Julius A. (1901)
Weiner, William (1913)
Weinstone, William (1913)
Weisbord, Albert (c. 1918)
Wicks, Harry (c. 1915)
Williams, Claude (c. 1930)
Wilshire, Henry Gaylord (1901)
Wilson, Lilith Martin (c. 1912)
Wolfe, Bertram (1917)
Wolfsohn, Leo (1913)
Work, John M. (1901)
Zack, Joseph (1916)
Zeidler, Frank P. (c. 1930)

## COMMUNIST PARTY (INCLUDES WORKERS PARTY AND COMMUNIST LABOR PARTY)

Abern, Martin (1919)
Allen, James (1928)
Amter, Israel (1919)
Bedacht, Max (1919)
Benjamin, Herbert (1921)
Berger, Meta (1938)
Bittelman, Alexander (1919)
Bloor, Ella Reeve (1920)
Briggs, Cyril (1921)
Browder, Earl (1920)
Budenz, Louis (1935)

Burlak, Anne (1927)
Cacchione, Peter (c. 1930)
Cannon, James P. (1919)
Carlson, Oliver (1921)
Charney, George Blake (1933)
Childs, Morris (c. 1927)
Connelly, Philip (1938)
Costigan, Howard (1936)
Darcy, Samuel (1921)
Davis, Angela (1968)
Davis, Benjamin (1933)
De Caux, Len (c. 1927)
Dennis, Eugene (1926)
Dodd, Bella (c. 1935)
DuBois, W. E. B. (1961)
Dunne, Vincent (c. 1910)
Dunne, William (1919)
Engdahl, J. Louis (1921)
Ferguson, Isaac (1919)
Flynn, Elizabeth Gurley (1925)
Ford, James (1926)
Foster, William Z. (1921)
Fraina, Louis (1919)
Freeman, Joseph (c. 1921)
Gannett, Betty (1923)
Gates, John (1931)
George, Harrison (1919)
Gerson, Simon (c. 1927)
Gitlow, Benjamin (1919)
Gold, Ben (1919)
Gold, Mike (c. 1925)
Goldman, Albert (c. 1925)
Green, Gil (1924)
Hall, Gus (1927)
Hall, Rob (c. 1929)
Halonen, George (1919)
Harris, Lem (c. 1930)
Hathaway, Clarence (1919)
Haywood, Harry (1923)
Healey, Dorothy Ray (1928)
Henderson, Donald (1931)
Herberg, Will (1926)
Herndon, Angelo (1930)
Hicks, Granville (c. 1934)
Hudson, Roy (1929)
Huiswoud, Otto (1919)
Jerome, Victor J. (c. 1930)
Johnstone, Jack (1921)

Konikow, Antoinette (1919)
Krumbein, Charles (1919)
Kruse, William (1921)
Lannon, Al (1931)
Larkin, James (1919)
Laukki, Leo (1919)
Lloyd, William Bross (1919)
Lore, Ludwig (1919)
Lovestone, Jay (1919)
McKinney, Ernest Rice (1920)
Miller, Bert (1919)
Minor, Robert (1920)
Morrow, Felix (1931)
Mortimer, Wyndham (c. 1932)
Nearing, Scott (c. 1927)
Nelson, Steve (c. 1921)
Olgin, Moissaye (1921)
Padmore, George (1924)
Patterson, William (1921)
Pepper, John (1922)
Perry, Pettis (1932)
Peters, J. (1924)
Potash, Irving (1919)
Poyntz, Juliet Stuart (1921)
Pressman, Lee (1934)
Puro, Henry (1923)
Quill, Mike (c. 1934)
Rahv, Philip (1932)
Reed, John (1919)
Richmond, Al (1928)
Ross, Carl (c. 1930)
Rustin, Bayard (1936)
Ruthenberg, Charles (1919)
Salutsky, J. B. (1921)
Scherer, Marcel (1919)
Schneiderman, William (1921)
Shachtman, Max (1922)
Skoglund, Carl (1919)
Spector, Frank (1919)
Stachel, Jack (1924)
Stokes, Rose Pastor (1919)
Swabeck, Arne (1919)
Taylor, Charles (1920)
Thompson, Robert (1933)
Toohey, Pat (1920)
Trachtenberg, Alexander (1921)
Wagenknecht, Alfred (1919)
Ware, Harold (1919)

Weiner, William (c. 1921)
Weinstock, Louis (c. 1924)
Weinstone, William (1919)
Weisbord, Albert (1924)
Weiss, Max (1928)
Wicks, Harry (c. 1919)
Wilkerson, Doxey (1943)
Williamson, John (1922)
Winston, Henry (1931)
Winter, Carl (1922)
Wolfe, Bertram (1919)
Zack, Joseph (1919)
Zimmerman, Charles (1919)

## INDUSTRIAL WORKERS OF THE WORLD

Abern, Martin (1913)
Benjamin, Herbert (c. 1915)
Bridges, Harry (c. 1921)
Cannon, James P. (c. 1905)
Debs, Eugene V. (1905)
De Caux, Len (c. 1921)
DeLeon, Daniel (1905)
Dunne, Vincent (1905)
Flynn, Elizabeth Gurley (1907)
Foster, William Z. (c. 1909)
Fraina, Louis (1913)
George, Harrison (1914)
Goldman, Albert (c. 1919)
Haywood, William D. (1905)
Hill, Joe (1910)
Johnstone, Jack (1906)
Jones, Mary Harris (1905)
Laukki, Leo (1914)
Lore, Ludwig (1905)
St. John, Vincent (1905)
Skoglund, Carl (1917)
Tresca, Carlo (1912)
Wicks, Harry (c. 1918)
Zack, Joseph (c. 1916)

## SOCIALIST LABOR PARTY

Bloor, Ella Reeve (1897)
Bray, John Francis (c. 1870)
DeLeon, Daniel (1891)
Fraina, Louis (1907)
Gronlund, Laurence (1870)
Grottkau, Paul (1883)

Harriman, Job (1889)
Haskell, Burnette G. (1879)
Hayes, Max S. (1897)
Hillquit, Morris (1887)
Kelley, Florence (1885)
Konikow, Antoinette (1893)
Lee, Algernon (1895)
London, Meyer (1898)
Maurer, James Hudson (1898)
McGuire, Peter J. (1876)
Nelson, Steve (c. 1920)
Parsons, Albert R. (1873)
Petersen, Arnold (1907)
Simons, Algie M. (1897)
Spies, August (1876)
Williamson, John (1918)

## SOCIALIST WORKERS PARTY (INCLUDES COMMUNIST LEAGUE OF AMERICA AND WORKERS PARTY)

Abern, Martin (1929)
Burnham, James (1937)
Cannon, James P. (1929)
Dobbs, Farrell (1934)
Dunne, Vincent (1929)
Farrell, James T. (1936)
Goldman, Albert (1933)
Howe, Irving (1938)
James, C. L. R. (1938)
Konikow, Antoinette (1929)
Lens, Sidney (1934)
Lore, Ludwig (c. 1929)
Macdonald, Dwight (1939)
McKinney, Ernest Rice (c. 1934)
Morrow, Felix (1933)
Muste, A. J. (c. 1934)
Novack, George (1933)
Shachtman, Max (1929)
Skoglund, Carl (1929)
Swabeck, Arne (1929)
Taylor, Charles (c. 1934)
Zack, Joseph (c. 1934)

## ANARCHISTS

Andrews, Stephen Pearl (c. 1850)
Berkman, Alexander (c. 1886)
deCleyre, Voltairine (c. 1887)

Day, Dorothy (c. 1932)
Goldman, Emma (c. 1887)
Lum, Dyer D. (c. 1877)
Most, Johann (c. 1880)
Parsons, Albert R. (1880)
Sacco, Nicola (c. 1908)
Spies, August (1880)
Spooner, Lysander (c. 1834)
Vanzetti, Bartolomeo (c. 1908)
Warren, Josiah (c. 1827)

## COMMUNITARIANS

Bellamy, Edward (1887)
Brisbane, Albert (c. 1830)
Collins, John A. (1840)
Noyes, John H. (c. 1840)
Owen, Robert (c. 1800)
Owen, Robert Dale (c. 1825)
Rose, Ernestine (c. 1830)
Wright, Frances (c. 1925)

## NEW LEFT

Berrigan, Daniel (c. 1964)
Berrigan, Philip (c. 1964)
Boudin, Kathy (c. 1965)
Carmichael, Stokely (c. 1960)
Cleaver, Leroy Eldridge (c. 1966)
Davis, Rennie (c. 1963)
Dellinger, David (c. 1960)
Dohrn, Bernardine (c. 1964)
Forman, James (c. 1961)

Goodman, Paul (c. 1960)
Hayden, Thomas (1961)
Hoffman, Abbie (c. 1967)
Lynd, Staughton (c. 1964)
Marcuse, Herbert (c. 1960)
Moses, Robert Parris (c. 1960)
Newton, Huey Percy (c. 1966)
Rubin, Jerry (1964)
Seale, Bobby (1966)

## FARMER LABOR PARTY

Benson, Elmer (c. 1920)
Marcantonio, Vito (c. 1934)
Williams, Howard Y. (c. 1929)

## OTHERS

Bliss, William D. P.
Bourne, Randolph
Dombrowski, James Anderson
Frank, Waldo
Holmes, John Haynes
Hook, Sidney
Horton, Myles
Mumford, Lewis
Phillips, Wendell
Phillips, William
Rauschenbusch, Walter
Steffens, Lincoln
Van Kleek, Mary
Woodhull, Victoria

# Appendix C: Place of Birth

**AUSTRALIA**
Bridges, Harry

**AUSTRIA**
Bartel, Heinrich L.
Berger, Victor L.

**CANADA**
Ferguson, Isaac

**CROATIA**
Nelson, Steve

**CURAÇAO**
DeLeon, Daniel

**DENMARK**
Gronlund, Laurence
Petersen, Arnold
Swabeck, Arne

**ENGLAND**
Larkin, James
Owen, Robert
Richmond, Al
Spargo, John

**FINLAND**
Halonen, George
Laukki, Leo

Puro, Henry

**GERMANY**
Ameringer, Oscar
Bedacht, Max
Germer, Adolph
Grottkau, Paul
Lore, Ludwig
Marcuse, Herbert
Most, Johann
Spies, August
Wagenknecht, Alfred

**HOLLAND**
Muste, A. J.

**HUNGARY**
Pepper, John
Peters, J.
Weinstock, Louis

**INDIA**
Scudder, Vida

**IRELAND**
Jones, Mary Harris
Quill, Mike

**ITALY**
Dodd, Bella

448

APPENDIX C

Fraina, Louis
Sacco, Nicola
Tresca, Carlo
Vanzetti, Bartolomeo

## JAMAICA
Domingo, W. A.

## LATVIA
Hillquit, Morris

## LEEWARD ISLANDS
Briggs, Cyril

## LITHUANIA
Benjamin, Herbert
Lovestone, Jay
Weinstone, William

## NEW ZEALAND
De Caux, Len

## POLAND
Gannett, Betty
Jerome, Victor J.
London, Meyer
Rose, Ernestine
Shachtman, Max
Stachel, Jack
Stokes, Rose Pastor

## ROMANIA
Abern, Martin
Scherer, Marcel

## RUSSIA
Berkman, Alexander
Bittelman, Alexander
Boudin, Louis B.
Cahan, Abraham
Charney, George Blake
Childs, Morris
Darcy, Samuel
Freeman, Joseph
Gold, Ben
Goldman, Albert
Goldman, Emma
Konikow, Antoinette

Olgin, Moissaye
Parken, Jacob
Potash, Irving
Rahv, Philip
Salutsky, J. B.
Saposs, David
Schneiderman, William
Spector, Frank
Trachtenberg, Alexander
Vladeck, Baruch Charney
Waldman, Louis
Weiner, William
Wolfsohn, Leo
Zimmerman, Charles

## SCOTLAND
Graham, James D.
Johnstone, Jack
Owen, Robert Dale
Williamson, John
Wright, Frances

## SLOVAKIA
Zack, Joseph

## SURINAM
Huiswoud, Otto

## SWEDEN
Carlson, Oliver
Hill, Joe
Skoglund, Carl

## SWITZERLAND
Claessens, August

## TRINIDAD
Carmichael, Stokely
James, C. L .R.
Padmore, George

## TURKEY
Bliss, William D. P

## UNITED STATES
### Alabama
Davis, Angela
Ford, James

Hall, Rob
Parsons, Albert R.
Perry, Pettis

## Arkansas

Cleaver, Leroy Eldridge

## California

Haskell, Burnette G.
McReynolds, David
Patterson, William
Steffens, Lincoln

## Colorado

Amter, Israel
Friedman, Samuel
Healey, Dorothy Ray

## Connecticut

Gilman, Elisabeth
McLevy, Jasper

## Delaware

Ware, Harold

## District of Columbia

Bray, John Francis

## Florida

Dombrowski, James Anderson
Randolph, A. Philip

## Georgia

Davis, Benjamin

## Illinois

Burnham, James
Dohrn, Bernardine
Farrell, James
Forman, James
Green, Gil
Harris, Lem
Hart, William Osborne
Krumbein, Charles
Lloyd, William Bross
Mooney, Thomas J.
Wicks, Harry

## Indiana

Budenz, Louis
Debs, Eugene V.
Harriman, Job

Oneal, James
Wayland, Julius A.
Wilson, Lilith Martin

## Iowa

Lee, Algernon
Lunn, George R.
Work, John M.

## Kansas

Browder, Earl
Cannon, James P.
Dunne, Vincent
George, Harrison
O'Hare, Kate Richards

## Kentucky

Matthews, J. B.
St. John, Vincent
Walling, William English

## Louisiana

Newton, Huey P.

## Maryland

Calverton, V. F.
Hoopes, Darlington
Lasser, David
Sinclair, Upton

## Massachusetts

Andrews, Stephen Pearl
Bellamy, Edward
Dellinger, David
DuBois, W. E. B.
Foster, William Z.
Hoffman, Abbie
Novack, George
Phillips, Wendell
Spooner, Lysander
Warren, Josiah

## Michigan

Benson, Allan L.
de Cleyre, Voltairine
Davis, Rennie
Hayden, Thomas
Ross, Carl

## Minnesota

Benson, Elmer
Berrigan, Daniel

Berrigan, Philip
Engdahl, J. Louis
Hall, Gus
Hathaway, Clarence
Williams, Howard Y.

### Mississippi

Winston, Henry

### Missouri

Dobbs, Farrell
Duncan, Lewis J.
Dunne, William
Harrington, Michael
Wilkerson, Doxey

### Nebraska

Haywood, Harry
Poyntz, Juliet Stuart

### Nevada

Hudson, Roy

### New Hampshire

Flynn, Elizabeth Gurley
Hicks, Granville

### New Jersey

Bourne, Randolph
Frank, Waldo
Freese, Irving C.
Gitlow, Benjamin
Kruse, William
Lens, Sidney
Weiss, Max

### New York

Billings, Warren K.
Bloor, Ella Reeve
Boudin, Kathy
Brisbane, Albert
Cacchione, Peter V.
Day, Dorothy
Eastman, Max
Gates, John
Gerson, Simon
Gold, Mike
Goodman, Paul
Henderson, Donald
Herberg, Will
Hook, Sidney

Howe, Irving
Hughan, Jessie Wallace
Laidler, Harry W.
Lannon, Al
Lash, Joseph P.
Lloyd, Henry Demarest
Lum, Dyer D.
MacDonald, Dwight
Marcantonio, Vito
McGuire, Peter J.
Miller, Bert
Morrow, Felix
Moses, Robert Parris
Mumford, Lewis
Ovington, Mary White
Phillips, William
Pressman, Lee
Rauschenbusch, Walter
Solomon, Charles
Van Kleek, Mary
Weisbord, Albert
Wolfe, Bertram

### Ohio

Blanshard, Paul
Block, S. John
Bohn, Frank
Hayes, Max S.
Herndon, Angelo
Rubin, Jerry
Ruthenberg, Charles
Thomas, Norman M.
Wilshire, Henry Gaylord
Winter, Carl
Woodhull, Victoria

### Oregon

Reed, John
Thompson, Robert

### Pennsylvania

Allen, James
Burlak, Anne
Connelly, Philip
Holmes, John Haynes
Kelley, Florence
Lynd, Staughton
Maurer, James H.
Mortimer, Wyndham

Nearing, Scott
Rhodes, George M.
Rustin, Bayard
Seidel, Emil
Stump, J. Henry
Toohey, Pat

### Rhode Island

Allen, Devere

### Tennessee

Horton, Myles
Mitchell, H. L.
Williams, Claude

### Texas

Minor, Robert
Seale, Bobby

### Utah

Haywood, William

### Vermont

Collins, John A.
Noyes, John Humphrey

### Virginia

Kester, Howard

### Washington State

Costigan, Howard
Dennis, Eugene

### West Virginia

McKinney, Ernest Rice

### Wisconsin

Berger, Meta
Heath, Frederic F.
Hoan, Daniel Webster
Krzycki, Leo
McCreery, Maud
Melms, Edmund T.
Quick, William F., Sr.
Simons, Algie M.
Taylor, Charles
Zeidler, Frank P.

# Appendix D: Birthdate (with Date of Death)

**1771**

Owen, Robert (1858)

**1795**

Wright, Frances (1852)

**1798**

Warren, Josiah (1874)

**1801**

Owen, Robert Dale (1877)

**1808**

Brisbane, Albert (1890)
Spooner, Lysander (1887)

**1809**

Bray, John Francis (1896)

**1810**

Collins, John A. (1890)
Rose, Ernestine (1892)

**1811**

Noyes, John Humphrey (1886)
Phillips, Wendell (1884)

**1812**

Andrews, Stephen Pearl (1884)

**1830**

Jones, Mary Harris (1930)

**1838**

Woodhull, Victoria (1927)

**1839**

Lum, Dyer (1893)

**1845**

Parsons, Albert R. (1887)

**1846**

Gronlund, Laurence (1899)
Grottkau, Paul (1898)
Most, Johann (1906)

**1847**

Lloyd, Henry Demarest (1903)

**1850**

Bellamy, Edward (1898)
Bliss, William D. P. (1926)

**1852**

DeLeon, Daniel (1914)
McGuire, Peter (1906)

**1854**

Wayland, Julius (1912)

**1855**

Debs, Eugene V. (1926)
Spies, August (1887)

**1857**

Haskell, Burnette G. (1907)

**1858**

Duncan, Lewis J. (1936)

**1859**

Kelley, Florence (1932)

**1860**

Berger, Victor L. (1929)
Cahan, Abraham (1951)

**1861**

Harriman, Job (1925)
Rauschenbusch, Walter (1918)
Scudder, Vida (1954)
Wilshire, Henry Gaylord (1927)

**1862**

Bloor, Ella Reeve (1951)

**1864**

Heath, Frederic F. (1954)
Maurer, James Hudson (1944)
Seidel, Emil (1947)

**1865**

Ovington, Mary White (1951)

**1866**

de Cleyre, Voltairine (1912)
Hayes, Max S. (1945)
Steffens, Lincoln (1936)

**1867**

Gilman, Elisabeth (1950)

**1868**

DuBois, W. E. B. (1963)

**1869**

Goldman, Emma (1940)
Haywood, William D. (1928)
Hillquit, Morris (1933)
Konikow, Antoinette (1946)
Work, John M. (1961)

**1870**

Ameringer, Oscar (1943)
Berkman, Alexander (1936)
Simons, Algie M. (1950)

**1871**

Benson, Allan L. (1940)
London, Meyer (1926)

**1873**

Berger, Meta (1944)
Graham, James D. (1951)
Lee, Algernon (1954)
Lunn, George R. (1948)
Oneal, James (1962)

**1874**

Boudin, Louis B. (1952)
Melms, Edmund T. (1933)

**1875**

Bartel, Heinrich L. (1968)
Hughan, Jessie Wallace (1955)
Lloyd, William Bross (1946)
Lore, Ludwig (1942)

**1876**

Larkin, James (1947)
St. John, Vincent (1929)
Spargo, John (1966)

**1877**

O'Hare, Kate Richards (1948)
Walling, William English (1936)

**1878**

McLevy, Jasper (1962)
Olgin, Moissaye (1939)
Sinclair, Upton (1968)

**1879**

Bohn, Frank A. (1975)
Holmes, John Haynes (1964)
Panken, Jacob (1968)
Stokes, Rose Pastor (1933)
Tresca, Carlo (1943)

**1880**

Block, S. John (1955)
Germer, Adolph (1964)

Johnstone, Jack (1942)
Laukki, Leo (date unknown)
Stump, J. Henry (1949)

## 1881

Amter, Israel (1954)
Foster, William Z. (1961)
Hoan, Daniel Webster (1961)
Wagenknecht, Alfred (1956)

## 1882

Hill, Joe (1915)
Krzycki, Leo (1966)
Mooney, Thomas J. (1942)
Ruthenberg, Charles (1927)
Salutsky, J. B. (1968)
Van Kleek, Mary (1972)

## 1883

Bedacht, Max (1972)
Eastman, Max (1969)
Freese, Irving C. (1964)
McCreery, Maud (1938)
Nearing, Scott (1983)

## 1884

Engdahl, J. Louis (1932)
Laidler, Harry W. (1970)
Minor, Robert (1952)
Mortimer, Wyndham (1966)
Skoglund, Carl (1960)
Taylor, Charles (1967)
Thomas, Norman M. (1968)
Trachtenberg, Alexander (1966)

## 1885

Claessens, August (1954)
Muste, A. J. (1967)
Petersen, Arnold (1976)
Quick, William F., Sr. (1966)

## 1886

Bourne, Randolph (1918)
McKinney, Ernest Rice (1984)
Pepper, John (1938)
Poyntz, Juliet Stuart (1937)
Saposs, David (1968)
Vladeck, Baruch Charney (1938)

## 1887

Briggs, Cyril (1966)
Dunne, William (1953)
Reed, John (1920)
Wilson, Lilith Martin (1937)

## 1888

Ferguson, Isaac (date unknown)
George, Harrison (date unknown)
Puro, Henry (1981)
Vanzetti, Bartolomeo (1927)

## 1889

Domingo, W. A. (1968)
Dunne, Vincent (1970)
Frank, Waldo (1967)
Krumbein, Charles (1947)
Randolph, A. Philip (1979)
Solomon, Charles (1963)
Wicks, Harry (1957)
Williams, Howard Y. (1973)

## 1890

Bittleman, Alexander (1982)
Cannon, James P. (1974)
Flynn, Elizabeth Gurley (1964)
Sacco, Nicola (1927)
Swabeck, Arne
Ware, Harold (1935)
Wolfsohn, Leo (1956)

## 1891

Allen, Devere (1955)
Browder, Earl (1973)
Budenz, Louis (1972)
Gitlow, Benjamin (1965)
Halonen, George (1954)
Miller, Bert (1973)
Patterson, William (1980)

## 1892

Blanshard, Paul (1980)
Fraina, Louis (1953)
Waldman, Louis (1982)

## 1893

Billings, Warren K. (1972)
Ford, James (1957)

456                                                    APPENDIX D

Gold, Mike (1967)
Huiswoud, Otto (1961)
Kruse, William (date unknown)
Weiner, William (1954)

**1894**

Hathaway, Clarence (1963)
Matthews, J. B. (1966)
Peters, J.

**1895**

Benson, Elmer (1985)
Mumford, Lewis
Spector, Frank (1982)
Williams, Claude (1979)

**1896**

Hoopes, Darlington
Jerome, Victor J. (1965)
Wicks, Harry (1957)
Wolfe, Bertram (1977)
Zimmerman, John (1983)

**1897**

Cacchione, Peter V. (1947)
Day, Dorothy (1980)
Dombrowski, James Anderson (1983)
Freeman, Joseph (1965)
Friedman, Samuel H.
Goldman, Albert (1960)
Perry, Pettis (1965)
Weinstone, William (1985)
Zack, Joseph (1963)

**1898**

Abern, Martin (1949)
Benjamin, Herbert (1983)
Gold, Ben (1985)
Haywood, Harry (1985)
Lovestone, Jay
Marcuse, Herbert (1979)
Rhodes, George M. (1978)

**1899**

Carlson, Oliver
De Caux, Len
Scherer, Marcel (1967)

**1900**

Calverton, V. F. (1940)
Padmore, George (1959)
Stachel, Jack (1965)
Weisbord, Albert (1977)

**1901**

Bridges, Harry
Hicks, Granville (1982)
James, C. L. R.

**1902**

Childs, Morris
Henderson, Donald (date unknown)
Hook, Sidney
Lasser, David
Marcantonio, Vito (1954)
Potash, Irving (1976)

**1903**

Connelly, Philip (1981)
Davis, Benjamin (1964)
Nelson, Steve
Weinstock, Louis
Williamson, John (1974)

**1904**

Costigan, Howard
Dodd, Bella (1969)
Farrell, James T. (1979)
Harris, Lem
Hudson, Roy (1982)
Kester, Howard (1977)
Shachtman, Max (1972)
Toohey, Pat (1978)

**1905**

Burnham, James
Charney, George Blake (1975)
Darcy, Samuel
Dennis, Eugene (1961)
Horton, Myles
Novack, George
Quill, Mike (1966)
Schneiderman, William (1985)
Wilkerson, Doxey

## 1906

Allen, James
Gannet, Betty (1970)
Green, Gil
Macdonald, Dwight (1982)
Mitchell, H. L.
Morrow, Felix
Pressman, Lee (1969)
Winter, Carl

## 1907

Dobbs, Farrell (1983)
Lannon, Al (1969)
Phillips, William

## 1908

Hall, Rob
Rahv, Philip (1973)

## 1909

Gerson, Simon
Herberg, Will (1977)
Lash, Joseph P.
Weiss, Max

## 1910

Hall, Gus
Rustin, Bayard

## 1911

Burlak, Anne
Goodman, Paul (1972)
Winston, Henry

## 1912

Hart, William Osborne
Lens, Sidney
Zeidler, Frank P.

## 1913

Gates, John
Herndon, Angelo
Richmond, Al
Ross, Carl

## 1914

Healey, Dorothy Ray

## 1915

Dellinger, David
Thompson, Robert (1968)

## 1920

Howe, Irving

## 1921

Berrigan, Daniel

## 1923

Berrigan, Philip

## 1928

Forman, James
Harrington, Michael

## 1929

Lynd, Staughton
McReynolds, David

## 1935

Cleaver, Leroy Eldridge
Moses, Robert Parris

## 1936

Hoffman, Abbie
Seale, Bobby

## 1938

Rubin, Jerry

## 1939

Hayden, Thomas

## 1941

Carmichael, Stokely
Davis, Rennie

## 1942

Dohrn, Bernardine
Newton, Huey P.

## 1943

Boudin, Kathy

## 1944

Davis, Angela

# Appendix E: Those Who Abandoned the Radical Movement

Benjamin, Herbert
Benson, Allan L.
Billings, Warren K.
Bittelman, Alexander
Blanshard, Paul
Block, S. John
Bohn, Frank A.
Boudin, Louis B.
Browder, Earl
Budenz, Louis
Burnham, James
Calverton, V. F.
Carlson, Oliver
Charney, George Blake
Childs, Morris
Cleaver, Leroy Eldridge
Collins, John A.
Costigan, Howard
Darcy, Samuel
Davis, Rennie
Dodd, Bella
Domingo, W. A.
Duncan, Lewis J.
Eastman, Max
Ferguson, Isaac
Fraina, Louis
Freeman, Joseph
Freese, Irving C.
Gates, John
Germer, Adolph

Gitlow, Benjamin
Goldman, Albert
Hall, Rob
Halonen, George
Haskell, Burnette
Hayes, Max S.
Herberg, Will
Herndon, Angelo
Hicks, Granville
Hoan, Daniel Webster
Hook, Sidney
Hudson, Roy
Kruse, William
Larkin, James
Lash, Joseph P.
Lasser, David
Lloyd, William Bross
Lore, Ludwig
Lovestone, Jay
Lunn, George R.
Matthews, J. B.
McLevy, Jasper
Miller, Bert
Morrow, Felix
Owen, Robert
Owen, Robert Dale
Padmore, George
Panken, Jacob
Phillips, William
Pressman, Lee

Puro, Henry
Quill, Mike
Rhodes, George M.
Ross, Carl
Rubin, Jerry
St. John, Vincent
Salutsky, J. B.
Saposs, David
Seale, Bobby
Simons, Algie M.
Solomon, Charles
Spargo, John

Waldman, Louis
Walling, William English
Weisbord, Albert
Weiss, Max
Wicks, Harry
Wilkerson, Doxey
Williams, Howard Y.
Wolfe, Bertram
Wolfsohn, Leo
Woodhull, Victoria
Wright, Frances
Zack, Joseph

# Appendix F: Ethnic Origin

## ANGLO-SAXON

Allen, Devere
Andrews, Stephen Pearl
Bellamy, Edward
Benson, Allan L.
Billings, Warren K.
Blanshard, Paul
Bliss, William D. P.
Block, S. John
Bloor, Ella Reeve
Bray, John Francis
Browder, Earl
Burnham, James
Collins, John A.
Day, Dorothy
De Caux, Len
Dellinger, David
Dobbs, Farrell
Duncan, Lewis J.
Eastman, Max
Freese, Irving C.
George, Harrison
Gilman, Elisabeth
Graham, James D.
Hall, Rob
Harriman, Job
Harris, Lem
Hart, William Osborne
Haskell, Burnette G.
Hayes, Max S.
Haywood, William D.
Heath, Frederic F.
Hicks, Granville
Hoan, Daniel Webster
Holmes, John Haynes
Hoopes, Darlington
Horton, Myles
Hudson, Roy
Hughan, Jessie Wallace
Johnstone, Jack
Kelley, Florence
Kester, Howard
Laidrel, Harry W.
Lee, Algernon
Lloyd, Henry Demarest
Lloyd, William Bross
Lum, Dyer D.
Lunn, George R.
Macdonald, Dwight
Matthews, J. B.
McCreery, Maud
McLevy, Jasper
McReynolds, David
Minor, Robert
Mitchell, H. L.
Mortimer, Wyndham
Nearing, Scott
Noyes, John Humphrey
O'Hare, Kate Richards
Oneal, James

Ovington, Mary White
Owen, Robert
Owen, Robert Dale
Parsons, Albert R.
Phillips, Wendell
Quick, William F., Sr.
Reed, John
Rhodes, George M.
St. John, Vincent
Simons, Algie M.
Spargo, John
Spooner, Lysander
Taylor, Charles
Thomas, Norman M.
Walling, William English
Ware, Harold
Warren, Josiah
Wayland, Julius A.
Wicks, Harry
Williams, Claude
Williams, Howard Y.
Williamson, John
Wilshire, Henry Gaylord
Wilson, Lilith Martin
Woodhull, Victoria
Work, John M.
Wright, Frances

## AUSTRALIAN

Bridges, Harry

## BLACK

Cleaver, Leroy Eldridge
Davis, Angela
Davis, Benjamin
DuBois, W. E. B.
Ford, James
Forman, James
Haywood, Harry
Herndon, Angelo
McKinney, Ernest Rice
Moses, Robert Parris
Newton, Huey P.
Patterson, William
Perry, Pettis
Randolph, A. Philip
Rustin, Bayard
Seale, Bobby

Wilkerson, Doxey
Winston, Henry

## DANISH

Gronlund, Laurence
Petersen, Arnold
Swabeck, Arne

## DUTCH

Muste, A. J.
Van Kleek, Mary

## FINNISH

Hall, Gus
Halonen, George
Laukki, Leo
Puro, Henry
Ross, Carl

## FRENCH

de Cleyre, Voltairine
Debs, Eugene V.

## GERMAN

Ameringer, Oscar
Bartel, Heinrich L.
Bedacht, Max
Berger, Meta
Berger, Victor L.
Calverton, V. F.
Germer, Adolph
Grottkau, Paul
Krumbein, Charles
Kruse, William
Lore, Ludwig
Maurer, James Hudson
Most, Johann
Mumford, Lewis
Rauschenbusch, Walter
Ruthenberg, Charles
Seidel, Emil
Spies, August
Stump, J. Henry
Wagenknecht, Alfred
Zeidler, Frank P.

## GERMAN/IRISH

Berrigan, Daniel
Berrigan, Philip

Budenz, Louis
Steffens, Lincoln

## IRISH

Cannon, James P.
Connelly, Philip
Farrell, James T.
Flynn, Elizabeth Gurley
Foster, William Z.
Harrington, Michael
Hayden, Thomas
Jones, Mary Harris
Larkin, James
McGuire, Peter J.
Mooney, Thomas J.
Poyntz, Juliet Stuart
Quill, Mike
Toohey, Pat

## IRISH/CANADIAN

Dunne, Vincent
Dunne, William

## IRISH/NORWEGIAN

Dennis, Eugene

## ITALIAN

Cacchione, Peter V.
Dodd, Bella
Fraina, Louis
Lannon, Al
Marcantonio, Vito
Sacco, Nicola
Tresca, Carlo
Vanzetti, Bartolomeo

## JEWISH

Abern, Martin
Allen, James
Amter, Israel
Benjamin, Herbert
Berkman, Alexander
Bittelman, Alexander
Boudin, Kathy
Boudin, Louis B.
Cahan, Abraham
Charney, George Blake
Childs, Morris

Darcy, Samuel
DeLeon, Daniel
Dohrn, Bernardine
Ferguson, Isaac
Frank, Waldo
Freeman, Joseph
Gannett, Betty
Gates, John
Gerson, Simon
Gitlow, Benjamin
Gold, Ben
Gold, Mike
Goldman, Albert
Goldman, Emma
Green, Gil
Healey, Dorothy Ray
Herberg, Will
Hillquit, Morris
Hoffman, Abbie
Hook, Sidney
Howe, Irving
Jerome, Victor J.
Lash, Joseph P.
Lasser, David
Lens, Sidney
London, Meyer
Lovestone, Jay
Marcuse, Herbert
Miller, Bert
Morrow, Felix
Novack, George
Olgin, Moissaye
Panken, Jacob
Pepper, John
Peters, J.
Phillips, William
Potash, Irving
Pressman, Lee
Rahv, Philip
Richmond, Al
Rose, Ernestine
Rubin, Jerry
Salutsky, J. B.
Saposs, David
Scherer, Marcel
Schneiderman, William
Shachtman, Max
Solomon, Charles

Spector, Frank
Stachel, Jack
Stokes, Rose Pastor
Trachtenberg, Alexander
Vladeck, Baruch Charney
Waldman, Louis
Weiner, William
Weinstock, Louis
Weinstone, William
Weisbord, Albert
Weiss, Max
Winter, Carl
Wolfe, Bertram
Wolfsohn, Leo
Zimmerman, Charles

## NORWEGIAN

Benson, Elmer

## NORWEGIAN/ENGLISH

Hathaway, Clarence

## POLISH

Krzycki, Leo

## RUSSIAN

Konikow, Antoinette

## SOUTH SLAVIC

Nelson, Steve
Zack, Joseph

## SWEDISH

Carlson, Oliver
Engdahl, J. Louis
Hill, Joe
Skoglund, Carl

## SWISS

Claessens, August

## UKRANIAN

Burlak, Anne

## WEST INDIAN BLACK

Briggs, Cyril
Carmichael, Stokely
Domingo, W. A.
Huiswoud, Otto
James, C. L. R.
Padmore, George

# INDEX

Abern, Martin, 1–2, 63, 233, 253, 354, 355, 356
Abolitionists, 73, 75, 76
Abraham Lincoln Battalion (Spanish Civil War), 150, 291
Accra, Ghana, 121
*Advance*, 84
Aero Service (World War I), 114
African Black Brotherhood, 219–220
African Blood Brotherhood, 45, 46, 190
African Friends of Abyssinia, 307
African Service Bureau, 307
Afro-American Information Center, 72
Agricultural Adjustment Agency, 318
Agricultural Workers Organizing Committee, 277
*Alarm*, 256–257, 310
Albion Hall Group (ILA), 44
All African Peoples' Conference, 308
All African Peoples' Organization, 308
All African Peoples Revolutionary Party, 67
Allen, Devere, 2–3, 383
Allen, James, 3–4
Alliance Placement Bureau (NY), 391
All-Race Conference, 46
Alwato universal language, 7
Amalgamated Butchers Union, 143
Amalgamated Clothing Workers, 35, 66, 208, 235, 308, 349, 435

Amalgamated Lithographers Union, 235
Amalgamated Meat Cutters Union, 158
Amalgamated Textile Union, 31, 285
Ambulance Corps (World War II), 183
American Academy of Arts and Sciences, 424
American Association for Labor Legislation, 317
*American Caravan*, 284
American Civil Liberties Union, 35, 53, 116, 134–135, 145, 211, 266, 279, 285, 392
American College of Trial Lawyers, 402
American Committee for Cultural Freedom, 56, 316
American Committee for European Workers Relief, 233
American Committee for Struggle Against War, 198
American Committee for the Defense of Leon Trotsky, 131, 389
American Committee on Africa, 338
American Commonwealth Political Federation, 417
American Conference on Democracy and the Terms of Peace, 179
*American Export Review*, 7
American Fabian Society, 34
American Federation of Labor, 20, 44, 48, 79, 96, 104, 122, 138, 139, 157,

189, 192, 198, 202, 204–205, 226, 251, 255, 257, 265–267, 280, 285, 354, 360, 385, 403, 433

American Federation of Labor-Congress of Industrial Organizations, 255, 329, 339

American Federation of Teachers, 112, 274, 415; Local 5, 112

American Forum for Socialist Education, 246

American Friends Service Committee, 84, 247

*American Guardian*, 6

American Labor Alliance for Recognition and Trade Relations with Russia, 388

American Labor Party, 33, 35, 70, 112, 239, 245, 262–263, 299, 309, 322, 364, 383, 384, 396, 402, 436

American Labor Press Association, 348

American Labor Union, 96

American League Against War and Fascism, 264

American League for a Free Palestine, 417

American League for India's Freedom, 3

American Legion, 165

American Letter-Mail Company, 368

American Negro Labor College, 220

American Negro Labor Congress, 46, 135

American Negro Labor League, 190

American Parish Among Immigrants, 378, 379

American Peace Mobilization, 77

American Railway Union, 21, 91–94

American Russian Famine Relief Association, 404

American Security Union, 243

Americans for Democratic Action, 143, 241–242, 436

*American Socialist*, 129, 294

American Socialist Society, 35

American Society for Technical Aid to Spanish Democracy, 143

American Student Union, 242

American Union Against Militarism, 379

American Unitarian Association, 122

American Workers Party, 2, 53, 55–56,

64, 66, 213, 233, 246, 269, 284, 286, 348, 356

American Writers Congress, 144–145

American Youth Congress, 169, 336

American Youth for Democracy, 336, 413

Ameringer, Oscar, 4–6, 295

Am Olam (Jewish Colonization Society), 58, 59

Amter, Israel, 6–7

Amtorg, 145

Anaconda Copper Co., strike at, (Montana), 124

Anarchist-individualists, 74, 367, 405–407

Anarchists, 24, 59, 73, 74, 161, 163, 249, 345, 389

Anarcho-Communists, 74, 162, 282

Anarcho-Socialist Society, 162

Anarcho-Syndicalists, 74, 107, 225

Anderson, Sherwood, 144

Andrews, Stephen Pearl, 7–9, 406, 425, 427

Anti-Anarchy Law (Massachusetts), 55

Anti-Conscription League, 88

Anti-Imperialist League, 30, 311

Anti-Semitism, 60, 111, 167

Anti-Slavery Society, 75, 315

Anti-Vietnam War movement, 167

A. Philip Randolph Educational Fund, 269

A. Philip Randolph Institute, 329–337, 339

*Appeal to Reason*, 97, 359, 362, 407–408

Aptheker, Herbert, 188

*Arbeiter Tsaitung*, New York (*Arbeiter Zeitung*) (Yiddish), 60, 105, 203

*Arbeiter Zeitung* (Buffalo), 283

*Arbeiter Zeitung* (Chicago and Germany), 11, 366

*Arbeiter Zeitung* (Milwaukee), 19, 172

Arlington National Cemetery, 387

Arvin, Newton, 201

Association of All Classes of All Nations, 335

Association of the Bar of the City of New York, 402

*Atheneum Illustre* (Amsterdam), 101
Atlanta Penitentiary, 99, 151
Augustine, Paul, 314
Australian Seamen's Union, 44
Authors League of America, 3
Auto Workers Union, 280

Baker, Charles, 341
Baker, Ella, 281, 338
Baldwin, Roger, 53, 182
Balfour Declaration, 396
Baptist Church, 273
Barnard College, 317
Barnes, J. Mahlon, 97–98, 205, 428
Baron, Victor, 152
Bartel, Heinrich, 11
Beal, Fred, 384
Beard, Charles, 41
Bedacht, Max, 11–12, 50, 343
Begun, Isidore, 154
Bellamy, Edward, 5, 12–14, 34, 77, 92,
    103, 171, 178, 185, 265, 270, 330,
    407, 419, 427
Bellevue College, NB, 257
Bellow, Saul, 358
Benjamin, Herbert, 14–16
Benson, Allan, 16–17, 98
Benson, Elmer, 17–18, 82, 182, 417
Berger, Meta, 18–19, 109
Berger, Victor, 5, 6, 11, 18, 19–24, 92,
    93, 94, 95, 97, 98, 99, 105, 106, 109,
    189, 197, 198, 204, 207, 245, 248,
    250, 266, 296, 298, 321, 334, 353,
    354, 360, 395, 403, 420, 427, 428
Berkeley, California Socialists Elected,
    97
Berkman, Alexander, 24–26, 74, 162–
    163, 165, 207, 257, 283, 371
*Berkshire Current*, 13
*Berliner Freie Presse*, 282
Bernstein, Eduard, 22
Berrigan, Daniel, 27–28, 90
Berrigan, Philip, 27–28, 90
Biemiller, Andrew, 382
Billings, Warren, 26, 28–29, 63, 165,
    278
Birth control, 164
Bittelman, Alexander, 29–31, 110, 297

Black House, 71
Black Liberation Army, 39
"Black Manifesto," 137
Black Muslims, 71
Black Panther Party, 66–67, 71–72, 84,
    291–292, 352
Black Panther Political Party, 84
Black United Front, 67
Blanshard, Paul, 31–33, 70, 146, 209,
    212, 381
*Blast!*, 26
Bliss, William, 33–34, 351
Block, S. John, 34–35
Bloor, Ella Reeve, 35–37, 404
Bogalusa, LA, Saw-Mill Workers Strike
    Committee, 123
Bohn, Frank, 38
Bolshevik Party, 26, 70
Bolsheviks, 29, 127–128, 159, 166, 207,
    362, 380, 403; seizure of power by,
    99, 238, 244, 251, 332, 342, 350,
    372, 388
Boni and Liberight, 26
Bonus Army, 144, 411
Bookkeepers, Stenographers and Ac-
    countants Union, 48
Boudin, Kathy, 38–39
Boudin, Louis, 39–41, 95, 142, 207
Bourne, Randolph, 41–42, 144, 284
Bray, John Francis, 42–44
Brewer, Roy, 79
Brewery Workers Union, 349
Bridgeport Federation of Labor, 270, 272
Bridges, Harry, 44–45
Briggs, Cyril, 45–47
Brisbane, Albert, 47–48
British Jamaican Benevolent Association,
    116
British Labour Party, 360
*Bronx Home News*, 81
Brook Farm, 47, 76
Brookings Institution, 142
Brooklyn Bar Association, 402
Brookwood Labor College, 265, 269,
    285, 349
Brophy, John, 100
Brotherhood of Carpenters and Joiners,
    290

Brotherhood of Labor, 327
*Brotherhood of Locomotive Engineers Journal*, 100
Brotherhood of Locomotive Firemen, 90–91
Brotherhood of Painters, Decorators and Paperhangers, 410
Brotherhood of Railroad Carmen, 363
Brotherhood of Sleeping Car Porters, 328
Brotherhood of the Carpenter, 351
Browder, Earl, 12, 30, 48–53, 54, 62, 63, 81, 82, 83, 109, 110, 113, 124, 136, 137, 138, 139, 140, 144, 145, 152, 169, 170, 182, 186, 190, 196, 217, 262, 275, 276, 357, 369, 370, 377, 384, 385, 386, 411, 418
Browderism, 110
Bryan, William Jennings, 14, 20, 34, 44, 93, 138, 140, 247, 408, 419
Buch, Vera, 412
Budenz, Louis, 53–54
Buffalo *Arbeiter Zeitung*, 283
Building Service Employees Union, 246
Bukharin, Nikolai, 50, 142, 253, 254
Bund, Jewish, 29, 251, 297, 334, 348, 393–394
Bureau of International Revolutionary Propaganda, 332
Bureau of Medical Economics, American Medical Association, 361
Burke, Kenneth, 145
Burlak, Anne, 54–55
Burned Over District, 255
Burnham, James, 55–56, 64, 213
*Butte Daily Bulletin*, 124

Caballero, Largo, 2
Cacchione, Peter, 57–58, 86, 154
Cahan, Abraham, 13, 58–61, 93, 104, 105, 203
California Department of Penology, 296
California Un-American Activities Committee, 196
Calverton, V. F., 61–62, 213
Campaign for Economic Democracy, 188
Cannon, James, 1, 2, 49, 50, 62–65, 124, 160, 186, 233, 246, 252, 253,

269, 279, 354, 355, 356, 369, 374, 411
Carlson, Oliver, 65–66
Carmichael, Stokely, 66–67
*The Carpenter*, 267
Castro, Fidel, 69, 144
Cathedral of St. John the Divine, 211
Catholic Peace Fellowship, 27
*Catholic Worker*, 89
Catholic Worker Houses of Hospitality, 89
Catholic Worker Movement, 88
Catholic Worker Organization, 180
Central Cooperative Wholesale, 177
Central Labor Union (Boston), 351
Centralia Massacre (WA), 78
*The Challenge* (Los Angeles), 419
Chambers, Whittaker, 12, 253, 314
Charney, George Blake, 68
Charter Revision Commission (NY), 383
Chartists, 42, 75
Chicago Bureau of Charities, 358
*Chicago Daily Socialist*, 129, 248, 310, 390
*Chicago Defender*, 136, 307
"Chicago Eight," 211, 337
Chicago Federation of Labor, 96, 139, 233, 374
Chicago Peace Council, 247
*Chicago Record*, 358
"Chicago Seven," 187
Chicago Stockyards Labor Council, 225
*Chicago Times*, 310
Chicago Trades and Labor Council, 310
*Chicago Tribune*, 145, 166, 247–248
Chicago Typographical Union, 310
*Chicago World*, 424
Child Labor Amendment, 214
Childs, Morris, 68–69
Christensen, Parley, 189
Christian Democrats, 255
Christian Science, 191
Christian Socialist Movement, 114, 155, 258
Christian Socialist Party (Germany), 282
Christian Socialists, 416
Christian Socialist Society in America, 33
Christian Social Justice Fund, 156

Christian Social Union, 351
Christian Utopian Socialists, 293
Church Association for the Advancement of the Interests of Labor, 33–34
Church League for Industrial Democracy, 351
Church Peace Mission, 287
Cigar Makers Union, 267
*CIO News*, 100
*The Citizen* (Schenectady), 258
Citizens Union, 381
City Affairs Committee (New York, NY), 32, 212, 381
Civic League (St. Louis), 53
Civil Defense, 90
Civil Liberties Committee, 154
Civil Rights Committee AFL/CIO, 436
Civil Rights Congress, 311
Civil Rights Defense Committee, 292–293
Civil War (U.S.), 8, 42, 303, 315, 335, 406–407
Claessens, August, 69–71
*Clarity*, 336
Classroom Teachers Association, 112
*Class Struggle*, 40
Cleaver, Leroy Eldridge, 67, 71–73, 292
Clergymen's Socialist Alliance, 31
Cleveland *Citizen*, 188, 189
*Cleveland Press*, 188
Cleyre, Voltairine de, 73–75
Coal and Iron Police, 265
Coalition Caucus, 181
College Settlement Association, 351
Collegiate Association for Research of Principles, 73
*Colliers*, 332
Collins, John, 75–77, 335
Colorado Fuel and Iron Company, 153
Cominform, 110
*Coming Nation*, 360, 408
Comintern. *See* Communist International
*Commentary*, 316
Commission of Inquiry into the Charges Against Leon Trotsky, 292
Commission on Industrial Relations, U.S., 347, 349

Committee for a Third International, 129, 317, 388
Committee for Nonviolent Action, 287
Committee for Non-Violent Revolution, 108
Committee for Unity of Agricultural and Rural Workers, 198
Committee on Economic and Social Justice, 231
Committee to Defend America by Aiding the Allies, 284
Committee to Defend Negro Leadership, 136
Committee to Support South African Resistance, 338
Commonwealth Builders, Inc., 78
Commonwealth College, 66, 416
Commonwealth Party, 296
*The Communist*, 30, 149, 176, 224, 253, 316, 342
Communist International (Comintern), 1, 15, 30, 48, 50, 51, 63, 82, 108–109, 110, 124, 139, 141, 142, 145, 146, 152, 156, 159, 177, 207, 219–220, 226, 233, 234, 252–254, 276, 307, 312, 313, 331, 342, 343, 350, 355, 369, 372, 374, 388, 389, 411, 418, 423–424
Communist International (Executive Committee), 12, 169, 241, 314, 331, 333, 388
Communist International (International Control Commission), 313
Communist International (Negro Commission), 219
Communist International (Seventh World Congress, 1935), 51, 54, 82, 169, 182, 350
Communist International (Sixth World Congress, 1928), 30, 63, 190, 226, 253–254, 311, 355
Communist Labor Party, 37, 40, 63, 65, 124, 156, 233, 241, 248, 252, 254, 331, 333, 342, 349, 374, 399, 404
Communist League of America, 1, 63, 159, 233, 246, 269, 279, 292, 356, 363, 374
Communist League of Struggle, 412

Communist Party, National Board, 170
Communist Party (China), 109
Communist Party (Finland), 177, 244
Communist Party (France), 170
Communist Party (Great Britain), 100
Communist Party (Hungary), 313
Communist Party (Majority Group), 157, 254
Communist Party (Marxist-Leninist), 191
Communist Party (Mexico), 423
Communist Party (opposition), 254
Communist Party (Philippines), 109
Communist Party (Puerto Rico), 387
Communist Party (South Africa), 109
Communist Party (Soviet Union), 50, 334, 413
Communist Party (Spain), 160, 384
Communist Party (U.S.), 1, 3, 4, 6, 7, 10, 11, 14, 17, 19, 29, 32, 35, 36, 44–55, 57, 62, 65, 68, 70, 77–79, 98–101, 108–111, 112, 119, 121, 123, 124, 125, 128, 131, 132, 133, 137, 139, 140, 141–146, 149–159, 169–170, 175–177, 180–182, 186, 187, 189, 195, 196, 197, 198–201, 208, 212, 217, 219–221, 224–226, 232–234, 239, 240, 241, 243, 245, 248, 252–255, 262–264, 269–270, 274–276, 279–280, 287, 289, 290–296, 297–298, 305–306, 308–309, 311–314, 316–320, 322, 325–326, 328, 333, 335, 336, 340, 342, 348, 350–351, 355–356, 362–363, 365–366, 368–370, 372–374, 377, 378, 382–389, 391–392, 396, 399–400, 404, 409–418, 421–424, 433, 435–436
Communist Party (U.S.), Finnish Federation, 320
Communist Party (U.S.): Hungarian Bureau, 313, 314; Hungarian Federation, 312
Communist Party (U.S.), Jewish Federation, 29
Communist Party (U.S.), Political Committee (Politburo, Polburo), 30, 51, 82, 124, 135, 151, 156, 169–170, 190, 276, 312

Communist Party (U.S.), Women's Section, 318
Communist Party of Britain, 418
Communist Party of Canada, 2, 166
Communist Political Association, 51, 52, 136, 140, 196, 217
Communisty Church (NY), 211
Communist Youth International, 355
Confederacion Nacional de Trabajos, 384
Confederate Army, 309
Conference for Progressive Labor Action, 284, 286, 348
Conference for Progressive Political Action, 53, 208–210
Congregational Church, 31, 33
Congress of American Artists, 284
Congress of Industrial Organizations, 45, 55, 100, 109–110, 141, 153, 157–158, 195, 199, 215, 269, 280, 318, 319, 322, 336, 369, 411, 416
Congress of Industrial Organizations, Los Angeles, 77, 196
Congress of Industrial Organizations in California, 77
Congress of Racial Equality, 287
Connecticut Federation of Labor, 270
Connelly, Philip Marshall, 77–78
Conservative Party (NY), 113
Consumers' Research, strike at, 264
Convention of the Infidels of the United States, 335
Convention People's Party (Ghana), 308
Cooperative Central Exchange, 319
Cooper Union, 29, 69, 267, 401
Copenhagen Conference, Socialist International (1910), 129
Corey, Lewis, 141–143, 213
*Correspondence*, 224
Cosmopolitan Club, 300
Costigan, Howard, 78–79
Council of African Affairs, 120
Council of Federated Organizations, 281
Council of Workers, Soldiers and Sailors (Portland, OR), 414
Court of Domestic Relations (New York City), 35
*The Crisis*, 118
*Crusader*, 46

Crusader News Agency, 46
Cumberland Presbyterian Church, 215
Cunard, Nancy, 306
Czechoslovakia, Soviet invasion of, 170, 197, 335, 366
Czolgosz, Leon, 74, 163–164, 283

*Daily News Record*, 147
*Daily People*, 101, 105, 106, 141
*Daily People's World*, 152
*Daily Worker*, 3, 30, 54, 62, 69, 83, 86, 110, 128, 129, 151, 154, 159, 182, 186–187, 200, 276, 279, 312, 317, 325, 334, 355, 370, 400, 421, 423
Darcy, Samuel, 81–83, 140
Darrow, Clarence, 73, 164, 179, 248
Davis, Angela, 83–85, 263, 422
Davis, Benjamin, 57, 85–87, 136, 176, 191, 200
Davis, Rennie, 87
*The Dawn*, 33
Day, Dorothy, 88–90, 180
Debs, Eugene, 5, 14, 16, 20, 21, 23, 34, 43, 90–100, 105, 147, 168, 171, 178, 189, 197, 198, 204, 205, 206, 207, 232, 245, 247, 248, 250, 268, 270, 278, 280, 298, 327, 328, 329, 360, 371, 408, 419, 421, 427, 428
Debs Caucus (Socialist Party), 180–181, 273
Debs Column (Spanish Civil War), 384
DeCaux, Len, 100–101
de Cleyre, Voltairine, 73–75
DeLacey, Hugh, 79
DeLeon, Daniel, 14, 20, 21, 34, 38, 92, 93, 94, 95, 96, 101–107, 178, 189, 192, 203, 232, 245, 249, 314, 347, 359, 360, 408
Dell, Floyd, 88, 127, 158, 164, 346
Dellinger, David, 107–108
Democracy '76, 181
Democratic Agenda, 181
Democratic Farmer Labor Party (MN), 18, 336, 417
Democratic front, 110, 186
Democratic Party, 82, 86, 178, 181, 210, 226, 242, 251, 259, 262–263, 271,

309, 334, 358, 373, 382, 395, 403, 407
Democratic Party (Terre Haute, IN), 90, 93
Democratic Party (WA), 78–79
Democratic Party of Los Angeles, 77
Democratic Socialist Federation, 180
Democratic Socialist Organizing Committee, 181, 197, 217
Democratic Socialists of America, 179, 181, 197, 216
Democrats for Eisenhower, 66
Dennis, Eugene, 52, 66, 69, 83, 108–111, 151, 152, 176, 187, 196
Dennison House, 351
*Dennis vs. U.S.*, 110
*Denver Labor Enquirer*, 185, 256
*Department of Agriculture (U.S.)*, 405
*Department of Labor (NY)*, 349
*Department of Labor (U.S.) (Women in Industry Division)*, 392
*Department of Labor (U.S.) (Women's Bureau)*, 392
*Department of Resource Development (WI)*, 434
*De-Stalinization*, 111
*Detroit Declaration of Principles (Socialist Party, 1934)*, 383, 401
*Detroit Journal*, 16
Detroit Presbytery, 417
*Detroit Times*, 16
Deutsch, Babette, 238
Dewey, John, 41, 127, 128, 131, 160, 212, 213, 292, 381, 389
*Dial*, 284
*Die Autonomie*, 162
*Direct Action*, 108
Disciples of Christ, 178, 295
*Dissent*, 216–217, 246
Distinguished Service Cross, 386
*Distributors Guide*, 52
Divine Light Mission, 87
Dobbs, Farrell, 64, 111–112
Dodd, Bella, 112–113
Dohrn, Bernadine, 113–114
Dombrowski, James, 114–115, 215
*Dombrowski vs. Pfister*, 115
Domingo, W. A., 46, 115–116

Douglas, Paul, 238
Douglass, Frederick, 75, 426
Dreiser, Theodore, 144
Dublin City Council, 241
DuBois, W. E. B., 117–121, 238, 268, 300, 301
Duclos, Jacques, 52, 83, 110, 140, 170, 217, 176
Dunayevskaya, Raya, 224
Duncan, Lewis, 121–123, 164
Dunne, Grant, 111, 123, 124
Dunne, Vincent, 123–124
Dunne, William, 123, 124–125, 129, 152
Dutch Reformed Church, 284

Eastman, Crystal, 127
Eastman, Max, 62, 88, 127–129, 213, 371
Ehrenreich, Barbara, 181
Eight Hour League, 310
Emancipation of Labor Group (Russia), 232
Emancipation Proclamation, 302, 315
Emancipator, 116
Emory University, 114
Emory University, Alumni Association, 114
Encyclopedia Africana, 121
Encyclopedia of the Social Sciences, 142
End Poverty in California Movement (EPIC), 78, 82, 185, 296, 363
Engdah, J. Louis, 129, 234, 311
Engell, George, 257, 310, 311
Episcopal Church, 351
Episcopal Church Socialist League, 351
Equal Rights Association, 335
Equal Rights Party, 426–427
Equitable commerce, 406
Esperanto, 7
Espionage Act of 1917, 99, 127, 207, 234
Esquire, 262
Eteenpain (Forward) (Finnish), 320
Ettor, Joe, 134
Euro-Communism, 151, 413
European Recovery Program, 349
Everett, Washington massacre in, 134

Fabian Essays, 420
Fabian Society (British), 16
Fabian Tracts, 407
Facts, 423
Fair Play for Cuba Committee, 144, 246
Farmer-Labor Association, 123
Farmer-Labor Movement, 186
Farmer-Labor Party, 139, 189, 233, 312, 377
Farmer-Labor Party (MI), 186
Farmer-Labor Party (MN), 17, 18, 83, 123, 336
Farmer-Labor Political Federation, 417
Farmers Emergency Relief Conference, 182
Farmers National Committee for Action, 37, 182, 405
Farmers National Relief Conference, 404
The Farmer's National Weekly, 176
Farm Holiday Association, 182
Farm-Labor-Progressive Party (WI), 434
Farm News Letter, 176
Farm Research, Inc., 182, 404, 405
Farm Research Bureau, 176
Farrell, James T., 131–132, 358
Fascists, 3, 37, 166, 306, 389
Federal Bureau of Investigation, 39, 54, 69, 79, 84, 113, 253, 386, 415
Federal Emergency Relief Administration, 271, 318
Federated Press, 100, 266
Federated Trades Council (Milwaukee), 21
Federated Trades Council of Reading, PA, 333, 373
Fellowship of Reconciliation, 2, 218, 230–231, 264, 285, 286, 287, 338, 379
Fellowship of Southern Churchmen, 230–231
Feminists, 18
Ferguson, Isaac, 132–133, 248
Ferrer, Francisco, 25, 74
Fielden, Samuel, 310, 311
Fight for Freedom Committee, 284
Finnish Socialist Federation, 298
First Congregational Church, Tampa, FL, 31

First Presbyterian Church, Schenectady, NY, 258
Fischer, Adolph, 257, 310, 311
Fish Committee, 140
"Five-to-Midnight" line, 196
Flynn, Elizabeth Gurley, 36, 133–135, 389
Fonda, Jane, 188
Force Ouvrière (France), 255
Ford, James, 46, 135–136, 142, 144, 201, 212, 220, 305, 306
Foreign Agents Registration Act of 1938, 120
Foreign Language Federations (Communist Party), 29
Forman, James, 136–137
*Fortune*, 261
Fort-Whiteman, Lovett, 220
Foster, William Z., 29–30, 37, 48, 49, 50, 52, 63, 65, 66, 68, 69, 82, 83, 85, 86, 109, 110, 111, 136, 137–141, 142, 151, 152, 156, 170, 191, 196, 201, 212, 225, 226, 233, 240, 252, 253, 305, 312, 313, 343, 369, 386, 410, 411, 418, 423
Fourier, Charles, 47
Fourierites, 76
Fraina, Louis, 141–143, 213
Frank, Waldo, 143–144, 284
Freedom Budget, 329
Freedom Democratic Party, 67, 137
Freedom Riders, 137
*Free Enquirer*, 303, 430
Freeman, Joseph, 145–146, 290
Freese, Irving, 146–147
*Free Thought*, 76
Free Trade League, 247
Free Trade Union Committee, 255
*Free Trade Union News*, 255
*Freie Arbeiter Shtimme* (Yiddish), 60, 73
*Freie Gemeinde* (German), 11
*Freie Wort* (German), 11
*Freiheit* (German), 282
*Freiheit* (Yiddish), 156, 297, 409
Frick, Henry Clay, 25, 162, 163, 257
Friedman, Samuel, 147, 383
Friends of Soviet Russia, 400

Friends of the Abraham Lincoln Brigade, 150
Friends of the Soviet Union, 7, 318, 350
Fund for the Republic, 180
Fur and Leather Workers Union, 317
Furniture Workers Union, 310
Gannett, Betty, 149–150
Garden Homes (Milwaukee), 424
Garland Fund, 182, 289
Garrison, William Lloyd, 75, 315
Garvey, Marcus, 46, 115, 116, 220, 327
Gastonia, NC, strike in, 37, 154, 400
Gates, John, 68, 86, 110, 111, 141, 150–152, 155, 196, 312, 370, 423
General Electric Co., 258–259
General Motors, 153
George, Harrison, 125, 152
George, Henry, 5, 102, 218
Georgia Insurrection Law, 200
German Socialist Federation, 252
Germer, Adolph, 99, 153, 207
Gernsback Publications, 243
Gerson, Simon, 153–155
Ghana, 121
Gilman, Elisabeth, 155–156, 231, 384
Gitlow, Benjamin, 63, 66, 156–157, 199, 342, 400
*Gitlow vs. New York*, 156
Glass Blowers Union, 77
Gold, Ben, 157–158, 317
Gold, Mike, 62, 128, 145, 158–159
Gold Coast Aborigines Rights Protection Society, 307
Goldman, Albert, 64, 159–160, 279
Goldman, Emma, 24, 25, 74, 94, 122, 161–167, 283, 296, 371, 419
Gompers, Samuel, 21, 92, 101, 104, 122, 189, 202, 206, 256, 265, 268, 372, 403, 408
Goodman, Paul, 108, 167–168, 261
Grace Church (Boston), 33
Graham, James, 168–169, 383
Grand United Order of Odd Fellows, 85
Grangers Cooperative League of America, 49
Great Northern Railroad, 91
Greeley, Horace, 8
Green, Gil, 83, 113, 169–171

Greenback-Labor Party, 36, 43, 256, 310, 366
Greenberg, Clement, 326
Green Corn Rebellion, 6
Greenpoint Settlement, 300
Greenwich House, 300
Gronlund, Laurence, 13, 92, 171, 185, 407
Grottkau, Paul, 172–173, 282, 310
Guardian Educational Scheme, 430

Hacker, Louis, 213
Hall, Gus, 85, 87, 110, 169, 170, 175–176, 335
Hall, Otto, 189
Hall, Rob, 176–177
Hall of Science (NY), 430
Halonen, George, 177
The Harbinger, 76
Harlem Liberator, 46
Harlem People's School, 220
Harlem Socialist Club, 133
Harriman, Job, 94, 95, 97, 178–179, 189, 204, 353, 359, 428
Harrington, Michael, 89, 179–181, 217, 273, 358
Harris, Lem, 176, 181–182, 404, 405
Harrisburg Eight, 28
Hart, William Osborne, 183
Haskell, Burnette, 183–186, 256
Hat, Cap and Millinery Workers Union, 369
Hathaway, Clarence, 186–187
Hayden, Thomas, 187–188
Hayes, Max, 178, 188–189
Haymarket Case, 24, 59, 73, 162, 247, 256–257, 310–311, 367
Haywood, Harry, 189–191
Haywood, William, 38, 48, 63, 97, 106, 122, 134, 191–195, 202, 205, 248, 275, 298, 341, 372, 389
Haywood, Pettibone, and Moyer case, 205
Headwaiters and Sidewaiters Society of Greater New York, 327
Healey, Dorothy Ray, 195–197
Hearst Newspapers, 265
Heath, Frederic, 197–198

Henderson, Donald, 198–199, 277
Henry Street Settlement, 230
Herberg, Will, 199–200
Herndon, Angelo, 85, 200, 421
Herndon vs. Lowry, 200
Herron, George, 361
Hicks, Granville, 201, 371
Highlander Folk School, 114, 215
Hill, Joe, 134, 201–203
Hillman, Sidney, 70, 235, 239
Hillquit, Morris, 40, 94, 95, 96, 97, 104, 105, 106, 145, 159, 178, 189, 203–209, 210, 235, 238, 245, 248, 250, 296, 298, 321, 359, 360, 371, 379, 382, 387, 395, 396, 401, 403, 428
Hiroshima, Japan, Atomic bombing of, 219, 385
Hoan, Daniel, 209, 210, 311, 321, 382, 383, 428
Hoehn, G. A., 103
Hoffa, Jimmy, 111
Hoffman, Abbie, 211
Hollywood Anti-Nazi League, 224
Hollywood Citizen News, strike at, 77
Holmes, John Haynes, 211–212, 384
Homestead Steel Company, 162
Hook, Sidney, 55, 62, 212–213, 224, 238, 326
Hoopes, Darlington, 213–214, 383, 421
Hoover Institute, 424
Horton, Myles, 114, 215–216
Hotel and Restaurant Workers Union, 336
House Committee on Un-American Activities, 4, 110, 140, 157, 201, 218, 225, 242, 264, 274, 319, 337, 409, 417, 433
Houston Telegraph, 309
Howe, Irving, 216–217, 246, 358
Hudson, Roy, 217–218
Hughan, Jessie Wallace, 218–219, 384
Huiswood, Otto, 46, 219–221
Hull House, 215, 229
Humphrey, Hubert, 18, 132, 417
Hungary; uprising of 1956, 85, 111, 141, 151, 170, 224, 290, 410; Soviet government in (1918), 312

Hunger March, National (1932), 55, 421, 422
Hunter College Instructors' Association, 112

Illinois Bureau of Labor Statistics, 229
Illinois Legislature, 230
Illinois Sedition Law, 414
Illinois Steel Company, 414
*Il Martello* (Italian), 389
Immigration Service, 415
Imperial Valley, CA, agricultural strike in, 195
Independence Party, 272
*Independent*, 403
Independent Communist League, 254
Independent Labor League, 254
Independent Labor Party (Britain), 240
Independent Miners Relief of Kentucky, 144
Independent Political Council, 327
Independent Socialist League, 180, 216, 357
Independent Trade Union Educational League, 139
Independent Voters of Illinois, 417
Indiana, House of Representatives, 91
*Industrial Solidarity*, 347
*Industrial Unionist*, 152
Industrial Workers of the World, 1, 15, 21, 38, 44, 48, 90, 96, 97, 100, 106, 107, 109, 122, 127, 133, 134, 138, 152, 159, 175, 189, 191–193, 195, 198, 201–202, 204–205, 225–226, 244, 327, 332, 341, 342, 346–347, 354, 360, 363, 365, 374, 384, 389, 414, 433
Institute for Social Studies, 359
Inter-Church World Movement, 349
Intercollegiate Socialist Society, 237–238, 352, 362, 365, 372, 379
Internal Security Act of 1950, 87
International, First, 9, 267
International, Fourth (Trotskyist), 64, 279, 357
*International African Opinion*, 307
International Association of Machinists, 186, 385

International Brigade (Spanish Civil War), 150, 190, 385
International Brotherhood of Electrical Workers, 124
International Brotherhood of Teamsters (Teamsters Union), 41, 63, 64, 111, 123, 363
International Bureau of Revolutionary Literature, 159
International Children's Committee, 82
International Communist Opposition, 254
International Conference of Negro Workers, 135, 306
International Congress of Culture, 146
International Congress of Negro Writers, Second, 221
International Convention of the Negro People of the World, 220
International Fur and Leather Workers Union, 157, 158, 316
International Labor Defense, 1, 63, 85, 129, 134–135, 159, 200, 262, 292, 311, 318, 355, 366
International Ladies Garment Workers Union, 143, 152, 199, 208, 254–255, 387, 435–436
International Longshoremen's and Warehousemen's Union, 44
International Longshoremen's Association, 44
International Publishers, 3, 388
International Red Aid, 355, 366
International Socialist Congress (1925), 60
*International Socialist Review*, 38, 40, 98, 293, 395
International Student Service, 242
International Trade Union Committee of Negro Workers, 220, 306
International Typographers Union, 188, 189
International Unemployment Day, 82
International Union of Electrical, Radio, and Machine Workers, 243
International Union of Socialist Youth, 180
International Workers Aid, 411
International Workers Order, 12, 16, 409

International Workingmen's Association, 9, 184, 267, 427
International Working People's Association, 172, 310, 366
Irish Labor Party, 241
Irish Socialist Party, 241
Irish Transport and General Workers Union, 241
*Irish Worker*, 241
Iron and Steel Workers Union, 298
Italian American Victory Council, 390
Italian Socialist Federation, 389

Jackson, George, 84–85
Jamaica Progressive League, 116
Jamaica Trades and Labor Union, 220
James, C. L. R., 223–224, 307
James Connolly Socialist Club, 241
Jefferson School of Social Science, 388
Jerome, V. J., 146, 224–225, 372
Jesse James Gang (SDS), 113
Jesuit Missions, 27
Jesuits, 27
Jewish Agitation Bureau, 393–394
Jewish Anarchist Federation of New York, 26
Jewish Cloakmakers Union, 59
*Jewish Daily Forward*, 60, 61, 93, 105, 239, 297, 382, 394, 422
Jewish Labor Committee, 436
Jewish People's Committee (Jewish Committee Against Fascism and Anti-Semitism), 409
Jewish Social Democratic movement, 70
Jewish Socialist Federation, 29, 93, 157, 203, 297, 348
Jewish Tailors Union, 59
Jobs or Income NOW (JOIN), 87
John Birch Society, 265
John Hancock Life Insurance Co., 87
John Reed Clubs, 145, 159, 201, 316, 325–326
Johnson, Tom, 340
Johnstone, Jack, 225–226
Joint Action Committee (ILGWU), 435
Jones, Mary Harris, 226–227, 295

*Der Kampf*, 29
Kangaroos faction of SLP, 178, 189, 204, 245
*Kansan Lehti (People's Tribune)* (Finnish), 244
Kansas City, MO, Central Labor Council, 49
Kautsky, Karl, 92, 206
Kaweah Cooperative Community, 183
Keep America Out of War Congress, 143, 424
Kelley, Florence, 229–230
Kester, Howard, 230–231, 277, 416
King, Martin Luther, Jr., 215, 281, 338, 339
Klonsky, Michael, 191
Knights of Labor, 43, 63, 103–104, 226, 256, 268
Konikow, Antoinette, 232–233
Kronstadt, Russia, uprising in, 26, 166
Krumbein, Charles, 233–234
Kruse, William, 99, 234
Krzycki, Leo, 235, 383
Kusbas Colony, 195

Labor, U.S. Department of, 34
*Labor Action*, 3, 53, 55, 64, 216
*Labor Age*, 285
*Labor Defender*, 355
Labor Department (U.S.) (Women's Bureau), 392
Labor Department (U.S.) (Women in Industry Division), 392
*Labor Herald*, 50
Labor Leadership for Peace, 247
Labor League for Thomas and Maurer, 235
*Labor on the March*, 100–101
Labor Party, 178, 360
Labor Press Association, 35
Labor Publications Society, 285–286
Labor Reform Party (MA), 315
Labor Research Association, 388
Labor's Chest to Aid Victims of Fascism, 403
Labor's League for Political Education, 365

Labor's Non-Partisan League, 195
Labor Sports Union, 336
Labor Temple (New York, NY), 286
*Labor Unity*, 186
Labor Zionists (Poale Zion), 251
Labour Party, Australian, 208
Labour Party (British), 40, 208
Labour Party (New Zealand), 208
LaFollette, Robert, 98, 100, 123, 155, 186, 189, 208, 238, 252, 264, 266, 299, 380, 396, 403, 428
LaGuardia, Fiorello, 32, 35, 154, 262, 309, 322, 346, 364, 383, 396
Laidler, Harry, 32, 70, 237–239
Lannon, Al, 240
La Plebe (Italian), 389
Larkin, James, 240–241
Lash, Joseph, 241–242
Lasser, David, 15, 242–243
Lattimore, Owen, 54
Latvian Socialist Federation, 298
Laukki, Leo, 244
Lautner, John, 410
*L'Avvenire* (Italian), 389
Lawrence, MA, textile strike in, 21, 25, 133, 193, 389
League Against German Fascism, 3
League Against Imperialism, 305
League for Cultural Freedom and Socialism, 131, 325
League for Democratic Control, 285
League for Independent Political Action, 3, 396, 417
League for Industrial Democracy, 3, 32, 156, 180, 198, 217, 237–240, 362, 380–381
League for Non-violent Civil Disobedience Against Military Segregation, 338
League of American Writers, 143, 144, 145, 201, 184, 363
League of Coloured People, 307
League of Hollywood Voters, 79
League of Professional Groups for Foster and Ford, 142, 201, 212, 279
League of Revolutionary Black Workers, 137

League of Struggle for Negro Rights, 135, 190, 313
League to Endorse Peace, 266
Lee, Algernon, 206, 244–246
Leeds Workingmen's Association, 42
Lehr und Wehr Verein (Learning and Defense League), 310, 366
Lenin, V. I., 49, 51, 128, 129, 142, 199, 208, 225, 275, 298, 371, 393, 395
Lenin School (Moscow), 69, 149, 157, 190, 220, 234, 291, 317, 433
Lens, Sidney, 246–247
Lewis, John L., 6, 30, 109, 125, 198, 199, 227, 318, 319, 387, 411
Liberal Club, 371
Liberal Party (NY), 70, 86, 239, 245–246, 364, 436
*Liberation*, 108, 246, 273, 284
*Liberator*, 127, 145, 158, 248, 332
*Liberty*, 73
Liebknecht, Wilhelm, 95
Lingg, Louis, 257, 310, 311
Lippmann, Walter, 238, 259, 371
Little, Frank, 123
Little Falls, NY, strike in, 259
Little Steel Strike, 175
Llano Colony, 179
Lloyd, Henry Demarest, 93, 94, 229, 247–248
Lloyd, William Bross, 132, 248–249
*Locomotive Firemen's Journal*, 90
London, Meyer, 98, 203, 249–252, 394
Longview Publishing Corp., 155
Lore, Ludwig, 142, 232, 252–253, 297, 318
*Los Angeles Herald-Dispatch*, 47
*Los Angeles Herald Express*, 77
Lose Angeles Newspaper Guild, 77
*Los Angeles Times*, 178
Lovestone, Jay, 12, 15, 29, 30, 37, 50, 63, 139, 142, 156, 157, 199, 220, 234, 253–255, 264, 274, 276, 297, 313, 343, 369, 411, 414, 423, 424, 435
Lowell, MA, textile strike in, 133

Lowndes County Freedom Organization, 67
*Lowry, Herndon vs.*, 200
Ludlow, CO, massacre of strikers in, 25, 227
Luhan, Mabel Dodge, 194
Lum, Dyer, 74, 107, 255–257
Lunn, George, 257–259
Lusitania, 98, 208, 360, 395
Lynd, Staughton, 188, 260

McAlister, Sister Elizabeth, 28
MacArthur Foundation, 281
McCarran Act, 176
McCarthy, Joseph, 4, 46, 54, 264, 265
*McClure's Magazine*, 371
McCreery, Maud, 266–267
MacDonald, Dwight, 89, 108, 132, 261–262, 326
McGuire, Peter, 267–268
Machinists Union, 278, 295
McKay, Claude, 48, 128, 158
Mackenzie-Papineau Battalion (Spanish Civil War), 385
McKinney, Ernest Rice, 268–269
McLevy, Jasper, 3, 146, 270–272
McNamara, James, 63, 165, 178–179
McNamara, John, 63, 165, 178–179
McReynolds, David, 273
*Madison Democrat*, 358
Madison Square Garden, riot in, 383
Magistrate's Court (New York, NY), 364
Marcantonio, Vito, 68, 262–263
March on Washington (1943), 260, 329, 338
March on Washington (1963), 329, 337, 339
March on Washington (1983), 339
Marcuse, Herbert, 84, 263–264
Marcy Center Settlement House, 183
Marine Workers Industrial League, 109
Marine Workers Industrial Union, 217, 334
Maritime Federation of the Pacific, 44
Marshall Plan, 140, 160, 262, 392
Marx, Karl, 43, 51, 92, 144, 171, 184, 205, 213, 267, 282, 331, 355
Marx-Engels Institute (Moscow), 212

Marx Memorial Library (London), 418
Massachusetts Institute of Technology, 243
*Masses*, 88, 127, 158, 332
Matthews, J. B., 264–265
Matusow, Harvey, 68
Maurer, James, 18, 206, 235, 265–266
Maurin, Peter, 88–89
Max Planck Institute (Germany), 264
Mayer, Milton, 108
May 19th Coalition, 39
Mazzini Society, 390
Meany, George, 255, 277, 329
Melish, William, 84
Melms, Edmund, 273–274
*Memphis Advocate and Western District Advocate*, 430
Merton, Thomas, 90
Mesabi Range, MN, mine strike in, 134, 152, 389
*Messenger*, 116, 269, 326
Methodist Church, 264
*Metropolitan*, 332
*Michigan Daily*, 187
*Midwest Daily Record*, 54, 182
*The Militant*, 63, 111, 279, 356
Militant faction (Socialist Party), 70, 209, 245, 299, 364, 373, 381, 382, 383
Miller, Bert, 274–275
Miller, Louis, 105
Milwaukee County Historical Society, 11, 198
Milwaukee Electric Railway and Light Co., 353
Milwaukee Federated Trades Council, 266
*Milwaukee Journal*, 197, 361, 424
*Milwaukee Leader*, 6, 11, 99, 197, 266, 274, 360–361, 424, 428
*Milwaukee Post*, 428
Milwaukee Public Enterprise Committee, 435
Milwaukee School Board, 18
*Milwaukee Sentinel*, 197
Mine, Mill and Smelter Workers Union, 196

Miners Relief Committee to Kentucky, 144

Minneapolis, Teamsters strike, 63, 175

*Minneapolis Daily News*, 129

Minneapolis Office Workers Union, 123

Minneapolis Trade and Labor Assembly, 186

Minneapolis Youth Council, 336

Minnesota and Midwest Youth Congress, 336

Minnesota Federation of Labor, 186

Minor, Robert, 82, 146, 275–276, 299, 363, 369

Mississippi Summer Project, 260

Missoula, MT, Free Speech fight in, 133

Missouri Bureau of Labor Statistics, 267

Mitchell, H. L., 276–277

Mobilization for Survival, 247

*Modern Dance Magazine*, 142

*Modern Monthly*, 213

*Modern Occasions*, 325

*Modern Quarterly*, 61, 62

Modern School (Shelton, NJ), 25, 74

Modern Times (Brentwood, Long Island), 8, 406–407

Montana Federation of Labor, 124, 168

Montana Selective Service Appeals Board, 168

Moon, Sun Myung, 73

Mooney, Thomas, 26, 28–29, 63, 165, 264, 275, 277–278, 366

Moore, Richard B., 46, 116

Morrow, Felix, 64, 279

Mortimer, Wyndham, 279–280

Moses, Robert Parris, 280–281

Most, Johann, 25, 162, 163, 172, 256, 281–283, 310, 366

*Mother Earth*, 25, 165

*Muller vs. Oregon*, 230

Mumford, Lewis, 283–284

Municipal Ownership League, 248

Murray, Philip, 319

Muste, A. J., 2, 53, 55, 64, 66, 108, 213, 233, 246, 269, 274, 284–287, 348, 356, 374, 378

Musteists, 160

Mystic Arts Book Society, 279

Nagasaki, Japan, atomic bombing of, 219, 385

*Naradnaya Volya (People's Will)*, 24

Nashoba, TN, Community, 303, 429

*The Nation*, 2, 32, 143, 380

National Agricultural Workers Union, 277

National Association for the Advancement of Colored People, 118, 120, 211, 230, 231, 268, 299–300, 329, 337, 339, 402–403, 421

National Black Economic Development Conference, 137

National Campaign Committee for Unemployment Insurance, 400

National Child Labor Committee, 230

National Citizens Political Action Committee, 18

National Civic Federation, 96, 237

National Civil Liberties Bureau, 134, 379

National Club (Jamaica), 115

National Committee for a Sane Nuclear Policy (SANE), 217, 385

National Committee for the Defense of Political Prisoners, 201, 292

National Committee to Aid Victims of German Fascism, 400

National Committee to End the War in Vietnam, 247

National Consumers League, 230

National Council of Senior Citizens, 387

National Economic Development Conference, 137

National Farmers Union, 182

National Farm Labor Union, 277

National Hunger March, 55, 421–422

National Clubs, 14, 103, 171, 185, 265, 419

National Labor Relations Board, 349

National Labor Union, 427

National Lawyers Guild, 35, 113

National Maritime Union, 217

National Miners Union, 37, 291, 387

National Mobilization Committee to End the War in Vietnam, 39

National Mobilization To End the War in Vietnam (MOBE), 87, 188

National Negro Congress, 136, 328–329

*National Review*, 56, 128, 200
*National Rip-Saw*, 98, 296
National Social Reform Union, 34
National Student Association, 136
National Student League, 176, 198, 413
National Textile Workers Union, 54, 55, 412
National Union of Dock Laborers, 240–241
National United Committee to Free Angela Davis, 85
National Woman Suffrage Association, 335, 425
National Women's Rights Convention, 335
National Women's Trade Union League, 402
National Workmen's Committee for Jewish Rights, 395
*Naye Velt* (*New World*) (Yiddish), 348, 394
Nazi-Soviet Pact, 19, 30, 51, 56, 77–78, 140, 151, 242, 243, 262, 284, 290, 298, 328, 356, 392, 400
Nearing, Scott, 35, 62, 145, 289–290
Neebe, Oscar, 310, 311
Needle Trade Workers Industrial Union, 157
Negro American Labor Council, 329
*Negro Champion*, 46
*Negro Liberation*, 190
*Negro Liberator*, 86
*Negro Quarterly*, 200
*Negro Worker*, 46, 220, 306
*Neie Tseit* (Yiddish), 59
Nelson, Steve, 290–291
*New America*, 180
New American Movement, 181, 197, 217, 375
Newark Community Union Project, 187
New Deal, 30, 70, 78, 109, 215, 249, 262, 277, 328, 381, 382, 383, 392
*New Democracy*, 9
New Harmony community, IN, 302–303, 405–406
*New Harmony Gazette*, 303
*New International*, 56, 64, 142, 223, 356
New Lamark, Scotland, 301, 303

*New Leader*, 208, 299
*New Leader* (British), 307
New Left, 4, 27, 84, 107, 108, 167, 180, 187, 217, 224, 260, 263, 280, 337
*New Masses*, 62, 143, 145, 158, 201, 279, 284, 316, 325
New Negro Movement, 116
*The New Republic*, 32, 41, 142, 144, 159, 284
*New Review*, 300
*News and Letters*, 224
Newton, Huey, 67, 71, 72, 84, 291–292, 352
New Workers School, 424
*New World*, 116
*New York Amsterdam News*, 45
New York Central Labor Federation, 104
New York City Charter Revision Commission, 35
New York City Housing Authority, 396
*New York Commercial Advertiser*, 371
*New York Communist*, 333
*New York Daily Call*, 35, 88, 99, 207, 275, 364, 380, 387
*New Yorker*, 262
*New Yorker Volkszeitung*, 105, 232, 252
*New York Evening Post*, 371
*New York Evening Telegram*, 381
*New York Evening World*, 275
New York Furriers Joint Board, 157
*New York Herald*, 145
*New York Herald Tribune*, 141
*New York Leader*, 380
*New York Post*, 13, 242, 253
New York School of Philanthropy, 391
New York State Bar Association, Committee on Civil Rights, 402
NY State Labor Relations Board, 41
New York Stock Exchange, 211, 337
New York Student League, 413
New York Teachers Union, 112
*New York Times*, 143, 300, 332
*New York Tribune*, 8, 47
New York Workers Committee on Unemployment, 243
*New York World*, 58, 166, 332, 401
Niagara Movement, 118

Niebuhr, Reinhold, 114, 215, 231
Nkrumah, Kwame, 67, 121, 307, 308
No-Conscription League, 26, 165, 218,
    379
No-Frontier News Service, 2
Non-Partisan Labor Defense, 292
Non-Partisan League, 123, 208, 377, 384
Nonviolent Action Group, 66
Non-violent Direct Action Committee,
    286
North American Alliance for Labor and
    Democracy, 372
North American Aviation Strike, 77, 280
North American Newspaper Alliance, 2
Northern Pacific Railroad, 168
Norwalk, CT, Socialists in, 145–147
Novack, George, 292–293
Novy Mir, 366
Noyes, John Humphrey, 43, 293–294

Oakland Tribune, 185
Ocean County, NJ, Democratic Commit-
    tee, 83
Office of Strategic Services, 263
Office of War Information, 424
O'Hare, Kate Richards, 98, 99, 165,
    209, 295–297
Oklahoma Leader, 6
Old Guard faction, Socialist Party, 32,
    70, 209, 245, 299, 309, 381–383
Olgin, Moissaye, 252, 297–298
Olson, Floyd, 17
Omholt, Andrew, 36, 37
Oneal, James, 298–299
One Big Union Club, 433
101st Airborn Division (U.S. Army), 151
Oneida Community, 293, 294
Orchard, Harry, 192–193
Order of Lenin, 36
Organization Committee for a Revolu-
    tionary Workers Party, 157
Oriental-Exclusion Act, 76
The Outlook, 32
Ovington, Mary White, 230, 299–301,
    403
Owen, Chandler, 116, 269, 327
Owen, Robert, 20, 75, 76, 301–302,
    303, 335, 405, 430

Owen, Robert Dale, 301–303, 430
Oxford Pledge, 165

Pan African Federation, 307
Panken, Jacob, 308–309
Pan-Pacific Monthly, 50
Paris Commune, 427
Parson, Albert, 256, 257, 309–311, 366
Parsons, Talcott, 238
Partido Obrero de Unificación Marxista
    (POUM), 254, 384, 412
Partisan Review, 56, 64, 131, 261, 316,
    325
Party Organizer, 149
Passaic, NJ, textile strike in, 274, 380,
    400
Paterson, NJ, textile strike in, 133, 194
Patterson, William, 311–312
Peacegrant, 120
Peace Information Center, 120
Peacemakers, 108, 287
Pearson's Magazine, 16, 36
Pennsylvania Federation of Labor, 265
Pennsylvania Old-Age Assistance Com-
    mission, 266
Pennsylvania Sedition Law, 291
People's Council of America, 179, 423
People's National Party (Jamaica), 116
People's Party, 14, 20, 34, 43, 63, 197,
    247, 353, 407; of California, 185
People's Printing Company, 373
People's Relief, 396
People's United Church, 258
People's World, 78, 149, 150, 334–335
Pepper, John, 312–313, 343
Perfectionists, 293
Perry, Pettis, 313
Peters, J., 313–314
Petersen, Arnold, 314
Phalanx, 47
Philadelphia, streetcar strike in, 138
Phillips, Wendell, 315–316
Phillips, William, 316, 326
Pinkerton guards, 162
Pittsburgh American, 269
Pittsburgh Coal Co., 111
Pittsburgh Congress (of 1883), 184
Pittsburgh Courier, 268

Pittsburgh Manifesto, 184, 282
*Plaebeian*, 47
Plumbers and Steamfitters Union, 233, 265
Poale Zion (Labor Zionists), 393
Pogroms, 29, 58
*Political Affairs*, 149, 413
*Politics*, 261
Poor People's Campaign, 339
Popular Front, 15, 30, 51, 54, 82, 124, 131, 136, 140, 169, 177, 182, 190, 201, 224, 225, 243, 262, 297, 363, 369, 402, 417; in Spain, 2, 17, 160, 356, 385
Populist faction of Socialist Party, 383
Populists. *See* People's Party
Port Huron Statement, 187
Potash, Irving, 316–317
Powell, Adam Clayton, 86, 339
Poyntz, Juliet, 252, 317–318
Prairie Socialists, 6
Preparedness Day Parade (San Francisco), 28
Presbyterian Church, 230, 257, 378
Pressman, Lee, 318–319
*Producers News*, 377
Professional Groups for Earl Browder and Ford, 144
Progressive Citizens of America, 18, 242
Progressive Labor Party, 374–375
Progressive Miners of America, 6
Progressive Mine Workers Union, 227
Progressive Party (1924), 208, 380, 403
Progressive Party (1948), 392
Progressive Party (1949), 17, 18, 110, 140, 196, 262; Labor Division, 100
Progressive Party (WI), 434
Proletarian literature, 13, 158, 165
Proletarian Party, 414
*Prolit Folio*, 325
Propaganda of the deed, 59
Protestant Episcopal Church, 33
Providence, RI, 2
Provincetown Players, 158
Provisional Organizing Committee for a Communist Party, 191
Public Enterprise Committee of Wisconsin, 321

Public Utilities Commission (NY), 259
Puerto Rico, 251
Pullman, Company, strike, 91–92, 247, 328
Puro, Henry, 182, 319–320

Quick, William, 321
Quill, Mike, 322–323

*Radical America*, 224
Rahv, Philip, 261, 316, 325–326
Railroad Brotherhoods, 208
Railway Labor Act, 328
Railway Union (Mexico), 423
*Raivaaja (Pioneer)* (Finnish), 177, 244
*Ramparts*, 71
Randolph, A. Philip, 116, 136, 269, 326–329, 338, 339; Educational Fund, 269; Institute, 329–337, 339
Rand School of Social Science, 69, 245–246, 299, 387, 423; Bureau of Labor Research of, 289–290, 317
Rapp-Condert Investigation, 112
Rappites, 302, 429
Rauschenbusch, Walter, 258, 330–331, 379
*Readers Digest*, 128
*Reading Daily Eagle*, 333
*Reading Labor Advocate*, 333, 373
Reagan, Ronald, 56, 84
Realignment Caucus (Socialist Party), 180–181
*Red Dawn*, 152
Red Family commune, 188
Red International of Labor Unions (Profintern), 37, 49, 50, 124, 135, 157, 194, 220, 305–306, 317, 435
Red Scare, 364, 380, 401
Red Special, 97, 168, 270, 278
Reed, John, 63, 127, 141, 142, 156, 194, 201, 241, 331–333, 342, 343, 371, 423
Regional Planning Association of America, 284
Reitman, Ben, 164
Rensselaer Polytechnic Institute, 201
Republican Party, 56, 85–86, 93, 185,

250–251, 262–263, 268, 271, 273, 309, 377, 395, 407, 421
Reserve Officers' Training Corps, 349, 413
Retail Clerks International Protective Association, 246
Reuther, Walter, 180, 216, 370
*Revolt*, 278
*Revolutionary Age*, 289, 333
Revolutionary Policy Committee (Socialist Party), 264, 383
Revolutionary Workers League, 246
Revolutionary Writers Federation, 325
Revolution of 1905 (in Russia), 3, 348, 387
Rhodes, George, 333–334, 382
Richmond, Al, 334–335
Riverside Church, New York, NY, 137
Robeson, Paul, 120, 191
Rochester Labor College, 31–32
Roman Catholic Church, 88; P. Blanchard and, 31, 33, 69, 70; Bella Dodd and, 113
Ronn, Eskel, 177
Roosevelt, Franklin D., 22, 30, 35, 52, 70, 78, 82, 83, 109, 110, 169, 235, 243, 262, 299, 309, 328, 329, 338, 348, 383, 384, 391
Rose, Ernestine, 335–336
Ross, Carl, 336
Rubin, Jerry, 337
Ruskin Colony (TN), 408
Russell, Charles Edward, 354
Russell Sage Foundation (Committee on Women's Work), 391, 392
Russian Socialist Federation, 298
Russian Soviet Recognition League, 388
Rustin, Bayard, 281, 329, 337–339, 358
Ruthenberg, Charles, 29, 40, 63, 99, 139, 156, 189, 206, 245, 253, 297, 312, 313, 340–343, 369, 411, 418, 435

Sacco, Nicola, 37, 63, 134, 135, 166, 201, 311, 345–346, 389
Sacco and Vanzetti Defense Committee, 345–346
Sailors Union of the Pacific, 183, 186

St. John, Vincent, 63, 106, 346–347
St. John Tucker, Irvin, 99
St. Louis Declaration (1917), 35, 179, 207, 245, 251, 341, 361
*St. Louis Labor*, 103
*St. Louis Post-Dispatch*, 276, 296, 424
St. Martha's Church (New York City), 34
St. Michael's College, Toronto, 27
*Sakenia (Sparks)* (Finnish), 177
Salutsky, J. B., 348, 355
*San Antonio Gazette*, 275
San Francisco, general strike, 44, 82
San Francisco Labor Council, 28
San Francisco Trades Assembly, 184
Sanial, Lucien, 103, 104, 105
San Quentin Penitentiary, 85
Santo, John, 322
Saposs, David, 349
Save the Union Movement, 374
Schapiro, Meyer, 132, 213
Scherer, Marcel, 349–350
Schlossberg, Joseph, 105
Schnaubelt, Rudolf, 310
Schneiderman, William, 350–351
*Schneiderman vs. U.S.*, 350
School Board (Milwaukee), 18
School for Workers, University of Wisconsin, 267
Schwab, Michael, 310, 311
Scottsboro Case, 150, 311, 313
Scudder, Vida, 351–352
Seale, Bobby, 71, 72, 291, 352
Seattle, WA, general strike in, 374, 418
Seattle Unemployed Citizens League, 78
Second Baptist Church, New York, NY, 330
Second Youth March for Integrated Schools, 281
Seidel, Emil, 5, 97, 353–354
Selective Service, 49
Self Determination of the Black Belt, 189–190
Senate Committee on Internal Security, 215
Senate Government Operations Subcommittee, 265

Sephardic Jewish Congregation of Curacao, 101
*Seven Arts*, 143, 332
Shachtman, Max, 2, 56, 63, 64, 131, 160, 180, 181, 216, 233, 253, 269, 279, 354–358
Shaw, George Bernard, 16, 164, 420
Sheboygan *New Deal*, 266
Sherman, Charles, 347
Shoeworkers Union (San Francisco), 28
Simons, Algie, 95, 358–361, 403
Sinclair, Upton, 36–37, 62, 82, 185, 296, 359, 361–363, 419
Single Tax movement, 102
Skaneateles Community, 75, 335
Skidmore, Thomas, 303
Skoglund, Carl, 123, 363–364
Smith, Vern, 125, 152
Smith Act, 7, 54, 55, 64, 68, 78, 85–86, 110–111, 124, 135, 141, 149, 151, 154, 160, 170, 176, 196, 225, 290, 291, 293, 313, 317, 334, 351, 363, 366, 370, 386, 388, 410, 411, 413, 433
Smithsonian Institution, 302, 303
Social Democracy of America, 14, 21, 93–94, 159, 197, 298, 427
Social Democratic Federation (U.S.), 70, 214, 245, 266, 272, 299, 309, 329, 364, 383, 384
*Social-Democratic Herald*, 198, 274
Social Democratic Party (Germany), 4, 7, 172, 209, 263, 282, 393
Social Democratic Party (Hungary), 312
Social Democratic Party (U.S.), 3, 21, 94–95, 178, 189, 197, 204, 205, 226, 249, 279, 298, 352, 359
Social Democratic Party of North America, 267
Social Democratic Party of Wisconsin, 353–354
Social Democratic Workers Party (Russia), 393
Social Democratic Youth (Sweden), 363
Social Democrats (Italy), 255
Social Democrats (U.S.), 147, 181, 273, 339, 353

Social Gospel movement, 31, 34, 257, 258, 264, 289, 330, 379, 416
*The Socialist Appeal*, 169, 223
*Socialist Call*, 147, 229
Socialist Club (CCNY), 253
Socialist Club, University of Illinois, 88
Socialist International, 60, 180, 207, 232, 296, 298, 341, 363
Socialist Labor Party (U.S.), 14, 20, 34–36, 38, 92, 94–95, 101, 103–107, 138, 141–142, 171–172, 178, 185, 189, 192, 203–204, 229, 232, 245, 249, 265, 267, 298, 310, 314, 359, 366, 408, 418
Socialist Party (Canada), 225
Socialist Party-Russian Federation, 366
Socialist Party Scandinavian Federation, 363, 374
Socialist Party-Social Democratic Federation, 180, 435–436
Socialist Party (Spain), 160
Socialist Party (of Switzerland), 11
Socialist Party (U.S.), 2, 3, 4, 6, 11, 12, 16–24, 29, 31, 32, 35–40, 48, 59, 61, 63, 65, 69, 70, 90–100, 116, 118, 122, 124, 127, 129, 138, 141, 145, 146–147, 152–153, 155–157, 160, 165, 168, 179, 181, 183, 186, 188–189, 190–191, 193–194, 197–198, 203–214, 216, 218–219, 229–235, 237–241, 243, 244, 245, 248, 250–252, 258–259, 261, 264–279, 300, 317, 318–319, 321, 327, 329, 331, 334, 340, 341, 348–351, 353, 355–366, 372, 373–374, 377, 378–385, 388, 393–396, 399–404, 407–408, 411, 412, 414, 416, 418, 421, 423, 427–428, 433–435; in Brockton, MA, 94; in Haverhill, MA, 94; in MT, 124; 168; in Reading, PA, 266; in Wisconsin, 18, 109, 183
Socialist Party, U.S., Left Wing (1919), 1, 29, 37, 63, 64, 99, 132, 142, 207, 232, 241, 248, 333, 340, 342
Socialist-Populist Coalition (Milwaukee), 20
Socialist-Progressive Coalition (OK), 6
Socialists, Austrian, 205

Socialists, British, 205
Socialists, European, 205
Socialists, Finnish, 177
Socialists, French, 205
Socialist Trade and Labor Alliance, 36, 104–105, 203–204
Socialist Workers Party, 2, 62, 111–112, 124, 131–132, 160, 216, 233, 261, 269, 279, 284, 292, 293, 356, 363, 374, 378
Socialist Zionists, 272
Social Problems Club (CCNY), 150, 154
Social Revolutionary Club, 310
Social-revolutionary Clubs, 282
Society of Christian Socialists, 351
Society of Friends, 285, 337
Society of Jesus, 27
Soledad Brothers case, 84
Solidarity (Poland), 224
Solomon, Charles, 32, 364–365, 383
Sorge spy ring, 234
*Sosialisti* (Finnish), 244, 319
Sotheran, Charles, 103
Southern Christian Leadership Conference, 281, 287, 339
Southern Conference Education Fund, 114, 115
Southern Conference for Human Welfare, 114, 115, 177, 215
Southern Negro Youth Congress, 83
*The Southern Patriot*, 115
Southern Tenant Families Union, 230–231, 277, 384, 416
*Southern Worker*, 3
Sovereign, James, 104
Soviet Union, 19, 32, 119, 121, 124, 128, 144, 149, 160, 165, 182, 191, 194, 196, 211, 213, 217, 223, 225, 233, 239, 242, 254, 276, 299, 306, 333, 369, 384, 387, 392, 404, 410, 415, 422
Spanish American War, 38, 257
Spanish anarchists, and syndicalists, 167
Spanish Civil War, 150, 160, 185, 254, 290, 363, 389
Spanish Loyalists, 144
Spargo, John, 97, 204, 300, 360, 365, 403

*The Spectator*, 309
Spector, Frank, 365–366
Spector, Maurice, 2
Spies, August, 257, 310, 311, 366–367
Spokane, WA, Free Speech Fight, 133, 138, 225
Spooner, Lysander, 367–368
*Spotlight*, 336
Springfield, IL, race riot in, 403
*Springfield Union*, MA, 13
Spring Mobilization to End the War in Vietnam, 108
Spring Street Settlement House, 378
Spring Valley, IL, coal strike in, 247
Stachel, Jack, 368–370
Stalin, Joseph, 12, 37, 48, 50, 51, 52, 83, 128, 141, 150, 151, 156, 160, 170, 177, 190, 239, 254, 291, 297, 299, 313, 328, 356, 369, 384, 393, 413, 424
State, County, and Municipal Workers Union, 112; Local 555, 112
State Insurrection Law (GA), 55
Steadman, Seymour, 99
Steel Workers Union, 175
Steffens, Lincoln, 179, 370–371
Steinmetz, Charles, 259
Stockholm Appeal, 120
Stokes, Graham, 372
Stokes, Rose Paster, 238, 372
Strasser, Adolph, 267
Student League for Industrial Democracy, 242
Student Nonviolent Coordinating Committee, 66, 72, 84, 115, 136–137, 187, 188, 281, 287
*Student Outlook*, 242
Students for a Democratic Society, 38, 87, 113, 180, 187
Stump, J. Henry, 372–373
Subversive List, 357
*Sunday Worker*, 4, 312
Supreme Court, U.S., 55, 121, 151, 153, 156, 164, 195, 196, 200, 260, 291, 334, 338, 386, 413
*Survey*, 32
Swabeck, Arne, 373–375
*Symposium*, 55

*Syndicalist*, 420
Syndicalist League of North America, 49, 138, 225

Tammany Hall, 32, 212, 247, 381
Taylor, Charles, 377–378
Teachers Union, NY, 112
Teheran Thesis, 169–170, 196
Telluride, CO, strike, 192
Tennessee Valley Authority, 383
Terre Haute and Indianapolis Railroad, 90
Third World, 263
*This Month*, 269
Thomas, Norman, 2, 3, 24, 26, 32, 35, 146, 147, 155, 156, 180, 183, 209, 212, 214, 216, 231, 235, 238, 239, 245, 266, 272, 277, 299, 321, 330, 334, 352, 364, 378–385, 396
Thomas for President Clubs, 380
Thompson, Robert, 52, 113, 170, 385–387
*Times* (London), 179
Time Store, 406
Tobin, Daniel, 111, 124
*The Tocsin*, 245
Toledo, OH, Auto-Lite strike, 53
Tom Mooney Defense Committee, 264
Toohey, Pat, 387
*Toveri (Comrade)* (Finnish), 319
Trachtenberg, Alexander, 355, 387–388
Trade Union Committee for Unemployment Insurance and Relief, 410
Trade Union Committee of Negro Workers, 306
Trade Union Educational League, 50, 139, 225, 232, 418
Trade Union Unity League, 55, 109, 112, 139, 157, 190, 226, 305, 318, 369, 400, 433
Trade unions. *See* Labor unions; American Federation of Labor; Congress of Industrial Organizations; Industrial Workers of the World; Socialist Trade and Labor Alliance; Trade Union Unity League; and *names of other labor unions*
Transport Workers Union, 322, 402

Trautmann, William, 106, 347
Tresca, Carlo, 133, 134, 318, 388–390
Triangle Waist Company Fire (New York City), 401
*Trinidad Weekly Guardian*, 305
Trotsky Archives at Houghton Library, Harvard University, 160
Trotsky, Leon, 2, 50, 54, 56, 63, 64, 88, 124, 128, 131, 142, 144, 145, 159, 160, 166, 213, 223, 233, 252, 253, 286, 292, 297, 312, 326, 355, 356, 357, 366, 374, 377, 389
Trotskyists, 54, 55, 62–65, 123, 127–128, 144, 159–160, 213, 216, 223, 231, 233, 253, 261, 279, 325, 354, 374, 384, 418, 433
Trotter, William Monroe, 118
Truman, Harry, 87, 329, 338
Truman Doctrine, 262
*Truth*, 184
Tse-tung, Mao, 373
Tucker, Benjamin, 73, 164, 256, 427
*Turnverein* (Turner Bund), 19, 366
Tydings Committee (U.S. Senate), 53
*Tyokansa (Worker)* (Finnish), 177
*Tyomies (The Worker)* (Finnish), 244, 319, 336
Tyovaen Opisto (Work People's College) (Finnish), 244, 319
*Tyovaen Osuustoimintalehti (Workers Cooperative Journal)* (Finnish), 177

Unemployed Councils, 7, 14, 15, 200, 243, 290–291, 421–422
Unemployed League, 277
Unemployment Day (March 6, 1930), 15
Unification Church, 73
Union Club, 271
Union for Democratic Action, 143, 417
Union for Democratic Socialism, 273
Union of Soviet Socialist Republics. *See* Soviet Union
Unitarian Church, 121, 201, 211, 299
United Automobile Workers, 153, 254, 279, 280, 370
United Brotherhood of Carpenters and Cabinetmakers, 267
United Cannery, Agricultural, Packing

and Allied Workers of America, 195, 198, 199, 277
United Communist Party, 29, 63, 342, 399
United Farmers League, 37, 377
United Farm Workers, 90
United Federation of Teachers, 269
United Front, 176
United Fund for Finnish-American Archives, 336
United Garment Workers, 435
United Hebrew Trades, 60, 203
United Jewish Charities of Rochester, NY, 161
United Labor Party of California, 204
United Mine Workers of America, 153, 226, 227, 374, 387
United Nations, 120, 311
United Negro Front Conference, 46
United Office and Professional Workers Union, 369
United Service Employees Union, 246
United Shoeworkers, 254
United Spanish War Veterans, 259
United States Army, 192, 386
United States Congress Against War, 264, 400
United States Immigration Commission, 317
United States Labor Service, Advisory Council, 392
United States Military Academy, West Point, 12
United States People's Anti-Imperialist Delegation, 72
United States Post Office, 368
United States State Department, Ideological Advisory Unit, 424
*United States vs. William D. Haywood et al.*, 194
United Toilers, 414
Universal Negro Improvement Association, 46, 116
University Books, Inc., 279
University of Bridgeport, 271
University of the Toilers of the East, 190, 311
University Settlement (NY), 402

Untermann, Ernest, 359, 420
Utah State Board of Pardons, 202
Utica, NY, textile strike in, 31

VanKleek, Mary, 391–392
Vanzetti, Bartolomeo, 37, 63, 134, 135, 166, 201, 311, 345–346, 389
*Vapaus (Freedom)* (Finnish), 319
Veterans Administration, 386
Veterans of the Abraham Lincoln Brigade, 291
Vietnam Day Committee, 337
Vietnamese National Liberation Front, 87, 113
Vietnam War, 27, 90, 108, 170, 188, 246, 260, 262, 273, 281, 385
Vladeck, B. Charney, 147, 209, 382, 383, 392–396
Vogt, Hugo, 105
Voice of America, 66
*Voice of Labor*, 333
*Vorwaerts* (Milwaukee), 11

Wagenknecht, Alfred, 341, 342, 399–400
Wage Workers Party, 138
Wagner Act (National Labor Relations Act), 41
Waldman, Louis, 147, 400–402
Wallace, Henry, 17, 100, 110, 140, 158, 199, 242, 319, 322, 384, 385, 392
Walling, William English, 204, 300, 360, 402–403, 420
Ward, Harry F., 114
War Department (U.S.), Ordinance Division, Women's Division, 392
Ware, Harold, 36, 37, 176, 182, 404–405
Ware Group, 405
War Labor Policies Board, 392
War Manpower Commission, 366
War on Poverty, 180
War Production Board, 243
Warren, Fred, 408
Warren, Josiah, 7, 8, 43, 405–407
War Resisters League, 218–219, 262, 273, 286, 338
Washington, Booker T., 118

Washington Commonwealth Federation, 78–79

Washington State un-American Activities Committee, 79

*Washington Times*, 16

Watchmakers' Union, 29

*Waterfront Worker*, 44

Wayland, Julius, 97, 407–408

Weathermen (faction of Students for a Democratic Society), 113

Weather Underground, 39, 113, 114

*Weekly People*, 101, 103, 359

Weiner, William, 409–410

Weinstock, Louis, 410–411

Weinstone, William, 50, 411

Weisbrod, Albert, 412

Weiss, Max, 412–413

Wellesley Summer Institute for Social Progress, 3

West, Don, 215, 416

West African Students Union, 307

West African Youth League, 307

Western Electric, 111

Western Federation of Labor, 193, 346, 347

Western Federation of Miners, 94, 122–123, 191–192

Western Minorities University (U.S.S.R.), 244

Western Union, 184

*Western Worker*, 149

Western Writers Congress, 363

West Indian Federation, 116

Wickersham Committee, 28

Wicks, Harry, 414–415

Wiita, John, 182, 319–320

Wilkerson, Doxey, 415

Williams, Albert Rhys, 31, 238

Williams, Aubrey, 115

Williams, Claude, 416–417

Williams, Howard Y., 417

Williamson, John, 52, 83, 418, 423

Williamstown (MA) Institute of Politics, 3

Wilshire, Gaylord, 164, 418–420

*Wilshire's Magazine*, 36, 361, 419

Wilson, Lilith, 214, 420–421

Wilson, Woodrow, 16, 29, 35, 41, 99, 145, 202, 206, 238, 351, 365, 378, 379, 403

Winston, Henry, 421–422

Winter, Carl, 422–423

Wisconsin Defense League, 361

Wisconsin Farmer-Labor Progressive Federation, 266

Wisconsin Loyalty League, 361

Wisconsin State Federation of Labor, 210

*Wisconsin Vorwaerts*, 19

Wolfe, Bertram, 199, 423–424

Wolfsohn, Leo, 424–425

Woman Suffrage movement, 18, 164, 226, 230, 266, 395

Women's Christian Temperance Union, 36

Women's International League for Peace and Freedom, 230, 352

Women's liberation movement, 73

Women's Militia (SDS), 113

Women's Trade Union League, 351

*Women's Wear Daily*, 147

Woodhull, Victoria, 9, 425–427

*Woodhull and Clathin's Weekly*, 426

Woodstock Jail, 92

Work, John, 427–428

*The Worker* (weekly), 129, 155, 298

*Workers Age*, 199

Workers Alliance, 15

Workers Alliance of America, 14, 15, 242, 243, 416

*Workers Call*, 359

*Workers Challenge*, 414

Workers Committee Against Unemployment, 318

Workers Communist League, 157

Workers Councils, 355

Workers Defense League, 180

Workers Defense Union, 36

Workers Ex-Servicemen's League, 57

Workers International Relief, 349, 400

Workers Liberty Defense Union, 134

Workers Party (Communist), 1, 37, 63, 81, 128, 139, 234, 342, 343, 348, 350, 388, 399–400

Workers Party (Shactmonist), 2, 64, 131, 160, 216, 223, 261, 269, 279, 357

Workers Party (Trotskyist), 56, 160, 246, 269, 286, 356

Workers School (New York, NY), 65, 290, 318, 388, 392, 410, 423

Working Class Union, 6

Workingmen's Cooperative Publishing Association, 35

Workingmen's Party of the United States, 267, 302, 430

*Workmen's Advocate*, 101

*Workmen's Circle*, 70, 394

Works Progress Administration, 143, 243, 271, 318

World Anti-Slavery Convention, 315

World Congress for Peace (Paris, 1949), 120

World Federalists, 417

World Federation of Trade Unions, 78

World Peace Brigade, 287

*World Tomorrow*, 379

World Tourists, Inc., 409

World War I, 2, 31, 45, 46, 49, 57, 61, 88, 98, 127, 134, 135, 137, 156, 165, 175, 194, 205, 206, 212, 230, 237, 241, 242, 244, 245, 251, 284, 298, 332, 333, 341, 342, 365, 372, 379, 389, 391, 399, 403, 420, 428

World War II, 2, 3, 32, 111, 136, 154, 176, 200, 218, 223, 235, 243, 246, 384, 386

World Youth Festival (Helsinki), 84

Wright, Frances, 303, 429–431

Wright, Richard, 190

*Yates vs. U.S.*, 334

Yiddish journalism, 59, 61

Yiddish language, 59, 69, 70, 73, 105, 145, 348, 394

Young Christian Workers, 27

Young Communist International, 1, 65, 82, 355, 413, 418

Young Communist League, 81, 149, 150, 153, 169, 175–176, 195, 200, 334, 336, 338, 385–386, 412–413, 421–422

Young Communist League (Canada), 418

*Young Democracy*, 2

Young Men's Christian Association, 146, 215, 230–231, 268

Young Men's Christian Association (Swedish), 201

Young Men's Municipal Reform League, 247

Young People's Socialist League, 1, 15, 81, 180, 216, 234, 279, 349, 409, 412

Young Socialist International, 65

Young Socialist League, 180

Youngstown Sheet and Tube (OH), 175

*Young Worker*, 65, 169, 413

*Young Workers League*, 65, 81, 169, 190, 290, 350, 355, 418

Youth International Party (Yippies), 211, 337

Zack, Joseph, 433

Zeidler, Frank, 210, 321, 428, 434–435

Zimmerman, Charles, 255, 435–436

Zionists, 145, 297

# CONTRIBUTORS

ROBERT ALEXANDER is Professor of Economics at Rutgers University. He is author of *The Right Opposition* (1981).

BARBARA BARTKOWIAK is a freelance writer and researcher.

JOHN BECK is Assistant Professor of History at Oklahoma State University.

JEFF BENEKE is a freelance editor, writer, and historian.

CASEY BLAKE is Visiting Assistant Professor of History and Humanities at Reed College.

CLAYBORNE CARSON is Associate Professor of History at Stanford University. He is author of *In Struggle: SNCC and the Black Awakening of the 1960s* (1981).

ART CASCIATO is an Instructor in English at Northeastern University. He is completing a dissertation on the American Writers Congress.

NORAH CHASE teaches English at Kingsborough Community College and is writing a biography of Elba Chase Nelson, one-time head of the New Hampshire Communist Party.

MACEO CRENSHAW DAILEY is Assistant Professor of History at Boston University.

LOWELL DYSON is Assistant to the Chief Historian, Center of Military History, in Washington, D.C. He is the author of *Red Harvest* (1982).

ROBERT FITRAKIS is a graduate student in political science at Wayne State University.

MICHAEL FURMANOVSKY is a graduate student in history at UCLA. He is completing a dissertation on the Communist Party in California during the depression.

DOROTHY GALLAGHER is a writer and former fellow of the New York Institute for the Humanities at New York University. She is the author of *Hannah's Daughters* (1976).

DAVID GARROW is Associate Professor of Political Science at City College of New York. He is author of *The FBI and Martin Luther King, Jr.* (1981).

JOHN GERBER has taught history at Northeastern and Tufts University. He is completing a biography of the Dutch Marxist Anton Pannekoek.

ALBERT GLOTZER was a founding member of both the Communist Party and the Socialist Workers Party.

MAX GORDON was an editor of the *Daily Worker*. He is a frequent contributor to scholarly and political journals.

JANET GREENLEE is Assistant Professor of Economics at Lake Forest College.

ROBERT L. HARRIS is Associate Professor of Afro-American Studies at Cornell University.

STEPHEN K. HAUSER teaches history at Milwaukee Area Technical College.

JOHN HAYNES is director of tax policy for the state of Minnesota. He is the author of *Dubious Alliance: The Making of Minnesota's DFL Party* (1984).

ROBERT HILL is editor of the Marcus Garvey Papers at UCLA.

JAMES INGBRETSON is a graduate student in history at the University of Wisconsin—Milwaukee.

MAURICE ISSERMAN is Assistant Professor of History at Smith College. He is author of *Which Side Were You On? The American Communist Party During the Second World War* (1982).

LILLIAN KIRTZMAN JOHNPOLL is a researcher and freelance writer.

MIKE KARNI is director of the Iron Range Interpretive Center in Minnesota and editor of *Finnish Americana*.

ISRAEL KUGLER is Professor of History Emeritus at City University of New York.

JUDY KUTULAS is a graduate student in history at UCLA. Her dissertation deals with American intellectuals and the Left.

DANIEL LEAB is Professor of History at Seton Hall University. Among his books is *A Union of Individuals: The Formation of the American Newspaper Guild*. He is editor of *Labor History*.

PAUL LEBLANC is a freelance writer and political activist.

HUGH LOVIN is Professor of History at Boise State University. He has written extensively on third parties in the 1930s.

CHARLES MARTIN teaches history at University of Texas El Paso. He is author of *The Angelo Herndon Case and Southern Justice* (1976).

DAHRL ELIZABETH MOORE is a librarian at Florida Atlantic University.

JOHN O'SULLIVAN is Professor of History at Florida Atlantic University.

ROBERT RUSHIN is a graduate student in political science at Emory University.

PENNY RUSSELL is a graduate student in history at Stanford University.

JAMES GILBERT RYAN is Assistant Professor of Political Science at Drexel College. He is completing a biography of Earl Browder.

ED SHOEMAKER is a graduate student in history at Emory University.

GERALD SORIN is Professor of American History and Director of Jewish Studies at the State University of New York, College at New Paltz. His latest book is *The Prophetic Minority: American Immigrant Jewish Radicals 1880–1920* (1985).

MART STEWART is a graduate student in history at Emory University.

PAT SULLIVAN is a fellow at the Carter Woodson Institute at the University of Virginia. She is completing a book on the Henry Wallace campaign in the South.

DOROTHY SWANSON is director of the Tamiment Library at New York University.

WARREN VAN TINE is Professor of History at Ohio State University.

ALAN WALD is Associate Professor of English at the University of Michigan. Among his books is *James T. Farrell: The Revolutionary Socialist Years* (1978).

KENNETH WALTZER is Associate Professor of History at James Madison College at Michigan State University. He is writing a book on the American Labor Party.

SETH WIGDERSON is Instructor in History at Dearborn Community College.

TOM WILLIAMS is Assistant Professor of History at Emory University.

ROBERT ZIEGER is Professor of History at Wayne State University. His latest book is *Rebuilding the Pulp and Papers Workers Union 1933–1941* (1984).

# ABOUT THE EDITORS

BERNARD JOHNPOLL is retired Professor of Political Science at the State University of New York at Albany. He is the author of *Pacifists Progress* (1970) and *The Impossible Dream* (1981).

HARVEY KLEHR is Samuel Candler Dobbs Professor of Politics at Emory University. He is the author of *Communist Cadre* (1978) and *The Heyday of American Communism* (1984).